A
Bloc
of
One

The Political Career of Hiram W. Johnson

RICHARD COKE LOWER

STANFORD UNIVERSITY PRESS
STANFORD, CALIFORNIA   1993

Stanford University Press
Stanford, California

© 1993 by the Board of Trustees of the
Leland Stanford Junior University

Printed in the United States of America

CIP data are at the end of the book

To my wife, Lou,
and to my mother, and
the memory of my father

Preface

If Hiram Johnson had had his way, this book would never have been written. That is not because he would have objected to its contents, although almost certainly he would have done precisely that. Throughout this work, I have tried to take Johnson seriously—to see and understand his world from his perspective as well as from my own. But while I have been sympathetic, I have also been critical, and criticism almost always brought out the worst in Johnson. Thin-skinned and suspicious, forever on his guard, he could discover in any criticism signs of a deeper malice. In addition, he most certainly would have found further reason to distrust historians in any work that did not conform totally to his own perceptions and judgments, for if he gladly culled history's lessons and grimly awaited its verdicts, historians themselves, he would insist, even when honest, too often got it wrong. With an almost unerring instinct, they misunderstood and misrepresented the times and the characters they purported to understand.

More fundamentally, however, if Johnson had had his way, this book would not have been written because there would have been no public life, no political career at all, to document and describe. Growing up under the shadow of his politically active father, Johnson was intrigued by the world of politics but hesitant to embrace that world. He knew the attractions of a public life, but saw too how it could corrupt. Thus early on, he chose not to follow in his father's footsteps. "I am not a politician in any sense of the word," he once announced. "I have never held and never will hold any public office."[1] But in 1910, at the age of 44, he chose again, running for and winning election as governor of California. For the next 34 years, until his death, in August 1945, he held elective office—6 years at the state Capitol in Sacramento and 28 years in the United States

Senate. And from the beginning, he cut his own political path. Stubbornly independent, Johnson almost invariably brought an apocalyptic intensity to the battles he waged. For him, politics was the art not of compromise but of confrontation. On his office wall hung a framed quotation from Abraham Lincoln:

> I am not bound to win,
>   but I am bound to be true.
> I am not bound to succeed,
>   but I am bound
> To live up to what light I have.
>
> I must stand with anybody
>   that stands right; stand
> with him while he is right,
>   and part with him when he goes wrong.[2]

He "walked alone," recalled Raymond Moley, of New Deal brain trust fame. Or as Johnson himself put it, he preferred to be a "bloc of one."[3]

As governor, Johnson provided the leadership for a progressive reform movement that both altered the mechanics of California's politics and fundamentally redefined the obligation of the state to its citizens. Nor was his mark limited to a single state. In 1912 he joined with others to push for the creation of a national Progressive party and, less eagerly, became that party's nominee for the vice presidency on a ticket headed by Theodore Roosevelt. In 1920 and again in 1924 he sought the presidency itself, campaigning unsuccessfully for the Republican nomination.

Johnson was elected to the United States Senate in 1916, midway through his second term as governor, and took his seat just as the United States entered World War I. In the Senate, he joined with fellow insurgents and continued thereafter to identify himself as a reformer, but he quickly embraced a second cause as well, becoming one of the nation's most adamant proponents of American isolation. An irreconcilable in his opposition to American entry into the League of Nations, Johnson continued to labor in support of American isolationism throughout the 1920s and 1930s, and from his deathbed cast his final vote in 1945 against American entry into the United Nations. Characteristically, he ended his political career as he had begun it—in opposition, as a bloc of one.

This book had its beginnings almost a quarter of a century ago, when, as a graduate student at the University of California, I chose

Hiram Johnson as a likely subject for a doctoral dissertation. But let me add as well that this book has not been 25 years in the making. Once the dissertation was out of the way, I turned my attention to other interests. My notes, which had ranged beyond the narrow focus of my dissertation thanks to a research grant from the John and Dora Haynes Foundation, were packed away. Occasionally I thought of returning to those notes and attempting a full-length biography, but until the last few years I always found reason for delay. And then one day all reason left me; I decided to supplement the research already in place, bought a word processor, and began.

Those responsible for encouraging such lunacy on my part would have to include my wife, Lou, who promised it would be fun; Larry Levine, who directed my dissertation at Berkeley and who has encouraged me ever since; friends of graduate school days, including Masao Matsumoto, Jerry Clarfield, Walt Stein, and Roger Sharp; and a host of good friends at California State University, Sacramento. Included in that latter category are Peter Shattuck, Jerry Tobey, and Richard Fauber. All three read the manuscript in its entirety; all three made it a far better work than it would otherwise have been. Larry Levine also read an early version of this work, making many useful comments. I also want to thank Nancy Atkinson, Norris Pope, and Peter Kahn of Stanford University Press for the work they did in preparing this manuscript for publication. I am grateful to them. My thanks too to Joseph Pitti, who shared with me his knowledge of California history and who helped with Chapter I; to Robert Long, who was similarly helpful on issues of foreign policy; and to my wife, Lou, who read and reread, and then read again, and didn't seem to mind.

Richard Coke Lower

Contents

22 pages of illustrations follow p. 200

A
Bloc
of
One

The
California
Years

Heritage and Legacy
1866–1916

Hiram Warren Johnson was born in Sacramento, California, on September 2, 1866, and grew up in this city on the make, a pioneer community eager to tap the flood of new opportunities unleashed by the opening of the American West. He grew up too in a household alive to the world of politics. In ways not always expected, both community and household helped shape the man. The city itself, resting at the junction of the Sacramento and American rivers, with a population of little more than 15,000 at the time of his birth, was one of the instant communities that had erupted in the wake of the Gold Rush less than two decades earlier. A commercial way station between San Francisco and the Mother Lode, it remained an economic center as agriculture came to displace mining and as population shifted from the foothills to the fertile valley in which it lay. From Sacramento, the capital of the state after 1853, emerged the "Big Four"—Collis P. Huntington, Mark Hopkins, Leland Stanford, and Charles Crocker—who in the 1860s oversaw the building of the Central Pacific Railroad linking California with the East; and the city, with its extensive repair yards and depot, increasingly came to serve the railroad and in turn was served by it. By the 1880s the company had come to dominate the region's economy, providing direct employment for almost 2,000 of the city's 22,000 residents and a payroll of $156,000 each month.[1]

Until 1902 Sacramento defined the setting of Hiram Johnson's world. Very much shaping the substance of that world was his father, Grove Lawrence Johnson. As ambitious as the city he adopted as his home, Grove Johnson was a native of Syracuse, New York, and the youngest son of Quincy Adams Johnson, a lawyer, active abolitionist, and minor participant in the founding of the Republican party in New York State. Quincy's death in 1856, only two years after the death of his wife, Juliette, left the fifteen-year-old Grove an orphan. Almost immediately, he found work as a teacher. Soon thereafter he began studying law in the offices of Sedgwick, Andrews, and Kennedy. He was admitted to the New York bar in 1862, just a few days after his twenty-first birthday. Earlier that same year, not yet old enough to vote, he was elected to the Syracuse School Commission, on which he represented the city's fourth ward, holding the seat his father had held at the time of his death.

Alert to every opportunity, Grove never hesitated to push his way forward. Though quick-tempered and often abrasive in manner, he was also eager to impress others. Photographs of him show a full-bearded, thin, and wiry man of less than average height who dressed with meticulous care—his boots well polished; his striped trousers, frock coat and black, broad-brimmed hat well brushed; a boutonniere kept fresh by a vial of water sewn to his lapel. In Syracuse he met Anne Williamson deMontfredy, a year his junior, who was attending the local finishing school. They eloped in January 1861, after her parents refused to sanction a marriage they deemed below her station. At the end of the year their first child, Albert, was born and a daughter, Josephine, soon followed.[2]

Like many of the upwardly mobile of the mid-nineteenth century, Grove was not always careful of the route he chose. In September 1863, caught in a tangle of debts, he hurriedly left Syracuse under indictment for falsifying two promissory notes. His case, the local newspaper lamented, was "a very sad one." He headed west, traveling to Sacramento on the overland stage. With the help of his brother who had earlier gone west under happier circumstances, he secured a position as clerk in the Quartermaster Corps and worked in Arizona, California, and Washington before being mustered out in April 1865. In May, not long after his twenty-fourth birthday, he was back in Sacramento, and in the fall of that year, after briefly returning to New York, he accompanied his wife and family across the Isthmus of Panama to their new California home. By the end of the year they had put down roots in Sacramento, and Grove quickly liquidated the debts owed to his Syracuse creditors. Hiram, their second son, was born the following year. Somewhat later, two more daughters arrived: Mary Adelaide ("Mamie") in 1871 and Mabel Anne in 1872.[3]

To make his way in Sacramento, Grove sold insurance, served for more than a decade as clerk of the county Swamp Land Board, and in 1867 joined the County Assessor's Office as chief clerk. A natural orator with a voice that, as one observer recalled, could vibrate "like the sting of a bee," Johnson sought elective office as he had in Syracuse.[4] In 1867 he ran for the position of county auditor on the Union party ticket, only to withdraw from the race when evidence was uncovered that implicated him in tampering with voter registration lists.[5] In 1871, shifting his allegiance to the Democratic party, he ran again, this time for the California State Senate, but scandal continued to plague him when charges were voiced in the aftermath of the election that invisible ink had been used to taint the ballots of his opponent; whatever the truth of the charges, Grove lost the election by a margin of three to two.[6]

As a Democrat, Grove spoke out for Horace Greeley in the presidential campaign of 1872, was elected to the Democratic State Central Committee in 1873, and was the party's candidate for the state Senate once again in 1875, running last in a four-man contest.[7] Shortly thereafter, he severed his adopted party ties and returned to the Republican fold. The timing could not have been better: in 1877, over the cry of "renegade" voiced by a handful of GOP regulars, Grove was nominated and won election to the California State Assembly. In 1879, his days of party wandering at an end, he was elevated to the state Senate.[8]

Though he shifted between parties, Grove always remained true to his own set of values. An activist and a reformer, he supported temperance, argued for Sunday closing laws, spoke out for free textbooks and compulsory education, and introduced legislation to enable women to practice law and to grant wives the right to sue their husbands for support. He was also an early advocate of woman suffrage.[9] But there were limits to his stance as a reformer. When running for state office, he quickly identified himself with the Central Pacific Railroad, stressing the concrete economic benefits the company provided for both Sacramento and the West. "The interests of the railroad and Sacramento are identical, and should always remain so," he announced in his first successful Sacramento campaign in

1877, repeating a theme he had voiced earlier. "They should labor together like man and wife, only to be divorced by death."[10] For those outside of Sacramento, however, it was an increasingly unpopular theme. As the company's operation expanded in the mid-1870s to include the Southern Pacific, the Western Pacific, the Northern Railway, and the California Pacific, finally embracing 85 percent of the transportation network in the state, antirailroad sentiment began to swell: Californians complained of monopoly, of discriminatory rates between regions and shippers, and of political manipulation at all levels of government.

Johnson was renominated for the state senate in 1882 but was defeated in the state Democratic landslide of that year.[11] For the next decade he continued to involve himself in party politics both at the local level and at the state level, as a member of the Platform and Resolutions Committee of the Republican state conventions in 1888 and 1892, but he devoted the bulk of his energies to the practice of law, dealing with both criminal and civil cases and building a reputation as one of the most able and aggressive of the region's attorneys. As one local newspaper observed, he might have lacked complete familiarity with the law, but he was always alert to any weakness in the arguments of his opponents, and his ability to organize testimony in an almost unbroken phalanx made him a "keen, shrewd, indefatigable, unwearying, untiring advocate, ever ready and always eloquent."* Of the seventeen accused murderers he defended during his career, he saved all but one from the gallows.[12]

A self-centered and often overbearing man, Grove Johnson was renowned for a quick temper and a talent better suited to making enemies than cultivating friends. He ruled his home with the same intimidating energy he devoted to politics and the law, seeking with a martinet's determination to shape his children in his own image.[13] Such measures as the posting of a daily schedule for the bathing of each of his children in the fully furnished bathroom he had installed in his house were directed to that end. Both Grove and his wife,

* *Sacramento Bee*, Nov. 14, 1887. Johnson, the *Bee* continued, "had a sarcasm as cutting as a December wind, a wit as keen as the edge of a Damascus blade, a knowledge of human nature that looks right through a man, a shrewdness that penetrates into every avenue of a case—and above and beyond all, an industry that never seems to know what weariness is." Winfield Davis, *History of Political Conventions in California, 1849–1892* (Sacramento, 1893), pp. 424, 537, 571. Johnson began to practice law in California in May 1874.

ambitious for their children's future, emphasized the importance of education and drew upon their home library, one of the largest in the city, to supplement the offerings of the local public schools. The outlines they prepared stressed history and literature, with special attention given to memorization and recitations. When the seven-year-old Hiram found it difficult to pronounce sibilants without a slight lisp, he was sent to the banks of the American River with a list of words provided by his father in hand, and ordered to place pebbles in his mouth in proper Demosthenes fashion to overcome the disability. In 1879, at the time of Ulysses Grant's visit to Sacramento, the thirteen-year-old Hiram made his public speaking debut with a recitation of Thomas Read's patriotic ballad "Sheridan's Ride."[14]

Hiram, called "Jack" by his playmates, apparently enjoyed a happy childhood as he played in empty lots and at the state Capitol, then under construction a few blocks from his home; survived the taunts of his brother, who chanted "Hiram, Hiram, Hiram," to humiliate him; and accompanied his father on various errands, once to see the incendiary Denis Kearney, of San Francisco sandlot fame, when he arrived in Sacramento to participate in the constitutional convention of 1879. But as Hiram much later recalled, the warmth and contentment of family life seemed to dissolve as the family grew more prosperous.[15]

In 1882, at age 16, Hiram graduated from public high school as class valedictorian. Judged too young to begin college, he spent the next two years in his father's law office, where, like his brother Albert before him, he learned shorthand reporting. In 1884, again following in the footsteps of his brother, he entered the University of California. At Berkeley he joined the Chi Phi fraternity, pitched on the university's baseball team, was a member of the rhetorical society, competed on the rifle team and the school's lawn tennis club, and was elected editor of the junior yearbook. Though not an especially diligent student, he proved to be a successful one, burning little midnight oil in the effort. But his college career was cut short at the beginning of his junior year by his marriage to Minnie McNeil, also a Sacramento resident, who was at the time attending nearby Mills College in Oakland.

Family legend has it that the timing of the marriage was prompted by Minnie's determination to travel abroad, where, as an aspiring operatic singer, she could obtain the training necessary to perfect her talents. Adelina Patti, the world-famous operatic star, had been impressed by the richness of Minnie's voice and had invited Minnie to journey with her on her return to Europe. Having secured the consent of her father, a successful Sacramento carpenter turned contractor, Minnie was busily packing when Hiram rushed to Sacramento and broke her resolve with his proposal of marriage. Others have suggested a far more prosaic explanation for the timing of the marriage, namely, that it was determined by Minnie's prenuptial pregnancy—their first child, Hiram Johnson, Jr., was born six and a half months later, on August 10, 1887.[16] Whatever the truth, it seems clear that the marriage was from the outset emotionally fulfilling. Minnie, who was somewhat plain in appearance, could be stubborn, outspoken, ambitious, and contentious. Indeed, in personality the two were much alike, and although they occasionally disagreed, they lovingly sustained one another for more than 58 years. Throughout, Minnie remained in the background, shunning the publicity Hiram later attracted. Early in their marriage he characterized her as "the boss," but it seems doubtful that she ever bossed him in directions he was unwilling to go.

*   *   *

Following their marriage, Hiram and Minnie remained in Sacramento, where they took up residence in a house built by Minnie's father next to his own. Meanwhile, Hiram worked in his father's law office and studied for the bar. In 1890 their second son, named Archibald for Minnie's father, was born. By then, Hiram had become a partner in the family firm—a firm that prospered as both he and his brother settled into the Sacramento establishment. Earlier, in 1885, Albert had become secretary of the Sacramento Board of Trade. Five years Hiram's senior, Albert bore a close physical resemblance to his father and was as meticulous with words as his father was with dress. He excelled both as an orator and as a legal scholar. Hiram, square-built and heavier of frame and lacking Albert's intellectual intensity, always considered his brother superior in talents. But Hiram was a skilled opponent in open court, having inherited from his father a quick tongue, earnest manner, and aggressive style, and a voice that could similarly "sting like a bee." Nor were his clashes always verbal; in one encounter, the younger Johnson came to blows with Sacramento District Attorney Frank Ryan.[17]

But if the firm of Johnson, Johnson & Johnson prospered, the partnership did not, and in 1893, Albert, as high-strung and temperamental as his father, left to begin his own law practice. The move freed him not only from his father's firm but also from his father's political convictions. By 1895 Albert was a public convert to the single-tax system of Henry George; in 1898 he actively supported the unsuccessful gubernatorial candidacy of James Maguire, the Democratic candidate, and in 1900 he spoke out forcefully for William Jennings Bryan.[18] He also became increasingly addicted to alcohol, a condition that contributed to his death less than a decade later.

In all probability Albert's decision to leave the family firm was influenced if not determined by his father's resolve to return to active politics. In 1892 Grove had pushed hard to obtain the Republican nomination to the House of Representatives but was passed over by the party, the nod going to John F. Davis, who was himself defeated by Anthony Caminetti, the Democratic challenger in the race.[19] Two years later Grove was given his chance. It was a good time to run; the nation slumped in depression while Grover Cleveland sought ineffectually to promote recovery by clinging to the gold standard. Opening his campaign in September of that year, Grove caustically compared the promises of the Democratic party in 1892 with the economic collapse that had followed. With true Republican zeal he emphasized the need to maintain the protective tariff that a Democratic administration had sought to undermine. With equal fervor he declared his support for "free silver," a position firmly held by the bulk of both Republican and Democratic politicians in the state. To his constituency in the Second District, which included the farmers of the Sacramento Valley and the miners of the foothills, he emphasized his concern about the growing problem of hydraulic mining debris that fouled the Sacramento River, thus restricting river commerce and flooding agricultural land, and his commitment to resolve the problem by securing funds from the federal government to restore navigation.[20] Hiram, himself increasingly involved in Republican party affairs, actively supported his father, charging in one speech that Caminetti was the candidate of the Southern Pacific. In fact, as Caminetti replied in an unsuccessful effort to promote a series of confrontational debates, it was a charge better made against Grove.[21]

At issue were the mechanics of repayment of the railroad's mortgage debt to the federal government, the Reilly bill, reported from the House Committee on Pacific Railroads of the 53rd Congress and quickly returned to committee following the eruption of public protest. Endorsed by Collis Huntington, the bill substantially reduced the company's debt, extending repayment over a 50-year period with interest held to 3 percent. Throughout the campaign, both Johnson and Caminetti denounced the proposal. Debts, Grove argued, must be paid, not passed on to the public as an additional burden. "Let's put the screws of law upon them," he said of the railroad, "and let us eventually foreclose, if necessary." William Mills, a Southern Pacific functionary and general manager of the *Sacramento Union*, privately expressed disgust with Johnson's position. Too many politicians, he growled, accepted railroad support and then denounced their benefactor.[22] But Mills, and perhaps the bulk of Johnson's audience, struck by the forcefulness of Johnson's presentation and diverted by the excitement of his many torchlight rallies, failed to appreciate the nuance of his position, for if he spoke righteously about the need to repay debts he also called into question the repayment schedule required by the act, implying that it was too stringent and could be met only by raising rates for California's shippers, yet another burdensome cost.[23] Reassured by Collis P. Huntington, Mills and the Southern Pacific worked energetically for Grove's election.[24]

Johnson won handily and in December 1895 was off to Washington for the opening of the 54th Congress, where he took a seat on the House Committee on Pacific Railroads. From that committee emerged the Powers bill—introduced by Horace Powers of Vermont—which while making some concessions to the antirailroad animus of the West was in many ways even more generous to Huntington's operations than the Reilly bill, requiring redemption of the full obligation at 2 percent interest over a period of 80 years.[25] Action on the measure awaited the second session of the Congress, but Grove quickly identified himself as a supporter of the bill; in fact he was its only supporter within the California delegation. By his advocacy, he gained notoriety throughout the state and was actively pilloried by William Randolph Hearst's *San Francisco Examiner*, which, via the caustic pen of Ambrose Bierce, had led a crusade against the Reilly proposal and continued in strident denunciations of the Powers substitute.²⁶ Long identified as a friend of the railroad, Grove seemed to many to have become its prostitute.

After serving as a delegate to the St. Louis Republican National Convention, which denounced the heresy of "free silver" and nominated William McKinley for president, Johnson returned to Sacramento to secure the unanimous endorsement of his party for a second House term. But he encountered almost insurmountable odds as he began his campaign in August, facing both Marion DeVries, the fusionist candidate of the Democratic and Populist parties, and a continuous fusillade from Hearst's *Examiner*.²⁷ Stressing the tariff issue, insistent that despite appearances the Republican party was still the party of bimetalism and a friend of silver, boasting of his achievements in securing additional appropriations for the cleansing of the Sacramento River, he could not finesse the railroad issue as he had done in 1894.²⁸ His defeat would be Huntington's defeat, William Mills privately acknowledged, and the company actively mobilized its resources behind his candidacy.²⁹

But nothing seemed to work. With growing irritation, Johnson demanded more and more support in behalf of his campaign. "He dont [*sic*] want friends," Mills sourly complained; "he wants slaves."³⁰ Unable to sidestep the issue of the railroad, Johnson sought to convert his constituency by reemphasizing the economic benefits it provided Sacramento. It was an effective appeal within the city, but it too often boomeranged elsewhere in his district.³¹ The campaign, Mills observed, was poorly run, and a stubborn Johnson, with his "ostentatious subserviency" to the railroad, had become his own worst enemy.³²

Johnson returned to Washington as a lame duck to become once again Huntington's California spokesman. Despite his defeat, he continued to endorse the arguments presented by the railroad's advocates that any settlement more demanding would be ruinous both to the company and to California's shippers. Ignoring overwhelming evidence to the contrary, he insisted that no one in California save William Randolph Hearst and Adolph Sutro, the Populist mayor of San Francisco, sought a foreclosure of the mortgage and government operation of the enterprise. The debt, he argued, would in fact be better canceled. But in the end, he was the only California representative to vote for the Powers bill. It failed decisively, losing by more than 60 votes.³³ In celebration, California's Democratic governor,

James Budd, declared a state holiday, which would be punctuated by bands, bonfires, and torchlight parades. Meanwhile, Grove had already taken his revenge. Just prior to the vote, anticipating the failure of the bill and bitter about his own election defeat, he replied to the Hearst attacks upon him in a House address that stands out as one of the most intemperate invectives of the late nineteenth century.*

★   ★   ★

As in 1894, so in 1896 Hiram stood behind his father. The voters, he charged, should not be swayed by the "blackmailing sheet" of William Randolph Hearst. Echoing his father's appeal, he pointed to the more than $80 million of railroad investment in Sacramento, arguing that any man in Sacramento who voted against Grove because of his position on the funding bill did "not deserve to live and prosper within its gates."[34] But if Hiram expressed public support, he perhaps entertained private doubts. Certainly with the coming of the depression of the 1890s he sounded a very different note from that of his father. In May 1893, delivering the city's Memorial Day address, he shifted from a rhetoric often florid with patriotic bombast to examine the social issues of the day:

We have seen of late years the concentration of the wealth of this country in few hands and the alarming increase of poverty in our midst. We have seen perhaps an aristocracy rearing its head amongst us, not of blood but of wealth. We have seen perhaps this aristocracy arrogating to itself the rights and the privileges that belong to the aristocracies of the older world, and we

* *Cong. Record*, 54th Cong., 2nd sess. (Jan. 8, 1897), pp. 592–93. Charging, as he had during the campaign, that Hearst was a "blackmailer" who turned against the railroad when his subsidy was discontinued, Grove commented: "We knew him to be a debauchee, a dude in dress, an Anglomaniac in language and manners, but we thought he was honest. We knew him to be licentious in his tastes, regal in his dissipations, unfit to associate with pure women or decent men, but we thought 'Our Willie' was honest. We knew he was erotic in his tastes, erratic in his moods, of small understanding and smaller views of men and measures, but we thought 'Our Willie,' in his English plaids, his Cockney accent, and his middle-parted hair, was honest. We knew he had sought on the banks of the Nile relief from loathsome disease contracted only by contagion in the haunts of vice, and had rivaled the Khedive in the gorgeousness of his harem in the joy of restored health, but we still believed him honest, though low and depraved. We knew he was debarred from society in San Francisco because of his delight in flaunting his wickedness, but we believed him honest, though tattooed with sin." The speech, the *San Francisco Examiner* reported, contained unprintable filth and was unparalleled in parliamentary history for its "insane fury and obscenity." Ladies, it observed, had left the gallery in shock. *San Francisco Examiner*, Jan. 9, 1897.

have seen the poor becoming poorer, until in some parts of this country they are little better than serfs. . . . It may be that ere long, as the classes among us become more distinct, as the poor become poorer, and as hunger drives men to desperation, that we will be confronted with a problem again as serious as that which confronted the statesmanship of this country at the opening of the rebellion. It may be that men in this country, driven to desperation by their wrongs, suffering for the common necessities of life, will go forth from their starving families and engage in another rebellion against wrong and oppression that will eclipse in its bloodshed and its fierceness, in its lawlessness and its slaughter, any the world has ever seen. . . . May God ward off from us any such contest as this. . . . But if such a contest does come . . . may we be found in the future, as you were in the past, struggling and if need be, yielding our lives as you did, in the right, in behalf of equality in man.[35]

It was not a speech designed to comfort or soothe nor an address his father would have made. Perhaps Albert's rebellious spirit had rubbed off; perhaps Hiram, then 26, was already moving in new directions. Four years later, in 1897, almost immediately after Grove returned from Washington to the practice of law and to a subsequent career in the California State Assembly, the partnership with his son was dissolved. Political differences, a contemporary observer wrote, had divided the family.[36]

Sacramento municipal politics further divided Grove from his two sons. In 1899, over the heated protests of some within the Old Guard, Republicans refused to endorse the reelection bid of Mayor William Land, turning instead to George Clark, who promised a crackdown on the city's vice and immorality. Both Hiram and Albert were actively involved in the contest, and Clark drew upon their legal talents when Land, having lost the election, refused to vacate the office, charging that Clark, by failing to list his election expenses fully, had violated the city charter and thus made himself ineligible for office. The case, which was ultimately appealed to the state Supreme Court, was resolved in Clark's favor, and Hiram Johnson joined the new administration as city attorney.[37]

In seeking reelection in 1901, Clark made no effort to obtain the Republican nomination, running instead as an independent. Party stalwarts charged apostasy while Clark's supporters denounced "boss rule." "Every force of evil is against him," Hiram Johnson cried out at one of the many bonfire rallies in support of the mayor.[38] Sticking with his party, Grove Johnson denounced Clark and reprimanded his sons. "Children make mistakes," he chided. "The old man never does."[39] But with the endorsement of the Sacramento Ministers Association, Clark was once again victorious, trouncing Land, the Republican nominee, by almost two to one.[40]

The following year Sacramento's Republican establishment rallied as Clark, together with his "lieutenants" Hiram and Albert Johnson, enlarged the scope of their insurgency by seeking to elect a slate of local delegates to the Republican State Convention in opposition to the renomination of Governor Henry Gage, a favorite of the Southern Pacific. Once again the issue was "boss rule." Clark's supporters lashed out at the "machine's" endorsement of Gage. In reply, Clark's opponents accused the mayor of seeking to become the "boss" of Sacramento. Both Hiram and Albert were named to an independent slate, while Grove took his place on the regular Republican ticket. All three actively participated in the campaign, the elder Johnson speaking at party rallies, his sons, "two of the choicest monologists that every 'kicked it over the pike,'" assuming the role of primary speakers for the opposition.[41]

Conducting a shoestring operation, the Clark forces, as in 1901, held evening rallies throughout the city. A large tent provided the setting, a bonfire drew the crowd, and musical entertainment leavened the audience. Unable to secure the backing of either of Sacramento's two major newspapers, the *Record-Union* and the *Bee*, they published their own weekly sheet. But they battled against impossible odds as the Republican party establishment, with far more at stake than a local election, mobilized their forces against the insurgents.[42] At first hoping that their independent ticket might win the support of labor, Hiram Johnson expressed growing distress when William Herrin, the political spokesman for the Southern Pacific, arrived in town and rumors began to circulate that railroad employees who failed to support Gage would be fired. The battle, Johnson protested, was not with the railroad; the interests of the city and the Southern Pacific were intertwined. But, he continued, if the railroad reached beyond its legitimate sphere, it would be time to "preach a new gospel of reform."[43] Soon thereafter, as the campaign neared its end, Johnson became a spokesman for that new gospel, angrily lashing out against the efforts on the part of the railroad's management to solicit votes both by threats and by the promise of cash to individuals willing to be trucked in vans to the polling stations on election day. His protests, however, made little difference. In the largest turnout to that time, the regular Republican ticket won in every precinct.[44]

Despite their involvement in reform politics, neither Albert nor Hiram sought out political careers. They would be full-time lawyers, not part-time politicians, and even before the conclusion of the 1902 Sacramento campaign Hiram had agreed, at the urging of Albert and perhaps of Minnie, to test his legal skills in California's largest city, San Francisco.[45] Forming a partnership, the two brothers opened their office in the Mills Building at the corner of Bush and Montgomery in the fall of 1902. Hiram enjoyed almost immediate success, and quickly became one of the stars of the San Francisco courts, his dramatic style, ready invective and earnest delivery providing good copy for the press. His tenor voice, first soft, then sharp and rasping, could provoke both tears and anger from a jury. No better trial lawyer ever entered a courtroom, an associate long afterward observed.[46] In 1904 he was appointed special prosecutor in one of the city's more lurid trials, that of George C. Collins, a fellow attorney indicted for bigamy. Having fled to Canada, Collins was extradited to face Johnson's wrath. There was, the *San Francisco Chronicle* reported, "no more scathing denunciation of a man accused than that pronounced yesterday by Hiram W. Johnson."[47] Albert, playing a less conspicuous role, was more and more absent from the office, a victim of alcoholism, and in 1905 the partnership was dissolved.

In 1906 San Francisco's newly elected district attorney William H. Langdon turned to Hiram Johnson, hoping to appoint him as chief prosecutor in a series of spectacular trials that would rock the San Francisco establishment. Facing indictment were the city's chief political boss, Abraham Ruef; Mayor Eugene Schmitz; and some of the city's most prominent business leaders. But Langdon was overruled when the appointment of Francis Heney, fresh from his federal prosecution of land and timber fraud in Oregon, was successfully urged by Fremont Older, the crusading editor of the *San Francisco Bulletin* who had initiated the investigation, and Rudolph Spreckels, heir to a sugar fortune, a millionaire by his own efforts, and the chief financial backer of the probe.[48] Having secured Theodore Roosevelt's agreement to release Heney and William J. Burns, the nation's foremost detective, to prepare the case, Older saw Heney as the logical man to see it through. Johnson was retained as an assistant to the prosecution.[49]

As a member of the prosecution team, Johnson was almost immediately involved in thwarting the effort on the part of the Board of Supervisors to replace Langdon with Ruef himself and thereby end the prosecution before it began. In addition, Johnson represented the city in the impaneling of the jury to try Ruef and Schmitz on a charge of extortion. The trial, set for April 1907 as the delaying tactics of the defense were gradually exhausted, opened with Ruef changing his plea to guilty, an act prompted by the success of the prosecution in inducing the city's Board of Supervisors to implicate themselves and to testify to a series of bribes that linked them and Ruef to the directors of some of the city's major utilities. For Langdon and his associates, the goal had always been to move against the corporate sources of corruption, not their willing agents in city hall. By promising immunity to the supervisors and limited immunity to Ruef if he agreed to cooperate, they had, they hoped, acquired the means necessary to win their goal. Ruef was bound over for further prosecution while the trial of Schmitz for extortion proceeded, ending with his conviction in June.* Meanwhile, Johnson helped draw up new indictments as the graft trials took shape. But nothing went right; the Schmitz conviction was later overturned on a technicality, and Ruef, key to the prosecution, refused to implicate directly the corporate bribers. In the end the net the prosecution sought to weave fell into pieces, trapping only Ruef himself. Other convictions followed but save for Ruef's, all were reversed on appeal.

Johnson spent the greater part of 1907 working in the background as a member of the prosecution team. Occasionally he assumed a fleeting prominence, as when, arguing the case against Theodore Halsey, of the Pacific States Telephone and Telegraph Company, tempers flared and he struck at Halsey's attorney, lunging wildly amid a wreck of overturned chairs in open court. Not so lucky as he had been in his encounter with Sacramento District Attorney Frank Ryan sixteen years before, Johnson was judged the aggressor and fined $25.[50] But Johnson was always loath to stay in the background and inwardly chafed under Heney's direction. Clearly jealous of each other, these two high-strung men found cooperation difficult, and

---

* *San Francisco Call*, March 20, 1907. Schmitz was found guilty on June 13, 1907. The same day, Albert Johnson, who had been admitted to an Oakland hospital, died. The press listed the cause as typhoid fever. *Sacramento Union*, June 14, 1907.

in October of that year, as the San Francisco municipal elections neared, Johnson resigned from the prosecution in order, as he said, to free himself from any taint of a conflict of interest in actively campaigning for the reelection of Langdon as district attorney. Thus once again, after an interval of five years, he found himself on the political stump preaching the "gospel of reform" and crying out against the corrupt power of corporate interests and the privileged who gave them succor.[51]

Langdon was returned to office, but the election illustrated a significant weakening in popular support for the continuation of the graft prosecutions as many within the business community rallied to their own. They could accept the indictment of Ruef and the self-confessed guilt of the supervisors—after all, they were leaders of the Union Labor party, which had emerged out of the labor strife within the city, and their guilt demonstrated the dangers of "class" politics and labor activism. But for the prosecution to reach out and indict the heads of powerful corporations seemed far more threatening, indeed destabilizing to the very social order of which they were a part.

Johnson did not return to the prosecution team following Langdon's reelection, preferring to return to his own private practice, which he had too long ignored. But in November 1908 he was catapulted back into the case when Francis Heney, pursuing a set of indictments against Ruef, was shot through the head in open court by a crazed ex-convict, only narrowly escaping death. Instantly interest in the trial mushroomed. The next evening, a crowd of ten thousand, tense with excitement, dazed by the sudden turn of events, and bewildered by rumors linking the attack to the attempted murder of a witness by dynamite earlier in the year, flooded into the Dreamland Rink. There Langdon, together with Spreckels and others, sought to temper emotions that seemed bent on mob revenge. There too Langdon announced the appointment of Hiram Johnson as Heney's successor.

Joining in the appeal for calm, Johnson promised to work without compensation and carry on Heney's efforts as a public duty. In the next three weeks, in cooperation with his close friend and fellow associate Matthew Sullivan, Johnson pushed the case against Ruef to conclusion.[52] His two-and-one-half-hour summation was a savage assault on the accused. Invective, one reporter wrote, poured from his lips in a continuous torrent as he faced a jury he feared might have been rigged. "We know he is guilty," he snapped, his glare riveting the jury. "You know he is guilty. . . . Dare you acquit him?" Twenty-four hours later, on their fifth ballot, the jury moved for conviction.[53]

★   ★   ★

Viewed within a wider context, the San Francisco graft trials, as well as Johnson's earlier insurgency in Sacramento, were part of a growing pattern of rebellion against boss rule and the subserviency of politics to the economic power of a few. In Los Angeles, the same dynamics were at work; reformers, largely middle class and professionals, organized to overthrow the existing political order, and came close to victory in the municipal elections of 1906. Elsewhere in the state similar efforts were under way.[54] Nationally the pattern was the same, symbolized by the career of Robert La Follette of Wisconsin, and by the actions of Theodore Roosevelt at the White House. Progressivism was on the rise as local and national currents combined, swelling into new tides of political insurgency. Indeed, for many Californians eager for change, it seemed clear that the continued success of the state's Old Guard depended less upon its own inherent strength than upon the lack of any organized opposition.

Edward Dickson, political editor of the *Los Angeles Express* and a participant in the municipal reform movement in Los Angeles, waxed optimistic in a letter to fellow Los Angeles reformer Meyer Lissner: "I think that a state movement for a refor[m] within the [R]epublican party would find instant support."[55] Together with Chester Rowell, editor of the *Fresno Republican*, Dickson sponsored a series of meetings, out of which came the League of Lincoln-Roosevelt Clubs, formed in 1907.[56] Identifying itself with the emerging national progressive movement, the league called for an open endorsement of Roosevelt's presidency and support for the continuation of his policies at the 1908 Republican National Convention. But the larger goal was closer to home: to build upon the emerging reform sentiment within the state and to shape an organization capable of wresting control of the Republican party from the Old Guard. Reformers sought to build their own machine to overthrow that of their enemies.

And as the league made clear, at the core of their task was the destruction of the Southern Pacific's political hold on California.

The dominant power in the city of Hiram Johnson's childhood, the Southern Pacific was the dominant power at the state Capitol as well. As the largest single employer and landholder in the state, it had the most to win, the most to lose, and by all odds the most to preserve through its manipulation of the political process. To that end William Mills had focused his energies; continuing that effort, William Herrin and Walter Parker had perfected the process, developing what was popularly known as the "Southern Pacific Political Bureau." Many of the state's politicos, Grove Johnson among them, had long been open allies; less overtly, many others at one or another point in their careers had sought out its favors.

Flexible and nonpartisan in its approach to politics, the railroad had drawn back from its involvement in Democratic party affairs as California in the decade of the 1890s increasingly moved toward Republican party rule. Within the GOP, however, its influence remained formidable. Long the foil of reform agitation, occasionally stumbling in its efforts to exercise political dominance, and compromising when it could not control, it had most recently demonstrated its power at the Santa Cruz Republican State Convention in 1906, where James Gillett became the party's gubernatorial candidate, and again in 1907 in the legislative session that began his term. But as reformers began to organize, both the railroad and its supporters proved vulnerable. At the 1908 Republican State Convention, league pressure helped to secure an open endorsement of Roosevelt's choice of William Howard Taft as the party's new standard-bearer. Outflanking the Old Guard, the league was successful as well in securing the nomination and election of a significant number of assemblymen and state senators to the California State Legislature that opened in 1909.

Johnson's participation in the San Francisco graft prosecution was the bridge that brought him into the inner circle of California's reformers. In January 1909 he represented the Direct Primary League, an organization sponsored by Dr. John R. Haynes of Los Angeles, before the new legislature. Speaking in support of legislation to institute a direct primary in the state, he again confronted his father. The 67-year-old Grove, tied to the Old Guard by habit and years of service, was by now a stalwart in the Assembly and chairman of the all-powerful Assembly Judiciary Committee. Identified by one unfriendly observer as "by far the ablest parliamentarian in the Legislature," he expressed his displeasure with his son while refusing to confront Hiram in direct debate.[57] But Grove's political career was near its end. Crusty and as abrasive as ever, lashing out against the host of "wicked innovations" that reformers sought to enact, he labored to preserve the old order that seemed about to dissolve around him.

In the 1909 legislature the conservative establishment succeeded in postponing its final defeat, but not in preventing it. Better organized than their opponents and controlling the strategic centers of power in both houses, they were able to turn back legislation to establish the initiative, to deflect measures aimed at eliminating some of the legal loopholes through which the indicted in the San Francisco graft trials had escaped conviction, and to weaken substantially legislation that would enhance state supervision over railroad rates and services. They succeeded too in thwarting the effort to adopt the "Oregon plan" for the nomination of U.S. senators by a direct-primary vote. But these were Pyrrhic victories, holding actions, illustrations not of strength but of weakness. The progressives had defined the agenda against which the Old Guard battled. "The machine," Meyer Lissner rejoiced, "was on the run."[58] Moreover, although the specific primary system that Hiram Johnson defended before the legislature was not adopted, a substitute was enacted that provided for the popular nomination of party candidates for state offices. The bill would open the door to Johnson's election as governor in 1910. It would also end the legislative career of his father.*

With the passage of the direct-primary bill the Lincoln-Roosevelt League set out to select a slate of candidates for the Republican nominations of 1910. As all agreed, central to that task was their pick of governor to head the ticket. Heney at first seemed the most likely choice. He was by all odds the best known of the league's advocates, having recovered from the attempted assassination of 1908.[59] An able and aggressive speaker, earnest in his reform com-

---

*In the 1910 primary election Grove narrowly lost the Republican nomination to C. A. Bliss—883 to 938. By a single vote cast in the Prohibitionist party column, he became the nominee of that party and thus appeared on the ballot in the general election—only to be swamped by Bliss. Johnson attributed his August defeat to the liquor interests, who opposed his effort to prohibit saloons within one and one-half miles of Stanford University, and to the fact that he was "a friend, not a follower or slave to . . . the Southern Pacific." "Every one who had a real or fancied grievance against that company or anything else hit me because they wanted to smite something, and I was the handiest mark." *Sacramento Bee*, Aug. 19, 1910.

mitment, he could rally many to the cause. But he could also repel. To some, his prior Democratic party affiliation boded ill. To others, his harsh, impulsive, abrasive style was off-putting. Often injudicious in his remarks, he had only recently failed one political test— his effort to secure election as San Francisco's district attorney in 1909. His selection, Chester Rowell predicted, would irreparably fragment the Lincoln-Roosevelt League.[60] In fact, as almost all were to conclude, the most obvious candidate for the position was Johnson. Meeting on February 7, 1910, the executive committee of the league voted overwhelmingly for his nomination.[61]

Even before that vote, however, Johnson made clear his determination not to run. Forty-three years old, established in San Francisco with an increasingly lucrative law practice, at home at 857 Green Street on Russian Hill overlooking the Golden Gate and the bay, he saw much to lose and little to gain by such an effort. As a vice president in the league, he had earlier taken the stump in support of the unsuccessful campaign by Heney and the reform element to retain power in San Francisco.[62] Though he stood ready to take to the stump again, he insisted that it be in support of another. But league officials remained adamant. Persistent in their solicitations, Rowell, Lissner, Older, and Dickson pursued Johnson for more than two months. Short of murder, Rowell confessed, he was willing to do almost anything to secure Johnson's consent.[63]

Minnie was the first to falter. When the subject was initially broached, she protested that she would "rather die" than agree to the scheme. Frightened as much by the possibility of victory as of defeat, she had no wish to return to Sacramento, disliked the demands of political life, and resented the material sacrifices involved.[64] Her reconsideration almost certainly rested on her realization that Hiram, although unable to admit it even to himself, very much wanted to run. Transforming ambition into duty would become one of Johnson's trademarks. In mid-February, at home in bed suffering from a cold and fever, he met with Fremont Older, who, he long afterward recalled, "begged, pleaded, cajoled, and exhorted."[65] Now free of Minnie's objections and able to convince himself of his indispensability, he grudgingly assented. It was, he publicly acknowledged, "with the utmost reluctance" that he was induced to enter the race.[66]

Doubtless contributing to Johnson's hesitancy to involve himself

in the contest were his tangled emotional ties with his father. They
had clashed before, but if Grove had freely lashed out at his sons,
Hiram had never publicly replied. Nor would he ever. Told that
Grove planned to campaign actively against him, he admitted to
Charles K. McClatchy, editor of the *Sacramento Bee* and an old boy-
hood chum, "It would be quite heartbreaking . . . if father should
personally assail me during the campaign."[67] He vowed to his sister
not to respond.* A private man with very private feelings, Hiram
sought unsuccessfully to hide the hurt of estrangement, and to what
must have been his obvious relief, Grove made no effort to carry out
his threat. But Hiram's enemies, among them William Randolph
Hearst and Harrison Gray Otis, the autocratic Republican publisher
of the *Los Angeles Times*, were far less restrained, linking Johnson
to his father in a series of personal attacks.

Otis, a spokesman for the Old Guard, hated both the railroad and
the reformers as threats to his own assortment of establishment values and to his hope for the unfettered economic development of
Southern California. His attacks recalled Hiram's earlier political
support for Grove and charged that he had withdrawn that support
and ended his subserviency to the railroad only when it became obvious that there was political gain in such a move.[†] Complaining

*HWJ to Mabel Dray, Feb. 26, 1910. Following his election, Hiram sought to mend
the relationship with his father, and urged that they meet personally. Letters tended
to exacerbate differences, he wrote, and were unnecessary since the two men lived
within blocks of each other. HWJ to Grove Johnson, Mar. 20, 1912. But both Hiram
and his father, despite occasional professions of affection, found reconciliation difficult. Hiram and Minnie, Grove complained, too often found reason to ignore his invitations. Writing in 1912, Hiram accused his father of expressing "a hatred the parallel of which we have never seen in sane human beings." HWJ to Grove Johnson,
Dec. 30, 1912. Grove's relationship with his other children appears to have been similarly strained. See Grove Johnson to HWJ, Apr. 12, 1911, Mar. 7, June 7, 1912, Dec. 21,
1913, Dec. 9, 1920. Ultimately, the breach between Hiram and his father was partially
healed, but only after Hiram's election to the Senate in November of 1916. In 1919
Grove actively supported his son's quest for the presidency and in 1921, as a result of
Hiram's intercession, was appointed to the U.S. Land Office Receivership at Sacramento, a post he held until it was discontinued in 1925. He died in February 1926.
See HWJ to boys, July 2, 1921. Clearly hurt by his estrangement from his father,
Hiram sought to ensure that the relationship with his own children never frayed.
Nowhere is that effort better reflected than in the frequent, usually weekly, letters
he wrote to his sons once they had left home. When either delayed in their reply,
Johnson mixed admonitions with assurances of support and affection, forging a rela-
tionship that at times could be suffocating.

†*Los Angeles Times*, July 27, 28, 31, Aug. 2, 7, 1910. Somewhat inconsistently,
the *Times* also charged that Johnson's promise to kick the S.P. out of California was

that the *Times* had attacked him on the one subject he would not discuss, Johnson responded to the charge with a savagery that made it clear that if he differed politically from his father he was still his father's son. The explosion came near the end of the primary campaign, when Johnson spoke before a crowd of 3,000 who filled Simpson Hall in Los Angeles. Midway through his speech, a voice cried out from the rear of the auditorium asking him what he thought of Otis. Pausing briefly to make sure he had properly heard the question, he lashed out in reply, his words cutting the air with their sharpness: "In the city from which I have come we have drunk to the very dregs the cup of infamy; we have had vile officials; we have had rotten newspapers; we have had men who sold their birthright . . . every debased passion and every sin have flourished." But, he continued,

we have nothing so vile, nothing so low, nothing so debased, nothing so infamous in San Francisco, nor did we ever have, as HARRISON GRAY OTIS. He sits in senile dementia, with gangrened heart and rotting brain, grimacing at every reform, chattering impotently at all things that are decent, frothing, fuming, violently gibbering, going down to his grave in snarling infamy. This man Otis is the one blot on the banner of Southern California; he is the bar sinister upon your escutcheon. My friends, he is the one thing that all Californians look at, when, in looking at Southern California, they see anything that is disgraceful, depraved, corrupt, crooked and putrescent—that is HARRISON GRAY OTIS.

His outburst, whether spontaneous or as some have suggested prearranged, shouted in anger and defiance, was more than reminiscent of his father.[68]

Indeed, as the campaign of 1910 made clear, Hiram Johnson resembled his father in many ways. Both men were fighters, hotly competitive, out to win the game they played. Grove had long prided himself on his pugnacious style, his ability not to make friends but to get things done and to succeed. Nor was his son any less adept either in the courtroom or on the political platform. The Lincoln-

---

a sham. The railroad's representatives, it noted, "view his progress with entire equanimity. The managers of the old Espee ring remember Hiram's service in the past. They do not forget whose son he is." The rumors of estrangement between Hiram and his father, it continued, "are put out for buncombe. They have had several conferences since the campaign began." On Otis, see Richard C. Miller, "Otis and His Times: The Career of Harrison Gray Otis of Los Angeles," (Ph.D. diss., University of California, Berkeley, 1961).

Roosevelt League had made him their candidate not only because he was least likely to fragment the reform movement but also because he possessed great energy, fighting skill, and intensity. "I have such a singularly peculiar temperament that obstacles and difficulties make me only the more obstinate, and when I have started to fight, the blackness of it, serves as a spur, rather than a deterrent," he once wrote.* To a colleague he confessed, "Perhaps more than most men I don't like to be whipped, but when a blow comes my head goes up higher in the air and I want to fight more."[69] When posing for newspaper photographers he often assumed the stance of the boxer, a stocky scrapper, his fists clenched in readiness, his feet firmly planted for the knockout blow. Thirty years later he still sought to project the image—by then a septuagenarian in the ring.

Johnson shared with his father not only a fighter's determination and an eagerness to personalize political contests and call into question the character of his foes, but also a jealous nature, a mercurial temperament, petulance, insensitivity to others, and self-absorption in any campaign he waged. Early in the 1910 race he made clear his reluctance to link his campaign with that of other league hopefuls. Too often, he complained, they wearied their audience. Albert J. Wallace, the league's candidate for lieutenant governor, was a "bore," after whom an effective speech was almost impossible, and too many others, lacking the fire of reform, merely scrambled for office.[70] "Of all the Damn Fool Leagues that ever existed, the LINCOLN-ROOSEVELT REPUBLICAN LEAGUE not only is the worst, but the worst that could ever be conceived," he exploded at one point as the league fumbled some of its publicity efforts.[71] Clearly the 1910 race would be his own, and Johnson quickly established his own independent operation, drawing upon the talents of Al McCabe, a skillful political operator and organizer from San Francisco, to help coordinate his campaign.[72]

*HWJ to Amy Johnson, Mar. 9, 1918. Explaining his campaign strategy, Johnson wrote, "I have found as I have ever found, when an issue is divorced from personality it lacks the heat of enthusiasm which stirs the electorate." HWJ to Otto A. Case, Apr. 18, 1916. See also HWJ to C. K. McClatchy, May 12, 1916. But Johnson's approach to political issues, as almost all recognized, was much more than a conscious strategy. "He seems built so that he has to personify things," Rowell observed. Senator William Borah apparently agreed. "When a man opposes Johnson he hates him," Borah allegedly remarked. Rowell to Katherine P. Edson, Oct. 10, 1919; Clinton Gilbert, *The Mirrors of Washington* (New York, 1921), p. 191; HWJ to Hiram Johnson, Jr., Apr. 2, 1928.

In what was certainly one of the most exhaustive efforts California's voters ever witnessed, Johnson toured the state for more than five months. His crimson Locomobile became a familiar sight, with his elder son, "Jack," at the wheel and an entourage in tow. He opened the primary campaign with a ten-day tour of Los Angeles and California's southern counties, beginning on March 10, then returned to the Bay Area for a short rest and a one-week series of speeches there. In early April he traveled to Yreka, near the Oregon border, and thence into the northern Sacramento Valley and the Sierra foothills, crisscrossing the area and stopping even in the smallest of hamlets, an aide ringing a cowbell to announce his arrival. After returning to his San Francisco home for another brief rest, he went back to the lower Sacramento Valley in late April to begin a tour that took him south into the San Joaquin Valley. Once again home in mid-May, he readied himself for a second ten-day tour of California's southern counties. In early June he addressed an overflow San Francisco audience and, between short rests, made a series of appearances throughout the Bay counties. Early in July, with Johnson making as many as fifteen speeches a day, his auto caravan headed into California's northern coastal counties, then returned after a week to the lower Sacramento Valley and a second push in the Bay Area. With almost a month remaining in the primary campaign, he had already driven approximately 8,000 miles and delivered almost 1,000 speeches. Back on the road in the first week of August, he made his third appearance in Los Angeles and the southern counties and, after a hurried trip to Sacramento, concluded his campaign in San Francisco.[73]

Johnson almost always drew enthusiastic audiences to hear his scheduled addresses. Invariably, he focused on a single theme: to kick William Herrin and the Southern Pacific out of California politics. It proved an effective theme, and he rarely complied with those who urged him to alter his focus, to move from attack to an elaboration of reform ideals. That was not his style, as he bore in on the Southern Pacific and its allies with the same fury with which he had attacked the bigamist Collins and the bribe-taker Ruef, taunting his Republican opponents for their failure to address the issue. The contest, he insisted, was one between the people and the privileged, and it was the outrage of the people on which he built his hopes. Decency and honesty confronted the "poisoned press" and "your big banker, your big merchant, sinning respectability joining hands with the criminal and the thug."[74] Disclaiming any attack on property, calling out as well for the support of the worker and organized labor, he sought to blur class divisions even as he appealed to them. He professed his Republican credentials but made it clear that he was an "insurgent Republican"—in the style of La Follette, of Iowa's Jonathan Dolliver, and of Indiana's Albert Beveridge—and a partisan of Theodore Roosevelt. It was a "bully fight" he acknowledged at one of his gatherings, echoing Roosevelt over the roar of applause and appreciative laughter that erupted. Taft, whose administration had quickly disenchanted progressive enthusiasts, went unmentioned.[75]

Both Johnson and the Lincoln-Roosevelt League won substantial victories in the primary election of mid-August. In the race Johnson secured the Republican nomination with 101,000 votes, almost twice the number cast for Charles Curry, his closest competitor. Curry, California's longtime secretary of state, had unsuccessfully sought out the support of both the Lincoln-Roosevelt League and the Southern Pacific. Alden Anderson, state superintendent of banks and the putative candidate of the railroad, trailed badly, receiving little more than 38,000 votes, while Philip Stanton, the Assembly speaker and favorite of the *Los Angeles Times*, limped far in the rear. The league enjoyed huge success, winning all but one of the statewide races; securing the nominations of William Kent and William Stephens as candidates to the House of Representatives and, more narrowly, the endorsement of John D. Works for the United States Senate; and, in the Assembly and state Senate races, winning strongly in the southern part of the state and making gains in the north.[76] The first battle had been won.

*   *   *

With its August primary victories in hand, the Lincoln-Roosevelt League once again demonstrated its effectiveness when the Republican State Convention met in San Francisco in September to hammer out the platform and select new party officers. During the primary campaign the party's Old Guard, in control of the State Central Committee, had sought to embarrass league candidates by calling for an endorsement of Taft, condemning insurgency, and demanding that all prospective candidates for the Republican nomination commit themselves in advance to support the full party slate. At the San

Francisco meeting the league quickly displaced the Old Guard and secured control of the party machinery, electing Chester Rowell as temporary chairman and Meyer Lissner as head of the new State Central Committee.

Unwilling to break completely with Taft and the national administration, the new majority made it clear that insurgency had its blessing. They cheered the mention of Theodore Roosevelt and applauded Gifford Pinchot, the onetime head of the Forest Service whom Taft had fired for insubordination. Pinchot had campaigned actively in behalf of Johnson and the league. Addressing national issues, they called on the state's representatives in Congress "to join with the progressive forces" and work for the passage of constitutional amendments to pave the way for an income tax and the direct election of senators. They pledged themselves to tariff protection for California's agricultural and industrial interests while calling too for the establishment of a tariff commission and a reform of the rate-making process. Turning to statewide issues, they both endorsed the progressive bills that had been beaten back in the 1909 legislative session and added to that agenda, defining a platform that was far and away one of the most advanced of its time.*

Now in control of the party, California's Republican progressives moved to secure control of the state. Once again, the coming battle would revolve around Johnson and the race for the governorship, for if a majority of California voters were Republican in most political contests they were less wedded to that party when it came to the selection of their governor. Although able to hold the office after 1898, the party's grasp was at best uncertain. In 1902 the Republican George Pardee, running well behind his party ticket, narrowly squeaked to victory over his Democratic challenger Franklin K. Lane, and in 1906 James Gillett was elected to the office only be-

---

*Specifically, the platform called for a variety of measures to undermine both party and machine control of California politics: the elimination of the party circle on ballots and the establishment of a nonpartisan judiciary, the initiative, the referendum, the recall, the short ballot, and a merit system. As a part of their campaign for direct democracy they called too for woman suffrage. In addition, the platform endorsed the establishment of an effective state railroad commission with the power to determine the physical valuation of railroad holdings, a public service commission to regulate the rates of all public utilities, prison reform, an employer liability act, and a "square deal for labor." Obligatory was the condemnation of Asian immigration. See Franklin Hichborn, *Story of the Session of the California Legislature of 1911* (San Francisco, 1911), pp. xiv–xxiv; George Mowry, *The California Progressives* (Berkeley, 1951), p. 131.

cause William Langdon, running as the candidate of William Randolph Hearst's newly created Independence League, and Theodore Bell, the Democratic hopeful, split the vote, thus allowing Republican success.

Theodore Bell, unopposed in the Democratic party primary in 1910, had fought the 1906 contest in opposition to both Hearst and the Southern Pacific. Continuing to identify himself as a reformer, he sought to prevent Johnson from monopolizing that label. But the political dynamics had changed in the four years since 1906. No longer backing an independent ticket, Hearst had returned to the Democratic party to become Bell's ally, and Bell's main chance for success in the general election depended on his ability to woo Republican conservatives frightened by Johnson's shrillness.

Bell assumed a posture of moderation, professing his progressivism while promising a "square deal to all." In so doing, he immediately opened himself to Johnson's charge that he gave only lip service to reform while seeking to placate the very interests he denounced. Bell had condemned Hearst in 1906, Johnson reminded his audience, but now welcomed his support. And if he could "crawl to Hearst" he could also crawl to Herrin and the Southern Pacific.[77] His promise of a "square deal for all" was little more than a platitude. "No just man would do otherwise," Johnson replied. "But no sane man would sit up all night figuring out a square deal for William F. Herrin and the Southern Pacific; they would take that and a great deal more without his valuable assistance."[78] Johnson's attacks had sting; they also brought results. Forced to choose between the two candidates, both the railroad and its associates made it clear that they favored Bell. Indeed, to James D. Phelan, onetime mayor of San Francisco and a fellow Democrat, it appeared that Bell had willingly affiliated with the railroad and its machine.[79]

As in the primary race, Johnson's campaign in the general election was as much a demonstration of his physical endurance as of his oratorical skills. On September 20, beginning near the Oregon border, he swept southward to Sacramento, circled east through the small foothill towns of the Sierras, then west and down the San Joaquin Valley. In early October he canvassed Los Angeles and San Diego, touring the state's southern counties. After returning north along the coast, stopping wherever crowds gathered, he rested a day in San Francisco, then sailed up the Sacramento River aboard a river steamer chartered for the purpose. From Sacramento he again took to the road, storming through the lower valley before returning to the Bay Area on October 13 for his first major address in San Francisco at the Dreamland Rink. Almost immediately thereafter, on board the "Johnson-Wallace Flyer," he made his way through the North Bay counties in a whistle-stop tour, crossed once again to the lower Sacramento Valley, then came back to the Bay Area to make speeches in Oakland and San Jose. After canvassing the San Joaquin Valley a second time, he visited Southern California once again, during the last week of October. In early November, as the election date neared, he returned to Sacramento before ending his campaign with a series of addresses in San Francisco.[80]

It was a killing pace. Johnson endured sixteen-hour days and the hoopla of bands, banquets, firecrackers, rockets, steam whistles, and parades. Repeating the theme of his primary campaign, he focused his attack on the Southern Pacific and its associates, drawing Hearst and Bell into its inner circle. Similarly, he continued to identify his campaign with Roosevelt and Republican insurgency. California, he insisted, must keep pace with the movement La Follette had pioneered and Roosevelt preached.[81] Large pictures of Roosevelt often decorated the halls in which Johnson spoke, and the ex-president's recent address at Osawatomie, Kansas, outlining a progressive agenda for a "New Nationalism," won Johnson's eager endorsement.[82] If Johnson hoped for Republican harmony, he made little effort to temper his remarks in order to cultivate it.

Fending off charges by Bell and his supporters that he was no more than an attorney for hire, willing to join the San Francisco graft prosecution for the $10,000 fee guaranteed by Spreckels but equally willing to lend his talents to the railroad or to the most notorious of embezzlers if the price were right, sidestepping the charges voiced by Republican dissidents that he was in reality a Democrat in disguise, Johnson won the governorship in the November 8th election. His large majorities in Los Angeles and the state's southern counties easily offset his more narrow losses to Bell in the Sacramento Valley and the foothills. Overall, his tally of 177,191, little more than 22,000 over Bell's, was almost 35,000 less than the total Republican gubernatorial vote cast in the primary election. Clearly, some Republicans had followed the advice of the *Los Angeles Times* to vote for those of the party whose orthodoxy could stand scrutiny, but not for the unworthy, the "false Republicans, Taft-hating Republicans."[83]

In the aftermath of the election, Johnson traveled east to confer with Roosevelt in New York and La Follette in Washington. Doubtless discussions centered on the hope that Taft could be displaced in 1912, and early in 1911 Johnson's name appeared as one of the charter members of the National Progressive Republican League to achieve that end. But of necessity, the primary task at hand lay in California—to realize the promises that progressives had so stridently voiced. During Johnson's absence in the east, Meyer Lissner, working with the newly reorganized Republican State Central Committee, sought to lay the legislative groundwork for that task by appointing a string of committees to prepare the agenda for the 1911 session. Reports were to be made the week before the opening of the session at a general conference, open to all, scheduled to meet in San Francisco.[84]

Johnson quickly made plain his displeasure with the scheme once he returned to the state. He had been pushed to assume leadership of the California progressives. Having accepted the responsibility, he now insisted upon the role. He pouted throughout the San Francisco conference, demonstrating his irritation by refusing to sit next to Lissner, and in later references to the event wrote sarcastically of "your famous San Francisco Conference."[85] Yet if Johnson's behavior reflected his acute sensitivity to any perceived slight, it reflected also an awareness of the limited effectiveness of the conference plan. "Nothing occurred that could be regarded as serious inharmony," acknowledged Franklin Hichborn, a sympathetic observer; but it was clear as well that there was no unity of purpose. Left to drift, the committees had too often compromised in formulating their recommendations. "Five days before the Legislature was to convene," Hichborn concluded, "the Progressives were without definite plan of action or recognized leadership . . . they were in doubt over some policies, and in a temper to divide over others."[86]

★   ★   ★

In early January 1911, forgoing any form of pageantry, Johnson walked with intentional Jeffersonian restraint the few blocks from his Sacramento hotel to the state Capitol to take the oath of office and deliver his first inaugural. A new era in California began as he outlined the tasks that lay ahead and demonstrated not only his willingness but his determination to lead. For Johnson, the problem was clear: "In some form or other nearly every governmental problem that involves the health, the happiness, or the prosperity of the State has arisen, because some private interest has intervened or has sought for its own gain to exploit either the resources or the politics of the State." The solutions were equally clear: to remove those in power who had shown themselves willing to serve private interests at the expense of the public; to establish within the state the necessary regulatory agencies capable of preventing abuses in the marketplace; and to create new mechanisms that would enable the public to oversee the political process.[87]

Johnson's inaugural address reiterated the platform pledges that had been announced earlier by Republican progressives when they assumed control of the party, but it also gave concreteness and specificity to those promises. Thus in calling for the initiative, referendum, and recall, he made it clear that the recall should include the judiciary—an issue that inflamed conservatives and deeply divided progressive ranks. Similarly, he insisted on the "Oregon plan" for the direct election of senators. Demanding legislation to give teeth to the Railroad Commission, he dismissed the "bogie man of unconstitutionality" that had stymied earlier efforts at reform and called too for an appropriation of $75,000 to enable the commission to begin the task of evaluating the financial worth of railroad properties. The speech touched upon almost all of the pledges included in the party platform. Noting that the Democratic party had more often than not pledged itself to similar goals, Johnson made it clear that they had become "administration measures" and that the legislature would be held accountable for their enactment.*

*The one measure ignored in the inaugural was that of woman suffrage, ironically the measure his father had long ago endorsed. Hiram, ambivalent at best on this proposal, had earlier refused to endorse it and had made no reference to it during the 1910 campaign. Even so, he privately insisted that the party make good its promise to allow voters to decide the issue; on one occasion he whacked the table with his fist to drive home his point. In October 1911 an amendment providing for woman suffrage was approved by a narrow margin. While actively campaigning for other amendments in the October election, he acknowledged that he would personally vote for the measure but voiced no argument in its behalf. It was not easy, Rowell later wrote, for Johnson "to take serious women seriously, especially in politics." Rowell to Katherine Edson, Aug. 29, 1913, Edson Papers; Edward A Dickson, "Susan B. Anthony," Dickson Papers; *Fresno Republican*, Sept. 27, 1914; *San Francisco Bulletin*, Sept. 22, Oct. 6, 1911. See also *Pacific Outlook*, Jan. 28, 1911, pp. 2–3, 6–7. Thereafter, Johnson became an active champion of woman suffrage in the 1912 presidential

From the beginning Johnson actively involved himself in the legislative process, letting it be known that he stood ready to rebuke publicly those who did not toe the line. By using his influence to help in the selection of committee chairmen and detailing the outline of proposed legislation in special messages, he gave both energy and direction to the California progressive movement. In fact, so dominant was his sway that at one point he found it necessary to dissociate himself from bills whose sponsors claimed executive sanction, protesting that such designation was appropriate only for those measures that had been included in the party platform.[88]

Under Johnson's determined leadership the state legislature moved with surprising speed, giving overwhelming support to almost all of the administration's proposals and adding many of its own.[89] Johnson withdrew the last-minute appointments of his predecessor, Governor Gillett. Charles Curry and Alden Anderson, whom Gillett had sought to reward following their defeat in the primary, were removed by abolishing the agencies to which they had been appointed. The Stetson-Eshleman bill giving the Railroad Commission the power to fix absolute rates became law; a workmen's compensation measure was passed; and a Conservation Commission was established to undertake a study of the state's resources. The "Oregon plan" for the election of senators was adopted, and the election of the judiciary and of school officials made nonpartisan. To ensure greater efficiency in government operations, a Board of Control was established to oversee and supervise state finances. Appointed to head the new agency was John Francis Neylan, an earnest 25-year-old newspaper reporter from the *San Francisco Bulletin* who had covered Johnson's primary campaign and who had obviously impressed him.[90] In 1913 California became the first state in the nation to submit a comprehensive state budget.

In addition, constitutional amendments were framed to provide for woman suffrage and the initiative, referendum, and recall; to establish an Industrial Accident Board that could implement the recently passed workmen's compensation act; and to reorganize the Railroad Commission as an appointive body with broad powers of

campaign and in his 1916 campaign for the United States Senate. In 1917 one of his first Senate committee assignments was to the Woman Suffrage Committee. But his conversion was less than complete. The entrance of women into the Senate, Johnson wrote in 1930, would lead to the "thorough breakdown and demoralization" of the body. HWJ to Archibald Johnson, Apr. 9, 1930.

control and jurisdiction over all public utilities. The amendments would come before the voters in October. In the meantime Johnson once again took to the stump, actively campaigning for more than three weeks and focusing his energies almost exclusively on the recall of the judiciary. For conservatives, the courts were the bulwark of stability and the defenders of property. Recall seemed little more than an invitation to anarchy. For Johnson, the judiciary represented the "last stand of privilege and corporate aggression." To deny that judges made law, he argued, was nonsense; thus, like other lawmakers, they must be made accountable. President Taft's recent vetoing of the Arizona statehood bill because its proposed constitution included judicial recall prompted Johnson's scorn. Unswerving in his determination, he forcefully championed the progressive concept of popular democracy. Sometimes, he acknowledged, the people make mistakes, "but in the long run they are always right."* Vindicated by the October results, he called a special session of the legislature in November to give legislative substance to the amendments.

In outlining their 1910 platform, California's Republican progressives had given lip service to organized labor but had been deliberately vague in their promises, limiting themselves to an endorsement of President Taft's call for a reexamination of court injunctions in labor disputes and to Roosevelt's earlier pledge of a "square deal" between management and labor. For Republicans such as Harrison Gray Otis, publisher of the *Los Angeles Times*, who was an avowed foe of unionization and a champion of the "open shop," any concession, however ambiguous, was inflammatory, a prescription for ruin. But while Otis distinguished himself by the fervor of his anti-union rhetoric, the substance of his position differed little from that of his progressive rivals in Los Angeles. In July 1910, little more than a month before Johnson's victory in the Republican primary, the pre-

---

* *San Francisco Bulletin*, Sept. 2, 18, 26, Oct. 6, 1911. At times, Johnson seemed carried away by his own enthusiasm. "The man who talks today of checks and balances is talking against popular democracy," he argued before a Berkeley audience. "No man is better able to govern than all others; no man is better in government than any other man." Yet he clearly saw some better able to govern than others, and despite his "Jacksonian" affirmation of the common man, not only accepted but championed the need for expertise in administrative positions. With less flamboyance, Johnson described the recall as an "admonitory and precautionary" device that would not be used once in a decade. See his Palo Alto address, *San Francisco Bulletin*, Oct. 6, 1911. Similarly, in his inaugural address, in which he affirmed the need for the initiative, referendum, and recall, he argued that the very existence of these measures would preclude the necessity of their use.

dominantly progressive Los Angeles city council, characterizing itself as "an honest business government," enacted one of the most
stringent anti-picketing ordinances in the nation in response to the
initiation of an organized campaign to unionize labor in that city. It
seemed an inauspicious beginning to the "square deal" California's
progressives had promised.

Moreover, if Southern California labor had little reason to celebrate the triumph of progressivism in Los Angeles, workers in San
Francisco, far better entrenched than their southern counterparts,
had reasons of their own to distrust California's progressive insurgency. Not all of San Francisco's union spokesmen had endorsed the
Union Labor party, described by one observer as a "medley of the
honest and the corrupt," which had initially evolved independently
of the city's labor leadership. In fact, many prominent union officials
had supported the graft prosecutions of Ruef, Schmitz, and their corporate bribers. Many others, however, saw in the trials an implicit
anti-union animus.[91] In 1907 Patrick McCarthy, powerful head of
the San Francisco Building Trades Council, voiced precisely such a
charge in his unsuccessful bid to become mayor, running as the candidate of the Union Labor party. Two years later, he won that office.
His victory, and the victory of other Union Labor candidates, effectively put an end to any further graft prosecutions in the city.[92]

In his campaign for a continuation of the graft prosecution in
1907, Johnson had argued against McCarthy's charge. The battle being waged, he noted, was not against unions but against their enemies, the corporate interests and their allies who pursued profits at
the expense of morality. William Langdon, the besieged district attorney, he insisted, represented the best of the Union Labor party
and stood as proof that labor could be entrusted with municipal responsibilities. "The union labor man who withholds his vote from
Langdon," he admonished, "is doing himself, his union and his
country a wrong."[93] And such was the text Johnson later repeated in
Francis Heney's unsuccessful 1909 campaign as he continued to focus his wrath on the city's corporate structure. Fighting his own
battle in the Republican primary in 1910, Johnson again courted labor's support. In Sacramento he appealed to "the honest workman,"
the employees of the railroad who constituted "the best citizens . . .
of the whole city," and reached out to "the men that toil with their
hands" as well as to "the great middle class."[94]

Johnson had little difficulty in winning the support of a majority of the "great middle class" in the 1910 election. He was, however, far less successful in blue-collar districts. There, much of labor's rank and file remained indifferent or antagonistic to his candidacy.[95] Even so, he was able to secure the endorsement of some of San Francisco's prominent labor leaders, chief among them Michael Casey and John McLaughlin, president and general secretary of the city's Teamsters' Union. Earlier, Johnson had acted as counsel for the union, beginning an association that bore political fruit in their 1910 endorsement. At McLaughlin's urging, Paul Scharrenberg, soon to become the executive secretary of the California State Federation of Labor, abandoned his Democratic ties to extend Johnson support.[96] Others would follow.

As governor, Johnson quickly cemented his ties with organized labor. He appointed McLaughlin to head the State Bureau of Labor Statistics, and placed Will French, a printer and onetime editor of the *Labor Clarion*, on the newly formed Industrial Accident Board. In time Scharrenberg too was brought on board. While the progressive leadership in Los Angeles shunned labor, Johnson provided the worker with both recognition and a forum in Sacramento. And there was more. Of the 49 measures endorsed by union labor in the 1911 legislative session, Johnson signed 39 into law, some, like the eight-hour day for women and minors in industry, over the strenuous protests of both Lissner and Edwin Earl, the progressive editor of the *Los Angeles Express* and *Los Angeles Tribune*, whose newspapers provided Johnson with one of his few outlets for favorable publicity in that city.[97] "Governor Johnson," the *Seamen's Journal* observed in the aftermath of the 1911 legislative session, "proved himself not only different from but better than any of his predecessors."[98] John Nolan, the Sacramento lobbyist of the San Francisco Labor Council, agreed. Johnson, he wrote, was entitled to and deserved the unanimous support of the state's labor movement.[99]

Nor did the pace of labor legislation slacken in the 1913 session of the state legislature, as Johnson pushed forcefully to strengthen the provisions of the workmen's compensation act of 1911 by requiring mandatory coverage, and demanded a new Industrial Accident Commission both to administer the provisions of the act and to provide the option of state underwriting of coverage. His "uncompromising" stand, Scharrenberg wrote, "should ever endear him to the men and women of labor."[100] In addition, at Johnson's urging, an Industrial Welfare Commission was established to investigate and set wage and working standards for women and children, and a Commission of Immigration and Housing created to facilitate the assimilation of immigrant populations in the state.[101] The goal, Johnson wrote, was to prevent the emergence in California of the "dreadful conditions of poverty" that prevailed in the cities on the East Coast—a threat that seemed increasingly probable with the imminent opening of the Panama Canal, which was expected to increase immigration from abroad.[102]

Organized labor's endorsement of Johnson added to the stridency of Harrison Gray Otis's accusatory rhetoric. The Johnson administration, the *Los Angeles Times* concluded, represented little more than an oligarchy of labor hoodlums and thugs bent upon the destruction of private property. From so bitter a critic, such diatribes were to be expected. In truth, they could almost be relished. If the *Times* ever found reason to praise him or his administration, Johnson observed, his whole world would be called into question. But if Otis and the *Times* could be ignored or openly denounced, divisions within progressive ranks could not. Here Johnson found himself buffeted not only by the Los Angeles wing of progressivism, which too often, as Rowell observed, defined their movement in businessmen's terms, but also by Fremont Older, who faulted Johnson for his failure to assume an even more activist posture in support of the worker.[103] Johnson was not always able to define a program to which all could subscribe and was especially irritated by those who sought to outflank him on the left. His goal, he complained, was "sane legislation" that would mute social discontent, not aggravate class division, while Older and those around him too often pushed for "extremes no sane man could justify."[104] Working to retain the support of labor and genuinely sympathetic to working class grievances, Johnson sought also to maintain some semblance of unity among the various factions that constituted the progressive coalition. It was rarely easy.

Factional discord most often erupted when the question focused not on humanitarian legislation to protect labor from abuse within the workplace but on the relationship between capital and labor, a far more fundamental issue. Like reformers elsewhere in the nation, the bulk of California progressives sought to provide safeguards for individual workers, not to enhance the power of organized labor, and while Johnson identified more closely with unions than with their enemies, he was careful to maintain his independence from both camps. Thus in 1911 he remained publicly aloof from the effort endorsed by many progressives to require the arbitration of labor disputes in public service industries. The bill, although it would not prevent strikes or lockouts, would delay their implementation until after a public review. Organized labor saw the proposal as a first step in a general campaign for compulsory arbitration of all labor disputes, and it was defeated in the legislature. The continuous efforts by organized labor to secure protection against the injunctive power of the courts in the 1911, 1913, and 1915 legislative sessions also failed. Enactment of such legislation, Meyer Lissner warned Johnson in urging him to sidetrack the 1911 measure, would destroy the progressive movement in Los Angeles.[105] Whether in fact Johnson was instrumental in the bill's defeat remains moot. Clearly, as with the arbitration bill, he refused to identify himself with it.

Yet Johnson could not always escape the animus between capital and labor that rumbled uneasily below the surface of California's maturing economy. In October 1910, little more than a month before his election as governor, the conflict had quite literally exploded with the dynamiting of the *Los Angeles Times* building. Twenty-one employees were killed in the blast. The following year labor unions rallied to the defense of John J. McNamara, secretary of the International Association of Bridge and Structural Iron Workers, and his brother James, both accused of the outrage. The unions charged a "frame-up," only to hear the brothers confess their guilt. It was a body blow for organized labor not only in California but throughout the nation. In Los Angeles the affair scarred both unions and the left, blunting the initiative of each.

Elsewhere in the state, among the unorganized and disaffected, unrest found expression in the revolutionary rhetoric of the Industrial Workers of the World. Appealing especially to the seasonal agricultural workers of California's large corporate farms, the IWW staged a series of "free speech" battles throughout the state between 1909 and 1913. They voiced incendiary rhetoric, invited arrest, and clogged the jails in the course of their campaign to demonstrate the irreconcilability of class divisions in a capitalistic society.[106] IWW members, more often the victims of violence than its architects, almost invariably prompted vigilante reprisals on the local level, and the organization gained a notoriety far in excess of its numbers, most especially in the wake of a riot in August 1913 protesting labor conditions at the Durst ranch near Wheatland, California, in which four participants were killed.[107]

Johnson's immediate response to the Wheatland riot was to dispatch units of the National Guard to police the area. One of government's central responsibilities, he insisted, was to protect life and property against disorder and the threat of intimidation and violence.[108] At the same time, however, he also insisted that a free society included the right of dissent and a just society necessitated the elimination of conditions that nurtured disaffection. Thus, in 1912 he authorized Harris Weinstock and Attorney General U. S. Webb to investigate the denial of constitutional rights in the wake of the San Diego IWW free speech fight, and in 1913 requested the Commission of Immigration and Housing to investigate the causes of the Wheatland riot. Both inquiries led to scathing indictments of the existing order.[109]

Convinced that the Wheatland disruption evolved out of the unsanitary conditions and inadequate housing afforded workers in California agriculture and that the unionization of agricultural workers was an impossibility, the commission undertook an extensive examination of labor camps throughout the state. It lacked the power to set or enforce regulations. Even so, it worked to define new standards and succeeded in securing some remedial change. But, as commission members argued, at the root of the problem was the very structure of California agriculture—"factories in the field" as one critic later observed—reliant on armies of migratory workers who lacked ties to the community, sustaining a social order that prevented the development of any real community. Inspired by an alternative vision, the commission members successfully pressed Johnson to endorse the creation of a Commission on Land Colonization and Rural Credits in the 1915 legislative session.[110] The new commission, pushed by Elwood Mead and Harris Weinstock, recommended that steps be initiated to reverse the concentration of landownership in California agriculture, but save for two pilot pro-

jects begun at the end of Johnson's term to demonstrate the feasibility of a less exploitive system, little was accomplished.[111]

*   *   *

In 1911 Johnson and the California legislature captured the attention of progressives throughout the nation—in no other state had so
bold a set of reforms been put into place in so short a span of time.
Two years later, in 1913, brushing aside the warnings of President
Woodrow Wilson, they galvanized a far larger audience by provoking
an international crisis with Japan. At issue was the effort to limit
the property rights of Japanese alien residents in the state by prohibiting their ownership of agricultural land, an effort that rested on
the economic fears of the state's farmers and on an entrenched anti-
Asian prejudice in the West that traced its roots to earlier times.[112]
It was a prejudice Johnson shared, although not one that he initially
sought to exploit. He was convinced that the state had the right to
discriminate in such matters, but agreed with Chester Rowell's observation that there was no urgency in pushing the issue.* Adding

* *California Outlook*, Apr. 26, 1913, pp. 5–6. The problem with the Japanese,
Johnson noted, was that they could not, or would not, assimilate into American society. HWJ to Roland Morris, Jan. 21, 1921. Whether he saw this as a racial "flaw," an
act of prideful defiance, or a condition shaped by white nativist prejudice remains
less clear. Johnson was by no means free of other prejudices reflective of his class and
background. In his mind, Jews were more often than not covetous and assertive, and
blacks indolent and slothful; but in both instances, he was drawn to environmental
explanations. Thus Jews were the victims of past injustices whose behavior had been
shaped by generations of discrimination. Johnson's anti-Semitism was largely uncon-
scious and unexplored and never publicly expressed; and clearly it did not prevent
him from working intimately with Meyer Lissner, Harris Weinstock, Simon Lubin,
or, in the early 1920s, Albert Lasker. But it did, in part, define his perceptions and in
rare instances soured them. When vacationing in Atlantic City in 1921, he was re-
pelled by the sight of "short, swarthy men [and] squatty, dumpy women." They talked
in foreign tongues and made him feel almost a stranger in a foreign land. There was
no need for a Zionist movement, he concluded. "Time, just as certain as it passes,
will make this country theirs." HWJ to boys, Sept. 10, 1921. See also HWJ to boys,
Oct. 1, 1921. Johnson's attitude toward black Americans would itself undergo trans-
formation as he assumed residence in Washington, a Southern city. Perhaps sharing
the abolitionist views of his grandfather (and of Grove himself, as far as can be determined), he had strongly objected to the overtly racist message of *Birth of a Nation*,
D. W. Griffith's 1915 film masterpiece, though he marveled at its technique. But once
in Washington, he began to make a distinction between the Northern and Southern
Negro, and found his prejudices confirmed by the behavior of the latter. Lissner to
HWJ, May 17, 1915; HWJ to Hiram Johnson, Jr., May 12, Dec. 7, 1918; HWJ to Archibald Johnson, July 25, 1918; HWJ to Amy Johnson, Aug. 31, 1918; HWJ to boys,

to his caution was the need to prevent any controversy that might threaten the success of San Francisco's 1915 International Exposition, planned to celebrate the opening of the Panama Canal. Thus, in his 1910 campaign, Johnson refused to reply when Hearst and the Democratic party branded him as pro-Japanese, and in the 1911 legislative session he worked effectively to sidetrack discriminatory legislation. Though unable to prevent passage of a bill in the State Senate, he managed to keep it from the floor of the Assembly.[113]

But there was political gain in exploiting anti-Asian prejudice on the West Coast, and in 1912, as in 1910, California Democrats sought to reap those benefits. Their target was Theodore Roosevelt, who, with Hiram Johnson as his running mate, had become Woodrow Wilson's chief rival in the 1912 presidential contest. Democratic party enthusiasts lashed out shrilly against Roosevelt's 1907 intercession to end Japanese discrimination in San Francisco's public schools and condemned his "Gentlemen's Agreement," put in place that same year, which altered but did not end the flow of Japanese immigration into the United States. Obviously wounded by the assaults, Roosevelt squeaked to a narrow victory in California. Wilson, Johnson observed, had almost captured the state by actively identifying himself with the anti-Japanese animus.[114]

Whether Johnson would continue to sidestep so politically popular an issue remained unclear. With the opening of the legislative session in 1913, he once again cautioned against any action but refused to tie himself down. He would not sponsor any anti-Japanese legislation, he informed a visiting delegation from the San Francisco Exposition, but could not promise what he would do if bills were presented in the legislature.[115] Predictably, as in 1911, bills prohib-

---

Oct. 29, 1921. Yet if Johnson was not free of cultural and racial prejudices, he exploited them only in one case, that of the Japanese. "I have no pride in Anglo-Saxon descent," he publicly observed. Such observations undeniably served the political purpose of strengthening his hold on San Francisco in a period in which cultural intolerance was rife nationwide; nevertheless they seem genuinely felt. Catholic, Protestant, and Jewish children of immigrants, he affirmed, could, and often did, become "the very best citizens." Throughout the 1920s Johnson remained steadfast in his opposition to the "national origins" scheme incorporated into the immigration legislation of the period. *Cong. Record,* 71st Cong., 2nd sess. (Apr. 25, 1930), p. 7710; U.S. Cong., Senate Committee on Immigration, *National Origins Provisions of Immigration Law, Hearings,* S.J. Res. 192, 70th Cong., 2nd sess. (1929), p. 90; HWJ to C. K. McClatchy, June 24, 1929.

iting Japanese aliens from owning land in California were indeed presented as the session began. By mid-March, sensing that some form of legislation was inevitable, Johnson began to work behind the scenes to eliminate any discriminatory features based upon race, pressing for a general bill applicable to all aliens. Initially optimistic, he found his efforts thwarted when the Assembly accepted the principle of Asian discrimination by a vote of 60–15, and the Senate, on which he had pinned his hopes, bowed under the pressure from European investment interests and followed the Assembly lead.[116]

As the legislation moved forward it became obvious to both Johnson and Wilson that a bill discriminating against Japanese aliens would be forthcoming. At first hesitant to act, Wilson had privately cautioned California's leadership against such a measure but had publicly stood aloof. He could not, he affirmed, interfere in the state's legislative process.[117] But on April 22, less than two months into his presidency, as Japanese protests mounted and both nations talked of war, Wilson dispatched Secretary of State William Jennings Bryan to California in an effort to defuse what was rapidly becoming a major international crisis. Whether the move was a symbolic act to mollify Japanese sensibilities or a genuine effort undertaken on the assumption that the legislature might be persuaded to reverse itself remains unclear. Certainly Bryan brought with him no new proposals, no inducements save his authority as an administration spokesman and his own personality.[118]

Nevertheless, it seems clear that if Bryan and Johnson had worked together the legislation could have been stopped. But Johnson was not about to cooperate with a Democratic administration that had stressed its anti-Japanese purity in 1912, nor was he willing to dilute the authority he exercised as governor. Instead, he moved to assert that authority by preparing a substitute bill that made minor textual concessions in wording while endorsing the principle of racial discrimination. The measure, the so-called Webb-Heney bill, was introduced on the second day of Bryan's visit, and Johnson marshaled the support necessary for its passage. Responding to Bryan's protestations before a closed session of the legislature in a brief, pungent summary, Johnson insisted that the question was not whether Japan would be offended by the action the state proposed but whether it would be "justly" offended.[119] But Bryan's appeal had made an impact. Democrats, persuaded by his efforts, and conservatives, less convinced of the need for immediate action and frightened by the developing crisis, moved to prevent the bill from reaching the floor.

In the end they failed when Johnson, rallying his supporters, reached out to derail their efforts. Many, he observed, followed his lead only out of personal loyalty.[120] Yet once it became clear that the alien-land bill could not be kept from the floor, almost all fell into line. In the Assembly the vote was 72 to 3; in the Senate 35 to 2.[121] Reflecting on the outcome, Johnson expressed both political and personal satisfaction. In addition to the merits of the legislation, he wrote, "it was the most fortunate thing that ever occurred from a political standpoint."[122] And he could not help but take a "malicious pleasure" in turning the tables on Wilson, revealing the hypocrisy of his state-rights posture and the vacuity of his past political demagoguery.[123] It was not Johnson's finest hour—nor was it Wilson's.

★   ★   ★

Developing the mechanics of popular democracy, enhancing the regulatory power of the state, curbing abuses in the workplace, and ensuring greater efficiency and economy in governmental operations were among the lasting contributions progressives achieved in California during Johnson's governorship. In each of these areas the problem revolved around special privilege and the need to check the abuse of power, and in each of these areas Johnson played an active, at times decisive role, focusing public attention on the ills that confronted society and identifying himself and his administration with their solutions. In yet another area of progressive concern, public morality, the issues were often more ambiguous and the solutions less clear. In 1911 Johnson signed bills to forbid racetrack gambling and to eliminate slot machines. In an effort to curb prostitution, a red-light abatement law was passed in 1913. Yet while Johnson shared the moral values upon which these efforts rested, he played no part in initiating such legislation and made little effort to identify his administration with it.[124]

In addition to being clearly more tolerant of social diversity than many of his progressive peers, Johnson was skeptical of the results that could be achieved through such legislation and always alert to the inherent political dangers involved. Similarly, he sought to distance himself from the temperance and prohibitionist sentiment that characterized part of the state's progressive movement. A moderate wet, he accepted the local option bill passed by the legislature in 1911 but refused to take any stand on the far more restrictive initiative measures endorsed by prohibitionists and their allies that went down to defeat in 1914 and 1916. "You can not make people be good faster than they want to be good," he once wrote.[125] But prohibitionists and their temperance allies continued to push, and in 1917, in his first year as a United States senator, Johnson found himself unable to escape what he characterized as the "infernal prohibition question."

Newly garbed in the patriotic buntings of wartime, prohibitionists moved successfully to secure a "bone dry" amendment in the House version of the Food Control Act that would prohibit the manufacture of all alcoholic beverages. Johnson was willing to outlaw the production of hard liquor, but hoped that nondistilled products would remain unaffected. To this end he joined with the Senate majority to modify the legislation by giving to the president discretionary control over the production of beer and wine.[126] Yet no sooner had the matter been disposed of than it reappeared in the demand for congressional passage of the Eighteenth Amendment.

Once again Johnson worked to limit the scope of prohibition, supporting an unsuccessful effort to substitute the term "distilled" for "intoxicating" and endorsing the provision requiring state ratification of the amendment within six years. The liquor interests, he wrote, were all but convinced that they could prevent ratification with such a requirement. Tempted to vote against final passage of the proposed amendment, certain that California's rejection of the initiative measures of 1914 and 1916 would justify the logic of such a stand, aware too that whatever position he took, the political costs would outweigh any possible benefits, Johnson remained undecided until the end. "Damn the liquor question," he exploded.[127]

At last, unwilling, as he wrote, to resort to holding his nose, "gagging, and voting with . . . the small unsavory crew who represent liquor," he agreed to accept the prohibition amendment. He had, he added, never yet flunked on a moral issue.[128] But in what he confessed was a "specious" public explanation, he sought again to sidestep the substance of that issue, arguing that the question was not prohibition, on which he expressed no opinion, but popular rule, and that he would willingly submit to the people any proposal for which there was a genuine demand.[129] Clearly, the effort to discipline the moral behavior of society was, for Johnson, less than compelling. A moral man but not a religious one, he willingly characterized himself as an "old fogey" as traditional standards of behavior began visibly to give way during and after World War I, but confined his occasional laments to his letters.*

* * *

Both the contours and the substance of California's progressive movement clearly bore the imprint of Hiram Johnson's personality. Old-fashioned in his values, at times limited in his vision, he accepted the basic structure of the social and economic order that had evolved during his lifetime in the wake of the nation's industrial revolution; but he also insisted that the power of the few be harnessed and made socially responsible. Too often he viewed his world as a simple contest between a corrupt few and the decent majority, for he was a sentimentalist by nature. Though intellectually quick, he was neither intellectually curious nor overly impressed by those who were. His interests lay in the concrete, not the abstract. He was intrigued by history—his heroes, perhaps significantly, were Lincoln and Napoleon—but more often he sought diversion in motion pictures and mystery novels. He had, he acknowledged, a "vitiated" literary taste.[130] A skilled poker player, he enjoyed an evening of cards, and in his first years in Washington joined the circle that included Philander Knox, Warren Harding, Joseph Frelinghuysen and Frederick Hale, all members of the Old Guard but companionable

*Was there not "a reversion of the race," he asked, complaining of the eagerness of women to attend the Dempsey-Carpentier heavyweight bout in 1921. "When I think of the transition from my younger days, when no woman would have dared either drink or smoke, to this era, when there is scarcely a young girl who dare not both drink and smoke, I know there has been some subtle change in womanhood. . . . I prefer the womanhood of old to the non-child-bearing, smoking, drinking, and neurotic creatures sitting at the ringside." HWJ to Hiram Johnson, Jr., July 2, 1921. In response to the "Fatty" Arbuckle case he noted, "I am unable to find anybody upon the screen or even upon the stage who hasn't been divorced several times, and who does not lead a rotten lecherous life. I wonder if there can ever come a readjustment." It was a wonder, he continued, how an "All-wise Providence can tolerate them"; but in writing of an "All-wise Providence" he was reminded of Arthur Brisbane's observation, "If camels had a god they would imagine him to have four legs and a hump." HWJ to Hiram Johnson, Jr., Sept. 17, 1921. See also HWJ to Raymond Robins, June 30, 1921; HWJ to C. K. McClatchy, Oct. 5, 1921. For Johnson's less than favorable review of Eugene O'Neill's *Strange Interlude*, see HWJ to Archibald Johnson, Dec. 24, 1928. The play, he remarked, was "prurient and rotten," and should have been "enacted in a lavatory, a tessellated lavatory, with exceedingly bright lights, red predominating." Perhaps, he continued, he was too old, too conventional, too narrow, to enjoy a presentation that was "vile, and vicious, erotic and degenerate on the stage."

nevertheless. He felt happiest at home, where he found the "warmth and contentment" that had eluded him in his own childhood, and both he and his wife sought constantly to protect their privacy.[131]

As an individual Johnson could be brusque and self-righteous, wry and satirical, warm and sympathetic. But no matter his mood, he was always candid and direct in his personal contacts, preferring the spontaneity of informal public encounters to the predictability of formal public gatherings. Whenever possible, he sought to avoid presiding at ceremonial events, choosing to delegate that task to others. As governor he demonstrated consummate political skills both in his mastery of the legislative process and in his relationship with the public, revealing an acute sensitivity to the pulse of both. He accepted too the need for expertise in government and drew freely on the energies of others, shaping a political structure far different from that which he had inherited. He both recognized and rewarded the talents of others, and his administration would have been far less impressive without the active involvement and contributions of those he appointed to positions of power.

But if others helped shaped the outlines and contributed to the success of his administration, Johnson remained at its center, determining its pace and direction, investing his energies, his emotions, his total self in California's progressive cause. He is not a "philosopher," acknowledged the *California Outlook*, unofficial organ of the insurgent forces; "he is a fighter, a crusader and an administrator."[132] As a fighter Johnson could be blunt, confronting his enemies in impassioned and accusatory rhetoric, but he was rarely impulsive, and almost always sought the advice and counsel of others, honing his understanding of the issues in the midst of free debate and discussion among his close political advisors.[133] Chester Rowell, a frequent participant in strategy sessions and certainly the most "intellectual" of the group, described Johnson as prudent and circumspect, willing to argue the conservative side of issues under discussion, and loath to accept programs that might be expensive to maintain. "You, with all your radical reputation, will be the most severely conservative and perhaps obstructive critic of the radical propositions made by us with less radical reputations," Rowell once chided Johnson.[134] But as Johnson made clear, once a debate had ended, he would make the final decision and others were expected to fall into line.

Johnson both relished and resented the political demands made upon him. By nature high-strung, competitive, and easily bored, he found in public life the excitement and applause he had earlier experienced as a lawyer in the courtroom, and he readily admitted that it fed his ego. There was as well, he stressed, a sense of accomplishment that could be found nowhere else.[135] But politics meant sacrifice of the far larger income he could earn as a lawyer and an end to the privacy both he and his wife cherished. It meant personal abuse, and although Johnson, like his father, excelled in ad hominem invective, like his father too, he was extraordinarily thin-skinned and sensitive to the personal attacks by his enemies. Moreover, politics always threatened the possibility of failure.

Even while savoring victory, Johnson was fearful of defeat and always ready to predict it. He confronted each election in a state of nervous agitation and invariably exaggerated the size of the obstacles to be overcome and the malevolence of his opponents. "Prophesying results of elections in which your own interests are concerned is absolutely the only question in life in which your judgment uniformly without a single exception has been mistaken," Rowell once reminded the gloomy governor.[136] He fretted continuously and was often sleepless before a major speech, unsure of his own ability to meet the test. Clearly he was not a happy warrior. Adding to his anxiety was his need for reassurance and his almost compulsive need to distance himself from the taint of his father and to prove both to himself and to others the probity of his intentions. An ambitious man, he worried lest he be seen as such. "You always scrutinize with extreme care and accept with the greatest caution any suggestion in accordance with your own desire," an associate complained, while "you give full faith to those who say your duty lies counter to your inclinations."[137] Given Johnson's temperament, it is clear why Rowell could often find him testy and cantankerous, swept by unpredictable moods that seemed to appear and disappear without reason.[138]

But in public Johnson gave no hint of doubt or indecision, projecting himself instead with both vigor and determination. "My only method of doing politics has been to state what I want to do and then, with a club, go out and endeavor to put it over," he once explained. Indeed it was on the political stump that he was most effective.[139] A rapid speaker, he crisply enunciated each word while outdistancing reporters who attempted verbatim notes. His somewhat high-pitched and occasionally rasping voice had a power that gripped his audience. On the stage he stood his ground, rarely bending or swaying his body, while emphasizing his points with emphatic gestures. His most characteristic move was a downward drive with his right arm and upraised fist.[140] "To hear him speak is to believe in his fundamental honesty and in the sincerity with which he takes his stand and advocates his beliefs," Oswald Garrison Villard reported.[141] Commenting on his exhortative manner, Chester Rowell discovered in Johnson an intense terror of boring any part of his audience or of releasing them, even for a moment, from the high tension to which they had been roused. Johnson used words as weapons and played upon his audience "as a great master plays on the organ."[142] His political gatherings characteristically generated the enthusiasm of a religious revival. Observing one such occasion, Edmund Norton wrote: "I have sensed a moral fervor fusing the assemblies into almost a spiritual frenzy for a few seconds; a mass-phenomenon rarely . . . witnessed outside of religious meetings."[143]

And it was precisely on the spiritual intensity he unleashed that Johnson built his hopes for the good society, for at the root of his progressivism was his conviction that if the bulk of his audience understood the plight of others they could be led to transcend their immediate self-interests and would, as he did, sympathize and respond. On the most fundamental of levels, Johnson sought the conversion of a people. His greatest asset, one observer wrote, was his impatience with injustice. His goal was to infect others with that same impatience.[144]

Chapter II

Armageddon and Back

The Politics of Progressivism
1912–1916

Initially, William Howard Taft, Roosevelt's handpicked successor, had seemed the guarantee that progressive policies would be carried forward at the national level, and in 1908 California's insurgent Republicans had rallied to his support. But by 1910 progressive faith in Taft had all but collapsed. Deficient in political skills, lacking Roosevelt's energy and magnetic appeal, unable to manage a party increasingly torn by its competing factions, the president instinctively drifted to the right, where he found himself most at home. Almost invariably his efforts to mute party divisions were counterproductive. In 1911, in an attempt to repair his declining fortunes prior to his 1912 reelection bid, he undertook a cross-country tour that brought him to California in mid-October. For California's progressives the visit did little more than confirm their existing doubts.

Hiram Johnson met Taft as his train entered the state and accompanied him throughout most of his California tour. He introduced him at his Sacramento appearance, joined with him in the groundbreaking ceremonies in San Francisco for the Panama-Pacific Exposition, and attended a banquet in his honor in Los Angeles. But their relations were frosty at best, contrasting sharply with the reception Johnson had extended to Roosevelt when the Colonel had visited the state in March of that same year. Then, both Johnson and Roosevelt had been profuse in the warmth of their mutual compliments. During Taft's stay, only the barest of formalities were exchanged.[1]

Throughout, Johnson complained, Taft "elbowed aside" progressives to surround himself with the Old Guard. Observing the president's performance, Johnson was not impressed: "I heard much about dollars and material prosperity and business. I never heard a single syllable of sympathy with human beings." There was, he added, "never any indication that [Taft] was governing for any but one class and for one purpose: business."[2] Clearly, Johnson and his associates would look elsewhere for their 1912 presidential choice.

For many, Oyster Bay, Theodore Roosevelt's home, was the most obvious place to look, and Johnson was not alone in urging the ex-president to enter the race. But the Colonel remained adamant in his refusals and cautioned against any move to draft him for the office. Although disappointed by Taft's record, he declined to run.[3] For California's progressive leadership, unwilling as they were to remain inactive, there thus seemed no alternative but to rally behind Robert La Follette, who had announced his own candidacy the previous June. Indeed, it was clear that if they did not act, others would. In late October, Rudolph Spreckels, never one to wait for others, had already sent out a call to organize a California conference in support of La Follette.

Irritated by this action, which trespassed on their own control in the state, Johnson and his associates quickly moved to take command of the La Follette campaign. They called their own conference, thus sabotaging Spreckels's, and on November 25, 1911, at a meeting in San Francisco, the California La Follette League was born with Chester Rowell as its temporary chairman. The die seemed cast, yet doubts remained. None questioned La Follette's progressive credentials, but few believed he could win the Republican presidential nomination. For most, La Follette was the available choice, not the preferred one. "Out of the many men in the movement, all of Presidential size, he is the one and only candidate," Rowell observed in his address before the 600 who gathered at the San Francisco conference. Applause followed, but his remark was as much a lament as a tribute.[4]

Lament gave way to confusion and the possibility of serious political embarrassment in the next six weeks when rumors began to circulate that Roosevelt was reconsidering his earlier decision and might agree to enter the race. Having embraced La Follette, California's progressive leadership suddenly feared that they might be saddled with him. The issue came quickly to a head in mid-January, when Roosevelt invited Johnson to Oyster Bay to discuss the political situation. After a series of hurried conferences, Johnson traveled east, carrying the proxies of his associates and empowered to drop La Follette if circumstances required. It was not a responsibility he relished.[5]

Having first stopped in Chicago to confer with Francis Heney, Johnson arrived in New York, where he closeted himself with Amos and Gifford Pinchot, Gilson Gardner, Medill McCormick, and George Record, all activists in the national progressive movement. Each voiced doubt about La Follette's chances, finding in the Wisconsin senator an idiosyncratic campaigner at best, one too often absent from the hustings and too busy writing his autobiography. His campaign, they agreed, had not caught fire. Indeed, their pessimistic assessment seemed shared by La Follette's own manager, Walter Houser, who, Johnson was told, had urged La Follette to abandon his campaign and enlist with Roosevelt. Still uncertain about whom he would support, Johnson lunched with Roosevelt on February 2 and learned that, in fact, the ex-president had become an active candidate. Still, Johnson remained unwilling to commit himself, wiring home that he would make no endorsement until after he conferred with La Follette the following week. Many in the Roosevelt camp, he added, were not progressives, and he preferred to delay any announcement.[6]

But Johnson's scheduled meeting with La Follette never took place. While speaking before a publishers' dinner in Philadelphia on the evening of Johnson's visit to Oyster Bay, La Follette, worried about his daughter's pending surgery and depressed by rumors of disaffection from his candidacy, lost emotional control. His rambling and repetitive two-hour address, a bitter tirade attacking his audience, would be characterized the following morning as evidence of his "breakdown."[7] To almost all it seemed apparent that his candidacy was at an end. Walter Houser confirmed that assessment when he privately informed a number of La Follette's backers that the senator would withdraw and that they were free to endorse Roosevelt. For many, whose first love had always been the Colonel, the release seemed almost a godsend, and Roosevelt organizations immediately mushroomed. But it soon became apparent that Houser had overstepped himself, and when La Follette insisted on continuing his campaign, Houser denied that he had ever authorized the release. Each side charged bad faith as the progressive movement splintered.[8]

Johnson remained in the East and delayed his own announcement for Roosevelt until February 19, carefully checking with a wide assortment of his California associates before making the move. Few saw any real alternative.[9] A postcard poll of California activists, conducted by Rowell, found a six-to-one majority for the Colonel, and on the same day that Johnson announced his endorsement, Rowell abandoned the La Follette League to call for a statewide meeting to organize the Roosevelt campaign.[10]

Heading the slate of delegates pledged to Roosevelt, Johnson kicked off that campaign less than a week after his return to the state. In a speech to an enthusiastic audience at the Temple Theater in Los Angeles, he lashed out at his favorite enemy, Harrison Gray Otis. The contest, he averred, was the same one that had been fought and won in the 1910 gubernatorial contest and the 1911 campaign for the state constitutional amendments—the battle between economic privilege and the common welfare. The line was once again drawn between progress and reaction. Echoing Roosevelt, he insisted that the nation "must control its big business . . . wealth in this nation must be made the servant of our people." Popular democracy, he added, was a means to that end.[11]

Johnson would repeat the themes of his Los Angeles address in appearances in San Francisco and Sacramento later in the month, but not until April did the campaign begin in earnest. As the contest evolved, its tone changed. Johnson continued to belabor Roosevelt's virtues and Taft's failures—"The child has been neglected, the legislation that was designed for humanity has been given little thought: it has been dollar diplomacy all along the line," he noted of Taft's administration—but increasingly he focused his attention on La Follette, the only Republican hopeful to campaign personally in the state.[12] Convinced that the Wisconsin senator could not possibly win the presidential primary, Johnson worried that divided progressive ranks would enable Taft to squeak to victory. And as Johnson continued to brood, he became increasingly sure that that was precisely La Follette's goal. La Follette had become a spoiler, ego-ridden and intransigent, willing to sacrifice the progressive movement to his own ambitions. He was, Johnson concluded, "totally crooked."[13]

In an effort to bridge progressive divisions rather than compound them, Johnson sought to temper his criticisms and restrain his anger in public; but restraint was not his forte.

Nor did La Follette encourage restraint. With funds provided by Rudolph Spreckels and an abundance of energy all his own, he almost totally ignored Taft in his California campaign to focus his wrath on Roosevelt, pounding hard on the theme that Woodrow Wilson would later repeat in his own contest against the Colonel. Roosevelt, he argued, was a pseudo-progressive. His insistence that big business be regulated and not destroyed made him the ally of the trusts rather than their enemy. Johnson, responding to La Follette with a mixture of anger, ridicule, and contempt, pointed to the political divisions within the state and reminded his audiences that Otis of the *Times*, John Spreckels of the *San Diego Union*, and Michael de Young of the *San Francisco Chronicle*, each solicitous of big business, had chosen Taft, not Roosevelt, as their candidate. La Follette, he charged, was playing the Old Guard's game. Quoting extensively from La Follette's own earlier praise of Roosevelt as a progressive champion, Johnson argued that La Follette had nothing to gain from the California contest save fodder for his own ego and urged progressives to rally to Roosevelt, the one candidate who could make a difference.[14] As the campaign neared its close, Johnson and his associates mobilized additional resources by calling upon Gifford Pinchot, Medill McCormick, and Albert Beveridge to stump the state. In May they reaped their reward: Roosevelt easily swept to victory in the California Republican primary, winning in all but three counties and polling more votes than the Taft and La Follette tickets combined.[15]

Nationally, the battle between Roosevelt and Taft waxed bitter as the two pronounced high principles and exchanged low blows. Roosevelt, trumpeting the outline of his "New Nationalism," stressed the need for a federal authority responsive to the public will, protective of the disadvantaged, and able to harness corporate power and prevent abuses in the marketplace. Taft, breaking precedent to campaign publicly for renomination, lashed out at Roosevelt's endorsement of judicial recall and popular democracy, emphasized the virtues of constitutional order, and complained of the "political emotionalists" and "neurotics" who vied for power.[16] Replying with insults of his own, Roosevelt made substantial progress in his quest for the Republican nomination, winning handily in nine of the twelve states that had adopted the presidential primary.[17] But where delegates were selected by more traditional means, both Taft and Roosevelt claimed victory, and it soon became obvious that the outcome of the Republican convention would hinge upon the certification of contested delegates by the Republican National Committee, dominated by Taft loyalists, which met for two stormy weeks prior to the convention opening.

Upon learning that the committee planned to displace two of the California delegates pledged to Roosevelt, Johnson rushed to Chicago to voice his objections, but on his arrival he refused to attend the hearings. He would not, he declared, participate in a trial in which thieves sat as judges.[18] Heney did attend, and his voice rasped with anger as he denounced the committee's decision on the California dispute. At times, violence seemed imminent as Heney vented his scorn. But the California decision was only one of a series of progressive defeats. Overall, of the 254 contested delegates, Roosevelt secured 19.

Predictably, the 1912 Republican National Convention, which began on June 18, roiled with passion, disorder, and near riot. Threats of party schism filled the air as Roosevelt, speaking before a frenzied crowd of 5,000 at the Chicago auditorium on the eve of the convention opening, rallied his forces and denounced boss rule. The battle, he exclaimed, was between "the rights of humanity" and the "sinister influences of moneyed privilege." His summons to his audience virtually precluded the possibility of compromise:

We fight in honorable fashion for the good of mankind; fearless of the future; unheeding of our individual fates; with unflinching hearts and undimmed eyes; we stand at Armageddon, and we battle for the Lord.[19]

Once the convention began, the debate over contested delegates flared anew. This time Johnson played an active role. His face crimson with rage, his voice, one reporter observed, like "a ripsaw going through a hard knot," he censured the ongoing proceedings and twice led the California delegation out of the auditorium. "I like that man," Mr. Dooley, Finley Peter Dunne's fictitious spectator, remarked from the sidelines. "He can get out iv a convention an' back in again as quick as any man iv his weight I iver see." On June 20, when it became clear that the Taft forces would triumph, Johnson walked out once again, the California delegation close behind. That evening he attended the gathering of Roosevelt and his lieutenants at the Congress Hotel. There, after spirited debate, the Progressive party was born. The next day Johnson was back once more before the Republican convention, but only to bid farewell in an address laced with denunciation and scorn, which nevertheless brought the crowd to its feet in a churning emotional display of cheers and thunderous applause. He was the "hero of the day," William Jennings Bryan remarked from his vantage point in the galleries.*

★   ★   ★

For Johnson and his associates, the initial hope had been that the California miracle might be duplicated on the national level: that the Republican party, captured by its insurgent wing, could be forged into an instrument of reform. But when it became clear that the Old Guard would retain control of the party machinery, Johnson and his California colleagues bolted with a clear conscience, convinced of their moral rectitude. They had, they insisted, fought the battle cleanly. Taft and his loyalists, defiant of the rank and file of their party and indifferent to common decency, had stooped to conquer. Already conservative in design, the Republican leadership had become conscienceless in method. Progressives bristled with indignation, and whether in fact their assessment was totally accurate mattered far less than the certainty with which they held to their convictions.[20]

Anticipating foul play, California's progressives had steeled themselves for action prior to the convention. An editorial in Edwin Earl's *Los Angeles Tribune* had earlier admonished progressives to stand by their principles and, if dishonesty prevailed, unite with others to form a Progressive party.[21] Lee Gates, speaking for the California

---

*Los Angeles Times, June 22, 1912; William Jennings Bryan, *A Tale of Two Conventions* (New York, 1912), pp. 72–74, 248, 303. One reporter wrote of Johnson: "The first notes of his voice keyed up your nerves to a fighting pitch. We can't imagine anyone's listening to Johnson for five minutes without wanting to fight—either to fight with or to fight against him. His voice sounds just as an east wind feels. It grates and snarls and pierces, and puts you all on edge. The whole man goes with the voice. Every posture and gesture is one of intensity. His hands are nearly always clenched. His jaw, a good strong fighting jaw, is set. His muscles are tense. He talks rapidly and with no gradation of volume or tone, without any embellishments of rhetoric, without any appearance of self-consciousness. He gives you the impression of a man carried away entirely on the flood of his own feelings." Anon., "Johnson of California: A Progressive in a Hurry," *Current Literature*, Aug. 1, 1912, pp. 156–59.

delegation as it left the Los Angeles Santa Fe station for Chicago, agreed, and promised his audience that whatever happened at the convention, Roosevelt would run in November. Arriving to learn of the final disqualification of two of their members, the state's delegates talked openly of a third party and adopted a resolution authorizing Johnson to take any steps necessary to ensure Roosevelt's candidacy.[22] It was a responsibility he readily assumed. "I think we may preside at the Historic Birth of the Progressive Party," Johnson had written Lissner on the day of his departure from California, and even as he fought at Chicago to secure concessions from the Republican party leadership, he privately complained that progressives were wasting their time by such efforts.[23]

On June 22 a dispirited Republican convention, winding to a close, easily renominated Taft for a second four years. Few believed he could be reelected. That evening, Roosevelt loyalists gathered at Orchestra Hall to chant for "Teddy," to listen to jeremiads by Johnson and others denouncing the events of the past weeks, and to pledge themselves to battle. In fighting trim, Roosevelt publicly agreed to accept a Progressive nomination if it were offered. The issue, he thundered, was no longer one of progressivism alone but of common honesty as well. Arrangements were made to gather in Chicago in August to inaugurate the new party and launch the crusade. There, Theodore Roosevelt, declaring himself to be as fit as a bull moose, would endorse a program of social reform far in advance of that proposed by either of the two major parties.[24] In the interim, Johnson was made chairman of the national organizing committee. After returning briefly to Sacramento, he was back in Chicago the following month to find himself pressed into further service in the Progressive cause.

At the same time that Roosevelt had launched his campaign for the Republican nomination, Johnson's followers, led by Edwin Earl, had initiated a campaign of their own in support of Johnson as Roosevelt's running mate.[25] The winning slogan, Earl enthused, would be "hands across the continent." Earl publicly boomed the governor and instructed his associates Edward Dickson and Harley Brundige to push the idea in their conversations with political activists and reporters in the East.[26] Others, including Chester Rowell and Meyer Lissner, endorsed the scheme, and many outside the state voiced their support. If Roosevelt were nominated at Chicago, the *New*

York Times speculated in early March, Johnson would in all probability be his choice for the second spot.[27] Johnson himself made no effort to encourage the boom, but neither did he try to suppress it. As in most instances where his own political ambitions were at stake, he vacillated. The idea was embarrassing; it was also attractive. It opened him to charges by his enemies that his endorsement of Roosevelt stemmed from his own ambitions; consequently, in his speeches during the California primary, he assured his audiences that he sought no higher office. Even so, as he admitted to Gifford Pinchot, "I would be hypocritical if I pretended I would not like the second highest office in this count[r]y."[28]

But if Johnson was receptive to the idea in June, when both he and Roosevelt still hoped that they might capture the Republican nomination, he found the suggestion far less appealing in August, for now it meant running on a third-party ticket. Woodrow Wilson's nomination by the Democratic party compounded the certainty of defeat by eliminating the possibility of any large-scale defection of progressive Democrats to the Bull Moose camp. Wilson's selection, Johnson wrote, was a "solar plexus blow" that all but guaranteed a Democratic victory.[29] Being under no illusions that the Progressive party could win in 1912, Johnson preferred to forgo an honor that promised much sacrifice and little reward. Thus when Roosevelt asked him to accept the nomination on August 5, the opening day of the Progressive convention, he declined and scurried to find a substitute. But Roosevelt was adamant, and the next day Johnson agreed to run on the condition that his nomination would be uncontested.[30] The following evening John Parker, who had himself often been suggested for the post because of his Democratic party ties, nominated Johnson, while Judge Benjamin Lindsey, whose candidacy had also been rumored, joined in seconding the nomination. By acclamation, Progressives chose the candidates to head their ticket. Both men proceeded to the platform to acknowledge the honor. Behind them unfurled a huge banner prepared by Lissner, on which was inscribed Earl's phrase: "Hands across the continent." Moved by the emotions of the moment, the candidates briefly addressed the crowd. "I have enlisted for the war," Johnson announced. And as the delegates' voices rang out in celebration, the convention came to an end.[31]

Though initially depressed by the task that lay ahead, Johnson quickly recovered his equanimity as he prepared for the battle. Given the foreordained results, he observed, "I shall hazard only my energy and my health."[32] In fact, as he rapidly learned, those who organized his itinerary were more than willing to sacrifice both. His tour outside the state, originally scheduled for four weeks, lasted ten, and he was not to return until after the election. It began with addresses in San Francisco and Los Angeles. From there, with a small group in tow, he headed east at the end of August aboard a public Pullman, making stops in Utah, Wyoming, Colorado, Kansas, and Nebraska. On discovering that his schedule included three afternoon speeches at the Nebraska State Fair and two additional addresses that same evening, he sought to cut back the demands made upon him, but instead the demands increased. Two days later, on September 5, he attended the Ohio State Progressive Convention at Columbus; the next day he was in Syracuse, New York, at a similar function. He spent the next three weeks on tour by special train, curving through Michigan, northern Illinois, Wisconsin, South Dakota, Iowa, southern Illinois, Indiana, and Ohio, making up to eighteen speeches a day from the rear platform of his car in the sticky heat of the Midwest. Temperatures sometimes soared over 100 degrees. With his train often running late and his itinerary constantly changing, he found himself increasingly irritated by the jerry-built nature of the enterprise. The whole campaign, he privately grumbled, had been terribly mismanaged, and it was impossible to meet every scheduled engagement. Publicly, he expressed much the same complaint: "I'd rather be a live Governor than a dead Vice-President." The countless rear-platform stops especially vexed him, and he gladly gave up his private railroad car to return to the public Pullman and the concomitantly reduced speaking schedule it guaranteed.[33]

Even so, his itinerary continued to expand. He set off for a whirlwind tour of New England in the last week in September, plunged into New York and New Jersey for nine days of speechmaking, then headed through Pennsylvania, Ohio, and Indiana for what he hoped was the wrap-up of his campaign. By this point his voice was often husky and his weight had dropped from 219 to 211. He would not, he advised Lissner, be able to continue the campaign upon his return to California.[34] But the hope of that return itself vanished in mid-

October when Roosevelt was seriously wounded in an assassination attempt in Milwaukee. With Roosevelt hospitalized, an exhausted Johnson, after some hesitation, agreed to meet the Colonel's commitments in the East. On board Roosevelt's private train, once again making the rear-platform appearances he had so come to detest, he moved back through New York, New Jersey, and Pennsylvania before concluding the campaign in New England on the eve of the election. All totaled, Johnson traveled more than 20,000 miles, gave at least 500 speeches, and addressed an estimated audience of one-half million in his ten weeks on the road. Yet again, the *San Francisco Bulletin* noted, Johnson had set a record of endurance.[35]

Throughout his tour, Johnson was well received. In Kansas City, the platform on which he spoke collapsed under the weight of those who surged forward to shake his hand. In Nebraska, William Jennings Bryan extended his blessing, though not his support, observing that the Progressive ticket would have been far stronger with Johnson at the head and Roosevelt as his running mate. In Columbus, Ohio, 1,500 delegates from the Progressive state convention sought Johnson out at his hotel after his speech, and two hours of handshaking followed. By the end of the campaign, his right thumb and forefinger had been thickly calloused by such ordeals.[36]

While preaching the doctrine of progressivism with his characteristic evangelical fervor, Johnson, like Roosevelt, ignored Taft—a negligible factor, Johnson insisted—to focus on Wilson. Occasionally his voice rang with anger, more often with sarcasm and scorn, as he dismissed Wilson's "superannuated, attenuated, academic discussions" of the issues. Wilson, he charged, was a "man of metaphors" whose pretensions to progressivism were belied by his states' rights posture and by his refusal to endorse federal intervention to protect the defenseless. The Progressive party, Johnson acknowledged, offered "no panaceas, no cure alls," but it was at least responsive to the first priority of any humane government, the conservation of men, women, and children: "We've exploited the government long enough to make a few men rich. Now we propose to exploit the government to make men better." He called specifically for the abolition of child labor and the establishment of a national minimum-wage law for women, framing his arguments to appeal to both the hopes and the fears of his audience, to their ideals and their self-interest. As citizens of the nation they had a responsibility for the well-being of their neighbors; to ignore that responsibility was not only morally wrong but socially dangerous. Echoing Roosevelt, Johnson preached reform as an antidote for revolution. The allure of socialism and the spread of anarchy, he reminded his audiences, grew from injustice.[37]

As expected, the Bull Moose insurgency, by splitting the Republican party, guaranteed a Democratic victory. Wilson, with 42 percent of the popular vote, obtained a commanding majority in the electoral college, and Democrats won control of both houses of Congress. The Progressive ticket took 27 percent of the national vote and triumphed in Pennsylvania, Michigan, Minnesota, South Dakota, Washington, and California, while Taft trailed with 23 percent of the vote and victories in Vermont and Utah. For Roosevelt and Johnson it was an impressive performance, but a defeat nevertheless. Back in Sacramento the second week in November, Johnson rested and readied himself for the opening of the 1913 California legislative session. But then and for the next four years, two interrelated goals absorbed his energies: to secure the triumph of progressive principles on the national level and to prevent the unraveling of the progressive coalition that had gathered around him in the state. Ultimately, both efforts ended in failure.

★　　★　　★

In California, strains within the progressive coalition continued to surface as various factions argued the merits of further reform. Some insisted that the progressive movement had run its course within the state, while others, like Johnson, were eager to push ahead—indeed, in the wake of the Bull Moose rebellion, determined to do so. In addition, the campaign of 1912 had taken its toll, further fragmenting the political order. La Follette's candidacy had left a legacy of smouldering resentment within progressive circles that was not easily extinguished. The Progressive bolt at Chicago had clearly nettled many others who were glad to call themselves reformers but remained staunchly Republican. And for those California Republicans who disdained the reformers, the sting of Taft's defeat was compounded by the refusal of the Bull Moose insurgents to relinquish control of the state's Republican party. Though Progressives nationally, Johnson and his supporters had remained Republicans at home. Confronting a situation that did not allow them to place a Progressive ticket on the California ballot, they had used their control of the Republican party machinery to select electors pledged to Roosevelt. In California, the Bull Moose rode the elephant.*

Conflicts over policies, personalities, and strategies flourished as well within the national Progressive organization. At Chicago, Roosevelt's policy of regulating trusts rather than prosecuting them had sharpened divisions between those who argued for a more stringent application of the Sherman Antitrust Act and those who demanded the act's repeal. George Perkins, one of the major financial backers of the new party, had graphically dramatized this conflict by stalking off the stage in protest when a Progressive platform endorsing the Sherman act was read to the convention. In the confusion that followed, Perkins managed to remove that endorsement, but bitterness endured.

Neither Johnson nor his California lieutenants disputed Roosevelt's position on trusts. Though clearly more willing than the Colonel to emphasize the malevolence of big business, and more willing as well to endorse the concept of public ownership as an alternative to regulation, Johnson held throughout his career that business should be judged not by its size but by its conduct.† But if the issue of corporate regulation did not place Johnson and his associates at

---

*In reviewing the California election laws, Progressives discovered that both presidential electors and legislative candidates would be forced to run as independents, indistinguishable from other splinter groups, unless they retained the Republican label. Faced with a situation that could not be remedied within the time available, even if a special legislative session were called, they much preferred that Taft electors choose the independent option. Lissner argued somewhat disingenuously that because the electors were to be selected by Republican legislators chosen in the September primaries, the Taft forces could field their ticket if they won control of the party. In the end, those who wanted to support Taft were required to write in his name on the November ballot. See *California Outlook*, July 6, 1912, p. 8, July 13, 1912, p. 4, July 27, 1912, pp. 6–7.

†In 1915 Johnson toyed with the idea of state ownership of the insolvent Western Pacific Railroad. It was, he noted, an "alluring" prospect. *Fresno Republican*, Mar. 11, 1915. See also HWJ to George Record, Nov. 27, 1916. On business ethics, Johnson was to note: "To lie, to misrepresent, to take false positions and bear false witness, to cheat, to defraud, to hurt and harm and ruin, when profitable, are but part of the 'business code.'" HWJ to Hiram Johnson, Jr., July 23, 1917. Commenting on Wilson's antitrust efforts, Lissner wrote: "I am absolutely out of sympathy with the national administration's idea of the regulation or forcing of competition. It can't be done." Lissner to M. H. Newmark, Mar. 15, 1915, Lissner Papers. See also Lissner to George Perkins, July 26, 1915, Lissner Papers. Similar comments can be found in the writings of Fremont Older and in the pages of the *California Outlook*. *San Francisco Bulletin*, Dec. 8, 22, 1913; *California Outlook*, Apr. 19, 1913, p. 2.

odds with Roosevelt, the prominence of George Perkins did. For many Progressives, the imperious and demanding Perkins was an anathema. As a member of the boards of United States Steel and International Harvester, Perkins personified the very corporate arrogance that Progressives hoped to discipline. But he was also Roosevelt's choice as chairman of the Progressive Executive Committee. Johnson and his associates, together with fellow dissidents, argued against the appointment when it was first made and continued thereafter to voice their objections in an effort to push Perkins to the sidelines. It proved an impossible task.[38]

Finally, if Progressives divided over personalities and platforms, all were forced to confront the overriding issue posed by the creation of the third party—its future in the aftermath of the 1912 defeat. Hurriedly built from the top down, the new party had recruited no more than a scattering of reform-minded incumbents from either major party to its national banner, and had also failed to prove its viability at the local and state levels. There, almost without exception, Progressive office seekers ran far behind their national ticket. Whether the new party could remedy these failings and establish the roots necessary for permanence remained uncertain. As early as February 1913, the publisher Frank Munsey, like Perkins a major financial contributor to the third party, withdrew his support and called for negotiations leading to an "amalgamation" of the Progressive and Republican parties. Few others in the new party followed his lead. Roosevelt rejected his proposal, insisting that a merger with either of the two traditional parties could come only on Progressive terms. But from the moment of defeat, talk of party reconciliation was in the air.[39]

Never one to back away from a challenge, Johnson signaled his own commitment to a permanent Progressive party by his active participation in the Massachusetts and New Jersey gubernatorial contests in the autumn of 1913. "We would rather lose with our principles than win without them," he defiantly exclaimed. And in fact, both Charles Sumner Bird and his New Jersey counterpart Everett Colby lost in their third-party bids.[40] But the true proof of Johnson's commitment to the third party was not his support of insurgency on the East Coast but his willingness to abandon control of the California Republican party and construct a new state Progressive party in its stead.

While a majority of Johnson's close associates acknowledged the logic of such a move, they nevertheless urged delay, hoping for some more definite guarantee that only time could bring. In the legislature, support was at best ambivalent. Some, for both emotional and ideological reasons, clung to their Republican ties; yet others, for practical reasons, feared that joining a new party would imperil their reelection prospects. In any case, they argued, because they had been elected as Republicans they had an obligation to serve out the session prior to any break. Within Johnson's inner circle, only Lissner and John Eshleman, chairman of the State Railroad Commission, appeared eager to bolt, while Earl, Dickson, Marshall Stimson, and Francis Heney all argued against the move.[41] Ultimately the decision fell to Johnson. He agreed to wait until the end of the legislative session but no longer, for he saw no real option but to quit the Republican party. Progressives throughout the state rallied to his call to do likewise.[42] On December 5, 1913, the progressive-dominated Republican State Central Committee dissolved itself. The following day, at a meeting in San Francisco, the California Progressive party was born. "The Progressive ship of state is launched and on her way," Lissner rejoiced, "and the old machine is welcome to what is left of the wreck."[43]

★   ★   ★

Earlier Johnson had expressed a wish to retire from politics following the conclusion of his term in 1914 and reassume his practice of the law, perhaps in partnership with his sons; he would speak out on public issues but no longer undertake an active political role.[44] The decision to create a state Progressive party seemed obviously to preclude that possibility. He could hardly lead California progressives out of the Republican camp and then abandon responsibility for the future of the enterprise. Even so, in the month following the announcement of the new party, Johnson refused to disclose his intentions. His inclination was not to run at all, Lissner wrote to Albert Beveridge. Encouraging Johnson to resist that inclination, Lissner stressed the necessity of his involvement. John Haynes agreed, not advising, he confessed, but rather begging Johnson to heed the counsel of his friends.[45] As in 1910, the pressure was on. Yet it seems clear that even without the added sense of obligation compelling him to help launch the California Progressive party,

Johnson had become so wedded to an active political role that his retirement was impossible. Once again, he both dreaded and delighted in the political chores urged upon him by his associates; but perhaps more than he consciously realized, he had come to see the California progressive movement as an extension of himself. To step away from active leadership would have been to do violence to his very being.[46] Irritated by the pressure put on him by others, Johnson would have been even more unhappy at being left behind.

But if Johnson for both practical and emotional reasons could not abandon a political role, he preferred to alter that role by announcing for the U.S. Senate. John Eshleman, a Johnson loyalist who had an impressive record as head of the Railroad Commission, could succeed him as governor. Both Earl and Lissner endorsed the plan.[47] Francis Heney firmly opposed it. Determined that he would not again be excluded from political office, Heney made it clear that he would campaign for whichever position Johnson left open. Heney's ambition contributed to the delay in Johnson's own declaration of candidacy and in the end crimped Johnson's plan to run for the Senate in 1914.

For many, Heney remained the same divisive force that he had been in 1910. He would "smash things utterly" if he ran for and won the Progressive gubernatorial nomination, Chester Rowell predicted. Johnson agreed, but his concurrence drew from far deeper roots. Intensely jealous of any potential rival, he could not help but vent his bitterness and anger toward both Heney and those who rallied to his support. Their goal, he petulantly concluded, was "to make Heney the central figure in the Progressive movement."[48] For Johnson, power, ambition, pride, and principles had become inextricably intertwined. To him, Heney's declaration was not a political event but a personal challenge. Ultimately, unwilling to risk the governorship, Johnson chose John Eshleman as his running mate for lieutenant governor and prodded a reluctant Chester Rowell to challenge Heney in the senatorial contest.[49]

Of the Progressive candidates for major office, only Heney faced opposition in the primary. John Eshleman, taking advantage of the recently created opportunity to cross-file in more than one party's primary, sought both the Progressive and the Republican nominations. Many others in the Assembly and state Senate races did the same, thus shielding themselves from the consequences of insurgency. Johnson, hopeful that his candidacy might encourage registration in the new party, ran only as a Progressive, and with Eshleman in tow, kicked off the campaign in mid-February. Thereafter, until the August primary, Johnson spent a part of each month on the road. He canvassed the whole of the state, twice visiting Los Angeles and the southern counties. Massive popular turnouts welcomed him wherever he spoke, but registration in the new party after the first flush of insurgency lagged far behind that for the Republican and Democratic parties. Although he was able to attract nonpartisan support, Johnson could not erase traditional party ties.[50]

Nor, with his characteristic pessimism, was he able to lay aside his own doubts about his chances for November. He had, he confessed to Roosevelt, "hit so many heads," been so uncompromising in his actions and so cavalier in his treatment of the standpat press, that his reelection was uncertain.[51] Yet even as he bemoaned the possibility of defeat, he rejected the Colonel's offer to aid in the campaign. Roosevelt's participation, Johnson explained to an associate, would distort the contest by transfiguring it into an attack on Wilson and a debate on national policies, thereby repelling potential Democratic support for the new party. But more important was the personal equation. The battle, Johnson wrote, would be his own. "Sentimentally," he admitted, that was the way he wanted it.[52]

Throughout the primary campaign Johnson hit hard at the Old Guard, which once again controlled the California Republican party. He focused his wrath on Otis, John Spreckels, and Michael de Young—the "Black Horse Cavalry of Privilege," the "three militant, marauding millionaire publishers" who alternately vied for power and exercised it within the state GOP. All three, Johnson observed, served as invaluable political guides: whatever policies they recommended, whichever individuals they endorsed, deserved public repudiation. So too did the party for which they spoke. Reciting the progressive accomplishments of his first four years, Johnson exhorted his audience to break their traditional party ties and make the Progressive party their new political home. The party of Lincoln, he charged, had forsaken its heritage, its commitment to humanity, but the spirit of Lincoln survived in new party guise. Only the timid, the "pussy-footing and hesitating" would fail to follow that spirit.[53]

From the outset Republican party strategists moved to blunt Johnson's appeals by staking out their own claims as reformers. At a meeting in Santa Barbara in early February, they pledged their support for "sane reforms" and somewhat awkwardly argued that the achievements Johnson called his own had been readied well before he became governor and owed little to his leadership. The Old Guard, Johnson retorted, were trying "the greatest double-back somersault, politically and intellectually, ever turned," in their effort to hold the liberal and moderate elements of their party in line. But in his attempt to recruit those same elements into the Progressive camp, Johnson turned his own intellectual somersault. Reciting the accomplishments of his administration, he invoked the past, not the future. He had, he argued, kept the faith; his 1910 pledges had been redeemed. His goal now was "to perpetuate that which has already been done." Clearly, the election of 1914 was to be a referendum on his record, not a mandate for bold new programs. His approach proved effective as a reelection appeal, but it was a feeble rallying cry for the building of a new party.

To Johnson's regret, though not to his surprise, Heney easily trounced Rowell in the August 25 primary to become the Progressive party candidate for the U.S. Senate. At the same time, Eshleman's nomination for lieutenant governor by both the Progressive and Republican parties seemed to all but guarantee that Johnson would draw similar support in the November tally. But if others saw his success as assured, Johnson did not. With the votes counted and the Progressive nomination now officially his, he stepped up his efforts, beginning an all but nonstop campaign, resting only on Sundays. Occasionally drenched by autumn rains, more often choked by dusty roads, he toured the state much as he had done in 1910, with Archibald, his younger son, serving as chauffeur.

Johnson's chief opponent was John D. Fredericks, a captain in the California Volunteer Infantry during the Spanish-American war and, since 1903, the district attorney of Los Angeles. Fredericks had wrapped up large majorities in the southern half of the state and swept to an easy victory in the GOP primary race. He was, Johnson conceded, an able and crowd-pleasing campaigner. A longtime foe of labor unions and chief prosecutor in the 1911 *Los Angeles Times* bombing case, he had powerful support in Los Angeles and in California's southern counties. He could profit as well from the friction within the Progressive camp sparked by the Heney campaign. Johnson, fearful that support for his own candidacy in Southern California was beginning to fray, undertook three separate tours of the south in the last two months of the campaign. "Formerly I used to worry about San Francisco," he acknowledged. "My worries this year are about Los Angeles."[54]

As the campaign continued, Johnson repeated the themes he had outlined during the primary, detailing the past achievements of his administration while hammering hard at the triumvirate of Otis, de Young, and Spreckels. Fredericks, whose campaign failed to catch fire, proved an easy target. Wrapping his campaign in clichés, the Los Angeles prosecutor sought to belittle Johnson's progressive accomplishments without at the same time alienating progressive Republicans. His attacks on "freak legislation" and "socialistic tendencies," heard during the primary, gave way to far blander generalities as Fredericks called upon Republicans of all hues to remain true to their party. Predictably, he equated the GOP with prosperity, pointed to the current national economic recession, and argued that with a Democrat in the White House and a Progressive in Sacramento, the economy was bound to suffer. California's businessmen, Fredericks charged, feared the Johnson administration and were reluctant to invest in so uncertain a political climate, but it was the political climate, he implied, far more than the substance of past legislation that was at fault. "All that we have that is good will be retained," he assured his audience, "and we will march on to the development of more and better things in the interests of humanity."[55] Glib, carping, and endlessly evasive, he became, in Johnson's words, "the distinguished shifty gentleman from Los Angeles."[56]

On the stump Johnson and Heney voiced mutual support, but the gulf between them remained unbridgeable. Suggestions that they coordinate their efforts prompted Johnson's profane refusal; only once, at the Los Angeles Shrine Auditorium, did the two men share the same platform. Their enmity was less than a well-guarded secret, so much so that at one point Johnson had to assure Rowell that rumors of his political alliance with James Phelan or Joseph Knowland, the Democratic and Republican U.S. senatorial hopefuls, were without basis.[57] But rumors continued to surface as Johnson campaign organizations blossomed throughout the state. Some supported the entire Progressive ticket, but many others were committed only to Johnson's own candidacy. Each candidate, Johnson explained in August to an angry Heney, had to reach out for bipartisan support. Just as William Stephens, running for reelection to Congress on the Progressive ticket, had drawn into his campaign individuals who supported the Republican Fredericks or the Democrat John Curtin in the gubernatorial race, so too he would invite support wherever he could find it.[58] In September, after the state Progressive party convention pledged itself to expand nonpartisanship to include all state offices, he could have added that his goal, at least in state contests, was no longer to recruit membership to the new party but to dissolve all partisan affiliations. Extending nonpartisanship from the municipal and county levels, where it had first been introduced, to the state level would serve nicely to finesse the-less-than-satisfactory showing in Progressive party registration within the state.[59]

Johnson romped to an easy victory in the 1914 general election. Not only was he the first governor in 60 years to win reelection, he also polled more votes than the total of his Republican and Democratic challengers combined. In the state's southern counties, over which he had most fretted, he made a strong showing: he ran well ahead of his overall state average in Los Angeles and lost to Fredericks only in San Diego.[60] But the election was not a victory for the Progressive party, either in California or nationwide. In the U.S. Senate race, Heney was defeated by James Phelan, the Democratic ex-mayor of San Francisco who had once helped to sponsor the graft trials Heney had led in that city. In Los Angeles only five of the fifteen Progressive Assembly candidates were victorious.[61] Nationally the results were a disaster. In the twenty states outside of California in which Progressives sought governorships, they lost in all twenty races, more often than not running a poor third against their Democratic and Republican counterparts. In some contests they ran fourth, behind various splinter factions. The Progressive party, Theodore Roosevelt concluded, had "come a cropper."[62]

★　　★　　★

Johnson feared that the party's national leadership, meeting at Chicago in the aftermath of the election, might abandon their struggle, and accordingly cautioned both Rowell and Lissner, attendant at the gathering, to hold the line. The situation, he wrote Benjamin Lindsey, was "not wholly hopeless."[63] In the volatile world of politics, conditions might change overnight; that being the case, Progressives should do little more than reaffirm their principles and await events. Most agreed, and although a handful of the more prominent within the party, including Medill McCormick, decided to return immediately to the Republican fold, the bulk at the Chicago gathering vowed to stand fast. But almost all recognized that the Progressive party had passed its prime. Trumpeted in 1912 as the party of the future that would reorient political divisions along clear ideological lines, it had become moribund, shying away from further disaster in local campaigns, while maintaining its independence primarily so that it might better negotiate concessions from a resurgent GOP. If Republicans remained unrepentant, Johnson warned, Progressives would have no other alternative but to resume their national crusade and in the process contribute to Wilson's reelection. Indeed, he confessed to Roosevelt, he would rather abandon politics than enlist under the "black banner" of those who had stolen the nomination at Chicago. His hope was that such a course would not be necessary.[64]

But if Johnson saw no alternative but to play a waiting game, he was not at all certain as to how it should be played. In May, in remarks to the departing members of the 1915 California state legislature, he indicated that he would not run again for state office. Coupled with his announcements of candidacy in 1910 and 1914, in which he had expressed his distaste for political involvement, the statement could be viewed as confirmation of his wish to retire to private life following the end of his term in 1918. But it also could be read as a bid for national office, perhaps for a seat in the U.S. Senate, perhaps for even higher stakes. In private conversations Gilson Gardner, representing the newspaper publisher E. W. Scripps, suggested one possible option. Rather than allow the Progressive party to collapse, Johnson should become its candidate for the presidency. Johnson could not win, Gardner acknowledged, and his campaign would ensure the reelection of Wilson, whom Scripps was also supporting, but the effort itself would help to resurrect the progressive cause. Johnson was not impressed. He would not campaign for the Progressive nomination, certainly not as a spoiler to ensure Wilson's reelection.[65]

From Lissner came a different suggestion; Johnson, he argued, should set his sights on securing the Republican party's vicepresidential nomination. The Progressive party, he reasoned, was about to fold, while the acrimony at Chicago foreclosed the possibility that Roosevelt could be nominated to head the Republican ticket. Nor would Johnson be any more acceptable than the Colonel as the Republican party's presidential nominee. But he would be perfect in the second spot, where he could reunite Progressives and Republicans, mending the breach of 1912. Roosevelt approved of the scheme, Lissner observed, and had already recommended that Johnson undertake a speaking tour in the East to broaden his support.[66] Others agreed. Nearly everyone he talked to, John Eshleman wrote, saw Johnson as the obvious choice for second spot on the Republican ticket.[67] Urging an active campaign in pursuit of that objective, the Progressive National Committee, in January 1916, recommended that Johnson campaign as a Republican in California's presidential primary and simultaneously run for the Progressive presidential nomination in other state primaries.

Johnson, however, adamantly rejected the strategy outlined by the Progressive National Committee. To acquiesce, he argued, would be to place himself in an equivocal position. Perhaps he was "oversensitive," he acknowledged, perhaps "illogical," but he could not in good conscience straddle the issues that divided the two parties by actively courting both camps. Many in his inner circle sought to convince him that his integrity was not at stake, but he refused to budge, declining, as Lissner lamented, to allow his name to be used in such a way.[68] Further hardening his resolve was Johnson's own ambivalence about the idea of fusion itself. Having helped create the Progressive party and having fought to ensure its permanence in 1913 and 1914, he now recognized that the end was imminent but could not bring himself to contribute to that end. His colleagues could bear that responsibility. Indeed, at times he consoled himself by blaming them for the collapse. They had too often lacked the enthusiasm necessary for the enterprise, "the singleness of purpose . . . the spirit of dying in the last ditch" that had defined the California crusade.[69] Clearly, Johnson found a certain grim satisfaction in contrasting his own role with that of his associates elsewhere.

Yet even in California, Johnson acknowledged, the Progressive party had failed to take root. Progressives held power not because of their party label but in spite of it. Party registration continued to lag behind that of the two old parties, and the persistence of traditional ties had once again been demonstrated when California's voters, in October 1915, rejected the plan passed by the legislature to eliminate partisanship in all state elections. The referendum marked Johnson's first serious setback in the state, for he had actively campaigned in support of the measure.[70] It seemed even at the time but a prelude to larger disaster. Fusion, Johnson had earlier insisted, should never come at the expense of progressive principles, but the momentum of events seemed to ensure that it would come in no other way. To return to the GOP, he now observed, would mean a generation of control by the reactionary element that had triumphed at Chicago. "I am really sorry," he added. "There was work for the new party to do."[71]

But while Johnson sought to dissociate himself from the fusion process, neither he nor his Republican adversaries could ignore its impact on California politics. Throughout the summer of 1915 rumors had persisted that Johnson would field his own slate in the state's Republican presidential primary as the first step toward reclaiming control of the party. In August, in an effort to stave off such a move, Willis Booth, a Los Angeles banker and Republican moderate, invited Lissner to discuss the possibility of compromise. The two agreed that the national Republican ticket should be Charles Evans Hughes and Hiram Johnson, and Booth felt certain that the state's Republican leadership would endorse such a package if Johnson took no steps to force the issue. Lissner was enthusiastic. Johnson was not. To wait for such an endorsement, he replied, "would write me a bigger ass than in my darkest moments I have ever dubbed myself." Though not yet certain whether he would involve himself in the effort to select a Republican delegate ticket, Johnson knew precisely how it should be done. To trust the word of those who had in the past been "false, treacherous and indecent politically" was lunacy. If Progressives wanted a Republican slate, they would put it together themselves.[72]

By the end of 1915, determined that he would not enter his name in the race, Johnson had all but decided to organize a slate of Republican delegates, uninstructed but sympathetic to the Progressive cause.[73] Again, Booth pressed for some sort of compromise, negotiating with Lissner to divide the delegate ticket between Republican regulars and Johnson loyalists with the understanding that the slate agreed to would support a Hughes-Johnson ticket at the Chicago convention. But as Booth made clear, there were conditions. If Johnson failed to win the nomination at Chicago, he would make no effort to seek the U.S. Senate post that Booth himself coveted.[74] Again, Johnson dissented. Willis Booth, he snorted, had the "usual cunning of his class."[75] Negotiations nevertheless continued, partisans on both sides maneuvering for advantage. In mid-January 1916, Walter Bacon, chairman of the State Republican Executive Committee, suggested the possibility of a conference with the Progressive leadership to work out some sort of arrangement. "He is all for harmony with a big 'H,'" Lissner wrote, and more than agreeable to a combination ticket if Johnson would stand for it.[76] But Johnson demurred, and the negotiations collapsed when Bacon brought the matter before the Republican Executive Committee. There, the idea was abandoned as Republican conservatives thundered their denunciations.[77]

From his comments it is clear that Johnson placed little faith in Lissner's diplomacy, and even before the negotiations with the GOP leadership collapsed, the effort to organize a Republican delegate ticket sympathetic to harmony on Progressive terms was nearing completion.[78] "We pulled the wires," Lissner later acknowledged. But almost from the beginning the wires became tangled. The United Republicans, the group on which Progressives pinned their hopes, meeting in San Francisco on February 27, moved to distance themselves from Johnson and his administration and agreed to open negotiations with Bacon and the Republican Executive Committee to select a compromise slate.[79] Their efforts fell through, and two slates, both uninstructed, were ultimately entered in the California Republican primary; but the United Republicans, feuding among themselves, continued to hang back from any association with Johnson or his administration.

Totally disgusted by the antics of the United Republicans, Johnson determined to wash his hands of the whole affair. "Stuffed respectability" was one of his more temperate descriptions of the group.[80] They could either fight or quit, he declared, but if they fought they would fight alone, without any help from his office.[81] Frantically, Rowell and others sought to mend the breach, and in mid-April, two weeks before the primary, a reconciliation of sorts was accomplished: the United Republicans agreed to solicit Johnson's endorsement, and Johnson, in a public letter, recommended that both Republicans and those Progressives who expected to rejoin the Republican party support the United Republican slate.[82] But it was not enough. In an extremely light turnout the regular Republican slate triumphed.* Jubilant, the Republican Old Guard celebrated the result as spelling the end of Johnson's reign in the state. "The Progressive party of California is as obsolete as the Greek kalends," the *San Diego Union* chortled. Both the party and Johnson, the *Oakland Tribune* agreed, were in discard.[83]

★   ★   ★

The triumph of the Old Guard in the California presidential primary shaped Johnson's mood as he readied himself for the Progressive National Convention, scheduled to coincide with the Republican convention meeting in Chicago.[84] He really did not want to go, he confessed, and was sure that the experience would be unpleasant.[85] He recognized the necessity of fusion, but still found himself emotionally unable to endorse it. Adding to his apprehension was his conviction that the Republicans at Chicago would make few real concessions, and that fusion would come at the expense of progressive principles. The Republican national convention, he predicted, would be the California delegation writ large—"as incapable of conscientious political action as so many swine."[86] Almost all agreed that the most logical choice to unite the two parties was Charles Evans Hughes, the onetime progressive governor of New York who had been appointed by Taft to the U.S. Supreme Court in 1911. Hughes had escaped the bitterness that had divided the two parties since 1912 and might bridge the gap between them in 1916. Johnson's private comments on Hughes were few. He would accept him, he confessed at one point, but was less than inspired by the prospect. More likely, he observed, Republicans would nominate "some timid, pussy-footed politician whose record is colorless." In fact, he was not at all certain that Hughes, "the mysterious, stuffed prophet" who refused to acknowledge his own candidacy and continued to

---

*Party registration was not a requirement for participation in the primaries. Thus, the *Fresno Republican* advised: "Don't bother about the Progressive primaries. There is no contest in them and a few votes will elect the delegates quite as well as a large number." *Fresno Republican*, May 1, 1916. But, upon examining the election returns in Los Angeles, Edward Dickson concluded that less than 500 Progressives had cast their vote in the Republican primaries. Dickson to HWJ, May 3, 1916. See also HWJ to Gilson Gardner, May 4, 1916; HWJ to George Knight, May 5, 1916; HWJ to T. S. Montgomery, May 8, 1916, HWJ to Irving Martin, May 11, 1916; Rowell to Theodore Roosevelt, May 21, 1916, Rowell Papers.

remain coyly aloof from the political hustings, did not fit that description.[87]

Roosevelt's own political priorities added to Johnson's woes. That the Colonel sought the Republican presidential nomination was clear to all; that he could secure it few believed. Indeed, even if Roosevelt were successful at Chicago, Johnson concluded, he would almost certainly lose to Wilson in the general election.[88] With the outbreak of the World War in August 1914, the onetime hero of San Juan Hill had quit his assaults on Republican conservatives to concentrate his fire on Wilson's foreign policies, lashing out at pacifists, pro-Germans, and those who refused to embrace his own belligerent nationalism. For the bulk of California progressives whose focus remained centered on reform politics, this was an unwelcome change. Most, including Johnson, concurred on the need for greater preparedness, but few were willing to endorse unreservedly the Colonel's most recent reinterpretation of the New Nationalism. Some, including Older of the *San Francisco Bulletin* and McClatchy of the *Sacramento Bee*, expressed growing distress.[89] The American people, Edwin Earl privately warned, feared electing a "war" president.[90]

But if Johnson was troubled by Roosevelt's substitution of national belligerency abroad for progressive militancy at home, he remained more than ready to enlist under the Colonel's banner at Chicago. Roosevelt was the "one outstanding American today," the "one man who approaches greatness as all of us have dreamed of it."[91] His nomination would of course eliminate any prospects that Johnson might have for the vice-presidential nomination, but it also would be Johnson's ultimate revenge on his California foes. Earlier, Phil Stanton, upon retiring from the Republican National Committee, had characterized the delegates selected at the California presidential primary as "real Republicans" because they stood for anybody but Roosevelt. Johnson was more than ready to take up the challenge. The Progressive party, he wrote, should "answer the refrain of 'anybody but Roosevelt' victoriously and vociferously and obstinately with 'NOBODY BUT ROOSEVELT.'"[92] It was not an attitude out of which compromises might be perfected.

Throughout the Chicago proceedings, Johnson remained a stubborn advocate of Roosevelt, but not a disciple, for the two men read from different texts. Roosevelt's priorities were clear—his own nomination or the nomination of a Republican candidate who shared his foreign policy views. In his mind, the fate of the nation hung on Wilson's defeat and a more militant defense of American rights abroad. Johnson's priorities were equally clear, and they focused not on international events but on affairs at home. Wilson's reelection, he observed, would be far less a calamity than the return to power of the Old Guard, and he feared that Roosevelt, preoccupied by the war, might try to obtain the Progressive party's endorsement of a "rotten reactionary" on a fusion ticket. Johnson's object at Chicago was to prevent such a result.[93] It was a task he vigorously pursued.

On his arrival, Johnson immediately objected to the tactics outlined by Perkins to hold off any Progressive nomination until after negotiations with the Republicans. Progressives must seize the initiative, he insisted, and Roosevelt should be nominated at the first opportunity.[94] Almost all within the Progressive camp agreed. Victor Murdock, chairman of the National Committee, voiced his disapproval of Perkins's scheme, as did John Parker of Louisiana. "They are right up in the air and it is as much as we can do to keep them from nominating you," John McGrath, Roosevelt's private secretary, reported to his chief over the private telephone line connecting Chicago to Oyster Bay.[95] But Perkins, with Roosevelt's public endorsement, prevailed, and the tactics that Johnson denounced as "stall and dicker" began.

On Thursday, June 8, 1916, the second day of the convention, Johnson reluctantly consented to enter into the negotiations pushed by Roosevelt and Perkins. The conference met late in the evening at the Chicago Club and argued until 3:00 A.M. the following morning.[96] Few cards being on the table, little was accomplished. Progressives insisted on Roosevelt's nomination. Republican spokesmen refused even to consider Roosevelt but made no proposal of their own. On Friday, Progressive delegates threatened open rebellion when Perkins again sought delay. Johnson, though reluctantly joining in support of Perkins, entered his protest as well. Only Roosevelt's expressed wishes, he affirmed, kept him at the task:

No matter what transpires tonight or tomorrow, a joint obligation or none, yours is the obligation to keep the faith. God finds us tonight—oh God help us—finds us sitting at the feet of Reed Smoot and Murray Crane. I make my protest against what has been done today and in the last two days of the

Progressive party. We've lingered so long, twenty-four hours will do us no more harm. But when that is over, you and I, my friends, will preserve the Progressive party.[97]

Once again the conference committee met; once again the meeting ended in failure.

Shortly after the second futile meeting, Nicholas Murray Butler, one of the Republican negotiators, hurried to Perkins's suite at the Blackstone Hotel to confer with Roosevelt over the private line from which the Colonel directed his operations. Neither Butler nor Roosevelt supported Hughes, the clear front-runner. Both talked of alternatives. Butler proposed Elihu Root, John Fairbanks, or Philander Knox. Roosevelt, at last aware of the impossibility of his own nomination, countered with Leonard Wood, and when Butler found Wood unacceptable, recommended Henry Cabot Lodge. Johnson's worst fears had come to pass—all were "rotten reactionaries." At Roosevelt's suggestion, Butler agreed to discuss the Lodge candidacy with Perkins and Johnson. "I should like to have Hiram Johnson included in the game," the Colonel observed. At five in the morning Perkins was back on the wire. Do you want me to talk to Johnson?, Roosevelt asked. "Not on your life; not for an hour or two," came the prompt reply.[98] Both Johnson and John Parker absented themselves that morning when the conference reassembled and did not participate in the debate that followed, out of which came the decision to recommend Hughes to both conventions. But there would be no joint nomination, at least not that day.

In a lengthy address, greeted by catcalls, hisses, and boos, Perkins announced the recommendation of the committee to the Progressive convention. Shouts of "No" filled the air. John Parker, loud in his protests, demanded Roosevelt's nomination. Bainbridge Colby, equally adamant, pushed Perkins aside to nominate the Colonel formally. Johnson, his face flushed in anger, vigorously seconded the proposal, calling on Roosevelt to rise to the responsibilities of leadership. Three minutes after the Republican party chose Hughes as its standard-bearer, Roosevelt again became the unanimous choice of the Progressives. Later that afternoon, shortly before John Parker received the nod as Roosevelt's running mate, the Colonel made his response. Declining to accept the nomination, he recommended that the matter be referred to the party's Executive Committee. If they agreed to accept Hughes, he would not object; if they disagreed, they could confer at further length. Perkins, anxious to avoid additional turmoil, sought to keep Roosevelt's reply secret until after the convention ended; but at Johnson's insistence, Perkins's plan was scotched. It was time, Johnson growled, that the leadership be frank with its members. As Roosevelt's telegram was read, delegates sat in stunned disbelief. Numbly, they voted to acquiesce. Katherine Edson's reaction to the events reflected the resentment of many: "I hate Roosevelt," she wrote.[99]

*   *   *

Johnson's attitude differed little. Never had Rowell and Dickson seen him in so peevish a mood. The two persuaded him to go east to see what might be salvaged out of the Chicago disaster, but once there, he at first declined to meet with Hughes. Under no circumstances would he visit Roosevelt, who twice extended him invitations. Johnson, Rowell explained, was "thinking with his liver." Ultimately Hughes and Johnson were brought together, but only after Johnson conferred with Gifford Pinchot, Harold Ickes, J. A. H. Hopkins, and James Garfield, all activists in the progressive cause. Others, among them Johnson's wife, urged Johnson to run in Roosevelt's stead, and both he and Pinchot toyed with the idea of an independent presidential candidacy. At last recognizing the impossibility of such an undertaking, they agreed to put together some sort of organizational network that would allow them to remain in touch.[100] Meanwhile, both Rowell and Dickson worked along more practical lines, seeking both to serve Johnson's interests and to secure what little advantage they could in their ongoing struggle with California's conservative Republican leadership.[101]

One scheme Rowell attempted was to obtain the substitution of Johnson for John Fairbanks, the Republican vice-presidential nominee. Earlier, prior to the defeat of the United Republicans in the California presidential primary, the possibilities of Johnson's selection for the second spot on a harmony ticket had been widely touted. It was, in Lissner's words, the "price" Republicans would pay for a joint nomination. During the Chicago convention Johnson had adopted an attitude that foreclosed such a possibility. Whether he now wished to reconsider remained unclear. Rowell was certain that he did, ascribing his "black dumps" to the failure of the effort to move forward.[102]

Once the Fairbanks scheme collapsed, Rowell, joined by George Perkins, approached John King and Murray Crane of the Republican Steering Committee about the possibilities of Johnson's unopposed candidacy for the U.S. Senate. Earlier, Johnson had privately spoken of such a race—the need for "one last fight" to put California's reactionaries to rout—but had not yet taken any steps in that direction, being still undecided in his own mind.[103] To Rowell he indicated that he had no interest in the office and very much doubted if either King or Crane could be trusted.[104] But negotiations continued, and Rowell returned home with what he thought to be an agreement. In addition, he secured his own appointment to the Republican National Committee (on which he would serve jointly with William Crocker), hoping thereby to clear the way for Progressive support of Charles Evans Hughes in California.

On June 26, by a vote of 32 to 6, with 9 abstentions, the Progressive National Committee endorsed the Republican ticket of Hughes and Fairbanks. The following day, from Sacramento, Johnson announced his own grudging endorsement, pointedly adding that he spoke only for himself and would not attempt to impose his choice on others. To Katherine Edson he privately confessed: "I don't know any reason . . . why we should break our necks in this campaign. . . . I never did submit to discipline and I am not going to now, politically or otherwise."[105] Acknowledging that the events at Chicago spelled an end to the California Progressive party, Johnson, in his endorsement, advised registered Progressives to return to their original parties and remake them along progressive lines.

Johnson's public declaration stridently reaffirmed progressive principles but made no mention of his intentions with respect to the Republican senatorial nomination. Only a handful knew of Rowell's efforts to pave his way in that race, but many had pointed to the contest as a way to restore progressive control of the California Republican party. His candidacy, Irving Martin had earlier argued, would "shake from the California electorate the dry rot of apathy which seems to have infected it during the past two years."[106] Even so, Johnson delayed his decision, fretting over the issue of his candidacy while complaining of his "poverty" and the obligation he owed his family. The understanding was that he would make his decision public on July 8, when the California Progressive party gathered at San Francisco's Palace Hotel for its last hurrah. Two days before the conference, Chester Rowell found him still undecided. His proposed speech left the matter unresolved.[107]

Just before leaving for San Francisco, Johnson prepared a news release explaining his decision. He would not run. He could do more for the state, he affirmed, by staying in Sacramento.[108] But of course the release was never issued. Predictably, when the choice had to be made Johnson could neither desert his ideals nor forego his ambitions. Once again he found himself pushed forward by his associates, and once again his declaration bore all the trappings of a sacrificial rite. "There is no lure for me in the United States Senate," he declared. "I have no desire to become a Senator and remove from this state that I love." He would remain a registered Progressive but would cross-file in the Republican race. His goal, he explained in announcing his decision to seek the Republican nomination, was not to win a Senate seat but to reclaim control of the Republican party, and if to some the rhetoric sounded self-serving, it formed precisely the context within which almost all of Johnson's enemies defined the coming battle.[109]

Johnson's speech before the Progressive conference echoed his continuing resentment toward Roosevelt and those who had contributed to the disaster at Chicago. While reaffirming his endorsement of Hughes, he again cautioned that he spoke only for himself and would not attempt to dictate his choice to others. But, he insisted, whether his audience joined with him to support Hughes or embraced Wilson, they had an obligation to defend California's progressive accomplishments from the assaults of Otis, de Young, John Spreckels, Hearst, and Joe Knowland—the reactionary pack who stood at bay, ever ready to destroy what reformers had built. By acclamation, the conference endorsed Johnson's candidacy. Chester Rowell's motion to engineer a unanimous endorsement of Hughes was tabled, and the meeting divided into two camps, a majority supporting Hughes, the minority Wilson. Once again, both groups endorsed Johnson.[110]

But as almost all agreed, Johnson would have to overcome tremendous obstacles in order to secure the Republican nomination. The opposition was well organized, and the aborted effort by the state's Progressives to eliminate partisan registration had created a situation in which 300,000 voters were ineligible to participate in the Republican primary. Running, Johnson mourned, would be "like going up against a braced game."[111] Earlier, prior to the Chicago conventions, he and his lieutenants had tried to remedy the situation by securing passage of legislation to create an open primary that would allow voters to declare their party affiliation at the voting booth, but the attempt had been held up by referendum. Thereafter, they fostered a quiet newspaper campaign in support of re-registration but could not publicly identify themselves with the effort; to do so would have weakened their bargaining position prior to the Chicago conventions. Moreover, as Edward Dickson observed, the rank and file of Progressives were reluctant to "flop" into the Republican party, knowing that the events of the next few weeks might require them to flop back.[112]

In desperation, Rowell and Johnson tried to call in the promise Murray Crane and John King had tentatively extended to clear the way for Johnson in the state, but the promise proved empty. William Willcox, Hughes's campaign manager, would do little more than urge that Californians settle their own problems without disrupting the national campaign. "We have acted decently and come out for Hughes," Johnson somewhat lamely complained. "The least that can be done by the Hughes managers in the East and those in charge of the Republican Party is to make our path easy, and a word from them would clear this situation."[113] But as Crocker made clear to Rowell when the two met to discuss the impasse, there were no words that could dissuade the Republican leadership from its bitter opposition to Johnson.[114]

Further contributing to Johnson's difficulties were the sectional tensions within the state between its northern and southern halves and the stubbornness of Edwin Earl, the progressive publisher of the *Los Angeles Express* and *Tribune*, in supporting greater political recognition for Los Angeles. From the beginning, California's progressives had been forced to cope with the problem of regional representation. John Works, now retiring from the Senate seat Johnson sought, had been acceptable in 1910 in part at least because he was from Los Angeles, and John Eshleman, Johnson's choice for lieutenant governor in 1914, had promised to change his residence to that city in order to satisfy the southern wing.[115] "Southern California has supported your administration nobly, and it hopes to receive proper recognition," Earl once wrote. No one, he later added, had done more for Johnson than he, and he did not want to be criticized if Johnson refused to give the south "what it was entitled to in connection with appointments to various offices."[116] But Earl often found himself on the outside, at odds with Johnson. He quarreled with Meyer Lissner over Los Angeles politics and resented Johnson's dependence on Lissner for guidance on state matters, arguing with the administration over both policies and personnel.[117] Whether he would support Johnson for the Senate remained in doubt. The seat, Earl insisted, was the property of the south.[118] In 1915 rumor had it that he would back Albert Wallace for the post. Later, Willis Booth claimed Earl's backing. Whomever Earl supported, Congressman Stephens was told, it would not be Johnson.[119]

But if Earl could not be wooed as a Johnson loyalist he could be won on his own terms: one only had to strengthen the influence of Los Angeles in California's political affairs. The death of Lieutenant Governor John Eshleman, in February 1916, provided just such an opportunity, and Earl quickly advanced the claims of the south.[120] During the next four months Johnson postponed his selection of Eshleman's successor as he sought to balance political demands against his own uncertainties and emotional needs. Perhaps, he confessed, he magnified the importance of filling the office, but he could not help himself. "I feel that my life was substantially barren before I became Governor and that the part that I have played in what has been done in California, is all that I have ever done. I know that it is all that I will ever leave."[121] Whomever he appointed would bear the responsibility for his life's work. He had chosen Eshleman in 1914 as his heir apparent, trusting in his capacity to carry the burden. He could find few others who met the test. Southern California, Chester Rowell observed, had a "first-class collection of second-class men."[122]

It was nevertheless clear that the post would go to the south, even clearer following Johnson's decision to run for the Senate that Earl would play a central role in the final choice. Johnson proposed H. L. Carnahan, of Riverside, chairman of the State Commission on Corporations. Earl pushed for William Stephens, the Progressive congressman from Los Angeles's Tenth District, and Earl, with the support of a nearly unanimous gathering of the southern leadership, would get his way. Traveling to Los Angeles, where he would participate in the decision and announce the selection, Johnson experienced what he characterized as the worst week of his political life.[123] The appointment ensured Earl's endorsement of Johnson's Senate candidacy, but it also set the stage for a final break both with Earl and with Edward Dickson, who had played a role in the arrangements and who, Johnson feared, exercised too great an influence over the congressman.[124] Within a brief period, Stephens himself was caught in the cross fire.

★   ★   ★

With the decision made and Earl's support secured, Johnson plunged into the campaign, opening with a massive rally at the Trinity Auditorium in Los Angeles. He spent the next five weeks on the road, concentrating on the south in three separate tours of that area. In their effort to beat back Johnson's challenge, the Republican party establishment branded him a heretic, "the most aggressive, the most dangerous, and the most intolerant enemy of Republicanism in California," and moved to prevent any division in their ranks by uniting behind Willis Booth, the Los Angeles banker who had earlier played a central role in the abortive "harmony" negotiations with Lissner.[125] Throughout his campaign, Booth stressed party loyalty and sectional comity, the need to respect the claims of the south to senatorial representation. He was, he added, a businessman rather than a politician, and would bring to Washington the "constructive, workable business principles" demanded by the times.[126]

Predictably, Johnson brushed aside both Booth and his claims. As governor he had spoken for the whole state; as senator he would do the same. Moreover, he had a "shrewd suspicion" that big business was already sufficiently represented at Washington. But of course, Johnson's main assault was directed not against Booth, whom he described as "a man lacking in vision," but against those who surrounded Booth, men whose vision was to restore the social and political order that had prevailed prior to 1910—"the same old rotten ranks": William Crocker, "with his inherited Southern Pacific millions," and Otis, de Young, and John Spreckels, the three "millionaire publishers." They claimed to be Republicans, Johnson charged, but their true loyalty was not to a party but to their reactionary principles, and when those principles had been threatened in the past they had willingly bolted. Party loyalty, he argued, was a sham issue.*

As Johnson's campaign continued, he rarely mentioned Booth save in ridicule. Claims made in Booth's behalf that he would be one of the most handsome senators ever elected prompted Johnson's mocking admission that in such a contest he could not compete. It was the only concession he made as he forcefully hammered home his attacks. Booth's election, Johnson warned, would open the way to the destruction of the progressive achievements already won within the state, while his own election would be a way to carry forward California's progressive movement to the national level.

While affirming his commitment to tariff protection for California's agricultural interests and his endorsement of woman suffrage, Johnson almost totally ignored the policies of the Wilson administration and refused to criticize those progressives who supported the reelection of the president. They had made their decision; he had made his. "I will support Charles E. Hughes both as a candidate and as president so far as I can do so and when I believe his views to be the right ones," he announced. He was, he continued, for "preparedness," the issue Roosevelt and Hughes trumpeted in calling into question Wilson's leadership and ability to meet the crisis of war abroad, but as Johnson defined it, preparedness was virtually synonymous with progressivism: it centered around the realization of a humane society rather than the mobilization of an American army. For the last six years, he argued, California's progressives had been pioneers of preparedness.

Clearly, Johnson's priorities revolved around California and the state's progressive movement. He would rather lose the election, he publicly avowed, than see the destruction of what he had helped to build. The priorities of California's Old Guard leadership were equally clear. They too saw the California primary as central. All

---

* *Stockton Record*, July 28, 1916; *Riverside Daily Press*, Aug. 2, 1916; *Fresno Republican*, Aug. 18, 1916; *Sacramento Bee*, Aug. 16, 1916; *San Francisco Bulletin*, July 22, 27, Aug. 12, 18, 1916; *San Jose Mercury Herald*, July 27, 1916. Booth's support, John Works observed, came largely from "that wing of the Republican party that made up the old corrupt Southern Pacific machine." Works was unsure whether Booth would, as he had privately promised, support progressive principles. Works had no reason to doubt Booth's assurances, he concluded, "other than some of the company [Booth] is keeping." John Works to Albert Searl, Aug. 14, 1916; John Works to Frank C. Roberts, Aug. 12, 1916, both in Works Papers. See also *Sacramento Bee*, Aug. 8, 1916.

else was subordinate, including the national presidential contest, and they promptly rebuffed efforts on the part of Hughes's managers to create some semblance of harmony prior to Hughes's campaign tour of the state. Chester Rowell, having been appointed to the Republican Campaign Committee, argued that the party's main task in the state was to reassure progressive voters. The Old Guard had nowhere else to go. But his continuing efforts were overruled by Crocker and Francis Keesling, chairman of the Republican State Committee, and the Hughes brigade chose to allow themselves to be identified with Johnson's enemies.[127]

Earlier, the Hughes committee had dissociated itself from the arrangement Rowell had tried to perfect, which would have enabled Johnson to run without serious Republican opposition. Now, refusing to "legitimate" Johnson's campaign for the Republican nomination, it rejected Rowell's proposal to allow the governor to appear jointly with Hughes in at least some Republican rallies.[128] Hughes, Johnson complained, had made no effort at all to identify his candidacy with the progressive movement. Reflecting on Hughes's apparent alliance with the Old Guard, Johnson privately elaborated on his public declaration that he would rather quit the campaign than imperil California's progressivism:

In 1910, we kicked the Southern Pacific out of the government of California. In 1916, through Mr. Hughes, the inherited Southern Pacific millions are again to control the state. . . . Mr. Hughes' election and Mr. Crocker's absolute control mean exactly what I say—that the Crocker millions inherited from Southern Pacific again dominate California. We can get along without a United States Senator; I can afford to be beaten. Can I afford, can I . . . permit that which I've so consistently fought . . . ? I'm not clear as to my duty; but my dear Rowell, and in this I'm very earnest, if I conclude my duty to California demands at any hazard, the defeat of Mr. Crocker and the prevention of the return to power of the old regime, and that only by defeating Hughes can these sinister influences be defeated in our State, I'll throw the Senatorship aside, and devote myself exclusively to the endeavor necessary.[129]

He was beginning to wonder if Bainbridge Colby, who had endorsed Wilson, was not right in his evaluation of political realities.[130]

Charles Evans Hughes confronted an impossible task—to be courageous and forthright without taking sides. His four-day California tour, just two weeks before the senatorial primary, was a disaster.

Surrounded by the Old Guard, courted throughout by Crocker and Keesling and in the south by Otis, he sought to distance himself from the state's political divisions but instead managed to exacerbate them. He had no concern with "local differences," he protested, while saluting William Crocker as "San Francisco's favorite son." Oblivious of an ongoing strike of San Francisco's culinary workers, he attended a banquet at the Commercial Club where he was served by scab waiters, and thereby unwittingly placed his imprimatur on the open-shop campaign then under way in the city.

Midway through his tour, in an incident long remembered, he rested at the Virginia Hotel in Long Beach, unaware that Johnson, about to begin his last canvass of the south, was himself a guest. Johnson arrived first, and upon discovering that Hughes was soon due, retreated to his room, convinced that he would be charged with trying to force himself on the Republican nominee. Doubtless he expected that Hughes, when informed of the situation, would assume the responsibility of initiating contact. But although many around Hughes knew of Johnson's presence, Hughes was not told and only learned of the incident the following day. He would have kicked down Johnson's door to exchange greetings, he later remarked.[131] Or perhaps he would have left that task to others, for while he sought to repair the public breach by appointing an aide to make amends and to suggest a joint appearance at Sacramento before he left the state, he made no personal effort to assure Johnson of his good will, and the fact that Keesling accompanied the aide scotched any possibility that Johnson would accede. Hughes had come and gone, Meyer Lissner wrote, leaving little more than a "trail of yellow smoke."[132] Franck Havenner, who later became Johnson's private secretary in Washington, estimated that Hughes had lost 100,000 votes during his tour. The visit, the *California Outlook* concluded, only reemphasized the "irreconcilable conflict" between progress and reaction.[133]

Throughout the campaign, Johnson demonstrated his ability to draw large, enthusiastic, sometimes record-breaking crowds, but whether such turnouts spelled victory in the primary contest was far less certain. Few doubted that he would roll up impressive majorities in the San Francisco Bay Area. The question was whether their numbers would offset southern returns. Meyer Lissner believed the margin would be close; with 300,000 ineligible to vote because of their failure to register, neither candidate, he predicted, would win by more than 20,000.[134] In fact, Johnson won the Republican nomination with a margin of only 15,000 while losing to Booth in the four Southern California coastal counties of Ventura, Los Angeles, Orange, and San Diego.[135] Still, given the odds, the outcome was, in Johnson's words, "truly marvelous." Not only did Johnson win the Republican nomination, but victories in Republican Assembly and state Senate contests ensured that progressives would reassume control of the party machinery they had abandoned two years earlier. They had returned from Armageddon in triumph.[136]

★   ★   ★

In the aftermath of victory, preparing for the September 19 Sacramento meeting of the Republican State Convention, Johnson toyed with the idea of reading Otis, de Young, and Spreckels out of the party. He could not, he had earlier declared, stand on the same platform with them.[137] But other counsels prevailed, and there would be no bloodletting at Sacramento. Rather, administration forces worked to consolidate their control without further exacerbating party divisions. Indeed, with a national election at stake, few on either side wished a public display of temper. Republican regulars silently acquiesced when the convention voted to endorse Johnson's gubernatorial reign, and some effort was made to accord them recognition in party appointments. Willis Booth was chosen as one of California's Republican electors. "The mean, nasty fellows, the irreconcilables—the stiletto men—we left off," Lissner observed; but harmony was the theme.[138] Johnson's address, a model of restraint, contributed to that theme. While avowing his own progressivism and cautioning against any backward step within the state, he ignored Crocker, Otis, de Young, and Spreckels, and for the first time in the course of his senatorial campaign strongly endorsed the presidential candidacy of Charles Evans Hughes.[139]

With both the Progressive and Republican nominations in hand, Johnson found it difficult to be pessimistic about his upcoming November election. Even so, he cautioned his lieutenants against overconfidence. George Patton, his Democratic opponent, was from Los Angeles and would make the same sectional appeal that Booth had employed during the primary. In addition, Johnson warned, Patton was almost certain to have the support, whether covert or not, of the reactionary Republican leaders who had played prominent roles in

Booth's campaign.* Yet, given the primary figures, there seemed no way Johnson could lose. In Sacramento over 32 percent of the Democratic electorate had written in his name on their primary ballots, and in San Francisco a significant if less impressive write-in campaign was evident. Clearly, Patton would be the loser in any widespread exchange of votes. But if, as Lissner remarked, Johnson would "win in a walk," he preferred to continue running, and accordingly again canvassed the state in a general sweep that took him from one end of California to the other.[140]

Once again, progressivism defined Johnson's theme. He reviewed the accomplishments of the past, boasted of California's standing as a leader in social reform and as a model of governmental efficiency, stressed his ability to transcend the state's sectional divisions, and vowed to carry forward the progressive movement in Washington. Repeating the message he had voiced at the Sacramento Republican convention, he warned against any progressive retreat. But he also continued to refrain from denouncing his longtime enemies by name; castigation of "millionaire publishers" and "reactionary politicians" was as close as he got as he celebrated a "reunited, rejuvenated, and progressive" Republican party.[141]

Moreover, despite his own reservations, Johnson no longer hesitated in his endorsement of Hughes but described him as a fellow progressive who had pioneered in the regulation of public utilities while governor of New York and who had been relentless in his assault on boss rule.† Hughes, he continued, had further proved his

*HWJ to Meyer Lissner, Marshall Stimson, Edward Dickson, Sept. 3, 1916. See also HWJ to E. A. Van Valkenburg, Sept. 5, 1916. Republicans, Frank Jordan announced, would prefer a "loyal Democrat" to Johnson. *Los Angeles Examiner*, Aug. 19, 1916. Just prior to the primary election, a proposal by John Bacon, the Republican Executive Committee chairman, to endorse whoever secured the nomination, lost by an overwhelming majority. *Bakersfield Californian*, Aug. 26, 1916; *Sacramento Union*, Aug. 24, 1916. The question, John Works wrote, was what kind of support, if any, Johnson would be given by Republican regulars. The "reactionary wing," he continued, would vote for Patton. Both the *Los Angeles Times* and the *San Francisco Chronicle*, he observed, were "keeping up the fight against Johnson, saying all the mean things they can about him." John Works to Curtis, Sept. 1, 18, 1916, Works Papers.

†But obviously the doubts remained. "The man I met in New York I thought was strong, alert mentally and brave. The man who came to California was cringing and cowardly and contemptible," Johnson wrote as he prepared for the final campaign. HWJ to E. A. Van Valkenburg, Sept. 5, 1916. See also HWJ to J. C. O'Laughlin, Sept. 12, 1916; HWJ to Frederick Davenport, Sept. 13, 1916.

credentials in the Supreme Court opinions he had written upholding both the California eight-hour law for women and the Illinois child labor law. He had been endorsed, albeit belatedly, by the Progressive party and, Johnson concluded, deserved the support of the state's progressives. Whether he would obtain that support was less clear. Initially, Johnson was doubtful. The memory of Hughes's California visit was too vivid. Further, once in office Wilson had strengthened his own support within progressive circles by adopting policies that he had earlier scorned.* Finally, Wilson had the support of those who opposed the more militant posture in foreign affairs that Roosevelt championed and Hughes seemed to echo. Many, both in California and in the nation, were relieved that Wilson had "kept us out of war." It was not a claim that Johnson sought to challenge. He continued as before to define preparedness in progressive terms, although he showed himself more willing than he had been during the primary to question the adequacy of the nation's defenses, and insisted that the government had an obligation to protect its citizens wherever they might be. While supporting Hughes, he made no direct attack on Wilson.

As the campaign continued, Johnson grew increasingly optimistic that Hughes could win the state.[142] On Tuesday, November 6, however, California's voters trooped to the polls to confirm his initial doubts. Early returns gave Hughes a comfortable lead in Los Angeles; on the basis of that tally Chester Rowell and William Crocker joined together to claim a Hughes victory by 40,000 votes. By Wednesday evening, as the national results were totaled, it became apparent that California would decide the contest. By Thursday it was evident that Wilson had won the state and had thereby been elected to a second term. His margin of victory over Hughes was less

---

*Once in office, Wilson accepted federal regulation of corporations and sponsored legislation creating the Federal Trade Commission and a model workmen's compensation bill for federal employees. In addition, by 1916 he supported woman suffrage and national child labor legislation. George Stone, Rowell's successor in the state's Progressive party, voiced the sentiments of many: "It seems to me that [Wilson] has been, and is now, doing for the Nation, just what our own Governor Johnson has been doing in California. . . . It would be to prove false to every sense of right and justice for me to condemn in Wilson what I profess to admire in Johnson." George Stone to Rowell, Sept. 8, 1916, Rowell Papers. Walter Lippmann agreed. Johnson's policies, he wrote, were far closer to Wilson's than to those of the Republican party. Walter Lippmann, "A Progressive View of the Election," *Yale Review* 6 (Jan. 1917), pp. 225–32.

than 4,000 votes. In contrast, Johnson had swept to an easy victory, winning over Patton by 296,000 and securing 61 percent of the total vote cast in the race. In San Francisco, Hughes lost by 15,000 while Johnson triumphed with an astonishing 72 percent of the electorate.

Almost immediately, the postmortems began. Johnson's foes charged treachery. In a flurry of editorial broadsides, the *Los Angeles Times* decried Johnson as the architect of a "crime unparalleled in the state's political history." He had joined with Democrats to divide the vote—Johnson for senator, Wilson for president. In no other way, the *Times* concluded, could the disparity be explained. The *San Diego Union* agreed. "The Republican party in California has been betrayed by the same political gangsters that sought to wreck it four years ago."[143] If Johnson had in fact desired a Hughes victory, noted Alfred Holman, writing for the *North American Review*, "one word" would have sufficed. Instead, the mainstays of Johnson's "subsidized press"—the *Sacramento Bee*, *Stockton Record*, and *San Francisco Bulletin*—had endorsed Wilson. In addition, Johnson had carried words of cheer to Democrats when he expressed doubts whether Hughes would be elected, while Rowell had provided false assurances to Republicans by predicting that Hughes would carry the state. George Harvey, editor of the *Review*, found Holman's argument persuasive.[144]

Johnson quickly countered with charges of his own. Harrison Gray Otis was a "journalistic ghoul," and Alfred Holman, editor of the *San Francisco Argonaut*, "the most snobbish journalistic flunky in California." If treachery explained Hughes's California defeat, it had been that of the Old Guard, which had consciously misguided him throughout his ill-fated tour of the state: "These little politicians, doing their little politics, preferred the gratification of their malice and the momentary triumph of their prejudice to the success of the Republican presidential candidate." The results in California, Johnson continued, were no different from those in Oregon, where the progressive Republican Miles Poindexter won easily in his U.S. Senate race but failed to carry the state for Hughes, or from those in Kansas, where Hughes also lost even though Republican Arthur Capper won the governship by 125,000.*

*News release, Part 2, Carton 43, HWJ Papers; HWJ to William J. Kunzie, Nov. 27, 1916. Roosevelt made many of the same points in a telegram expressing confidence

Johnson never completely lived down the accusations of his enemies. Nonetheless, he clearly had the better of the case. As all but
the most reactionary agreed, Hughes's tour of California had alienated large numbers of progressives and lost him whatever labor support he might have had, and the national campaign committee had
done little to repair the loss.[145] Rowell had harped on the need to
win the progressive vote and had continuously complained about
the "uncompromising anti-progressives" sent to canvass the state in
the aftermath of Hughes's visit, but his advice had been largely ignored.[146] Johnson, of course, was the most vocal progressive in the
state, and he had, despite charges to the contrary, strongly endorsed
the national ticket. In San Francisco during the wrap up of the campaign, he had, as the *San Francisco Bulletin* reported, repeatedly eu-
logized Hughes and was one of the few who had not been heckled
for the effort.[147] Yet rarely was his endorsement featured in the Old
Guard press, which largely ignored Johnson and his senatorial race.[148]

Johnson had not intentionally sabotaged the national campaign.
William Kent came closer to the truth when he observed that Wilson's California majority would have been far larger if Johnson had
not actively supported Hughes.[149] But if Wilson's own appeal and
Hughes's public image, tarnished as it was both by the Old Guard
and a flawed campaign strategy directed out of New York and Chicago, were the determining factors in shaping the outcome of the
election, it also can be argued that the political convulsion in California caused by the progressives' capture of the Republican party
after the August primary indirectly contributed to the result.

In the one-month interval between the primary and the selection
of a new Republican State Central Committee at the end of September, conservative regulars did little to sustain the national campaign on the local and district levels. Party literature accumulated
at Republican headquarters and sat undistributed; the national cam-

in Johnson's good faith. "I tried to read it to the Governor," Rowell wrote, "and by
reading rapidly I managed to get over about twenty words of it within the limits of
his patience. He did not indicate indignation but merely such complete indifference
that six seconds was the limit of the attention he could continuously give to the mere
question whether Colonel Roosevelt was friendly or hostile. This, of course, is not
his public attitude, but you are familiar with it as his private attitude." Rowell to
Lissner, Nov. 18, 1916, Rowell Papers. See also Theodore Roosevelt to Edwin Earl,
Dec. 20, 1916, in Elting Morison, ed., *The Letters of Theodore Roosevelt* (Cambridge,
Mass., 1954).

paign languished.[150] At the same time Johnson's campaign, organized independently and supported by progressives from both the Republican and Democratic camps, continued unabated with a flurry of rallies, promotional billboards, and posters.[151] In the midst of the transition, Johnson cautioned that anti-Hughes spokesmen should not be allowed to assume positions of leadership in the coming campaign; but there was no purge, and Johnson neither dissociated himself from his Democratic supporters nor assaulted Wilson's presidency.[152] Viewing the transition from the sidelines, John Works became convinced that Wilson sympathizers dominated the new Republican operation.[153]

Works was wrong, but many who did take part in the campaign were obviously less than enthusiastic in their support of Hughes. Like Johnson, they harbored doubts about his character; unlike Johnson, they could not as easily mask them.[154] Francis Keesling, conducting his own survey of the ongoing campaign in mid-October, was told that Johnson's senatorial battle was in full swing while Hughes's effort seemed paralyzed.[155] But just as Johnson could not with a word dictate the editorial policies of the *Sacramento Bee*, *Stockton Record*, or *San Francisco Bulletin*, neither could he or Rowell, who had replaced Keesling as chairman of the Republican Executive Committee, easily pump life into a presidential campaign that had too often disappointed the very groups that now controlled California's Republican party. No one, Katherine Edson observed, felt worse about Hughes's defeat than Johnson.[156] Her observation rings true, but in more subtle ways than might be apparent at first glance. Though he expressed regret, Johnson demonstrated no real distress over the presidential election results. What stung him was not Hughes's loss per se but the charge of personal betrayal, for hidden in this slander was a grain of truth. He had not betrayed Hughes; rather he had betrayed his own sense of integrity by supporting Hughes. All we succeeded in doing, Edson wrote, was "discrediting in a large measure our own leadership and losing the confidence of the people in our independence."[157] For Johnson, that was the hardest blow.

★   ★   ★

Between 1912 and 1916 the bulk of California's progressives had come full circle, first abandoning their Republican ties, then returning in triumph to control the state party organization. Johnson found the last lap of the journey the most trying. The ordeal had begun with the tragedy at Chicago, when Roosevelt refused to take up once again the Progressive banner. It had been aggravated by the charges that Johnson had betrayed Hughes along the way. But for Johnson, the most wrenching aspect of the journey was of his own making. Having been elected to the United States Senate, he found himself emotionally unprepared to withdraw from the governorship and abandon to others the body of accomplishments with which he identified himself. "The fact is," he mourned, "I don't want to leave here. This is where whatever in my life [that] had been worthwhile has occurred."[158] For six years, his success as a leader had hinged on his willingness to invest not only his energy but his total self in the progressive crusade and to require that others follow his lead. In the aftermath of his election to the Senate, his possessiveness and his obsessive insistence upon continued loyalty from his subordinates became major impediments in the transfer of power, and the fact that his successor, William Stephens, was an outsider whose selection had been demanded by Earl and the Los Angeles faction compounded his innate suspicions.[159]

In December, prior to Johnson's anticipated retirement, Stephens met with him to discuss the transition, only to be told that Johnson would retain the governorship at least through the first half of the 1917 legislative session. As that session began, rumors circulated that Stephens's friends would seek court action to test whether Johnson as senator-elect could continue as governor. Edward Dickson, who had helped to sponsor Stephens, actively courted Johnson's wrath by assuming the role of kingmaker, the role that Johnson continued to regard as his own.[160] In any transfer of power friction is inevitable as new patterns of deference and dependence emerge within a governing circle. Almost automatically, Johnson suspected the worst, increasingly more certain that the southern faction gathered around Stephens was not truly progressive. To Rowell, Johnson confessed that he was "like a jealous woman with hysterical paroxysms" as he contemplated the destruction of his legacy.[161] Stephens, he complained, lacked the force of character necessary to the task. "I would much prefer," he continued, that Stephens be "cranky and cross with me than that he . . . ever be Pecksniffian."[162] But in mid-

February, when Stephens demanded his resignation, Johnson responded with profanity and the relations between the two were severed. *"He wanted the job, and he wanted the money,"* Johnson concluded.[163]

Wilson's proclamation calling for a special session of Congress following the termination of diplomatic relations with Germany cut short any plans Johnson might have had to remain in Sacramento, and on March 11 he announced his intention to resign his governorship. In the interval between his announcement and the formal ceremony before a joint session of the legislature, scheduled for March 15, no words passed between Johnson and Stephens. Ten minutes before the session began, a reporter handed him a copy of Stephens's inaugural address. Five minutes later Stephens arrived to accompany him to the Assembly chamber. Grimly and silently Johnson stalked ahead of the small group of officials in tow. His voice occasionally breaking as he struggled to control his emotions, he delivered his valedictory address—a plea for the preservation of the reforms that had been put in place during his tenure. His departure, he acknowledged, was the most difficult task of his life. The following day he described the scene to Chester Rowell:

As I looked about at the strongest characters of the State of California, sitting in front of me with no attempt to conceal their feelings, I glanced at my successor. His sluggish pulse had not quickened a single bit—his cold heart was untouched by the stimulus of any human emotion. . . . I have left in control a man without heart or emotion or any fine perceptions or any decent impulse—a man without a soul. . . . Vain and egotistical, unfeeling, without [the] instincts of a gentleman, without the breeding of a thug—he has but one conception now and that is that his nose is in the trough and that he must maneuver to keep it there.[164]

In fact Johnson misread his successor. Although Stephens was somewhat colorless in personality and lacked the combative militancy that the state had grown to expect, he nevertheless fought to maintain Johnson's legacy. Californians elected Stephens to a full term in 1918, and during this tenure he successfully pushed for higher corporate taxes, battling against a conservative tide that would triumph in 1922.[165] But Johnson remained adamant. He rebuffed Stephens's efforts to heal their breach, finding in the governor's various appointments evidence to confirm his suspicions, and hatched plots to secure his removal in 1918.*[166]

Taking his leave of California, Johnson left behind a legacy of far-reaching reform, but by leaving the state he contributed as well to the very process his Senate candidacy had sought to prevent: the disintegration of the progressive coalition upon which the future of the reform movement depended.

*Neither Rowell nor Lissner would become part of Stephens's inner circle, and both found reason to be disappointed in the new governor's leadership. Stephens, Rowell remarked, was a "well-meaning dub" doing the best he could. Others expressed similar displeasure. Yet, save for John Neylan, who resigned in protest from the Board of Control, none endorsed Johnson's bitter appraisal of Stephens's character. Johnson, Rowell advised, should reach out to Stephens and thereby capture him, creating "a sort of constitutional monarch" and restoring the real power to Johnson's partisans. Rowell to HWJ, May 11, 1917. But, whether Rowell's scheme was practical or not, Johnson would have no part of it. In mid-December, observing that Stephens might find some pretext to come east to Washington, he urged Rowell to take steps to prevent such action. He had no wish for reconciliation. Instead, he moved to organize a full-scale rebellion by urging the calling of a conference of "fifty or sixty" of the state's leading progressives to force Stephens out in 1918. He would, he promised, actively campaign for the candidate the conference selected. No conference was in fact called, and when it became clear that some progressive dissidents might challenge Stephens in the primary, Johnson drew back, stating that only if Rowell entered the contest would he give his active support. Rowell, reluctant to run, nevertheless threatened to announce his candidacy, hoping thereby to secure Stephens's commitment to a progressive agenda. In the end, Stephens's chief opponent in the Republican primary would be James Rolph, Jr., mayor of San Francisco. Rolph lost to Stephens on the Republican ticket while edging out Francis Heney for the Democratic party nomination. The result was that Stephens had no organized opposition in the general election, for, as a Republican, Rolph could not legally run on the Democratic ticket unless he won the nomination of his own party as well. Although sympathetic to Rolph, Johnson remained publicly silent throughout the campaign. In the aftermath of the election, Stephens would tighten his control by removing from office those who had lagged in their support of his candidacy. On the election, see H. Brett Melendy, "California's Cross-Filing Nightmare: The 1918 Gubernatorial Election," *Pacific Historical Review* 33:3 (Aug. 1964), pp. 317–30.

Chapter III

War,
Peace,
and
Politics

The Confirmation of an Isolationist
1917—1919

For Hiram Johnson, as for many others who had invested their energies in the Progressive party, the continuing goal in the aftermath of the 1916 Chicago debacle was to salvage what they could from the wreckage of the national party. A handful would continue to repudiate fusion, arguing that the endorsement of Hughes by a majority of the Progressive National Committee amounted only to a setback, not a final end to their third-party hopes. To protest that endorsement, they met in rump convention in Indianapolis on August 2, where they vented their anger toward Roosevelt and refused to endorse either Wilson or Hughes. Individually most chose Wilson; some, like Bainbridge Colby, actively toured the nation in support of his reelection.[1]

Following that reelection those who still believed in the viability of the third party readied themselves to renew the struggle and began preparations for a conference scheduled to meet in St. Louis in early 1917. Matthew Hale, recalling Johnson's outspoken objection to fusion at the Chicago convention, urged him to attend. He was, Hale wrote, their "natural leader," the obvious successor to Roosevelt as the Progressive party's presidential candidate in 1920. The date for the conference, he added, would be set at Johnson's convenience.[2] Clearly tempted, Johnson nevertheless declined, albeit with the assurance that he would "fight anybody and break with any crowd" to keep alive the progressive spirit.[3]

In fact, Johnson had no real alternative but to respond as he did. To agree to Hale's proposal just after having successfully led California Progressives back into the Republican party would have been an impossibly foolhardy act. Still, he could not help but quietly salute those who persisted in independent political action. They marched to the tune to which he had once marched, refusing to compromise even in the face of defeat.[4] The trouble with Hale and his group, he wrote to Rowell, was that they confused the progressive movement with the Progressive party. But whether they were any less realistic than those who argued that the national Republican party could be captured and transformed into an instrument of reform was doubtful. That task, Johnson acknowledged, was an all but hopeless dream.[5]

Nor did the efforts to realize that dream alter Johnson's pessimism. After the election Chester Rowell journeyed east to meet with William Allen White, Raymond Robins, James Garfield, and Gifford Pinchot at the Chicago home of Harold Ickes. There they reaffirmed their endorsement of fusion and sought to advance the progressive cause. Much to Johnson's satisfaction George Perkins, the *bête noire* of the movement, had purposely not been invited, but to his chagrin the politics of compromise that Perkins had come to symbolize won the day.[6] The group ignored issues to concentrate on tactics: they called for the establishment of "Progressive Leagues" to push for reform on the state level, announced plans for a general conference of progressive Republicans to meet sometime in March, and demanded that the fifteen-member Republican Campaign Committee, which had been reorganized during the 1916 contest to include six progressives, be substituted for the Republican Executive Committee. No other demands were made.[7] The agenda clearly disappointed Johnson, who had earlier written of the importance of focusing on substance, not tactics, and who had found merit in George Record's suggestion of government ownership of corporate monopolies. "We talk of making progressive the Republican party," he complained, but the Chicago gathering failed to present even the outline of a program. What progressives needed to do, he continued, was not to follow in the footsteps of Perkins, to run back and forth to Republican standpatters under the assumption that the enemy would give way, but, as in California, to fight and subdue that enemy.[8]

The situation further deteriorated when Perkins, ignoring his exclusion from the Chicago gathering, seized its proposal and made it his own by calling upon national chairman Willcox to convene the Republican Executive Committee and to take the steps necessary to implement the change. Willcox complied, but the scheme almost immediately went awry when the conservative majority of the committee, in an obvious rebuff, further consolidated their control by electing John T. Adams of Iowa as vice chairman and heir apparent. Pushing himself further into the fray, Perkins conferred with Roosevelt, then joined with Everett Colby of New York to issue ultimatums demanding that the full National Committee be assembled and threatening to revive the Progressive party if the actions of the Executive Committee were not rescinded. He had heard from over 90 percent of the nation's leading progressives, he announced, and they were unanimous in their support.[9]

For Johnson the only real accomplishment of the Chicago gathering—namely the exclusion of Perkins—had been negated. "Perkins is in command again," he growled.[10] When pressed by Rowell to endorse the proposal for a convention of progressive Republicans, Johnson demurred: "With Hale, Heney, Bainbridge Colby, and Parker, and the others holding one conference, with Ickes and yourself and the rest of us holding another conference, and with Everett Colby and Perkins and Roosevelt in volcanic eruption in New York, our reactionary friends can well afford to laugh, and laugh they undoubtedly will." Perkins, he cautioned, should be ignored, not attacked, and the conference postponed unless its organizers were able to attract a substantial following of liberal Republicans as well as onetime Progressives. Moreover, even if the conference were called, he continued, he would almost certainly find himself in disagreement over the proposed agenda.[11] Meanwhile Ickes moved ahead, securing various endorsements, including that of Senator George Norris of Nebraska, and issuing the call for April 22, 1917.[12]

Johnson faced a dilemma. He could not endorse the efforts of those who championed an independent Progressive party, however great the temptation. Nor could he agree to cooperate in negotiations with the Republican national leadership even though such negotiations, as sponsors of the plan argued, might obviate the need

for independent political action. Thus when Raymond Robins proposed a third option, a proposal almost tailor-made to fit his needs,
Johnson eagerly embraced it. Visiting Johnson in Sacramento on the
eve of his departure in mid-March, Robins proposed a plan whereby
progressive Republicans would jointly subscribe $15,000 annually
over a three-year period. Approximately one-third of the money
would go to paying Johnson's travel expenses; the remainder would
be paid to Johnson himself at the rate of $200 per speech. For John-
son, who was already toying with the idea of returning to the practice of law to supplement an income reduced by $2,500 as a conse-
quence of his elevation to the Senate, the prospect of an additional
$10,000 annually was not unwelcome.[13] More importantly, the pro-
posal allowed him to sidestep the institutional demands pressed
upon him by Rowell and Ickes while providing a forum from which
to spur on a waning progressive movement.

Further, despite his reluctance to acknowledge his own political
ambitions openly, Johnson found Robins's proposal attractive in that
it provided as well a stepping-stone to the presidency. The broaching
of such an idea always flustered Johnson—"there is no more chance
in a presidential fight for me than for that proverbial snowball in the
proverbial torrid place"—but he was nevertheless obviously willing
to explore the possibilities. It was far too early to move seriously in
such a direction, he had advised Rowell prior to his talk with Robins, but it would not be amiss to publicize the California record.[14]
After Robins's visit, both Rowell and Lissner began to collect materials and prepare outlines for the proposed series of speeches.
Among the selected topics, Lissner wrote, "What California has
done" would be their *"pièce de résistance."*[15]

★   ★   ★

But as Johnson and the various progressive factions looked to the
past and grappled with the future, German-American relations exploded in crisis, shattering the expectations on which they had built
their plans. In February 1917, following the German announcement
of unrestricted submarine warfare, Wilson severed diplomatic relations and called upon Berlin to reconsider its new policy. In March
the sinking of American merchant ships began. As the crisis deepened, Perkins gave up his demand to reconvene the Republican National Committee. Shortly thereafter, Ickes announced the post-

ponement of the conference he had labored to organize.[16] Robins's scheme, reformist in aim but partisan by design, was also put aside. Domestic issues would soon be swallowed by the realities of war, and progressivism would lose much of its urgency, eclipsed by the new challenge from abroad. To engage in any sort of partisan appeal, Johnson discovered on his arrival in Washington, was no longer feasible. To suggest a program of social reform, he wrote, would "simply afford an opportunity to those who believe in none to boll [*sic*] you over."[17]

Prior to the election and his elevation to the Senate, Johnson had largely ignored international events in his public statements and refused to enter into the ongoing debate over Wilson's management of foreign affairs. The Republican Old Guard, joined in 1914 by Roosevelt, had pressed the attack, focusing on what it characterized as Wilson's vacillation both in Mexico, where he tried by intervention to shape the direction of the revolution in progress, and overseas, where he tried through diplomatic accord to secure Germany's respect for the nation's commercial rights as a neutral. His Mexican policy, they charged, was quixotic at best, for it contributed to a disorder that risked the lives of resident Americans and imperiled American corporate investments in that country. His efforts to induce Germany to abandon the submarine as an instrument of stealth and to accept the right of American citizens to trade and travel unmolested on the high seas, they contended, were undercut by his appeals for national self-restraint, by his unwillingness to press the issue to a conclusion, to draw the line by forcefully threatening retaliation. Adding to the cacophony of charges, some, like Roosevelt, called into question the policy of neutrality itself and stridently insisted that the nation had a responsibility to join with Britain and France in the war against Germany. Finally, almost all argued that the United States lacked woefully in its capacity either to enforce its will on Mexico or to stand up to Germany's threat. Wilson's reluctance to embrace military preparedness, they concluded, underscored his inability to understand the dynamics of international relations.

Insistent that property rights were subordinate to human rights and that the government's responsibility was to safeguard its citizens, not to serve as the handmaiden of corporate interests, Johnson instinctively found himself at odds with much of the Republican indictment. Perhaps Charles McClatchy put it best. Those who argued for a more militant posture in Mexico, he remarked in 1915, were the Otises and Hearsts, not innocent Americans but "plunderers . . . Hessian-Americans who invaded Mexico for the purpose of squeezing out of Mexico all they could get."[18] And the European war, "the great international crime of the age," was similarly understandable only within the framework of the nationalistic ambitions of the great powers,which had reverted to barbarism in an effort to secure territory, trade, and imperial status.[19] But if Johnson agreed with McClatchy's overall assessment and privately extended his blessings to the movement Henry Ford naively championed to bring peace to Europe, he could not reconcile himself to a policy that seemed to undermine respect for the nation's image abroad.[20]

A self-styled patriot, Johnson echoed Roosevelt's description of Wilson as the "Buchanan" of the twentieth century—even as he rejected Roosevelt's larger vision. "Any man's life may be very peaceful if he is always a poltroon, and any nation can have peace at the price of its men murdered and its women and children outraged," Johnson privately complained in March 1915 upon reading of the attacks on American residents in Mexico. The United States, he grumbled, condemned German atrocities in Belgium but ignored Mexican atrocities against its own citizens.[21] It was true, Johnson admitted, that he could not frame a specific policy that might resolve the nation's ongoing differences with Mexico. Still, he reasoned, a "strong government, without the necessity of war, or invasion of Mexico, could supply the remedy."[22]

In May came the sinking of the British liner *Lusitania* and the deaths of more than 120 of its American passengers. Wilson, Johnson complained, had spoken of "strict accountability" following the German announcement of submarine warfare, but in response to the *Lusitania* outrage he showed himself to be "the great pacifist who was too proud to fight."[23] In so doing, Johnson concluded, Wilson once again projected an image of timidity rather than resolve, thereby inviting rather than deterring further attack. For Johnson, the parallel was clear. The same remedy needed to settle differences with Mexico would work just as well in determining relations with Germany: "a strong government, without the necessity of war."*

*If Wilson, after 1914, "had thought of his country at all or had had a single heart beat for its youth and its manhood," Johnson later observed, "it would never . . . have

But the domestic battle Johnson sought to wage in 1916 precluded any direct assault on Wilson's foreign policies. He aimed to reanimate progressives, not to divide them further, and to belabor Wilson's failures would undermine this goal by providing comfort to the Republican Old Guard and to Harrison Gray Otis, who, as Johnson charged, with "trumpet blasts for all the panoply of war" strove to bludgeon progressives into submission. Those who led in the battle for preparedness came largely from conservative circles.* Moreover, by the time of the election Wilson had effectively sidestepped most of the charges voiced by his critics. Reversing direction, Wilson moved in early 1916 to co-opt the preparedness movement that he had earlier scorned. In so doing, he distressed the more pacifistic of his party and failed, of necessity, to satisfy his more militant Republican detractors. But by demonstrating both resolve and restraint, Wilson strengthened himself politically.

In other ways as well Wilson managed to shape international events to his own advantage. When Francisco Villa attacked American border towns in early March, Wilson first brandished the sword by dispatching American troops into northern Mexico, then defused the emerging war crisis by calling for a peaceful settlement that paved the way for mediation through a joint high commission. Similarly, despite the efforts of some within his own party to avert the controversy with Germany by altering the nation's definition of its neutral rights, he continued to insist that Germany respect those rights, and in the aftermath of the submarine attack on the French

---

been necessary to have shed our best blood and to have risked, as we are now risking, transmuting our republic." HWJ to Theodore Roosevelt, Aug. 16, 1918. See also HWJ to Amy Johnson, July 27, 1918.

Sacramento Bee, July 8, 1916. See also Michael Pearlman, *To Make Democracy Safe for America: Patricians and Preparedness in the Progressive Era* (Urbana, Ill., 1984). In San Francisco, leadership in the preparedness movement had been assumed by Thornwell Mullally, whom Paul Scharrenberg characterized as a "successful union buster." Mullally was the nephew of Patrick Calhoun, one of the major figures indicted in the San Francisco graft trials. In the spring of 1916, the city's downtown business community began preparations for a preparedness day parade, scheduled for July 22. Among those on the executive committee organizing the effort were William Randolph Hearst, William Crocker, and M. H. de Young. Organized labor in San Francisco voiced its bitter opposition, as did Fremont Older and Rudolph Spreckels; all described preparedness as the first step to war abroad and labor repression at home. The parade itself came to grief following the explosion of a bomb, which killed 10 participants and injured 40 others. See Richard H. Frost, *The Mooney Case* (Stanford, Calif., 1968), pp. 61–70, 80–87.

packet steamer *Sussex* in late March 1916, he appeared to secure German assent to American demands.

By such actions, Wilson effectively outflanked his critics. More often than not, Republican attacks during the 1916 campaign sounded carping and irrelevant. Johnson shared Charles Evans Hughes's conclusion that Mexico and Germany could have been earlier brought to heel and made to respect the nation's rights by a more resolute and determined posture on the part of the administration, but he saw little to be gained by belaboring the point. Neither progressivism nor his own senatorial candidacy would profit by such an endeavor, and during the primary campaign he ignored the bulk of Hughes's charges, agreed on the need for "adequate preparedness" in order to keep America at peace, and argued that progressive legislation to further social justice was itself the most important element of preparedness.[24]

Only in the last weeks of the campaign after the August primary, which had assured both his November election and progressive control of the California Republican party, did Johnson begin to emphasize the military side of preparedness and move more directly to question Wilson's leadership. Echoing Hughes's slogan, "America first; America fit; America efficient," Johnson defined the flag as each American's "shield and buckler, and his absolute protection wherever he might be," warned that "a nation that will not protect its women and defend its men will cease to be a nation," and, with a series of patriotic flourishes which included among other historic illustrations Roosevelt's demand for "Perdicaris alive or Rassouli dead," called upon the nation "to arise and awake with the spirit of America" and protect its own.[25]

★   ★   ★

Johnson repeated that theme in March 1917 in a speech before a mass patriotic rally at Philadelphia's Independence Square on the weekend before he took his oath of office as California's junior senator.[26] He was sworn in on April 2, as the first session of the 65th Congress began. That evening he watched and listened as Wilson reviewed the dispute between the United States and Germany and called for a declaration of war. An observer rather than a participant in the two-day Senate debate that followed, he then joined with an overwhelming majority of his colleagues in support of the war resolution. It was with "sorrow and regret" that he voted as he did, he privately acknowledged, but to act otherwise would have been inconsistent with the nation's honor.[27]

But if Johnson was now a resolute warrior, he was also a reluctant one. Wilson's address, with its injunction to make the world safe for democracy, failed to impress him. "I do not [t]hink he had a quickened pulse beat," Johnson observed of the president. "He spoke from the head and not once from the heart."[28] Senate debate struck him as equally uninspired; most noteworthy was Robert La Follette, who in his four-hour address shrilly denounced both the administration's lack of impartiality in defining American neutral rights and the president's decision for war. Certain that La Follette's charges could have been answered, Johnson complained that no one had been prepared for the task. On the whole, the speeches were "mediocre," and the expressions of enthusiasm for war too often forced. Many in the Senate, Johnson concluded, were little more than rubber stamps of the White House. Indeed, he added, if Wilson had asked for peace at any price, Congress would have willingly complied. In letters home Johnson complained of "the superficiality, the hollowness, the pretense and hypocrisy [*sic*]" of those about him. In short, he found his introduction to the Senate a depressing experience.[29]

But the primary cause of Johnson's distress upon his arrival in Washington was his own ambivalence toward the war itself, not Wilson's manner in addressing Congress or the quality of Senate debate. Unlike Roosevelt, Johnson could not invest war with romance and adventure or see it as an ennobling experience. Nor could he, like Wilson, define American belligerency as a means to realize a progressive new world. Initially he tried that latter course, lamely observing that Germany's defeat was essential if the doctrine that might makes right was to be repudiated and if world civilization was to continue to advance, but this attempt to cloak the war with some higher purpose was little more than an afterthought.[30] For Johnson, American belligerency was a grim duty, not a noble adventure, and it is doubtful whether his pulse beat any faster than Wilson's on the evening of April 2.

The nation, Johnson reasoned, had an obligation to defend its flag, its honor, and its self-respect, and Germany's assault on American neutral shipping made conflict all but inevitable. It was true, he acknowledged, that a war in defense of the nation's neutral rights could never generate the fervor and popular zeal that the Civil War had once inspired. Even so, he concluded, there was really nothing else to do but to respond as if head *and* heart were engaged "and every fibre of our being was aroused."[31] But almost from the beginning, Johnson found himself unable to sustain that pose. At first emphatic that the only way to fight was "with both hands and in every conceivable fashion" and suspicious that Wilson's real goal was to avoid combat by fighting "with our dollars to the last Frenchman and Englishman," within weeks he had begun to hope that the war would end without the necessity of landing American troops in Europe.[32] He was, he admitted, "unpatriotic enough to long for . . . peace without being insistent as to all its terms."[33]

Heightening Johnson's apprehension was the fear once common in progressive circles that reform itself would become one of war's chief casualties. Following America's entry into the war, many who had initially opposed participation on the basis of such fears set aside their doubts, justifying their turnabout by redefining war as a creative tool, a catalyst capable of hastening domestic reform and shaping a more efficient and humane society. A war fought for democracy abroad, they reasoned, would necessarily enhance democracy at home. Johnson remained skeptical. The plan that he and Raymond Robins had earlier devised for a series of addresses on progressive themes had already been set aside. Still, Johnson was not willing to abandon hope entirely, and in mid-April, working with Robins, he helped to organize an informal conference of fellow progressives. They met at the home of Gifford Pinchot to outline a fourteen-point program of mobilization around which reformers might unite.

In part, their object was tactical; by endorsing the decision for war, they sought to ensure that Robert La Follette and George Norris, who opposed American intervention, would not be taken as representative of progressivism. But they hoped too that by seizing the initiative they might help shape mobilization along progressive lines. The goal, they affirmed in their published declaration, was to achieve a "broader democracy, [a] more equitable distribution of wealth, and greater national efficiency, thus [to raise] the level of the general welfare." Overall, Johnson confessed, it was doubtful if much of the program would get far, but it would serve as a basis for future action.* It would serve as well to underscore publicly his standing within progressive circles. Pleased by the publicity the declaration generated, Johnson repeated the themes of the fourteen-point program in June 1917 at a bond rally in St. Louis. Out of the war, he cried, must come a "broader democracy" that would substitute "the spirit of social service for the spirit of gain . . . protect the weak against the strong . . . relieve the economic burden upon men and women and children, and help them to secure a larger share in the products of their toil."[34]

On the Senate floor Johnson just as forthrightly expressed what the philosopher John Dewey described as the "social possibilities of war." Wilson's assumption of control over the nation's railroad, telegraph, and telephone operations, he argued, was a desirable first step toward government ownership of all public utilities.[35] Similarly, government controls over the production and marketing of food and fuel that had been authorized by the Lever Act, controls characterized by opponents as "socialism," would continue in peacetime if they proved beneficial to the public.[36] In other ways as well war could establish precedents out of which future policy might evolve. Just as the nation was obliged to rehabilitate those injured in battle, so too it had a responsibility to care for the victims of industrial accidents at home.[37] "We are upon new and untrod paths," Johnson declared, "and only the demonstration whether they bring us good or ill will determine what governmentally our course will be in the future."[38]

But if war forced the nation to experiment with new programs and held within itself the potential to spur further social progress, it

---

*HWJ to Hiram Johnson, Jr., Apr. 15, 1917; HWJ to Rowell, Apr. 21, 1917; HWJ to boys, Apr. 23, 1917. The fourteen-point document included a call for woman suffrage, support for conscription, price supports to encourage agricultural production, "universal industrial service," conservation, guarantees to ensure the rights of wage earners, and price controls to halt the rising cost of living. To finance the war, it emphasized the need to draw from current revenue, particularly revenue to be generated by the graduated income tax and an excess-profits tax—wealth, they noted, must bear its fair share. Those present at the meeting, in addition to Johnson, Pinchot, and Robins, were Ickes, Donald Richberg, Ogden Reid, and Gilson Gardner. Those who signed the statement were William Draper Lewis, Miles Poindexter, E. A. Van Valkenburg, Rowell, and William Allen White. *California Outlook*, May 1917, p. 29. When Lissner reviewed the program, he concluded that if it were implemented the war would certainly be worth its costs. Lissner to HWJ, Apr. 23, 1917.

also could hamper reform, perhaps even threaten the roots of democracy itself. Though unwilling to deny the proposition that war could be turned to progressive purposes, Johnson was characteristically far more demonstrative in expressing his fears. "I am considerable of a radical today," he wrote little more than a month after war was declared, "but I prophesy to you that a year from now I will be a conservative, endeavoring to stem the tide of a people roused to frenzy by burdensome, repressive and coersive [sic] laws."[39]

★   ★   ★

Johnson was at first reluctant to join in Senate debate, for he recognized his own unfamiliarity with the rules and procedures of the body and felt sure that his colleagues expected him to make an "ass" of himself. His initial intention had been to "go slow," to observe Senate proceedings rather than actively participate in them. The first session, he predicted, probably would end in June 1917 after endorsing the president's program, and he would not withhold anything necessary to the war effort. At some point, he acknowledged, he would doubtless clash with the "truculent" Democratic majority, certainly with the "blue stocking" representatives of the Republican Old Guard, men like Lodge of Massachusetts and James Wadsworth of New York, but he would await the proper moment, and would in all probability remain inactive until the beginning of the second session.[40] In addition, he noted, he would maintain his independence from partisan ties and from his colleagues, who, while personally cordial, too often tailored their remarks to fit their audience and only rarely voiced their honest reactions.* Predictably, his jaundiced im-

*HWJ to boys, Apr. 18, July 2, 1917; HWJ to Archibald Johnson, Apr. 18, 1917. Johnson's independence from partisan ties had already been demonstrated on April 12, when, in executive session, he took issue with Boies Penrose to actively support the administration's nomination of William Kent and Edward Costigan to the U.S. Tariff Board. HWJ to Archibald Johnson, Apr. 14, 1917. Of his colleagues, he later wrote: "If there could be such a thing as punishment of intellectual dishonesty, our representative bodies would be depleted, and there would be mighty few men in public life." HWJ to boys, Oct. 1, 1921. But neither his independence nor his suspicions, he acknowledged, prevented him from being viewed by most of his colleagues as "a pretty good Republican." HWJ to Amy Johnson, May 5, 1918. Johnson found companionship within the Senate among both liberals and conservatives but formed few lasting friendships. Oddly, his closest friend in the Senate, until his death in 1921, was his seat mate, Philander Knox, of Pennsylvania. They shared nothing in common politically, Johnson noted, but between them was an intimate bond of real friendship. HWJ to boys, Oct. 21, 1921.

pression of the bulk of his colleagues endured for the next 28 years, but his resolve to go slow gave way within the month as his concerns with the social costs of American mobilization mounted and his doubts whether the nation could long stand the strain of the enterprise took root.

Perhaps no measure could have been better designed to alert Johnson to the dangers the nation faced at home or to project him into Senate debate than the Espionage Act, introduced in early April and pushed through the House by a determined president. The legislation prescribed fines and imprisonment for those who attempted to interfere with the armed forces, prohibited the use of the mails to disseminate "treasonable" material, and authorized government censorship of the press. Focusing his attention on the call for press censorship—"the most outrageous, shameful and tyrannical measure" ever sought by a free government—Johnson joined in the battle that enlisted the American Newspaper Publishers Association, Republican partisans concerned with preserving the press as an instrument to censure Wilson, and a cross section of both conservatives and liberals in opposition to the White House.[41] War, he conceded, required an extraordinary enhancement of presidential power, but, he warned, "we must stop short of [a] successful assault upon democracy's basic principles." The measure, he charged, was unnecessary, nebulous, and elastic, little more than an "excursion into autocracy."[42] Johnson quickly assumed a leadership role in the ongoing battle. He met nightly with members of the Washington press corps to listen to their proposals and hear their complaints. Arthur Brisbane, director of the Hearst-owned *New York American*, lent his support by providing a substitute amendment prepared by his legal staff, but Johnson found the substitute wanting. No better able to frame an alternative of his own, Johnson ultimately decided to move for the total elimination of the censorship clause. Only if this failed, he wrote, would he agree to compromise.[43]

On May 11, Johnson introduced his amendment to eliminate the censorship clause in what Lewis Seibold of the *New York World* described as one of the most impressive speeches heard on the floor in years. He pled not in behalf of the press, he announced, but rather in support of the "transcendent" right of all Americans to exercise free speech, a right especially critical in periods of stress, when too often emotions overrode judgment. Censorship was unnecessary, Johnson argued, for no battles raged on American borders. It would make truth a crime. It would inhibit if not prevent legitimate criticism of government and its operations and thus hamper rather than encourage needed efficiency. And finally, Johnson concluded, it would undermine democracy at home at the very time the nation sought to advance democracy abroad.[44] The next day his amendment passed by a single vote, and the legislation, stripped of the censorship provision, proceeded to conference, where a stubborn Wilson renewed his campaign for control over the press. Wilson's efforts succeeded in the conference committee but ultimately failed when the House rejected the committee action. "Verily, it was turning defeat into victory," Johnson crowed.[45]

At best it was a modest victory, however, and the Espionage Act, which passed in mid-June, contained provisions drastically curtailing the right of free speech. Although Johnson voted to support the final bill, he continued privately to voice his misgivings. "Hundreds of men," he complained little more than a month after the bill's passage, were being imprisoned for expressing even "mild criticism" of the president, while more and more newspapers and periodicals were being barred from the mails because of their "philosophic discussions" of the merits of the administration's war program. "We are making the *world* safe for democracy with the enthusiasm of Peter of Servia and the Mikado," he concluded.*

"The convictions of a lifetime were involved in this censorship fight," Johnson privately affirmed.[46] Many of those same convictions informed his tepid response to the Selective Service Act, which also came before the Senate in April. Johnson conceded the necessity of the draft but shared the not uncommon fear that conscription would prove unpopular, perhaps so much so as to provoke riot and disorder as it had during the Civil War.† Yet even if conscription were imple-

---

*HWJ to Hiram Johnson, Jr., July 23, 1917, emphasis in original. In November, following the end of the first session, Johnson returned to California to make a series of speeches. I would not attempt to do anything more than state facts, he confessed to McClatchy, for "if I were to express my opinion of the facts I would be guilty of treason and liable to twenty years imprisonment." HWJ to C. K. McClatchy, Nov. 21, 1917.

†HWJ to boys, Apr. 10, 1917. "The only expression of satisfaction I find about the war is that it will at least train our boys into shape to keep the Japs at bay," Joseph

mented without incident, it nevertheless represented a system resting on coercion and regimentation and thus turned the proper relationship between the government and the governed on its head, thereby threatening "the last proud tradition that made us a nation of sovereign free men, instead of a nation of mere military units."[47] Conservatives, he complained, had no difficulty supporting the draft. They viewed with "equanimity and cheerfulness and even with great enthusiasm, any law which will send men into battle and blow to pieces humanity."[48]

For the most part Johnson kept silent in the Senate debate on the main motion. He played an active and enthusiastic role only in supporting the amendment sponsored by Warren Harding to underwrite the martial ambitions of Theodore Roosevelt by allowing the ex-president to organize and command a corps of 100,000 volunteers. In his arguments in support of the amendment, Johnson stressed the importance of volunteers as a supplement to conscription, not as a substitute for it, but he clearly hoped that a volunteer system might postpone the day when the draft would be needed. The Senate accepted the Roosevelt amendment as part of the Selective Service Act, but in conference the amendment was rejected and the act modified to give the president the option of authorizing volunteer enlistments, an option he had no inclination to pursue. Thus modified, the bill became law in mid-May.[49] For Johnson, Wilson's refusal to satisfy Roosevelt's ambitions only confirmed his earlier impression of the president as a small, selfish, petty man, "carping and ungenerous," able to control the Democratic party majority but lacking any real qualities of leadership.[50]

Almost immediately the implementation of the Selective Service Act, touching as it did his immediate family, heightened Johnson's antagonism toward the draft. In July 1917 Johnson's older son, "Jack," 29, who had a wife and two small boys, received his notice. Pressed repeatedly by his father, Jack filed for exemption.[51] Everyone assumed, Johnson wrote, that married men with dependents would

Scott, district director of the draft for Southern California later reported. Joseph Scott to HWJ, June 30, 1917. See also Hiram Johnson, Jr., to HWJ, July 11, 1917. Writing to Archibald, his younger son, who had volunteered for service, Johnson observed: "All the stuff you read of patriotic young men loving to serve their country, waiting outside the door to be admitted to the Army, and praying to God that they might not be rejected, is the veriest rot." HWJ to Archibald Johnson, Aug. 2, 1917.

be the last to serve. But that assumption was almost immediately dashed when General Enoch Crowder, the Selective Service administrator, issued regulations permitting the induction of men whose dependents would not become public charges. Johnson exploded. The new rules were outrageous, an illustration of Prussianism unchecked, of a military mind preoccupied with a single goal and indifferent to the human costs and consequences involved. If not stopped, he predicted, the "crazy men" running the war would come close to precipitating revolution.

Embarrassed by the personal ties linking him to the matter but clearly prompted by those ties, Johnson labored hard to secure a modification of the draft regulations: he made the rounds of the Senate, peppered Crowder with his objections, conferred with Secretary of War Baker, and sought an appointment with Wilson.[52] Much to his relief, the administration overrode the military, issuing new regulations that seemed, at least in part, to set the matter to rest. For once Johnson found reason to applaud Wilson. "He has done me really a big favor and I feel grateful to him for it," he acknowledged. After meeting and chatting with the president at a dinner that followed the announcement of the new regulations, Johnson observed: "I really could get along with him very well indeed, I think."[53] The mood would quickly pass. In truth, Johnson could no more set aside his distrust of Wilson than abandon his fear of the potentially corrosive impact of war on American life. He was willing, he wrote, to give Wilson "all the autocratic powers" he sought, but would hold him as well to "strict accountability": "while his shall be the power, his, as well, shall be the responsibility."[54]

Throughout most of 1917 Johnson's fears remained tempered by the hope that American belligerency would provide an opportunity to advance progressive causes. War was necessarily an expensive enterprise, and wartime an opportune moment, as John Randolph Haynes urged, to put taxes where they belong, "upon the backs of the rich." Somewhat more temperately, Johnson had expressed similar sentiments, and the fourteen-point program to which he had subscribed in mid-April called for financing the war as much as possible out of current revenue by increasing the tax rate on higher incomes and imposing a war-profits tax on the nation's corporations.[55]

Corporations, of course, feared precisely such a result and bitterly denounced the $1.8 billion tax bill passed by the House in May, which placed additional burdens on them. Corporate representatives paraded before a sympathetic Senate Finance Committee and induced it to lop $200 million from the proposed schedule before reporting the measure to the Senate floor in August. There, La Follette, a member of the Finance Committee and author of a minority report highly critical of the inadequacy of the proposed bill, was expected to lead the opposition. But because of his antiwar stand, La Follette appeared to many as little more than a "traitor," more interested in subverting than supporting the nation at war. His advocacy, Johnson lamented, tainted even the best of causes. After meeting with Senators Borah, William Kenyon, Henry Hollis, and other sympathetic colleagues to plot a strategy that would draw attention away from La Follette, Johnson himself fired the opening gun for the insurgent cause, calling for an increase in surtaxes and the elimination of consumer taxes on all goods except alcohol and tobacco. In addition, he argued forcefully for the adoption of his own amendment to tax war profits by 80 percent. "Those who coin the blood of war," he insisted, "are the ones best able to pay the expenses of war."*

During the long, sometimes bitter debate over taxation, Johnson fought vigorously, his summer suits often soaked through with perspiration. At times he was sarcastic; occasionally he was pleading; always he was adamant. In his arguments he contrasted the eagerness of the Senate to conscript the nation's youth with its reluctance to touch corporate wealth. Answering those who charged that higher taxes would erode popular support for the war, he replied that the failure to tax windfall profits would destroy morale both at home and abroad.[56] His arguments had sting, and in the wake of his assaults, and those mounted by La Follette, Borah, Hollis, and others, the leadership of the Senate Finance Committee partially gave

* *Cong. Record*, 65th Cong., 1st sess. (Aug. 20, 1917), pp. 6183–86; HWJ to Hiram Johnson, Jr., Sept. 2, 15, 1917; HWJ to C. K. McClatchy, Sept. 17, 1917. La Follette, Rowell observed, "was an outright traitor." Rowell to Theodore Roosevelt, Dec. 1, 1917, Rowell Papers. The debate over taxes took place at the time when the first draftees were being sent to training camps and patriotic demonstrations were being held throughout the land to cheer them on their way. On September 4, Wilson led a parade down Pennsylvania Avenue with Congress in tow. Reluctant to join the march, certain that it was inconsistent with the dignity of the Senate and beyond the physical capacity of many, himself included, Johnson nevertheless participated, unwilling to be classed with La Follette. "What a cowardly lot we all are," he concluded. HWJ to Archibald Johnson, Sept. 5, 1917.

way, agreeing to increase both income tax rates and the war-profits levy. Not a progressive victory, neither was it a defeat. Johnson's own amendment to tax war profits at 80 percent was, as expected, easily scuttled, as were successive amendments by La Follette proposing rates of 70 percent and 60 percent. The financing of war, as Johnson feared, would continue to depend heavily on government borrowing, an arrangement that placed the ultimate burden on middle-class taxpayers. But gains had been made. Clearly pleased as much by his own prominence in the battle as by the outcome itself, Johnson tallied up the results. We raised hell, he wrote, and half a billion dollars in extra revenue.[57] In addition, he noted, while alienating the "predatory rich," he had clearly benefited himself politically. And there was more. It all reminded him of California in 1910. "It will require a long time and a greater effort," he observed, "but ultimately we'll Californianize the nation."[58] Not until after the armistice would he again express such a hope.

★　　★　　★

Throughout 1917 Johnson remained alert to the potentially destructive impact of war on American society but managed to keep his fears in check. In 1918 that task, never easy, became all but impossible, and though he continued occasionally to express the hope that war could be turned to progressive ends, it was more often than not an empty hope, overshadowed by what he saw to be threatening new patterns evolving in the wake of the nation's belligerency. Economic and industrial mobilization enhanced the power of the very corporate interests progressives had sought to discipline. Initially, Johnson saw the modest increases in tax rates that he and his associates had been able to force upon the nation's business community in 1917 as but the first in a string of victories yet to come. But there were no more victories, at least during the war. Congress delayed consideration of a second tax bill until after the armistice, and both Congress and the administration proved more than generous in their treatment of corporate America.

For Johnson that generosity was nowhere better demonstrated than in the legislation, passed in March 1918, that underwrote Wilson's takeover of the nation's railroads. Johnson found much to complain about in the pledge contained in the authorizing legislation to return the railroads to private management after the war, but he focused his wrath on the system of compensation provided by the act. This system guaranteed to the railroads returns equivalent to the profits earned in the three previous years. Using tables provided by Senator Albert Cummins of Iowa, Johnson calculated that the act would afford returns in excess of 20 percent to many of the nation's rail companies. To this figure he contrasted the $30 per month paid to the nation's draftees and the 4 percent return promised to investors in liberty bonds. Those who answered the country's call, he charged, did so at a sacrifice, whereas the railroads were to be rewarded at the highest possible level.[59] The measure, he wrote, was a "gross outrage," worse than the 1917 Revenue Act, for it was intentionally framed to provide windfall profits. Nonetheless, by large majorities the Senate held firm, successively rejecting proposals to limit profits to 5 percent, 6 percent, and 7 percent of capital stock. The final bill, he privately complained, "is the most outrageous and indefensible thing, and the most shameless thing that has been done by this subservient body since I have been here."[60] To Charles McClatchy he growled, "I don't know how better you can create a bolsheviki in this country than by [such] legislation."*

The guarantee of inordinate returns to railroads and the refusal to tax the war-related profits of American industry at the highest possible levels defined the pattern of economic mobilization. The negotiation of federal contracts such as that at Hog Island, on the outskirts of Philadelphia, where government and industry sought to develop the largest shipbuilding facility in the nation—"a saturnalia of extravagance," Johnson fumed, all conceived under "a brilliant phantasmagoria of patriotic pretense"—was yet more of the same.[61] Government did not conscript wealth; wealth conscripted govern-

---

*HWJ to C. K. McClatchy, Mar. 18, 1918. Nevertheless, Johnson initially remained hopeful that government management would pave the way for government ownership. But his hope vanished when William Gibbs McAdoo, directing the operation, announced substantial increases in freight and passenger rates in May 1918. McAdoo, Johnson wrote, seemed to be mismanaging the operation "almost by design" to arouse popular opposition to government ownership. His actions, Johnson concluded, had probably set the movement back a generation. Johnson himself remained committed to the cause but was no longer an active advocate after 1920. Much to his regret, he was absent from the Senate at the time the Esch-Cummins Act, which returned railroads to private management, was passed. He would have opposed the bill. HWJ to Lissner, June 4, Nov. 2, 1918; HWJ to Hiram Johnson, Jr., Dec. 13, 1918; Hiram W. Johnson, "What of the Nation?," *Sunset* (Nov. 1919), p. 13; HWJ to Doherty, July 15, 21, 1922.

ment to serve its own needs at the expense of others. Business, Johnson wrote, saw the war as a "sort of commercial enterprise where it is perfectly legitimate for great fortunes to be made out of our peril and disaster." Wartime profiteering, he added, was "open and shameful."[62]

Nor did Congress or the administration exercise effective oversight. Wilson, Johnson observed, was aloof and disengaged, spending his hours on the golf links, motoring, or attending an evening of theater. "He *never* goes to the office," Johnson complained.[63] On the Hill, the leadership of both parties, underneath a façade of partisan bickering, were united in their zeal to protect the power and enhance the profits of corporate enterprise and stood ever ready to scorn with charges of treason and disloyalty anyone who dared object. Even the most innocent of inquiries, Johnson wrote, triggered abuse. War had "warped and distorted" peoples' minds, leaving them "mentally inert and intellectually barren," creating an atmosphere in which the public was not only unwilling to exercise free speech but hostile to those who tried.* And it was this crimping of democratic rights, far more than the success of business in exploiting their new economic opportunities, that increasingly shaped Johnson's mordant appraisals of the war's impact upon American society. In the mobilization of the nation's economic resources progressives had lost the initiative to their conservative counterparts, but that initiative might in time be regained. Whether it would be possible to recover the right of free expression and restore the nation's prewar tolerance for dissent was far less certain.

When honest disagreement was no longer tolerated, Johnson argued in an address before a San Francisco audience in late 1917, American democracy would be lost.[64] It was a theme he had voiced during the debates over the Espionage Act at the beginning of the war; it was a theme he would reiterate thereafter as America's involvement abroad generated a new hysteria at home. At times, he observed, that hysteria found vent in mob violence or the angry de-

---

*HWJ to Theodore Roosevelt, Mar. 16, 1918. "The Wilsonian mode of government," he complained to his daughter-in-law, "is suppression, repression, and oppression; to stifle any criticism; to denounce as pro-German and disloyal, any individual who makes a legitimate, embarrassing inquiry; and, in every fashion, to prevent and preclude free expression and fair discussion." HWJ to Amy Johnson, Jan. 12, 1918. See also HWJ to Amy Johnson, July 12, 1918.

nunciation of neighbor by neighbor. It infused the rhetoric of a growing army of "patrioteers," those who "eat raw bones and drink hot
blood, all of whom neither go to war themselves, nor send their
own." Often it centered in the courts, where state or federal prose-
cutors, denying the legitimacy of free speech, secured convictions
by equating dissent with disloyalty. Attorneys, Johnson added, had
even been known to forsake their clients and thus debase their profession, because of their fear of being branded as disloyal.[65] In the
fury of war American society was being transfigured, and rather than
trying to check abuses, federal officials joined in the frenzy, dashing
constitutional rights in the process. Under threat of government intimidation, free speech and free press, the nation's "bulwarks," had
been extinguished. Sooner or later, Johnson wrote in March 1918,
he would explode upon the subject.[66]

The explosion came the following month when Wilson, seeking
greater authority to control dissent, proposed the Sedition Amendment to the Espionage Act. The legislation forbade "uttering, print-
ing, writing, or publishing any disloyal, profane, scurrilous, or abusive language" with reference to the government. It was, Johnson
announced on the floor, a "villainous measure," one he never could
accept.[67] Others balked as well, and before the bill went to conference the Senate modified it by including a provision sponsored by
Senator Joseph France of Maryland, to reaffirm the right to "publish
or speak what is true, with good motives, and for justifiable ends."
In conference, under pressure from the White House, the amendment was eliminated. Angrily denouncing that action, Johnson reiterated his opposition to the entire bill. The measure, he charged, put
a premium on hypocrisy, abrogated constitutional rights, shielded
incompetence, and, by breeding distrust of neighbors, further inflamed popular hysteria and aggravated social discontent. Rebuking
Albert Fall for asserting that in war different standards were required, he snapped, "Good God, . . . when did it become war upon
the American people?"[68] But that war too would continue. His protests served to extend the debate on the bill, but only briefly, and it
passed easily by a vote of 47 to 27.*

*HWJ to Hiram Johnson, Jr., May 5, June 30, 1918. To Charles McClatchy, who
endorsed the legislation, Johnson replied: "We are peculiarly in a state of hysteria
at present. Brave men flinch at the charge of 'disloyalty,' and when a prosecuting
officer stands before a jury asserting that patriots do their duty against one, who is

Just as war enhanced the power of the state and enabled it to abridge constitutional rights, so too it enhanced the power of the president and in so doing further compounded Johnson's fears for democracy. Modern wars, he had argued in 1917, necessitated the concentration of executive authority, and he stood ready to invest the president with "the most extraordinary and autocratic powers ever before conferred" in order to ensure the efficient mobilization of the nation's resources. "The short cut to victory," he had conceded, "is organization."[69] Yet from the beginning Johnson distrusted Wilson, and both the president's manner—cold, aloof, intensely partisan—and his exercise of power quickly fanned that distrust. Wilson had once defined the British parliamentary system as a model of political excellence, but as Johnson remarked in comparing him with Britain's prime minister, David Lloyd George, Wilson did not cooperate with his Congress or his party but sought rather to dominate, pressing demands but offering no explanations, seeking power but refusing accountability, continually declining to take others into his confidence.[70] As an administrator, Johnson observed, Wilson was a disaster, with "no more conception of administrative duties than a man in Kamchatka or Timbuctoo." He was little more than a political animal, and would willingly cover up any inefficiency rather than remedy it by exposure.[71]

Johnson joined in the clamor that erupted in the winter of 1917 as coal supplies ran short, the nation's shipbuilding stalled, the armaments program faltered, and reports surfaced of inadequate facilities in military training camps. He supported the efforts of George Chamberlain, the renegade Democratic chairman of the Senate Military Affairs Committee, to force upon the president a council of three to take charge of the mobilization process.[72] Wilson was quick to react, outflanking his critics by securing passage of the Overman Act, which enabled him to reorganize executive agencies without congressional consultation. Certain that no real changes would result, that Wilson sought only to still public criticism, Johnson nevertheless opposed the bill. The President's request, he conceded, was little more than a shrewd political maneuver. Even so, he confessed,

'disloyal,' there is mighty little chance for the fellow charged." HWJ to C. K. McClatchy, June 3, 1918. See also HWJ to C. K. McClatchy, May 13, July 16, 1918; C. K. McClatchy to HWJ, July 9, Aug. 8, 1918.

he could not rid himself of a gnawing fear that Wilson in his disdain for Congress was tempted to abolish it. The idea, he admitted, was incredible, but each day some act or event added to his "black impression."[73]

As the weeks passed, Johnson's suspicions grew. The passage of the Sedition Act in May 1918 had all but convinced him that the administration aimed to cripple freedom of speech and press. In June, Oscar Underwood, an administration stalwart, proposed a Senate rule to limit discussion of any bill to one hour and of any amendment to twenty minutes. The proposal, Johnson predicted, would lead in time to a total muzzling of the Senate. Taking the floor, his voice ringing in anger, he denounced Underwood's motion. With the press and public already cowed, and so too much of Congress, he charged, retention of unrestricted Senate debate was essential for the battle yet to come, the battle "to bring back this Republic into its own . . . to make the fight for democracy in this land."[74]

Underwood's motion failed, but Johnson's fears continued to fester as Wilson actively intervened in a series of Democratic party primary contests, seeking to purge candidates who had opposed his leadership. The president's goal, Johnson concluded, was to make Congress appointive.[75] Increasingly agitated, tempted "to throw caution to the winds" and begin his battle to restore the nation's fundamental freedoms, Johnson awaited further evidence of Wilson's grand design. He was sure the president would misuse the conscription law to draft dissenters and thereby subject them to military courts-martial. Indeed he believed Wilson would not hesitate to place the whole nation under military rule. The forms of democracy would remain, he conceded, but the nation would no longer have "a government representative of the people, or a government by law."[76] In September, Attorney General Gregory gave substance to that prophecy by launching a massive "slacker raid" in New York City. A chorus of outrage erupted as Gregory sought to discover draft evaders by wholesale detention and arrest. The action, Johnson charged on the Senate floor, was an act of terrorism: "The same sort of terrorism that makes it impossible to-day for any newspaper . . . to print what it desires, the same sort of terrorism that makes it to-day a crime for any man in this Nation loyally, legitimately, and honestly to speak his sentiments upon the rostrum or to his neighbors. Terrorism!" Reminding the Senate of his earlier call to preserve free debate so that democratic freedoms might in time be restored, he vowed that he would no longer remain silent but would speak out "whenever terrorism is attempted or militarism runs rampant."[77]

*   *   *

The war, Johnson had written in 1917, was a "bloody, murderous thing, . . . a frightful nightmare" that touched the nation in ways that would have been unimaginable but a few years before. Then, no one would have conceived of landing American troops in Europe.[78] It was a nightmare that shattered progressive hopes. War had not weakened the power of the wealthy; it had strengthened that power. It had not broadened democracy but debased it. And in the effort to enhance national efficiency, a "querulous autocracy" had emerged, indifferent to the democratic process, indeed, as Johnson came to believe, threatening its displacement.[79] It was a nightmare too that touched Johnson personally, endangering as it did the life of his younger son, Archibald, who joined the U.S. Army, fought at Château-Thierry, and almost immediately thereafter suffered a serious emotional breakdown. Paul Herriott, Johnson's onetime private secretary, was yet another casualty of the war, killed in a training accident in Texas.[80]

Johnson never questioned the nation's war declaration. America's belligerency was and remained an affair of honor—"our cause was just and our provocation ample." Yet almost from the outset he was increasingly troubled by Wilson's tendency to blur that fundamental truth.[81] The president's remark at the dedication of the Red Cross building in May 1917 that the nation was the friend and servant of mankind and had entered the war while entertaining no specific grievances prompted Johnson's immediate dissent. Wilson, he privately moaned, "muddles everything" and had failed to clarify "the reasons for the war, our aims and our purposes, and what ultimately we expect to achieve." Putting the question to various senators, he asked what action the United States would take if Germany abandoned submarine warfare, apologized, and agreed to make reparations. A perfect babel followed. Perhaps it was too early to talk of peace, he acknowledged, but it was clearly not too early to define the nation's wartime goals.[82] Yet, even as he hoped that the rumble in Congress for a discussion of war aims would intensify, he remained unwilling to initiate the discussion himself and thereby risk being associated in the public's mind with opponents of the war. In his public comments he touched the issue only obliquely and never in such a way as to precipitate debate.[83]

With the coming of the new year, Wilson himself brought the issue of war aims into sharp public focus in his celebrated Fourteen-Point address, delivered to a joint session of Congress on January 8, 1918. Seeking to capture the attention of the world, seeking as well to restore the faltering resolve in revolutionary Russia and thereby prevent a German victory on the eastern front, the president sketched out his vision of a peace worthy of war's sacrifice. Many applauded; Johnson did not. In detailing his objections, Johnson ignored the general objectives outlined in Wilson's first five points and ignored as well Wilson's endorsement of an association of nations, a proposal that would preoccupy him long after the armistice was concluded, to concentrate on the broad strokes with which the president remade the map of Europe. To his younger son, he wrote:

Today, we are told, substantially, that we can never make peace until Alsace-Lorraine shall be returned to France; until the frontiers of Italy shall be readjusted; until the people of Austro-Hungary shall be accorded the freest opportunity of autonomous development; until Servia shall have secured access to the sea; and the Balkan boundary lines shall be established, and an independent Polish State erected. I do not think that our people, if they understood, would wish to expend their blood and their treasure that Italy may have Trieste and the Trentino, and a couple of islands in Greece, and though my sympathies are wholly with France, and I would gladly have Alsace-Lorraine restored to her, I would not wish to send our boys across the sea alone for the purpose of wresting those provinces from Germany; nor would I waste a single American life in marking the boundary lines in the Balkans.[84]

Wilson's declaration, he insisted, by linking peace to conditions that could be obtained only by Germany's total defeat, would prolong the nightmare of war. In addition, the substance of those conditions and the fact that Lloyd George had outlined similar terms only three days prior to Wilson's address suggested that American policy was in fact being determined by the nation's cobelligerents. "We seem to have forgotten making the world safe for democracy," Johnson mused. "I am very sorry because I did love the phrase."[85]

From the outset Johnson had doubted whether the war could be ended by decisive victories on the battlefield.* Each side had tried, but in their efforts they had managed only to bleed themselves to a point of physical and psychological exhaustion. Nor was it at all certain that the United States, as a participant, would be any better able to tip the balance. As Americans were forced to assume more and more of the economic and military burdens their allies could no longer shoulder, Johnson observed, dissent at home was sure to intensify, and it would be voiced not only by liberals and the left but also by conservatives, who in any prolonged enterprise would be forced to sacrifice first their profits and ultimately their property. While decrying the success of the nation's corporations in reaping the profits of war, Johnson nevertheless predicted that ultimately it would be the nation's "rich and the well-to-do" who would demand peace; they would lead a revolution from the top down once they were forced to sacrifice.[86]

But as events in Russia made clear, other kinds of revolution were also possible, and Wilson's Fourteen-Point Declaration, by rejecting the opportunity for negotiations, furthered the possibility that socialist uprisings abroad would destroy Europe's ability to wage war. It was an undoubted fact, Johnson wrote on the eve of Wilson's address, that people everywhere were "seething and anxious" for peace. The one great question, he continued, was "how long can the people—that is the common people of the world—be kept in suppression and subjection. When they burst forth it may be as Bolsheviki, but until the explosion comes from them, in my opinion, there will be no peace."[87] A satisfactory settlement that would have vindicated American honor and ended German militarism had been possible, he insisted. Quite deliberately, Wilson had turned his back on that opportunity, choosing to pursue victory instead.[88]

And the president's choice, Johnson discovered, was a popular one. His initial hopes that Wilson's Fourteen Points would spark public and congressional protest quickly faded. Many in the Senate, he wrote, were "war mad," eager to see the Central Powers dismembered and the German people destroyed. At first Johnson had been

*In December 1917, in conversations with Medill McCormick and Bainbridge Colby, who had just returned from Europe, Johnson found confirmation of his doubts. The war, McCormick predicted, would end in a negotiated settlement. If this is true, Johnson reflected, why not negotiate now, "before the slaughter of all our young men?" HWJ to Amy Johnson, Dec. 29, 1917.

tempted to publicize his objections, but within days he reconsidered. Sooner or later, he lamely concluded, the Senate would take up one or another of the pending resolutions on war aims, and then he would be heard.[89] In the meantime, friends of the administration, aware of Johnson's growing misgivings, offered reassurance. From Roy Howard of the United Press, an admirer of Wilson, came word that the territorial provisions of the Fourteen-Point address were meant only to fortify Allied morale and did not fasten the United States to any concrete terms. Over lunch, Edward House, the president's occasional alter ego, echoed Howard. Wilson, he confided, had intentionally used "should" rather than "must" in describing postwar territorial alterations.[90]

Wilson's declaration on February 11 that the United States had no desire to act as an arbiter in Europe's territorial disputes and that peace did not depend upon the acceptance of any specific suggestion found in the Fourteen-Point address seemed further to confirm House's demur. Somewhat relieved, Johnson noted that the president had drawn back from his announcement of January 8. Nevertheless, without more specific disavowals and exacting declarations, the war aims of the nation remained dangerously ambiguous and misleading. One could choose, he complained, between the purpose as originally stated, the disavowal of that purpose announced in Wilson's Red Cross speech, the declaration of the Fourteen-Points, the assurances of Roy Howard and Colonel House, or the disclaimer of February 11. Increasingly plagued by insomnia, his suspicion of Wilson's "mental honesty" exacerbated by House's disclosures, Johnson continued to wait for the congressional debate on war aims—which never came—and to hope for a military victory that would at last put an end to the slaughter.[91]

Further contributing to Johnson's distress was his concern lest a prolongation of the war not only further erode democratic values at home but also, by enhancing Japanese power, threaten American security abroad. The Japanese, he wrote, were the "Prussians of the Pacific," insidious, cunning, and far more treacherous and cruel than the Germans. Japan had easily overrun German possessions in China and the Pacific in 1914 and 1915, and stood poised following Russia's withdrawal from the war in March 1918 to annex Siberia and Russia's eastern provinces. In time, Johnson predicted, Japan would change sides in the war, joining with Germany and reaching out to menace America itself.[92] Given his concerns, Johnson was understandably disturbed by the growing clamor voiced by the nation's allies for military intervention in Russia to restore an eastern front and eliminate Bolshevik power, fearful lest the United States by word or deed condone such a policy and thereby further whet Japan's imperial appetite. With mounting fascination and dread he watched the dynamics of international politics and hoped that Wilson would stand firm against Allied demands.[93]

In the summer of 1918, however, Wilson acceded to those demands by dispatching American troops to Siberia and north Russia to join with Allied forces. The argument that the war-weary Russians might be prodded back into the lines clearly did not impress Johnson, who sympathized with their plight. They were looked upon with scorn and disdain, he wrote, "because after losing eight millions of their people they did not lose eight millions more for Constantinople and the Dardanelles." He distrusted Lenin and Trotsky and the emerging Bolshevik leadership, but was nevertheless certain that a "faintly budding bloom" of democracy could be found in the Russian ferment and equally convinced that Allied and American intervention would blight its growth.* For Johnson, Wilson's acquiescence to intervention revealed the hollowness of his democratic rhetoric. It provided as well a cloak under which Japan could justify its imperial designs. Most importantly, it again demonstrated the president's inability to pursue a course other than one charted by the nation's cobelligerents. The French, Johnson was told, had threatened to "quit the game" if Wilson refused to cooperate.[94]

*   *   *

Ultimately, it was Germany and her cobelligerents who quit the game. The German 1918 spring offensive, which pierced but failed to break the Allied lines, left German forces vulnerable to Allied and American counter-thrusts that had begun in mid-July and continued into the fall. Reeling under the impact, Berlin, in early October,

---

*"Their cry for bread, and for land, is as little understood by the majority of our people as our original cry for decency in California was understood by the old line politicians." HWJ to Amy Johnson, July 20, 1918. Johnson's initial comments on Lenin and Trotsky can be found in HWJ to Amy Johnson, Jan. 12, 1918. Trotsky, he wrote, was a "little east side Jew waiter."

1918, began negotiations for the armistice that was concluded on November 11.* The nightmare of war had ended. But the dynamics unleashed by that nightmare persisted. America's military leaders, Johnson warned, were ready to use almost any excuse to retain a large, standing army. Equally troubling, the assault on free speech continued, its tempo quickened by fears of Bolshevism. In addition, Wilson's decision to attend the Paris Peace Conference, his selection of accompanying delegates, and his refusal even to discuss the terms of the settlement he planned to propose again underscored the irrelevance of Congress.[95] Finally, American troops remained in north Russia and Siberia, and there the killing continued. Failure to withdraw those troops, Johnson protested, once again belied the administration's profession of democratic principles and illustrated its chronic willingness to subordinate the nation's own interests to those of its allies. More ominously, American involvement in Russia seemed a harbinger of the future, a catalyst welding into permanence the corrosive dynamics undermining democratic values at home.

Johnson's understanding of the Russian imbroglio was largely shaped by Raymond Robins, who as a member of the American Red Cross Commission had viewed at first hand the Bolshevik revolution. Upon his return to the United States in June 1918, Robins had unsuccessfully sought an audience with Wilson to impress upon him the possibility of accommodation with the new Bolshevik leadership. He knew more about Russia than any foreigner, Johnson observed, and told a story "amazing and startling, and of but little credit to our co-belligerents."[96] Working closely with Robins, a frequent visitor at his home, Johnson mounted the first of his public attacks on the administration's foreign policy in December 1918. The attack took the form of a resolution requesting both information and an explanation of the reasons for America's continued involvement in north Russia and Siberia.[97] Using documents provided by Robins and notes supplied by Louis E. Browne of the *Chicago Daily News*, Johnson raised a series of questions implying that the United States had intentionally rebuffed efforts on the part of the Bolsheviks to secure a Russian-American rapprochement prior to

*When his daughter-in-law Amy Johnson died from tuberculosis on September 7, 1918, Johnson returned to San Francisco, where he remained until the first week in November. His correspondence during this period is scant.

Russia's withdrawal from the war and suggesting that the present
policy of economic blockade and military intervention intensified
that nation's woes by feeding Bolshevik terror.

Contrasting official explanations of American policy with newspaper reports of American deeds, Johnson insisted that the government had embarked upon an undeclared war against Bolshevik Russia. The armistice and the collapse of Germany invalidated whatever
justification there might once have been for such involvement, and
those who now shifted their ground to argue that it was America's
duty to restore order by rescuing the Russian people from the anarchy of revolution outlined a task of infinite scope. Concealed in
such a policy, he warned, was the danger that intervention in Russia was but a prelude to "war against revolution in all countries,
whether enemy or ally." A League of Nations built upon such foundations, he predicted, would necessarily degenerate into a bankrupt
"Holy Alliance." Johnson's own prescription was clear: "I want no
policy in our Republic of subjugating or subduing nations or peoples
who do not think as we do. I want no American militarism to impose by force our will upon weaker nations." Those who argued
otherwise, he added, endorsed a policy no different from that attempted by the now discredited Germany.[98]

In asking for an explanation of American policy in Russia, Johnson carefully wrote out and read the text of his speech, fearful that
any chance remark might brand him as a defender of Lenin and
Trotsky. Indeed, he acknowledged, the very truth seemed to make
him such. Documents provided by Robins gave plausibility to the
charge that the United States and its allies had first rebuffed invitations from Russia's revolutionary leadership when acceptance
might have kept Russia in the war, and thereafter had ignored
opportunities for cooperation. At the heart of the matter, Johnson
privately observed, was the fear on the part of the international
banking community that their enormous investments in prerevolu-
tionary Russia would be lost unless the Bolshevik government were
overturned. He could not prove such an accusation, he admitted, but
was nevertheless convinced of its accuracy. The bankers, he explained, encourage armed intervention "in support of some dictator
or representative of the old imperial family, so that a strong government, by which they mean a government at once recognizing their
debts, may be set up."[99]

Johnson was unwilling either to voice such a charge in public or to reveal the documents provided by Robins. He toed the line and kept his distance from the left. Even so, he was pleased by the results of his speech. Everyone had shunned the issue, he wrote, fearing identification with radicalism. But the response had been gratifying. If nothing else, he boasted, he had demonstrated that wartime restrictions no longer limited congressional discussion and debate, and had established his own preeminence as a vocal critic of administration policy. Moreover, his conviction that the American people would protest the nation's participation in an undeclared war seemed vindicated. To answer the flood of mail pouring into his office he found it necessary to prepare a form letter. His resolution, he cheerfully wrote, had "kicked up a beautiful mess" in the Senate. The Senate Foreign Relations Committee divided evenly and thereby delayed action. Yet, whether they acted or not, he added, he was determined to press forward his attack.*

In the weeks that followed, Johnson maintained his assault with comments on the floor and in press interviews.[100] In mid-January he introduced a second resolution, this time calling for the withdrawal of American troops from Russia. Notwithstanding the warnings of those around him, including his wife, to go slow and steer clear of the Robins documents lest he be painted as a Bolshevik, Johnson openly cited the documents to substantiate his accusations. American policy, he charged, was "weak and vacillating, stupid, and ignorant . . . a miserable misadventure, stultifying our professions, and setting at naught our promises." The United States and its allies bore the blame for much that had gone wrong in Eastern Europe. Indeed, he insisted, the policy pursued was counterproductive, for it had enabled the Bolsheviks to consolidate their power by appealing to Russian nationalism to oust foreign invaders.

But, as in his initial address, it was not past blunders but present dangers that worried him, not conditions in Russia but policies at home that prompted his wrath. The introduction of American troops into Russia, he argued, demonstrated the disparity between

---

*HWJ to Hiram Johnson, Jr., Dec. 13, 26, 1918; HWJ to Rowell, Dec. 27, 1918, Rowell Papers. While sympathetic to the Russian revolution, Johnson, unlike Robins, was not enamored of Bolshevik leadership. Since his speech, he wrote, "I've had to steer clear of big black-bearded male Russians, and slant-eyed female Russians. I am afraid of them all and don't want to become entangled with any of them, revolutionist or reactionary."

Wilson's promises and his performance. He had vowed not to intervene and then, "prating of our love for the Russian people," he had
done so. He had defined the nation's task to be custodial in nature,
ensuring that military supplies would not fall into German hands,
but, at the behest of the nation's cobelligerents, he had allowed
American forces to advance inland in an undeclared war. Wilson's
eloquent but ambiguous words had cloaked malevolent deeds.

In other ways as well, Johnson charged, the Russian misadventure
illustrated the vacuity of Wilson's rhetoric. "Open diplomacy" devolved into a policy shrouded in secrecy, developed and pursued
through undisclosed arrangements with our cobelligerents. "Self-
determination" meant in practice "determination by ourselves of
the kind of government others should have and then impressing that
kind of government upon an unwilling and a rebellious people."[101]
Joined by La Follette and Borah, Johnson maintained his attack
throughout the closing days of the 65th Congress, but was unable to
bring his resolution directly to the floor of the Senate and thereby
circumvent the Senate Foreign Relations Committee, which still refused to report his earlier resolution. On February 7, with the Senate
sharply divided along partisan lines, he lost by a margin of five votes,
and on the 14th only the tie-breaking vote of Vice President Thomas
Marshall prevented action.[102]

But as Johnson well recognized, the division in the Senate was
deceptive. Republicans rallied to oppose Wilson, not to support the
substance of his resolution. Many were critical not of intervention
but of Wilson's restraint, his refusal to join boldly with the nation's
allies and muster sufficient force to overthrow the Bolshevik regime.
Such was the position of Lodge, soon to become chairman of the
Senate Foreign Relations Committee, as well as of Lawrence Sherman of Illinois; Porter McCumber of North Dakota; and Charles
Townsend of Michigan. The Russian revolutionary government,
Lodge had earlier sniffed, was "no more fit to be dealt with in negotiations, no more capable of carrying out agreed terms, than a band
of anthropoid apes." Far from being able to withdraw American
troops, he predicted, Wilson would find it necessary to increase their
number.[103]

In an atmosphere supercharged with the emotions that would
shortly seethe forth in the Red Scare, few were as willing as Johnson
to dismiss the threat of radicalism. The Bolsheviks, he insisted,

were a symptom, not a disease, a product of tyranny and social injustice too long ignored. Their existence was an impetus to reform, not an excuse for reaction. "So long as we cherish liberty and preserve democracy, we need fear in our Nation no such noxious growth," he had affirmed in his first address on Russia.* Nor did he seem troubled by the fear that radicalism might spread westward into Central Europe, Austria, and Germany in the wake of the dislocation wrought by the war. Wilson's hurried appeal from Paris for an appropriation of $100 million in food relief was premised on the need to turn back such a threat. In the Senate, the relief measure won strong support from Lodge and a majority in both parties, and passed easily by 53 to 18. Johnson took his stand with the minority. The "imperious" manner of Wilson's request troubled him. He was certain too that the real motives behind the bill had less to do with hunger than with profits—the administration's goal, he argued, was to relieve American packers and other suppliers of their huge and unmarketable inventories. But above all, Johnson insisted, Americans should look first to their own needs and develop a comprehensive program to cope with the problems of demobilization and industrial dislocation, mounting tensions between management and labor, high rates of inflation, and the danger of widespread unemployment. Only then would he agree to consider foreign aid. "While building castles in the air in Europe," he cautioned, "let us make firm the foundation of our house at home."[104]

In defining his stand Johnson drew upon familiar isolationist themes. The tradition of American isolationism, long a commonplace in the nation's lexicon of values, rested as much on faith as on reason. It had been shaped both by the nation's geographic remoteness from threatening powers abroad and by a belief in the country's unique moral and political institutions, a heritage potentially vulnerable to Old World intrigue and infection. Germany's aggression, Johnson acknowledged in 1917, had impelled the nation

---

*In one of the early drafts for this speech, Johnson had been more specific: "The curse of the laborer's home is the fear of unemployment, of sickness and accidents unprovided for, of old age without a competence, and of sudden death without adequate protection for the home. Let us consider the right in a free land for industry to be free, and the right of capital to organize, the right of labor to organize and share in making the terms and conditions under which labor gives its life, a day at a time, to feed and house and clothe the people." Russia draft, misdated Nov. 1917, Part III, Carton 25, HWJ Papers.

to set aside that tradition, to abandon the Founding Fathers' "solemn injunction" against entangling alliances and to discard their warnings against American meddling in the political quarrels of Europe, for only by so doing could the menace of German militarism be thwarted. But that abandonment, he publicly cautioned, was "temporary," and as the war continued into 1918, further disfiguring American institutions at home and assuming new dimensions abroad, Johnson quickly found additional confirmation for his isolationist faith.[105] His concern lest Wilson lose sight of the immediate events that had provoked the nation's declaration of war, his hope for a precise definition of American war aims, his objections to the territorial provisions of Wilson's Fourteen Points, and his strident dissent from U.S. policy in Russia were all cut from a common cloth—his faith in isolationism, and his fear that American power was being subverted to serve the interests of Britain, France, and Japan at the expense of the American people.[106]

Nor did the end of the war eliminate that threat, as the Russian misadventure proved. The nation, Johnson observed, stood at a crossroads, and both Wilson and his Republican opposition seemed eager to turn in bold new directions. In the Senate, Henry Cabot Lodge, outlining his objections to a League of Nations, argued forcefully for the retention of the nation's wartime alliance. The United States, together with its allies, he insisted, bore an obligation to ensure the peace by guaranteeing the territorial settlement that would emerge out of the Paris Peace Conference. Other Republicans, including Philander Knox of Pennsylvania, appeared to agree.[107] It was a path Johnson refused to travel. "I do not want an American army policing the world and quelling riots in all peoples' backyards," he stated to Theodore Roosevelt. To the Senate he declared: "Let us have peace and get out of Europe."[108]

Chapter IV

New
Directions

*The League, the Treaty, and the
Campaign of 1920*

On December 4, 1918, Woodrow Wilson sailed from New York harbor, en route to France and the Paris Peace Conference, which was scheduled to begin in mid-January. Apprehensive from the beginning, Hiram Johnson awaited the conference results with growing impatience, all but certain that, as in war so in peace, Wilson's idealistic rhetoric would fall victim to Old World realpolitik. The nation's allies, Johnson observed, had already substituted closed hearings and press censorship for the open diplomacy championed in the first of the Fourteen Points. Others of the president's conditions for a just and lasting peace—the freedom of the seas and the removal of discriminatory trade barriers between nations—seemed destined to be ignored, while the secret treaties of America's wartime partners, dividing the territorial spoils of victory, predetermined that settlement.

Amidst the wreckage of Wilson's grand vision, little survived save the concept of a League of Nations. Here, Johnson was convinced, Wilson would get his way. But whether the league was meant to be taken seriously remained far less clear. The allies, Johnson predicted, would agree to its creation not because a league was essential to the peace they sought but because it was irrelevant to that peace. The concept itself, he remarked, was but another of Wilson's rhetorical flourishes, superficially attractive but almost entirely devoid of substance. Once again, Wilson deceived himself, captured by his own words, and in his vanity willing to rest content if those words were echoed by others. In fact, Johnson added, the president's determination to attend and participate actively in the Paris negotiations was a product of his conceit, and the league proposal itself was little more than an excuse for his triumphal tour abroad.[1]

Europe's leaders would happily exploit Wilson's vanity by embracing the league, "a paper organization of little or no consequence," and perhaps even by accepting some mild concession with regard to freedom of the seas, if in return Wilson would agree to their primary goal, namely, to underwrite the settlement at Paris with the guarantee of American power. Wilson, an innocent abroad, was certain to give way, and the United States, Johnson predicted, would end up "holding the bag," a bag woven from European ambitions and dyed with American blood.[2]

Johnson's assessment of European intentions remained constant; not so his evaluation of the League of Nations. Indeed initially, despite his readiness to dismiss the idea, Johnson found himself briefly tempted by the prospect of such a league. As an abstraction, he confessed, the concept of an organization able to prevent wars was "alluring and enticing." The difficulty, of course, was in translating hope into reality, and to rest the league upon Wilson's faith in the power of moral suasion would be to rest it on "the most empty of promises."[3] The war had already proven the frailty of that foundation, just as it had illustrated the dangers inherent in linking American fortunes to European designs. In an effort to strike a positive note, Johnson floundered. Wilson would have his enthusiastic support, he awkwardly announced to the Senate in late January, if he could secure a league "which does not relinquish our sovereignty and which in reality will be a preventive of future wars."*

On February 14, 1919, while still in Paris, Wilson disclosed the draft terms of the League Covenant, thereby adding new voices to the chorus of denunciations in Congress that had earlier been expressed by senators Borah of Idaho, and James Reed of Missouri. League membership, they charged, compelled the nation to become the world's policeman, hampered its ability to act in its own inter-

* *Cong. Record*, 65th Cong., 3rd sess. (Jan. 29, 1919), p. 2262. Instantly, James Reed, Democratic senator from Missouri and one of the earliest opponents of the league, interrupted to ask whether an effective league was possible without an infringement of national sovereignty. It was a question Johnson preferred for the moment to postpone.

ests, and invited outside interference in its domestic affairs. In the Western Hemisphere the league endangered the Monroe Doctrine. Globally it locked the United States into an international structure that guaranteed British domination by allowing India and the British Commonwealth countries equal voting rights.

Though Johnson kept silent in public, he was tempted to agree. No longer innocuous, no longer incidental to the Paris settlement, the league had become the means to harness American power to underwrite that settlement. He would wait for Wilson's own explanation of some of the league's more "abhorrent" provisions before making any public comment, he wrote, but Borah seemed closest to the truth when he described the league as a major triumph of British diplomacy.[4] Minnie Johnson was certain that he would soon join with Borah and Reed to denounce the proposal, but he continued to delay. "I am waiting, and really hoping, to be convinced," he wrote to Charles McClatchy; "and I'm not like the individual who made that remark, and then added that he would like to see the fellow who could convince him."[5]

But little that Wilson said was convincing. Returning briefly to Washington in the closing days of the 65th Congress before departing again for Paris to wrap up the negotiations, he seemed more intent on bludgeoning his critics than on converting them. "Blind and little, provincial people," he snapped on one occasion. Thirty-seven equally blunt Republicans who would hold seats in the next Senate, a number sufficient to prevent ratification of the finished treaty, signed their names to a round robin prepared by Lodge and Frank Brandegee of Connecticut, pledging their opposition to the league "in the form now proposed."[6] Johnson's name was included. As "a provincial patriotic American first," he explained, he would find it impossible to vote either for the covenant as presented or for an amended version if it contained provisions similar to the "obnoxious parts" of the original.[7]

Johnson's doubts, fed by rumors from abroad, intensified following the conclusion of the 65th Congress in March 1919. From Lincoln Colcord, of the *Nation*, and Judson Welliver, of the *New York Sun*, came word that the first task of the new league would be to use American troops to destroy the Bolshevik government of Russia. The design was consistent with Johnson's fears.[8] The more he studied the league, he confessed, the more he was convinced of its perils.[9] It was time once again for Americans to look to their own. To Chester Rowell he wrote:

Every morning as I read the dispatches—Egypt aflame; allied troops on the Dalmatian coast; the French pressed back from Odessa; Americans fighting valiantly at Archangel; a new allied army to be sent to maintain the boundary of Poland; Americans keeping peace between the Jugo-Slavs and Italians; Korea in revolt; China demanding justice as against Japan . . . I confess I am unable to understand an American father or an American mother who would wish to enter into any arrangement with the bankrupt nations of the earth to maintain their tottering governments with American blood.[10]

And it was precisely that role, he insisted, that the nation was being groomed to play. Article X of the covenant, which pledged American support to maintain the territorial integrity of member states, was "the most vicious thing in the whole scheme." The nation's wartime allies, Johnson remarked, will agree to almost any change in the text of the treaty "if we'll guarantee their territorial integrity for all eternity."*

For Chester Rowell, Johnson's mordant observations, while not unexpected, were nevertheless disappointing. In reply, he admonished Johnson to avoid identifying himself with the "parochial" Americanism preached by Wilson's critics. The time had come, he argued, for a "real" league even though it might substantially impair American sovereignty.[11] Others, though less enamored of Wilson's vision, warned of the political damage Johnson would incur by refusing to compromise. If, as they expected, Johnson planned a presidential campaign for 1920, it was imperative that he temper his antagonism. The flood of petitions from civic organizations, women's groups, organized labor, and church assemblies underscored the widespread appeal of the league throughout the nation.[12] Some doubted whether he could win even in California while standing on the unpopular side of the issue.[13] If Johnson enlisted in the opposition, Rowell warned, his only hope would be for the Senate to ratify the League Covenant in time to remove it as an issue from the coming campaign.[14]

*HWJ to Rowell, Apr. 9, 1919. To John R. Haynes, Johnson wrote: "How any man of liberal tendencies, any individual, whose thoughts are with ordinary humanity, can deliberately advocate such a provision as Article X passes my understanding." HWJ to John R. Haynes, May 16, 1919, Haynes Papers.

Already beginning to weigh his political prospects for 1920, Johnson agreed.[15] Yet he could no more set aside his opposition to the league than relinquish his hopes for the presidency. Unless major changes resulted from the ongoing negotiations at Paris, he affirmed in April, he would fight against American entry into the league to the very utmost of his ability.[16] At the same time, however, he tried to prevent his proposed candidacy from becoming entangled with the league issue. On May 7, 1919, in a letter to Lissner to be shared with his friends, Johnson signaled his interest in campaigning for the Republican presidential nomination. Totally ignoring foreign affairs, he stressed the need to renew the effort begun in 1910 to make the Republican party progressive. Those in California who had rallied in 1912 and 1916, he wrote, should begin to shape the outlines of his 1920 campaign, but they should do so informally and without publicity. Only later need the effort begin in earnest.* And to eliminate any doubt, in a subsequent letter to Lissner, Johnson reiterated his instruction to go slow, to delay the development of the campaign until after the League of Nations question had been decided.[17] Committed to doing his best to oppose American membership in the league but sure that the Senate would ultimately bow to Wilson's will, he envisioned a campaign far different from the one that ultimately emerged.[18]

★   ★   ★

Johnson was appointed to the Senate Foreign Relations Committee—the "one great committee," his wife exclaimed—at the opening of the special session of the new 66th Congress in May 1919.†

---

*HWJ to Lissner, May 7, 1919. In a second letter the following day, so that there would be no confusion, he acknowledged that he would oppose the league whatever the consequences. But it was clear that progressivism, not the league, would shape the content of the campaign. HWJ to Lissner, May 8, 1919. As late as May 1919 the League to Enforce Peace considered Johnson in the "doubtful" class with regard to the league but not inextricably opposed to it. Ralph Stone, *The Irreconcilables: The Fight Against the League of Nations* (Lexington, Ky., 1970), p. 89.

†Minnie Johnson to Hiram Johnson, Jr., May 28, 1919. Republican party leaders had worried that progressives would join with Democrats against the slim Republican majority in the Senate to prevent Boies Penrose from inheriting the chairmanship of the Senate Finance Committee. Borah utilized such leverage to secure Johnson's appointment to Foreign Relations. Opposition to Penrose was confined to the party caucus, and Penrose was assured of his chairmanship. Earlier, Johnson had declined the position of president pro tem. See HWJ to boys, May 27, 1919; HWJ to Hiram Johnson, Jr., Nov. 23, 1918, May 14, 19, 1919; Minnie Johnson to Hiram Johnson, Jr., May 19, 1919; Stone, *Irreconcilables*, pp. 94–99.

On May 20, the second day of the session, he offered a resolution calling on the State Department to transmit the full text of the peace settlement to the Senate. Copies of the document had been leaked by Germany and circulated widely abroad, but Wilson, who was still in Paris, refused to release anything more than a general synopsis. It was the sort of situation that was to be expected in the new context of open diplomacy, Johnson sarcastically observed.[19]

Two weeks later, with his resolution still pending, he took to the floor to deliver a ringing denunciation of the league and the Paris proceedings. Little of his message was new, but the delivery was characteristically pungent. The terms of the league covenant, Johnson observed, were loose, uncertain, and ambiguous. Membership placed the Monroe Doctrine at risk and threatened outside interference in the nation's internal affairs. The league itself was a triumph of British diplomacy, designed to enable Britain and its empire to secure a dominant status. It served well the needs of America's wartime allies, which were now gorged on the spoils of war, but it served no American interest that the nation could not better defend alone. Article X, the most "astonishing and outrageous" of the league's provisions, would require the United States to become a party to "the sordid quarrels and the diplomatic duplicity of Europe and Asia." By committing American power to the defense of the status quo, Article X, like the Holy Alliance in the aftermath of the Napoleonic wars, sought to freeze the world into immutability. It both victimized the weak—the Irish, Koreans, Chinese, and other subject peoples—and legitimized that victimization.

Examining the provisions of the peace agreement, Johnson focused on the Shantung settlement, which sanctioned Japanese control of that nominally Chinese province. A product of the secret treaties on the part of America's wartime allies, the settlement symbolized the immorality of "Old World Diplomacy" and made a mockery of Wilson's celebration of the principle of self-determination. If the United States could not prevent the robbery, Johnson argued, at least it ought not to sanction it. Turning finally to the constitutional implications of league membership, Johnson warned his colleagues against any move that would transfer control over the nation's foreign policy first to the president or his delegates abroad and ultimately to the league with its decrees from Geneva. He made it clear throughout his address that he would oppose the league however it might be amended, the *New York Tribune* observed. The issue, he emphatically concluded over the roar of applause that rocked the chamber, was not a partisan issue. "The issue is America. And I am an American."[20]

Having publicly taken his stand, Johnson readied himself to push forward. He would, he wrote, go to bat as forcefully as he could on every possible occasion.[21] In the Senate Foreign Relations Committee he joined with Borah to guard against any concessions to internationalism. Too many Republicans seemed ready to back away from the main issue, he moaned. Such was the case with Philander Knox, who proposed a five-part resolution that would allow an early vote on the peace treaty by disentangling Wilson's package, which tied the treaty and the league together. Unhappily for Johnson, section five of Knox's resolution pledged that the United States would consider any future threat to Europe's peace as a cause for concern and would consult with those threatened. In a stormy session of the committee, section five was deleted at the insistence of Johnson and Borah, who made clear that they would accept no obligation, however circumscribed, which linked the United States to political events abroad.[22]

Johnson was active on the floor in securing passage of his own resolution to obtain the full text of the finished treaty, and immersed himself as well in the proceedings of the Foreign Relations Committee. But his most hectic involvement over the next few months was on the stump, where he publicly lashed out at the league and the Paris settlement.[23] On June 28, joined by Reed of Missouri, he spoke at New York's Carnegie Hall. The audience, described by the *New York Times* as pro-Irish in sympathy, responded with high exuberance, booing any mention of Wilson's name. Johnson thought he had never had a more enthusiastic crowd.[24]

From New York, Johnson traveled to Detroit for the Fourth of July celebrations to welcome home some of the troops earlier sent to Russia. Three days later, he began a one-week tour of New England planned and financed by the recently formed League for the Preservation of American Independence. At the time of Wilson's final return from Paris, Johnson was in Boston, where he spoke in the morning before the Massachusetts State Legislature, attended an afternoon meeting at Faneuil Hall, and delivered two evening addresses, the first of them to a capacity audience at Tremont Temple, the city's largest auditorium. Still active as midnight neared, he stood atop an automobile to speak to the large crowd that had gathered. The rest of the tour continued at much the same pace, and Johnson returned to Washington in a state of near collapse. Sheer nerves, he wrote, had sustained him during the last lap of his journey, during which such an intense heat wave had enveloped the region that he had been unable to eat and had suffered occasionally from dizziness. But, he noted, it was all worthwhile. It had been a triumphant tour.[25]

Back in Washington, Johnson joined the ongoing hearings before the Senate Foreign Relations Committee and proceeded to turn the testimony of Secretary of State Robert Lansing to good advantage. The questioning had gone on for an hour, and the secretary seemed about to conclude. Then, in what Johnson's wife described as a "pussy cat mew voice," Johnson began his own interrogation. For one and one-half hours in the morning and two hours in the afternoon, he put Lansing through an exhausting examination that centered primarily on the Shantung settlement. Lansing not only acknowledged that the agreement was inconsistent with the president's Fourteen Points but also contradicted Wilson by concluding that the settlement had been unnecessary and that Japan would have endorsed the treaty without such a concession. "It's *great stuff* to fire at the League supporters," Minnie Johnson crowed.[26]

Shortly thereafter, at Lodge's request, Wilson invited the committee to meet with him at the White House on August 19. Though pleased by the invitation, Johnson expected little of substance to come out of the meeting. He was not to be surprised. Much of the discussion revolved around an attempt to clarify the nation's obligations under Article X, an enterprise that left Wilson's critics as baffled as they had been on first entering the room. Borah and Johnson probed the president's knowledge of the secret treaties that had been revealed in American newspapers as early as 1917 and widely discussed at that time, only to be told that he had known nothing of their existence prior to his arrival at Paris. Wilson admitted his disappointment with the Shantung settlement but insisted nonetheless that it had been necessary. When the committee asked him for the documents on which the league and the treaty had been based, he demurred.[27] Overall, Johnson wrote, the president had been courteous, pleasant, and extremely forbearing, more so than he himself would have been on such an occasion. Yet it was clear as well that Wilson made no converts.*

Later that month, Wilson announced preparations for his long-promised tour to take his case directly to the public. If he could not make converts in the Senate, then he would try to make them in the nation at large. He left on September 3, planning to speak in 23 states on a circuit of over 8,000 miles. Johnson too had returned to the stump on August 28, when he joined James Reed for a public rally in Baltimore. Having already decided that if Wilson took to the road he would follow, Johnson readied himself for the journey—only to be told that the League for American Independence would not underwrite his tour.[28] Because officials of the organization depended on funding provided by industrialists Andrew Mellon and Henry Clay Frick, they refused to support an undertaking that Johnson might turn to his political advantage. "They are ever remembering politics, and even in a fight for a principle, making their politics the main thing," he complained.[29]

But Johnson had not neglected politics either. Despite his earlier desire to divorce his candidacy from the League of Nations issue, he had, during his New England tour in July, recognized campaign possibilities "not seen before," and regretted that he had not had with him someone able to put together the skeleton of an organization in the area.[30] When the League for American Independence refused to sponsor and finance his proposed trip, he turned to other sources. Raymond Robins promised to fund the enterprise. Closeting himself with Borah and Medill McCormick, Johnson spent the next week organizing his itinerary. Only after his tour was assured did the league reverse itself and offer to fund it, an offer Johnson heatedly rebuffed. On September 9, one week after Wilson began his journey,

---

*HWJ to boys, Aug. 23, 1919. If he had been the president, Johnson confessed, he would have seen the committee "in Halifax before I would have sat there for three hours permitting a lot of asses to question me." Johnson ascribed Wilson's denial of knowledge of the secret treaties to forgetfulness rather than deception. Describing Wilson, Johnson wrote: "His face in repose is hard, and cold, and cruel. When he smiles, he smiles like certain animals, curling his upper lip and wrinkling his nose. His is not the infectious laugh of the red-blooded individual. His ponderous lower jaw gives a very strange appearance to his ordinary talking, and his brow, which is like the receding brow of a vicious horse, has in connection with the lower part of his face a singular sort of fascination. As one watches his profile, it is not of the intellectual man you think, but of some mysterious ill-defined monster."

Johnson set out on his own cross-country trek. Accompanying him was Al McCabe, who had been recruited from California for the occasion.[31]

Johnson assured himself of a successful beginning by opening his campaign in Chicago, a city Wilson had intentionally bypassed because of its reputation for Anglophobia. Joined on the platform by Borah and McCormick, he spoke before a capacity audience wild with enthusiasm. It was a "bully start," he observed.[32] From Chicago, while Borah and McCormick fanned out in different directions, Johnson traced the path pioneered by Wilson the week before. Often he took the same parade route and spoke from the same platform. Before crowds no less impressive than the president's, Johnson reiterated the objections he had voiced in his initial Senate address, drawing on materials garnered from Senate testimony and the foreign press to punctuate those objections. Whenever possible he sought to turn Wilson's arguments to his own advantage. Thus the president's characterization of his critics as "contemptible quitters" prompted Johnson to note that the real quitter was Wilson, who at Paris had quit fighting for his Fourteen Points. To Wilson's call for the nation to choose between the league and "Germanism," he replied that the real choice lay between the league and Americanism. Never disappointing his audience, Johnson swept westward, to St. Louis, where he was welcomed by an eighteen-minute ovation, to Kansas City and a crowd of 17,000, then to Des Moines, Sioux Falls, Lincoln, and Duluth—all "wonderful meetings." In Minneapolis a crowd of 10,000 packed the auditorium and trailed into the street, reminding one reporter of the Bull Moose campaign of 1912.[33]

Whether Johnson would extend his tour to the West Coast had depended from the beginning upon the progress of the treaty in the Senate, where debate had already begun on the various amendments included in the September 10 majority report of the Senate Foreign Relations Committee. He worried lest his own amendment to the treaty, devised to ensure that the nation's voting power in the league would not be eclipsed by that of the British Empire, might be decided before his return. More worrisome still was the possibility that the vote on the final treaty itself might take place during his absence, thereby leaving him "high and dry"—a comic end to his ongoing crusade. In view of these concerns he cut short his travels and returned to Washington on September 23. The interruption, he wrote, was "heartbreaking," yet also something of a relief. Since the beginning of the tour he had slept in a bed but three nights. "I presume there is such a thing as total physical exhaustion and that I'll never be nearer to it than I am now," he wrote en route to Washington. But the trip had been an obvious success, he added, and perhaps it was just as well to stop "at the very zenith" rather than tempt the fates by continuing to the coast. All he wanted was "sleep and rest."[34]

Johnson got little of either. Three days after his arrival in Washington he set out for California, having received assurances that debate on his amendment would be postponed until his return.[35] Only the day before Johnson's departure, at Pueblo, Colorado, a physically exhausted Wilson had been forced to cut short his own tour, and had begun the journey back to Washington. There, within a week, he suffered a debilitating stroke. But only those closest to the president knew of his condition, and there was no worrisome news from Washington to dampen the ardor of Johnson's reception in California. Arriving in San Francisco three hours behind schedule, Johnson was greeted by the shrieking of sirens and the cheers of an enthusiastic crowd massed at the Ferry Building. The next evening, following a luncheon address to 1,500 at the Palace Hotel, he filled the Coliseum where, as the Hearst press's Annie Laurie gushed, he spoke "everyday American to an audience which was first, last and all the time a typically American crowd."[36]

In Los Angeles, where enthusiasm for the League of Nations was perhaps most ardent, the reception was more restrained, but even Johnson's critics had to admit the zeal with which the 7,000 who filled the Shrine Auditorium applauded his indictment of the league. "His manner is that of a man tremendously in earnest," said the *New York Times.* "He drives his thoughts into the minds of his audience with a sledge hammer blow of utterances; he moves, rouses, and controls men who listen to him."[37] After a northward sweep through Portland, Tacoma, Seattle, and Spokane, Johnson concluded his junket before an audience of 15,000 at the Mormon Tabernacle in Salt Lake City.[38] He arrived in Washington once again exhausted. While attempting to make a short speech on Shantung, he found his voice partially gone and quickly retired from the Senate chamber. He returned briefly in the afternoon to cast his vote in an unsuccessful effort to amend the treaty. A night of vomiting followed, forcing him to cancel his scheduled appearance at Madison Square Garden the next evening.[39]

★   ★   ★

From the beginning Johnson believed that the broadsides he, Borah, Reed, and others launched against entanglement abroad were instrumental in persuading the public away from its initial uncritical acceptance of the league. Men such as Chester Rowell, he sneered, would doubtless support the president even if he ceded New England to the British Empire, arguing that the league would ultimately correct the infamy, but many others had substantially modified their views. Elihu Root, one of the elder statesmen of the Republican party, had at first been willing to accept Article X on a five-year trial basis, but now called for its total rejection. Even "puzzle-headed" William Howard Taft agreed that the Senate should place restrictions on their acceptance of the treaty so as to protect American interests. Imitation was the sincerest form of flattery, Johnson observed, as he examined a recent speech by Lodge that seemed to echo his own objections.[40] But it was also clear that while many Americans entertained doubts about certain provisions of the League Covenant, a majority remained committed to American membership, drawn by the very ideals the league symbolized, ideals to which Wilson had effectively appealed during his September tour. Americans had died in Europe's trenches, the president had argued, not just to defeat Germany but to realize a new and better world, a world free of strife—a world without war. It was, Johnson conceded, an effective appeal, even though it masked the true meaning of the league.

In addition, he insisted, it masked much more, for just as European spokesmen manipulated American idealism to serve their own ends, so too an international banking community did the same. In Russia they sought to restore the old order; in Germany they worked to impose an economic bondage that would guarantee the repayment of the Allied war debts that they had earlier financed.* Wall

*HWJ to Hiram Johnson, Jr., May 20, 31, 1919. It was hard to feel sorry for Germany, Johnson admitted when the terms of the treaty were first announced. But by August he would describe the terms imposed on Germany as "the wickedest thing since civilization." Moving beyond punishment, the Allies sought "to steal her trade and destroy her economic life, and take from her her industries." Rather than ensure

Street—the House of Morgan, Kuhn, Loeb, and Guaranty Trust—
certain to make billions in profit, was behind much of the pro-league
propaganda, Johnson wrote.[41] But since he lacked the evidence to
prove his suspicions and feared that without facts he could be made
to appear ridiculous or perhaps worse, he tempered his attacks in
public, focusing on the perils of the league rather than on the avarice of those who financed the crusade.[42] Nonetheless, he predicted,
given the power of the bankers and the obvious popular sentiment
for some sort of international agreement, ratification of the treaty
was assured. Clearly the Senate would not endorse American membership in the league on Wilson's terms—they would encumber
their acceptance with restrictions, and for that, Johnson and other
of the president's more determined critics took credit—but American membership in the league was inevitable. Events soon proved
him wrong.

If all the "pernicious" features of the league could be eliminated
by Senate amendments, Johnson had assured Harold Ickes in early
June, he could in good conscience accept American membership.[43]
But it was evident from the outset that amendments had little
chance of passing. Many senators, although sympathetic to the need
for some restrictions, balked at a device that would require a reopening of the Paris negotiations and a further delay of the formal
termination of the war. This resistance became obvious when the
Senate, in early September, began debate on the 45 amendments appended to the treaty in the majority report of the Senate Foreign
Relations Committee. All failed to pass, most by substantial margins. Johnson's own amendment, which would have altered voting
procedure in the league to ensure that Britain and its dominions
would not hold their advantage, came closest to passage, losing by
only two votes.[44]

On November 6, the Senate abandoned the effort to amend the
treaty and began to consider reservations, a far more appealing instrument for all save the league's most intransigent foes. Convinced
that reservations would be ignored once the nation entered the

peace, the treaty laid the foundation for future wars. It was in many ways, he concluded, worse than the league itself. Given the temper of the times, however, Johnson
was not about to plead Germany's cause. He had no quarrel with those who insisted
that Germany "pay the full price," he publicly observed. HWJ to Archibald Johnson,
May 22, 1919; HWJ to Hiram Johnson, Jr., May 31, 1919; HWJ to boys, Aug. 1, 1919;
Sacramento Bee, Sept. 16, 1919.

league, Johnson dismissed the developing contest as "a sham battle." Wilson's much-reiterated promise not to accept reservations was a bluff, and Lodge's assurance that reservations would safeguard American interests a ploy to catch the unwary.[45] The settlement that would emerge, Johnson observed, would allow "the Republicans to claim a great victory, the President to shout in triumph that he had a league of nations, and the international bankers to walk off with the . . . spoils."[46]

Nevertheless, on the slim chance that reservations might afford at least some measure of protection, Johnson joined in the debate, supporting the passage of the fourteen reservations proposed by Lodge and his lieutenants as well as those offered from the floor. Only the least restrictive, he complained, were successful. He was especially dissatisfied by the reservation adopted to ensure American voting equality with Britain and its empire and proposed a substitute of his own but was defeated by a narrow margin.[47] Proposals by Borah and Reed met more decisive defeats. On November 19, the process concluded, the Senate readied itself to approve the treaty. Having long since despaired of the outcome, Johnson watched first with delight and then with increasing glee as the "sham battle" devolved into a partisan stalemate. Urged on by Wilson, Democrats refused to endorse the treaty with reservations. Solidly behind Lodge, all but the most adamant of Republicans refused to ratify the treaty without reservations.

Johnson took his place with the "irreconcilables," voting against the league on all ballots, but it was clear that even if the irreconcilables had refrained from voting altogether the Senate could not have mustered the two-thirds necessary for passage. "It was the most ridiculous and laughable situation I have ever encountered," Johnson wrote, and only his fear of bringing the contending factions together prevented him from laughing aloud.[48] Tragedy had turned to farce. Certain that the victory was only temporary, Johnson awaited the reconsideration of the treaty that was sure to come in the second session. In the meantime he turned his attention to his own presidential ambitions.

*   *   *

By November 1919, the outlines of Johnson's campaign for the presidency differed markedly from those he had first proposed six months before. In May, skirting the issue of the league and urging his supporters to go slow until the Senate had acted, he had stressed familiar themes—the need to revitalize the Republican party along progressive lines and build on the foundations of the past. But even before the defeat of the treaty in November, which guaranteed that the league would be a central issue in the 1920 presidential contest, Johnson had realized that international affairs could not be sidestepped. Cautioned by his lieutenants to mute his intransigence and warned that his enemies were seeking to undermine his political prospects by encouraging an uncompromising stand, he characteristically pushed forward.[49] Indeed, he acknowledged, given the intensity of his convictions he had no real alternative.[50] Moreover, while he recognized the perils of his choice, he began also to discover the possibilities. If his enemies had been trying to "cats-paw" him, he commented in the aftermath of his successful New England tour in July, "they have been hoisting [themselves with] their own petard." And in September, after tracking Wilson westward with Al McCabe in tow, he had returned to Washington with a variety of contacts on which to build a campaign that did not ignore the issue of the league but instead capitalized upon it.[51]

In other ways as well the league defined new political dimensions. Rejection of his candidacy by California's progressives would be "absolutely fatal," Johnson had said when he first announced his intention to run for the presidency, but under the weight of the league issue the progressive foundations on which he had rested his hopes crumbled.[52] John R. Haynes, who claimed he would not endorse his own brother on an anti-league platform, withheld support. Mary Gibson, long an activist in progressive circles and chair of the California Federation of Women's Clubs, did likewise. Johnson's position, Katherine P. Edson remarked, would be fatal as far as the women's vote in California was concerned.[53] Marshall Stimson, quickly moving to embrace Wilson's dream—the "biggest idea that has yet been evolved that has a practical operative chance"—was yet another early defector, while Chester Rowell teetered precariously, torn between his friendship for Johnson and his commitment to the league ideal.[54] Lissner himself was at first uncertain, willing to "try on the dog" in the hope that it would do little harm and perhaps much good, but ultimately he stood with Johnson. Franklin Hichborn, Frank Devlin, H. L. Carnahan, and John Francis Neylan, now editor of William Randolph Hearst's *San Francisco Call*, quickly did the same.[55] But the impact of the league was undeniable: in its wake a multitude of old loyalties were shattered.

Adding to the political disarray, many formerly adamant enemies stepped forward to profess their friendship and proffer their support. Some guideposts, of course, remained. The *Los Angeles Times*, which had been directed by Harry Chandler since the death of his father-in-law, Harrison Gray Otis, continued to denounce Johnson, while Edward Dickson, who assumed control of the *Los Angeles Express* after Edwin Earl's demise, demonstrated that he was no longer a friend.[56] But even before Johnson launched his attack on the league, Michael de Young of the *San Francisco Chronicle* signaled support for his candidacy, as did bankers Herbert Fleishhacker and I. W. Hellman; George Cochran, of the Pacific Mutual Life Insurance Company; and J. A. Britton, of Pacific Gas and Electric.[57] In time others would follow. Given their willingness to support his candidacy, Charles McClatchy noted, Johnson's plan to place onetime Progressives at the forefront of his campaign was folly. The Progressive party itself, he continued, was "as dead as the proverbial mackerel," and the veterans of that party were no more useful to Johnson's organization than Republican stalwarts who had never strayed. At issue, McClatchy emphasized, were the mounting tensions between capital and labor emerging in the aftermath of war. American business, frightened by labor strikes at home and mass unrest abroad and worried that class divisions in the United States would soon come to replicate those of Europe, looked to leaders who could steer a middle way. Johnson, McClatchy concluded, was their man.[58]

Although Lissner was less enamored of the idea of an "emulsion" between progressives and their longtime adversaries (most people compelled to drink emulsions, he remarked, usually held their noses), he agreed wholeheartedly with McClatchy's assessment of the trends within the business community. Business now stood ready to endorse what they had once opposed, Lissner explained. They looked upon Johnson as a "radical with a balance wheel," and at last recognized the truth of the doctrine progressives had always preached, that "only through sane progressivism may they save their bacon."[59] Drawing upon similar perceptions, Johnson's lieutenants sought to construct the broadest possible base for the conference to endorse his candidacy, scheduled to meet at San Francisco's Palace Hotel on June 14. And as Johnson made clear, harmony had his blessings. He had no wish to alienate would-be supporters by dwelling upon past differences, he acknowledged, nor did he intend by his references to progressivism to move beyond what had been achieved in California during his governorship.[60] As in 1916, so in 1920: "What California has done" would be his *pièce de résistance*. But the task of perfecting harmony he willingly left to others. While he agreed to ignore past differences, Johnson could not forget them. Asked whether Governor Stephens should be invited to attend the Palace Hotel conference, he replied that he would "cheerfully acquiesce" but would not himself extend an invitation. Overall, he noted, he preferred to divorce himself from the mechanics of the operation and would neither hamper, hinder, nor veto the decisions of his friends.[61]

Nor was he displeased by the results. The Palace Hotel assembly sidestepped the issue of the league—the only sane thing to do, Rowell observed, until it had to be faced—and instead stressed "Americanism" and Johnson's achievements as governor.[62] GOP ex-senator Frank Flint, following an outline prepared by Lissner, performed flawlessly as chairman. Grove Johnson, still active despite his 78 years, attended to endorse his son; representatives of organized labor and California's women extended their approval; and in a conference described by Neylan as "overloaded" with conservatives, business too gave its assent.[63] Observing the events from Washington, Johnson found himself emotionally moved. "If I could quit the game right now, I'd feel it had been all worth while. . . . Pride, gratitude, affection, all the soft and sweet emotions are commingled as I go through the accounts. That meeting should be my epitaph."[64]

In the next six months the organizational efforts of Johnson's California committee floundered, and he had to wonder whether it had not in fact quite literally written his epitaph. Unwilling to be relegated to a favorite-son status, he called for a determined push to win support in California's neighboring states. Harold Ickes, he advised, could provide the western mailing lists from the 1916 presidential contest. After first wrapping up the west, his campaign would march eastward.[65] But little activity ensued. In July, Philip Bancroft, secretary of Johnson's organization, left for a month's holiday. Then and thereafter, out-of-state supporters experienced difficulty contacting the California group.[66] Explaining the disarray, Al McCabe recalled

Johnson's initial strategy. Only when the league was out of the way, he observed, would the campaign begin in earnest. It was a strategy Johnson no longer cared to pursue.[67]

In other ways as well the operation began to falter. Johnson had suggested that the campaign initially be funded from his own pocket—to do otherwise, he self-deprecatingly wrote, would be like taking money under false pretenses. His supporters, however, confident that finances would be no problem, unanimously overrode the proposal. In April, while Johnson toyed with the idea of his candidacy, Meyer Lissner predicted that $500,000 could be collected. They could raise $100,000 within a week, Johnson's younger son affirmed at the time of the Palace Hotel meeting. But "the plutes were out of town," Al McCabe discovered when he attempted to raise $50,000 by mid-October.[68] Johnson's lieutenants manifestly too often deceived themselves in predicting an enthusiastic outpouring of support for his candidacy on the part of prominent California businessmen. Some onetime enemies were possibly drawn to his standard in the hope that he could "save their bacon." Others doubtless found common cause in his isolationist stance. But perhaps the majority of former enemies who now enlisted in Johnson's campaign did so on the advice of Will Hays, the peripatetic chairman of the Republican National Committee, who exhorted party activists to avoid friction whenever possible. They were willing to ride with Johnson in California even though they had little heart for his candidacy. By endorsing him as California's favorite son, they conceded little.*

Unable to run the campaign single-handedly from his Senate office, Johnson returned to California in mid-December to attempt to breathe life into his organization. "I must either get some activity or quit altogether," he admitted.[69] Two weeks of hectic labor followed: strategy was discussed, an itinerary was planned, and personnel were recruited for the work that lay ahead. Only his personal

---

*The plan of the politicians, Johnson wrote, was to have as many favorite sons as possible from the various states, each selected on the basis of harmony. Thus standpatters would have no objection to his candidacy in California. HWJ to Neylan, Nov. 24, 1919. See also *New York Times*, May 26, 1920. Francis Keesling, in recalling the campaign of 1920 long afterwards, noted that word was sent down from Republican national headquarters to do nothing that might anger Johnson. Francis Keesling, "The Virginia Hotel Incident," 1947 Epilogue, Keesling Papers.

presence was necessary to muster the campaign, he explained, for a "splendid spirit" existed just waiting to be tapped.[70] But Johnson was never optimistic when his own political fortunes were at stake, and he had few illusions about the eagerness of the conservative establishment to support his candidacy. "Those who make presidents," he affirmed, "will have nothing of me." For them, Leonard Wood, whom Roosevelt had recommended in 1916 to bridge party divisions and who commanded the lead in the 1920 Republican race, seemed a more obvious choice. Wood stressed conservative themes, cried out for "law and order," and attacked the postwar militancy of labor.[71] Somewhat more moderate in his views, Governor Frank Lowden, the favorite son of Illinois Republicans, also had nationwide appeal. Warren Harding, soon to enter the primary in his own state of Ohio, was yet another of a host of favorite-son activists. "A suave, pleasant personality," Johnson noted of Harding, "without an atom of principle," the very sort of "spineless" individual the Republican party would most like to nominate, given that 1920 would surely be a Republican year.[72]

*   *   *

Johnson formally opened his presidential campaign with an address at the Kismet Temple in Brooklyn, New York, on January 13, 1920. Identifying "Americanism" as his theme, he focused on the dangers of international entanglement and on Wilson's recent declaration, in his Jackson Day letter of January 8, that the election should provide a "solemn referendum" on the league. Only if Wilson had announced that he was running for a third term would Johnson have been more pleased. Touching too on domestic issues, Johnson denounced the ongoing assault on free speech, notably the recent action of the New York State Assembly in denying seats to five of its members because of their Socialist party affiliations and Attorney General A. Mitchell Palmer's just-concluded nationwide roundup of left-leaning radicals. Once again, Johnson charged, reactionaries "wearing the livery of patriotism" were promoting national hysteria. What the country needed was a "just" government, a "balanced" government. "And because so much stress has been laid lately upon law and order," he continued, "I take this occasion to lay some stress upon the principles of liberty. . . . The right of any citizen within the law to express his opinions and air his beliefs is as sacred as the right of property." The real threat facing Americans, he concluded, was not revolution but reaction.[73]

Elsewhere on the road, Johnson emphasized other themes—inflation, the collapse of farm prices, the rights of organized labor—but always the league remained at the forefront of his campaign. At the prompting of his advisers he tried to sound an occasional positive note among his otherwise shrill denunciations. He would not oppose the development and strengthening of the nation's arbitration treaties, he acknowledged, and would welcome an "international forum" where the public could discuss and debate world issues— but there the nation's international obligations ended. Moreover, as Chester Rowell despairingly observed, while agreeing to an "international forum" Johnson hedged as to whether the United States ought to participate in such an enterprise.[74]

In his discussion of affairs at home Johnson was similarly vague in his prescriptions, whenever possible reminding his audience that the problems they faced had international roots that required isolationist solutions. He knew of no sovereign remedy for the soaring spiral of inflation, he conceded, but the issue could not be divorced either from the avarice of wartime profiteers and speculators or from the inefficiency and extravagance of the Wilson administration. Nor could it be divorced from the issue of the league, for only if the nation restrained its ardor for involvement abroad could economies be realized in government expenditures. Already, he charged, the military was demanding an army five times its prewar size to meet league obligations. Throughout his campaign, isolationist arguments eclipsed earlier progressive themes, but the latter were never wholly forgotten: Johnson called for the realization of Roosevelt's "square deal," cried out against the "arrogant power of exploiting wealth," absolved labor of responsibility for the high cost of living. In short, he made few concessions to those who stressed the need to win business support.[75]

Two days after Johnson's January 13 campaign kickoff, Henry Cabot Lodge, under pressure from Republican moderates, began discussion with Senate Democrats on the possibility of defining league reservations satisfactory to a two-thirds majority necessary for ratification. The results were "encouraging," Lodge announced on the first day, and within a week speculation was rife that a compromise had nearly been perfected.[76] To prevent such a turnabout, Johnson returned to Washington, where he collaborated with Borah and other irreconcilables to hold the line. Summoning Lodge to meet with them in Johnson's office on the morning of the 23rd, they threatened rebellion if Lodge retreated from the reservations he himself had once characterized as the "irreducible minimum." Three "corking hours" followed, Johnson reported, with "bitterness and indignation on our side and apologies on his."[77]

With the threat scotched, Johnson set out once again on the campaign trail, beginning with a one-week tour of Missouri. The state could be won with only the slightest effort, he had earlier written. At the end of the tour he was more doubtful. "If God had given me six bodies instead of one I'd have as good a chance as Wood with his six hundred millionaires behind him," he remarked. The Missourians had been friendly, but nothing had been done to advance his campaign since September, when he had visited the state while pursuing Wilson across country. Furthermore, if he hoped to win delegate support, he would have had to negotiate with politicians "accustomed to dicker and deal and profit," an occupation he was fitted neither emotionally nor financially to undertake.[78] Back in Washington, Johnson began preparations for a swing northward into Minnesota and the Dakotas, where primaries were scheduled for mid-March. But the Missouri junket had taken its toll, and he spent the next two and one-half weeks in bed on the verge of pneumonia, losing time he could ill afford.[79]

By the last week of February, Johnson set out for the Dakotas and Minnesota in a somewhat pessimistic mood, dreading the cold of winter that might undo him physically and doubting that the results could be at all helpful to him politically. His time, he complained, could be better spent elsewhere. The Minnesota primary would be little more than a farce. The polls would be opened only briefly, and the state's Republican party retained the option of ignoring the results. His expectations for South Dakota were no better. There, both Wood and Lowden had firmly entrenched themselves by blanketing the state with money and advertisements. Johnson's last-place finish was thus virtually guaranteed. From the outset he had hesitated to file; only at the urgings of others had he finally done so. North Dakota presented complications of its own. Johnson's original plan had been to identify his candidacy with Republicans opposed to Governor Frazier and the Non-Partisan League and thereby mute his reputation as a radical. But if the strategy was sound, North Dakota's party alignments were not, and on the eve of Johnson's departure, a divided North Dakota Republican party called upon all prospective candidates to withdraw from the primary race. When Johnson refused, the Non-Partisan League itself endorsed his candidacy. A pawn in the game of state politics, he tried to distance himself from his newfound sponsors but was less than successful. "In a region infested with rude forms of socialism," the *New York Times* queried, "why should he not advance with hope and with authority?"[80]

Despite the drawbacks he confronted, Johnson's canvass of the upper Midwest was not without value. As the sole candidate in the North Dakota race, he won the state's ten delegates by default. In his tour of South Dakota, he stressed his underdog position in the fight against "organized wealth and organized politics," and managed to draw large crowds despite subzero temperatures, a blizzard in Sioux Falls, and a minor train wreck, which interrupted his schedule. As predicted, he ran third in the race, but a surprisingly strong third, which enabled political commentators to emphasize his underlying strength. If he had had only one-fifth of Wood's resources, Mark Sullivan observed, he would have swept the state.[81] In Minnesota too Johnson could claim victory after winning majorities in the industrial centers of Minneapolis and St. Paul. Predictably, the state's Republican establishment ignored the vote, and the official tally was never published.[82] Continuing his campaign, Johnson swung from Minnesota into Michigan's Upper Peninsula and thence into the heart of the state. Winter storms and subzero temperatures plagued him, but his crowds were invariably enthusiastic. In Saginaw the audience waited almost two hours when his train was delayed, and in Detroit five thousand flocked to the armory to hear his address. A wonderful meeting, he exclaimed.

With his campaign gathering momentum, it was only with reluctance that Johnson broke off his tour to return to Washington for the balloting scheduled to begin once again on the Paris treaty and the Lodge reservations.[83] Few believed the league would pass even with reservations, and Wilson had already vowed not to ratify the treaty if reservations were attached. Meyer Lissner, still hopeful that Johnson could win back those who had strayed from his candidacy because of his opposition to the league, had earlier advised him to accept the treaty with reservations. The advice, of course, went unheeded, and on March 19 the treaty, winning a majority vote but not the necessary two-thirds, once again failed of passage.*

Johnson had little time to celebrate what proved to be the final futile effort to secure ratification of the treaty. Hurriedly retracing his steps, he resumed his canvass of Michigan. At Kalamazoo, the 399th Regiment, recently returned from Russia, stood at salute as he entered the town. Overflow audiences greeted him at Battle Creek and Grand Rapids. The campaign was "white-hot" and Johnson a "seasoned hypnotist in platform dynamics," the *Grand Rapids Herald* observed. Off to New York for a one-week tour, he then returned to Michigan for a four-day siege just prior to the primary. The siege ended in victory: Johnson defeated Wood, his closest competitor, by more than 44,000 votes.[84]

Buoyed by his success in Michigan, Johnson awaited the tests still to come—the Nebraska primary on April 20, New Jersey's the week following, then those in Indiana and Maryland in early May. He headed off to New Jersey for four days of speeches in the second week of April, traveled thence to Nebraska and Indiana, returned to New Jersey only days prior to that state's balloting, dipped briefly into Maryland, then headed west again to Indiana, where he remained until the primary. Winning in Nebraska, he rolled up a clean margin over Wood. That victory, coupled with his three-to-one triumph in the Montana primary and a write-in vote of more than 64,000 from Chicago's wards on the Illinois ballot, seemed to many to transform Johnson from an outsider into a front-runner. Of the six primaries he had entered, he had won five. He was gaining fast, Albert Beveridge wrote to his wife.[85]

In New Jersey, which political observers had characterized as a critical test of his eastern support, Johnson suffered his second defeat, but as in South Dakota, it was a defeat that revealed greater strength than weakness. In a race in which more than 100,000 votes were cast, Johnson trailed Wood by fewer than 1,300, and only the lack of a required $50,000 deposit prevented him from calling for a

---

*Lissner to HWJ, Jan. 24, 1920; Lissner to C. K. McClatchy, Jan. 31, 1920. Johnson ignored Lissner's advice on other issues as well. Regarding the presidential campaign, Lissner had advised him to tone down his condemnation of U.S. Russian policy and mute his harpings on First Amendment freedoms. Johnson's stand, Lissner wrote, "gives the impression of undue sympathy with the ultra-radical element." Lissner to HWJ, Apr. 17, 1919, Rowell Papers.

recount. As expected, he lost in Maryland, having spent only two days in the state. Indiana was another setback, but not a devastating one. Winning four of the state's thirteen districts and 35 percent of the vote, he lost to Wood by fewer than 6,000 votes.[86] Overall, given the extraordinarily slim resources on which Johnson depended, both his victories and his defeats were impressive. Funds never materialized, and almost without exception he found himself opposed by the local press and at odds with the regnant political machines in the states he visited. In Michigan, he relied entirely on unpaid volunteers. His New York headquarters, coordinating the campaign in the east, was described by one observer as a "one-man and one-woman affair." Senators Borah and William Kenyon took to the road to speak in behalf of his candidacy, as did Raymond Robins, but the campaign was almost entirely Johnson's own.[87]

★　　★　　★

As Johnson pushed his way forward, he continued to look over his shoulder, dogged by his fear that the whole enterprise would collapse if he lost to Herbert Hoover in California's May 4 primary. Wartime activities had made Hoover a popular figure with genuine grass-roots appeal. Even Johnson had been initially impressed.[88] Widely lauded by periodicals as diverse as the *New Republic* and the *Saturday Evening Post*, Hoover had been encouraged by both Democrats and Republicans to campaign nationally. He declined to do so, but allowed his name to be entered in the California Republican primary and quickly found a following, especially in the southern part of the state, where political ties to Johnson were weakest and enthusiasm for the league most intense. In all probability, Johnson predicted, Hoover would win in Los Angeles by a margin of five to one.[89] Edward Dickson, of the *Los Angeles Express*, rallied to his side; so too did the *Los Angeles Times*. A "delightful mixup," Meyer Lissner cynically noted, and whether they joined with Hoover because of his willingness to accept the league, or whether they saw in Hoover a useful club with which to bludgeon Johnson, it was a dangerous mixup as well.[90]

For Chester Rowell, the temptation was almost too great. Practically every person at the *Fresno Republican* supported Hoover, he acknowledged, and nine-tenths of the people he came into contact with were similarly inclined. Even his wife had become a convert.

Indeed, he admitted, if he were to dig down far enough into his own soul, he probably would do the same.[91] Writing to Meyer Lissner, Rowell wistfully recalled happier days when he and Lissner had worked behind the scenes, helping to shape the content of Johnson's campaigns. Johnson's chief blunder in the present campaign, he concluded, was that he had strayed from his "intellectual guardians." To William Kent, Rowell wrote, "I wish some previous accident had thrown Johnson and Hoover together, with Hoover to originate policies intellectually, with Johnson to criticize and sift them."[92] Rowell continued to support Johnson—"with reservations," as one observer remarked—while lauding Hoover in his editorials.[93]

Adding to Johnson's woes were the tactics employed by his California lieutenants paving his way in the California primary. Harmony had been the keynote of the Palace Hotel meeting that launched his candidacy, and Johnson had willingly acquiesced, delegating the task to others. He would do the same in the selection of his delegate ticket. Al McCabe and John Neylan assumed the job. The resulting slate, Franklin Hichborn later wrote, "had as strange an assortment of personalities as were ever assembled."[94] The delegate list included, among others, William Crocker; Joseph Knowland, of the *Oakland Tribune*; Michael de Young, of the *Chronicle*; John Miller, of Southern California Edison; George Cochran, head of the Pacific Mutual Life Insurance Company; and Herbert Fleishhacker.* The inclusion of such names, Johnson exploded, was a "rotten surrender to what I've always opposed." He had sent cautioning notes about the selection and had singled out Joseph Knowland by name for omission, but his objections had been ignored. As a result, a critic reminded him, he now had the support of men he swore could never be on the same political platform with him.[95] The reminder was unnecessary. "The strongest men on this delegation (so

---

*De Young had hoped to speak at the Palace Hotel meeting in June, but had been persuaded instead to write a letter in support of Johnson that would be read at the conference. De Young's selection as a delegate, Archibald Johnson later wrote, would "be a stench in the nostrils of every decent fellow in the state." Neylan disagreed. "To have thrown away the *San Francisco Chronicle* and the *Oakland Tribune* in the present fight would have been plain suicide." Neylan to Hiram Johnson, Jr., Apr. 6, 1920, Neylan Papers. See also Neylan to Hiram Johnson, Jr., Mar. 26, Apr. 8, 1920; Neylan to HWJ, May 8, 1920; Hiram Johnson, Jr., to Neylan, Mar. 22, 1920, all in Neylan Papers; Hiram Johnson, Jr., to HWJ, Mar. 6, 1920; Archibald Johnson to HWJ, Feb. 28, Mar. 1, 2, 1920.

far as National Republican politicians are concerned) are the men who have ever denounced me, and whom I have ever denounced," he moaned. The slate amounted to a confession of political weakness, and thus invited rather than precluded a contest in California. Moreover, even if he won the primary, he could expect no more than perfunctory support from his delegates at the Chicago nominating convention. But the wound went deeper:

In all my political life I have never felt as I felt when I read that list. I have had just one asset, and that was, my unyielding independence. I have reached such position as I have had with the people . . . because of their belief in my sincerity and my obstinacy for the right, and because they think I never would compromise with dishonesty or dishonest men. . . . I can afford to lose the nomination for the presidency. I never had much hope in that respect, as you know. . . . This delegation marks the loss of whatever possibility there was. But it does much more. It marks the beginning of a new policy on my part of compromise, intrigue, and perhaps surrender. . . . The severest blow to my political career has now fallen upon me, perhaps not so far as the general public may be concerned, but so far as I myself am concerned.[96]

The announcement of the slate, coming just on the eve of his first success in North Dakota, cast a pall on his victories then and thereafter.

As the Hoover forces mobilized in California, Johnson grew increasingly worried that the challenge would force him to break off his campaign in the East to preserve his favorite-son status at home. And as he recognized, a favorite son who had to "fight like hell" to remain a favorite son would have little impact on the Chicago convention.[97] Hoover, without even setting foot in the state, had become a spoiler or perhaps worse. Hoover's real goal, Johnson insisted, was not to win the Republican presidential nomination at Chicago but to cripple Johnson's own candidacy in order to clear the way for the nomination of a candidate from the Old Guard. Faced with such a nominee, Democrats, in their determination to retain the presidency, would rally to Hoover. Behind the complex maneuver, Johnson wrote, stood big business and the House of Morgan, but in addition the British government. They want the league, Johnson concluded, and Hoover, a modern day "Benedict Arnold," was their man. Indeed, he added, only after Sir Edward Grey, the former British Foreign Secretary, at the end of January signaled British willingness to accept reservations to American ratification of the treaty had Hoover conceded the need to protect American interests.[98]

Johnson was unwilling to make such charges in public, but became increasingly bitter and abusive in his philippics against Hoover as he awaited the call he was certain would come imploring his return to California. But the call never came. In mid-March, in an attempt to shore up his campaign in the state's southern counties, Johnson turned to Meyer Lissner, who, because of personal jealousies and antagonisms within his organization, had been kept to the sidelines. By late April political pundits were giving two-to-one odds that Johnson would win the state and even money that he would beat Hoover by between 35,000 and 50,000 votes.[99] On the eve of the balloting Lissner predicted victory by 50,000.[100] Exceeding all expectations, Johnson won by more than 160,000. "What a glorious victory it was!" he exclaimed. But it was also the most expensive of his campaign efforts, costing $98,000, a sum larger than the total expended in all his other contests combined. Even so, Lissner remarked, Johnson had been outspent by the Hoover camp, which had "money to burn" and spent it "like drunken sailors." Hoover's Los Angeles endeavor alone, Lissner estimated, had cost $100,000, much of it to finance an extensive advertising campaign in the area. Although Johnson lost to Hoover in Los Angeles, Lissner had managed to hold down Hoover's majority despite what he described as the "nastiest campaign I ever saw in politics."[101]

Johnson's political successes after the California victory were anticlimactic. Since he was on the ballot in Oregon, he considered going there to campaign, but he decided not to out of fear that if he lost, as the only candidate to stump actively in that state, his larger prospects would suffer. He won nevertheless, slipping by Wood with a margin of fewer than 2,500 votes and winning that state's 10 delegates. After dipping into North Carolina for a two-day tour, he won again in an exceedingly light turnout on the eve of the Republican convention. En route to Chicago and the convention, he ended his campaign as he had begun it, reiterating the centrality of the league. His goal, he announced, was to ensure that the Republican party "neither sulks nor 'pussyfoots' on the central issue."[102] On his arrival, five days before the convention opening, he was greeted by a noisy crowd of five thousand, who rallied outside his elaborate headquarters at the Auditorium Hotel to cheer his denunciation of the league. It was the only thing he talked about at Chicago, Walter Lippmann commented.[103]

At issue was the question of the party platform, specifically the plank submitted by Murray Crane that endorsed the league with reservations. Adamant irreconcilables, such as Johnson, Borah, and McCormick, threatened rebellion if the measure was adopted. Johnson was already prepared for battle, having placed himself, after some initial hesitation, on the California delegation as an alternate—a maneuver allowing him access to the floor.[104] But after eight years of fractious divisions, the Republican party had had its fill of schism, and in the end adopted a compromise plank—a masterpiece of equivocation, satisfactory to few but acceptable to almost all. Among the more apprehensive was Johnson himself; only after assurances from both Borah and McCormick did he give his assent.[105]

Such was the extent of Johnson's victory in 1920. The party establishment opposed him; he possessed only a fraction of the delegates needed for the nomination; and many of those delegates frankly expressed their preference for others—in short, he could not hope to stampede the convention into support for his candidacy. Nevertheless, he tried. Preparations were made to organize mass support among Chicago's citizens, who would fill the galleries and cheer mightily. Charles Stetson Wheeler, who had been forcefully removed from the California delegation in 1912, was back in 1920 to rouse the convention with his oratory. But it all fell flat, and Wheeler, in his speech nominating Johnson, opened old wounds by calling upon the "hand-picked delegates" of the south and the "political slaves" of the north, "lashed into line by the blacksnake of some party Legree, . . . to scourge the last of the bosses from this great temple of the Republican party." "The worst speech that ever was," Irving Cobb reported.[106]

Balloting began on Friday, June 11, the fourth day of the convention. Trailing both Wood and Lowden, Johnson reached the peak of his strength on the third ballot, on which he received 148 votes, far short of the 493 required. On the fourth and last ballot of the day, five of Oregon's ten delegates defected, leaving him with 140.5 to Wood's 314.5 and Lowden's 289. The evening was one of confusion. "1912 was a Sunday school convention compared to this," Johnson observed. His supporters toured hotel lobbies to decry the excessive monies spent by Wood and Lowden in the primaries. Speaking before a packed hall, Borah threatened to bolt if either was nominated.

At his fifth-floor Blackstone Hotel suite overlooking Michigan Avenue, Johnson was bombarded by requests that he accept the vice-presidential nomination. George Moses, renewing an offer made earlier in the campaign, sought to construct a Knox-Johnson ticket, while Warren Harding proposed a Harding-Johnson ticket. Early the next morning, Moses, together with Harry New and James Watson, was back at Johnson's suite once again to plead that he join with Knox. Johnson declined, reaffirming what he had long ago announced, that he would not allow himself to be nominated "for a hitching post."*

The deadlock earlier predicted between Lowden and Wood continued when the balloting was resumed on Saturday. Johnson opened on the fifth ballot with 133.5 votes, the same number he had started with the day before. On the sixth ballot Nebraska and Michigan broke, leaving him still in third place with 110 votes. On the seventh ballot, with 99.5 votes, he dropped to fourth place as Harding's strength began to show. Three more ballots followed as Harding swept to victory. Only California and Montana stood united in their support of Johnson to the end.

★   ★   ★

After voicing a few sharp words on the use of money and bribes and a system that "enables a few to disregard the will of the many as manifested in the primaries," Johnson quit Chicago to return to California. Whether he would actively support Harding remained in doubt. His plan, he remarked, was to sit on his front porch and look down on San Francisco Bay. "Whatever you do, don't ditch," William Wrigley pled. Albert Lasker, who with Wrigley had supported Johnson in the primaries, joined the appeal, as did Harding himself, ac-

---

*Hiram Johnson, Jr., "Notes for Article on Republican National Convention, 1920," Part VI, Carton 6, HWJ Papers; HWJ to boys, Oct. 29, 1921; *New York Times*, Apr. 19, May 7, 1920; HWJ to Neylan, May 7, 1920; HWJ to Fremont Older, Aug. 30, 1933. The 1920 vice-presidential nomination, as Calvin Coolidge discovered, would prove to be more than a "hitching post," and if Johnson had run on a ticket headed by either Harding or Knox, he would have become president. In all probability he had moments thereafter when he regretted his decision, but there is no evidence that he dwelt on it. Being made president in such a way would hold little "charm," he noted at the time of Knox's death. HWJ to boys, Oct. 29, 1921.

knowledging that he would be "under very great obligation" if Johnson consented to speak in his behalf.[107] In reply, Johnson defined his terms publicly. If Harding would endorse the irreconcilable position and forge the election into a referendum on the League of Nations, he would participate in the campaign. If not, Johnson privately added, "if he acts, as he has acted all his life, squirms and straddles and endeavors to be upon both sides of this vital problem—well, I won't speculate as to what may happen." A possible "political earthquake" loomed in California, the *New York Times* remarked.[108] Yet even this partial concession in support of Harding, Johnson discovered upon reading his mail, disturbed the "common folks who believe in me."[109]

Reiterating his terms two days before Harding's scheduled acceptance speech, Johnson once again warned against equivocation. If Harding evaded the issue, he declared, "a most difficult situation will be presented to men like myself."[110] But Harding did evade. His address did little more than echo the party's platform. Publicly Johnson beamed. The speech, he announced, was a "complete vindication" of the irreconcilables. Privately he remained apprehensive. Harding, he remonstrated, could not get by "with generalities and platitudes," and would soon have to make clear whether he intended to send the treaty back to the Senate, accept reservations, or reject it outright.[111] Hoping to push Harding into a more forthright stand in opposition to the league, Johnson temporized throughout the month of August. He expected to take an active part in the campaign, he assured a beseeching Lasker. However, he lamely continued, "I don't think the time is quite ripe for activity such as mine."[112]

With the Democratic party formally committed to American entry into the league, Harding's goal throughout the campaign was to secure support from the irreconcilables while preventing a party hemorrhage and the defection of Republican supporters of the league to the Democratic camp. The task was not easy, and the irreconcilables feared that Harding would make concessions to those who desired the league, leaving the irreconcilables with nowhere else to go. But Harding, a master of imprecision, continued to hedge. On August 28, in what was billed as a major foreign policy address, he condemned Wilson's league as having "passed beyond the possibility of restoration" while hinting that it could be restored, perhaps to serve as a model for a revised "association of nations." Lasker be lieved that Harding's proposal was as complete an endorsement of Johnson's position as could be expected. The suggestion that some of the league machinery be used to construct a new body, he wrote, was "a branch he had to extend to those who had been pro-League." Climbing out on that branch, the *New York Times* interpreted the address as a major concession to league supporters. So too did Harold Ickes. Others were not so sure. Chester Rowell, writing to Hoover, wondered whether it did not justify a repudiation of Harding by league advocates.[113]

In mid-September, circumstance as much as conviction forced Johnson to speak in support of Harding before the California Republican State Convention meeting in Sacramento. Insistent that the league dwarfed all other issues, he argued that Harding and James Cox, his Democratic opponent, had taken "plain and unambiguous" positions—the one against American membership, the other in support. Efforts by pro-league Republicans to keep Johnson off the platform in Los Angeles projected him once again into the debate. Word reached him that Edward Dickson, of the *Los Angeles Express*, when lunching with Elmer Dover, of the Republican National Committee, had threatened to endorse Cox if Johnson were allowed to speak. Dover thereupon tried to dissuade Johnson from speaking and in so doing all but guaranteed that he would. "We cannot permit the party, the candidate and above all ourselves to be put in the position of opposing the League in San Francisco and favoring it in Los Angeles," Johnson growled.[114]

Meanwhile, Harding, still calling for the creation of an "association of nations," continued to equivocate. But on October 7, at Des Moines, he seemed to move toward the irreconcilables. "It is not interpretation, but rejection, that I am seeking," he asserted; Cox favors "going into the Paris League and I favor staying out."

Thereafter, as the campaign wore to a close, Harding emphasized his anti-league stand. In response, a handful of pro-league Republicans, including Rowell and Marshall Stimson, bolted to endorse Cox.[115] Most, however, stood by their party. Little more than a week after Harding's change of tack, Elihu Root put together a document, signed by 31 prominent Republicans, announcing that the party accepted the league with reservations. Johnson chose, at least for the moment, to ignore the announcement. Pleased by Harding's new emphasis, he accepted invitations to address audiences in the East, and in October, three weeks before the general election, he began the campaign that had been urged upon him four months earlier.

By then it was obvious that Cox had no chance. "If it were a prize fight," Johnson remarked, "the police would interfere on the grounds of brutality."[116] But even the experts were surprised by the sweep of the November results. Winning 60 percent of the vote, the largest popular mandate given to any candidate to that time, Harding took all but eleven states; for the first time since Reconstruction, the "solid south" was broken. In the new Congress, Republicans would enjoy a majority of 172 in the House, the largest in the party's history. In the Senate, Republicans picked up 10 new seats, ensuring a majority of 22. As he summed up the results, Johnson predictably ignored the crosscurrent of forces that had shaped the landslide victory and turned his attention instead to the league. Wilson's "solemn referendum" was over; the American people had spoken. "The League is forever dead," he publicly announced. "Americanism has triumphed."[117] But as he well recognized, there were good reasons to doubt the accuracy of such a finding, and even if it were true, more than sufficient reason to lament the costs of such a triumph.

Chapter V

The
World
at
Bay

1921–1929

When Katherine Philips Edson met Hiram Johnson in
early December 1920, as he prepared to leave California for Washington and the lame duck session of the 66th Congress, she found him in fine spirits, promising to be "more progressive than he had ever been in his life."[1] But his outward posture was
only a pose. He had never left California more reluctantly or with
greater misgivings, he privately confessed.[2] Four years earlier, during
his senatorial race, Johnson had symbolized a reformist tide within
the state; his announced goal had been to reanimate progressivism
elsewhere—to "Californianize the nation." And in 1919 he had once
again emphasized that theme as he tentatively outlined his proposed
presidential campaign, stressing the pivotal role California progressives would play in initiating and underwriting his effort. But in the
wake of war new issues had emerged, and while Johnson found a
common tie between nonentanglement abroad and progressivism at
home, many others did not. Neither Johnson nor Rowell was able to
resolve their quarrel over the league, and their friendship quickly
foundered. Elsewhere as well, old loyalties collapsed under the
weight of changing times.

In Southern California a majority of Johnson's once prominent
associates, clearly restive following his rupture with his Sacramento
successor William Stephens, openly repudiated his presidential bid
and moved almost en bloc to the camp of Herbert Hoover, where

they remained for the next decade. To fill the gap, Johnson found himself relying more and more on new faces, many once unfriendly. In Los Angeles, Frank Doherty and ex-senator Frank Flint, previously spokesmen for the Old Guard, became his primary contacts. Meyer Lissner, whom Harding would soon appoint to the U.S. Shipping Board, remained a loyalist but was increasingly isolated from the intimacies of California politics.[3] Elsewhere too, older political alignments gave way. Around the personalities of Hoover and Johnson new coalitions emerged, drawing support from both progressive activists and their former adversaries and remolding the contours of politics in the one-party state.* "We have gone down hill and down hill very rapidly," Johnson mourned in the aftermath of the 1920 election as he surveyed the California scene.[4]

Prospects in Washington looked equally bleak. It was not at all clear whether Harding's landslide victory spelled an end to the ongoing league debate, and even if it did, Johnson could not ignore the wider implications of the 1920 Republican sweep. "During our generation," he lamented, "it cements in power the old standpatters. It is the end of Progressivism."[5] It was possible that the reform movement might in time recover, he conceded, but it was doubtful that he would live to see the day. The prospects were galling, doubly so perhaps because of the irony of circumstances that had led him to endorse and actively campaign for the Republican ticket. His alliance with Harding, he privately maintained, was only "temporary," having been prompted by the need to ensure American independence from foreign ties and commitments; but much had been sacrificed both in California and the nation in the attempt to realize that end.[6]

Personal and family concerns compounded Johnson's woes. De-

*Richard Dale Batman, "The Road to the Presidency: Hoover, Johnson and the California Republican Party" (Ph.D. diss., University of Southern California, 1965). See also HWJ to William Hard, May 25, 1926. Cultural and nativist tensions in the new era created additional inroads. Johnson had succeeded, Franklin Hichborn wrote, because "he was able to keep all classes—wets and drys, Nordics and Mediterraneans, and the good and the bad—pulling together. It was a curious team, but it got California out of the ruts. One of the penalties that Johnson is suffering is that now when the team has stopped pulling, the Catholic is looking askance at Johnson's Protestant ally and the Protestant at Johnson's Catholic ally. And so with the Nordics and the Mediterranean, the wet and the dry, the good and the bad, and the Republican and the Democrat—each is asking himself, is it possible that I ever pulled in that disreputable team?" Hichborn to Hilda W. Korsgren, June 6, 1921, Hichborn Papers.

spite the inevitable irritations of the office, Johnson relished his role as a United States senator, frankly admitting that it appealed to his vanity.[7] For Minnie, however, a political life had long since lost any appeal it might once have had. It required residence in second-rate cities—first Sacramento and then Washington. It incurred the frequent household disruption of seasonal shiftings back and forth across the continent. It intruded on the privacy she savored. Above all, it meant an end to her hopes for real wealth, for the good life that had once seemed attainable. Annoyed by these various sacrifices, she repeatedly urged Hiram to retire from the Senate and resume his career in the courtroom. San Francisco had defined her ambitions at the turn of the century. New York City, with the glamor and excitement of its shops and theaters, became her new focus. The time had come, she insisted, for Hiram to devote his attention to the well-being of his home and family. They lived well, but by Minnie's standards not well enough.

Neither Johnson nor his wife belonged to the social set in Washington; they partied little and entertained less. But the relative privacy of their lives did little to ensure economy in their lifestyle. Eager to mollify his wife, Hiram readily consented to impractical expenditures. In their first year in Washington they made the circuit of some of the capital's more expensive hotels, their expenditures exceeding their income by $300 per month. Minnie, Hiram wrote, would not be content with a small apartment or a second-rate hotel.[8] Thereafter, from 1918 until 1929, they lived seven miles north of Washington in Riverdale, Maryland, in the 28-room Georgian mansion built by the heirs of Lord Baltimore at the beginning of the nineteenth century. Tied to the main highway by an unimproved and weed-choked road, the Calvert Mansion had only recently been restored and made habitable after years of neglect. Damp and drafty in winter, and far too large for their needs, it was nevertheless in many ways an ideal retreat. For Minnie, who had chosen the property, the spacious brick and stucco mansion provided an outlet for her own abundant energies, a multifaceted challenge to her talents for renovation and refurbishment. For Hiram it was a refuge from the bustle of Washington, a place of ease and relaxation where he could spend his Sundays planting in the garden, playing with his dogs, reading, or, with a small group of friends, playing cards or watching movies, which he showed on his two home projectors. But while the $1,500 per year lease of the property was well within their means, the upkeep and continuous repairs necessary for occupancy far exceeded what they could afford on his salary of $7,500 per year. A chauffeur, cook, and houseboy added to the expenses. They led a much too extravagant existence, Johnson privately commented to his elder son.[9]

To supplement his income Johnson resumed his practice of the law in 1918, returning to the courtroom for the first time since 1910. Ironically, William Randolph Hearst became his first client when he unsuccessfully defended Hearst's International News Service before the Supreme Court in a suit initiated by the Associated Press. William Borah, Hearst's original choice as counsel, had initially accepted the brief but then found himself otherwise engaged. Johnson had demanded a fee of $10,000, more than three times Borah's price, and was surprised when Hearst's representatives agreed to his terms. Clearly, he was less than eager for a case that linked him to his longtime antagonist. Even so, he rationalized, the employment was both legitimate and lucrative, and he did not have to associate personally with Hearst.[10] Other cases followed; he represented the city of San Francisco in its battle over streetcar franchises and collaborated with his elder son in a reclamation dispute in Sacramento. But his income was never more than a fraction of what he might earn if he abandoned politics, as his wife wished. Under pressure at home, he agreed to return to private life and to practice law in San Francisco, but Minnie, increasingly unwilling even to travel to California, was determined that he should begin his new career in New York.[11]

In December 1920, upon their return to Washington, just such an opportunity appeared when representatives of the motion picture industry, prompted in part by the efforts then under way in several states to enact film censorship laws, offered to finance the opening of a law firm in New York City with Johnson at its head. The proposal guaranteed a minimum of $40,000 per year and included provisions for a branch office in San Francisco under the control of his two sons. Minnie urged him to accept, but he declined. "Should I resign and enter into this thing," he confessed, "I would feel that my life was ended."* Instead, he continued to divide his time be-

*HWJ to Archibald Johnson, Dec. 30, 1920, Jan. 13, 16, 1921; HWJ to boys, Jan. 1, 1921; Minnie Johnson to Hiram Johnson, Jr., Dec. 30, 1920. Earlier, again over the objections of his wife, Johnson had turned down an offer, which would not have required his resignation from the Senate, to lend his name to a banking venture put

tween the Senate and the courtroom, and the Hearst connection was renewed when he accepted employment under Mayor Hylan and Tammany Democrats in New York City's tangled effort to maintain control of the city transportation system. The case, Johnson wrote, satisfied both his ever-present need for additional funds and his sympathy for public ownership.[12] But at the same time the employment required frequent commutes between Washington and New York and heavily drained his time and energy. In 1922 he withdrew from further practice. He could be either a lawyer or a senator, he had earlier remarked to his sons, but he could not successfully be both.[13] Not unexpectedly, his differences with Minnie continued. Though known affectionately as "the boss," she could not get her way. "I think I have been pretty selfish," Johnson once admitted.[14]

All of these factors, both personal and political, plagued Johnson following his return to the Senate in December 1920, and for more than two years thereafter he regularly complained of a general malaise, of periodic vertigo, and of an inexplicable indifference to Senate proceedings. Thoughts of his own death occasionally surfaced. Perhaps, he once mused, he was going through some metamorphosis. One observer, who ascribed Johnson's behavior to the collapse of his presidential hopes in 1920, described him as "a pale fat man, moping in and out of the Senate," bored by debate, and both listless and suspicious in his personal associations.[15] In an effort to restore his vitality, the naturally sedentary senator began a program of exercise and diet, going regularly to the Senate gym to be mauled by masseurs and pummeled by medicine balls. He lost almost 40 pounds in the ordeal.[16] His difficulties during this period, perhaps prompted by overwork, or by the hurt of defeat in 1920, perhaps illustration of a recurrent psychological malady, or related to a series of real if apparently minor physical illnesses he experienced at the time, cannot be completely divorced either from the taxing political and personal

---

together by friends in California. As outlined, the project would have provided a minimum yearly income of $5,000, plus returns on stock. It was, he was told, a sure thing. "In California, your name would mean millions of deposits from people who would have faith in a 'Johnson bank.'" But there was a chance of failure, Johnson observed, and "if failure did come, and if, because of my only treasure, my good name, the stock were sold, which, subsequently, turned out valueless and unprofitable, there would be nothing left for me, but to die; and if I did not speedily die, all my remaining days would be dark, and clouded, and unhappy." C. F. Stern to HWJ, Jan. 22, 1918; HWJ to Hiram Johnson, Jr., Feb. 4, 1918.

compromises he found it necessary to make or from the not always well-controlled irritation expressed by his wife.[17]

* * *

One compromise Johnson refused to make. For the next quarter century, until his death, in 1945, he stood fast in the struggle to maintain the nation's independence from political commitments abroad. "America First," his refrain in 1920, continued to be his battle cry thereafter. With a conviction sharpened by the experience of World War I, Johnson insisted that the United States could not participate in European events yet remain aloof from European quarrels and their consequences. At a minimum, involvement in controversy abroad would aggravate schisms within the nation, fragmenting American society and creating endless friction. The experiences of so-called "hyphenated Americans" during the war and the social divisions apparent in the league struggle dramatically illustrated a truth that was evident as well in the everyday politics of San Francisco. Under stress, the nation's "melting pot" refused to melt.[18] At the extreme, World War I and its Russian aftermath demonstrated to Johnson the disfiguring consequences of American participation in world affairs. Civil liberties had been imperiled and humane goals trampled by greed. Executive authority grew unchecked while American power became the tool of European ambitions. For Johnson, the major threat to the nation's well-being, to its underlying values as well as to the progressive ideals he embraced, came from abroad.

In his quest for political isolation, Johnson often discovered dire threats in the most innocent circumstances. Those who disagreed with his prescription, he charged, were either wicked or naive. The wicked, indifferent to the multitude of dangers inherent in their programs, were eager to extend American commitments abroad in their selfish pursuit of economic gain and political advantage. They scarcely differed from those who sought to thwart progressive goals at home. The naive, by far the larger of the two groups, victims of misplaced idealism and too often blinded by the propaganda of those with more concrete ends in mind, failed to realize the obvious realities of international politics or to respect the limits of the possible. Los Angeles, long the home of frenzied enthusiasms and utopian crusades, was the stronghold of league support in California.

Within this demonology Johnson clearly simplified the nature of the controversy over American foreign policy and often crudely misrepresented his antagonists. Too eager to ascribe sordid or impractical motives to those with whom he differed, he was temperamentally unable to heed, let alone accept, the assurances of those who called for modifications in the nation's traditional posture of isolation. He was and remained an outspoken isolationist. At the root of his conviction lay an unquestioned faith in the uniqueness of the American experience. The nation's citizens might not be inherently better, he argued, but they were fundamentally different from those abroad. Distanced by ocean moats, they had perfected a society and shaped a set of attitudes that set them apart from their European counterparts. In contrast, the Old World remained a victim of its past, irrevocably tied to its heritage of national rivalries, territorial ambitions, and class resentments.[19]

Voicing such beliefs, of course, did not distinguish Johnson from his contemporaries. Those who shaped the nation's postwar policies, men such as Wilson, Hughes, and Hoover, were equally convinced of the axiomatic truths of America's uniqueness.[20] All shared too a recognition of the nation's economic ties to the larger world. For Johnson, isolation described a political imperative, not an economic posture. No less than Hoover or Wilson, he stressed the importance of world markets and resources in determining American prosperity. In pursuit of that goal, he vigorously supported an enlargement of the nation's merchant marine. In 1922 he broke with many of his liberal colleagues to endorse legislation, proposed by the U.S. Shipping Board and endorsed by Harding, that would have provided lavish subsidies to the nation's shipping interests, and in 1928 he joined with a majority in the Senate to extend a more modest program of aid. It was difficult to be generous to the shippers, he confessed, and it would have been far preferable for the federal government itself to operate the merchant fleet it had built during the war, but the nation's commercial needs overrode less important considerations.[21]

Of necessity, Johnson asserted, the United States was a major sea power and international trade the lifeblood of American prosperity. Resources from abroad fueled the American economy; access to oil, manganese, rubber, jute, and tin was essential. And as postwar economic dislocations gave way in the mid-1920s to a period of sus-

tained economic growth, Johnson emphasized too the nation's enhanced dependence on international markets. America's ability to
produce far exceeded its capacity to consume, he argued. "We must
of necessity market much of this surplus abroad, if our general prosperity and our standards of living are to be maintained and privation
and hardship are to be kept from great masses of our people."[22]

But if Johnson shared with his antagonists a faith in the nation's
uniqueness and a belief that commercial dynamics tied the United
States to the world, his differences from them were equally fundamental. For "internationalists," World War I marked an end to the
era of American political isolation. A new age dawned, Wilson reasoned, not because Americans willed it but because they could no
longer prevent it. Technology and commerce welded the world together. Only those with "pigmy minds," he added, could ignore the
changed circumstances. For Wilson the league was, among many
other things, the only alternative to an even more perilous balance-
of-power system from which the nation could no longer escape. Under American instruction, the Old World would in time be shaped
in the image of the new.

In the decade of the 1920s Wilson's Republican successors, less
enamored than Wilson of the concept of collective security and
more willing to concede the persistence of international rivalries
and the inevitability of power balances, defined a more modest role
for the United States. Nevertheless, sharing the perception that the
United States could no longer escape the world, they concluded that
American self-interest required that the nation accept new responsibilities abroad to aid the establishment of a more stable world order. Johnson, who too often blurred the real differences between Wilson and his Republican successors, denied the assumption common
to both that the nation's vulnerability in a new and modern age necessitated the abandonment of political isolation. He argued from a
very different premise, namely, that the United States' participation
in the First World War proved not the futility of continued political
isolation but the ineptness of Wilson's prewar diplomacy.

Johnson differed from his antagonists not only in his denial of
the need for political involvement abroad but also in his vision of
the consequences that would result from the nation's participation
in international agreements, understandings, and alliances. Looking
overseas, he was more impressed by conflict than by community,

more by the permanence of national rivalries than by the possibility of international harmony. European statesmen, he observed, continued to subordinate hopes for peace to their own national ambitions. Turmoil in Russia, the Middle East, and Central Europe; growing friction between France and Great Britain; conflict between Germany and her neighbors; and the reemergence of Franco-Italian rivalry all reflected not just temporary postwar dislocations but the persistence of Old World antagonisms.

No policy, Johnson agreed, could completely immunize the nation from the risks of international conflict and their inevitable consequences, but to enter willingly into foreign disputes, he insisted, heightened rather than lessened the probability of American involvement in sacrificial and unnecessary wars. Convinced of the duplicity of most foreign spokesmen and certain that even given the best of intentions events could rapidly outstrip the ability of individuals and nations to control them, he preferred the hazards of a world he felt he knew to the promises and hopes that others held before him. To those who contended that the United States could not escape the world, Johnson replied that it could not remake the world either, and that to try was not only futile but ultimately destructive of the very uniqueness that defined the nation's life and set it apart from societies abroad.[23] Few who argued for America's fuller participation in international affairs wished to dwell on the proposition that the contours of American society might be inwardly disfigured as a consequence. For Johnson, that inevitability seemed as clear as the fundamental axiom of American exceptionalism on which he premised his opposition.

*   *   *

Harding's election in November 1920 did little to diminish Johnson's anxiety over the direction of America's role abroad. He was certain that the fate of the nation still hung in the balance, and certain too that the initiative rested with a man of extraordinarily pliable principles. From the beginning, Johnson observed, Harding's attitude toward the league had been shaped more by political expediency than by reasoned conviction. While still in the Senate, Harding had carefully measured the feelings of his Ohio constituents before endorsing the Lodge reservations. During the presidential campaign Johnson had tried to pressure Harding to embrace the position of the irreconcilables and to forge the election into a referendum on the league. Once the results were in he readily ignored the multitude of crosscurrents that had shaped Harding's landslide victory in order to describe it as a mandate for isolation. Indeed, given the intensity of his convictions, Johnson could see it in no other way. "The man on the street," he privately concluded, "made up his mind on the League of Nations."[24]

But Harding's own statements during the contest made clear that the final determination of the nation's policy abroad had been postponed, not resolved. In 1919 and 1920 the efforts to secure membership in the League of Nations had failed less because of opposition by the irreconcilables than because of Wilson's own stubbornness and his ability to retain the support of his party. With Harding in office the opportunity for American participation in a modified league was by no means scotched. And even if the new president rejected the existing league, his ambiguous but oft repeated suggestions that the United States might join in building an "association of nations" as a substitute posed endless possibilities for renewed entanglement abroad. It remained unclear whether the proposal was an evasion, as his Democratic opponents charged, or an outline, as his pro-league supporters maintained. Harding's intentional vagueness made him an enigma to all in the months between his election and inauguration. "Nobody here seems to know what the new President's course will be," Johnson commented. "He is all things to all men, and I rather think he is getting away with the attitude."[25]

To find a common denominator that might harmonize the multiple differences within the Republican party had been Harding's hope during the campaign; it remained his hope thereafter. On December 6, 1920, at the opening of the lame-duck session of the 66th Congress, the president-elect met with his fellow senators at the Capitol. The following day he met privately with Johnson at the Washington home of Edward McLean. In the course of their conversation, Harding cordially chided Johnson on his past political irregularity, stressed the need for cooperation in the future, professed his own liberal inclinations, and flatteringly mentioned the possibility of Johnson's future elevation to the presidency. In search of that illusive harmony, he tentatively suggested that negotiations could be opened with Britain and France to secure the promised association of nations within a modified league. Predictably, Johnson objected.[26]

The meeting, one of many that Harding held prior to his inauguration, illustrated the difficulties the new president would have in moving from campaign platitudes to concrete proposals.

The uncertainty of the situation coupled with Harding's obvious unwillingness to fragment party ranks prompted Johnson to adopt a policy of watchful waiting. Political considerations heightened Johnson's wariness. The public, John Francis Neylan warned, was eager for an end to the turmoil of the Wilson years and would be impatient with any effort that might thwart Harding's leadership. A premature rupture with the new administration would endanger Johnson's ability to secure legislation favorable to California's interests and damage his chances for reelection in 1922. Further complicating the situation, Neylan added, was the tenuousness of the bond between Johnson and many of the newfound supporters who had rallied to his cause in 1920. Patronage could serve both to strengthen his position within the state and rebuild progressive ranks.[27]

Yet if Republican control of the White House made patronage available for the first time, the 1920 defeat of James Phelan, California's Democratic senator, and the election of the Republican Samuel Shortridge as his successor seriously impaired Johnson's patronage options. Shortridge's deep ties to the Old Guard and his platform repudiating the league and endorsing tariff protection for California's interests had helped him win the primary, but so too had the fact that progressive ranks had split between his two competitors in the race—William Kent and A. J. Wallace, Johnson's onetime lieutenant governor. Johnson had never been close to either of these two progressives and had remained steadfastly aloof from all three candidates during the primary despite various efforts on the part of both Kent and Shortridge to entangle him in the contest.* Although John-

* HWJ to Lissner, July 30, 1920; HWJ to Al McCabe, July 8, 1921. George West, an active participant in Kent's campaign, would tell a different tale, as would William Kent himself: both claimed that Johnson had supported Shortridge and was responsible for his nomination and election. See West, "Hiram Johnson After Twelve Years," *Nation*, Aug. 9, 1922, pp. 142–44, and the reply by Franck Havenner, *Nation*, Aug. 16, 1922, pp. 166–67; William Kent to Ickes, Sept. 27, 1920; William Kent to Francis Heney, Sept. 4, 1920, both in Kent Papers. But neither Wallace, a good man of the "Sunday School type," as Rowell described him, campaigning in support of unfettered American adherence to the league, nor Kent, a "reservationist," could have expected Johnson's pre-primary endorsement. Neither could Shortridge, despite his having endorsed the Johnson ticket in 1920 and his obvious attempt to link himself to Johnson in his senatorial campaign. But if, as West argued, Johnson aided Shortridge, it was

son endorsed Shortridge as a part of the Republican ticket in the general election, he entertained few illusions about the willingness of his new colleague to cooperate in matters either of patronage or of policy. Within weeks following the inauguration, the two men clashed. Shortridge, Johnson wrote, had converted his office into a headquarters for Robert Armstrong, the Washington correspondent of the *Los Angeles Times*, and was "as low a scrub as I have ever known."[28]

Few in California believed that Johnson could maintain cordial ties with the new administration, and friends of Shortridge waited confidently for the rupture that neither Johnson nor his associates sought.[29] Initially it seemed that they would not have long to wait. Harding's selection of Charles Evans Hughes as his secretary of state and Herbert Hoover as secretary of commerce sorely tested Johnson's restraint. It would have been difficult to find two less satisfactory nominees. Both were among the 31 Republicans who had signed the declaration prepared by Elihu Root in the closing days of the campaign, pledging their support to Harding as the key to American entry into a modified league. Both were men of strong personality, able to shape the direction of the new administration. Hughes, Johnson wrote, had ability and astuteness but also a "diabolical cunning."[30] Hoover, possessed of no apparent virtues, was an "intellectual crook" who had to be closely watched.[31] Indeed, Hoover's California residency, coupled with his ability to capture the loyalties of Johnson's enemies, whether standpat or progressive, compounded the importance of his selection. When Hoover's nomination was announced, reports circulated that Johnson would collaborate with Republican regulars in the Senate, who had been alienated by Hoover's participation in Woodrow Wilson's 1918 call for a Democratic Congress, to oppose confirmation. Johnson quickly denied the rumors but made no effort to disguise his distaste for the selection.[32]

---

only by his failure to be more vocal in denying the link Shortridge sought to forge. Kent secured the endorsement of Rowell, who privately described him as "erratic," as well as that of Charles McClatchy, of the *Sacramento Bee*, and Fremont Older, but as Kent later complained, the support of each was tepid at best. See William Kent to Rowell, May 5, 1920; Rowell to David Starr Jordan, June 23, 1920, both in Rowell Papers; Lemuel Parton to Katherine Edson, June 7, 1920, Edson Papers; William Kent to Lemuel Parton (copy), May 9, 1921, Hichborn Papers; HWJ to Lissner, Sept. 1, 1920, Lissner Papers; HWJ to Al McCabe, July 8, 1921.

But if Johnson was disgusted, he was not surprised. He had predicted Hoover's nomination almost from the day of Harding's election, and had personally stressed his objection in his December 7 meeting with the president-elect. Harding had refused at the time to commit himself, and subsequently proposed a second meeting in St. Augustine in mid-February to undercut Johnson's expected wrath. But Johnson, ill at home and perhaps too recognizing the futility of any further discussion, declined the invitation, and despite Harding's effort to soften the blow, viewed the Hoover appointment with anger.[33] In the end, however, he grudgingly acquiesced in the confirmation of both Hoover and Hughes, thus avoiding the rupture his associates so feared.

Johnson similarly held himself in check in his public response to Harding's inaugural address. In his answers to reporters' questions, he diplomatically ignored the new president's readiness to "associate ourselves" with the nations of the world and focused instead on Harding's promised rejection of Old World entanglements. "Having been kicked over the capitol dome," Johnson explained, "I parachuted down by clinging tenaciously to the one thing I had, [the issue of] the League of Nations."[34] For Neylan, who had earlier expressed the hope that Johnson could preserve his self-respect and avoid a break, at least until the mid-term elections in 1922, this temperate response was a good beginning.[35] Yet less than four days after the April opening of the special session of the new Congress, which had been called to deal with the pressing problems of tariff and taxation, Johnson found himself at odds with the new administration in its first major foreign policy initiative.

*   *   *

Ironically the break came not over any attempt by Harding to perfect an "association of nations" but over White House endeavors to secure economic advantages in Latin America. To realize those advantages the administration lobbied for passage of the 1914 Thomson-Urrutia treaty, which authorized a $25 million payment to Colombia for its loss of Panama during the 1903 revolution. Strongly supported by the Wilson administration, the agreement had prompted a series of spirited protests by Theodore Roosevelt and had faced stiff Republican opposition throughout the seven years that it had remained bottled in the Senate. Roosevelt's death, in

1919, removed one major impediment to ratification. That same year, the Senate further smoothed the way by eliminating a clause expressing "sincere regrets" for any actions by the U.S. that might have marred cordial relations between the United States and Colombia, but the treaty still rested firmly on the implied culpability of Roosevelt and the policy he had pursued at the time of the Panamanian revolution.

Viewed within a partisan framework, the treaty constituted an obvious embarrassment for the Republican party. It was, however, an embarrassment the party was willing to endure, as quickly became apparent once debate began in April 1921. Amendments specifically designed to absolve the Roosevelt administration of any taint of impropriety failed, opposed not only by the bulk of Democrats but by a significant cross section of Republicans as well. Attempts to reduce the amount to be paid were equally futile. Johnson, standing with the opposition, vigorously defended Roosevelt while caustically attacking the "marvelous mutations," the "flexible and elastic" opinions, of those Republicans who now gathered in support of the treaty. Reading from a 1917 committee report authored by Lodge and signed by Fall, Brandegee, McCumber, and Borah in opposition to ratification, Johnson scornfully quoted Lodge and his associates against themselves. Of the signatories, only Borah stood firm. How, Johnson asked, did an act of wickedness under a Democratic administration suddenly become an act of virtue when undertaken by its Republican successor? The money involved, he asserted, violated Harding's pledge of economy and might better be used to relieve distress at home. The nation had an obligation to its own, he acknowledged, but that obligation did not include the payment of blackmail to governments abroad in order to expand opportunities for American enterprise.[36]

With the full force of the administration pushing for ratification and with Theodore Roosevelt, Jr., undersecretary of the Navy, lobbying in support, opposition proved fruitless, and on April 20, 1921, the treaty was approved by a vote of 69 to 19. The majority included 40 Republicans. Almost certainly, the *New York Times* remarked in celebrating the outcome, a majority of Republicans would similarly reverse themselves when the Versailles treaty once again came up for debate. From his very different perspective, Johnson agreed. Indeed, that had been his fear from the beginning, for if he had expressed solicitude for Theodore Roosevelt and contempt for Latin American regimes—Colombia, he sarcastically commented, was ruled by an "opera bouffe" government—throughout the debate he was far less concerned with the substance of the Colombian agreement itself than with the European implications of the Senate's turnabout.

The ease with which the treaty passed after seven years of determined opposition clearly demonstrated the willingness of the vast bulk of Republicans to follow in Harding's footsteps even if it meant personal embarrassment and repudiation of their past declarations. If Harding resubmitted the Treaty of Versailles to the Senate it too would be ratified, Johnson gloomily predicted.[37] "We have now a Senate more subservient, more servile, and more contemptibly sycophantic than the Senate has ever been during my residence here."[38] With a peace still to be formalized between the United States and Germany, with wartime debts still to be negotiated, and with the nation's relationship to the league and to Europe still to be determined, the action of the Senate and of the Republican majority both foreshadowed the dangers inherent in future administration action and afforded Johnson an opportunity to reaffirm his position publicly. "I wish indeed that I had opinions so flexible and so elastic that overnight they could change. It would be easier sailing for me," he remarked, but "some of us can not do that thing when our country is at stake and when there is a great policy to be determined. So, however hard may be the road, we have got to travel it and travel it to the end, no matter where it may lead or what may happen on the way."[39]

Johnson was reluctant to initiate a public break with the new administration, recognizing as he did the wisdom of those who urged restraint. Yet he had little choice. "Perhaps the Lord made me a normal rebel, perhaps I'm just an obstinate ass; but I just have to go my own way," he confessed to his sons.[40] But while his opposition to the Colombian treaty was forcefully expressed, it was also carefully crafted. In his address he all but ignored the predominant role played by American oil interests in seeking ratification of the treaty, foregoing the opportunity to pillory the Harding administration as a tool of big business.[41] Further, he directed his attacks not against the White House, which had initiated the ratification effort, but against those in Congress who had reversed their previous stand. Lodge bore the brunt of Johnson's wrath, whereas Harding went unscathed. While breaking with the administration, Johnson remained on satisfactory terms with the president. Whether so fragile an arrangement could endure ultimately depended on Harding's response to the outstanding foreign policy problems generated by the war. The contours of American foreign policy had yet to be defined. They would provide the test for Johnson's support.

*   *   *

During the presidential campaign Harding had promised that a separate peace with Germany would be the first order of business in his administration. Wilson, unwilling to forsake what he had labored so tenaciously to achieve—a peace treaty tied securely to the league—had vetoed the Knox peace resolution passed by Congress, which would have ended the war while circumventing the Versailles obligations. The new session and a Republican president again created the opportunity for joint congressional action, and the Knox resolution was quickly reintroduced. But instead of appealing for its passage, Harding called for delay, cautioning Congress against any precipitate act. Meanwhile, Secretary of State Hughes announced that the United States would officially reenter the Supreme Council and unofficially attend sessions of the Reparations Commission.[42]

As viewed by the administration, such actions were necessary in order to ensure international recognition of American rights arising out of its participation in the war.[43] As seen from Johnson's perspective, against the backdrop of the recent passage of the Colombian treaty, both the delay in the passage of the Knox resolution and the State Department announcements were part of a larger scheme to undo the verdict of 1920. "It is only a question of time until the storm breaks," he remarked. "With or without the League of Nations we'll be carried into the European maelstrom."[44] He remained publicly silent, but vowed to take to the stump in a repeat of 1919 if his fears proved correct. Borah promised to stand with him, but to Johnson's disappointment, other erstwhile irreconcilables stood mute. They complained in private, he grumbled, but no longer had the will to resist. The Senate Foreign Relations Committee, Johnson wrote, was little more than an arm of the executive. Even Brandegee and Knox, he continued, were "supine, subservient, miserable, contemptible lackeys of power."[45]

Johnson's fears that Hughes, Hoover, and the Republican "internationalists" might push a pliant president and an acquiescent Congress to overturn "the verdict" of the 1920 election, while not without foundation, were plainly exaggerated. Hughes, far more realistic in his political assessment, quickly came to understand the limits that defined his options. He would not turn his back on Europe, yet he recognized full well the dangers inherent in pushing for league membership. One reckless act, he later acknowledged, would have undermined the administration's ability to accomplish anything, and like the grin of the Cheshire cat, the promise of American entry into a modified league quickly dissolved. In early July, after a delay of two months, the Knox resolution, partially rewritten to reflect White House concerns lest American rights be abridged, was passed by both Houses and quickly signed by the president.[46] Thereafter the administration proceeded with the final negotiations of the Berlin treaty with Germany, drafted around the Versailles settlement but carefully designed to avoid any commitments arising out of that settlement and specifically repudiating the league.[47]

In the Senate Foreign Relations Committee only William Borah regarded the treaty as unsatisfactory and fought against ratification. His outspoken dissent placed Johnson in an awkward position. Johnson shared Borah's distaste for the many references to the Versailles settlement that were contained in the Berlin treaty, but did not find in them sufficient reason to oppose the overall settlement.[48] The ranks of irreconcilables continued to splinter as Johnson admitted his inability to understand either Borah's arguments or Borah himself. He sought to heal their breach, but made little progress. Borah, he noted, was "a very strange and very uncertain individual . . . as responsive as cold marble." Ultimately the Senate Foreign Relations Committee reported the treaty favorably with one reservation and with Borah the lone dissenter. The reservation provided the key to Johnson's support. At the first meeting of the committee he had demanded that the United States stand aloof from membership in the Reparations Commission, toward which Hughes seemed to lean. That demand was incorporated into the Lodge reservation accompanying the treaty. Only Congress could authorize American participation in those agencies arising out of the Versailles settlement. With that position clearly stated, Johnson gave his assent.[49]

From the beginning of the struggle over the league, Johnson had spoken out against what he felt to be the two cardinal goals of Allied diplomacy—first, to use the power of the United States to underwrite the postwar territorial settlement with its division of spoils, and second, to use the power of the United States to guarantee the collection of reparations imposed upon Germany. Membership in the league defined such an obligation; participation in the Reparations Commission implied similar duties. The Berlin treaty, with the addition of the Lodge reservation, guarded against such threats. "By the ratification of this treaty we do not desert our allies," Johnson announced with satisfaction on the Senate floor; "we abandon certain international bankers."[50] For him, the settlement constituted a major victory. Borah remained dissatisfied, saying little but looking, as Johnson noted, like a "sullen child grieving over a supposed wrong."[51] Even more grieved were Wilson loyalists who quite rightly saw in the Senate action the repudiation of all that Wilson had worked to achieve. During the debate the ex-president attempted to mobilize his party against the treaty, and in defeat requested a list of Democratic defectors so that he might scorn them thereafter.[52]

*   *   *

Johnson hoped that the United States, by insulating itself from any formal responsibility for the calculation or collection of German reparations, had insulated itself as well from the conflicts that would almost certainly arise between the vanquished and victorious of Europe. The reparations provisions of the Versailles treaty, he argued, "are revolting to every advocate of future peace and every lover of liberty." New wars would inevitably evolve out of the spoils of the past.[53] But if Johnson wished to distance the United States from the repercussions of Versailles, he could not shield the country from the economic consequences of the four years of belligerency that had culminated at Versailles.

As a belligerent, the United States government had extended credits to its European associates both for the prosecution of the war and for immediate postwar reconstruction. From its prior status as a debtor nation, the United States was transformed by the war into the world's creditor. Loans abroad, totaling $10 billion, necessarily tied the United States to the governments of Europe. Economically those obligations could not be divorced either from German rep-

arations or from the larger assortment of inter-Allied debts that
weighed upon the European victors. Politically they remained distinct. Neither Wilson nor his Republican successors accepted the
Allied contention that a common cause required reciprocal self-
sacrifice: the cancellation of the intergovernmental debts generated
by the war. That proposition, first broached to Wilson while at Paris
and repeated by the British government in the Balfour notes of August 1922, continued to dominate the thinking of Allied spokesmen
throughout the 1920s.[54]

The policy of the United States, first announced by Wilson, rested
on the inviolability of contracts and the realization that debts owed
to the government did not disappear upon cancellation but rather
became an additional obligation to be met by the nation's taxpayers.
It was a position Johnson readily endorsed. In fact, few at home
could be found on the other side of the argument. Even those who
stressed the importance of European economic reconstruction in
order to expand American trade opportunities muted their calls
for a modification of the nation's debt policy, reluctant to argue
that American taxpayers should absorb the whole of the burden.[55]
Among the more vocal and clearly the most vulnerable of those who
proposed a loosening of American policy were international bankers, at whom Johnson aimed his wrath. They spoke not for the nation, he charged, but for themselves, hopeful that by reducing the
level of intergovernmental debts they could more easily underwrite
future foreign loans and ensure repayment of their own private
obligations.[56]

Nor was Johnson any more tolerant of those outside the banking
community who argued that the United States might use the promise of a reduction or cancellation of claims as a tool to prod Europe
to embrace a general program of arms reduction. Abandonment of a
debt that Europe had no intention of paying, William Jennings Bryan
observed, might help shape a lasting peace.[57] Brushing aside such
hopes, Johnson denied that peace was the primary goal of the European powers. But his fundamental objection went far deeper, and
denied the very premise on which such proposals rested, namely,
that the war had been a mutual effort. The nation's associates had
professed a common cause, he declared, but had in reality fought
for selfish gain: "I recall Balfour and Viviani . . . telling us how
they were making war to preserve civilization, unselfishly, with-

out thought of gain or profit, and I remember how at the very time they were talking to us, their pockets were stuffed with secret treaties dividing up peoples and territories."[58] The Versailles settlement with its transfer of empires and its imposition of punitive reparations vividly displayed the reality of Allied hypocrisy. Americans, Johnson concluded, should learn from deeds and not be led astray by words, for to accede to European wishes by cancelling or reducing outstanding claims would demonstrate both the naïveté of the idealist and the greed of those, both at home and abroad, who cloaked their selfishness in the rhetoric of a common cause.

Convinced that misconceived idealism and narrow self-interest exerted tremendous pressure in shaping the nation's foreign policy, Johnson paid keen attention to the initial efforts by the Harding administration to manage the debt settlement. Economic ties, he recognized, could undermine the nation's desire for political isolation. Even so, economic ties could not be eliminated unless the United States forgave its European debtors. To cut through this dilemma without risking American political entanglement abroad required caution and a well-defined policy spelling out the mechanics of repayment. But the draft bill creating the World War Foreign Debt Commission, proposed by Secretary of the Treasury Andrew Mellon in the summer of 1921, included no specific guidelines for settlement. It was a "Hoover-Morgan scheme," Johnson charged, and was "as clear as mud."[59] Under the proposal, Allied debts could be reduced and interest forgiven. European obligations could be refinanced by the sale of new bonds, an approach that would shift the original obligation from public to private hands. "Do that," Johnson warned, "and you will not require a League of Nations to be mixed in every brawl, every controversy, every war and every difficulty abroad."[60] More dangerous still was that German reparation bonds could be substituted for Allied obligations, a tactic that would make the United States an unwitting guarantor of the reparations settlement.

Neither Johnson nor Congress would accept so open-ended an authorization, and the legislation creating the World War Foreign Debt Commission was heavily laced with restrictions. Nevertheless, Johnson remained dissatisfied, and called for an amendment specifically requiring congressional approval for each settlement. His attempt failed by a margin of nine votes, but in fact the amendment proved unnecessary since none of the agreements negotiated were compatible with the rigid guidelines established by Congress.[61] All would have to come before the Senate.

In defending an American policy intent upon allied repayment of debts, Johnson minimized the economic difficulties facing European debtors. "We ought not . . . to be exercising the part of the inhuman or cruel creditor," he granted, but he remained convinced that Europeans could pay the full amount they owed.[62] Even so, he acquiesced when the World War Foreign Debt Commission, in its first settlement, ignored the stipulations set by Congress both by extending the period for British repayment of its debt and by reducing the interest payments required. He had initially hoped that the settlement could be modified so that interest rates would be maintained at the same level as that required by United States bondholders, but when that effort failed, he ultimately voted for the agreement as negotiated. Ending the controversy on less than satisfactory terms would be better, he reasoned, than allowing it to fester unresolved.[63] The British settlement was the last that Johnson endorsed, however. The leniency of American terms, he argued, did not significantly alter the nation's image abroad as a Shylock, and the even less demanding terms set by the Debt Commission in the settlement of the outstanding claims with other nations were both improper economically and demeaning to the nation. It would be far better, he insisted, to forgo immediate settlement than to accept the tokens agreed to.[64]

Overall, Johnson was disappointed by the efforts on the part of the Harding and Coolidge administrations to liquidate the economic consequences of the war. He agreed with Charles Evans Hughes that European recovery hung upon the economic recuperation of Germany but dissented when Hughes, circumventing the spirit of the Berlin treaty, proposed that the Reparations Commission call upon private American experts to provide advice and extend additional credit. American participation, even in a private capacity, Johnson warned, might bind the United States to commitments abroad. More fundamentally, Europe's pressing need was not to make reparations work but to repudiate a policy based upon spoils.

But Hughes prevailed. His suggestion, first publicly broached in December 1922, just prior to France's retaliatory seizure of German coal mines in the Ruhr Valley as a result of Germany's default on reparation payments, was unanimously accepted by the Reparations Commission in November 1923. Charles Dawes headed the committee of experts called into being by the commission, and Hughes, keeping in the background, mobilized the American banking community to underwrite the resulting settlement, making clear that it had the support of the United States government.[65] Ironically, the insistence of Johnson and his fellow isolationists that the United States government avoid any direct involvement in the rehabilitation of Germany provided new opportunities for the international banking community. But as Johnson grudgingly conceded, given both the unwillingness of the European victors to forgo German reparations and the determination of the nation's policymakers to ease European tensions by participating in the German imbroglio, there was no other alternative. Clearly, for the United States government to assume direct responsibility for the reparations settlement constituted a far greater threat.

Indeed, nothing was more dangerous, Johnson warned, than formal American involvement in the tangle of reparations, and in early 1925 he voiced alarm that American representatives, by participating in the Paris Conference allocation of reparation payments, had taken that fateful step by linking German funding of United States occupation expenses to the Dawes program. Compounding the blunder, Frank Kellogg, head of the delegation and soon to be secretary of state, had bowed to foreign pressure by withdrawing a proviso declaring that the United States government accepted no obligation to guarantee reparation payments agreed to at the meeting. Kellogg's action provoked Johnson to sponsor a resolution of inquiry asking for a clarification of American policy. Not satisfied with Hughes's response, denying that the government was either "legally or morally bound" to ensure German reparation payments, Johnson warned again of the perils that lurked abroad.* Whether or not American

---

* *Cong. Record*, 68th Cong., 2nd sess. (Feb. 4, 1925), pp. 2984–93; *New York Times*, Jan. 18, 20, 22, Feb. 5, 1925; HWJ to boys, Jan. 21, 1925; HWJ to C. K. McClatchy, Jan. 21, 1925. Johnson described Kellogg as follows: "He is not a bad man, but he is weak and timid, and absolutely subject to the influences of great financial power and big business. His greatest ambition while here was to sit upon the steps of the British Embassy, and if he could but be invited to the functions of the Embassy he was ecstatic." HWJ to C. K. McClatchy, Jan. 14, 1925. Kellogg, he noted, could

spokesmen saw the event as a reversal of national policy, he stated, European diplomats did. The United States was slowly becoming entangled in a web of Europe's making, he wrote, and over time, without any recognition of it on the part of most Americans, they would become entrapped.[66]

★   ★   ★

If economic ties could entangle, political agreements could bind, and Johnson's most forceful dissent in the 1920s focused on the agreements emerging out of the Washington Naval Conference, which met in the winter of 1921–22. In his Fourteen-Point Declaration of January 1918, Wilson had spoken of the need for a mutual reduction of armaments. The hope for such a reduction had struck a responsive chord both at home and abroad, and Wilson had played upon that hope in his campaign for American adherence to the league. Only by abandoning isolation, he argued, could the United States avoid becoming a nation in arms, a garrison state dependent solely upon itself in a hostile world. The cost of such independence, Assistant Secretary of the Navy Franklin Roosevelt added, might amount to $1 billion a year in naval expenditures alone.[67] Following the Senate's rejection of the Versailles settlement in November 1919, the administration, as if to underscore the point, called for a resumption of battleship construction as authorized in the Naval Act of 1916, broadly hinting that an even more extensive armaments program might become necessary if the Senate persisted in opposing the league. Internationally the outlines of a naval arms race began to unfold.

For the Harding administration, eager to restore some approximation of "normalcy," the situation would cry out for solution. For league irreconcilables, who were vulnerable to the charge of obstructionism voiced both from Geneva and from home, the task became that of finding some workable alternative outside the framework of the league that could reduce world tensions by eliminating the threat of renewed naval competition. In pursuit of that end William

---

bend to power "with the flexibility of a courtier and the servility of a sycophant." HWJ to boys, Jan. 13, 21, 1925. Johnson's first impressions had been no better. Kellogg, he wrote in 1917, "is not a man of any parts. He is oily and he crawls, and every man that is in a position of power here he whines about, and ingratiates himself by his servility." HWJ to Hiram Johnson, Jr., Aug. 13, 1917.

Borah, assuming leadership in the Senate, proposed a resolution in the lame-duck Congress in December 1920 to suspend temporarily the American naval building program, and called upon the president to invite Britain and Japan to a conference on arms limitation.[68] The moves proved popular, but action was postponed. None questioned the desirability of a naval limitation accord, but many argued that the action was premature and that it might needlessly hamper the incoming Harding administration. Borah's efforts were thwarted, and the lame-duck session ended in a filibuster over naval appropriations. There the matter rested, for Harding, who entered the White House in March 1921, continued to delay until swayed both by public demand for action and by British moves that provided new incentives.[69]

In July 1921 the Harding administration assumed the initiative by broadening the scope of the Borah resolution and extending invitations to eight nations to attend a naval arms conference at Washington. Johnson, having been in New York during much of the prior debate, had taken little part in the proceedings. While sympathetic to the hopes of almost all Americans for some resolution to the emerging arms race, he was predictably far more demonstrative in expressing his fears. Neither the agenda, which included discussions of problems in the Far East, nor the selection of American delegates was reassuring. Harding, hoping to avoid the kinds of self-inflicted wounds that Wilson had incurred, looked to the Senate for delegates and chose Lodge, the Republican majority leader, and Oscar Underwood, Lodge's Democratic counterpart. Those two, joined by Elihu Root and Hughes, composed the American negotiating team. With the possible exception of Hughes, Johnson complained, none of the appointees was truly interested in disarmament.*

For Johnson, the intentions of the administration and its representatives and the motives of the nations attending the conference were equally dubious. Only if a "righteous" public opinion oversaw

---

*HWJ to Lissner, Oct. 5, 1921. From third-hand sources, Johnson heard that Lloyd George considered Underwood a "cipher," deemed Lodge "wholly partisan, without initiative," and likened Root's presence to "Great Britain having another member on the Conference." But Hughes was of another stamp. Lloyd George did not actually fear him, Johnson was told, but did see him as the only possible impediment to British designs. Johnson passed the information on to Harding. HWJ to boys, Oct. 21, 1921.

the proceedings at every stage, he wrote, was success possible, and even then it was not assured, for a similar tide of "righteous opinion," heedless and misinformed, had earlier carried the nation to the very brink of league involvement. Once again the pulpit and press cried out for action, and in so electric an atmosphere the opportunities for misadventure were limitless. Almost anything, he groaned, might be put over.[70]

In the interval between the issuance of invitations to the conference and its assembly in November, Johnson persistently demanded open meetings and full publicity. If secrecy prevailed, he warned, the results would be much as they had been at Versailles.* Privately he claimed credit for the passage of the resolution proposed by Democratic senator "Pat" Harrison of Mississippi endorsing open sessions and full publicity for the negotiations in progress. When Harrison first introduced his resolution, Lodge, with the apparent acquiescence of the Republican majority, had objected. Quick to respond, Johnson joined with his Democratic colleague, passionately arguing for Senate endorsement of open diplomacy. Success in negotiations, he declared, would be impossible behind closed doors.[71]

Johnson attended the Arlington ceremony and the burial of the unknown soldier that preceded the opening of the Washington Naval Conference. It was an emotionally moving moment. The pageantry of the diplomats and warriors arrayed in their elaborate uniforms, he wrote, contrasted oddly with the crowds of nameless spectators in attendance: "The puzzling and perplexing thought kept twisting my mind of how some way could be devised to divert the homage from the unknown dead to the inarticulate and unknown living."[72] Attending the opening session of the conference the following day, he was again moved when Hughes, in his welcoming address, dramatically outlined specific reductions in the fleets of the world's major powers. No better homage could have been conceived. Setting aside his undercurrent of suspicions that some secret agreement had already been arranged among the negotiators, Johnson expressed pride that by insisting on open diplomacy he had perhaps played a part in the success of the first day. "The open session, the

---

*HWJ to boys, Aug. 13, 1921. Commenting on the dangers of closed doors and the persuasiveness of English diplomats, especially Lloyd George, Johnson wrote: "After a secret session, when the key is turned in the door, and the representatives of the nations file out, [Lloyd George] generally occupies the position of the cat in the argument with the canary." HWJ to C. K. McClatchy, Oct. 29, 1921.

frank avowal to the world at large, and the proposition publicly and directly made, all won my admiration," he confessed. Thereafter, he continued, the conference degenerated into the very closed and secret sessions he had feared.[73]

Johnson had hoped for a single agreement incorporating some variant of the naval limitations outlined by Hughes. Instead, what emerged from the proceedings was an assortment of treaties placing limits on naval construction but addressing as well political questions about the Far East. Johnson was disappointed but not surprised. The conference could have been concluded in a week, he observed, if the participants had been sincerely interested in disarmament.[74] The announced results did little more than confirm his conviction that their interests lay elsewhere. Predictably, he refused to accept the administration's argument that a successful arms limitation treaty depended on the resolution of outstanding political issues in the Pacific. When Harding met with him privately to reassure him and urge him to set aside his doubts, Johnson was unmoved, finding in the president's words only evidence of his gullibility.[75] Any political settlement, he argued, invariably imposed political commitments on the United States. Both national honor and national security were thereby imperiled. Arguing from that premise, Johnson became one of the administration's most forceful antagonists.

Of the various agreements concluded at the conference, two were potentially vulnerable to Senate rejection. The first, an agreement with Japan, provided for United States control over cable facilities on the island of Yap. This relatively minor treaty ended a dispute that had arisen at the conclusion of the war, when Japan gained possession of Germany's island empire in the western Pacific north of the equator. Far more critical was the treaty to end the Anglo-Japanese alliance and substitute a Four-Power pact in its stead. Both the Yap and Four-Power treaties were controversial; both were sure to provoke extended Senate debate. In contrast, little opposition could be expected either to the Nine-Power agreement pledging the signatories to self-restraint in China and reaffirming the Open Door objectives of the United States, or the Five-Power pact limiting the world's major naval powers in the construction of capital ships. The administration, aware of the difficulties that centered on the Four-Power agreement, tested Senate support by moving first on the Yap treaty, insisting as it did so that arms limitation would fail if the Senate refused to accept the totality of the conference results. Consideration of the Five-Power arms limitation agreement, seen by most as the centerpiece of the proceedings, was placed last on the agenda to ensure maximum support from the undecided.

Johnson was not among the undecided. The Yap treaty, he argued, was a tacit acceptance of Japanese imperialism. Japan's title to the island and to the territories of the western Pacific rested on secret agreements negotiated by America's cobelligerents prior to the United States' entry into the First World War. Senate ratification, he argued, would constitute the "first surrender." It would mark the "first time that the United States of America [had] recognized secret agreements dealing with territories and peoples."[76] The cable facilities of Yap, he admitted, were not worth the price of conflict with Japan, but neither were they worth the price of forsaken principles. Moreover, he maintained, an alternative existed. The United States could have stood its ground as Wilson had once demanded, and secured the internationalization of the island through joint Allied agreement. Instead it had contracted with a nation whose history of imperial cruelty was notorious. "I am not ready," he cried, "with the lesson of Korea before me, to turn over fifty, sixty, seventy, eighty, or a hundred thousand human beings to the rule of Japan."[77] Johnson articulated the qualms of many. Joseph France, a fellow irreconcilable, echoed his objections. So too did Key Pittman and Joseph Robinson, from the Democratic side. But it was not enough. The treaty, needing a two-thirds majority, passed on March 11 by a margin of seven votes.

Even before the conclusion of the Senate debate over Yap, the first battles had already been fought over the Four-Power treaty. The agreement, which would abrogate the Anglo-Japanese alliance of 1902 and substitute a consultative pact among the United States, England, France, and Japan to protect their respective interests in the Pacific, had not been part of the formal agenda of the Washington conference, even though most observers recognized that modification or abandonment of the alliance was key to any successful conference. James Reed of Missouri, one of the first to object to the proposed substitute, quickly branded the agreement as "treacherous, treasonable, and damnable."[78] Johnson, in California at the time the terms of the Four-Power treaty were announced, refrained from comment for almost three weeks before condemning the arrangement as a device that in essence underwrote the Japanese empire. The Senate, he observed, would have to "study every word and phrase before we commit our country to this unexpected and extraordinary contract."[79] Back in Washington, he devoted himself to that end, terminating further legal employment to concentrate his energies on the task.[80] "What I thought harmful and dangerous under wilson [sic] is no less harmful and dangerous under Harding," he sourly remarked.[81]

The Four-Power treaty, defended by the administration as a necessary first step in the armaments negotiations, quickly became the source of Johnson's greatest anxiety. The treaty's ambiguous text, Johnson noted, failed to clarify the new role the United States would play in the Far East. Article One pledged the signatories to respect one another's insular possessions in the Pacific. Again, the spoils of war would be recognized. Article Two required the signatories to "communicate with one another fully and frankly in order to arrive at an understanding as to the most efficient measures to be taken" if their interests in the Pacific were threatened by an outside power. To Johnson and his irreconcilable colleagues it sounded as if the administration had constructed a military alliance, a miniature League of Nations in the Pacific.

Harding minimized the nation's obligations and stressed instead the importance of the pact in securing arms limitation. The treaty was, he emphasized, an accord, not an alliance, and it implied no entanglement or surrender of traditional American independence. Johnson disagreed. Harding's assurance that the United States remained free of obligation in the aftermath of any conferences called under the second article, he argued, was belied by the ambiguous stipulation that an "understanding" was to be reached by the joint endeavors of the powers involved. If Harding were correct, if there were in fact no obligations on the part of the United States or its associates collectively to act, that fundamental point, he reasoned, should be spelled out fully in the treaty. But the logic of the situation suggested otherwise: without the promise of force to underwrite territorial possessions, the document was a "useless and futile fulmination" and Japan would have refused to forgo its alliance with Britain.[82]

The contrast between the administration's refusal to make available the minutes of the Four-Power negotiation on the one hand and the wealth of background materials provided for the less significant agreements reached at the conference on the other convinced Johnson that the United States had assumed wide-reaching commitments.[83] In the Senate Foreign Relations Committee, Frank Brandegee, echoing many of Johnson's fears, proposed a comprehensive resolution both incorporating Harding's assurance that the United States recognized no legal or moral obligation to maintain the rights of other nations in the Pacific and reaffirming congressional control over any American action taken under the pact. It was, Johnson optimistically wrote, a pretty good reservation. Six days later, over Johnson's bitter protests, Lodge proposed a far milder substitute. And Lodge would have his way. After meeting with the president, Brandegee altered the text of his resolution to satisfy administration guidelines, and the modified Brandegee resolution, which omitted the guarantee that any action agreed to in future conferences required congressional assent, passed by a vote of ten to three over the heated objections of Johnson, Borah, and France.[84]

On the floor Johnson persevered in his opposition, questioning the alleged threat of the Anglo-Japanese alliance to American interests while stressing the inherent peril of the Four-Power treaty. Lodge, speaking for the administration, had emphasized the dangers of the now abrogated alliance and minimized any obligations arising out of its substitute. Johnson argued the reverse. English and Japanese representatives, he observed, had long professed the benign, defensive nature of their pact. One could either accept or reject their assurances; both pointed to the same conclusion. If they were to be believed, no substitute was in fact necessary. If they had misrepresented their earlier alliance, they could hardly be trusted in the future. Nor, he insisted, could Lodge and the administration have it both ways, stressing the centrality of the Four-Power agreement in securing British and Japanese acceptance of arms reduction while minimizing its import with respect to American responsibilities and obligations. And even if it were possible to accept administration assurances, he argued, those who favored the pact failed to recognize that alliances by their very nature bred fear and suspicion among those excluded. Once involved in a Pacific alliance, the United States would find itself invariably embroiled in conflicts abroad. International tensions would be exacerbated as counteralliances formed.[85] The treaty did not lessen the chances of friction in the Far East; it enhanced them, for it provided no mechanics to include outside parties to disagreements that might arise. Overall, its purpose seemed to be not to resolve disputes but to win them.

Moreover, Johnson added, even if the treaty were specifically limited to insular possessions in the Pacific, its implications necessarily extended beyond this immediate focus. Russo-Japanese tensions on the Asiatic mainland would inevitably broaden to include Japan's insular possessions, and the United States would ultimately find itself drawn into a far wider arena. Reviewing the British parliamentary debates, Johnson found the impetus for the Four-Power pact in the hopes of the British government to rid itself of its Japanese ally. British attendance at the Washington conference, he insisted, had revolved around that goal. "Britain was determined to get rid of an obnoxious alliance and succeeded." Japan, he continued, "was determined to get something as good, and got something better," for the alliance had not really been abrogated but rather enlarged to include the United States. If the Senate agreed to ratification, he warned, the United States would enter into an Anglo-Japanese partnership that, in its brief existence, had "aided cruelty, sheltered wantonness, justified destruction, and [had] been the incentive to bloodshed and the enslavement of peoples."[86]

At the heart of Johnson's opposition to the Four-Power agreement was the very ambiguity of the pact and the parallels that could be drawn between Article X of the rejected League Covenant and the present proposal. Both the *New York Times* and the *New York World* saw in the agreement a regional version of the league. Johnson agreed. The obligations, he admitted, might be "vague, indefinite, inchoate," but they remained obligations, and they threatened both the nation's independence and its security. To those who argued that any agreements reached under Article Two of the pact could be ignored by Congress, Johnson replied, quoting the Henry Cabot Lodge of 1919, that the United States was morally bound to honor the promises it had made. "Our proud boast has ever been that in letter and in spirit we have maintained our faith and have ever redeemed our pledges."[87] So proud a boast required more than caution; it required that the United States hold back from even the gesture of a pledge, for gestures promised future commitments.

Johnson recognized from the beginning of the debate that he

would be no more successful in his opposition to the Four-Power treaty than he had been in his remonstrations over Yap. Partisan loyalty, Harding's acceptance of the modified Brandegee reservation, and overwhelming popular endorsement of a package that included arms reduction ensured the administration's success. Attempts to mobilize popular opposition collapsed for lack of press support.[88] On the Republican side only three joined with Johnson in dissent, and Johnson found reason to be disappointed in the efforts of each. Borah, he commented, would not "fight worth a damn"; La Follette, tainted by his wartime stand, was ineffectual; and Senator France, refusing to accept any of the Washington conference results, was rightly regarded by his colleagues as "abnormal."* On the floor, efforts to attach additional reservations failed, and the treaty was brought to a vote on March 24. It passed, with the 4 Republican holdouts and 23 Democrats opposed. "If this treaty had been sent to the Senate by President Wilson, there would have been forty Republican votes against it instead of four," Johnson angrily charged.[89] In his private comments, sorrow displaced anger: "Of course I do not believe that our country is ruined or that our people will be immediately destroyed. I do believe that we have entered upon a policy, which if continued to its logical conclusion, will mean an end to the Republic we have known and of which we have boasted."[90] The nation's ultimate decline might take generations, he acknowledged, "but just as certainly as it has proven the end of every democracy since civilization began, an alliance with imperialism will prove our undoing."[91]

In arguing against the Four-Power pact Johnson had contrasted the ambiguous phrasing of Article Two with the more direct wording of the Nine-Power agreement. In the latter case, nations were to meet and confer when questions arose but there was no obligation, either stated or implied, to reach agreement or to undertake joint action. Nevertheless, when the Senate turned to discussion of the Nine-Power agreement, Johnson made clear that he was suspicious of any meeting, however circumscribed. He would vote for ratifica-

*HWJ to boys, Mar. 16, 26, 1922. Of Borah, Johnson noted, "He acted like a man who wanted to keep his record straight, and yet had little stomach for the position he was taking. He really made no sequential effort, no stirring appeals, no careful analysis—indeed, no extended fight."

tion, he explained, but only because an endorsement of the Open Door and the pledge of self-restraint might tend to moderate some of the dangers inherent in the Four-Power pact.[92]

With equal misgivings Johnson supported the Five-Power arms limitation agreement. He could not overcome the suspicion that the United States had lost more than it had gained in the exchange, but neither could he document it. Joint pledges of nonfortification of specific island outposts seemed at first glance to entail abandonment of the Philippines and retreat from the Pacific, but naval experts convinced him of the contrary.[93] The details of arms limitation itself, he had earlier confessed, included highly technical matters, and he was unable to question the decisions of experts.[94] In the future Johnson would seek to become his own expert, cultivating contacts within the navy to underwrite his suspicions.

Johnson's enthusiasm for arms limitation agreements ended in 1922. The events that followed only strengthened his conviction that the nation's rivals were not sincerely interested in an effective program to curb their militaries. "While America scrapped warships," he later charged, "Britain scrapped blueprints."[95] The Five-Power agreement did not, as Hughes had promised, put an end to the naval arms race. Rather, it altered the terms of the race by eliminating the nation's advantage in capital ships while increasing its disadvantage in destroyers and cruisers by quickening the pace abroad in building in those categories. In response Johnson became an outspoken proponent of accelerated American naval construction, an unofficial spokesman for the Navy League, and a foe of any future disarmament program. In 1927 he viewed with satisfaction the collapse of negotiations at Geneva to extend the reach of naval limitation, and in 1930 he organized and participated in the only real filibuster of his Senate career in an unsuccessful effort to prevent ratification of the London naval accord.[96]

★   ★   ★

To counter the charge of obstructionism had been part of William Borah's motive when he assumed leadership in the call for an American initiative to end the naval arms race. Ironically, the fight over the Four-Power pact only strengthened the accusation. Johnson's stand had been politically costly in California. Among the major newspapers in the state, only the *Sacramento Bee* and the Hearst press provided support.[97] The best way to avoid the charge of negativism, Frank Doherty advised, was to oppose by proposing, by endorsing something "equally if not more constructive."[98] It was a familiar refrain, echoing the advice given at the time of the league contest. Borah easily mastered that craft, blending and balancing contradictory ideas with a wizard's skill. Johnson found it impossible; he not only lacked the talent but despised the art. Borah, he later complained, "can dance a jig on Wall Street with Dwight Morrow . . . [and] can scowl with Wheeler and La Follette, and he even may pursue a third policy and march with the southern democrats for States rights."[99] Johnson excelled as a crusader, not as a magician, and his own repertoire was accordingly far more limited.

In December 1922, little more than nine months after the conclusion of the Washington conference, Borah again assumed the initiative, calling for yet another international conference, this time to consider the world's economic problems. "I would have staked my life that Borah would stick in the great fight in which we have been standing together during the last four years," Johnson lamented. "It was a solar plexus."[100] The proposal, Johnson argued in the Senate, contained all the potential for American entanglement that the league entailed. Indeed, he continued, the league, with its rules of procedure and with its members bound to some core of agreement, was far less dangerous than Borah's "omnibus endeavor which has neither limitations nor specifications."[101] Economic issues, he again insisted, could never be divorced from their political roots, and to accede to Borah's request would tie the United States to the very maelstrom it ought to avoid, ultimately bringing the nation into the "most repulsive" of all postwar bodies, the Reparations Commission. Opposed by the administration, the Borah initiative came to naught, and Borah himself, having dramatized the issue and argued forcefully in its behalf, characteristically let the matter drop. For Johnson, the maneuver left a bitter aftertaste. Borah, he wrote, is acclaimed as "a great statesman . . . while I am still a nasty little demagogue."[102]

Though he scorned Borah's initiative, Johnson was not indifferent to the political and economic dislocations of postwar Europe. "The world is in a whirl again, and Europe apparently is seeing red," he observed in January 1923, as French and Belgian forces invaded the Ruhr following Germany's reparations default.[103] At the root of such ills, he maintained, lay the Versailles treaty and the spirit on which it rested. The United States, he wrote in a lengthy article solicited by the *New York Times*, could attempt to defuse the crisis in three different ways: by providing advice, money, or military guarantees. But none of the remedies would work. Americans had no monopoly on wisdom and could offer no suggestions that were not already known to Europe. Money, either an extension of new government loans or the reduction of inter-Allied debts, would do little more than fuel international rivalries:

If a European government becomes richer this year than it was last year, does it thereupon reduce its army and contract its diplomatic adventures? Does it cease with new revenue to hate its rivals and to prepare to resist them and to ruin them? If Poland were solvent instead of bankrupt, would she cede to Russia the Russian territory which she now occupies? If Britain received from us a total cancellation of her debt to us, would she retire from her perilous situation with the Turks . . . ? If France had all the money in the world, would she cease her armaments or love the Germans or ask them to unfurl the German flag once more over the German soil on the left bank of the Rhine?

Military guarantees, the last of the three alternatives, would perpetuate the very injustices on which resentments rested. What was required, Johnson concluded, was not American rescue but European regeneration. American involvement would only hamper the efforts necessary to realize Europe's recovery, efforts that could be undertaken only by Europe's own.[104]

★   ★   ★

In February 1923, slightly more than a month after Borah introduced his abortive proposal for a world economic conference, the Harding administration proposed American entry into the Permanent Court of International Justice, the World Court, arguing that that body, though a child of the League of Nations, was nevertheless independent of its founders. To forestall the predictable opposition, the administration itself recommended the attachment of reservations defining the conditions of American participation and providing the mechanics by which the United States would join with league members to elect judges and finance the nation's share of World Court expenses. In addition, the administration specifically affirmed that membership in the court would not entail obligations to the league and that the protocol of the court could not be amended without the consent of the United States. Summing up the administration's package, Johnson derisively remarked: "If we now do what is asked, the situation is this: We are wholly out of the League. We are in part of the League. By reservations we are out of the part of the League we are in. The part of the League we are in, and from which by reservation we get out, functions as a part of the League with our assistance."[105]

For Johnson the proposition was more than stylistically awkward. It was fraught with peril. In itself, he acknowledged, the World Court was innocuous; submission of claims was voluntary—no nation was subject to jurisdiction without its own consent. And clearly he would have had it no other way. In an effort to outflank the administration, Borah called for the codification of international law and the compulsory adjudication of international disputes within a new World Court entirely independent of the league. Borah's proposal, Johnson observed, was folly.* But Johnson and Borah agreed that the ties between the existing World Court and the league could not be severed by Senate reservations. Both believed United States membership in the World Court would provide, however remotely, the back door through which the nation would ultimately enter the league itself.[106] With Johnson's help, the effort to entomb Harding's new initiative in the Senate Foreign Relations Committee succeeded.

In fact, the battle was postponed for almost three years. Harding's death, in 1923, and Coolidge's tepid endorsement of the proposition enabled opponents of the World Court to carry on with their delaying tactics, but in the interim public support for the proposal continued to grow. Both the Republican and Democratic parties endorsed American membership in the World Court in their 1924 platforms, and in early 1925 the House, by an impressive majority, passed a resolution supporting adherence.[107] In 1926, when Senate debate began, it was clear that the administration would prevail. To further the chances of passage, the original administration reserva-

---

*Borah's proposal can be found in *Cong. Record*, 67th Cong., 4th sess. (Feb. 14, 1923), p. 3605. Johnson commented: "The codification of the law of nations is the sheerest bunk. It would take a world legislature (an utter impossibility) to do this and a century would not accomplish the result." HWJ to C. K. McClatchy, Dec. 24, 1926. See also HWJ to C. K. McClatchy, Mar. 5, 1923.

tions were strengthened to include the right of the United States to withdraw its membership at any time and a clause was inserted re-affirming American independence from foreign ties. In addition, at the urging of John Bassett Moore, professor of international law at Columbia University and the only American jurist serving on the World Court, a fifth reservation was added, which prohibited the court from entertaining, without the nation's approval, requests for advisory opinions on matters in which the United States had or claimed an interest.

Upon counting the votes before the contest began, Johnson found no more than twenty opposed to American membership, far fewer than the one-third plus one necessary to defeat the measure. Passage was inevitable, he concluded, but given the circumstances he refused to become "overly excited."[108] In part, those circumstances were shaped by William Borah, who had become chairman of the Senate Foreign Relations Committee following the death of Henry Cabot Lodge. While leading the fight against the administration's proposal, he continued to promote his own remedy, a new court wholly out-side the league. In so doing, Johnson grumbled, Borah transformed the contest into a sham battle over reservations and thus obscured the central issue.[109] One of the few irreconcilables in the debate, Johnson, as in 1919, was willing to accept any reservation in order to cripple the administration's proposal but unwilling to crusade for Borah's utopian substitute. With defeat a forgone conclusion he lim-ited himself to a single Senate address decrying the dangers of court membership. To join the World Court, he claimed, was unnecessary; the nation could always arbitrate controversies using traditional channels. Further, for the United States, the world's creditor, to place itself at risk before a court dominated by its debtors would invite endless discord. More significantly, he argued, even though the World Court was itself impotent, it could entangle the United States in the league, for the possibility of league sanctions to enforce court rulings existed, and out of sanctions sprang war.[110]

But if Johnson stressed the entanglements of the court and the potential dangers entailed by United States membership, his central fear was that success on the part of court advocates might erode the nation's commitment to isolationism and embolden league advo-cates to renew their efforts. Entry into the court constituted the "first false step," he had earlier written. "Thereafter, easy would be the descent to Hell."* Seeking to forge the contest into a referendum on the league, Johnson made a last, moving appeal prior to the final vote: one by one he called the roll of Republican senators who were veterans of the league battle to ask if any would vote, with or without reservations, for league membership, then paused dramatically in the silence that followed.[111] As expected, the Senate thereupon moved to adopt the court resolution, and did so by a vote of 76 to 17.[112] But in the end the very reservations that Johnson had dismissed as insignificant came to serve his cause. Member nations of the court, unwilling to accept the fifth reservation relating to advisory opinions, called for direct negotiations to secure an acceptable compromise. Refusing to accept such an invitation, a cautious Coolidge let the matter drop. It remained in limbo for another nine years.[113]

★   ★   ★

In his diatribes against American membership in the league, in his bitter denunciation of the Four-Power pact, and in his outspoken opposition to involvement in the Reparations Commission and the World Court, Johnson never minced his words in publicly emphasizing the need for American political isolation. In those very rare instances when events forced him to consider the nation's involvement in the Western Hemisphere, he was somewhat more circumspect. Ideally, of course, the United States should refrain from imposing its will on others, and in the early 1920s Johnson joined with a handful of Senate liberals to call for the withdrawal of U.S. military forces from Haiti, Nicaragua, and the Dominican Republic.[114] In 1923, bitterly criticizing the nation's presumption in denying the right of revolution to others, he protested the State Department's decision to sell American military equipment to the government of Mexico while refusing arms sales to rebel forces seeking to overthrow that government. The policy, he declared, was "immoral if not illegal," akin to Old World diplomacy, the very antithesis of American ideals. By its actions the United States had become an indirect participant in Mexico's internal affairs, supporting the status quo

---

*HWJ to C. K. McClatchy, Mar. 5, 1923. "There is an absolute determination upon our pro-leaguers and pro-British Americans to carry on the fight, and to carry it on with patience and skill," Johnson wrote. "They are constantly and persistently boring in, making converts, and preparing for 'Der Tag' when America will be redeemed and will become a part of the League of Nations dominated by Great Britain." HWJ to C. K. McClatchy, Mar. 19, 1927.

and generating needless resentment throughout Latin America.[115] Decrying the imperialism of Europe and Japan, he warned against Americans succumbing to the same infection.

But if Johnson could be shrill, he could also be silent. At no time, either publicly or privately, did he express any misgivings over the events that had led to American control in Panama. Rather, he defended American action in his opposition to the Colombian treaty and later, near the end of his career, fought doggedly, if unsuccessfully, against the modification of U.S. rights in the Canal Zone.[116] The posturing of Latin America's leaders amused Johnson; he could never really take them seriously. On a voyage through the canal in the summer of 1925, he was impressed by the accomplishments of American enterprise. Similarly, in his intransigent defense of U.S. rights to the waters of the Colorado and Rio Grande, he was indifferent to the impact American action would have on Mexican holdings.[117] Clearly, when the interests of the United States clashed with the claims of others, Johnson's "American First" posture assumed a less than benign character.

Perhaps the Nicaraguan policy pursued by Calvin Coolidge and Secretary of State Frank Kellogg in 1927 best revealed Johnson's ambivalence in dealing with affairs in the Western Hemisphere. Withdrawal of American troops from the area had sparked disorder almost immediately, and the administration quickly responded with the reestablishment of American authority. As in Mexico in 1923, so in Nicaragua: the United States mixed in the internal affairs of another country, seeking, in Johnson's words, "to keep a tottering, ineffective government, responsive to us, alive with the bayonets of Marines."[118] But although he privately complained, reminding correspondents of his almost singular protest in 1923, he was publicly silent and voted against amendments to cut off funds sustaining America's military presence.[119] Public agitation, he noted, would not aid the country's cause. Once again, isolationist convictions clashed with nationalist pride. We were wrong to be there, he acknowledged, but like the man who has a bear by the tail, once engaged we had little option but to hold on. Mexican support of Nicaraguan rebels made that country a proxy in a larger contest that in time might threaten American holdings in Panama, and to withdraw, Johnson concluded, would risk American prestige throughout the area.[120] In 1931, when American marines suffered casualties at the hands of

Nicaraguan rebel forces, Johnson demonstrated his resolve to hold fast; he would not, like Borah and La Follette, run at the first sign of trouble. The issue had been transformed to a higher plane. "A nation is scarcely worthy of the name that declares, not only its inability, but its disinclination to protect its own."[121]

*   *   *

Johnson voiced only scorn toward the Coolidge administration's last major diplomatic venture, the ratification of the Kellogg-Briand Pact. The agreement grew out of French efforts to harness the United States to a bilateral treaty strengthening France's security in Europe. Wanting no part in such an undertaking, Secretary of State Kellogg, working closely with Borah, transformed the proposed agreement into a multilateral pact pledged the renunciation of war for aggressive purposes; in its new form the agreement generated tremendous enthusiasm among peace groups in the United States and popular applause worldwide.[122] Some saw the pact as a symbol of the nation's acknowledgment of its international responsibilities, perhaps a stepping-stone toward membership in the league itself. Many more viewed it as a substitute for the league, a demonstration of the nation's ability to forge a peaceful world, not through the rancor of Old World diplomacy but by affirmation of the very principle of peace itself. For Johnson it was nothing more than a farce—"a great big piece of American bunk."[123]

Unlike the Four-Power agreement, the pact made no provision for future international conferences; unlike the World Court, it had no connection with the league. Testimony before the Senate Foreign Relations Committee and statements from abroad made clear that no sanctions would be forthcoming in the event the treaty were breached. In committee deliberations Moses and Reed sought further assurance by proposing a set of reservations specifically safeguarding American interests. Both Borah and Kellogg agreed with the substance of the reservations, but feared that if they were formally attached to Senate acceptance they would hamper the moral force of the pact. Johnson, certain that the pact had no force, moral or otherwise, was indifferent. For the first and only time in his career, he stood outside the ranks of the irreconcilables. The treaty, he observed, was like a character in a Henry James novel—"analyzed by its proponents into disintegration." It was a meaningless treaty and thus reservations were unnecessary. In the Senate hearings and the floor debate that followed, Johnson remained for the most part silent, waiting until the eve of the vote to accurately characterize the pact with a poem by François Villon: [124]

> To Messire Noel, named the neat
> By those who love him, I bequeath
> A helmless ship, a houseless street,
> A wordless book, a swordless sheath,
> An hourless clock, a leafless wreath,
> A bed sans sheet, a board sans meat,
> A bell sans tongue, a saw sans teeth,
> To make his nothingness complete.

With only one dissenter, the Senate accepted the treaty. The pity, Johnson remarked in the aftermath of the vote, was not the pact itself but the fact that so many Americans had been taken in by the ruse, naively convincing themselves that ratification would somehow bring forth a new era. [125]

Contemptuous of those who rested millennial hopes on self-denying pledges, Johnson found at least partial consolation in the administration's 1929 naval construction act, which came to the floor little more than a week after the passage of the Kellogg-Briand Pact. The bill authorized the construction of fifteen light cruisers and one aircraft carrier. In debate Johnson mocked the various public groups who questioned the need for naval preparedness, scornfully dismissing the "pacifists ladies' associations, Friday morning clubs, Tuesday noon clubs, Wednesday 9 o'clock clubs, and Thursday 6 o'clock in the evening clubs." Borah, who sponsored a resolution to codify the rules of the sea during war, felt his sting as well. In the real world, Johnson argued, no nation could be expected to endanger its perceived interests voluntarily by subscribing to abstract principles. Britain had not refrained from interfering with rights claimed by neutrals during the war, nor had the United States, once it became a belligerent. In peacetime, rights were a function of laws and convention; in war, they depended solely on the power of nations to enforce compliance through threats of retaliation.

Power lay at the center of international relations, Johnson insisted; hence the United States should protect its interests not by denying the centrality of power or by seeking to harness American power to the designs of others in leagues, alliances, and international agreements, but by maintaining sufficient means to counter any threat. Lulled by the results of the Washington Naval Conference and hopeful that its own restraint might be reflected in the policy of others, the United States had too long ignored its growing inferiority in auxiliary vessels. If anything, Johnson concluded, the administration's bill fell short of present needs. He joined in the overwhelming Senate majority in support of the building program while calling as well for the establishment of naval parity with Great Britain.[126]

*   *   *

Throughout the 1920s Johnson tried to temper his image as an isolationist. The United States, he insisted, was not, nor could it be, a hermit nation. It was tied to the outside world by trade, and American prosperity could not be divorced from foreign markets. So too, the American people were bound to the wider world by their multinational heritage. Such economic and cultural ties, however, necessitated political autonomy rather than political involvement in that wider world. In an effort to appear less the obstructionist, Johnson agreed that Americans had to be "ever alive to humanity's cry or civilization's call." The United States, he promised, would always be willing to attend international conferences free of intrigue and open to the world's peoples. Indeed, the nation's very aloofness from the machinations of Europe afforded it the opportunity to organize such assemblies.[127]

Yet in practice Johnson's observations were little more than empty gestures. "He abounds in melting charity," the *New York Times* remarked.[128] In his universe humanity's cry too often concealed selfish national ambition; conferences by their very nature invited abuse and intrigue. His perception of the world was colored by distrust both of nations abroad and of American leadership at home. "I am suspicious of diplomats," he once confessed.[129] Distrust led him to question the motives of his adversaries and to predict catastrophe from any new initiative. Patriotism, his protectiveness of American rights, often blinded him to the consequences of America's role abroad. But if he was too ready to see the dire in the innocuous and to ignore the many economic and political problems that Europe faced, he did recognize the centrality of power in foreign relations, a reality that many of his contemporaries too often denied.

In the decade of the 1920s Congress played an active role in the shaping of foreign affairs, often hampering the president and his subordinates, at times compelling them to action, but never fundamentally challenging their overall policy goals. Senate and House pressure was instrumental in the calling of the Washington Naval Conference and hastened both the negotiation of the Berlin Treaty in 1921 and the withdrawal of American troops from Germany in 1923. Senate suspicion undercut the possibility of formal United States participation in the Reparations Commission, forced the passage of an explanatory reservation to the Four-Power agreement, indirectly led to the failure of the United States to join the World Court, and sharply limited the discretion of the World War Foreign Debt Commission.

Nevertheless, Johnson found the record disappointing. The Senate had failed to maintain the dominant role it had assumed in the waning years of the Wilson administration. Partisanship, he averred, had diluted the steadfastness of some irreconcilables. Pacifism shaped the attitudes of others. Borah, sometimes vigorous, always unpredictable, rallied to a number of causes but proposed policies no less dangerous than those of the administration. Despite congressional efforts, the executive's reliance on informal and unofficial observers could and did circumvent restrictions on American participation in the tangled web of reparations. Where seemingly strict guidelines existed, they were ignored, as in the settlement of war debts. Out of the Washington conference had come an arms limitation agreement that Johnson distrusted and soon defined as detrimental to national security. Even more threatening in his view was the Four-Power treaty, which, however modified by the Brandegee reservation, linked the nation's fortunes to the possibility of wider involvement in an unstable world. Convinced of Hoover's insincerity, of Hughes's shrewdness, and of Kellogg's timidity in the face of British pressure, Johnson felt sure that the executive branch stood poised to implement by degrees Wilson's grand design.

In this, Johnson was clearly wrong. The foreign policies outlined in the 1920s were no more satisfactory to the disciples of Wilson than they were to Johnson and the other irreconcilables. Accepting Wilson's conclusions that the United States could no longer remain aloof from global affairs, Hughes, Hoover and Kellogg, with various degrees of skill, worked to preserve the status quo, to ease frictions between the world powers arising out of the recent war, and to secure American economic advantages through the continuation and extension of the principles of the Open Door. They maintained, however, that these goals could be realized without compromising the nation's traditional political independence in world affairs. While endorsing international cooperation, they denied the wisdom of collective security, firm in their belief that cooperation could be effective without binding commitments or a radical limitation on the nation's freedom of action. Like Wilson, they were internationalists in their acceptance of shared values and in their assertion of American responsibility to an international community; they differed from him in their refusal to accept overt political entanglements. Their often ambiguous statements during the debates over the league and their eager promotion of international cooperation led Johnson to doubt their sincerity and to misrepresent their position. To him, they appeared Wilsonians in disguise.

Yet even if he had trusted their motives, Johnson would have objected to their solutions and feared the consequences of their actions. If not Wilsonians by design, they would become Wilsonians by default. Cooperation to secure the status quo and to advance the principle of the Open Door, assistance in the resolution of international tensions, threatened political entanglement while benefiting an economic elite who ignored the dangers to American society that flowed from the pursuit of their private ambitions. Congressional obstruction remained for Johnson the first line of defense against such threats; latent public antipathy to involvement abroad, galvanized by the disillusionment growing out of the war, provided the ultimate safeguard of the nation's independence.

Grove Johnson, sometime in the 1870s. After being forced to flee his hometown of Syracuse, New York, to avoid prosecution, Grove settled in Sacramento, where he quickly made a place for himself both as a lawyer and as a politician. Reproduced courtesy of the Bancroft Library, University of California, Berkeley.

The *San Francisco Examiner* lashes out at Grove Johnson as a pawn of Collis P. Huntington and his railroad empire. In 1910, in a speech long remembered, Hiram Johnson excoriated Harrison Gray Otis, the autocratic publisher of the *Los Angeles Times*, in similar terms, calling him a blot on the state's escutcheon. The cartoon is by Swinnerton, *San Francisco Examiner*, Mar. 2, 1896.

HUNTINGTON'S HANDIWORK.

The Grove Johnson Blot on the California 'Scutcheon.

Hiram Johnson (second from left) relaxing with his Chi Phi fraternity brothers in 1885. Johnson left the University of California at the beginning of his junior year in order to marry Minnie McNeil, herself a Sacramento resident, then attending nearby Mills College in Oakland. Whether the marriage was forced by Minnie's prenuptial pregnancy, or by her determination to take up an operatic career in Europe, remains unclear. Reproduced courtesy of the Bancroft Library, University of California, Berkeley.

Hiram Johnson as a Sacramento lawyer sometime in the 1890s. Though his older brother, Albert, left the firm of Johnson, Johnson, & Johnson in 1893, Hiram remained in partnership with his father until 1897. Reproduced courtesy of the California Room, California State Library, Sacramento.

With the 1910 general election two days away, Johnson relaxes at home, having just concluded a grueling eight-month campaign for the governorship. Johnson defeated Theodore Bell, his Democratic opponent, by 22,000 votes. Reproduced courtesy of the Bancroft Library, University of California, Berkeley.

LIKE FATHER LIKE SON

Hiram Johnson's dubious connections. The primary election of 1910 as viewed by the *Los Angeles Times*, July 27, 1910. The *Times* had been a vigorous opponent of the Southern Pacific railroad, but it was even more vigorous in its opposition to the California progressives. Here, Johnson is depicted as carrying on in the tradition of his father, a tool of the Southern Pacific.

HIS REPERTOIRE

The election of 1910 as viewed by the *San Francisco Examiner*. The *Examiner* endorsed Theodore Bell, the Democratic party candidate, who had pledged to elimnate railroad abuses in state politics long before Johnson picked up the issue. It was an old note, no longer fresh, yet Johnson knew no other. Chopin, *San Francisco Examiner*, Oct. 24, 1910.

THE OSTRICH

Johnson, preoccupied by the single issue of the railroad, ignores the more important issues of the day, including Asian exclusion, while Theodore Bell and the Democratic party march proudly past toward victory. Chopin, *San Francisco Examiner*, Oct. 24, 1910.

The Johnsons—Hiram and Minnie. Minnie relished Hiram's political victories but bemoaned his political career. It required residence in second-rate cities (first Sacramento and then Washington), intruded on a privacy she cherished, and undermined her hopes for the wealth that Hiram's career in law had once seemed to promise. Periodically she urged Hiram to abandon politics and return to the courtroom. But although she was known affectionately as "the boss," she would not get her way. The top picture shows the two relaxing at Lake Tahoe after the election of 1910. The second picture was probably taken during their European tour in 1923. The identity of the third person is unknown. Both pictures reproduced courtesy of the Bancroft Library, University of California, Berkeley.

Chester Rowell (1867–1948). Co-founder of the Lincoln-Roosevelt League, Rowell was a moving force in the rise of the progressive movement in California and was one of Johnson's closest associates until differences over foreign policy ended their friendship. Reproduced courtesy of the California Room, California State Library, Sacramento.

John Francis Neylan (1885–1960). Neylan was appointed in 1911 to head the newly created Board of Control, where he remained throughout Johnson's governorship. At times Johnson complained of Neylan's ego, but he always listened willingly to Neylan's advice. Reproduced courtesy of the California Room, California State Library, Sacramento.

Alexander McCabe (1873–1950). A skilled political operator, McCabe helped organize Johnson's 1910 campaign and played a central part in all of his subsequent campaigns. During Johnson's governorship, McCabe served as Johnson's private secretary. Reproduced courtesy of the California Room, California State Library, Sacramento.

Meyer Lissner (1871–1930). Active in Los Angeles reform circles, Lissner helped organize the Lincoln-Roosevelt League and went on to become Johnson's chief political mainstay in southern California. Reproduced courtesy of the California Room, California State Library, Sacramento.

In the governor's office. As governor from 1911 to 1916, Johnson provided the leadership for a progressive reform movement that totally revamped California's political order, creating a legacy that can still be felt today. Reproduced courtesy of the California Room, California State Library, Sacramento.

In June the California delegation to the 1912 Republican national convention gathers for a portrait. Elected in the California presidential primary, they were pledged to Theodore Roosevelt. Once it became clear that President Taft's forces controlled the Chicago convention and would determine its outcome, they decamped. The three men on Johnson's right are (from left to right) Chester Rowell, Charles S. Wheeler, and Francis Heney. Isabella Blaney and Jesse Hurlbut sit to Johnson's immediate left. Directly above Blaney is C. C. Young. Reproduced courtesy of the Bancroft Library, University of California, Berkeley.

In August 1912, many of the same delegates returned to Chicago to form the Progressive party and nominate Theodore Roosevelt for president and Hiram Johnson as his running mate—note the bandana covering the "Republican" designation on the Roosevelt standard. Seated to Johnson's immediate right is ex-Governor George Pardee. Reproduced courtesy of the Bancroft Library, University of California, Berkeley.

Standing at Armageddon. Theodore Roosevelt and Hiram Johnson. As vice-presidential candidate in 1912, Johnson campaigned energetically, traveling more than 20,000 miles and giving an estimated 500 speeches in ten weeks. But as Johnson recognized, it was a hopeless task. The Progressive insurgency allowed Wilson to win the White House and the Democratic party to control Congress. Reproduced courtesy of the Library of Congress.

Johnson meets with Secretary of State William Jennings Bryan (left) on the steps of the Governor's Mansion, May 3, 1913. Woodrow Wilson had sent Bryan to Sacramento to try to dissuade the legislature from passing the Alien Land Act prohibiting the sale of agricultural land to Japanese nationals. Bryan's mission failed when Johnson made it clear that passage of the measure had become one of his administration's chief priorities. Reproduced courtesy of the Library of Congress.

In 1914 Hiram Johnson ran for reelection as governor on the Progressive party ticket, seeking thereby to root the new party permanently. As in 1910, he canvassed the state in an exhaustive campaign. In November he romped to an easy victory, polling more votes than his Republican and Democratic challengers combined. It was just about the only success Progressives could point to nationally. In this photo, Johnson's younger son, Archibald, sits at the wheel of the auto. Reproduced courtesy of the Bancroft Library, University of California, Berkeley.

The 1914 campaign. Left: Not all of Johnson's speeches were scheduled in advance. Here he stops just outside Los Angeles for an impromptu address. Right: Yet another unscheduled stop. Both photos reproduced courtesy of the Bancroft Library, University of California, Berkeley.

BY HOOK OR CROOK

Following the collapse of the Progressive party in 1916, the bulk of California's insurgents returned to the Republican party. Campaigning for the United States Senate as a Progressive, Johnson is pictured as he reaches out to grab the Republican nomination as well. The move proved successful, and in a close election, Johnson won the Republican primary. Bronstrup, *San Francisco Chronicle*, Aug. 16, 1916.

The first governor in sixty years to win reelection, Johnson takes the oath of office for the second time in January 1915. Appellate court justice E. C. Hart administers the oath. Lieutenant Governor John Eshleman, who would die midway through the term, is seated center. Reproduced courtesy of the California Room, California State Library, Sacramento.

Hiram and younger son Archibald, 1917. Disregarding Johnson's advice, Archibald, then 26, volunteered for service once America entered the war. He fought at Château-Thierry and later underwent a serious emotional breakdown. Johnson had hoped that neither of his sons would be sent off to war, and when his elder son (then 29, married, and with two children) received his draft call, Johnson protested vigorously, demanding a change in the administration of the draft laws. Reproduced courtesy of the Bancroft Library, University of California, Berkeley.

There were, Johnson once wrote, "working" senators who were actively involved in the legislative process, and "social" senators who left the work to others. Johnson preferred to be a working senator and rose rapidly in the Senate, his talents readily apparent to his colleagues. Early on he was appointed to the Military Affairs Committee. This photo was taken in August 1919, as Johnson strides past the Capitol. Reproduced courtesy of the Library of Congress.

A trio of Republican irreconcilables: Senators Medill McCormick (Illinois), William Borah (Idaho), and Johnson, 1919. All three actively campaigned against American membership in the League of Nations, with Borah and Johnson more frequently on the stump, while McCormick helped organize the itinerary. Reproduced courtesy of the Bancroft Library, University of California, Berkeley.

Johnson's isolationism as viewed by Gale, *Los Angeles Times*, Oct. 26, 1919.

At home: the Calvert Mansion. Johnson and his wife always managed to live beyond their means. Arriving in Washington in 1917, they first took up residence in expensive hotels before finally settling into the 100-year-old Calvert Mansion, located in Riverdale, Maryland. Reproduced courtesy of the Library of Congress.

Both Hiram and Minnie took pleasure in their retreat from the bustle of Washington. Here Hiram sits contentedly on the steps of the Calvert Mansion. Reproduced courtesy of the Bancroft Library, University of California, Berkeley.

Johnson in typical fighting pose, chin down, fists ready for the knockout blow. For Johnson, politics almost always meant confrontation, not compromise. "Perhaps more than most men I don't like to be whipped," he once wrote, "but when a blow comes my head goes up higher in the air and I want to fight more." Reproduced courtesy of the Library of Congress.

After a four-month holiday tour abroad, Johnson returned to New York in July 1923 where he was greeted by a police band, a motorcycle escort, and a crowd of more than 2,000 well-wishers. His hat was not yet in the 1924 presidential ring, but it was clearly doffed. Reproduced courtesy of the California Room, California State Library, Sacramento.

ANNOUNCED FOR JUNE.

Johnson could always count on the support of C. K. McClatchy and the *Sacramento Bee*. Here the *Bee* promotes Johnson for president. In fact the road proved far less easy than depicted, and in the end, the groom was jilted. Wahl, *Sacramento Bee*, May 8, 1920

Johnson and the *Los Angeles Times* shared a mutual hatred until almost the end of Johnson's political career. If the *Times* ever found reason to support him, he once remarked, his whole world would be called into question. Here the *Los Angeles Times* contrasts Hiram Johnson with Charles C. Moore, his opponent in the August 1922 Republican primary. Johnson won easily, with almost 57 percent of the vote. Gale, *Los Angeles Times*, Aug. 19, 1922.

OUR WORST FEARS ABOUT THE SCARCITY OF GAME BEING REALIZED

Although most Americans considered the League of Nations a dead issue following Senate rejection of U.S. membership in November 1919 and March 1920, Hiram Johnson clearly did not, and he rarely allowed an opportunity to pass without lambasting the League. Darling, *Sacramento Union*, Dec. 24, 1923.

The Johnson presidential boom, 1924. A determined Johnson beats his own much-patched drum, but few gather to listen. In fact, Johnson's 1924 presidential campaign was a disaster from the beginning as Coolidge coasted to an easy victory in almost all the primary states, winning even in California. Sykes, *Philadelphia Evening Public Ledger*.

Hiram Johnson and Harold Ickes. Fast friends since Bull Moose days, both men were active reformers. Both were also petulant, stubborn, and strong-willed, and in the mid-1930s their friendship rapidly soured. Until that point, however, Ickes had been constant in encouraging and supporting Johnson's political ambitions. Reproduced courtesy of the Bancroft Library, University of California, Berkeley.

Hiram and sons Archibald (left) and "Jack" (right), probably in 1926.
Johnson's relations with his sons were close, and both Archibald
and Jack worked to further their father's political career. Reproduced
courtesy of the Bancroft Library, University of California, Berkeley.

From 1922 through 1928, Johnson fought for passage of a bill to dam the
Colorado River at Boulder Canyon. It was the most important domestic
legislation he sponsored during his 28 years in the Senate. Here Coolidge
signs the bill at a White House ceremony, Dec. 21, 1928. Reproduced courtesy of the Bancroft Library, University of California, Berkeley.

Hiram Johnson rescues the Boulder Dam bill from the power trust and assorted lobbyists who sought to destroy it. Smith, *San Francisco Examiner*, May 25, 1928.

NO JOB FOR A WEAKLING

Hiram Johnson with C. K. McClatchy in Sacramento in the early 1930s. McClatchy, eight years Johnson's senior, was publisher of the *Sacramento Bee* and one of Johnson's closest personal friends. They rarely disagreed, but when they did, they clearly valued their friendship more. Reproduced courtesy of the Eleanor McClatchy Collection, Sacramento Archives and History Museum.

Often pictured together, Hiram Johnson and William Borah shared both a common isolationist commitment and an ability to forcefully articulate their views. Both were members of the Senate Foreign Relations Committee yet they were personally never close. In January 1935, the two collaborated to successfully prevent U.S. entry into the World Court. Here, they examine the final Senate tally. Reproduced courtesy of the Bancroft Library, University of California, Berkeley.

Johnson, Senator Key Pittman, Chairman of the Senate Foreign Relations Committee (center), and Secretary of State Cordell Hull (right) meet to discuss the merits of neutrality legislation, probably in 1936. Willing to accept the Neutrality Act of 1935 which outlawed the sale of American arms to warring nations abroad, Johnson fought adamantly against additional restrictions on the nation's trading rights. Reproduced courtesy of the Bancroft Library, University of California, Berkeley.

Not yet recovered from the stroke he suffered the previous year, Johnson returns to California, Sept. 1, 1937. Meeting him at the Oakland mole are his son "Jack" and grandson, Hiram Johnson III. Reproduced courtesy of the Bancroft Library, University of California, Berkeley.

Johnson campaigned actively for Roosevelt in 1932 and supported the bulk of New Deal legislation in FDR's first term, but by 1937 the two were bitterly at odds. Here Johnson and FDR briefly exchange greetings in San Francisco during Roosevelt's tour through California in July 1938. George Creel sits at Roosevelt's right. Reproduced courtesy of the Bancroft Library, University of California, Berkeley.

Johnson shares a secret with Senator Tom Connally (Dem.–Texas) at the Senate Foreign Relations Committee hearings in May 1939. During the hearings, the 72-year-old Johnson played an active role in helping to derail Roosevelt's effort to repeal the arms embargo. Reproduced courtesy of the Bancroft Library, University of California, Berkeley.

The Campaign of 1940. Cross-filing in the state's Republican, Democratic, and Progressive primaries, Johnson won all three. Meanwhile Willkie, facing a more difficult challenge, actively sought out Johnson's support, something (the cartoon reminds us) Charles Evans Hughes might have profitably done back in 1916. Willkie lost California in the general election while Johnson won a fifth senate term with 82 percent of the vote. Berryman, *Evening Star* (Washington, D.C.), Sept. 20, 1940.

Chapter VI

At
Home

The Decade of the 1920s

In his opposition to foreign entanglement Hiram Johnson could appeal to the American public by capitalizing
on the nation's historic isolationist impulse. When dealing with domestic issues, however, the popular mood served to impede rather
than advance his hopes. An era had ended as a majority of Americans,
turning away from adventures abroad, seemed equally unwilling to
join progressive crusades at home. The United States, Johnson lamented in the aftermath of Harding's inauguration, had become the
most conservative nation on earth.* Reporters who had fed muck-
raking fires a decade earlier now spouted "sycophantic slush" and
refused to question conservative orthodoxies. Every major journal-

---

*HWJ to C. K. McClatchy, Apr. 16, 1921. See also HWJ to C. K. McClatchy, Mar.
9, June 21, 1921; HWJ to Fremont Older, Jan. 17, June 15, 1921. When campaigning
in 1912, Johnson had stressed that reform was necessary to ensure against more radical alternatives. In the decade of the 1920s he expressed similar views: "I do not
delude myself with the idea there will be any *sudden* change; but I am . . . certain . . .
that this administration is sowing to the wind and some day perhaps after we have
passed, because of it, the American people will reap the whirlwind." HWJ to boys,
May 29, 1921, emphasis in original. "I do not despair by any means of the future. I
simply think that we're in an era that comes in cycles . . . from which we will unquestionably emerge. The only fear I have is that we will swing so far in the one
direction, that we will swing too far back in the other when the revulsion comes."
HWJ to boys, Jan. 13, 1925. See also HWJ to boys, Apr. 10, May 29, 1921; HWJ to
Arthur Brisbane, May 27, 1924. Fremont Older reflected the disillusionment of many
once earnest reformers: "Why should you make yourself unhappy? I long since lost
all hope of the [human] race. It simply can't make the grade. Its appetites, its vanities,
and its cruelties are too deep-seated to be anything more than superficially lessened.
I suppose one ought to be big enough to pity the poor fools, but that is a height I
haven't yet been able to reach." Fremont Older to HWJ, Jan. 20, 1923.

ist, Johnson complained, was "crawling on his belly to the White House." Mark Sullivan, William Allen White, Norman Hapgood, and David Lawrence were little more than "lick-spittles and prostitutes" to the new era. Even the best of journals, such as the *New Republic*, he added, seemed to temper its mood to fit the times.[1]

Critical of the tone of American journalism, Johnson lashed out at other aspects of the nation's changing society as well, specifically decrying the ongoing assaults both on organized labor and on the mechanics of the direct primary.[2] In California, as Katherine Edson reported, the newly formed Better America Federation, under the leadership of Harry M. Haldeman, branded every worker who joined a trade union as an "anarchist and a socialist."[3] Similar organizations, born out of the dislocations of the war and the Red Scare, took root throughout the nation, and by the summer of 1920 the National Association of Manufacturers had established an open-shop department to coordinate the various endeavors under way to eliminate the advantages labor had realized during the war. Highly successful, the open-shop campaign gained further impetus when federal and state courts imposed tight restrictions on union rights, upheld the legitimacy of the yellow-dog contract prohibiting union recruitment, and expanded the injunction into a major tool of employer protection. All good law perhaps, Johnson mused, but baffling to the man who labors and repulsive to those who value humanity above property.[4]

Equally distressing to Johnson was the continuing assault on the direct primary. Between 1901 and 1917 the concept of popular nomination of party candidates had swept the nation. Thirty-nine states had abolished party nominating conventions and had enacted direct-primary laws for state and federal representatives; some had included the opportunity for presidential primaries as well. But in the aftermath of war the backlash began: party stalwarts inveighed against the expenses of the primary, the fragmentation of party responsibility, and the elevation of personality above party. Throughout the nation attempts to repeal or fundamentally alter the mechanics of direct nomination gathered support. Those efforts, Johnson protested, struck at the very roots of progressivism. Primaries did not guarantee good government, he conceded, but they remained the only solid foundation on which good government could rest. The need was to perfect the primaries, to control expenses in state and federal contests, and to remove the impediments to a truly national presidential primary.[5] Fearful that public apathy would enable the Old Guard to restore the earlier convention system, Johnson sought throughout the 1920s to emphasize the centrality of the direct primary. When that system is abolished in California, he predicted, "our movement . . . will be so dead that another generation will be unable to revive it."[6]

Johnson's concerns with the ongoing assaults on organized labor and the direct primary extended beyond his own immediate political needs but clearly were not divorced from them. California's unions, though ambivalent at best toward the progressive rebellion of 1910, had become an important factor in Johnson's success in the 1914 gubernatorial race and in his Senate victory in 1916.[7] His strength in San Francisco and his relative weakness in Los Angeles in part hinged on the differing power of union labor in those two cities.

He benefited as well from both the faults and the virtues of the primary system. It was a device that complemented his talents, his oratorical skills, his almost magnetic ability to shape and mold an audience. Above all, it fitted his temperament. Unwilling to subordinate himself to any superior, stubbornly insistent upon his independence, and demanding of others what he could rarely give of himself—a personal loyalty that transcended policy differences— Johnson found in the direct primary the guarantee of his own success. The retention of the California primary, upon which his career had rested since 1910, and the reform of the presidential primary system, which had marred his ambitions in 1920, were deeply tied to his own interests.

But if Johnson's concerns with regard to organized labor and the direct-primary system were self-serving, they were also rooted to a larger theme that transcended his own political needs. In both instances, wealth sought to reassert its power; privilege sought to enhance its dominance. The central issue in the 1920s, he argued, remained what it had been in California prior to the progressive insurgency: would business control government and society for its own ends or would government harness business for the ultimate welfare of the whole society?

★   ★   ★

Given the popular mood and Warren Harding's background, there seemed little doubt on which side of this question the new administration would fall. Pledged to government retrenchment and the restoration of "normalcy," Harding called for a special session of Congress to meet in mid-April 1921. In anticipation of the event, political observers predicted that Johnson would quickly become one of the president's most adamant critics, as outspoken in his assault on the administration's domestic agenda as in his promotion of isolationism. He would surely break with the White House, they concluded. In fact, the break never came.

Although Johnson and Harding found themselves at odds over both foreign and domestic policies, they did not allow their differences to dominate their relationship. The president, affable and generous, eminently likable as an individual and instinctively wary of conflict, tried throughout his administration to remain on good terms with all factions of his party, and both Hiram and Minnie were welcomed dinner guests at the White House. Occasionally Hiram participated in the stag poker sessions Harding so enjoyed. Johnson would never alter his mordant appraisals of the president—he had no more appreciation of the big questions than the "Man on the Moon." Indeed, participation in such social gatherings only strengthened that perception by affording Johnson the opportunity to contrast himself with Harding and his inner circle. If Johnson sometimes doubted his own abilities and was occasionally overwhelmed with a sense of his own limitations, he confessed, he easily found himself "intellectually" superior to those around him.[8]

But Harding's outgoing effusiveness made association easy, and the relationship between the two remained amicable on both the social and the political levels. It was difficult not to feel kindly toward the president, Johnson admitted.[9] In Johnson's increasingly acrimonious conflicts with Shortridge over California patronage, Harding sought to be accommodating. At one point he went out of his way to secure an ambassadorial position at The Hague for Richard Tobin, of the Hibernia Bank, as a personal favor to Minnie. In his own way Johnson too found it possible to be accommodating.[10] Though privately grousing, lending his vote but rarely his voice to the efforts on the part of Senate insurgents to chip away at Harding's domestic programs, he almost never took the lead in opposition to those programs, content more often to carp than to participate actively in floor debate.

The nomination of William Howard Taft as chief justice in July

1921 provided a rare exception. The appointment, Johnson wrote, was one of the most sinister acts of the administration. This man "devoid of learning, judicial temperament, and of principles," long the *bête noire* of progressive reform, was to be given the opportunity to consolidate conservative gains at the highest level. Many in the Senate spoke privately against the selection, but in the executive session called to confirm the appointment, Johnson angrily observed, only three joined him in casting dissenting votes. On returning home that evening, he described himself as being as low in spirits as he had ever been. It took all his determination, he continued, not to contemplate retirement to private life.*

More often, however, Johnson reacted to Harding's proposed domestic agenda with irritation rather than outrage. In part, his relative indifference to that agenda was shaped by his ongoing legal involvement with the transit battles in New York. Frequent commutes to and from the city took much of his time and left him both physically and intellectually drained. Absorption in the contests over the administration's international policies further taxed his energies. He began to wonder if he did not share the limitation Woodrow Wilson had once confessed to: a one-track mind.[11]

Perhaps political considerations also played a part. While convinced that he could help determine the foreign policies of the Harding administration, Johnson saw little chance to alter or fundamentally redefine a domestic program that seemed politically popular. His only real opportunity, he wrote, was to make a record for the future.[12] That record would allow him to maintain his status as a progressive but would not impair his political standing in a new and more conservative era. Thus in 1921, in the wake of the Newberry election scandal, he sponsored a constitutional amendment to control excesses of spending in primary contests and proposed a second amendment to establish a uniform system of presidential primaries,

*HWJ to boys, July 2, 1921. See also HWJ to Raymond Robins, July 1, 1921; HWJ to Ickes, July 2, 1921; *New York Times*, July 1, 1921. Taft was not the only Harding nominee that Johnson opposed. David H. Blair, nominated to head the Internal Revenue Service, was another. Pledged to Johnson as a delegate from North Carolina to the 1920 National Republican Convention, he had bolted and in so doing had earned Johnson's wrath. Johnson's persistent efforts to block the appointment were unsuccessful. See HWJ to boys, May 1, 10, 29, June 8, 1921; HWJ to Hiram Johnson, Jr., May 27, 1921; HWJ to Jake Newell, May 10, 1921; HWJ to Ickes, May 10, 1921; *New York Times*, May 4, 1921.

but he made no effort to launch a campaign in support of either of those measures, and both died in committee.[13]

The same year, angered by the exploitation of West Virginia mine workers, Johnson successfully pushed for a Senate probe of the matter. In 1922, in response to the decision of the Supreme Court in *Bailey v. Drexel Furniture Company*, he sponsored a constitutional amendment to enable Congress to reimpose limits on child labor.[14] He criticized government economies that denied a "living wage" to low-level federal workers, and in 1923 reaffirmed his support for state minimum-wage laws for women, condemning the Supreme Court's negation of that principle.[15] To black Americans he pledged his support for anti-lynching legislation; to immigrants, he declared his belief that the United States should continue to offer asylum to the politically and religiously persecuted.[16] All of these issues were significant, but none received more than Johnson's limited attention.

Above all, his reticence in floor debate, his reluctance to lay siege to Harding's domestic programs, was shaped by his inability to design any compelling alternative to the policies sponsored by the White House. In foreign affairs his goal was to ensure American independence from foreign entanglements. The need was to defend what had already been won, and his posture of obstructionism was an appropriate strategy to that end. In domestic affairs a policy of negation could blunt the initiatives of the White House, perhaps postpone the further triumph of conservatism, but that was all. Liberal instincts made an inadequate substitute for concrete programs. Observing Johnson's dilemma, Chester Rowell recalled his own unsuccessful effort to put together some sort of "kitchen cabinet" that could have served Johnson in the Senate in much the same way a similar operation had served him as governor. Rowell was certainly correct; without concrete programs progressivism could only flounder. At the same time, however, Rowell failed to come to grips with his own inability to develop an agenda independent of the administration's. Instead, Rowell defined cooperation with Hughes and Hoover as the test for progressivism, a test Johnson easily failed.[17]

★   ★   ★

The dilemma confronting Johnson plagued the whole of progressivism in the decade of the 1920s as the movement splintered over both means and ends.[18] Although liberal by instinct and genuinely sympathetic to the plight of others, he had no answers of his own for the nation's domestic ills and could discover no answers in the proposals urged by his colleagues. Thus, in the battle over tax policy, he found himself opposed to the administration's endeavor to shift taxes from the wealthy but was also wary of the alternatives presented. The original bill, authored by Secretary of the Treasury Andrew Mellon, called for the elimination of the excess-profits tax and a halving of the maximum surtax rate to 32 percent. The administration managed to keep the measure intact both in the House and in the Senate Finance Committee, but their work unraveled once the bill reached the floor of the Senate. There, insurgent Republicans joined Democrats in a scathing attack on the proposal.

The measure, Johnson agreed, was "a tribute to big business," but in sharp contrast to his active participation in the 1917 battle over wartime taxation, his involvement here was minimal; he sponsored no amendments and remained almost silent in floor debate.[19] Clearly sympathetic to the administration's critics, he endorsed their attempts to retain the excess-profits tax, to open tax returns to public scrutiny, and to modify the deep cuts sought by the administration in the surtax rates. But privately, he voiced qualms that high rates were often a sham, encouraged tax evasion, and were, whatever their merits, unpopular not only among the wealthy but among the American population at large. Seeing no way to remedy the evils associated with the tax structure, he found himself tempted by what he conceded to be the least palatable alternative, a regressive sales tax, and at one point broke with liberal ranks to consider such an alternative.* Ultimately, the revenue bill that emerged in 1921 blunted the designs of the administration by holding surtax rates to 50 percent. For Johnson, it was a less than satisfactory settlement. Perhaps, he mused, he would vote against "the whole dirty scheme." In fact, he missed the final vote altogether.[20]

Johnson's dilemma showed itself as well when farm groups thrust

---

* *Cong. Record*, 67th Cong., 1st sess. (Nov. 4, 1921), p. 7298. "A tax scheme which requires one army of experts to teach honest people how to pay what is due the government, and which creates another army of experts to teach the dishonest how to cheat the government, is an abominable thing," he remarked in supporting the Smoot amendment that would have eliminated various nuisance taxes and established a 2 percent sales tax. See also HWJ to boys, Oct. 1, 29, 1921.

their concerns before Congress. During the war the nation's mid-western farmers had eagerly expanded their output, encouraged by the government to do so, but in the war's aftermath they faced depressed markets and a sharp fall in prices. Wishing to help them, Johnson joined in the progressive move to strengthen the provisions of the Packers and Stockyards Act and symbolically sat next to George Norris when the Nebraska senator angrily attacked administration policies that had sidetracked his bill to create a government board to market farm surplus abroad. Yet, even as he signaled his support, Johnson privately concluded that none of the proposed remedies would solve the farm problem.[21]

Throughout Harding's presidency Johnson confessed his indifference to domestic legislation. Foreign affairs, he wrote, constituted the only really interesting enjoyable part of his work.[22] Undoubtedly his relative inattention to affairs at home, while shaped in part by political considerations in a conservative era, reflected even more his own uncertainty, his inability to discover any compelling cause in which to invest his energies. In time that situation would change, but not until midway through the decade.

Until then, the only legislative measure that prompted any significant activity on Johnson's part was one that followed the direction outlined by the White House—reestablishing a high protective tariff. Industries will be amply taken care of, Frank Doherty observed from California, and "while they are getting theirs, we ought to get ours."[23] Johnson readily agreed. The tariff, he concluded, was not really a progressive issue even though some had once argued otherwise. Rates could never be determined in any but a chaotic fashion. That being the case, the battle over tariff protection was essentially a game of get and grab, and in any game he played, his object was to win.[24] Thus freed from any self-imposed philosophical constraint, Johnson moved forcefully to test his persuasive skills as an attorney for the interests of his state: he lobbied and logrolled, pleaded and cajoled, devoting long evenings and endless hours to the cause of shelled almonds, walnuts, olive oil, raisins, and lemons both before the Senate Finance Committee and on the floor of the Senate. He skated on "very thin ice" and worked "like a damn dog," he complained, but it was worth it.[25] He could not be himself in a fight where principles were not at stake, he self-consciously confessed to his sons, but he found satisfaction in the demonstration of his skill at the game. Perhaps too, he found even greater satisfaction in the political benefits he derived from the contest, for as Frank Doherty correctly noted, Johnson was able to reach out to elements in California who could have been reached in no other way.[26]

★   ★   ★

Johnson's need to reach out to additional groups was clear to all, for in 1922 his first term in the Senate would end, and despite his wife's long-standing irritation and his own occasional expressions of distaste for continued political involvement, few doubted that he would seek reelection.* His obsessive attention to every hint of possible challenge made his intentions clear. The real question was whether he would be opposed in the primary. Almost without exception his California associates assured him that there would be no significant contest, and even those less than friendly tended to agree.[27] In the summer of 1921 Chester Rowell informed Johnson's supporters that the Hoover camp had no claim on the office, either for Hoover himself or for a surrogate. If a contest developed, he added, it would be launched by the Better American Federation and others of the far right.[28]

Skeptical of the Hoover people even "on oath," Johnson ignored the optimistic predictions of his lieutenants, certain that a hard primary fight was brewing and that Rowell and Hoover would join in the opposition, and perhaps lead it.[29] And as both friends and enemies recognized, Johnson's outspoken assault on the Four-Power pact in the winter of 1921–22 had quickened just such a prospect. "He didn't have to do it," Rowell observed. "The road was all macadamized before him and the traffic cops had cleared everything off of it. From his personal standpoint the obvious strategy would be, like Br'er Rabbit, to 'lay low an' say nuffin'."[30] For Johnson, the only question was whom his enemies would anoint—Rowell himself;

---

*Johnson and his wife repeatedly discussed the possibility of retirement, but the question whether they would reside in San Francisco or New York could not be resolved. "I wish I was out of the damn game, and living again in San Francisco," Johnson noted at one point. Politics had lost its luster. "I am sick of the abuse of it, and the constant fighting." But, of course, he would not quit, and fears that he might be defeated in the primary began to haunt him. Given his personality, he confessed, nothing would be so "humiliating" as defeat. HWJ to Hiram Johnson, Jr., Apr. 20, 1922; HWJ to boys, May 11, June 23, 1922; HWJ to Archibald Johnson, Feb. 14, 1922.

Francis Keesling; William Kent; Superior Court Judge Gavin Craig; Professor James Hyde of Stanford University; or David Prescott Barrows, president of the University of California.[31]

As the filing date drew near, and as Johnson for the first time began to breathe more easily, his pessimistic instincts were confirmed.[32] In mid-June, after a series of setbacks, Hoover loyalist Ralph Arnold finally persuaded a reluctant Charles C. Moore to take up the challenge.* Moore, a strident critic of Johnson's isolationism and head of Hoover's California ticket in 1920, was not especially well known in the state, and unlike more politically prominent figures had little to risk. But Johnson was not about to underestimate the threat. Eager though he was to return to California, he was forced to wait until the battle for California's tariff protection was won, in mid-July. Once in California, he devoted a month to continuous campaigning, plunging first into Los Angeles and the state's southern coastal counties, where his support was weakest; traveling thence to the Bay Area and the hot, dry Sacramento valley, back through the valley towns of the San Joaquin, and into southern California once more before concluding his campaign in Berkeley and San Francisco.

A whirlwind of activity, Johnson attracted two thousand cheering supporters to the high-school auditorium in San Jose and a crowd estimated at nearly three thousand in Vallejo. In Bakersfield seven thousand people, the largest assembly in the city's history, gathered in the city hall square, and more than four thousand turned out for Johnson's "home town" rally at the Sacramento armory. In San Fran-

---

*C. C. Moore to Harry Chandler, Nov. 7, 1922; Ralph Arnold to T. T. C. Gregory, Aug. 15, 1922, both in Arnold Papers. "If we don't lick Johnson we have very little chance of ever doing anything for Hoover in the bigger things we have in mind," Arnold observed. Johnson saw the Hoover strategy in much the same way. "I must be literally destroyed politically, in order that [Hoover's] ambition may see its fruition." HWJ to boys, June 23, 1922. Many years later Arnold recalled his effort. See Ralph Arnold, "Laying Foundation Stones," *Historical Society of Southern California Quarterly* 37 (Sept. 1955), pp. 243–60. Rowell too had been given the opportunity to run. "I could have had the support of the public service corporations, of the Southern Pacific politicians, and of all the gang that I helped Johnson kick out of politics. I am also offered the support of the *Los Angeles Times*, and might have that of the *San Francisco Chronicle*. You will agree that it is not an inspiring prospect." Rowell to Milo Rowell, Mar. 31, 1922, Rowell Papers. See also Rowell to Edward Hamilton, June 23, 1922, Rowell Papers; Hichborn to HWJ, Mar. 27, 1922; Al McCabe to HWJ, June 21, 1922; HWJ to boys, June 17, 1922; HWJ to Doherty, June 23, 1922; Lissner to John R. Haynes, Mar. 30, 1922, Haynes Papers.

cisco during the conclusion of his campaign, an estimated eighteen thousand wedged their way into the Civic Auditorium and overflowed beyond. Even the south responded enthusiastically. Johnson filled Spreckels Theater in San Diego, turning hundreds away. In Los Angeles a crowd estimated at between seven and eight thousand jammed the streets in front of the Philharmonic Auditorium, unable to gain entry into the packed hall, and in Long Beach the municipal auditorium was overrun by what was described as the largest public gathering in the history of that city.[33]

On the stump Johnson voiced a familiar theme. The present battle, he charged, was but a continuation of the contest he had waged since 1910:

It's the same old fight, with the Chandlers, and the *Los Angeles Times*, and the Harry Haldemans, and the Better America Federation, and little Dicksons, and John D. Spreckels and the *San Diego Union*, and all the rest of the reactionary crew, who, by fake stories, sham issues and daily malice and mendacity, hope to regain the Senate from those whose government they were scourged, twelve years ago, by an indignant and resentful people.[34]

Throughout the campaign Johnson bitterly denounced his enemies but never mentioned Moore by name, referring to him rather as "Chandler's vicarious candidate."* His rhetoric ever shrill, Johnson reviewed the state's progressive past and pilloried Harry Chandler, stressed the importance of the direct primary and again pilloried Harry Chandler, emphasized his support of child-labor legislation, his opposition to Japanese immigration, and his advocacy of the Boulder Dam project, and pilloried Harry Chandler.

At the same time that he lashed out at the vested interests that sought to undermine California progressivism, Johnson appealed to many of those same interests, boasting of his achievements in the recently concluded tariff battle and declaring California "the best

---

*If Johnson saw Moore as something of a cipher, so too apparently did Rowell. Moore, he observed, is no more intellectual than Johnson but has the advantage of "teamwork," which means "that if men like Hughes and Hoover supply the initiative he can be trusted to co-operate intelligently and efficiently." Rowell to William Kent, July 12, 1922, Rowell Papers. For a breakdown of the various political factions that supported Moore, see HWJ to Doherty, June 23, 1922. Haldeman's endorsement of Moore, William Kent lamented, handed labor to Johnson. Delighted by the endorsement, Al McCabe agreed. Los Angeles labor, he wrote, saw the Senate contest as their fight. William Kent to Rowell, June 22, 1922, Rowell Papers; Al McCabe to HWJ, June 29, 1922.

protected State that there is in the Union."[35] Turning to foreign affairs, he sidestepped Moore's attacks by minimizing the significance of his opposition to the Four-Power pact. His stand, he protested, had been the right one, but more importantly, it was "for weal or woe" a part of the past, a deed accomplished. What was essential, he argued, was the future, and to a chorus of cheers he reiterated his faith in an America unsullied by foreign ties.[36]

Moore, having few substantive issues on which to build his campaign, made Johnson himself the issue by calling into question his Republican credentials.[37] Johnson, he charged, was a maverick, little more than the lackey of William Randolph Hearst, certainly not a Harding loyalist.[38] But while Moore struggled to embrace the banner of Republican orthodoxy and to identify himself with the president, Johnson held tight to that banner, firmly tying himself to the Harding administration. He was not a rubber stamp, he conceded, but he hewed much more closely to the Republican mainstream than did his opponent. It was Moore, he replied, who was not a "real" Republican. Moore's insistence in 1919 that the United States ratify the League Covenant without reservations placed him firmly in the Democratic camp. The "real" Republican position, Johnson declared, was the one he pronounced and Harding shared, namely, that the nation should remain aloof from foreign commitments.

Nor did the White House deny Johnson's claim to fraternity. Throughout the campaign the Harding administration, recognizing the obvious dangers of an unsuccessful bid to unseat Johnson and doubtless hopeful that Johnson might reciprocate in 1924 by helping to clear the way for Harding's own reelection, worked behind the scenes to undercut Moore. In after-dinner conversations with Johnson just before the 1922 campaign, Harding had expressed himself "in the friendliest fashion."[39] Whether by design or default, the U.S. Shipping Board, headed by Albert Lasker, a longtime Johnson enthusiast, and including Meyer Lissner, held hearings in the state. Neither showed the slightest qualm in expressing their views. "My interest in Hiram is so deep that I do not want to feel that I have left anything undone," Lasker privately acknowledged.[40] Johnson secured additional support as well. Vice President Calvin Coolidge, in San Francisco to attend the American Bar Association convention, extended Johnson a warm verbal embrace in his speech before the Commonwealth Club. Johnson, he affirmed, was a "credit to his state and to the nation."[41] Assistant Attorney General Mabel Walker Willebrandt agreed. The Harding administration, she publicly affirmed, must reluctantly remain neutral during the primary, even though Johnson was a close personal friend of the president's.[42]

Winning in all but four counties, losing significantly only in Los Angeles, Johnson bested Moore in the April 29 Republican primary by more than 74,000 votes in a total turnout of almost 553,000.[43] The victory was not, however, unalloyed. In the state's gubernatorial election conservatives triumphed as William Stephens narrowly lost an upset race to Friend Richardson, California's state treasurer. Johnson, no friend of Stephens's, had distanced himself from the governor during the campaign, but his hostility to Richardson flared even more intensely. Rumors that Johnson might endorse Thomas Woolwine, the Democratic candidate for governor, proved groundless. Both Johnson and Richardson gave lip service to Republican unity; both called for the election of the full Republican ticket. But the antagonism between the two men and their two different political philosophies repeatedly surfaced as Johnson worked successfully to deny Richardson control of the Republican State Central Committee.[44] Herbert Hoover, stressing the support of his California "friends" for the Republican ticket, complained to Harding that the Johnson "machine" was not on line.[45] Hoover's complaints were echoed by Johnson's own—almost all of the Hoover organization, he charged, remained tepid toward if not antagonistic to his senatorial candidacy. His goal, he stated, was to heal the party wounds inflicted by Hoover and Richardson.[46] Yet as Johnson continued his winning campaign against William Pearson, his Democratic opponent in the general election, he made it clear that Republican harmony and the healing of wounds did not include the abandonment of the state's progressive legacy, and cautioned his audience to stand fast against reactionary tides.[47]

★   ★   ★

Following his reelection Johnson returned to Washington, where he eagerly awaited the end of the lame-duck session of the 67th Congress and a temporary respite from politics. For the first time since the beginning of his Senate career, Congress would not be in nearly continuous session, and both he and his wife looked forward to a holiday abroad prior to the organization of the new Congress in December. The trip, tentatively scheduled for two months but later extended by Minnie to more than four months, was, at Minnie's behest, characteristically in the grand style.[48] Accompanied by their older son, "Jack," and by Alex Moore, the newly appointed ambassador to Spain, they sailed on the *George Washington*, toured France, Spain, and Italy, crossed the Channel to England, then recrossed to visit Holland, Belgium, and Germany before returning aboard the *Leviathan* in late July. Throughout, Johnson played the tourist, turning down the opportunity to write newsletters for publication. He would not attempt to interpret America to Europe or Europe to America, he noted.[49] But if the doughty isolationist felt more comfortable viewing country scenes and relaxing on the Riviera than attending ambassadorial functions, he did not insist on his isolation from such events but took time out to lunch with Marshal Foch in Paris, meet Mussolini, and visit The Hague to observe a session of the World Court.[50] To the *New York Times* Johnson appeared to be silently gathering more evidence to bolster his isolationist convictions. Perhaps too, the newspaper suggested, he was readying himself for a second presidential bid.[51]

In fact, Johnson did plan a political campaign in 1924, but not for the White House. His presidential ambitions, he wrote not altogether candidly, had been laid to rest in 1920, and in any event, to attempt to displace a sitting president would be futile. If Harding wanted the nomination, it was his for the taking. But that did not mean that Hoover and the Old Guard should be allowed to walk away with California's Republican delegate slate. There Johnson would make his fight.[52] Moreover, despite his professed lack of interest in the presidency, he was not about to take himself out of the national race publicly until it became necessary to do so. Too much was at stake. The elections of 1922 had weakened the hand of the Old Guard and of the president himself, sending a scattering of Harding's more prominent supporters, including McCumber in North Dakota and Kellogg in Minnesota, down to defeat. To some, the Harding presidency appeared increasingly unpopular and thus vulnerable. Almost anything could happen. Perhaps Harding would refuse a second term. Indeed, as Bert Meek commented, he might always "drop dead."[53]

In Washington, Senator George Moses, the maverick conservative from New Hampshire, encouraged Johnson to run and tested the waters for his candidacy in an article published under the pseudonym "Polis" in the March 1923 edition of the *Forum*. Johnson, he wrote, had matured during his years in the Senate. "It is not that he is less determined now, but that he is more suave. It is not that he is less sincere now, but that he is more experienced. It is not that he is less courageous now, but that he is more wise."[54] Whether Moses played the game merely to oust Harding or whether he sincerely believed in Johnson's prospects, the drift seemed clear. Progressive, but not of the La Follette stripe, Johnson might secure the support of many conservatives if he chose to run.[55]

The welcome given Johnson upon his return from Europe graphically illustrated the possibilities. A reception committee organized and underwritten by George Harvey Payne, the New York banker and editor of the *Forum*, in conjunction with Mayor Hylan, met Johnson on his arrival. Two thousand supporters gathered at the Battery; the police band played, and a motorcycle escort moved up the avenue.[56] The following evening Johnson was the featured speaker at what was billed as a "non-political" banquet at the Waldorf Astoria. Twelve hundred attended, representing a spectrum of political faiths. Johnson would later describe the affair thus:

Some of its contrasts might be indicated to you when I say that Stoddard, proprietor of the *Mail*, rank reactionary, was with Arthur Brisbane of the Hearst papers; Kirkwood of the *Kansas City Star*, supposed to be Progressive, was close by Jimmie Williams, editor of the *Boston Transcript*, a representative of blue-blooded New England; the Democratic Mayor of New York, Hylan, sat next to Sam Koenig, the Republican leader of New York; . . . Charles M. Schwab, reactionary steel man, of great wealth, sat with Irving K. Taylor, wealthy business man, who has always been Progressive. Frank Hitchcock, the man of mystery in national politics and Republican regular, was close by the New Jersey delegation who stood with me and by their guns in 1920; Eugene Meyer of the present administration, its financial leader, in fact, and Thomas W. Miller, regular Republican, Alien Property Custodian, sat with Mayor Carlson of Youngstown, Progressive Republican ever since 1912, and Harold Ickes, Progressive leader of Chicago; and so the story went all along the lines, and in the gathering were politicians of national fame or notoriety, and newspapermen and magazine editors of all classes and kinds.[57]

In his address to this diverse audience, Johnson unleashed an assault on the World Court, seeking to thwart the administration's efforts then under way to secure American entry into that body. The nation's energies, he charged, should be devoted to problems at home, not to futile and inherently dangerous gestures abroad. "If one tenth of the effort now being made to take us into Europe were devoted to taking our own out of their distress . . . we would have a contented and prosperous people." Carefully disclaiming any presidential ambitions and avoiding any direct attack on Harding, he took aim at Hughes and Hoover, and later wrote to his sons that while the possibility that he might seek the presidency for himself remained slim, he might still "raise Cain with others."[58]

If Johnson's goal in the fall of 1923 was to ensure that Hoover and the Old Guard did not control the California delegation to the Republican National Convention and to force the administration to retreat from its advocacy of the World Court, Harding's death, in August 1923, totally altered the situation. The presidency itself once again beckoned, and although Johnson privately confessed that his presidential ambitions were no longer "so fierce and so keen" as they had once been, they could not be stilled. Publicly silent, he wrestled with the consequences of the new situation. His earlier eagerness to return to California in order to undercut Hoover gave way to a desire to remain in the East, to await events, and, if conditions developed, to build the organization for a national candidacy.[59]

But California would not wait. Quickly convinced of the difficulties he might encounter in his home state, he headed west, stopping in Chicago to confer with Harold Ickes, Albert Lasker, and William Wrigley about his possible presidential candidacy. Both Lasker and Wrigley, though at first hesitant, promised financial help.[60] Even so, Johnson refrained from any public announcement of his candidacy during the next two months, perhaps still ambivalent, still uncertain of his course. Once back in California he took to the road to make a series of speeches reaffirming his dedication to progressive principles and his faith in American isolation.[61] He showed "all the symptoms of a man suffering from the suppression of a Presidential ambition," the *New York Times* observed. Meanwhile, organizational efforts elsewhere lagged. "For God's sake, come east," Harold Ickes admonished, and in mid-November Johnson acceded, returning to Chicago to announce his candidacy formally.[62]

★   ★   ★

From the outset Johnson approached his task with caution, seeking to ensure political support prior to his formal announcement, perhaps waiting for a draft, though none developed. The defection of George Moses to the Coolidge camp immediately after Harding's death came as an unexpected blow, and Johnson worked to prevent further embarrassments.[63] His choice of Frank Hitchcock as general manager reflected his prudence. Hitchcock, past manager of the Taft and Wood campaigns, was a master of political stealth and intrigue with a proven ability to ferret out support. A skilled insider, appearing and disappearing unexpectedly, he seemed, as one observer noted, "to know somebody everywhere." "My distinguished manager moves with care and caution," Johnson remarked. "Perhaps for this very reason, he will move with certainty and success."[64]

Yet commitments were almost impossible to nail down in the fluid situation created by Harding's death—various favorite sons began to surface tentatively while others held back to await events. Gifford Pinchot, recently elected governor of Pennsylvania, voiced private sympathy for Johnson's candidacy but refused to involve himself. Borah, predictably playing his own game, endorsed Coolidge in the hope that the new president could be brought to share his views.[65] So too did Raymond Robins, who had become an activist champion of a proposal, first advanced by Salmon Levinson, to secure world peace by outlawing war. At an earlier meeting with Johnson in Europe, Robins had promised political support if Johnson would join with Borah in endorsing the scheme. Johnson had declined on the grounds that the proposal was unworkable. "I'm willing to try almost anything to prevent war . . . but I'm a rotten hand at tilting at windmills," he wrote to Ickes.[66] Follow-up efforts to mollify Robins collapsed for the same reason.[67]

To Meyer Lissner, Johnson's selection of Hitchcock seemed a masterstroke illustrating the seriousness of his challenge. But for Johnson the appointment quickly turned into a disaster. The campaign went awry from the outset. Organizational efforts floundered as Hitchcock pursued his mysterious ways. He failed to understand the importance of a popular campaign, Johnson complained. The headquarters, "the poorest . . . I have ever seen anywhere," lacked organization, authority, a speakers bureau, circulars, and publicity.[68] Hitchcock was shuttled to the sidelines after quarreling with George Payne, his initial sponsor.[69]

But even without Hitchcock, Johnson's campaign failed to find its stride, for it was flawed less by an incompetent manager than by the very strategy Johnson embraced. The goal was to draw together, as he had at the Waldorf Astoria banquet, a spectrum of political voices, a coalition of conservatives and liberals, that might be led to endorse the dictum he and Roosevelt had long championed that reform was not a threat to the social order but the very key to social stability. Effectively implementing his strategy proved far more difficult than defining it. During his stopover in Chicago, where he formally announced his candidacy, Johnson did no more than hand out a typed statement replete with generalities, and refused any interviews.[70]

When he returned to Chicago the following week Johnson was no more forthcoming. His speech, though rhetorically impressive and earnest in tone, merely rehashed the Waldorf Astoria address, emphasizing foreign affairs and alluding only vaguely to domestic programs.[71] Whereas the progressivism of 1912 had been brazen and militant, the *New Republic* chided, Johnson's performance in Chicago was a parody, circumspect and calculated. Progressive rhetoric, it continued, made an inadequate substitute for positive programs.[72]

Throughout the campaign, however, Johnson almost always seemed a half step behind in defining his position, too often hesitant, too often responding to the agenda set by Coolidge and only rarely developing his own. His hope had been to occupy the middle; instead, he found himself caught in the middle. Urged by some of his backers to be more radical, by others to be more restrained, he was unable to heed the criticisms of either side. To the many conservatives he intended to woo he sounded increasingly shrill and strident. To ardent progressives, he appeared dull and uninspired. Recalling his support for higher tariffs and his refusal to attend a progressive conference La Follette had put together in Washington in the aftermath of the 1922 elections, *The Nation* rejected his progressive credentials.[73] Many others did the same.

To make matters worse, the Coolidge forces, which controlled the mechanics of the national party organization, moved skillfully to blunt his appeal. Rallying to the White House, the Republican Central Committee dropped plans to reduce the size of the southern delegations, which had long been overrepresented in party conventions, and relocated the 1924 convention site from Chicago to Cleveland, where Johnson's crowds would be thinner. Johnson bitterly protested, but to no avail.[74] Coolidge's program, outlined in his first message to Congress on December 6, 1923, centered on domestic issues and called for economy and frugality to solve the nation's domestic ills. His budget recommendations proposed a reduction of the maximum surtax rate to 25 percent, a figure many in the corporate community found attractive.

In early December, William Randolph Hearst called on the White House, where he discovered that Coolidge really wasn't an ultraconservative after all. Henry Ford, earlier at odds with the administration, now gave his blessing, perhaps wooed by the tax proposal or by Coolidge's apparent willingness to endorse Ford's effort to obtain title to the federally owned Muscle Shoals property in Alabama as the site for a new manufacturing center.[75] Republican newspapers flocked to the president.[76] For Coolidge, the lines of support continued to grow. "Perhaps the time is proper for Emma Goldman and Bill Haywood to return, declare for Mr. Coolidge, and be acclaimed," Johnson cynically observed.[77] In fact the Coolidge appeal wafted even into Johnson's own camp. William Wrigley, one of Johnson's central backers, found himself tempted. If Coolidge's tax bill passed, Wrigley admitted, "nothing could stop the Republican party in 1924 from the President down to the Constable in a small town." Indeed if Secretary of the Treasury Andrew Mellon announced for the presidency, Wrigley stated, he would be elected almost unanimously.[78] Manifestly, Johnson needed to shape an alternative to the administration's tax bill that was equally appealing.

*   *   *

Following some preliminary press sparring with the White House, Johnson took to the road in early January, braving the first major storms of winter to launch his campaign with speeches in Cleveland and Chicago. Privilege, he charged, dominated the White House; it sought to maintain itself unfairly by the manipulation of the nominating process and to enrich itself unjustly by a tax bill that benefited the few at the expense of the many.

Who is it that is indulging in this propaganda that is sweeping over the country today, that is filling every newspaper and at the head of which are our bankers and the United States Chamber of Commerce? Do you imagine that it is the man who, by a reduction of taxes, will save $10 or $30 or $100? . . . The concern of this tax scheme is not for the man of small income, who can least bear the burden, but the concern is for those of large incomes, who can best bear the burden.

Like Coolidge, Johnson promised tax reduction, but a reduction that would respond to the needs of the less affluent. The uncertainty he had expressed during the 1921 tax fight vanished. Great riches and big business, he charged, "have a happy faculty of looking out for themselves." Johnson differed from Coolidge too in his support for a veterans' bonus; economy, he observed, should not come at the expense of the nation's commitment to its ex-servicemen, nor need it do so. Taxes could be reduced on all incomes under $10,000 and sufficient revenue would still be available to meet the nation's obligation to its veterans.[79]

While critical of Coolidge's domestic policies, Johnson tried from the beginning to forge the contest into a debate over foreign policy. Invariably he devoted the second half of his addresses to upbraiding the president on America's role abroad, particularly the administration's participation in the German reparations imbroglio and its endorsement of America's entry into the World Court. Both, he charged, were but steps on the road to entrapment in the web of Old World diplomacy. The League of Nations, he averred, was not a dead issue, nor could it be so long as Hughes and Hoover remained in the administration to determine the nation's course abroad. However much they might deny it, they had not abandoned the cause for which they had fought in 1919. Johnson found additional reason for complaint in the State Department's recently announced decision to sell arms to the Obregón government in Mexico, which was then under attack by rebel forces. By that policy, he charged, the United States became a party to the conflict, and by that policy the nation embraced an ambition, characteristic of European powers, to force its will upon others.[80]

It is doubtful if Johnson's essay on foreign policy advanced his candidacy; 1924 was not 1920. In the interval the emotions, fears, and hopes that had earlier divided the country had stilled. In arguing against the nation's entry into the League of Nations, Johnson preached to the converted; in decrying the nation's Mexican policy and attacking the World Court, he preached to the indifferent. Nobody gives a damn about the World Court, William Wrigley commented.[81] Yet the larger problem was that few seemed to care passionately about the presidential contest itself. Charging into Michigan, Illinois, and Indiana in mid-January, returning to Illinois, Nebraska, and the Dakotas in February and again in March, Johnson almost always attracted overflow crowds and enthusiastic audiences, but failed to seize the initiative or to find the issue that might galvanize the electorate. A day after a mass meeting the excitement seemed to die away, wrote Arthur Evans, political reporter for the *Chicago Tribune*.[82]

In rural areas Johnson's initial inability to define a farm program that differed substantially from the president's plagued him. Coolidge's formula, he charged, was inadequate—farmers needed more than the admonition to help themselves with the development of cooperatives and additional credit facilities. Government must not only promote cooperation among farmers but "sympathetically cooperate with them." His attack was strident, his prescription bland. Government, he cautioned, could not enter the grain business; legislation could not alter economic laws. The answer to the farm problem lay in traditional progressive remedies: lower freight rates and the expansion of inland waterways.[83] Not until February, at the urging of his advisers, did Johnson commit himself to the McNary-Haugen plan, whereby farm prices would be raised by government purchase and the dumping of surplus abroad. What Johnson must do, Doherty observed in promoting a more aggressive stance, was to recognize that Americans had moved beyond the radicalism of 1912.[84] While clearly willing to move, Johnson nevertheless hesitated, for he was not sure of his direction.

The eruption of the Teapot Dome scandal in late January gave a temporary boost to Johnson's campaign. As evidence developed by the Senate Lands Committee tainted the cabinet Coolidge had inherited, Republican regulars massed in defense of the administration.[85] Johnson was one of the few of his party to support the Robinson resolution demanding an immediate cancellation of the lease contracts and the dismissal of Secretary of the Navy Edwin Denby. Every individual who "innocently or ignorantly has been a part of the filching of the public domain" must go, Johnson cried.[86] Yet when his advisors encouraged him to press the matter home with a direct attack on Coolidge, Johnson initially wavered, fearful that the effort might backfire and generate sympathy for the beleaguered president. His later militant calls for stronger executive leadership to put an end to government corruption were ably finessed when Coolidge eased both Denby and Attorney General Daugherty out of his cabinet.[87]

As the campaign sputtered, finances became an increasingly severe problem.[88] Critical to Johnson's election hopes were the primaries in North and South Dakota, Michigan, Illinois, and Nebraska,
but no more than $11,000 was available for the North Dakota race,
and Ickes, in charge of the Illinois campaign, had little more for that
contest.[89] With a campaign both underfunded and incapable of at-
tracting additional support, Johnson dug in for the fight.[90] The North
Dakota primary, scheduled for March 18, afforded the first test.
There, Coolidge had the support of both the federal bureaucracy and
the state's party establishment. Robert La Follette posed a second
challenge. In anticipation of an independent candidacy soon to be
launched nationally he had withdrawn from the Republican race.
But his supporters pushed him back on to the ticket. Encouraged
and financially aided by the Coolidge camp, they distributed more
than 200,000 La Follette stickers that could be attached to the Republican ballot.[91] In the final tally Coolidge won with 41 percent
of the vote. La Follette ran second and Johnson third, with a scant
25 percent.

A week later Johnson narrowly squeaked to victory in the South
Dakota primary, but considering the energy he had expended during
his tour of the state and the active support provided by both Governor William McMaster and Senator Peter Norbeck, the victory demonstrated greater weakness than strength.[92] Winning the Dakotas,
Frank Doherty had earlier stressed, was essential to his candidacy,
and once the returns were in, the jerry-built structure that supported
Johnson's campaign collapsed. William Wrigley, who had been rest-
less from the beginning, publicly withdrew his support.[93] On April 7,
Coolidge won Michigan with an overwhelming 70 percent. In Illinois the following day the tally was less crushing but equally devastating: Coolidge secured 59 percent of the vote in a heavy turnout.
By winning Nebraska the same day, Coolidge came within 25 votes
of the nomination.[94]

Without funds but unwilling to withdraw and forsake those who
had lent their energies to his campaign, recognizing too the futility
of continued activity, an exhausted Johnson after a brief rest resumed his campaign in New Jersey and Ohio. Finally, at the end of
the month, he called a halt.[95] At the same time, however, he refused
to accept Lasker's advice to concede formally. Hoarse, his voice
trembling with emotion and at times breaking, he ended his cam-

paign with defiance, once again castigating the "unholy alliance between crooked big business and crooked politics."[96] In May came the coup de grace: he lost to Coolidge in California.*[97]

"From the announcement of the candidacy and the selection of a crook like Hitchcock as manager, to the very end, it was a series of blunders and disasters," Johnson concluded. But perhaps, he philosophically mused in an effort to heal the hurt, it was all for the best. His California defeat meant in all probability that his political career would end following the conclusion of his Senate term in 1928, and he could then return to the private life for which his wife had so often pled. Until then, he affirmed, he would persevere in the battle for progressive causes.[98] For Minnie, the pain went deeper. "It's terrible to be so bitter," she confessed to her older son; "as the days go on I was in hopes it would ease up a bit—but it grows harder. . . . Your father says he is going out [to California] the 1st of June. Don't expect me, sweetheart, because I'm never coming if I can help it. Our whole lives, the ambition for my children, all of my desires for comfort and riches and ease have always been sacrificed for that State and now defeat. Don't even bury me there."[99]

★   ★   ★

In April 1924, prior to the California election debacle but with his presidential campaign already in tatters, Johnson resumed his Senate seat. There, as the first session of the 68th Congress wound to a close, he helped dismantle the president's legislative program. The first battle centered on the administration's proposal to place Japanese immigration under a quota system similar to that for European immigrants. By including such a provision in the pending immigration act, Secretary of State Hughes argued, Congress would

*HWJ to C. K. McClatchy, Apr. 29, 1924. Almost from the beginning it had been clear that California could not be won unless Johnson succeeded in his midwestern campaign. When it became obvious that the campaign had collapsed and that he had no chance to secure the nomination, his supporters urged him to return to canvass the state. Johnson refused, and instead sent an appeal to the California voters admitting that he could not win the nomination but calling on the electorate to support his slate as a symbol of their progressive convictions. HWJ release, "Statement to the People of California," no date, Part III, Carton 25, HWJ Papers. See also John L. Shover, "The California Progressives and the 1924 Campaign," *California Historical Society Quarterly* 51:1 (Mar. 1972), pp. 59–74. As Shover notes, even though all recognized the futility of his campaign, Johnson won in Northern California, carrying 36 of the state's 58 counties. In San Francisco he swept to victory with 60 percent of the vote.

set at rest past antagonisms with Japan while actually reducing the level of current Japanese immigration allowed under Roosevelt's 1907 Gentlemen's Agreement.

The House was the first to object. It rejected both Hughes's proposal and the Gentlemen's Agreement itself, insisting for the first time on total Japanese exclusion. In the Senate, administration prospects looked brighter. But once debate began all hope vanished. Henry Cabot Lodge mounted the attack by charging that Japanese ambassador Masanao Hanihara had introduced a veiled threat in warning of "grave consequences" that would follow if the administration's proposal were not accepted. Avidly siding with Lodge, Johnson actively participated in the Republican caucus and in the subsequent closed session of the Senate, to repeat his long-standing opposition to continued Japanese immigration. By overwhelming margins, the Senate adopted exclusion and rebuffed follow-up efforts by the administration to secure a two-year delay in the implementation of the measure.[100]

Coolidge was equally unsuccessful in mobilizing congressional support for the economy program that formed the core of his campaign. With Johnson eagerly participating, the Senate shredded the Mellon tax proposal by setting surtax rates at 40 percent, far above the administration's 25 percent goal, by raising the estate tax from 25 percent to 40 percent, and, in the wake of Republican scandals, by opening tax returns to public scrutiny.[101] Finally, at the urging of both liberals and conservatives, the veterans' bonus was passed and Coolidge's veto of the measure narrowly overridden. The actions of Congress obviously consoled Johnson for the hurt of defeat.

Johnson did not attend the Cleveland Republican convention. Releasing his South Dakota delegates and withdrawing his name from consideration, he remained in Washington and listened to the lackluster proceedings on the radio. His gloom brightened considerably when Herbert Hoover failed to secure the nod as Coolidge's running mate. "The anti-Johnson California delegation left the hall with its idol shattered and its hero repudiated," he crowed.[102] But there was little else to cheer. The results at Cleveland, he concluded, once again demonstrated that the Republican party leadership marched to the drum of big business. Nor were they alone. In New York City the explosive Democratic convention, ruptured by what seemed an unbridgeable chasm between urban and rural America, as symbolized by the rival candidacies of Al Smith and William Gibbs Mc-Adoo, almost disintegrated before coalescing around John W. Davis, the Democratic equivalent of Coolidge. The only issue of the campaign, Johnson privately wrote, "was whether we enter the House of Morgan by Wall Street or Broad Street. . . . Big business is thoroughly satisfied. The rest of us can fight the usual sham battle."[103] Given the nature of the contest, he preferred the sidelines.[104]

Nor was his determination to sit out the 1924 presidential campaign altered by the independent candidacy of Robert La Follette. Throughout the primary contest Johnson had affirmed both publicly and privately that his fight was within the Republican party. Even if he fully believed in La Follette, he confessed, he could not now alter his declaration.[105] Doubtless his personal dislike of La Follette, spawned by the events of 1912, hardened that resolve. But even without Bull Moose memories the two men would have been rivals, distanced as much by what they shared as by disagreement over specific measures. Each recognized the need for an activist government that would respond to the problems of the disadvantaged, differing more often in detail than in overall design. Both defended the nation's isolationist traditions although they disagreed more profoundly on other foreign policy matters. In personality as well the two were similar; charismatic and able to attract loyalists, they also could repel. For both, conviction could dissolve into self-righteousness, ambition could degenerate into self-preoccupation. Each sought to dominate others and neither would accept a subordinate role. In many ways they clashed because they were so much alike.*

Despite these factors and despite his recognition of the impossibility of the task, Johnson was not unsympathetic to the campaign La Follette waged. The bulk of Johnson's rank and file supporters, Frank Doherty noted, were indifferent to party ties and would either openly embrace La Follette or quietly vote for him in November.[106] Franck Havenner, a Johnson stalwart in the California primary fight, became co-manager of La Follette's California campaign, while Charles K. McClatchy reluctantly but effectively massed his news-

---

*Johnson was rarely complimentary in any of his personal observations, but he clearly respected La Follette even if he did not like him. La Follette demonstrated some "atrocious" character flaws, Johnson wrote, but "he's fundamentally sound, an indefatigable worker and of absolute honesty and integrity." HWJ to boys, Nov. 1, 1921.

papers in support of the Wisconsin senator.[107] Johnson himself remained publicly aloof notwithstanding solicitations from both the La Follette and the Coolidge camps. He broke his silence only once, to condemn the action of the California State Supreme Court in its four-to-three ruling that denied La Follette an independent slot on the ballot, and thus forced him to run as the candidate of the Socialist party in the state.[108] La Follette, Johnson asserted, was no Socialist, and the actions of the court violated both the letter and spirit of the state's election code.[109]

Privately Johnson fed materials to McClatchy useful in answering Coolidge's campaign assault.[110] La Follette's proposal to place limits on the Supreme Court's power to invalidate congressional acts, he wrote, was far less radical than the scheme proposed by Theodore Roosevelt in 1912. Johnson was especially angered by the arguments proffered by Rowell and Robins in an effort to anoint Coolidge as a progressive and to mobilize onetime progressives in support of the administration, and had to fight back the urge to participate actively in the campaign.[111] In the end he did nothing. Coolidge swept to an easy victory, winning 54 percent of the national vote. John W. Davis trailed with less than 29 percent, and La Follette ranked a poor third, with little more than 16 percent.* Johnson brooded over the outcome but found solace in it as well; in Illinois, he noted, La Follette with his greater resources had been no more successful than had he with his handful of loyalists. But it was a limited consolation at best. In the aftermath of the election the Republican leadership moved to discipline La Follette and his supporters. Johnson and Norris, who had remained silent, were unaffected, but over their objections, La Follette, Smith Brookhart, Edwin Ladd, and Lynn Frazier were stripped of their committee chairmanships.[112] Once again, reaction had triumphed. Less than a year later La Follette himself was dead, his place in the Senate taken by his son and namesake.

*   *   *

As president, both before and after the election of 1924, the unaggressive Coolidge was more often a figurehead than an energetic par-

---

*In California, Coolidge did equally as well, although there the tallies of Davis and La Follette were reversed, with La Follette second in the race and Davis at the bottom with little more than 16 percent. Daniel P. Melcher, "The Challenge to Normalcy: The 1924 Election in California," *Southern California Quarterly* 60:2 (Summer 1978), pp. 155–82.

ticipant in the legislative process.* While lacking Harding's faults, he lacked his warmth and generosity as well. Invariably aloof and reserved in his dealings with others, he preferred to await events rather than shape them, and when forced to act, allowed his distrust of government activism and his commitment to economy to determine his responses. His appointments of William E. Humphrey and Charles W. Hunt to positions on the Federal Trade Commission reflected his conservative instincts. Johnson opposed the appointments, as did other progressives, but to no avail.[113]

Anti-administration forces did succeed in defeating the nomination of Charles Warren as attorney general. A onetime ambassador, Warren had served Coolidge as a floor leader at the 1924 convention. He was also a central figure in the sugar industry then under indictment on anti-trust charges. His reputation, Chief Justice Taft privately remarked, was that of a man who resorted to "evasion and concealed methods."[114] Johnson shared that assessment. Warren, he wrote, "was not a lawyer. He was [a] negotiator, connubiator, manipulator, fixer," a man who had "devoted his talent, his abilities, his activities wholly to making life a little harder for the great mass of the people for the very sordid purpose of making a little more money for a very few overrich."[115] On the first vote, while Vice President Dawes napped at the New Willard Hotel, the Senate tied 40 to 40, and before Dawes could resume the chair the nomination was defeated. With uncharacteristic determination Coolidge later tried again, only to be rebuffed by a vote of 46 to 39. For the first time since Reconstruction, a cabinet nominee had failed to secure confirmation. For Johnson, it was a pleasant moment.†

*Donald R. McCoy, *Calvin Coolidge: The Quiet President* (New York, 1967). Johnson noted of Coolidge: "I really believe there never was a man in high position so politically minded. I do not think there is any principle or policy of government that for one instant will sway him when he believes his personal political fortunes may be influenced. I can not conceive of any conjuncture in our affairs, any crisis in which he would passionately espouse a particular course because of his belief in it, or because it was right. He weighs, I think, his every word and every action by the effect they may have upon his personal political future." HWJ to boys, Nov. 13, 1926.

† *Cong. Record*, 69th Cong., 1st sess. (Mar. 10, 16, 1925), pp. 101, 275. Perhaps even more pleasant to Johnson was his success in blocking the nomination of Wallace McCamant of Oregon as judge on the Circuit Court of Appeals. When McCamant ran as a delegate at large in the Republican presidential primary of 1920, he had pledged to support the winner of the Oregon primary. Johnson won that primary, but McCamant consistently supported Wood during the convention and led the stampede

Tax legislation, farm relief measures, and the battle over the development of public power defined the core of Republican insurgency in the years following Harding's death. In 1926, Coolidge won the tax battle when the administration's bill—which cut surtaxes by up to 50 percent, halved the estate tax, and eliminated both the gift tax and publicity of income tax returns—passed overwhelmingly in both houses. Johnson's own participation in the fight was minimal. A case of near pneumonia kept him bedridden for almost a month. Absent from the Senate, he paired his vote in support of the efforts of Norris, James Couzens, and other Republican insurgents to hold the line, and joined with them in opposition to the final bill.[116]

Congress was far more divided over farm relief legislation, a persistent topic of debate in the decade of the 1920s. Midwestern anger had flared up in the off-term elections of 1922 and would do so again in 1926. Johnson's own position remained consistent. Having taken his stand during his presidential campaign in 1924, he continued to support the McNary-Haugen program, and took every opportunity available to contrast American largess abroad with the government's parsimony at home. "The very men who have . . . so generously scattered our money all over Europe, cynically and contemptuously say we must not devote a very small fraction of the amount . . . to aid those who are suffering in our own land," he exclaimed. Arguing that the priorities should be reversed, he affirmed his willingness to try any experiment that might promise relief for America's farmers.[117] To California agriculturalists who complained that the McNary-Haugen proposal would not help them, and might in fact be harmful to their interests, he bitingly replied that having secured tariff protection for themselves they should not begrudge government intervention on behalf of their midwestern counterparts.[118]

As Johnson expected, the 1926 McNary-Haugen bill, opposed by the administration, went down to defeat, losing in the Senate by a vote of 39 to 45.[119] The following year the measure was widened to include additional commodity interests, and in this form won congressional endorsement. Coolidge predictably responded with a

---

for Coolidge as vice president. During his hearings before the Senate Judiciary Committee, McCamant made his fatal blunder under grilling by Johnson: he characterized Theodore Roosevelt as "not a good American." See HWJ to boys, Jan. 16, 30, 1926; HWJ to Hiram Johnson, Jr., Mar. 14, 20, 1926; HWJ to C. K. McClatchy, Mar. 17, 1926; *New Republic*, Mar. 17, 1926, pp. 96–98.

veto, citing both practical and constitutional arguments. The sponsors of the bill rewrote it in an effort to meet the constitutional
objections, and in 1928 it was repassed by large majorities as both
Democrats and Republican insurgents maneuvered for political advantage in the upcoming elections. As expected, Coolidge once
again exercised his veto.

The success of the McNary-Haugen bill on the Hill, while
prompted by election-year politics, reflected also a growing liberal
temper that defined the dynamics of Congress during the last two
years of Coolidge's presidency. "I imagine there never has been a
time during our recollections at least, when what for want of a better word we term 'big business' has been so openly and avidly in
control," Johnson had lamented in early 1926, echoing the refrain
he had voiced repeatedly since 1920.[120] Three months later, following the spring primary elections, his tone had considerably changed.
In rural areas, the discontent that he had tried to exploit in his 1924
presidential bid exploded, bringing down Republican stalwarts such
as William McKinley of Illinois, George Pepper of Pennsylvania, and
Irvine Lenroot of Wisconsin. Among the new Republicans entering
the Senate were Smith W. Brookhart of Iowa, who had been unseated
the preceding year in a disputed election and now returned trium-
phantly; Gerald Nye of North Dakota, who had requested and secured Johnson's endorsement; and John Blaine, replacing the defeated Lenroot. "It begins to look like a 'new deal' is here," Johnson
cheered. The prestige of the Coolidge administration, he added, was
falling "as rapidly as the French franc and Italian lira."[121] And the
slide continued, spilling over into Democratic success in November.
William Butler, the Republican national chairman and a close con-
fidant of Coolidge, lost his Massachusetts seat to David Walsh, and
James Wadsworth, Jr., succumbed to Robert Wagner of New York.
Overall, the Republican majority in the Senate was cut from sixteen
to two, a reduction that considerably increased the leverage of Republican insurgents. For Johnson the future seemed to brighten; he,
Norris, and Couzens, he wrote, "smile at one another and go around
looking like the cat who swallowed the canary."[122]

The changed makeup of Congress was important not only in
strengthening the demand for significant farm legislation but also in
providing additional support for those who argued for development
of public power. Throughout the 1920s the power debate centered

on the endeavors of George Norris to secure federal development and operation of the government facilities at Muscle Shoals, Alabama, which had been constructed during the war to eliminate American dependence on Chilean nitrates.[123] In order to end federal involvement, both the Harding and the Coolidge administrations solicited bids from the private sector. Henry Ford was among the first to come forward, promising to produce an abundance of fertilizer to restore depleted farm lands if he were guaranteed a 100-year lease of the property. Other bids followed, and the issue quickly became bogged in contending claims.

Constant in his vision, Norris saw in Muscle Shoals the key to federal development of the hydroelectric resources of the entire Tennessee watershed. Pursuing that goal, in 1924 he successfully turned back the attempt by Henry Ford to secure title to the Muscle Shoals facility. The following year Norris came close to defeat when the Senate passed the Underwood bill providing for the lease of the property to private interests, but he managed to regain control on a technicality. By including materials in the bill that had not existed in either the House or Senate versions, Norris argued, the conference committee had exceeded its authority. His point was narrowly sustained, and the session expired before a vote on a revised bill could be taken. "It is a pretty good thing to have one body that moves deliberately and slowly, and where there is unlimited debate," Johnson observed.[124]

The battle persisted. In 1926 those who pushed for private development still seemed to hold the upper hand, but confusion over the competing bids for the property prevented any action. The following year, with the convening of the more liberal 70th Congress, the tide turned, and as the first session of that new Congress neared adjournment, the Norris bill, acknowledging the principle of public ownership, passed. In the Senate, after more than 24 hours of continuous debate, the vote was 43 to 37. Coolidge responded with a pocket veto, and the contest was resumed when Hoover entered the White House. In 1930, by significant majorities, the Senate once again endorsed the measure, and early the next year both houses reached agreement. No matter what the ultimate fate of the bill might be, Johnson noted in tribute to Norris, "this is his hour of triumph."[125] Characterizing the proposal as not liberalism but degeneration,

Hoover promptly replied with a blistering veto. Muscle Shoals would wait for the coming of the New Deal.

★ ★ ★

Throughout the long ordeal, Johnson remained unswerving in his support for his Nebraska colleague. He was, he noted at one point, plugging along as best he could in opposing the "Muscle Shoals steal."[126] Norris might be "dreaming dreams," he argued in reply to one attack, but dreams had built the nation, and Norris's dream would ultimately prevail. "I chant no requiem over a lost cause. That cause will survive every one of us here."[127] But in the fight over public power Johnson did more than follow in Norris's wake. While supporting the Muscle Shoals project, he led his own battle for the development of the Colorado River, a battle that brought him into direct conflict with his two chief political antagonists, Herbert Hoover and Harry Chandler.

The proposal Johnson championed had its origins in the attempts of the settlers of California's Imperial Valley to end their dependence on an irrigation system that by flowing first through Mexican territory held them in thrall to events below the border. In 1905 and 1906, the system put together by valley residents had given way, flooding a portion of the valley, and from 1910 to 1915 the U.S. government had undertaken flood control works in Mexico to prevent a repetition of the disaster. Those efforts, sustained by the recently formed Imperial Irrigation District, enabled the owners of lands south of the border to benefit without cost. Seasonal scarcity of the valley's water resources and increased water usage by holders of Mexican property, together with the disorder caused by Mexico's ongoing political revolution, created additional complications.

Prompted by the complaints of valley residents, Congress in 1920 authorized a detailed study of the lower Colorado by the Department of Interior. Responsibility for that project fell on Arthur Powell Davis, head of the Reclamation Service. Davis, the nephew of John Wesley Powell, the pioneer explorer of the region, had long expressed enthusiasm over the possibilities of the Colorado; his report, issued in conjunction with Interior Secretary Albert Fall in 1922, transformed the project from one of regional concern to one of national significance. The report recommended the construction of an "all-American" canal, the construction of a high storage dam at or near Boulder Canyon, and the development of hydroelectric power to finance the latter project. As proposed, the dam was to be the largest of its kind ever built. The recommendations of the Fall-Davis report were incorporated in the authorizing legislation introduced in April 1922 by Johnson and Phil Swing, a founder and chief counsel of the Imperial Irrigation District before his election in 1920 to the House of Representatives.[128]

Eager to tap both the water and power resources of the Colorado, California's southern cities supported the project. Other parties found reason to object. Agricultural interests outside the basin wanted assurance that reclamation in the southwest would not add to the surplus plaguing the nation's farmers. The seven states constituting the Colorado watershed sought protection from each other, fearful that those states first able to develop the river's resources would establish claims detrimental to the rest. To overcome this problem, Congress, in 1921, authorized the seven involved states to enter into a compact to divide the waters. Unable to agree among themselves, the states compromised by dividing the region into an upper and lower basin, each with its own water allocations—the upper basin comprising Wyoming, Colorado, New Mexico, and Utah, the lower basin comprising California, Nevada, and Arizona. But Arizona, concerned that California's use of Colorado water would exhaust the lower basin's resources, refused to ratify the compact and in so doing threatened the whole enterprise. Not bound by the agreement, Arizona retained the right to perfect its claims at the expense of its northern neighbors.

The disposition of lands below the border further complicated the undertaking, for development of the river could adversely affect rights claimed by Mexico.[129] Moreover, much of the Mexican property benefiting from the existing system and threatened by the new proposal was owned by Harry Chandler and the *Los Angeles Times*. Development of an "all-American" canal would force the owners of Mexican properties to assume the costs of irrigating their lands. Finally, the proposed development of hydroelectric power, which was essential to the financing of the dam, posed yet another problem in that it pitted public and private power interests against each other.

In the face of the many obstacles to the project, the administration offered tepid support at best. Interior Secretary Fall had endorsed the plan and Harding seemed sympathetic, but in March

1923 Fall had resigned and in August Harding was dead. Hubert Work, Fall's successor, after some hesitation, endorsed the outlines of the proposal, as did Coolidge, but both declined to take an active role, leaving the initiative to others.[130] Hoover was a study in ambiguity. He was involved from the outset, having been selected by Harding to chair the conference of state delegates brought together to hammer out the interstate compact dividing the waters of the Colorado. While he professed support, he continually found reasons for delay. Cautious and noncommittal in his public pronouncements, he seemed more intent on curbing than promoting the project. Only the need for flood protection had his ready acknowledgment, and that end could be achieved by the construction of a low dam that neither produced power nor threatened the Chandler holdings in Mexico. In 1924, while campaigning for Coolidge in California he privately recommended such a course, and the following year Representative John Fredericks of Los Angeles, with the endorsement of the Los Angeles Chamber of Commerce, formally introduced the proposal.[131] It quickly died in committee.

Hoover was equally unsuccessful in preventing the California State Legislature in 1926 from adding to its ratification of a revised six-state compact a condition that required the construction of a high dam large enough to hold twenty million acre feet. Nevertheless, Hoover persisted, advising Phil Swing in 1927 to revamp his legislation along the lines outlined by the Fredericks bill.[132] Whether Hoover's actions stemmed from his well-known distrust of state enterprise, from technical considerations concerning the feasibility of the project, from political considerations revolving around his reluctance to alienate Chandler and the *Times*, or from his personal dislike of Johnson, the results were the same. In 1925 Hoover and Johnson met in an attempt to reach some sort of understanding. Their only accomplishment was confirmation of their mutual distrust. Johnson's goal, Hoover complained, was to reap political advantage and embarrass him personally.[133] Hoover's ambition, Johnson concluded, was to undermine the project. And the division persisted. "Whenever I uncover a foe of our Boulder Dam bill there I find Hoover," Johnson groused.[134]

A Swing-Johnson bill was introduced in each of the four Congresses between 1922 and 1928, and for Johnson passage of the measure became an obsession, as much so as his battles against entanglement abroad. He would rather pass the bill than anything else and would sacrifice anything for that end, George Norris commented.[135] To participate fully in the effort, Johnson secured his own appointment to the Senate Irrigation and Reclamation Committee even though California was already represented on that committee by Shortridge. With Phil Swing in attendance he helped to orchestrate committee hearings in the fall and winter of 1925 both in Washington and in the Southwest, skillfully questioning the various witnesses to prod the measure forward without provoking additional opposition.[136] Shortridge, he complained, was of no help at all, and except for John Kendrick of Wyoming, committee members were either hostile or indifferent.[137]

By 1926, however, all sides appeared ready to make concessions. Heretofore, the Swing-Johnson bills, while explicitly requiring that municipalities be given preference over private companies in the marketing of hydroelectric power, had been intentionally vague about who should construct the power plant itself, giving to the secretary of the interior the option of assigning that task to the federal government. At Hoover's insistence the bill was revised; the new version retained the option of a federally built plant but modified the language concerning the marketing of the power generated. Municipal preference was retained but in a more ambiguous form that cited the provisions of the Federal Water Power Act of 1920. In addition, the bill was altered to make the construction of the "all-American" canal contingent upon the failure to secure an agreement with Mexico over the existing irrigation system.[138]

With these modifications agreed to, Johnson was able to get his bill reported in the spring of 1926, but in the House the measure remained bottled in committee until late December, when it was again delayed by a hostile Rules Committee.[139] Taking the floor in early January 1927, as the second session of the 69th Congress neared its end, Johnson sought both to publicize the issue and to pressure the House Rules Committee into action. Hoover and the administration gave lip service in support, he wrote, "while stabbing us in the back."[140] Arizona, afraid that its rights to Colorado water would be forfeited, adamantly opposed the project, while rumors circulated that if the provisions of the bill were altered to eliminate the option of federal construction of the power plant the bill would pass. "We're up against the most powerful, concentrated and influential trust in the world, the electric power trust," Johnson asserted.[141] In desperation he called on the White House, but heard only platitudes.[142] Determined to move ahead, he kept his bill before the Senate for ten days—one session ran continuously for more than 30 hours—and when that failed, he abandoned his long-held commitment to free debate to call, unsuccessfully, for cloture.[143] The session finally ended in chaos and confusion as Arizona's senators continued to filibuster against the measure.

Johnson returned to the battle in December 1927, with the opening of the 70th Congress. Though pessimistic about final passage, he hoped that something might turn up to tip the balance.[144] Midway through the session, his hopes were realized. Progressives had sought authorization at the start of the term for a Senate investigation of the power trust. Administration supporters quickly thwarted the move by shifting responsibility for the inquiry to the Federal Trade Commission. The action, Johnson snorted, was equivalent to "chloroforming" the probe.[145] But to his surprise and to that of many others, the FTC diligently pursued the investigation. In April it revealed that the National Electric Light Association had raised more than $400,000 to defeat the Swing-Johnson bill and that the National Utility Association had paid $7,500 to Richard Washburn Child, the former ambassador to Italy, for preparing a pamphlet in opposition. Among those on the payroll of the utilities were Stephen Davis, onetime solicitor in Hoover's Commerce Department, and Irvine Lenroot, who had received $20,000 for lobbying against the proposed investigation by the Senate. Additional revelations continued to undermine the opposition by calling into question the reasons for their dissent.

In May the House Rules Committee, under pressure, allowed the Swing-Johnson bill to go to the floor, where it was passed by a voice vote. Using the FTC revelations to good effect, Johnson called for another continuous session to force Senate action, sharply challenging his colleagues to stand up to the power trust.[146] With Vice President Dawes casting the deciding vote, the motion for continuous sessions carried, but Johnson was unable to extend the session into June. All the while, Arizona filibustered.[147] So disorderly was the clash between Johnson and Henry Ashurst of Arizona, that the Senate went into executive session in its final hours to prevent a public display of its bad temper.[148]

With the assurance that the Boulder Dam project would be the first order of business when the Senate reassembled in December, Johnson was fairly confident of victory as Congress adjourned in preparation for the 1928 elections.[149] Yet doubts remained. Neither the Republican nor the Democratic party endorsed the project in its platform, and Hoover, soon to become president, was less than effusive in his public remarks during the campaign. Nor was Coolidge's message that opened the second session of the 70th Congress encouraging. While endorsing the project, he questioned government development of its hydroelectric potential. But Johnson was well positioned, and the fact that his bill was first upon the floor provided the leverage necessary to success. Given the situation, another filibuster by Arizona was all but impossible, and after two weeks of stormy and often acrimonious debate—"two weeks of hell," as Johnson described it—the bill passed easily, with only eleven opposed. Later that month, while Congress prepared for its Christmas recess, Johnson watched as Coolidge signed the legislation.

As enacted, the measure provided for the creation of a high dam to hold 26 million acre feet. Over Johnson's objections, a limitation of 4.4 million acre feet was placed on California's allotment of water, and funds were provided to Arizona and Nevada to compensate for tax revenue that would have been available to them if private interests had been allowed to develop the resources. In addition the secretary of the interior retained the option to build the power facilities, and municipal preference, although less explicitly called for than in the original version of the bill, was retained.[150]

The provision for municipal preference in the allocation of hydroelectric power continued to stir debate once the Hoover administration began. Johnson, hopeful that Congress would stand firm and force the administration to construct the optional power plant, made it his goal "to prevent the power trust from undermining the bill's provisions."[151] It was not an easy task. Ray Lyman Wilbur, the new secretary of the interior, quickly secured a "clarification" from the Interior Department solicitor that allowed the government to ignore municipal preference if "a more secure and businesslike contract" could be made. He proposed to allocate 25 percent of the generating power to Southern California Edison. Wilbur's actions,

George Norris angrily remarked, meant that the president had determined that he could repeal acts of Congress.

Both Swing and Johnson vigorously protested, but in the end all sides gave way.[152] Wilbur, who had earlier insisted that participating municipalities must purchase and install their own generating equipment, thereby increasing their costs, rescinded that demand and agreed to full federal construction of the power plant; in return, Southern California Edison secured 9 percent of the marketable power. In July 1930, with the contracts signed, construction began, and in September Wilbur drove the silver spike for the railroad connecting the site with Las Vegas and, without a hint of embarrassment, named the dam for the "great engineer who really started this greatest project of all times," Herbert Hoover.[153]

★　　★　　★

Johnson's political battles in the mid-1920s were not limited to Washington and the floor of the Senate. California was a second front. In part, his involvement with the politics of the state revolved naturally around his own political fortunes—he would be up once again for reelection in 1928. But his concern was not bound solely to that end. At stake too was the fate of progressivism in California. Friend Richardson, elected governor in 1922, held a slim conservative edge in the state assembly and had moved swiftly to undercut past reforms, where possible terminating progressive administrators of state agencies and appointing conservative successors. By means of the newly acquired line-item veto, he cut deeply into the funding of educational programs and social agencies, bringing with him the spirit of the accountant, measuring all by a single yardstick.[154] In 1923 California's progressive leaders rallied, forming the Progressive Voters League in an effort to regain control.[155]

Johnson shared the goal of the league but remained on its periphery, as much perhaps from the desire of its organizers as by his own wishes. A decade earlier he had personified the drive for state reform; California's progressive movement had coalesced around his personality. But times had changed—his isolationist stand had alienated many who shared his domestic views; his political independence within the Republican party alienated others. To some his ambition appeared disruptive, his personality too dominant, his enemies too numerous. Once a unifying force, Johnson had become a divisive influence in progressive circles. All wished to identify with his accomplishments as governor, most appreciated his denunciation of progressives' enemies, but many were reluctant to request his direct endorsement. To be known as a "Johnson" candidate in some parts of the state could bring as many enemies as friends.[156]

The ambiguous role Johnson played in state politics was evident in the 1924 elections. After the collapse of his own candidacy he held aloof from the presidential contest, but he was determined to take to the stump in support of progressive candidates in various Assembly and state Senate districts then under attack by Richardson.[157] But the plan fell through, and he had to content himself with a general statement attacking Richardson and supporting progressivism as his contribution to the primary and general elections. A more active campaign, he was told, might backfire.[158]

In 1926 the stakes were higher and the obstacles larger. Both Richardson and Shortridge sought reelection. Focusing on the gubernatorial contest, the Progressive Voters League, after some bickering, selected Lieutenant Governor C. C. Young to challenge Richardson in the primary.[159] Johnson had no trouble with the choice. Though a somewhat colorless candidate, Young had been a progressive from the moment he entered politics. The Senate contest posed greater difficulties. Eager for Shortridge's defeat, Johnson had urged those who shared his sentiments to agree on the selection of an opposition candidate.[160] Their choice was not inspired. Robert Clarke, a Los Angeles judge, could campaign on the slogan "Southern California needs a Senator," a slogan Johnson would as soon deflect from his own race two years hence, but Clarke was a weak candidate with few visible assets and with limited name recognition.[161]

On arriving in California at the end of July, Johnson quickly discovered the pitfalls that awaited. The primaries, he asserted, offered a straightforward contest between progress and reaction, and he was determined to participate "with a smash and bang," by devoting the month to an active campaign in support of both Young and Clarke.[162] But not all shared his perception. Clarke, though eager for Johnson's aid, nevertheless ignored his advice to deemphasize foreign affairs and focus on domestic issues, preferring instead to shape his campaign around an attack on American membership in the World Court.[163] Young, seeking to broaden his support, hoped to distance himself from Johnson and those issues extraneous to the state campaign. When Young's lieutenants met Johnson's train at the state border, they made it clear that they did not want their campaign to become entangled with Clarke's.[164]

But Johnson was determined to proceed, even under conditions that he characterized as "sickening and disgusting, embarrassing and humiliating," and spent the month of August actively campaigning for both candidates with broadside attacks on the records of Richardson and Shortridge.[165] In the primary election Young squeaked to victory in the gubernatorial race by a margin of less than 15,000, and politicos argued whether Johnson's advocacy had helped or hurt.[166] Johnson's exertions to unseat Shortridge ended in disaster. With almost no newspaper support and with many of Johnson's closest associates working against him, Clarke lost in the primary by 100,000.[167]

The difficulties Johnson encountered in the 1926 elections spelled danger for his own renomination in 1928. Further contributing to his anxiety was the policy of "harmony" pursued by Governor Young in the wake of his success, and by Charles Neumiller, a longtime Johnson associate and chairman of the California Republican Central Committee. Both men supported progressive policies but, unlike Johnson, their goal was to blur divisions within the party rather than aggravate them.[168] It was not too early to start preparations for his own 1928 campaign, Johnson advised Frank Doherty, his chief Southern California strategist, in November 1926.[169] A strenuous contest lay ahead and he did not relish being dependent upon "those whom [sic] I think, whether justly or unjustly, sold me out [in the Clarke race]."[170]

But it was Calvin Coolidge, not Frank Doherty, who set the stage for Johnson's reelection in 1928. Certain that Coolidge planned to seek reelection to a second full term, Johnson was as surprised as the rest of the country when in August 1927 the president announced that he would not again run.[171] Hoover quickly stepped forward as the heir apparent, and his aides as quickly signaled their willingness to deal. If Johnson cooperated in their effort to put together a united Hoover delegation in California, they would clear the way for his renomination to the Senate.[172] The situation, Rowell reminded Hoover, "had to be steered rather than forced."[173] Johnson bristled with objections. He recognized that Hoover held the advantage in that the selection of the California delegate ticket would be in May and the Senate primary not until August; he hoped too that Dawes or some other candidate might displace Hoover at the convention. He would not commit himself; clearly, given his temperament and his loathing for Hoover, such a commitment would have been impossible.*

But in fact no direct commitment was necessary as long as Johnson remained silent, allowed events to run their course, and made no attempt to undermine the Hoover boom in the state. This much he was willing to do. Indeed, he insisted, he had no real choice; he had not been able to control the actions of his lieutenants in the Clarke race in 1926, and all seemed eager to pursue a policy of harmony and exploit the situation created by Hoover's candidacy.[174] The bargain was struck when Hoover's managers asked for the unanimous backing of the California Republican House delegation. Five of the members balked, and agreed only after they had been assured that Johnson would run unopposed.[175]

Certain that the arrangement would collapse following Hoover's nomination, Johnson awaited the announcement of an opposition candidate backed by the Hoover forces and told his associates to delay the filing of his own candidacy papers until after the Kansas City convention.[176] The idea of yet another campaign was "nauseating," he confessed, and even success would be tempered by the fact that he would be serving under Herbert Hoover. That prospect, he acknowledged, was "anything but exhilarating." Perhaps, he mused, it was time to quit the game.[177] "One moment I feel so sick

*HWJ to Hiram Johnson, Jr., Dec. 3, 1927; HWJ to Archibald Johnson, Dec. 3, 1927; HWJ to C. K. McClatchy, Dec. 9, 1927, Feb. 8, 25, 1928, Feb. 18, 1930; HWJ to boys, Feb. 3, Mar. 2, 1928; HWJ to Ickes, Feb. 13, 25, Mar. 2, 1928. "He is the foremost candidate and will express himself on no issue," Johnson remarked of Hoover. "People are quite content with this attitude, and every international sheet, and they are the most important of the press, praise him to the skies for differing reasons, and dogmatically assert, where their politics are at variance, that he believes in their particular creed. There is no embarrassment in a wet international sheet saying he is wet and a dry international rag saying he is dry; in a public ownership paper averring he is for public ownership, and a conservative one cackling over the fact that public ownership is anathema to him. The League of Nations people regard him as their hero and say he will take us into Europe, while the Moseses and Edges who are making his fight blazon forth he has become the greatest isolationist in the nation. He simply sits tight, with enormous wads of money behind him." "Every rogue, every unconvicted thief, every scoundrel, politically, gravitate naturally to his banner," he added. HWJ to Hiram Johnson, Jr., Mar. 11, 1928; HWJ to boys, Mar. 17, 1928.

of the whole thing that I think I do not wish to remain longer in Washington, and then again I wonder . . . if, after all these years I have spent in public life now, I could be happy in doing anything else exclusively." Contributing to his uncertainty was the ever pressing problem of finances. Whether he remained in Washington or not, he acknowledged, he would have to seek additional income and would once again be forced to practice law. Moreover, much to his distress the lease on his Maryland home would soon expire and could not be renewed.*

Johnson had often expressed a desire to escape the demands of politics, a desire that intensified prior to each of his bids for reelection. But now, with his third senatorial race impending, the desire seemed for the first time more than simple posturing. Minnie, despite her long-standing resentment of the sacrifices of political life,

*In 1926 Senator Caraway of Arkansas, without Johnson's knowledge, purchased the Calvert Mansion and then demanded possession. Johnson refused, sought unsuccessfully to purchase the property himself, and at his wife's urging insisted on remaining until the expiration of the lease, in 1929. After the election, the Johnsons, with characteristic extravagance, purchased a large, $40,000, three-story home in Washington, D.C., at 122 Maryland Ave., NE, convenient to the Capitol. The building had been a lodging house before their purchase and required extensive repairs; thus for many months Johnson's peace was disturbed by "carpenters, steamfitters, plumbers, paper hangers, tile men, and plasterers." Overall, the refurbishment added $25,000 to the price. Almost immediately after the purchase, the home was threatened by the plans for the construction of the Supreme Court building. Chief Justice Taft, going out of his way to warn Johnson personally, remarked that he wasn't a "Caraway." In the end, much to the Johnsons' relief, the Supreme Court building was constructed across the street from their home. See HWJ to Hiram Johnson, Jr., Mar. 1, 1926; HWJ to boys, Mar. 5, 18, Apr. 6, 1929; HWJ to Archibald Johnson, Mar. 6, 1929. Johnson had spoken throughout the 1920s of his need to return to the law to supplement his income. The purchase of the house added to that need, but the final arrangements for his new practice were delayed by the special session called by Hoover in 1929. For a breakdown of Johnson's financial holdings, see HWJ to Hiram Johnson, Jr., May 9, 1935. In 1930 Johnson entered into a law partnership with Theodore Roche and Matthew Sullivan in San Francisco. Johnson confined his practice almost exclusively to those times when Congress was not in session, and excluded from his caseload any matter that might come before Congress. In declining one case, he wrote to Theodore Roche: "There isn't anything about this matter that would in the slightest degree militate against my employment as an attorney, but I have been so scrupulously careful in matters where the government was interested that I err on the safe side." HWJ to Theodore Roche, Sept. 6, 1938. See also HWJ to Hiram Johnson, Jr., Apr. 18, 1942. On Johnson's chronic concern about his financial status and the need to return to the practice of law, see HWJ to Hiram Johnson, Jr., Feb. 6, 1925, Mar. 11, 1927, Dec. 24, 1928; HWJ to Archibald Johnson, Oct. 16, 1926; HWJ to boys, Feb. 2, 1927, Feb. 2, 1929; HWJ to C. K. McClatchy, Jan. 29, 1927, Mar. 7, 1929, July 15, 1931.

remained silent; she refused to offer any advice, fearful that she would be blamed for any decision he made.[178] But in the end events made the decision for Johnson. The truce held. Buron Fitts, California's lieutenant governor, explored the possibility of entering the race but was unable to gather sufficient support; his candidacy, Edward Dickson cautioned, would be unwise.[179] Friend Richardson, who earlier had tentatively announced for the position, withdrew his name from consideration, citing his obligation to Hoover.[180] For once, the California Republican party seemed united. In July, a month before the primary, Johnson sat down to lunch with Hoover at the presidential nominee's Palo Alto home. Smiling as he emerged with Hoover at his side, Johnson endorsed the Republican ticket and announced the themes of his own reelection bid: his support for the still-pending Boulder Dam bill and his opposition to the power trust.[181]

In what all predicted would be a walkaway victory, Johnson limited his primary campaign to a brief Southern California tour, during which he emphasized Boulder Dam and the power trust and quoted extensively from the revelations of the Federal Trade Commission. And if he supported Hoover, it was from a distance. "No man on earth is so sacrosanct but that his position on the power trust and Boulder Dam should not be made plain to the American people," he pointedly observed as Hoover continued to hedge.[182] On the advice of Charles McClatchy to find a way to endorse the Republican ticket without stultifying himself, he stressed the importance of the tariff in protecting California agriculture and, though rarely mentioning Hoover by name, exhorted his audience to rally to the common cause by supporting the entire ticket.[183] His only opponent in the Senate contest, Charles Randall of Los Angeles, a Prohibitionist cross-filing in the Republican race, was swamped as Johnson won the Republican primary in every county, sweeping to victory by a margin of almost five to one.[184]

Upon returning to the stump in October, Johnson continued to distance himself from Hoover and ignored suggestions that he campaign nationally for the ticket in the East and Midwest. His activity was minimal; he made no speeches in California's largest cities and contented himself with luncheon engagements in a scattering of the state's smaller communities.[185] In his speeches, which he characterized as "non-political," he belabored Boulder Dam and berated the power interests, as he had during the primary. While others "toadied" and "bowed" and "crawled" in the Hoover campaign, he wrote, he kept his self-respect. He was elected to his third Senate term by a margin of almost 868,000 votes.[186]

Chapter VII

Hoover, Roosevelt, and the New Deal

1929–1937

Hiram Johnson found little to cheer in the Republican triumph of 1928. Assured of a third term, he returned to Washington for the opening of the lame-duck session of the 70th Congress to negotiate final passage of the Boulder Dam bill and to await the coming of the new administration. The prospect of Hoover in the White House especially galled him, dampening whatever pleasure he might have taken in his own reelection success. Hoover had swept to victory with 58 percent of the popular vote in his race against Al Smith, winning 40 of the 48 states in a contest that reflected both the nation's economic hopes and its cultural fears.

Throughout the campaign Hoover had identified himself with the prosperity of the times while also championing his own vision of an American system of cooperative enterprise that promised even greater abundance. In addition, he projected an image embodying traditional "Protestant" values that many Americans felt to be threatened. After the inauguration, Johnson ruefully quipped, "God will reign."[1] And that His hosts would be many there seemed little doubt. On the Hill, Republicans had increased their majorities in both houses. The progressive edge, Johnson lamented, had been eliminated, for the Old Guard found reinforcement in a "young guard" of eager novices.[2] To compound his irritation, both the press and public seemed to fawn over the new president, gushing in praise of his every platitude:

The understanding here is that next month he will make a soul-stirring appeal upon the text "Honesty is the Best Policy," and the following month will arouse our people to a frenzied enthusiasm upon "Virtue is its own Reward"; and succeeding that within four weeks, he speaks upon "Truth Crushed to Earth will Rise Again"; and then in a great climax, wherein all of the people of the United States will be listening in, and on tiptoe with excitement, he will plead for "Let Us All Be Up and Doing."*

Contemptuous of what he characterized as "the moronic era of the age of bunk," Johnson sought solace in acidic humor but was instinctively drawn to more doleful forecasts. The new political configuration, he predicted, coupled with Hoover's strong ties to the nation's press and his mastery of public relations, would enable him to determine policies and dominate Congress far more effectively than had his predecessors. In style if not in substance the beginnings of "something of a dictatorship" were emerging in which the "king can do no wrong."[3]

But in fact Hoover's political honeymoon proved short-lived. He had succeeded in overawing the Republican party at the 1928 convention but not in capturing the loyalty of its legislative factions. The Old Guard distrusted him both because of his activist reputation and because of his wartime involvement with Woodrow Wilson and the Democratic party. Senate liberals distrusted him because their commitment to legislative rather than administrative remedies for the nation's ills set them at odds with the "American system" he championed. His difficulties became apparent almost immediately as the special session of the 71st Congress, called to meet in mid-April 1929 to cope with the persistent issue of agricultural relief, began its deliberations.

Hoover was unalterably opposed to the McNary-Haugen scheme, which had been twice vetoed by Coolidge. During the campaign

*HWJ to C. K. McClatchy, Apr. 25, 1929. Earlier Johnson had remarked: "From Wilson to Hoover, I have watched the press of the Nation gradually degenerate into a lickspittling aggregation. With each succeeding administration, it has become more pliant, more subservient, and more truckling. It would seem at present to have reached the bottom of the pit, but in my observation of the last fifteen years, I have noticed that now in comparison it is capable of reaching a hitherto unthought of and unplumbed depth of degradation." HWJ to C. K. McClatchy, Apr. 16, 1929.

Hoover had appealed to rural America by calling for the creation of a Federal Farm Board that would work in tandem with agricultural cooperatives to stabilize seasonal prices and facilitate commodity marketing. In addition, he promised to modify tariff rates for agricultural products in order to enhance farm income. "The indications are that harmony will be the rule," the *New York Times* observed at the beginning of what many thought would be a short special session to accomplish these ends.[4] But disharmony reigned, and when the session ended in late November, its tasks remained unfinished.

The administration's farm bill prompted the first major controversy. In the Senate, debate revolved around the complaint of farm spokesmen that Hoover's solution ignored the core of their problem, the agricultural surplus. In response, Republican insurgents and Democratic regulars proposed adding an "export-debenture" provision to the bill as an option available to the president; this device, a variant of the McNary-Haugen plan, would allow the government to underwrite commodity prices and dump surpluses abroad. Johnson backed the move, perhaps inspired as much by the opportunity to needle the White House as by his faith in the proposed remedy.* With sarcastic public references to Hoover as "the greatest executive in all the world," Johnson scorned those who argued against government interference in the marketplace. The president's own proposal, he insisted, did precisely that, or it did nothing. Certain in his own mind that Hoover offered little more than a gesture in support of farm interests—"insincere," "sham," and "bunk" were the terms that peppered Johnson's private correspondence[5]—he pushed for the inclusion of the debenture provision. Hoover's predecessors, he argued, had not been moved by "misfortune, catastrophe or devastation" to take effective action to meet the farm crisis, and the administration's bill, with its vague terms, seemed only to perpetuate that legacy.[6]

---

*Put off by the retreat of McNary and others from their original proposal, Johnson admitted that "the farmer leaves me rather cold." But the "canny crew" running the "White House propaganda machine" and the "lousy press" with its support of "big interests" warmed him considerably. "I get a real kick in fighting them all," he wrote, "and really, my son, the only kick there is in public life to me now is in doing just as I damn pleease [sic] and as I think is right." Indeed, Johnson had always relished the "kick" of battle, but Hoover's occupancy of the White House clearly enhanced the enjoyment. HWJ to boys, May 4, 1929; HWJ to Hiram Johnson, Jr., June 13, 1929.

Hoover lost the first round: the Senate by a narrow margin turned back his attempt to eliminate the debenture option. Regaining the initiative, he secured its removal in the House-Senate conference, but again the Senate rebelled, rejecting the conference report. It was, Johnson crowed, "a declaration of independence."[7] But as he expected, the rebellion proved short-lived. Better able to control the House, the administration succeeded in thwarting Senate rebels. The final bill, without the debenture provision, passed in June with only eight opposed and with Johnson among the majority.

Hoover's difficulties were similarly evident in the prolonged battle over tariff revision that began in the summer of 1929. Having promised action during the presidential campaign, Hoover stood aloof as the Senate by a single vote defeated Borah's proposal to limit revision to agricultural schedules and as the contest subsequently devolved into a wild scramble for higher rates. Even Johnson, an unashamed advocate of protection who had voted against Borah's initiative, found the display irritating. California, he grumbled, was asking more than any other three states and had degenerated into the "gimme class."[8] But, as in the past, he scrambled with the rest. After a brief trip to San Francisco to complete arrangements to enter into a law partnership, he returned to Washington in mid-September to immerse himself in the "miserable tariff bill" and in the fight for California's interest.[9] Moreover, if Johnson had once predicted that Hoover would dominate the legislative process, he now increasingly complained both publicly and privately of Hoover's reticence, his indecisive posturing, his unwillingness to lead. During the entire proceeding, he charged, the president could not be pinned down. To the public Hoover hinted that the emerging tariff bill was harmful to consumers and filled with inequities, but to the Republican leadership he recommended even higher rates.[10] "He has not the guts to take a stand on anything," Johnson remarked.[11]

As the ordeal of tariff making ground drearily on into the second session of the 71st Congress, senators sustained their rebellious mood. They appended the already rejected export-debenture plan to the proposed tariff bill and refused to comply with Hoover's request to continue the "flexibility" provision adopted in the 1922 tariff act, which gave the president the authority to alter individual duties by 50 percent. Again Johnson stood with the majority in defiance of the White House. Presidential power to adjust rates, he argued, was both improper and dangerous. It did not, as its proponents claimed, take the tariff out of politics; it merely altered the political dynamics of ratemaking by shifting control from Congress.[12]

Johnson acknowledged that tariff protection should reflect the differences in production costs between American and imported goods. He admitted as well that too often that principle was overlooked as the ratemaking process degenerated into a game of grab. Yet even as he conceded the unsavory nature of the legislative mechanics out of which tariffs emerged, he insisted that it was the best system that could be devised.[13] It was, however, a laboriously slow system; not until late in the second session and only after the onset of the Great Depression was an exhausted Congress finally able to pass the tariff bill. Once again Hoover ultimately prevailed. Asserting himself in the conference settlement between the two houses, he secured the elimination of the export-debenture provision and salvaged the principle of flexibility.

In other ways as well Johnson found himself at odds with the new administration. When, in early 1930, Hoover nominated Charles Evans Hughes to succeed William Howard Taft as chief justice, Johnson kept silent in the confirmation debate only because of the connection that had existed between him and Hughes since the 1916 presidential contest in California, but he voted against the confirmation. The 26 votes gathered in opposition to the "bewhiskered myth," he wrote, were a "healthy sign."[14] Even healthier was the Senate's rejection of John J. Parker of North Carolina as nominee to the Supreme Court. The nomination, pushed by a stubborn president against the advice of the party leadership, generated opposition both from those sensitive to Parker's defense of racial discrimination and from those angered by his support of labor injunctions and the yellow-dog contract.[15] Ignoring the first complaint, Johnson focused on the second. Parker's character was not at fault, he argued, but neither was it distinguished. In being politically ambitious, a perennial candidate for office, Parker was no worse than many others on the bench. But his rejection, Johnson emphasized, will strike a blow against "this inhuman, this cruel, and this wicked [yellow-dog] contract that rests upon the necessity of human beings and the hunger of innocent and helpless children." The nomination was defeated by a single vote. Before the end of Hoover's term, Congress by overwhelming margins outlawed the yellow-dog contract itself.*

★   ★   ★

Hoover's initial ventures in the shaping of American foreign policy predictably raised Johnson's rhetoric to a fortissimo level. In his inaugural address the president had spoken only briefly of the nation's involvement abroad, urging both United States participation in the World Court and a new initiative to further the reduction of naval arms. Alert to the ever-present possibility that the battle over the court might be renewed, Johnson strove to mobilize the opposition, calling upon prominent isolationists to make known their objections while voicing his own dissent in broadside attacks on the floor of Congress and in a radio address. Hoover, he insisted, had not abandoned his internationalist convictions; rather he pushed for American entrance into the World Court as the first step in his larger design to secure American entry into the League of Nations.[16] But in fact Hoover made no real effort to pry the court resolution from the Senate Foreign Relations Committee until near the end of his term, when chances for its passage were all but nil.

To Johnson's regret, however, Hoover quickly took the lead in promoting a new naval limitations accord, working with Ramsay Mac-

* *Cong. Record*, 71st Cong., 2nd sess. (May 1, 5, 1930), pp. 8103, 8476–78; *Cong. Record*, 72nd Cong., 1st sess. (Feb. 29, Mar. 1, 1932), pp. 4938, 5019. See also HWJ to boys, May 3, 7, 1930; HWJ to C. K. McClatchy, May 3, 1930. The vote on the Parker nomination was 39 to 41. Johnson had little to lose by taking the stands that he did. Clearly he had no expectation of securing patronage from the White House. He would, he noted, have as much influence with Hoover as he had had with Coolidge, "exactly none at all." HWJ to Fremont Older, Feb. 18, 1929. From California, Rowell urged Hoover to crack down: "Johnson has clearly made himself personally impossible. He has openly declared war on you, and announced himself ready to take the consequences. You will know best how to impose those consequences." Rowell to Herbert Hoover, June 22, 1929, Rowell Papers. See also Rowell to C. C. Young, June 11, 22, July 2, 1929, Rowell Papers, advising Governor Young to demonstrate that his loyalty lay with Hoover and not Johnson, and HWJ to C. K. McClatchy, Jan. 26, 1930. Perhaps unintentionally, the breach between Johnson and Hoover was publicized when, in November 1929, Johnson was not invited to accompany other members of the Senate Foreign Relations Committee to a White House dinner in honor of Charles Dawes. Hoover apologized when the slight was made public and called it an oversight. Johnson accepted Hoover's apology but remained convinced that the slight had been intended. In 1930, when Johnson's office was broken into and his files rifled, he believed Hoover was somehow implicated. See *New York Times*, Nov. 6, 7, 8, 1929; Herbert Hoover to HWJ, Nov. 6, 1929; HWJ to boys, Nov. 8, 1929, May 9, 17, 1930.

Donald, Britain's recently elected prime minister, to prepare the way for the London Naval Conference, which opened in January 1930. The conference, a follow-up to the Geneva failure of 1927, was carefully crafted to avoid the pitfalls of Geneva by subordinating the role played by naval authorities in the negotiating process. From the beginning Johnson feared that the administration might bow to France's desire to link the United States to a European security treaty or to Japan's hope to alter the nation's exclusionist immigration policy. Such concerns further underscored his call for open diplomacy. As always, he attended to any sign that American interests might be compromised.[17] His worst fears, of course, were not realized. What emerged instead from the negotiations was an agreement establishing guidelines for the construction of British, Japanese, and American cruisers and other auxiliary vessels.[18] Though admittedly skeptical of the settlement, Johnson initially styled himself as "open-minded" and promised to withhold judgment until Senate hearings on the treaty began; but it is doubtful if any agreement could have won his approval. Certainly he had no difficulty in finding allies within the naval establishment to underwrite his suspicions.[19]

Concessions to Britain limited America's ability to build the kinds of heavy cruisers that U.S. naval experts had unsuccessfully pressed for at Geneva, while concessions to Japan drew back from the 5-5-3 ratio that had been established at the Washington Naval Conference in the allocation of tonnage allowed respectively to Britain, the United States, and Japan. As the ratification hearings opened, Johnson quickly became the acknowledged leader of the opposition. His strategy was to delay action in the Senate Foreign Relations Committee by extending the proceedings, in the hope that the final vote on the floor could be put off until after the November midterm elections. Sharply cross-examining proponents of the treaty, he condemned the concessions that had been made. Summoning his own string of witnesses from within the naval establishment, he led them through their endless objections. The settlement, he wrote, was "wicked," an "outrage" that should never have been allowed.[20] As in the past, he sought access to the background materials on which the treaty was based, only to be rebuffed.[21]

Johnson successfully prolonged Senate consideration of the treaty during the regular session but could not prevent Hoover's call for a special session to meet in July 1930 to conclude the business. With only a handful of senators joining him in dissent, Johnson doggedly pressed his attack both on the Senate floor and on a nationwide CBS radio broadcast. The agreement, he conceded, did provide adequate protection for American home waters but failed to protect the nation's lines of trade beyond those waters. Overseas trade was critically important to American prosperity, he emphasized, and consequently so were the military instruments upon which the preservation of the nation's commercial rights as a neutral rested.*

Perhaps Johnson hoped that even without the votes to defeat the treaty he had the resources to outlast the majority and prevent a quorum as the off-term elections neared. In any case, intending, as he wrote, to "leave a record" for the future, he took the floor frequently and held it persistently in the closing days of debate in what amounted to the only filibuster he ever attempted.[22] It was, however, a charge he intemperately denied. Too many senators, he protested, "who are gagged and lashed and bound, and who sit here without the nerve and without the intelligence to discuss this treaty, assume to say that anybody who dares discuss it upon this floor is filibustering or is wasting time."[23] But popular enthusiasm for additional limits on naval construction could not be stilled. Outgunned, outvoted, Johnson lost his battle by overwhelming margins. The Senate, characterized by the *New York Times* as "wilted and weary," rejected the resolutions he and the small band of holdouts proposed in order to cripple the treaty and voted 58 to 9 in favor of the agreement.[24]

★   ★   ★

The Republican sweep of 1928 had rested on the nation's prosperity. For many Americans, Hoover symbolized the emergence of a new economic order, engineered through mass production, that held out the promise of ever greater abundance. It would be an "irony of fate," Harold Ickes perhaps half-wishfully observed shortly after the inauguration, "if this superintellect, this great engineer and administrator would have to face during his administration a business and

---

* *New York Times*, June 18, 19, 29, 1930. Johnson's normal pace of 100 words per minute was exceeded in his radio address as he fought for time. The *New York Times* clocked him at 150. Even so, he went over his time limit of 22 minutes by an additional 5. HWJ to Hiram Johnson, Jr., June 20, 1930; HWJ to Archibald Johnson, June 20, 1930.

financial depression."[25] The fates were in fact unkind. In October 1929, less than a year into Hoover's term, the economy began visibly to crumble.

At first Johnson seemed indifferent. The only explanation he had heard for the market slide, he sarcastically wrote in late October, was that Hoover, or rather "God," had been temporarily absent from Washington, "sailing o'er the Ohio river."[26] He had little doubt that the slump would be short-lived. Indeed, he predicted, the situation would ultimately rebound to the president's advantage. If Al Smith had occupied the White House, Johnson wrote, the press would have instantly conspired to blame him for the panic. In contrast, Hoover would be given undeserved credit for the market's natural recovery.[27] But the economy failed to respond to the president's entreaties. For Johnson, the crisis quite literally began to strike home. Although he himself went unscathed thanks to his chronic shortage of funds and ingrained distrust of the stock exchange—he defined investment in the market as but another form of gambling—both of his sons suffered serious financial losses.* Then in 1933 his younger son, Archibald, committed suicide, under a weight of personal and emotional problems to which the economic collapse had clearly contributed.†

---

* "There are some advantages in being too poor to speculate," Johnson had earlier noted. But it was doubtful if he would have played the market even if he had had the money to do so. "I never bought a share of stock in my life," he stated, "and I never walked through a stockbroker's office and looked at a blackboard but what I have the same feeling I used to have when I was a boy, when I sneaked into the crowded room where the Keno players were anxiously watching the drawings and keeping tab upon their cards. I always have a sort of feeling that I am somewhere where I ought not to be, and a part of some enterprise my presence in which I would rather conceal." HWJ to Archibald Johnson, Jan. 4, Apr. 11, 1926. See also HWJ to Hiram Johnson, Jr., Apr. 28, 1922; HWJ to Archibald Johnson, Apr. 13, 1929. Both Johnson and his wife dreamed of better times. Throughout the 1920s they hoped that oil might be found on some Redondo Beach property owned by Minnie, but as Johnson explained, "if anything were discovered that brought me financial success I should feel that the whole scheme of the universe had gone wrong." HWJ to Doherty, Apr. 3, 1929. See also HWJ to boys, Apr. 19, 1929.

† Archibald, who had always been high-strung, had suffered a psychological breakdown at the end of World War I. With the coming of the economic depression his income was dramatically reduced and he unsuccessfully sought various government positions. In 1933, six weeks prior to his suicide, Martha Leet Johnson, his wife of eleven years, was granted a Reno divorce, and remarried in the same week. Archibald, alone in the library of his Hillsborough mansion, shot himself through the heart with a .38 revolver. After his debts were paid, his estate totaled $759.00. Hiram Johnson

Throughout the remainder of 1929 Johnson predicted that the market would soon rebound, but with the coming of the new year he began to reflect the emerging pessimism of the new decade. He still hoped for a miracle, he acknowledged, but doubted its coming.[28] Slowly at first and then more rapidly, the nation plunged into depression; industrial production fell and unemployment mounted. On returning to California in the summer of 1930 following the special Senate session called to ratify the London naval agreement, Johnson found "everyone" suffering financially. Disillusioned, they were searching for an answer that they no longer trusted Hoover's promises to provide.[29] The November midterm elections bore out his observations: the Republican party gains of 1928 were eliminated. In the new Congress, Republicans would control the Senate by a single vote; in the House they were no longer the majority.

From the onset of the economic crisis Hoover tried to exclude Congress from an active part in meeting the challenge. Relief, he insisted, depended on a public spirit willing to respond spontaneously and voluntarily to the hardships of others, and the government's role should be confined to mobilizing that spirit and coordinating the resultant endeavors of the private sector. In Congress the leadership of both parties offered little resistance. They hoped that Hoover might find the key to recovery and were unwilling to assume responsibility for an alternative course—in fact they were unable to define any alternative.[30] But as the president's efforts floundered, his political authority, never more than tenuous at best, continued to erode. Distrusting Congress, he was increasingly distrusted by Congress. "On the Republican side he is practically friendless," Johnson observed upon his return to Washington at the end of 1930. When

---

was close to both of his sons, at times holding both in almost suffocating embrace, but he had often assured Archibald that a special psychological tie linked the two of them together. Johnson must surely have been devastated by the suicide; however, because he refused to share his grief with others, it is impossible to assess the impact of the loss. Perhaps Johnson blamed himself for not having been there when he was needed, or for not pushing hard enough to find his son some federal sinecure; perhaps he blamed Martha, the ex-wife, or perhaps Archibald himself, who was too often impractical, too often the romantic. Or perhaps Hiram and his wife were too numbed by a tragedy they could not fathom to feel anything like guilt or blame. Archibald Johnson to HWJ, Sept. 28, 1918, Feb. 16, 1933; *San Francisco Chronicle*, Nov. 24, 1922, Aug. 2, 1933, July 13, 1935; *Sacramento Bee*, Aug. 1, 1933; HWJ to Archibald Johnson, May 28, 1933.

Hoover had first taken office, Johnson had stood out as one of the president's most vocal critics; now he had been joined, indeed at times outdistanced, by his colleagues.[31]

In part, as Johnson saw, Hoover was a victim of economic forces over which he had no control. The real problem, he admitted, was that neither the president nor anyone else knew what to do.[32] All were overwhelmed by the vast scale of the crisis. But increasingly Hoover was a victim as well of his own actions. Seeking to restore public confidence, he filled his economic forecasts with expressions of optimism, ineffectually preaching what Johnson characterized as "a sort of psychological Christian Science."[33] Insistent that the federal government could not assume responsibility for public relief, he minimized the hardships countless Americans faced. "The fact is, there is not a damn thing that comes from this administration that you can believe," Johnson wrote, echoing a growing tide of public disillusionment.[34]

But while Johnson was critical of Hoover and the Republican party, he was no more impressed by the Democratic party leadership. They trailed along, subservient to the president's wishes, and in those rare instances when they did make their presence felt, they masked the central problems unleashed by the depression, no more willing than Hoover to accept federal responsibility for aiding the distressed.[35] For Johnson, the struggle over drought relief in early 1931 demonstrated the bankruptcy of both parties.[36] Hoover, adamant that federal outlays of funds be limited, insisted that no public monies could be used to provide food relief for those in need. To do so, he argued, would constitute a dole. Ultimately the issue was resolved to allow a minimum allotment for food relief but only for those who were financially eligible to secure emergency loans. The Democratic party had pushed Hoover to make concessions, Johnson observed, but had played a "shell and pea game" by obscuring the one real issue—"whether in times of great emergency and sudden catastrophe, the Government should appropriate money to feed the suffering and starving."[37] They argued over means, and if in the end they provided relief, they did so only for a few.

Overall, the last session of the 71st Congress, lumbering without direction, disappointed both Hoover and Johnson. From Johnson's perspective it appeared vacillating, hesitant, and uncertain. To the president it seemed willful and headstrong, as evidenced by its passage once again of the Muscle Shoals project, which he vetoed, and by the large majorities that overrode his veto of the veterans' bonus. The experience doubtless strengthened Hoover in his resolve not to call a special session of Congress but instead to allow himself nine months of respite before the regular session of the new Congress assembled. Johnson was no more eager than Hoover for a special session, and looked forward to the opportunity to supplement his income by returning to California to begin his long-delayed practice of law.[38]

In the interval the economic crisis deepened both at home and abroad. In June 1931, seeking to shore up a structure of international finance that pressed hard upon the nation's domestic banking institutions, Hoover proposed to European governments a one-year moratorium on all intergovernmental debts. After securing assent abroad, he made the moratorium the first order of business when the new Congress met in December of that year. Damning the arrangement from the moment the plan was first announced, Johnson for once found himself eager to return to Washington.[39] Hoover's action, he charged, was legislation by fiat. Unwilling to call a special session, the president had sought legislative agreement by polling individual congressmen. Worse still, 68 senators had pledged their support. The arrangement too much resembled the suggestions current in some circles to short-circuit the legislative process by investing additional power in the executive. "Why do we need a representative body at all," Johnson scornfully asked from the floor, if Congress stood willing to acquiesce in decisions already made?[40] The measure itself, he argued, was unnecessary and burdened the American taxpayer at a time when the administration called for economy. Nor had the promise of a moratorium halted the European collapse; it had merely enabled investment bankers to continue to draw interest on their private lending. Emphasizing the alterations the French had insisted upon before agreeing to the proposal, he urged his colleagues to release themselves from their earlier pledges of support.

Above all, Johnson argued, the moratorium should not be allowed to become the first step in the scaling down or cancellation of those debts owed to the United States government. The European states, he maintained, could be made to pay. Moreover, even if they refused, he emphasized, the debts should not be forgiven, for while the nation would clearly benefit if payments continued, it would benefit as well from default. More than balance sheets were at stake in pressing for payment. "Once they have defaulted," Johnson publicly observed, "we will know just where we stand and we will not again commit the errors which have been committed in the last fifteen years in this country." In no better way might the nation's isolationist resolve be fortified.[41]

As he expected, Johnson lost his fight in Congress.[42] The administration pushed hard, emphasizing the need for haste to meet the emergency. The joint resolution emerged intact from the House and moved smoothly through the Senate Finance Committee after ten minutes of study. The attempts to amend the measure on the floor were quickly and easily defeated. Those pledged to Hoover stood firm, and on December 22, the Senate by a vote of 69 to 12 agreed to the moratorium. Yet, despite his defeat, Johnson found reason to cheer, for both the resolution itself and the debate it generated reemphasized congressional determination to hold Europe to its obligations. Hoover's recommendation that the World War Foreign Debt Commission be reestablished was scotched and with it the possibility for the renegotiation of existing debts.[43]

In addition, the moratorium prodded Johnson to undertake an examination of the marketing of foreign securities in the United States; this study would ultimately lead to the passage of the Johnson Act of 1934. At his urging, the Senate agreed to an investigation to be conducted by the Senate Finance Committee. Although Johnson was not a member of that committee, he nevertheless participated in and promptly came to dominate the inquiry. With no resources save an attentive and supportive press, in an unfriendly committee made up, as he put it, of the "puppets of big financiers," confronting as well a series of hostile witnesses, Johnson made headlines from the outset by demonstrating links between the State Department and Colombian oil concessions and by revealing a host of abuses in the marketing of both European and Latin American securities within the United States.[44] He was "raising hell," Secretary of State Henry Stimson growled. Hard at work, occasionally sleepless, he was also having a "bully time."[45]

★   ★   ★

Agreement to the moratorium was only one of a number of actions that Hoover pressed upon the new Congress that met in December 1931. Accelerating bank failures, which dashed any hope for economic recovery, forced him reluctantly to set aside his distaste for legislative remedies and to call upon Congress to increase bank liquidity and to extend emergency loans to the nation's financial institutions. The Glass-Steagall Act and the Reconstruction Finance Corporation quickly followed. While hopeful that the RFC might do some good, Johnson was predictably suspicious of its Wall Street origins. Endorsements by financiers Otto Kahn, Eugene Meyer, and Bernard Baruch—the "Israelites," as Johnson sourly wrote—deepened his distrust. Under pressure from the White House, the Senate rejected an amendment sponsored by Royal Copeland of New York to enlarge the scope of the RFC by allowing it to provide loans to states and municipalities as well as to financial institutions. The final bill, pushed by the administration, passed easily in both houses. In the Senate the vote was 63 to 8. Johnson, who had supported the Copeland amendment, abstained.[46]

Hoover called too for economy—for a balanced budget that required both a reduction in government expenditures and the adoption of a national sales tax. Only with such a package, the administration reasoned, could business confidence be restored and the process of recovery be instigated. Johnson took an active part in the debate, seizing every opportunity to criticize an administration that could forgive its debtors abroad while demanding greater sacrifice from its own at home. He vigorously protested the cutback of federal programs. It was too easy, he argued, to speak of economy and ignore the social costs involved; some economies were "dearer than the dearest extravagance."[47] Unsuccessfully he urged that the proposed 10 percent salary reductions for government workers be limited to those earning more than $2,500 per year. The White House, he claimed, was pursuing a "false economy" that destroyed the very parts of the public service that ought to be fostered.[48]

Johnson rejoiced when the House, in March 1932, turned back Hoover's drive for a national sales tax. To almost all, the action came as a surprise, for although Republicans had lost control of the House as a result of the 1930 elections, the new Democratic leadership seemed no more willing to challenge Hoover than had their Republican counterparts. Both parties, Johnson wrote, belonged to the same special interests and marched to the same tune.[49] But when the House Democratic leadership pushed for a vote on the national sales tax, it quickly lost control. Pandemonium erupted on the floor and shouts and whistles echoed from the walls as a Democratic majority, joined by a handful of Republican insurgents, soundly defeated the measure. The Democratic rank and file, Johnson cheered, "declared its independence, and voted itself in favor of common humanity."[50] The Senate contest was less dramatic—despite the first extended performance of Huey Long of Louisiana—but equally decisive.[51] Ultimately, the revenue bill that emerged from Congress restored tax rates approximating those in place during World War I. Johnson's effort to eliminate the many nuisance taxes included in the final package proved unsuccessful; even so, he was not dissatisfied by the result.[52]

Johnson's support for tax increases during a period of economic collapse was not unusual for the times. Indeed, it would have been difficult in 1932 to find anyone, whatever their political persuasion, who would argue in support of major budget deficits, and if some in the decade of the 1930s came to see deficit spending as a positive good, a regenerative tool that could counter cyclic swings of the economy, Johnson always remained suspicious of the fiscally unorthodox. But he was willing to spend, and he firmly believed that one of government's primary responsibilities was to aid those in need. Unhesitatingly he supported legislation introduced in the 72nd Congress to provide public works and unemployment relief.

The first major proposal, the La Follette–Costigan bill, authorizing a $375 million grant to the states to underwrite relief efforts and a similar amount for public road building, died in the Senate in February 1932, a victim of the administration's displeasure and the Senate's own uncertainty over the use of loans rather than grants.[53] The fate of the bill, Johnson angrily remarked from the floor, once again dramatized the "irreconcilable conflict" between a standpat majority, content to support privilege, and a progressive minority, attentive to the needs of the people. Under Hoover, government was receptive to "every whispered request" by big business but deaf to the clamor of the public for general relief. Administration policies, he continued, had broken from the shibboleths of the past to intercede actively in the marketplace. The president's Farm Board speculated in the wheat pits and cotton markets; his Reconstruction Finance Corporation extended aid to banks and railroads. Yet all the while administration spokesmen voiced the pieties of the past, emphasizing economy, denouncing doles, and charging socialism in their opposition to proposals to relieve public distress.[54]

By the spring of 1932, however, as the economy continued to collapse and as election year politics began to quicken, it became clear that the White House would agree to federal funding of state relief programs if they were financed by federal loans rather than by outright grants. Hoover, Johnson remarked, had turned a "remarkable somersault," and increasingly the contest revolved around what form public relief would take.[55] Congress labored well into the summer, holding sessions late into the evening, as tempers flared in the ever more fractious body. "We're all ragged here, physically and mentally," Johnson wrote, noting that if he had been 40 years younger he would have had a dozen personal confrontations. "Everybody is sick, sore, sour and sullen."[56]

Contributing to that mood was the massing of 20,000 unemployed veterans in Washington's Anacostia Flats in the summer of 1932 in support of an immediate payment of the soldiers' bonus. They ought not to have come, Johnson sadly commented, and no legislator should respond to their numbers or their veiled threats. Yet many were palpably in need. Johnson sympathized with their plight but could not support their cause. "My heart was with them," he privately acknowledged, and he fought his own battle between heart and head before finally voting with the large Senate majority to reject the proposal.[57] What was needed, he insisted, was a program of general relief, not one limited to a single group. He was certain that the bonus army itself posed no immediate threat either to the nation's capital or to the processes of government, but he nevertheless saw in the assemblage a possible harbinger:

If they change their cry, and if they put their demands solely upon the ground of the right to work, and the right to live, and the right to eat, and if they are without work without any fault on their part, as is undoubtedly the fact, and if they can bring here to the capital of the nation some hundreds of thousands of those similarly situated, who are nearly begging for bread today, because jobs are denied them, and if with these, the agrarian population, losing now their farms and facing ruin, unite, then the old cadavers like myself in the halls of the legislature will be pretty roughly tossed upon the common in front of the Capitol, and the Englishman sitting in the White House, and governing us upon the theory of relieving the misery of Europe, will betake himself with a celerity and an alacrity most amazing to another and healthier clime. What saves us in this country is the farmer's love for law and order. This, doubtless, arises from the fact that he has something in the shape of a shelter over his head, and something in his yard, and in his field, that he may gather for food for himself and his family. When he reaches the depth of despair of the urban dweller in this country, and when feeling as the city unemployed do, he unites with them, we can say goodnight to the present government.[58]

Meanwhile, the battle over relief raged on, in part fueled by the clamor from Anacostia. In July the Wagner-Garner bill enabling the RFC to extend loans to the states and providing $300 million for self-liquidating public works was passed by Congress, but as expected, the bill was promptly vetoed. A week later Congress passed a revised bill designed to meet Hoover's objections. The resulting Emergency Relief and Construction Act, while eliminating provisions in the vetoed bill that authorized unsecured loans, allotted almost the same RFC funding to states as well as support for self-liquidating public works.[59]

Looking back over the first session of the 72nd Congress as it finally wrapped up its affairs in mid-July, Johnson described it as the worst he had experienced. Congress had "done more things with less knowledge . . . than in any other session ever held." And neither the president, the financial experts, nor Congress, he admitted, knew what was happening or in what direction the nation was moving. "We have simply taken innumerable shots in the dark," he conceded.[60] Even more troubling, at least some of his colleagues were beginning to wonder whether economic recovery was possible using democratic means. "If this country ever needed a Mussolini it needs one now," Pennsylvania's conservative senator David Reed had earlier remarked. Johnson increasingly feared that that was precisely Hoover's design: "The administration has but one thought," he privately concluded, "to get by until the November election in any way, no matter what, and after the election, the deluge."[61]

★   ★   ★

Johnson's assessment of Hoover's reelection prospects varied with his mood. In early 1932 he was convinced that the president had no chance.[62] But by the spring his own instinctive pessimism, coupled with Hoover's readiness to endorse policies he had once scorned, prompted growing uncertainty. A tough fight was in the making, Johnson came to believe, and by no means a sure one.* Equally uncertain was the role Johnson might play in that fight.

Earlier, his own presidential candidacy had been rumored. Upon his return to Washington in November 1931, at the beginning of the 72nd Congress, Johnson had been pleased by the response to his off-the-cuff remark that Hoover could best serve the nation by following Coolidge's example and declining a second term.[63] To reporters who sought a declaration of his own candidacy, he cryptically responded that he would tell them when he was ready. His prime objective, both then and thereafter, was to ensure Hoover's defeat in 1932. Convinced at that point that Hoover could renominate himself but that he could not be reelected, Johnson was inclined to remain uninvolved.[64]

But if Johnson was reluctant to make yet another try for the presidency, he did not dismiss the idea entirely. Harold Ickes, having canvassed progressive ranks, encouraged him forward with a flurry of appeals. La Follette seemed sympathetic, Ickes eagerly reported, as did Bronson Cutting, Gifford Pinchot, Smith Brookhart, Gerald Nye, and Charles McNary.[65] In addition, Johnson could easily secure the endorsement of Robert McCormick and the *Chicago Tribune*.[66] "I wish to God I had either the power or the ability to come to you and prove to you that you ought to run," Ickes pleaded in mid-December.[67] Once Johnson announced his candidacy, he added, the funds necessary to his campaign could easily be raised. Liberals stood ready to contribute, as did conservatives, who were increasingly aware of Hoover's inadequacy. Johnson would win the primaries of North Dakota, Illinois, and Ohio with little trouble and had an excellent chance in Michigan, Wisconsin, Minnesota, Nebraska, and South Dakota.[68] Though tempted, Johnson preferred to wait in the background "looking wise and mysterious," if only to worry the "yellow man in the White House."[69] Yet the prospects sounded increasingly attractive, and he was not averse to further exploration of the subject.

As an announced candidate, Johnson could chose between two

*HWJ to boys, May 1, 1932; HWJ to C. K. McClatchy, May 7, 12, 28, June 5, July 3, 1932. Johnson commented: "If Hoover with four billion of dollars practically granted him by Congress can not elect himself, he is more unpopular than Judas Iscariot." HWJ to C. K. McClatchy, July 17, 1932.

courses of action. First, he might adopt the strategy pushed by Ickes and make an aggressive bid for the nomination. To weigh this option, he met with McCormick in Washington, where the Chicago publisher pledged his support.[70] In letters home he sounded out his strength in California.[71] He quickly determined that he could win the primary states of the Midwest but felt less certain of his home state. Ultimately, he concluded that even if he were successful in the primaries he would hold no more than 20 percent of the delegates and could not hope for his party's nomination. He would have become the instrument by which conservatives eliminated Hoover only to select another of their own.[72]

A second strategy, more limited in scope but gratifying in its own way, would be to confine his candidacy to California, to become a spoiler, demonstrating Hoover's unpopularity in the state and almost certainly at the national convention as well. Clearly, there would be more than a hint of sweet revenge in adopting the very tactic that Hoover had used against him in 1920, and Johnson seemed briefly to toy with the idea before finally relinquishing it.[73] Perhaps if favorite sons had announced elsewhere, perhaps if he had been more sure of his own strength in California, he would have done otherwise. In the end Johnson turned down the offers of support and decided against any sort of candidacy. Yet even with the limited prospects for overall success—owing to the hostility of party regulars and the recognition that 1932 was not likely to be a Republican year—the decision was not an easy one. If he had been younger than his 66 years and less debt-ridden, he confessed, he would have proceeded despite the difficulties.[74] As it was, he centered his hopes on Hoover's defeat in the general election.

Crucial to those hopes was the candidacy of Franklin Roosevelt. None of the other Democratic possibilities, Johnson asserted, differed substantially from Hoover. In fact, he continued, the Democratic party leadership really preferred Hoover to Roosevelt, and if they failed in their attempt to deny Roosevelt the nomination at Chicago they would doubtless move to undercut him in the general election.[75] Roosevelt, he acknowledged, might be far from the ideal candidate, perhaps too vacillating as his critics charged, but he had positive strengths and his faults were too easily exaggerated. One could love him for the enemies he had made.[76] In contrast, Al Smith, his major rival, was in essence a lackey of big business, and his attacks on Roosevelt's alleged "demagoguery" were themselves an exercise in the art.[77]

Drawn to Roosevelt even before the New York governor's public disavowal of his 1920 endorsement of American entry into the League of Nations, Johnson was elated by his early primary successes and distressed when his campaign seemed to falter in Massachusetts, Pennsylvania, and California.[78] But Roosevelt's candidacy survived, and his nomination at Chicago, followed by his dramatic flight from Albany to Chicago to deliver his acceptance speech, fired Johnson's imagination and prompted a public cheer. There was, Johnson announced, "something fine and gallant and exhilarating" in the scrapping of the tradition that a candidate must wait to be notified of his selection.[79] In July, sure of nothing except that he could not support Hoover, Johnson awaited the end of the congressional session and his return to California. There he would determine his own course of action and his "very uncertain future."[80]

Prudence dictated a low profile, and prudence became Johnson's political guide in the summer of 1932. Just prior to his departure from Washington, he met with William Gibbs McAdoo, who was in the process of launching his bid for Shortridge's Senate seat; Pat Harrison, Democratic senator from Mississippi; and Senator John Cohen of Georgia, vice chairman of the Democratic National Committee, thereby stirring up rumors that he might endorse Roosevelt. The meeting had no real significance, Johnson assured his family and close friends; but rumors of a possible bolt persisted.[81] Upon his return to California, Johnson declined interviews and remained publicly silent as the presidential campaign evolved. In September, in his annual Labor Day address before the State Federation of Labor, meeting at Modesto, he briefly broke his silence to reemphasize his differences with the Republican Old Guard and the president, but whether he would move from disapproving generalities to an open endorsement of Roosevelt remained unclear.[82] Roosevelt actively courted progressive Republican support throughout his campaign, and in a speech in Sacramento the day after Johnson's Modesto address, singled Johnson out as "a warrior in the ranks of true American progress."[83] The senator gratefully acknowledged the compliment but gave no hint of his future intentions.

Though apparently immune to Democratic party courtship in September, Johnson was roused by Republican party obtuseness in

October to inject himself into the race. In a transparent attempt to embarrass Johnson politically, Ernest P. Clarke, publisher of the *Riverside Press*, after conferring with Louis Mayer, chairman of the Republican State Central Committee, dispatched an open telegram asking Johnson to make an "emphatic declaration" for Hoover. It was, Chester Rowell moaned, a stupid blunder that immediately backfired. In a prompt, lengthy, public reply, Johnson outlined his position. He was a progressive; Hoover was not.

The Progressive believes this government belongs to all its people . . . the stand-patter, paying lip service to common humanity, makes a mock of his words, by his court of special classes. . . . The Progressive thinks in terms of human beings; the stand-patter has little thought or concern for them. . . . I would not taint my record nor stultify myself now by abandoning the principles for which I have battled unceasingly during my career. . . . I cannot and will not support Hoover.[84]

The following week Harold Ickes, newly appointed as director of the Western Division of the Roosevelt-Republican Progressive League, arrived in San Francisco to confer with Johnson. Whether he persuaded Johnson to endorse Roosevelt or whether Johnson had already decided to do so is unclear. Working with Ickes, Johnson scheduled addresses in San Francisco, Los Angeles, and Chicago. "We are again standing at Armageddon," he joyfully wrote.[85] While Chester Rowell scurried to create a ragtag California Hoover Progressive Club, Johnson took to the road, kicking off his campaign efforts at San Francisco's Dreamland Rink before a crowd of 14,000 cheering enthusiasts and a nationwide radio audience.[86]

In his address, Johnson hit hard at the failures of Hoover and his administration, vividly contrasting the promises of 1928 with the realities of 1932. The president's stand on prohibition, Johnson argued, was an evasion, his farm program a farce. Unemployment, initially ignored by Hoover, had been neither halted nor even reduced, while human misery had been met with empty gestures. With malicious delight Johnson savaged Hoover's moratorium and denounced the midsummer federal assault on the Bonus Army at Anacostia—"a cruel and cowardly act." He laced his accusations with the venom that had welled since 1920. Hoover was the creature of big business and the utility interests; his formative years had been determined abroad and his philosophy shaped "in gambling on the stock exchange in London." Concluding with a call for the rebirth of progressive idealism, Johnson identified Roosevelt as a part of that rebirth. With much the same message, he pounded Hoover in Los Angeles and Chicago on the eve of the election.[87]

★   ★   ★

Elated by Roosevelt's November success, Johnson quickly dispatched congratulations both to Roosevelt and to his campaign manager, Jim Farley—"the greatest political general of our times."[88] To William McAdoo, newly elected Democratic senator from California, he expressed a ready willingness to be of service in any way he could.[89] But if the elections bolstered Johnson's hope for a more aggressive program to meet the nation's ills at home, events during the presidential transition also raised fears that even in defeat Hoover might succeed in determining Roosevelt's course abroad by securing his agreement to a prolongation of the moratorium and a renegotiation of foreign debts. In pursuit of that goal, Hoover invited Roosevelt to meet with him at the White House on November 22 in preparation for the transfer of power. The meeting was a trap, Johnson warned Roosevelt. Both the public and Congress had shown their determination that debt payments would be resumed in December following the end of the moratorium; it was folly, he observed, for Roosevelt to make any commitment prior to his inauguration.[90] Much to Johnson's relief, the conference between Hoover and Roosevelt proved inconclusive, but Johnson continued to voice his concern, reemphasizing his opposition to any modification of debt policy both on the floor of the Senate and in his first meeting with Roosevelt in mid-January.[91]

The meeting, at the Mayflower Hotel on January 19, was both brief and pleasant. Roosevelt was in the process of selecting his cabinet. Earlier, he had made it known that he desired Johnson as his secretary of the interior. Johnson, although pleased by the offer, had already determined to refuse. The job itself, he wrote, was not attractive. More importantly, he would not place himself in a position that might require him to subordinate his views to that of a superior. He had never been a team player and was not about to forgo the political independence he had cultivated over a lifetime.[92] Thus even as Roosevelt renewed the offer with the suggestion that the scope of the Interior Department would be broadened, Johnson graciously declined and turned the conversation to foreign affairs, emphasizing the need to select a secretary of state who was not from the triumvirate of offices represented by Hughes, Root, and the House of Morgan. Congratulating Roosevelt on having side-stepped Hoover at their first meeting, he warned against entrapment at the conference Hoover and Roosevelt had scheduled for the following day.

Throughout the meeting with Johnson, Roosevelt was characteristically vague and charming, making no promises but apparently sympathetic. Johnson left the room very much liking the man.[93] Yet he remained apprehensive, still fearful that Roosevelt might succumb to the internationalists. Roosevelt's willingness to hold a second meeting with Hoover, coupled with his private conversations thereafter with the British ambassador at Warm Springs, compounded his fears. "That he is putting himself in a position where he will get his fingers burned I think there is little doubt," Johnson pessimistically concluded.[94]

Meanwhile the lame-duck 72nd Congress, having begun its short session in December, moved ineffectually toward its conclusion. Hoover, again calling for a balanced budget, renewed the cry for retrenchment and pushed once more for the adoption of a sales tax, while Robert Wagner, Edward Costigan, and Robert La Follette, Jr., who had led the battle for relief in the first session, continued to press their initiatives. Almost nothing was accomplished. The session, Johnson complained, limped aimlessly along, muddled and without purpose. He was ready to try "almost anything" to relieve the visible distress in the land, yet found little before him on which to act. He supported efforts that would have allowed the RFC to extend grants rather than loans to states in need, but these failed. Next he joined with a majority to increase the lending power of the agency to $600 million, but the bill died in the House. A similar fate awaited the banking bill, which was filibustered by Long of Louisiana before its Senate passage. Despite the massiveness of Roosevelt's victory, or perhaps because of it, Congress preferred delay.[95]

If the election failed to galvanize Congress into greater activity in addressing the nation's economic ills, it did nonetheless help to shape the environment out of which came the repeal of prohibition. Demands for repeal had intensified with the coming of the depression. Proponents of repeal, drawn in part from conservative ranks, stressed the revenues from taxes on alcohol that might substitute for higher income taxes. Proponents of prohibition were already on the defensive, for the debate over law enforcement had become more strident during the Hoover administration; and they now found themselves increasingly under assault. Hoover, who had paid lip service to the cause of prohibition during his presidency, waffled during the election campaign, while the Democratic party overwhelmingly endorsed repeal in its party platform.*

Never an enthusiast, Johnson had accepted prohibition as a political fact of life and had been more critical of its advocates than of the principle itself.[96] In California support for prohibition had cut across liberal and conservative lines, but the active leadership of the movement, after the accession of Arthur Briggs in 1920 to head the state Anti-Saloon League, had been almost without exception conservative, and the organization had shown little hesitancy in subordinating its principles to other causes.[97] Few of Johnson's close associates were avid prohibitionists, and Charles McClatchy and Matthew Sullivan, among his closest friends, were ardent wets. So too were his sons. Johnson had been largely content to ignore the issue in his public statements and to take an occasional holiday drink in private. He was of course aware of the multiple abuses wrought by prohibition, and he deplored the excesses it spawned, but he also believed prohibition had accomplished some good. He had supported the punitive legislation sponsored by Wesley Jones in 1929 to increase penalties for violation of the Volstead Act and confided to his sons in early 1930 his willingness to accept further punitive measures.[98]

But as the mood of the country changed, Johnson shifted to meet it. In 1932 he joined a Senate minority in support of legislation to legalize the manufacture of beer and wine and strongly endorsed the demand for repeal in the Democratic party platform. The misplaced congressional priorities that placed prohibition ahead of relief as the focus of legislative concern earned his derision, as did those who called for a referendum to decide the issue of repeal. He supported the resolution sponsored by Senator John Blaine that effectively circumvented the dry forces entrenched in state legislatures

---

*The Republican party's prohibition plank, Johnson observed, was a perfect reflection of Hoover's mind—"timid, weak, vacillating, uncertain, ambiguous, indirect, deceitful, uncandid, and dishonest." HWJ to C. K. McClatchy, June 19, 1932.

by requiring ratification of the repeal amendment by state conventions. The measure passed both House and Senate. The nation might continue to suffer from depression, but the days of prohibition were numbered.[99]

★   ★   ★

It would have been difficult to find a more dramatic setting for the beginning of Roosevelt's presidency and the onset of the New Deal than that provided by the banking crisis of 1933. In the few weeks prior to the inauguration the banks of 38 states had halted operations as the nation's financial system tottered on the brink of insolvency. Johnson, attending a presidential inauguration for the first and only time, found Roosevelt's indictment of the money changers particularly apt. No Republican, Johnson observed, would have dared to express such a truth.[100] Of necessity, the banking situation was the first item on the agenda of the new Congress, which was hastily called into special session in mid-March. A participant even before the opening day, Johnson attended the March 5 meeting of Roosevelt and the Democratic party leadership in which the administration outlined its banking program. Late in the evening of March 8, he met again at the White House with Roosevelt; Secretary of the Treasury William Woodin; Ray Moley, of the brain trust; and the Democratic congressional leadership to review the still incomplete draft legislation to deal with the crisis. Caught up in the discussion, he found himself standing before the president, passionately exhorting him to exclude the existing financial establishment from the new banking system. If public confidence were to be restored, he argued, the Mitchells, the Morgans, and the Wall Street crowd should be kicked "into oblivion" and a Federal Reserve Board selected that would regulate bankers and not be regulated by them.[101]

The administration's bill that emerged, designed to reassure rather than remake the banking establishment, was far less than Johnson had hoped for, but he quickly joined the overwhelming Senate majority in support of the measure. The following Monday, upon learning that Federal Reserve officials in San Francisco had advised against the reopening of the Bank of America, Johnson and McAdoo hurried to the Treasury Building to confer with Secretary of the Treasury Woodin. The California enterprise, under the control of A. P.

Giannini, was the nation's largest banking chain, with 410 branches throughout the state. In their discussions with Woodin, Johnson set aside his own suspicions that the decision to shut down the corporation was political in nature, reflecting the distaste of the banking establishment and of California's Old Guard for Giannini, who had always been somewhat of a political and economic maverick, and instead stressed the economic repercussions that would follow if the bank remained closed. While acknowledging that Woodin had perhaps already made up his mind, Johnson was nevertheless pleased when the secretary, in the presence of the two men, signed the order for reopening.[102]

In the 100 days of the first session of the 73rd Congress, and in the second session that met from January through June of 1934, Johnson, with rare exceptions, lent his support to New Deal initiatives. Drawing from his own experience as governor, he had offered Roosevelt unsolicited advice at their first meeting: define a program, present it with a bang, stand by it, and push it through. Because no clear remedies existed, he observed, it would be necessary to experiment with "hundreds of millions of dollars, or perhaps billions, and if necessary waste it, in even *endeavoring* to find a solution for relief."[103] Eager to see the administration succeed, Johnson for once set aside his doubts, ignored what he found distasteful, and endorsed legislation that extended unprecedented powers to the executive. From the beginning of his legislative career, congressional subservience to executive leadership had provoked his strident dissent. But what he had condemned in the past he now accepted, necessitated as it was by the economic crisis and made palatable by his faith in the president. Roosevelt might occasionally blunder, he admitted, but he had the "guts" to act, and if he stumbled, he stumbled in the right directions. "We're nearer our philosophy of government than we have ever been in my lifetime," Johnson enthusiastically wrote.[104]

Often when he did dissent from the administration it was to object to the parsimony of New Deal initiatives rather than to their revolutionary character. Thus, although as the 100 days began Johnson supported the president's budget bill seeking to pare down government expenses, he soon found reasons to object: economies were being made at the expense of veterans and the disabled. The fault, he insisted, lay not with Roosevelt but rather with the Executive

Budget Office. Its director, Lou Douglas, "was born to the purple, loves the English and their ways, and has a heart of stone." His actions, Johnson concluded, were shameless, outrageous and cruel.[105] The following year Johnson stood with a majority to override the president's veto of the independent-offices bill, preferring, he wrote, to err on the side of liberality by providing an additional $6 million for the nation's disadvantaged.[106] Johnson ignored administration guidelines on other issues as well; notably, he endorsed the legislation sponsored by Senator Hugo Black to reduce unemployment by limiting the work week to 30 hours and opposed an administration substitute. He was, he declared, "prepared and ready, desirous and enthusiastic" in his support of Black's proposal. The 30-hour bill passed easily by a vote of 53 to 30.[107]

To derail a similar move in the House, the White House worked to construct an alternative to the Senate's Black bill. Out of this effort came the most far-reaching legislation of the 100-day session, the National Industrial Recovery Act. Title I of the act provided for the creation of the National Recovery Administration, which sought to end the ongoing economic slide by establishing a framework of economic controls in the form of codes of "fair competition" underwritten by the government. Title II authorized the development of the Public Works Administration, which, with an appropriation of more than $3 billion, would inject life into the stagnant economy. In the Senate, the NRA proposal incited one of the most heated debates of the session. Liberals argued that the proposed codes would enable big business to circumvent antitrust laws. Conservatives objected to the guarantees extended to workers, which, in addition to providing both wage and hour protection, endorsed the right of labor to organize. On the floor Johnson enlisted with a majority to prevent a weakening of labor's rights within the proposed industrial codes and sought to strengthen the provisions against monopolistic practices on the part of industry. When the conference committee eliminated the latter safeguards he voted with many of his liberal colleagues against final passage. The moved proved futile, and the bill squeaked by with six votes to spare.[108]

Despite serious reservations, Johnson supported the administration's farm program with its provisions for production controls, confessing to his sons that it was the "most bizarre thing that was ever suggested to a set of sentient beings." If it had not had Roosevelt's endorsement, he remarked, it would not have had "a corporal's guard" in its favor. His distrust of "bizarre financial adventures" notwithstanding, he supported the Thomas amendment to the Agricultural Adjustment Act giving to the White House discretionary authority to alter the value of the dollar. Doubtful that inflation would work and fearful that it could too easily get out of hand, he placed his faith in the President.[109] Predictably, he opposed the various additional measures sponsored by his Senate colleagues designed to inflate the currency and in fact voted against provisions of the administration's gold bill as a symbol of his belief that the government should not violate its pledges to redeem the dollar in gold.[110]

Roosevelt's endorsement of Muscle Shoals had Johnson's enthusiastic support. Having committed himself to the project during the campaign, the president now set to work with Norris to redevelop the Tennessee watershed. Johnson too pushed for further development of public power, seeking both to establish a separate NRA code for public power projects and to eliminate taxation of municipally owned power facilities. He successfully argued against Senate rejection of Norris's attempt to secure such immunity only to be defeated in the conference settlement.[111] His own amendment to enable the RFC to lend money to municipalities for the acquisition of power plants narrowly lost on the Senate floor.[112]

Johnson's campaign to restrict the jurisdiction of the courts in rate cases before state utility commissions was more successful. The power interests, he argued, delayed compliance with commission decisions on rates by exhausting state court remedies and then shifted their appeals to federal courts, where the action had to begin anew. Johnson proposed to limit jurisdiction on such cases to the state courts. If utilities lost on the state level, they would have no further appeal save to the U.S. Supreme Court. The bill was pushed through the Senate after a fierce fight, but was then held up in the House Judiciary Committee. Johnson helped pry it out, entreating his House colleagues to ignore legal arguments and concentrate their attack on the power trust. To his delight, with neither warning nor urging, Roosevelt volunteered his endorsement at a news conference.[113] With almost no opposition voiced on the floor the bill moved forward, and the measure was signed by the president.[114] This bill was one of two "Johnson Acts" passed during the second session of the 73rd Congress.

★   ★   ★

The second and far more significant Johnson Act evolved out of Johnson's investigation into the marketing of foreign securities initiated at the time of the Hoover moratorium. Three proposals emerged from that inquiry. The first required full disclosure of the content of foreign loans available to the investing public. The second and third, both far more controversial, were Johnson's call for a government commission to which holders of defaulted obligations might turn for redress, and his proposal to prohibit further private lending to foreign governments that defaulted on their obligations.[115] These measures, originally proposed in 1932, were reintroduced as the New Deal began. Provisions for full disclosure were quickly adopted as a part of the Securities Act of 1933. To provide protection for American holders of defaulted foreign bonds, Johnson campaigned for the creation of a Federal Corporation of Foreign Security Holders. The Senate accepted his measure as an amendment to the Securities Act, but the bill was held up in conference at the urgings of the State Department, which feared that the proposed government corporation would infringe upon its own prerogatives and needlessly entangle the government in private disputes that would be best settled through less formal means. Echoing the State Department's criticism, Roosevelt, despite Johnson's entreaties, refused to endorse the project. Ultimately Congress resolved the issue by giving the president the option of creating such a body—an option he would choose to ignore. Johnson, a member of the conference committee putting together the final version of the Securities Act of 1933, only reluctantly agreed to the compromise.[116]

The "Johnson Act," which was later characterized as a major facet of the nation's determination to isolate itself from Europe, was also a result of compromise between Johnson and the White House. Introduced in early 1932, as Hoover began his last year in office, the legislation prohibited the extension of private loans to governments that had defaulted on any of their obligations, whether owed to the government of the United States or to private American investors. The governments in question at the time were not those of Europe, which, despite their complaints, had continued to pay war debts, but those of much of Latin America that had defaulted on their obligations to private investors. Only if the European nations refused to resume payments following the termination of the Hoover moratorium would the law apply to them. Johnson believed they would refuse, but the legislation he proposed was not meant to single them out. His bill, broad in scope, covered both intergovernmental debts and government bonds held by private investors. In shaping the proposal he drew from the precedent that the Department of State had itself established in the mid-1920s in pressing European governments to negotiate the settlement of their war debts.

Johnson's bill assumed a new urgency in December 1932, when the moratorium ended and the defaults that Johnson had predicted began. Only Finland continued to meet its obligation in full. France refused payment altogether, while Britain and Italy repaid only token amounts. With his characteristic shrillness Johnson once again arraigned Old World perfidy, at one point clashing hotly with Borah, who argued that debt renegotiation could be used as a tool to promote European disarmament. It was time, Johnson insisted, for the nation to give up such illusions and act in its own interests. But his proposal remained locked in committee, and the session ended with no action taken.[117] As the New Deal began, Johnson reintroduced his bill, and it was quickly reported to the floor. But surprisingly, given his fears that Roosevelt might follow Hoover's lead by acquiescing in default or accepting token payments in lieu of the obligations due, he made no effort in 1933 to push his legislation to a vote.

Johnson's uncharacteristic restraint stemmed less from White House pressure than from his own reluctance to provoke international debate on the eve of the World Economic Conference, which was scheduled to meet in London in the summer of 1933 in an effort to promote currency stabilization. He had no wish either to embarrass Roosevelt or to be held personally responsible if the conference collapsed. But the delay, he made clear, was only temporary. Raymond Moley and William Bullitt had earlier met with Johnson, in mid-April 1933, to sound him out and to outline some sort of compromise acceptable to the White House. Roosevelt, they began, believed him to be one of the most knowledgeable people in the country on the problem of international debts. "The amenities having been thus established, and presumably the wild animal having been stroked into an affectionate purring," Johnson wrote, they then went on to suggest the possibility of a renegotiation of European war debts. In reply Johnson made clear that he would accept no deals and that he would oppose an extension of the moratorium, a renegotiation of war debts, or token payments in lieu of the obligations owed.[118] Nevertheless he held his bill in abeyance, and made no protest either in June or December of 1933, when Roosevelt accepted token payments from Britain and Italy.

With the opening of the second session of the 73rd Congress, in early January 1934, Johnson at last pressed for passage of his bill. Little more than a week later it was adopted in a nearly empty chamber without a roll-call vote. The administration, hopeful that Johnson could be persuaded to abandon or at least alter his proposal, successfully moved for reconsideration. Working closely with Assistant Secretary of State R. Walton Moore, Johnson reluctantly agreed to modifications that would restrict the scope of the legislation to debts owed to the federal government. The public, if they dared, might still invest in the bonds of Latin American governments that were already in default to private investors. In addition, Moore pushed hard for provisions that would allow nations to escape default altogether if, like Great Britain and Italy, they continued to make token payments on their war debts, but here Johnson drew the line and refused to make any concession. Thus modified to meet the administration's main objections, his bill was once again brought to the floor in early February. Once again it passed without either debate or a roll-call vote.[119]

Roosevelt had good reason to limit the scope of the Johnson Act to loans owed to the federal government. To include obligations owed by Latin American countries to private investors would not only threaten the Good Neighbor policy promoted by Secretary of State Cordell Hull but also entangle the government in an endless web of claims and counterclaims on the part of the various groups involved. Roosevelt's earlier refusal to endorse Johnson's proposal for a government Corporation of Foreign Security Holders had rested on similar reasoning. But once modified to exclude such provisions, the legislation could prove useful to the White House. For Johnson, the act settled past accounts. European states could either resume full payments on what they owed or repudiate their debts. Whichever option they chose, he reasoned, the United States would benefit. In contrast, Roosevelt, who was clearly willing to renegotiate war debts, almost certainly saw the Johnson Act as a useful prod to spur European governments toward some acceptable compromise. So far, the president complained, Britain had offered only $460 million as full settlement of its $8 billion debt. They talked such ridiculous sums, he added, "that no self-respecting Congress and, for that matter, no self-respecting President, could go on with the discussion."[120] Cooperating with Johnson even though working at cross-purposes, Roosevelt publicly distanced himself from the proposed legislation while clearing the way for its passage in the House. In his testimony in support of his bill before the House Committee on Foreign Affairs, Johnson was careful not to publicize Roosevelt's behind-the-scenes support. With almost no opposition, the bill swept to an easy victory and was signed by the president on April 13, 1934.[121]

In other battles as well Johnson drew the line in his compromises with the White House, and nowhere was that line more firmly held than in the 1934 fight over the administration's proposed Reciprocal Trade Agreement Act. His dissent from this measure was consistent with his record. He had opposed presidential discretion in the setting of tariff rates in the 1922 act and had argued forcefully against the flexibility provision included in the Hawley-Smoot tariff of 1930. The pending bill, far wider in scope than earlier measures, transferred the determination of tariff rates from Congress to the executive. That power, Johnson asserted, should be left to Congress; he would not entrust California's interests to others, certainly not to Secretary of State Cordell Hull or Secretary of Agriculture Henry Wallace. Hull, he argued, is a free trader, opposed to all tariffs, while Wallace's views are often incoherent, going through "such peculiar and rapid gyrations that I cannot follow them at times." Drawing from earlier tariff battles, he reminded Democrats of their own past opposition to executive encroachment and quoted the Democratic leadership against itself. But the administration prevailed. Johnson's proposal to exclude agricultural goods from the reach of the legislation failed, as did his amendment to allow Congress the right to reject individual trade agreements. In fact, none of the many attempts to weaken the act succeeded, and the bill passed easily by a vote of 57 to 33.[122]

*   *   *

With the New Deal came the initiation of public works under the auspices of the Public Works Administration, and much of Johnson's time was taken up in efforts to secure endorsement of California projects. Earlier, when Congress had adopted the Emergency Relief and Construction Act at the end of the Hoover administration, he had successfully attached amendments enabling the Reconstruction Finance Corporation to lend money to San Francisco's Bay Bridge and Golden Gate Bridge projects and to Southern California to aid in the construction of the California aqueduct bringing water from the Colorado.[123] With the coming of the PWA new sources of funding became available that Johnson sought to tap. Johnson's close relationship with Harold Ickes, director of the PWA as well as secretary of the interior, brought delegations throughout the state to Johnson's doorstep more avidly than they might otherwise have come to request his active intervention, and in time his friendship with Ickes became as much a burden as an asset.[124] While in California between sessions he found his telephone constantly ringing. To curb the inevitable scramble for government favors, he urged the various proponents of California projects to coordinate their efforts, but few seemed ready to subordinate their hopes to others. To Senator McNary he confessed that he contemplated an early return to Washington to escape their pleading.[125] Those who sought out his help, he discovered, held him responsible for the projects they proposed and blamed him if they were not funded.[126]

Harold Ickes further added to his discomfiture by insisting that Boulder Dam appropriations and RFC loans be counted in determining future PWA projects in California. To include past projects, Johnson objected, was unfair, and even accepting Ickes's accounting, the state's allotments had been "few and far between."[127] But Ickes held firm. Authorization for the development of the All-American Canal, a project included in the Boulder Dam bill but long delayed, was initiated not by Ickes but by Roosevelt. "We skated on pretty thin ice," Johnson commented to Phil Swing.[128] The president was instrumental as well in securing federal funding for California's Central Valley Project.[129] Meanwhile, much to Johnson's displeasure,

Ickes sought to expand programs in the eastern states, which had benefited proportionately less from government expenditures, and continued to deemphasize California.[130] In time, the friendship between the two would cool, their relationship marred by differences over public projects, by Johnson's intense desire to win, and by Ickes's refusal to let him win. Outwardly the two men remained cordial but their earlier intimacy no longer existed.*

As the New Deal evolved, Johnson continued on good terms with both the Republican and the Democratic party leadership. To his surprise his outspoken support of Roosevelt in 1932 had not lost him standing with his fellow Republicans. In early 1933, responding to rumors that he would be kicked out of the Republican party, he jocularly replied that it would be he who would do the kicking.[131] Senator David Reed did threaten to move in caucus to deny him committee posts in the lame-duck session that followed the election, but the threat quickly backfired, and Johnson's assignments were increased to include membership on the Naval Affairs Committee and, ironically enough, the Republican Legislative Steering Committee.[132] Most of the Republicans, Johnson wrote, were madder at Hoover than at him.[133]

In addition, Johnson's affection for Roosevelt remained strong, and he continued to marvel at the president's personality, his driving force, his penchant for hard work, his ability to relax, his informality, and his unfailing good humor. "Does he ever get mad?," Johnson once asked the president's wife.† Sailing with Roosevelt and a small party on the Chesapeake Bay one hot July day in 1935, he watched as the president clipped the stamps off of incoming mail to save for his collection. He seemed totally free of worry, without a care. As he hoisted himself from his wheelchair, Johnson was again struck by his determination: "As I looked at that great body of his, strong, vigorous, and powerful, and then at the helplessness of his

---

*Ickes, Johnson grumbled, "is as pigheaded as I am." HWJ to Hiram Johnson, Jr., Feb. 25, 1934. Minnie Johnson was first to evidence coldness, perhaps because Ickes's hesitancy in endorsing a proposal for a yacht harbor at Sausalito put together by her son angered her, perhaps because Ickes's wife, "aggressive, militant, of the grenadier type," Hiram observed, was off-putting. See HWJ to Hiram Johnson, Jr., Dec. 19, 31, 1933, Feb. 11, Mar. 3, 22, Apr. 23, Dec. 30, 1934, May 26, 1935, Jan. 21, 1936; *The Secret Diary of Harold L. Ickes* (New York, 1953), entries for Oct. 30, 1934, Aug. 10, Aug. 27, 1935, Feb. 21, 1936.

†HWJ to Hiram Johnson, Jr., Apr. 1, 1933. The answer was no.

extremities, and his inability to do what the rest of us could do, I realized more than I ever had before, something of a will power about him that very few human beings possess."[134]

Though aware of Roosevelt's manipulative skills, Johnson was not immune to them.* The president's kindness toward both him and his wife was often demonstrated—in his adoption of the epithet "the boss" in reference to Minnie; in his invitations to gather at Warm Springs; in the many dinners and receptions they attended; in Roosevelt's intercession to obtain acceptance of the All-American Canal and federal funding for the Central Valley Project; in the warmth of his consolation following the suicide of the Johnsons' younger son, Archibald; in the offer of a cabinet post and his inclusion of Johnson in early policy planning; and in the frankness of private conversations.[135] More so than at any time since Harding's death, Johnson had access to the president on an informal basis, and Roosevelt, with what seemed to be a shared commitment to progressive ideals, was a far more congenial host.

Johnson had no illusion that he was part of an "inner circle," but he could believe that his influence made a difference. Certainly, Roosevelt, with his blend of charm and cunning, of affection and calculation, sought to "use" Johnson; but the uses to which he was put were congenial to his own interests. Thus, during the first 100 days, Roosevelt attempted to persuade Johnson to accept an appointment as a delegate to the World Economic Conference scheduled for that summer.[136] Johnson found the proposal tempting, not because he was eager to attend the conference but because it provided the opportunity to take Minnie abroad. But a number of factors stood in the way of his acceptance. He had earlier voted against the appropriation for an American delegation, out of distrust of international conferences and in the belief that most negotiations led to American capitulation. In addition, he knew that if he attended he would quickly become an obstructionist, torn between his responsibility to the administration and his own beliefs. Finally, the offer contradicted his long-held and publicly stated principle that senators should not participate in the negotiations of treaties that they would

---

*"He has an extraordinary cunning," Johnson remarked of the president. "With his delightful smile, he looks you in the eye and proceeds rather deliberately about half way with what he has in his head, and awaits the expression from you as to whether he shall proceed further." HWJ to Hiram Johnson, Jr., Feb. 4, 1934.

then be asked to judge at the time of ratification. Unwilling to reject the offer outright, however, Johnson postponed his decision.

Roosevelt offered encouragement, emphasizing that the conference would deal not with foreign debts but with economic stabilization, and assured Johnson that he could be his own man, that he had in fact been chosen for his ability to say "no."[137] At home his wife urged him to accept; at one point she secretly telephoned Harold Ickes to request more time so that she might plead her case more fully.[138] But ultimately his doubts overrode his desires, and he declined. It would have been fun, he sighed. He owed Minnie a holiday, and this probably would be their last chance to go abroad. He might have enjoyed the pageantry of the proceedings, the formal attire, perhaps even the plug hat. But the trip would have cost much more than they could easily afford, and the study and preparations required for serious participation in the proceedings far exceeded what he was willing to undertake. As for the conference itself, he added, it might succeed or it might come to nothing. Indeed, when he met with Moley and Bullitt over dinner, he had the distinct impression that they wanted him on the delegation to sabotage the whole enterprise. Yet even if all went well, there was no guarantee that he would not find himself in a position of defending the conference results while bitterly opposing other initiatives of the president in foreign affairs. Perhaps, he concluded, he was just a "crank."[139]

★   ★   ★

Johnson had endorsed Roosevelt in the election of 1932 despite his recognition of the political fallout that would threaten his own reelection bid in 1934. Almost immediately, he had begun to take steps to circumvent the expected opposition. The danger, of course, lay in the persistent hostility of the state's Old Guard, but it was compounded by a revolution that was taking place in partisan registration in California. The state's Democratic party expanded explosively in the wake of the New Deal, reshaping the contours of California politics by tapping support from the very groups on which Johnson had traditionally depended. Thus Johnson had cause for concern about his chances in a Republican primary; yet he was unwilling to register as a Democrat. To solve the problem he plotted to alter California's election code by substituting an open primary for the direct primary system then in effect. An open primary, affording the voter the opportunity to select either party ballot on election day, would virtually guarantee his renomination. The effort to alter the code began in December and continued into the spring.[140] McAdoo, after some prompting, gave behind-the-scenes support, and the requisite legislation passed the state Assembly. But in the state Senate, Lieutenant Governor Frank Merriam cast the deciding vote to kill the measure, and attempts to secure reconsideration failed.[141] Whether the scheme could have worked remains unclear. Any change in California's election laws would have affected not only Johnson's political fortunes but those of countless others, and the legislation could have been held up by referendum by any group displeased by its consequences.

Having failed to alter the election code, Johnson's lieutenants talked of forming a new Progressive party, limited almost solely to his reelection. If he registered as a Progressive and won that party's nomination, he would be assured a place on the final ballot. Retaining his Republican label threatened those chances, for a candidate was required to win the nomination of the party in which he was registered in order to run in the general election. Thus as a registered Republican Johnson might cross-file in the Democratic contest and win there, yet lose in the Republican race and thereby forfeit his opportunity to appear before the voters in November. Hoping to defer any decision, Johnson cautiously probed his various options in the summer and fall of 1933. In addition he encouraged the formation of both nonpartisan "Johnson-for-Senator Clubs," to establish a roster he might draw upon when the time for a decision came, and of the third party, a paper organization that he hoped might be limited to 20,000 or so registrants.[142]

On January 26, 1934, speaking for the administration, Postmaster General Jim Farley put an end to the hopes of California Democrats that Johnson might register as a Democrat and thereby strengthen their party ticket by announcing that Johnson would doubtless win the Democratic nomination in any case and thus should not be opposed. The announcement, a "bolt from the blue," cleared the way for Johnson's nomination in the Democratic primary but did not end his dilemma, and he continued to lean toward the idea of re-registering in the third party.[143] A straw poll, hurriedly taken, indicated that he would obtain 60 percent of the vote of Northern California in the Republican primary but only 43 percent in the south. If these figures were accurate, he noted, he had no alternative but to change his registration.[144] Yet he hoped to delay the day, and he found reason to do so in the threat, dismissed by many of his supporters, that his enemies would not remain quiescent if he changed. Caution was required, he believed, for to move too openly in forming a Progressive party might encourage the Republican Old Guard to mount an all-out challenge by thrusting forward a strong candidate of their own.

Nonetheless, by the end of March Johnson had all but decided to register as a Progressive.[145] McClatchy encouraged him on. Johnson, he wrote, would have no more chance than "a cat in hell without claws" in the Republican primary.[146] But as the date for his filing drew near Johnson began to have second thoughts. His political allies, in cooperation with Paul Scharrenberg and California's labor leaders and aided financially by A. P. Giannini, had put together a Progressive party, but it was pitifully small. San Francisco had fewer than 400 registrants, and in many counties there were no more than 40 or 50.[147] With no announced candidates, the new party had little popular appeal. To compound the problem, Upton Sinclair's entry into the Democratic race for governor focused attention on that contest, further reducing the attraction of the new party. In addition, San Francisco's labor leadership, who were involved in putting together the third-party operation, suddenly found themselves embroiled in the city's 1934 waterfront strike.

With little more than a paper organization in hand and with many onetime participants now fighting other battles, the possibility loomed that Johnson might find himself a stranger in the very party he had created. He had to make his decision by June 23; California's voters could register until mid-July. It would require little effort for a small, organized group to capture the new party. They might, as Frank Doherty had warned much earlier, be "nit-wits," or they might, as others suggested, be recruited from the Old Guard in order to sabotage Johnson's ambitions.[148] To be defeated in the Progressive party, Johnson moaned, "would be a worse and more ridiculous ending than plugging along with the Republican party and ultimately meeting defeat in a hard-fought primary there."[149] Hurriedly returning to California to view events at firsthand, he declared himself a

"Roosevelt-Progressive-Republican," cross-filed in the Democratic, Progressive, and Commonwealth parties, and maintained his registration as a Republican.[150]

Ironically, after months of indecision and torment, Johnson found his opposition in the 1934 Republican race to be negligible. By early March his enemies had given up their efforts to defeat him. They had been unable to find a candidate of substance, and seemed unwilling to risk a major breach in the party.[151] Rowell, Richardson, and Shortridge had all been rumored as possible candidates but none would run.[152] In the Republican primary Johnson faced a single opponent; in the Democratic primary, two filed against him. All were political unknowns and none had organized backing.

Always suspicious, Johnson cautioned his lieutenants to stay alert in their communities, for he believed there must be some "deep, dark conspiracy" afoot.[153] Ultimately he concluded that any activity on his part would only galvanize his enemies into action, and he remained silent for most of the campaign.[154] He also refused to play any role in the gubernatorial race—which pitted Upton Sinclair, the Democratic nominee, against Frank Merriam, on the Republican ticket, and Raymond Haight, candidate of the Progressive and Commonwealth parties—ignoring Jim Farley's urgent request that he publicly endorse Haight. In August, almost by default, Johnson won the Republican nomination by a margin of more than two to one and the Democratic nomination by more than six to one. Since no one opposed him in the Progressive and Commonwealth parties, in which he had also cross-filed, he would face only the Socialist party nominee in the November general election.[155] In September Johnson broke his silence for the only time in the campaign—at a Labor Day rally in support of Roosevelt and the New Deal.[156] In November he swept to victory, winning more than 94 percent of the vote.

*   *   *

Johnson's relationship with the administration struck a sour note when he returned to Washington following his reelection. In part his attitude toward the president was clouded by the role Roosevelt had played in the U.S. senatorial reelection campaign of Bronson Cutting of New Mexico. Cutting, like Johnson, had broken with the Republican party in 1932 to campaign for Roosevelt; but while Roosevelt helped clear the way for Johnson's California victory in 1934, he promoted the candidacy of Cutting's opponent, Dennis Chavez, on the New Mexico Democratic ticket. The election results, tangled in controversy, were brought for resolution before the Senate, where Chavez and the Democratic leadership pressed their case to unseat Cutting. Eager to protect Cutting, Johnson secured a position on the Senate Elections Committee.[157] In an after-dinner conversation with Roosevelt at the White House in mid-December, Johnson's first meeting with the president following the election, he brought up the dispute and expressed his sympathies for the embattled incumbent. Roosevelt, in his reply, totally ignored Cutting's sacrifice in 1932, and remembered only that Cutting had been unnecessarily acid in his criticism of Roosevelt's veto of veterans' benefits. In the spring of 1935 on a return trip to Washington with additional affidavits in support of his cause, Cutting was killed when his plane crashed in dense fog, and when Dennis Chavez, appointed by the governor of New Mexico to fill out the term, took the seat, Johnson, Norris, La Follette, Nye, and Shipstead walked out of the chamber in protest.[158] From beginning to end, Johnson believed, the administration's behavior had been shoddy.

Roosevelt's decision to call for a vote on American adherence to the World Court furthered Johnson's rift with the administration. The issue had apparently died after member states refused to agree to the Fifth Resolution attached to the Senate acceptance of the court in 1926, but had resurfaced during the Hoover administration when Elihu Root conceived a new formula to safeguard American interests. No longer did the United States claim veto power to prevent the issuance of advisory opinions. Rather, it reserved the right to protest such contemplated action and to withdraw from the court if its protests went unheeded. Johnson had already shown his determined opposition by objecting to any formula that might break the stalemate and bring the United States into the court. Hoover, obviously reluctant to push the issue, allowed the matter to rest in the Senate Foreign Relations Committee, taking no action until late in his term. Finally, in May 1932, long after any realistic expectation for Senate action, the measure was favorably reported out of committee by a narrow margin. During the election, both parties endorsed American membership in the court with "adequate safeguards," but the issue continued to hang fire. In 1933 Roosevelt casually assured Johnson that no attempt would be made to push the court that year, but the following year, in March 1934, the issue was joined when Key Pittman, the chairman of the Senate Foreign Relations Committee, commenced hearings.[159]

In January 1935 the court became the first major order of business before the new 74th Congress. Roosevelt, at their first meeting following his return from California, assured Johnson of his indifference to the outcome, confiding that he acted only to fulfill the Democratic platform pledge. Disappointed, Johnson promised to fight and readied himself for the battle.[160] In early January the measure, including the Root formula further buttressed by additional reservations, was voted out of committee.[161] On the floor both Johnson and Borah worked behind the scenes to organize the opposition while launching out as well with their own broadside attacks. Much of Johnson's argument was a rehash of his earlier speeches. The court was a plaything of Europe, a pawn of international intrigue; it served no American interest that could not be better served through traditional channels of arbitration. Although largely impotent, the court might undermine the nation's immigration policies or call into question state land-use policies discriminating against Asians who lacked the opportunity for citizenship. Most importantly, it was a creature of the League of Nations. Accept the court, he argued, and you whet the appetite of those seeking American entry into the league. But if Johnson laced his arguments with the bromides he had voiced in the 1920s, he drew too from the very different world of the early 1930s to drive home his point. Europe "sits over a volcano," he charged; Japan had invaded Manchuria and raped China; Mussolini lunged toward Africa. The world was in turmoil, and the nation should take heed lest it be drawn into foreign conflict.[162]

From the beginning, Johnson recognized the futility of his protest. The *New York Times* initially counted only twelve against the court proposal, and a White House poll in early January estimated no more than fifteen or twenty in opposition.[163] The fight was a very difficult and lonely one, Johnson wrote.[164] On the floor, additional reservations to restrict further the conditions of American entry were uniformly defeated. So too was the single amendment sponsored by George Norris, which would have required two-thirds approval by the Senate before any matter could be submitted to the court for adjudication. Yet as the contest went on, opposition intensified. In a series of vitriolic attacks, the Hearst press roared its disapproval.

On the air, Father Charles Coughlin, the fiery radio priest, thundered his denunciations.[165] As the possibility of administration defeat began to loom, Roosevelt belatedly began to act. Proponents of the court criticized him at the time and thereafter for playing a far too passive role. Johnson damned his activity. Having been assured by Roosevelt of his indifference to the outcome and told by Pittman that the president would not participate in the battle, Johnson was outraged when Roosevelt publicly endorsed American membership on the very day he began his Senate presentation and incensed when the White House started to pressure Senate holdouts. Only his fear that an assault on the administration might backfire and cost him Democratic votes prevented him from attacking Roosevelt directly.[166]

As the contest wore to a close at the end of the month, the opponents, who had dominated the debate, awaited their defeat. Johnson counted 28 votes against the court measure—a substantial number, but not enough for victory. But almost immediately he collected the pledges of 5 more from a spokesman of disgruntled Republicans. At once eager to proceed, he waited on tenterhooks over the weekend and through Monday, fearful that the arrangement might fall apart. But on Tuesday, as the galleries cheered, the Senate turned down American adherence to the World Court by a vote of 52 to 36, 7 short of the two-thirds required. Johnson held another pledge in reserve to use if needed.[167] A disappointed Ickes, telephoning his congratulations, found him as "happy as a boy."[168] Even so, Johnson remained apprehensive, for rumors circulated that the administration planned to circumvent the Senate action by calling on Congress to provide for entry into the court by joint resolution. "The snake is merely scotched," he pessimistically wrote. But nothing came of the rumors and the issue of court membership was finally concluded. In a private lunch the following month, Roosevelt and Johnson agreed that their conflict had left no scars.[169] Doubtless both dissembled.

*   *   *

The contest for Cutting's seat and the battle over the World Court soured Johnson's relationship with the administration. Roosevelt's proposal for an emergency public-employment program costing almost $5 billion aroused additional concern. When the president had alerted him to the proposal at their initial meeting after his return to Washington, Johnson had been dumbfounded. At first blush, he wrote, the scheme seemed "as bizarre as anything Upton Sinclair had suggested."[170] Both the open-ended delegation of congressional purse strings to the executive and the enormousness of the appropriation distressed him. Although he accepted the need for additional relief, he joined with an overwhelming majority to reject La Follette's proposal to double the appropriation and in fact lent his support to an unsuccessful effort to halve the appropriation and limit the duration of the experiment to one year.[171]

Complicating the debate was Roosevelt's threat to return the bill to committee if he were not given the authority to pay less than prevailing wages to those employed in the proposed work-relief programs. Industries, Johnson protested, were not required to reduce the price of materials sold to the government; labor should not be required to make such a sacrifice. Conservatives hoping to defeat the legislation joined with liberals seeking to meet labor's objections to narrowly pass the McCarran amendment, which mandated prevailing wages. The Senate majority, Johnson conceded, included many on "the preferred financial list of Morgan and Company," but he voted with the majority nevertheless, ignoring Roosevelt's telephoned appeal to support the administration. Ultimately, with Johnson still opposed, the Senate compromised by giving the president discretionary control of relief wages while maintaining prevailing wages on major building projects.[172]

As the session continued into the spring Johnson privately voiced growing concern about the escalating costs of government initiatives and what seemed to be a lack of direction on the part of the administration. If he had a talent for rhyme, he observed, he would compose verse around such themes as "'Everybody is Nutty'; 'We are all on the way to the Bug House'; 'We are raising hell and we don't know What. We are going Far but we don't know Where.'" Totaling government outlays for current and proposed programs, he anxiously pointed to the $10 billion debt that at some point would have to be paid.[173] The restraints had broken down, he complained, as every interest scrambled for federal funds and special favors. Yet even as he complained, he himself scrambled. Ever alert to California's interests, he continued to push hard for reclamation and argued in support of greater benefits for the state's farmers, seeking to include flax seed and asparagus in the administration's farm program.

"I wish I could sing a song that I want to be a statesman, but I cannot sing it for I am destined to be a dirty little driven errand boy," he confessed.[174] Acknowledging that such tasks were a senator's duty, he found himself immersed in a host of issues about which he cared little. Roosevelt, he grumbled, offered no direction, no real leadership. The president was fundamentally right on the great issues, but seemed to have lost touch and was no longer altogether in control.[175]

In early June, as tempers frayed in the summer heat, Roosevelt began to take command, pushing for congressional passage of old-age assistance, new banking controls, regulation of public utilities, safeguards for labor, and a revised tax bill. The proposed legislation, perhaps the most far-reaching of any single congressional session, would dramatically redefine American society. Johnson readily endorsed the package. The president, he wrote, was "eternally right" in his insistence on the dismantling of public-utility pyramids. "Crookedness is as natural to exploit[ative] big business as sinuosities are to a snake," he noted as he enlisted with the slim majority that prevented the invalidation of the "death sentence" provision in the Senate's version of the Public Utility Holding Company Act.* The Wagner National Labor Relations Act, passed in the Senate even before Roosevelt's call, had Johnson's approval, as did the Social Security Act with its provisions for unemployment insurance and old-age assistance, and the Banking Act with its emphasis on centralized management and enhanced federal regulation. Johnson refused to support La Follette's attempt to define a far more steeply graduated income tax than the one endorsed by the White House, and stood with the majority in support of the administration proposal. The result, hardly the "soak-the-rich" package its critics charged, increased taxes on capital gains, on estates, and on incomes over $50,000. Approval of the tax bill and a much-compromised Public Utility Holding Company Act brought an end to what was increasingly a "sick, tired, and nasty tempered" Congress, and Johnson was more than happy to return to San Francisco.[176]

In contrast to the previous session, which was long, strenuous, and exhausting, the short session of the 74th Congress, which as-

---

*HWJ to Hiram Johnson, Jr., Aug. 1, 1935. "Of course," he continued, "all big business is not crooked, but the exceptions prove the rule, and whenever you delve into their hidden practices, it is like exhibiting maggots in turning over an apparently polished stone."

sembled at the beginning of the election year of 1936, was relatively inactive. Both Johnson and his wife, once again lunching with Roosevelt on their return from San Francisco, found the president worried about the upcoming national contest; he fretted in particular about the bias of the press and the war chest that the Republicans had amassed in anticipation of the campaign.[177] Johnson felt fairly confident that Roosevelt would win reelection, but conceded that the battle would be perhaps the most divisive he had ever witnessed. To his son he wrote of a "class war"—a war well within the confines of the political system, but a class war nevertheless, with the "lackeys of power and wealth on the one side, and just plain, ordinary Americans upon the other."[178] Assaults on the New Deal by Al Smith, John Raskob, and Hearst, he observed, did more to help than hurt Roosevelt. Indeed, he added, Roosevelt's own impetuosity was the only possible stumbling block to his success.[179]

Careful to mend his political fences in his annual message to Congress, Roosevelt launched a strident attack on the "entrenched greed" of his opponents but recommended no new initiatives and moved to cut government spending. Congress was called upon to recreate a farm program in the aftermath of the Supreme Court's invalidation of the AAA. Johnson, closely following its impact on California's agricultural interests, endorsed the legislation. In addition, he supported an unsuccessful effort to increase appropriations for the Interior Department and opposed the move to reduce the proportion of PWA funding of state and local projects. Yet even as he cultivated government largess for his constituents, he complained of the costs and applauded Roosevelt's veto of the soldiers' bonus bill. The Senate's subsequent override of that veto he characterized as "cowardly" given the nation's growing indebtedness.[180] Johnson labored as well, more actively in committee than on the floor, to restrain those who sought to develop neutrality legislation in a world increasingly more perilous.

★　★　★

On June 6, 1936, two weeks before the close of the 74th Congress, Johnson suffered a severe cerebral vascular stroke. Recovery was slow. After a month in bed, he began therapy at Washington's Naval Hospital. By August he dressed each day, but even a short walk left him fatigued, and his speech, while improved, remained halting.

His wife, herself partially incapacitated by a fall that required 25 stitches in her upper arm, worked with his office staff to hide his condition from the press and public. Fearful that word might get out, the two kept to the house save for an occasional automobile ride and short walks. "He has seen no one, and by *no one* I mean *no one*," Minnie wrote in mid-August.[181] Under doctor's orders, he lost 28 pounds by October. He looked haggard and worn; his clothes no longer fit him; his face was far thinner, and deeply lined. "He has become an old man," Ickes observed the next year at their first meeting following his stroke.[182] His voice lacked its earlier timbre; his old energy and fighting spirit had ebbed away. "I think I am a rotten old shell," Johnson groused in early September shortly after his seventieth birthday.[183] In October he suffered a setback with a serious infection of his lymphatic glands, flu, and a bout of colitis. Impatient and often depressed, he worried about his responsibilities to his law firm. The death of Charles McClatchy and the fatal illness of "Uncle" Matt Sullivan, one of his law partners, added to his burden. His doctors forbade him to participate in the 1936 political campaign, and he chafed under the restraint when solicitations for his participation in the contest poured in from the administration, from Roosevelt himself, and from Roosevelt's opponents. He was, he wrote to Jim Farley, "decidedly upon the inactive list" for the time being, but he held out the possibility of future participation.[184]

But as the campaign progressed, Johnson began to voice a growing mistrust of Roosevelt. Minnie, harboring no doubts at all, was convinced that the president could no longer be trusted. His participation in the World Court battle had angered her, and she felt certain that he would not hesitate to involve the United States in further adventures abroad. Thus persuaded, she was determined to cast her vote for Alf Landon, the Republican presidential candidate. Landon wasn't much, she admitted, but at least he wasn't Roosevelt.[185] Under siege at home, Johnson increasingly echoed his wife's criticisms. In March 1936 he had thought that a rematch of Roosevelt and Hoover would clearly define the issues. The differences between the two, he wrote, were the differences between himself and Harry Chandler. But by October he found much of Hoover's indictment of Roosevelt persuasive.[186] The "class war" that he had visualized at the beginning of the year had come, but it no longer seemed as alluring. Labor's growing militancy and Roosevelt's apparent endorsement of that militancy disquieted Johnson. There were "too damned many [Harry] Bridges, John L. Lewises, [David] Dubinskys, and [Max] Zaritskys . . . in this fight," he noted.[187] The president, he charged, decried the vastness of the war chest available to his opponents but had no scruple in buying the support of farmers and relief workers with an open checkbook.[188] Given a second four years, he might try to pull the United States into the League of Nations or its equivalent.[189] Despite his misgivings, however, Johnson voted for Roosevelt, albeit with little enthusiasm and considerable apprehension.*

Roosevelt's 1936 landslide victory added to Johnson's unease. In the aftermath of the 1934 off-term elections he had expressed concern over the growing tide of administration supporters in Congress who balked at subjecting executive proposals to close analysis. Such an attitude, he noted, was "an evil thing in a democracy."[190] In the wake of the 1936 election, those concerns swelled into alarm. Increasingly distrustful of the president's intentions and fearful of mounting budget deficits, he worried about the possibility of "all sorts of experiments . . . some of which will give us the cold shivers," and mourned that there would be none in Congress to stop the president and few even to protest. He hoped that Roosevelt could resist his love of the dramatic, the lure of the grandiose, that might lead him, as it had Wilson, to seek to become "arbiter of the world."[191] Slowly improving from his stroke, Johnson left Washington for Miami Beach with his wife in early December and missed the opening of the 75th Congress. They returned in early February to confront the fears they had come to share.[192]

*HWJ to Hiram Johnson, Jr., Oct. 24, 1936. Johnson had expressed misgivings with regard to the consequences of Roosevelt's reelection prior to his stroke but with far less intensity than during his period of confinement. See HWJ to Hiram Johnson, Jr., May 31, 1936. It is possible as well that a sense of his own diminishing capacities intensified Johnson's fears about the future.

Chapter VIII

In
Opposition

1937–1945

By no means fully recovered from his stroke, Hiram Johnson returned to the Capitol on February 5, 1937, one month after the beginning of the 75th Congress. That same day President Roosevelt inadvertently defined the central issue of the session by suddenly and without warning calling for a reorganization of the judiciary. Emphasizing an overcrowded docket and judicial inefficiency, he proposed legislation that would enable him to appoint 44 new judges to the lower bench and 6 additional justices to the Supreme Court. Johnson immediately dissented.

No less than Roosevelt, Johnson had protested against the political nature of the American court system and its power to thwart legislative initiatives. In 1911 he had championed the fight in California to subject judges to popular recall and in 1924 had viewed without qualm Robert La Follette's proposal to give Congress the power to override Supreme Court rulings. In the Senate he had voted against the court confirmations of William Howard Taft, Charles Evans Hughes, and John J. Parker. Like Roosevelt too, he had been distressed by the actions of the judiciary in overturning New Deal programs. The National Recovery Administration, he wrote following its invalidation in 1935, had done well under trying circumstances. It was odd, he continued, that a modern, progressive, sensible, presumably intelligent government rested on "the veto power of nine old men" and on an interpretation of the constitution's commerce clause that had not changed since the 1780s. And while not particularly sympathetic to the program of crop controls introduced and administered under the Agricultural Adjustment Act, he was nevertheless bewildered by Justice Owen J. Roberts's 1936 decision denying the constitutionality of that program. The whole system of judicial review, he concluded, had to be reexamined. Judicial self-restraint was an inadequate safeguard in a modern democracy.[1]

But for Johnson, Roosevelt's proposed solution was itself a far more serious threat to the nation's democratic institutions than the antiquated court system it aimed to repair. The president's actions confirmed his suspicions and focused them in sharp relief: Roosevelt sought not a more efficient court but a compliant one, subordinate not to Congress or to the principles of popular review but to the executive. His emphasis on judicial efficiency was "hypocritical pretense." The president's proposed actions, Johnson warned, would establish dangerous precedents for the future—when the country shifted directions, Roosevelt's successors could take similar action. But of far greater concern to Johnson were the uses to which Roosevelt would put the legislation. With huge party majorities in both houses of Congress and a subservient court, he would effectively exercise dictatorial control. Even if the president had no such ambitions, Johnson reasoned, the very pressures of the office, unchecked by court or Congress, would lead to that result.[2]

All but certain that Roosevelt harbored exactly such designs, Johnson found additional confirmation for his fears in the president's tepid response to the rash of sit-down strikes that erupted in industrial plants across the land in the winter and spring of 1937. Labor, Johnson wrote, had become "arrogant and cruel," indifferent to the law and to its own abuses in trespassing on the property of others.[3] A balance might have been struck between unions and management, he maintained, but Roosevelt had ignored that opportunity, and by condoning or at least tolerating the sit-down strikes led by John L. Lewis and his Congress of Industrial Organizations had further enhanced his power.

Looking to the future, Johnson predicted catastrophe. It would come in one of two forms. Militant unions might continue to grow and eventually forge an alliance with the president that would allow them jointly to dominate.[4] More frequently he wrote of a second possibility. Neither Roosevelt nor Lewis would be able to keep their ambitions in check. Ultimately they would clash, and the president would turn against both Lewis and the tide of labor militancy. By exploiting the very situation he had helped to shape, Roosevelt would win acclaim as a stabilizing force both from a frightened middle class and from the nation's business elite. The result, Johnson predicted, would be a fascist dictatorship. The lessons were there for all to read in the recent history of Europe—in Mussolini's march on Rome, in Hitler's rise to power.[5] For Johnson, the fate of the nation hung in the balance. Once an impediment to the democratic process, an independent court had become a bulwark against impending tyranny.

The battle over the court-reorganization bill began in February and was not concluded until July. Burton K. Wheeler, Montana's insurgent Democrat, led the opposition to the White House while the Republicans kept to the sidelines, seeking to defuse any effort to turn the contest into a partisan debate. Though eager to participate, Johnson was forced as much by reasons of health as by concerns over political strategy to remain on the periphery and concentrate what little energy he had in a brief, scathing attack on the sit-down strikes. He raised the issue in mid-March, upon learning that the Senate had yet to take a stand. Professing his sympathy for union labor and still insistent on his liberal credentials despite the first favorable reference to him in the *Los Angeles Times*, he urged congressional condemnation in what one reporter called the shortest speech of his career. The real issue, he argued, was not the right of labor to organize but the threat to public order and the erosion of the rule of law such strikes symbolized. "Down that road lurks a dictatorship."[6]

The impact of his stroke was clearly visible. Any sustained activity rapidly tired him. Words no longer came easily, and he often had to pause, groping for the right expression. He found it nearly impossible, he mourned, either to organize his thoughts or to follow the arguments of others. The cross-country tour of senators Black and La Follette sponsored by the Labor's Non-Partisan League in support of the court bill especially angered him, and he longed for the energy to follow them as he had followed Wilson in 1919. "A man could not die in a better cause," he affirmed.[7] Though frustrated by his own incapacity, he was pleased by the reaction to his few words condemning the sit-down strikes.[8]

In April, Senator James Byrnes of South Carolina furthered the attack on the sit-down strike by introducing an amendment to the pending Guffey coal bill to outlaw the use of such strikes in the coal industry. Later the proposal was modified to apply to all industry and brought before the Senate, where Johnson eagerly voiced his endorsement. The president, he charged, could have put an end to the situation with six words: "I will not tolerate sit-down strikes."[9] The White House successfully sidetracked Byrnes's initiative but only by promising that the matter could be brought up later in a separate resolution. That resolution, far less peremptory than the original, condemned the abuses of both labor and management. It passed easily. For Johnson it was a most inadequate substitute, so diluted, he complained, as to be without value. Indeed, by condemning as well management's abuse of labor, it opened itself to interpretation as condoning the actions of the strikers.[10]

Meanwhile the court-reorganization battle continued. The twelve-vote difference that Roosevelt had mobilized against Byrnes's proposal, Johnson predicted, would define his margin of victory in the larger contest as well. Though an improvement over his mid-February prediction of defeat by ten to one, the new forecast was nevertheless disheartening. The president, he glumly observed, could pick off the weak and undecided with projects and patronage. Yet Johnson found reason as well to hope. He was delighted when the annual reports of the attorney general and the solicitor general failed to sustain Roosevelt's charge of judicial delay, and overjoyed when Chief Justice Hughes, in a public letter to Wheeler, denied the charge of judicial inefficiency and shifted the burden to the White House by explaining that too many New Deal enactments had been ill-written and ill-argued in court.[11]

Critical of any action that might enable the president to obtain by indirection what he sought through more direct means, Johnson voted against the judicial retirement bill passed by Congress that allowed elderly judges to leave the bench with full pay. Only three others joined him in the gesture. At any other time, he conceded, he would have gladly supported the legislation, but the professions of its sponsors could not mask their true intent. He would, he added, feel contempt for any on the bench who retired before the court-reorganization battle was ended. For Johnson, almost all else was subordinate to that fight.[12] When Justice Willis Van Devanter, one of the Supreme Court's most conservative stalwarts, did in fact resign, Johnson was incensed; and when members of the court seemingly shifted ideological ground to affirm the constitutionality of the

Wagner National Labor Relations Act he was "nauseated."[13] The majority decision was the right one, he admitted, but they had made it for the wrong reasons. Johnson realized that the vacancy left by Van Devanter and the interpretative shift embraced by the court undercut congressional support for the president's bill; nevertheless he saw both events as demonstrating Roosevelt's ability to bludgeon his way to victory even without congressional assent.

By May the Senate Judiciary Committee had split ten to eight against the administration's court-reorganization proposal, and Democratic congressional leaders, never more than reluctant supporters at best, began to search for a compromise. Johnson once again revised his estimates, now hopeful that the original bill could be defeated on the Senate floor, if only by a bare majority. When the Democratic party leadership endorsed a substitute measure sponsored by senators Pat McCarran, Carl Hatch, and Marvel Logan that would enable the president to increase the size of the Supreme Court each year by one justice for each member over the age of 75, Johnson denounced the move. The difference between the original and the new bills, he charged, was the difference between grand and petty larceny. But in another sense the new measure was worse than the original bill, for it would enable the Senate to obscure the moral issues of the debate.[14] Worse still, the new proposal might snare just enough support to succeed. Roosevelt, he observed, was "doing his damndest" in its behalf. While in Atlantic City for a brief, not altogether successful respite to renew his strength, Johnson predicted a tough fight and the possibilities of a filibuster. The administration, he wrote, claimed 53 sure votes for the substitute, and it was doubtful if the president could be stopped.[15]

In July debate on the substitute began, led by majority leader Joe Robinson, to whom the president had promised a place on the Supreme Court. A week later Robinson was dead of a heart attack, and Democratic support for the substitute, which had been secured out of loyalty to Robinson, collapsed. Now facing all but certain defeat, Roosevelt tried to escape political embarrassment by calling off the vote. Congress, he could argue, had not rejected his leadership; it had merely postponed action. But Wheeler, who had led the opposition, seeking a demonstration of his victory, demanded that the bill be recommitted, shorn of any reference to an enlargement of the Supreme Court, and then returned to the floor. Having no real op-

tions, the administration gave way, but secured Wheeler's pledge
that the move for recommittal would be without a roll-call vote and
that no direct reference to the Supreme Court would be made on the
floor. Neither pledge was kept. From the Republican side Charles
McNary demanded the tally, and the bill was recommitted by a vote
of 70 to 20. Johnson broke the second pledge by raising the question
of the court. "Is the Supreme Court out of the way?" he persistently
asked. Told that it was, he concluded the Senate debate that had
begun six months earlier. "Glory be to God!" he exclaimed, his arms
raised in triumph and thanksgiving.[16]

To fill the vacancy left by Justice Van Devanter's resignation, Roosevelt looked to the Senate and chose Hugo Black. Deaf to appeals
for senatorial courtesy, Johnson dissented, blocking immediate confirmation and forcing consideration by the Judiciary Committee. He
owed a courtesy to the American people, he remarked. Black, he
privately growled, was a "witch-burner," totally unfit to be a judge,
let alone a justice of the high court.[17] In public too he questioned
the suitability of Black's temperament—albeit less caustically than
in private—but concentrated his focus on constitutional objections,
emphasizing the argument he had prepared when it appeared that
Robinson would be placed on the court. By voting for the retirement
bill, he insisted, Black had increased the emoluments of the office
and was thus ineligible. Only later, after his successful confirmation, did it come out that Black had been a member of the Ku Klux
Klan at the beginning of his political career. The revelation further
substantiated Johnson's judgment, but clearly it was Black's ties to
the White House and the active role he played in campaigning for
the court-packing plan that had shaped Johnson's reasoning.[18]

*   *   *

The battle over the court marked a turning point in the history of
the New Deal. The underlying divisions within the Democratic
party between rural and urban, conservative and liberal factions,
never far from the surface, began to rupture more rapidly, and the
domestic initiatives of the administration were blunted more frequently as a conservative Democratic leadership asserted itself in
opposition to the White House. The court-reorganization battle was
a turning point as well for Johnson, a parting of the ways with the
president.[19] Prior to 1937, Johnson had criticized the consequences

of New Deal programs, the mounting budget deficits, the permanence of projects once deemed experimental, but despite growing qualms, he had retained his faith in Roosevelt's intentions. If a break came, he once predicted, it would grow out of disagreement over the shaping of the nation's foreign policy. Eventually the two men did indeed find themselves bitterly at odds over the direction of American policy abroad, but it was the president's initiatives at home that precipitated their irreconcilable split.

With few exceptions, Johnson had supported almost all the domestic programs pushed by the administration in Roosevelt's first term. Without exception, he opposed each new initiative in the second. Writing in 1939, Harold Ickes commented that Johnson had moved much further to the right than he had ever been to the left.[20] But Ickes was wrong; fundamentally Johnson had not moved at all. He had not repudiated his progressive convictions, his sympathy for the nation's needy, his belief that government had a role to play in relieving human distress. What he repudiated was Roosevelt and a New Deal that, for all its professions of progressivism, seemed increasingly threatening to the very progressive values he had always embraced.

Three overlapping themes shaped Johnson's course in Roosevelt's second term: his distrust of the president's intentions, which some might argue bordered on paranoia; his belief that continued budget deficits could only lead to economic ruin; and his conviction that neither a sound economy nor a healthy society could be built within the framework of the New Deal. For Johnson, Roosevelt's unmasking had come with the introduction of the court-reorganization plan. The president's dogged persistence in pushing the scheme together with his tepid resistance to the sit-down strikes measured the character of the man. A political animal, Roosevelt built and destroyed political coalitions not to serve the nation's needs but to serve his own unquenchable ambitions. An opportunist, he would run with labor when it served his interests but might betray them for the same reasons. When the Senate thwarted him in the court-reorganization fight, he sought indirectly what he had been unable to achieve by a single stroke—unhampered control of the nation's destiny. Johnson never completely shared his own apocalyptic vision with the public, limiting his worst fears to his private correspondence, but he returned to that vision often, and premised many of his actions upon it.[21] Thus, while conceding the need to protect unorganized workers by establishing federal minimum wage and maximum hour standards, he voted against the Fair Labor Standards Act. Never again, he wrote, would he delegate power to the administration; never again would he risk "turning over the economic life of the country to the President for him to exercise at his own sweet will."[22]

Johnson was even more adamant in his opposition to Roosevelt's executive-reorganization bill, introduced in 1937 and debated on the floor in 1938. The measure, he asserted, was neither an economy bill nor an efficiency bill. It was a bill to delegate undefined power to the White House. It made no difference who the president was, he publicly argued. Giving to the White House the power to reorganize the executive branch was an emasculation of congressional rights. The need was to retrieve what had already been delegated, not to delegate more. No president, he insisted, should ask for such powers and no president should be given them. To acquiesce was to step toward dictatorship.*

But of course for Johnson it made a great deal of difference who the president was. He would have opposed similar legislation in any administration, he privately acknowledged, but would have accepted its passage with some equanimity. In itself, he conceded, the bill was not that important, but seen within a wider context it was a companion to the court-reorganization plan—yet another scheme to give unlimited powers to the executive.[23] Johnson endorsed any effort to restrict that power, but was discouraged by how few restraints the Senate seemed willing to impose. Changes had been made, but not nearly enough. Most depressing was the narrow rejection (39 to 43) of the Wheeler amendment requiring prior congressional assent to any specific reorganization proposed. The votes to ensure its passage were there, Johnson grumbled, but under intense White House pressure they had been lost. And the pressure continued. In what all recognized as a major test of Roosevelt's leg-

---

*HWJ to Hiram Johnson, Jr., May 7, 29, 1937; *Cong. Record*, 75th Cong., 3rd sess. (Mar. 16, 18, 22, 28, 1938), pp. 3461–65, 3644, 3817–18, 4196–97. Roosevelt, Johnson argued in the Senate, will "send for his Attorney General, who will distort a word here and twist a phrase there, and then write an opinion that will enable the President to accomplish the results he wants." Ibid., p. 4197. See also Richard Polenberg, *Reorganizing Roosevelt's Government, 1936–1939* (Cambridge, Mass., 1966).

islative skills, he prevailed upon the Senate to pass the executive-reorganization bill by a margin of seven votes.[24]

The battle did not end there, however. Celebrating his victory, Roosevelt publicly observed that the vote proved that the Senate could not be bought by organized telegrams based on misrepresentation. Johnson protested hotly to his colleagues and urged a response. When no one seemed willing to reply, he erupted in a stinging public rebuke of both Roosevelt and the Senate. Did the president mean that Congress could only be bought by projects and White House favors?, he asked.[25] Roosevelt's press comment, he added, revealed a personality "complex" that in itself justified Senate distrust. Others rose to respond, and a stormy debate followed.

In reply, Roosevelt publicly denied that he had any dictatorial ambitions. His statement, Johnson snorted, didn't mean a "damn thing." Indeed, the very phrasing of his denial, with its constant references to himself, belied the content. But for Johnson the prompting of a public discussion of Roosevelt's imperial ambitions and the president's apparent need to deny the charges were themselves salutary events.[26] Even more gratifying was the dramatic rejection by the House of the executive-reorganization bill. When the House leadership told Johnson that they had the votes for recommittal, he had at first doubted them. But the prediction proved accurate, and Johnson delighted in telling any colleague who would listen that he had been unable to sleep the evening following the House action—he had been too busy laughing.[27]

New Deal spending programs compounded Johnson's distrust of Roosevelt. Large, open-ended appropriations gave the administration the power to reach beyond Congress and shape a new political landscape of constituencies that owed their allegiance to the White House. In addition, control of the purse enabled the president to work within Congress by using promises of federal projects to generate support he might not otherwise have enjoyed. But Johnson's concern with mounting deficits predated his distrust of Roosevelt. He had always been wary of the economically unorthodox and had never seen large-scale federal outlays as anything more than a temporary expedient in response to the emergency of the early 1930s.

As the sense of crisis waned, his fears of government reliance on spending and his concerns with the consequences of budget deficits grew proportionally. Even as he supported New Deal programs and pushed for additional federal funding for California projects in the flush of the so-called "second 100 days" of 1935, he expressed his doubts, warning of the dangers of runaway inflation or the possibility of government repudiation of its debts if spending were not checked. In Roosevelt's second term he took his stand. There was a time, he warned the Senate, when half a million dollars was considered significant: "Now we pass, with a supercilious sneer, an appropriation of half a million dollars, and nobody thinks it is of sufficient consequence to occupy the time of the Senate for a quarter of a second."[28] Not only did he vote against the bulk of appropriations requested by the administration, he voted too against most of the appropriation bills tailor-made by the president's conservative Democratic foes. "I wish I could rid myself of the idea that everything that happens in the Senate has to receive my approval, and that every fight in the Senate is my fight," he wrote. But of course he could not. For Johnson the stakes were too high.*

In the fall of 1937 the "Hoover" depression gave way to the "Roosevelt" recession. An economy seemingly on the way to recovery once again began to collapse. Roosevelt initially hesitated to act, but in April 1938 proposed a multi-billion dollar program of public spending and work relief. Congress, facing an election year, readily complied. Johnson did not. The proposal, he wrote, was intended as much to divert attention from the executive-reorganization bill that had just failed in the House as to deal realistically with the nation's economic woes. While acknowledging those woes and the need for public relief—between ten and fifteen million Americans, he esti-

---

*HWJ to Hiram Johnson, Jr., Apr. 23, 1938. In the 75th Congress, Johnson voted to override Roosevelt's veto of the veterans bill (veto overridden 69 to 12) and his veto of an increase in appropriations for the Federal Land Bank (veto overridden 71 to 19). In both cases, Johnson let his opposition to Roosevelt take precedence over questions of economy. In opposing the administration's housing program sponsored by Senator Robert Wagner of New York, he supported amendments to limit spending and voted against final passage of the measure (bill passed 64 to 16). In addition, he voted against the rivers and harbors public works bill (bill passed 51 to 32) and against appropriation for the National Resources Committee (bill passed 59 to 18). In the 76th Congress Johnson voted against the $1.2 billion farm bill (passed 61 to 14), against an increase in appropriations for the Department of Commerce (bill passed 41 to 23), and against the program, crafted by Roosevelt's critics following his call for a $3.86 billion program of self-liquidating projects, for a $2.4 billion program focused primarily on rural projects (bill passed 52 to 28). The latter, the so-called "Lend-Spend" bill, died in the House.

mated, required such aid—Johnson brooded over the political dynamics that had shaped the bill. Ostensibly the plan aimed to prime the economic pump, but in fact it aimed to "prime the polls." In the end his sympathy for the needy gave way to his distrust of the president, and Johnson enlisted with a minority of ten in symbolic opposition to the administration's bill. He would have supported a more limited program providing direct relief to those in need, he wrote, but could not endorse the omnibus measure proposed.[29] The following year a far less compliant Congress cut $150 million from the $875 million budget request for Works Progress Administration relief funds and rejected by a single vote the motion by Senate majority leader Alben Barkley to restore the full amount. Johnson took pleasure in the outcome. In the course of his career he had rarely involved himself in backroom debate, but in this case he had actively interceded with some of his undecided colleagues to shore up their resolve, and now he boasted of his own role in determining the result. Absent from the floor at the time of the vote, he paired in support of the relief bill as it passed the Senate while continuing to oppose the bulk of appropriation measures that came before Congress.[30]

Johnson's antagonism to the White House stemmed not only from his ever more demonic image of Roosevelt and his mounting fears of the economic and political consequences of unrelieved budget deficits but also from his shattered faith in the ability of the New Deal to establish a foundation on which any sound economic recovery might rest. From the outset of the depression he had underscored the need to act while admitting that no one knew what to do. He was prepared, he had stated, to try "almost anything," and the New Deal, similarly inclined, had become his temporary home. But if Roosevelt's initial ardor to experiment had attracted Johnson's support, the experiments themselves had not succeeded in bringing recovery. New Deal economic gains appeared transitory from the perspective of 1938. By then the momentum of recovery had sputtered and then died, and those in command seemed no more able to understand the causes of the collapse than they had been at the beginning of their tenure. Roosevelt, Johnson commented, was drifting, uncertain of his economic policies, while others within the administration called out for contradictory remedies—some demanded an open assault on the power of big business; others argued vehemently for a restoration of government ties with the business community. The administration, Johnson observed, was awash in confusion, and the president's decision in early 1938 to resume spending amounted to a confession of failure. Large-scale spending might, as in the past, provide a temporary respite, but its inadequacy had already been demonstrated. Roosevelt had relied on spending for five years, and "finds himself just back where he commenced," Johnson concluded.[31]

Fundamentally, Johnson's early ties to the White House had been based on his trust in Roosevelt and his faith that the New Deal was a lineal descendant of progressivism. The president's manner, the warmth of his fireside chats, his very willingness to act, had seemed to demonstrate that kinship. If the bankers had not been cast from the nation's financial temples, they had at least been chastised, and the ranting of the economically privileged could be taken as further evidence of Roosevelt's progressive soundness. By moving to protect the poor, he had demonstrated his compassion. By endorsing the public-power campaign, which George Norris had begun in the 1920s, he had seemed to embrace the progressive ideal itself. Initially delighted by these signs, and assured by his faith in Roosevelt's integrity, Johnson had managed to set aside his doubts about the merits of specific New Deal programs.

Once that faith dissolved, however, Johnson opposed White House programs even when he accepted their merits, for without that faith, he found in Roosevelt and the New Deal only a grotesque caricature of his own progressive vision. Federal programs, Johnson charged, had distorted the nation's constitutional balance by shifting power from Congress to the White House. They had corrupted the political process by whetting Roosevelt's imperial ambitions while providing him the means to advance those ambitions. They had created an atmosphere in which both Congress and its constituencies reached out for gifts and favors, indifferent to the wider consequences of their actions. Finally they had spawned the social violence of the CIO. The caring government Johnson had always championed had given way to a manipulative government; the progressive society he had hoped to see flourish was rent by anger and social division. A free society, he concluded, was giving way to social regimentation.*

* The best single account of the relationship between progressives and the New Deal is Otis L. Graham, Jr., *An Encore for Reform: The Old Progressives and the New Deal* (New York, 1967). As Graham points out, Johnson was by no means alone in his growing disenchantment with Roosevelt and his view that the New Deal was

For Johnson, the outlines of that regimented society were nowhere better defined than in the administration's farm bill, introduced in 1937 and passed in 1938. In an effort to boost farm income, the White House once again endorsed a policy of scarcity, calling for permanent legislation that limited farm output by establishing acreage allotments and marketing controls. In 1933 Johnson had set aside his doubts and had supported the creation of the first Agricultural Adjustment Act. In 1938, in the fight over the second AAA, he rebelled. He was not opposed to farm relief, he avowed, and had a twenty-year record of support for measures to relieve rural distress, but he would not "take the farmers of this land by the scruff of the neck and tell them what they must do and how they shall do it."[32]

In the contest over the administration's 1938 farm bill, Johnson fought to retain price supports, but at the same time he strove to eliminate production controls, joining in an effort to amend the bill to include the concept of "cost of production," a scheme that drew its inspiration from the principle of McNary-Haugen. The amendment, introduced by William McAdoo, failed by a vote of 40 to 46. By far more decisive majorities, supporters of the White House turned back an attempt, led by McNary of Oregon, to limit the duration of the measure to two years. Once again, Johnson found himself in the minority. Yet despite his opposition to the measure and his support for these efforts to weaken it, Johnson remained alert to the demands of California farm interests to be included in the new farm program, and worked diligently to satisfy their hopes even as he prepared to vote against the final bill. Defeat of the measure, he believed, would ultimately serve those interests far better than any short-term gains they might derive from its passage. The legislation,

---

a betrayal of progressivism, not its fulfillment. My opposition to Roosevelt's more recent policies, Johnson wrote, does "not mean that I want to see back in power the old masters whom we drove out of California, and Roosevelt drove out of here in the early part of his career. I don't think thoughtful men trust Roosevelt now, and I mean men just like myself, who were in sympathy originally with what he was trying to do, but who have reached the conclusion, first, that he did not know how to do it, and secondly, that he would take whatever means he could, however disgraceful and dishonorable to gain his ends. His ends even when good were marred by this sort of procedure, and when his ends sought were bad, as frequently they were, he endeavored to attain them by downright bribery, and the most corrupt practices politically." HWJ to Hiram Johnson, Jr., July 4, 1940. See also Ronald A. Mulder, *The Insurgent Progressives in the United States Senate and the New Deal, 1933–1939* (New York, 1979), and Ronald L. Feinman, *Twilight of Progressivism: The Western Republican Senators and the New Deal* (Baltimore, 1981); HWJ to Frank Snook, June 7, 1937.

he warned, was the first step toward regimentation not only of America's farmers but of the whole social order. It was, he wrote to his son, a "wicked bill" that would in time generate resentment and rebellion from the very groups it succored. It passed by a vote of 56 to 31.[33]

★   ★   ★

By 1938 Johnson was no more certain in his own mind of the remedies for the economic depression than he had been in 1930 or 1932. He was only certain that Roosevelt and the New Deal had failed. The visible erosion of Democratic congressional support for the White House pleased him, and he hoped that the 1938 midterm elections might further undercut the president's power. In an effort to recoup past losses, Roosevelt seized the initiative, interceding in select Democratic primaries to defeat his conservative detractors. The so-called "purge" of 1938 had begun. Four years earlier Johnson had been pleased by Roosevelt's involvement in his own reelection bid and in that of other Republican supporters of the administration, angry only that the president had refused to endorse Bronson Cutting. In 1938 Johnson's priorities changed. The president's most recent involvement in elections, he wrote to Harry Byrd, one of Roosevelt's prominent Democratic critics, constitutes "compelling proof that he has reached such a despotic and unreasonable state of mind that he will tolerate no man who disagrees with him at all."[34] Johnson closely followed the primary election returns, and rejoiced as the president's purge proved abortive.[35] The results of the November general election, which for the first time since the onset of the depression reduced Democratic majorities and enhanced conservative ranks, pleased him even more.

Only the California returns were disheartening. McAdoo, up for reelection, had earlier requested Johnson's endorsement, only to be rebuffed. From the beginning their relationship had been chilled by differences over patronage and power, and the rift had deepened as Johnson's distrust of Roosevelt mounted.[36] McAdoo, Harold Ickes observed, although often independent of the White House, generally lined up with the administration. Johnson, from his very different perspective, agreed, and on that basis refused support. McAdoo, he wrote, had become a "groveling, crawling, lousy stooge."[37] Hoping for McAdoo's defeat in the general election, Johnson was overjoyed when he lost in the Democratic party primary.

At first, Johnson interpreted the primary election results to reflect his hopes: McAdoo's defeat, he believed, was a popular repudiation of the White House. McAdoo had, in Johnson's words, fastened on Roosevelt "like a leech" during the campaign, and had won the president's endorsement, only to be rejected by the voters. But in fact, as Johnson quickly realized, the election was a repudiation of McAdoo's moderation and of his refusal to endorse the pending "Ham & Eggs" proposition, a somewhat bizarre pension scheme to be voted on in November.[38] The state's Democrats had moved away from the political center rather than toward it by nominating Sheridan Downey, an eloquent champion of Upton Sinclair, Francis Townsend, and "Ham & Eggs." Downey, Johnson wrote, had a reputation as a man of few principles and many "isms." Yet if the Democratic candidate spoke for the left, Philip Bancroft, the Republican electorate's surprise choice in 1938, spoke for the political right. He was a member of the executive committee of the ultra-conservative Associated Farmers of California and a rabid opponent of organized labor.[39]

Although Johnson held aloof during the primary fight, he endorsed Bancroft in the general election. He did not share Bancroft's attitude toward labor, he claimed, but he had to admire him for not pulling any punches.[40] Certainly Bancroft would not be swayed by Roosevelt's charm. Johnson played at best a secondary role in the race, but he did ask John Townsend, chairman of the National Republican Senatorial Committee, to contribute additional funds to the California campaign; solicit, albeit unsuccessfully, an endorsement for Bancroft from the *Sacramento Bee*; and deliver a radio address in his support. But just as "Ham & Eggs" helped beat McAdoo, so too it contributed to Bancroft's defeat at the hands of Downey. Another stumbling block was the massive increase in party registration and voting that enabled the state's Democratic party to make substantial gains in the November elections. For Johnson this Democratic surge was a disappointment, contrasting sharply with the national trends on which he built his hopes.[41]

*   *   *

On his return to Washington for the opening of the 76th Congress, in January 1939, Johnson found himself caught up in a series of fights. He opposed the nomination of Harry Hopkins as secretary of commerce and took the opportunity to flay him in the Commerce

Committee hearings for his participation in Roosevelt's abortive purge of conservative Democrats.[42] Senators La Follette and Elbert Thomas, both of the Civil Liberties Committee, came in for a sharp rebuke for employing what Johnson regarded as intimidating tactics in their investigation of corporate efforts to cripple organized labor. Their request that the committee's appropriation be doubled in anticipation of hearings soon to begin in California received his heated opposition. The question, Johnson argued, was not whether corporate wrongdoing should be probed but whether the investigation should be conducted fairly and objectively.* In addition, he opposed a much modified executive-reorganization bill, which, to his displeasure, passed in Congress, and he continued to vote against most major appropriations bills with the exception of those for defense. But it was defense, or more precisely the nation's posture in response to growing instability abroad, that began to overshadow all else both for Johnson and for the nation.

With the exception of the fight over the World Court, foreign policy issues had played a marginal role in Roosevelt's first term, and Johnson's relationship with the administration had been relatively tranquil, more so perhaps than he had initially expected. When, in early 1933, Prime Minister Ramsay MacDonald of Great Britain and ex-premier Edouard Herriot of France met with Roosevelt to discuss the tangled web of international debts, disarmament, and economic stabilization, Johnson had sniffed suspiciously, fearful of some broad new commitment on the part of the United States. But his fears, if not unfounded, had not been realized. The president had accepted his solution to the war-debt problem and facilitated the passage of the amended Johnson Act through Congress.

---

* *Cong. Record*, 76th Cong., 1st sess. (Aug. 4, 1939), pp. 11043–51. "If there is any man on earth . . . who is not observing the law, who does things which are not proper and fit to be done, then investigate him to the full; but, for God's sake, give him a square deal. . . . If he is wrong, find it out and punish him. If he is right, for the love of God acquit him and say that he is right." See also HWJ to Hiram Johnson, Jr., Aug. 5, 1939; Philip Bancroft to HWJ, Aug. 24, 1939; HWJ to Doherty, Nov. 9, 11, 21, 22, 23, 1939, Jan. 6, 1940. In fact, Johnson found himself in a position similar to that which Roosevelt confronted in dealing with the sit-down strikes; neither the committee nor its opponents merited support or encouragement. Certainly Johnson was not about to become the defender of the Associated Farmers of California or other corporate groups bent on labor exploitation. "To hell with them all," he wrote in exasperation. HWJ to Doherty, Nov. 23, 1939. Johnson was absent when the final appropriation for the committee was approved.

And a second, far more significant issue had been at least temporarily defused when Roosevelt dropped administration plans to push for a discriminatory arms embargo against nations at war.

The proposal, growing out of the Kellogg-Briand Pact, had been seen by some as a way to give teeth to that pact. If international aggression was outlawed, aggressors should be denied access to arms.[43] It was an appeal that acquired greater urgency as the futility of the pact was demonstrated. In the Pacific, Japan moved onto the mainland of Asia in the early 1930s, carving out a new empire in Manchuria. In Europe too, the old order visibly began to crack. Globally, the signs of international discord multiplied. At Geneva in 1933, delegates to the international disarmament conference, caught between the fears of France and the ambitions of Hitler's Germany, stumbled toward failure. Seeking to break that deadlock, Roosevelt, in May, authorized Norman Davis, the head of the American delegation, to propose that the United States would make no effort to interfere with collective sanctions imposed on an aggressor if an adequate program of disarmament could be achieved. In short, Roosevelt agreed that the United States would cooperate with the League of Nations as an associate; it would retain the right to make its own independent judgment but alter its traditional definition of neutral rights.

In the House, agreement to a discriminatory arms embargo had already been secured, and hearings had begun in the Senate Foreign Relations Committee. Apprehensive, certain that the bill would be favorably reported, Johnson determined to fight it on the floor. But Johnson was wrong, for even before Davis delivered his bombshell message at Geneva on May 22, a majority of committee members had already begun to express concern that the United States would be drawn into conflict abroad if the president were given the power to designate aggressors. Certainly Davis's Geneva proposal, linking the pending legislation to cooperation with the league, hardened Johnson's resolve. This was, he wrote, the most momentous issue America had faced since the league controversy of 1919.[44] Two days after the Davis announcement, Johnson offered an amendment to eliminate the discriminatory features of the proposed arms embargo, arguing forcefully and successfully for its adoption. When chairman Key Pittman told Roosevelt that the resolution could not be passed without the modifications Johnson had pushed in com-

mittee, the president promptly capitulated, and the amended resolution was reported favorably by a unanimous vote. To Johnson a
dissimulating Roosevelt privately confided that Davis had exceeded
his instructions. And there the matter ended, for Johnson stifled his
urge to denounce Davis publicly and Roosevelt, unwilling to push
for the emasculated proposal, allowed the bill to die on the Senate
floor.[45]

But as international tensions escalated, the issue of American
neutrality was rekindled, not by the administration but by a growing
popular demand that the United States find some way to insulate
itself from world disorder. Throughout 1934 peace movements rallied to the cause, anxious for the nation to avoid the pitfalls that had
dragged it into war in 1917. In the Senate, the Nye Committee was
formed to investigate the role of international arms dealers in provoking conflict, an investigation that broadened to include an examination of the role of American bankers in shaping Wilsonian diplomacy prior to American intervention. Increasingly vocal, Nye
often moved beyond the available evidence to define the lessons of
World War I. Arguing that traditional neutral rights had been out-
moded by modern technology, he sponsored legislation in April
1935 to prohibit American sale of contraband goods to belligerents
and to forbid American travel on belligerent vessels. Other resolutions, similar in intent, followed.[46] The White House, unable to stop
the gathering momentum, sought to shape it to its own designs,
again calling for presidential discretion to discriminate against aggressors in the application of the act. The administration's goals,
international law specialist John Bassett Moore correctly observed,
were the very reverse of Nye's—the president wished not to isolate
the United States from international disorder but to project the
United States into controversies abroad.[47]

No more willing in 1935 to delegate power to the president than
they had been two years before, the Senate Foreign Relations Committee ignored White House solicitations and insisted that the legislation be uniformly applied to all belligerents. But for Johnson the
victory was only partial. Adamantly opposed to any delegation of
power to the president, he was only slightly less opposed to any
compromise of American neutral rights. If Nye argued that the
events preceding American entry into World War I illustrated the
need to abandon or modify rights no longer defensible, Johnson ar-

gued that those rights could be sustained if the nation made clear its determination to do so. He still believed, as he had in 1917, that the government had an obligation to protect its citizens in the pursuit of their legitimate activity abroad and remained willing to accept war itself as a last resort in defense of those principles.[48]

Throughout the 1920s Johnson had repeatedly underscored both the importance of global markets in sustaining prosperity at home and the need for a strong naval presence to ensure that American rights were respected. The world might be more perilous in the 1930s, but little had changed with regard to American rights or the nation's economic requirements. Certainly foreign markets were no less important in a period of depression. The whole thrust of Nye's efforts ran counter to Johnson's perception of America's role in the world. Acceptance of the legislation, he privately observed, would "denature us as a nation."[49]

With the Senate committee's refusal to invest the president with discretionary authority, Johnson hoped that the pending legislation, as in 1933, would be dropped. But neither he nor Roosevelt could withstand the growing popular clamor for action. Abroad, Mussolini readied his forces to invade Ethiopia, and fears mounted that the world would once again be thrust into war. On April 6, the eighteenth anniversary of American entrance into World War I, 50,000 veterans paraded in Washington in a march for peace. A week later, university students across the land undertook a one-hour "strike for peace."

Unable to delay Senate action in support of Nye's proposal to redefine the nation's neutral rights, Johnson sought instead to restrict the materials that the bill would make subject to embargo; specifically, he proposed to substitute the phrase "arms, ammunition and implements of war" for the detailed list of contraband goods that Nye had originally included. The move succeeded, but Johnson, still dissatisfied, continued to call for restraint. The whole matter, he complained, was being rushed through without any real time for discussion.[50] But the momentum could not be stayed. On the floor proponents of Nye's revised neutrality act promised more than discussion, threatening a filibuster if the measure were further delayed. Bowing to popular pressure but recognizing too that the proposed legislation worked to the disadvantage of Italy in its pending war with Ethiopia, Roosevelt acquiesced, asking only that the provisions of the resolution be limited to six months. Eager to adjourn, pressed by an increasingly more articulate public for action, unopposed by the White House, Congress quickly responded with a nearly unanimous assent.[51]

In his own remarks prior to the Senate vote on the Neutrality Act of 1935, Johnson set out his objections. Congress, he charged, was acting out of haste and fear, seeking to anticipate events rather than realistically respond to them. The act outlined a policy whose logic led to the total abandonment of the nation's traditional rights as a neutral. Denial of arms to warring nations did not guarantee a peaceful world; it merely added to the advantage of those bent on aggression by denying weapons to their victims. Nor did it guarantee that the United States could avoid international strife. Those who believed the contrary were "doomed to disillusionment, disappointment, humiliation and regret." But despite his reservations and his hope to see American rights endure unabridged, Johnson voted with the majority in support of the measure. He accepted it, he explained, not for the prohibitions it defined but for its underlying intent to ensure nonentanglement in the affairs of nations abroad. Passage, he observed, marked the "triumph of the so-called isolationists." Whatever its limitations, the resolution constituted a "declaration of American policy, of keeping out of Europe and European controversies, Europe's wars, and remaining just American."[52] Indeed, in light of the rejection earlier that year of American membership in the World Court, Johnson was right.

Congress had to face the issue of neutrality once again when it reassembled in early 1936. Hoping for quick passage of permanent legislation, the administration prepared a bill conceding the impartial embargo of arms and ammunition. The aggressor theory, Assistant Secretary of State R. Walton Moore assured Johnson in his testimony before the Senate Foreign Relations Committee, had been interred.[53] But in fact this bill did not eliminate presidential discretion but only altered it. In response to the outbreak of war the president was required to embargo arms and implements of war to all belligerents. At the same time, however, he could at his discretion restrict trade in other commodities to their prewar levels. The bill's label of neutrality, John Bassett Moore commented, "was a swindle of a low order."[54] In effect, the proposal sought to underwrite the informal program of sanctions the administration had already unsuccessfully attempted under the guise of a "moral embargo" at the time of Mussolini's invasion of Ethiopia.

Johnson had been uncharacteristically silent when the moral embargo was announced between sessions, but he was determined to defeat the president's new bill. Hearings began in mid-January, and Johnson insisted that the testimony in the executive sessions of the Senate Foreign Relations Committee be transcribed so that a record could be retained for posterity. The transcription was also retained for John Bassett Moore of Columbia University and Edwin Borchard of Yale, experts in international law who shared Johnson's vision of American rights untrammeled.[55] Secretary of State Hull testified first. Under badgering by Johnson, he proved a poor witness as he argued that the administration's goal was to remain impartial in the event of war and that the moral embargo against Italy demonstrated that impartiality. The administration's proposal, Johnson wrote, contained a great deal of "hypocrisy and a tremendous amount of hocus-pocus."[56]

Contributing to the clamor in the committee hearings was the introduction of a substitute bill sponsored by Nye and Bennett Clark in the Senate and Maury Maverick in the House that denied presidential discretion in the application of the law while further circumscribing American trade in times of war. This measure too Johnson opposed, having already insisted on the unencumbered retention of the nation's commercial rights.[57] With the multiple divisions in the Foreign Relations Committee between administration adherents, partisans of the Nye-Clark proposal, and supporters of Johnson, arguments grew heated, and as the deadlines set by the expiration of the 1935 act drew near it became clear that any major initiative would provoke extended debate. Few on the committee, indeed few in Congress, endorsed Johnson's demand to retain traditional maritime rights, and Borah, who came the closest to Johnson's view, was a less than dependable ally, impulsive and often contradictory in his remarks. It was a lonely position, Johnson acknowledged, but he would make his fight not only in committee but if necessary on the Senate floor.[58] There he would not be alone, for even if only a handful supported his prescription, a majority might be mobilized to oppose the discretionary powers desired by the president.

Aware of the political realities and anxious to end an increasingly fractious and potentially unmanageable situation, the administration gave way, and endorsed a substitute proposal sponsored by Senator Elbert Thomas to modify the existing program of neutrality by including a ban on loans to all belligerents. For Johnson it was a satisfactory settlement, but Nye and those who favored additional measures to guarantee American insularity persisted in their demands.[59] On the floor they moved to limit the duration of the proposed resolution to three months, thus threatening another round of debates at the close of the session. The Senate soundly defeated their effort, and rejected as well their attempts to amend the existing resolution to include trade quotas that would further impair the nation's traditional commitment to freedom of the seas.

Johnson was delighted by the outcome, but remained apprehensive. The final battle, he warned, had only been postponed. Pacifist groups were developing into a "militant and aggressive army" both in Congress and throughout the country, while internationalists continued to "skulk," seeking some way to shape the popular mood to their advantage.[60] But there was time as well to relish the victory of the moment. Most journalists singled out Johnson and his threat of an active filibuster as the decisive factor in the defeat of the administration's original bill. The consensus, he remarked, "was that my wickedness prevailed."[61] The tribute, though surely an oversimplification, nevertheless pleased him.

★   ★   ★

The various efforts on the part of the administration in 1933, 1935, and 1936 to invest the president with discretionary power in the application of American neutrality legislation had distressed Johnson but had not precipitated a break in his relationship with Roosevelt. For Johnson, the villains resided at the State Department, not at the White House. Hull, Norman Davis, Newton Baker, the old League of Nations crowd, endeavored to shape the president to their will. During Roosevelt's first term, Johnson had become convinced that the president was fundamentally sound on domestic issues; he had also tried to persuade himself that the president was equally sound in matters of foreign policy. It was true that Roosevelt could be impulsive—his actions abroad were much like his actions at home, "swiftly without warning taken, and in some respects in defiance of his previous utterances," he had written in 1933—but even after the 1935 contest over the World Court, Johnson believed that Roosevelt had met the test. In time he might break under the pressure of the internationalists, might find himself unable to resist the dreams of a Caesar, a Napoleon, or a Wilson to remake the world, but that time had not yet come.[62]

As international tensions multiplied and as his irritation with the New Deal grew, Johnson's faith in Roosevelt waned. Still, he could rejoice when the president, at San Diego the day before Mussolini's invasion of Ethiopia, defined American policy as free from European entanglements. Only in 1936, following the announcement of the moral embargo and the fight over the Neutrality Act to underwrite that embargo, did his doubts begin to pull even with his hopes; perhaps Roosevelt was "hamstrung" by the administration's unwillingness to repudiate Norman Davis's Geneva declaration formally; perhaps he had at last given way to the suasions of the internationalists.[63]

When in 1937 Congress returned once again to the issue of neutrality, Johnson had already broken with Roosevelt. But the so-called cash-and-carry act, hammered out while the battle over the Supreme Court raged, was not an administration bill. The president had stayed in the background, seeking to salvage what he could but leaving the initiative to Congress. There, the cry for the United States to eliminate any possibility of being inadvertently drawn into war because of its ongoing trade with belligerents was almost deafening. Adopting many of the features Nye and Clark had earlier championed, Key Pittman, chairman of the Foreign Relations Committee, sponsored a package in which the ban on arms, loans, and travel was retained and the perils of trade in other commodities were eliminated by the cash-and-carry formula popularized by Bernard Baruch. By that device title to goods would be transferred to belligerents prior to shipment and such trade denied to American vessels. For Johnson, who insisted on the preservation of the nation's traditional neutral rights, the proposal was a cowardly surrender. In addition, the legislation was complicated by concessions to the president. In the Senate version of the bill, the determination to implement the "carry" portion of the act was left to the executive, who retained an option in selecting materials to be excluded from American vessels.

As eager to deny presidential discretion as he was to defend traditional rights, Johnson found himself in a two-front war, and in the aftermath of his stroke ill-prepared to undertake either. In the Senate

Foreign Relations Committee, hearings were brief. With Johnson as the sole dissenter, the bill was favorably reported in mid-February.[64] On March 3 Johnson voiced his protest from the floor. He scorned the "peace at any price people" willing to "take the profits and then hug ourselves because somebody else has to take the risk," and denounced the discretion afforded the executive. Both the policy itself and the procedures for flexibility in its application, he argued, had the potential for incalculable harm. Any departure from an impartial stance would generate resentment on the part of nations disadvantaged and would enhance rather than decrease the possibilities that the United States would find itself, inadvertently or intentionally, drawn into international conflicts. But even if the law were applied evenhandedly, he reasoned, it did little more than strengthen the authority of those nations who controlled the seas. By forsaking traditional neutral rights the United States in effect allied itself with Japan in the Pacific and Great Britain in the Atlantic. The arrangement comported neither with neutrality nor with the best interests of the United States. Recognizing the unpopularity, both in Congress and throughout the land, of a return to the defense of traditional neutral rights, Johnson pleaded for an extension of the 1936 legislation.[65]

By his own admission, Johnson's speech, just over an hour in length, was poorly delivered. It was his first major effort on the floor since his stroke the previous June. He found himself unable to concentrate and occasionally confused in the interchange with his colleagues, and his pulse raced past 100. At times he managed to display a flash of his famous oratory, the *New York Times* reported, but as Johnson privately lamented, he lacked his earlier fluency.[66] Even so, he acknowledged, it was unlikely that he could have made a difference. The votes were not there. Attempts to amend the legislation uniformly failed, and only six joined him in opposition to Senate passage. That number increased to fifteen in the final tally after the Senate consented to the conference report that further enhanced presidential discretion by making all the cash-and-carry provisions optional. Again, a weary Johnson took the floor, but only briefly to repeat his earlier objections.[67]

The international perils that the United States hoped to escape became more acute in 1937. Mussolini had already bombed his way to empire in Africa, and Spain was rent by civil war. In Asia, Japan renewed its advances in a bloody undeclared war against China, and in Europe, Hitler continued to agitate, promising peace while demanding new concessions. When, at the end of May 1937, Borah demonstrated his talent for mischief by suggesting that the cash-and-carry act be invoked against Germany for its participation in the Spanish civil war, Johnson predictably exploded. "Our people have one thing to do," he snapped—"keep out."[68]

Roosevelt ignored Borah's proposal, but on October 5, 1937, in an address in Chicago, he condemned the "reign of terror and international lawlessness" abroad, called for a "quarantine" against the spread of international anarchy, and affirmed the need for "positive efforts for peace." The quarantine speech, then and thereafter, provoked speculation as to Roosevelt's intentions. To some, the speech seemed a bellwether, a testing of isolationist sentiment, the beginnings of a radical shift in policy from Roosevelt's earlier public espousal of nonalignment and nonentanglement. Coming on the eve of the League of Nation's condemnation of Japanese aggression, it seemed to portend more active participation by the United States in world affairs. Johnson refused to see it that way. Though angered by the address, he was nevertheless convinced that Roosevelt's speech was prompted less by design than by impulse, shaped less by a preoccupation with foreign affairs than by the demands of domestic politics. The speech, he surmised, was essentially intended to divert public attention from the embarrassment of the revelation that Hugo Black, Roosevelt's Supreme Court nominee, had once belonged to the Klan.[69]

But if Johnson saw no bold new departure in Roosevelt's public confession of an internationalist faith, the announcement did heighten his already existing concern that the president, impulsive by nature, might enlist with others abroad in a program of sanctions against aggression or, equally dangerous, seek to initiate sanctions on his own. To follow in the path of others was to enter the trap long posed by the League of Nations; to attempt to lead in the development of sanctions was to create your own trap, to embrace Wilsonian illusions. The United States, Johnson wrote, "cannot strut as a knight-errant to reform the world."[70] The attempt would be both provocative and futile: provocative in that the United States would rouse the hostility of nations against which it discriminated; futile in that no other nation could be trusted to maintain sanctions once it had realized its own national ends.

Diplomacy, Johnson had earlier observed, was a "hypocritical game," and sanctions were a part of that hypocrisy.[71] France spoke earnestly of "democracy" and scrambled frantically to shape alliances with Germany's totalitarian neighbors in the east; similarly, France and Great Britain had called for sanctions against Japan and Italy and then stepped aside to cut their own deals with the aggressors. In 1932 Secretary of State Stimson had taken the lead in condemning Japan's expansion into Manchuria and had then been left, as Johnson noted, "holding the bag."* In 1935, while the Roosevelt administration encouraged a "moral embargo" against Italy, both France and Britain had hung back, secretly prepared to concede what they publicly denounced. And in the wake of Roosevelt's quarantine speech came British recognition of Italy's African spoils, the resignation of Foreign Secretary Anthony Eden, and the ascent of Prime Minister Neville Chamberlain as an apostle of appeasement. Though sympathetic to Eden, Johnson did not decry the cabinet shuffle. In truth, in some ways he relished it as yet another example of Old World diplomacy, of Europe's indifference to moral values in the high-stakes game of international intrigue—a game that the United States had no business entering, but a game that Roosevelt seemed eager to play.[72]

*   *   *

When Congress reassembled in early 1938 Johnson went on the offensive by presenting a resolution calling on the administration to define its foreign policy. In his remarks, he contrasted the president's "quarantine address" with the recently concluded Brussels conference, in which the United States and the other signatories of the Nine-Power pact met to consider Japan's moves in Asia. The nation needed to know, Johnson stated, whether American policy had

---

*HWJ to John Bassett Moore, Oct. 7, 1937. See also *New York Times*, July 15, 1939. At the time, Johnson had objected to Stimson's effort. It was not necessary, he noted, to join the League in order to write a note to Japan "about the Kellogg-piffle pact." *New York Times*, Oct. 31, 1931; *San Francisco Examiner*, Oct. 16, 1931. See also HWJ to Mary Connor, Sept. 22, 1931; HWJ to C. K. McClatchy, Oct. 25, 1931; HWJ to F. M. Stevenson, Oct. 20, 1931; HWJ to Hiram Johnson, Jr., Feb. 13, 1932; HWJ to Archibald Johnson, Feb. 29, 1932; HWJ to E. T. Williams, Nov. 15, 1933; *New York Times*, Oct. 16, Nov. 20, 21, Dec. 15, 18, 1931; *Cong. Record*, 72nd Cong., 1st sess. (Jan. 19, 1932), p. 2233. Johnson was not indifferent to Japanese expansion but saw it as a threat to legitimate American enterprise abroad. In 1932 he suggested American recognition of the Soviet Union as a possible counterweight. "Japan should not be made to feel that Russia's downfall would be applauded in the United States," he observed. *New York Times*, Apr. 24, 1932.

changed—whether the president's earlier professions of the principle of noninvolvement had given way to a policy of intervention.
If Roosevelt was bent upon quarantine, he argued, implementation
of that new policy would require sanctions, and sanctions, whether
undertaken alone or in conjunction with others, implied the use of
force and the threat of war. But sanctions, Johnson noted, had not
been forthcoming at Brussels. Having called for a quarantine, Roosevelt had then backed away from the idea. All he had managed to
do, Johnson concluded, was to place the United States in a "pusil-
lanimous" position.[73] Manifestly it was time for an official clarification of what seemed to be incoherence in the defining of American policy.

The administration's call for a $2 billion naval expansion bill to
increase tonnage by 20 percent underscored the need for a clarification of American policy. As in the past, Johnson supported the building program. The navy, he agreed, was far below the strength necessary to protect the nation's interests. But he feared the uses to which
a more powerful navy might be put. "We may need it to whip the
Japs," he confided to his son, the Panay incident fresh in his mind,
"but we don't need it as an auxiliary of Great Britain."* Voicing his
misgivings, he proposed a second resolution calling on the administration to disclose any agreements or understandings with Britain
or any other nation involving naval cooperation.[74] Hull promptly
denied the existence of any such arrangements, and Johnson publicly accepted the disavowal, despite his private conviction that an
unwritten understanding did exist.[75] When Hull later charged that
there were too many irresponsible people making too many irresponsible statements, Johnson replied that he knew of only one—
Roosevelt, in his quarantine speech.[76]

Johnson had hoped in 1938 to focus public attention on the nation's foreign affairs in a major policy address, but, he wrote, the

---

*HWJ to Hiram Johnson, Jr., Jan. 29, 1938. See also HWJ to Hiram Johnson, Jr.,
Feb. 19, 1938; HWJ to John Bassett Moore, Apr. 17, 1938. In response to the Panay
incident, Johnson announced: "I will not subscribe to the idea that a gunboat of
America may be blown to pieces because somebody may see fit to take a shot at her
and then, subsequently, with tongue in cheek, say that he is 'sorry' and apologize."
Cong. Record, 75th Cong., 2nd sess. (Dec. 13, 1937), p. 1357. In 1938, he seemed again
to rattle the sword at Japan, but made it clear that he would endorse the use of force
only to protect U.S. interests, not to underwrite Chinese independence. *Cong. Record*,
75th Cong., 3rd sess. (June 16, 1938), pp. 9524–25; *New York Times*, June 17, 1938.

time never seemed quite right. He was reluctant to feed the fears of the pacifists, who saw in naval construction a provocative act.[77] Perhaps too he doubted his ability to undertake such an exertion. He was recovering his strength and outwardly appeared more fit, but he still tired easily and felt compelled to write out his comments before delivering them if time allowed. By 1939 opportunities for debate seemed better, and Johnson's health, though never completely restored, had gradually improved. Meanwhile, his perception of Roosevelt further deteriorated. Johnson feared that the administration might seek some settlement of the debt debacle to circumvent the Johnson Act and thus enable Americans to invest in Europe's wars. He was alert as well to the undercurrent of agitation set loose by the administration to shape a more flexible neutrality policy that would allow the president to designate aggressors once the existing cash-and-carry act expired. Nervously Johnson awaited the confrontation.[78]

The first clash came in January 1939 with the disclosure that America's military aircraft were being made available to France. The arrangement, while entirely legal, had been wrapped in secrecy, but became public following the crash of an experimental bomber under construction by North American Aviation in California. The incident sparked an angry debate in Congress that gathered fire when Roosevelt, in off-the-record remarks to the Senate Military Affairs Committee, reportedly asserted that America's first line of defense lay in Europe.[79] Johnson quickly condemned the secrecy of the arrangement between the United States and France and questioned whether sales of aircraft abroad did not weaken the nation's defenses at home. In back of it all, he privately concluded, was the administration's effort to get us into a war with Germany.[80] A wandering Roosevelt had set his course.

That fear defined the unstated premise for Johnson's long-delayed speech, prepared well in advance, which he delivered on March 2, 1939, before a crowded Senate chamber. Roosevelt's earlier professions of isolationism made at San Diego in 1935 and Chautauqua in 1936, had been contradicted, Johnson argued, by his Chicago "quarantine" address of 1937, and by his recently delivered State of the Union message, which called for measures to discourage aggression short of war but more effective than mere words. Harshly critical of the administration's new initiatives, Johnson outlined his own test for the nation's foreign policy. America, he stated, wants no war, no entangling alliances, no commitments, understandings, or agreements. A policy of sanctions, he continued, was inherently wicked—more horrible than the bombing of cities, for it destroyed the innocent in foreign lands, "the weak, the sick, the lame, the halt—those who never did a wrong." He denied the quixotic illusion that the world could be remade and predicted a dictatorship at home if the nation ever undertook the attempt—and dictators are detestable "whether they are actual or potential, and wherever they may be," he pointedly added.*

Johnson returned to that theme in early May in a brief, impromptu address that had all the flair of an earlier time. Congress, he admonished, should remain in session as a watchdog to guard against "mad adventures" that might be launched by the White House. The United States would be neither eased into war nor driven to it, for just as the Senate had held firm twenty years earlier by turning back Wilson's entreaties for the league, so too it would meet the challenge of the 1930s. Concluding his address over a roar of applause that erupted from the galleries, he urged the nation to be itself and to remain aloof from international conflict. If the Congress were to adjourn, he privately noted to John Bassett Moore, Roosevelt would look for some excuse to project the United States into war.[81]

The deepening of the European crisis in March 1939 intensified Johnson's concern over possible presidential misbehavior. Czechoslovakia, dismembered at Munich the previous September, was occupied by German forces, and the whole of Western Europe seemed poised on the brink of war. Those same events set the stage for Congress and the administration to reexamine once again the nation's neutrality laws and the soon-to-expire cash-and-carry provisions of 1937. Hearings in the Senate Foreign Relations Committee, after a three-months postponement, began in early April with a cacophony of voices in support of a host of proposals. Greatest atten-

* *Cong. Record*, 76th Cong., 1st sess. (Mar. 2, 1939), pp. 2131–39; HWJ to Hiram Johnson, Jr., Mar. 5, 1939. According to the *New York Times*, Johnson started off well but tired after an hour. *New York Times*, Mar. 3, 1939. In 1919, denouncing the nation's Russian policy, Johnson had made much the same point about sanctions: "When we put that ring of steel about a country, do you realize what it does? It doesn't starve your horrible Bolsheviks at all; it starves your weak and your sick and your infirm and your mothers and your babies." League speeches, no date, Salt Lake City?, Part III, Carton 25, HWJ Papers. See also *Cong. Record*, 74th Cong., 1st sess. (Jan. 17, 1935), p. 575.

tion centered on the so-called "Peace Act of 1939," introduced by
Key Pittman and endorsed by the administration, which repealed
the arms embargo and allowed all trade on a cash-and-carry basis.
While still professing to favor the elimination of every infringement
on American trade, Johnson nevertheless cooperated with advocates
of the arms embargo to oppose the change.[82]

By June the chances that the administration might succeed in removing the arms embargo, never strong, began to erode further. Hull
endorsed the proposal but declined to testify in the Senate hearings,
reportedly fearful of cross-examination by the committee's isolationists and especially of Johnson's inquisitorial skills.[83] Johnson
doubted whether he and his colleagues could keep the Pittman resolution bottled in committee but felt certain that it could be stopped
on the floor. There were, he observed, between 20 and 25 senators
determined in their opposition, more than enough for an extended
filibuster as the session neared its close.[84]

By the end of the month White House hopes were further damp-
ened when a rebellious House insisted on retaining the arms embargo. Unwilling to concede defeat, Roosevelt renewed his endeavors to pry the legislation out of the Senate committee. Twenty years
earlier isolationists had met in Johnson's office to plan strategy for
the league battle. The scene was repeated in July 1939. More than a
score of senators gathered to pledge their support.[85] Joining with Nye
and Clark, Johnson plunged into the fray, working to prevent committee action and preparing for a possible floor fight. But the floor
fight never materialized. Within a week the battle was averted and
the matter concluded when the committee by a single vote agreed
to postponement. Concerned that an unpredictable Borah might
bolt, Johnson, sitting next to him, assumed his sternest posture and
riveted him with a stare as the roll was called. Neither Borah nor
the vote disappointed him. It was, he cheered, a "beautiful fight,"
and even if Roosevelt renewed the struggle he was sure that he and
his colleagues would "go the limit."[86]

*   *   *

From the beginning, attempts to shape American neutrality legislation had faced a battery of complications. Neutrality, Johnson
had noted on the Senate floor in 1935, "is the most complicated and
difficult subject with which statesmen have ever dealt."[87] Congres-

sional isolationists had largely succeeded in denying discretionary powers to the president, but they had to face the fact that neutrality necessarily had discriminatory results. Whatever policy the United States adopted, whether it retained traditional rights, imposed an arms embargo, or settled on cash-and-carry, there would be an impact abroad, advantageous to some, harmful to others. Many in the isolationist camp tried to sidestep these difficulties by emphasizing that their sole aim was to immunize the United States against international perils. Their position rested on two central assumptions: that the American people could remain morally indifferent to overseas aggression, and that the security of the United States would remain unaffected by changes wrought abroad by war. But as international tensions multiplied, many isolationists came to question these assumptions and began to share Roosevelt's view that with greater flexibility the United States would be able to remain at peace and at the same time either deter aggression or alter its course. Ultimately the question was whether the nation ran greater risks by seeking to insulate itself from the world or by attempting to shape the direction of world affairs. It was a question that continued to rankle as Germany, in September 1939, marched into Poland and peace gave way to war in Europe.

Throughout the 1930s Johnson had been no more able than most Americans to remain morally indifferent to aggression abroad. He condemned the "bloody cruelties of Shanghai" and publicly deplored the bombing of civilian populations in China and Spain.[88] He tried to be openly cynical in his approach to European affairs and was undeniably eager to discount the "decadent British Empire" and the "so-called democracies" of France and Great Britain, who voiced high principles and practiced low deeds.* He attributed Hitler's rise to power to the punitive and unjust settlement of Versailles and sympathized with Germany's quest for the exercise of full sovereignty in the Rhineland. Still, he could not escape the moral issue.

*HWJ to Hiram Johnson, Jr., Mar. 22, 1936, Apr. 2, Mar. 5, 1939. The references to "so-called democracies" can be found in *Cong. Record*, 76th Cong., 1st sess. (Mar. 2, 1939), p. 2133, and in HWJ to Hiram Johnson, Jr., Mar. 5, 1939. Roosevelt, Johnson satirically noted in 1939, had made clear that he preferred England and France and their allies, "those great democracies, Russia, Roumania, Poland and Turkey." See HWJ press statement, July 14, 1939, Part III, Carton 26, HWJ Papers; Senate Committee on Foreign Relations, Hearings, *Neutrality, Peace Legislation, and Our Foreign Policy*, 76th Cong., 1st sess. (Apr.–May 1939), p. 65.

Hitler was "a brute, ruthless, cruel and utterly unprincipled," and the persecution of the Jews shameful. Nor could he agree with Charles Lindbergh, once the war began, that it made no difference which of the two sides won.[89] But if Johnson recognized a moral dimension in the conflict abroad, he continued to maintain that that conflict did not threaten the nation's essential interests.

Johnson had hoped that the European war could be averted, but argued that even if it came, Hitler could never secure mastery of the Continent. It had been tried before, but never successfully. Nor could Germany physically threaten the Western Hemisphere; those who spoke of fleets of planes bombing American cities voiced "moonshine" and "bunk."[90] Johnson could understand why some U.S. citizens might plead for a more vigorous American policy in response to the assaults on their friends and families abroad, but nevertheless resented such pleas. He had never been free from an undercurrent of anti-Semitism common to his class and generation, and his private references to American Jews became sharper and more frequent as the nation's commitment to noninvolvement began to crumble. Like League of Nations enthusiasts, idealists, and internationalists, "the snobs and snoots" who wallowed before the king and queen of Britain, American Jews, he asserted, subordinated the needs of the United States to foreign causes.[91] And it was the nation's needs, or more precisely his conviction that entry into war would undermine democracy at home, that lay at the very core of his isolationist faith. Clearly Johnson's fear of Roosevelt's designs contributed to that conviction, but they did not create it. Under the most benign of presidents, war would bring in its wake repression and ruin, restrictions on free speech, and financial bankruptcy.[92]

With the outbreak of the European war in September 1939, Roosevelt called for a special session of Congress to revamp the neutrality laws and thereby aid the Allied cause. Once again seeking the elimination of the arms embargo, he spoke of a return to the traditional tenets of international law. But the proposed legislation, mandating as it did the adoption of cash-and-carry regulations for all commodities, including arms, was much the same as the Pittman bill earlier tabled by the Senate Foreign Relations Committee, not a return to the traditional practices Johnson had always defended. Yet it seems clear that he would have refused his support in any case since for him, Roosevelt's determination to take sides in the war overrode all other considerations. Thus Johnson joined with what he had once branded the "peace at any price" group, reversing himself to adopt the very rhetoric he had earlier scorned. With the fate of the nation hanging in the balance, he explained to John Bassett Moore, there was really nothing else to do. Americans, he publicly declared, must choose between profits and peace, and retention of the arms embargo was crucial to the nation's destiny. Eliminate the embargo, he argued, and the United States would find itself gradually absorbed into the European war. Once involved, American democracy would collapse.[93] But the same dynamics that hardened Johnson's resolve weakened the nation's commitment to nonparticipation. Though still isolationist, a majority of Americans had come to believe what Johnson firmly denied—that there were steps short of war that could affect the outcome of events abroad.

On September 26 the administration's bill came before the Senate Foreign Relations Committee. Two days later, it was approved by a vote of 16 to 7. On the floor Senate isolationists readied themselves for battle, hopeful that they could mobilize public opinion to sway the undecided. Once again they worked out their strategy in Johnson's office, and Johnson himself assumed a central role in the coordination of the fight.[94] But as he realized, unless there was some "lucky break," the cause was lost.[95] There were no lucky breaks. Across the country, advocates of the existing arms embargo massed to support their position and to inundate Congress with their appeals, but those who called for revision were equally active in launching crusades and in staging popular rallies.

In the Senate, administration supporters remained in the background, allowing the opposition to dominate the debate and exhaust their reserves. Taking the floor to conclude what he realized was a lost cause, Johnson spoke for more than an hour. At times his voice dropped almost to a whisper as he addressed a hushed and unusually crowded chamber.[96] Every instinct, he admitted, encouraged Americans to condemn Germany, but Americans should take care lest they repeat the mistakes that had led them once before into war. Then Americans had been misled by propaganda from abroad; at present they were being deceived by propaganda from the White House. Still adamant in his belief that the nation had no real stake in the war and that it remained invulnerable to foreign attacks, Johnson refused to accept the contention that the United States could shape the outcome of the conflict abroad without becoming militarily involved. Perhaps it was conceivable, he granted, but it involved an enormous gamble. At risk were not only the lives of American citizens but American democracy itself.[97] But as he feared, a majority proved ready to gamble. The following week, after the efforts to attach a series of crippling amendments failed, the administration's bill passed with 63 in the majority and 30 opposed as impatient cries of "Vote! Vote!" rang in the chamber.[98]

In the weeks that followed, the sense of urgency that had shaped the national debate seemed belied by events. At war, none of the belligerents fought. In many ways it seemed yet another great diplomatic dance, a "phony war" of bluff and bluster. If the warring powers stopped their army maneuvers and began to draw blood, attitudes might change, Frank Doherty reported from California. As it was, advocates of aid to Great Britain had begun to grow silent.[99] But in the spring of 1940 that sense of urgency returned with a vengeance as the "phony war" gave way to blitzkrieg. In a period of three months, between April and June, Germany was able to accomplish what it had failed to realize in four years of bloody struggle between 1914 and 1918—the mastery of Western Europe. Only Britain stood fast, under attack from the air.

Johnson sympathized with Britain's plight but held firm to his earlier convictions, still protesting that the United States must distance itself from the conflict. Indeed, in some ways the changing fortunes in Europe strengthened his determination. Perhaps because the blitzkrieg had shaken his belief in the invulnerability of the United States to foreign attack, he increasingly stressed the importance of home defense and the need to retain armaments that Britain sought for its own needs. "We could not fight a war now to save our necks with a tenth-rate country," he observed.[100] At the same time, however, there were limits to his support for preparedness. In July 1940 he voted against the confirmations of Frank Knox and Henry Stimson to head the Navy and War departments, and the following month he fought earnestly if unsuccessfully against peacetime conscription, supporting any amendment that might cripple the legislation. It was, he charged, a "sinister bill" motivated less by defense than by Roosevelt's intentions abroad.[101]

★   ★   ★

During his fight in 1940 to ensure American isolation, Johnson fought too for his own reelection to the Senate. As in 1934, his goal was to win the nomination of both the Republican and Democratic parties, but this time the potential stumbling block was the Democrats. Republicans, Frank Doherty observed, had nowhere else to go but to his candidacy, and his visible break with Roosevelt made their path much easier.[102] Many who had never previously supported him now volunteered their help. Harry Chandler and the *Los Angeles Times* cautiously extended their endorsement, and even Friend Richardson was rumored to favor his reelection.[103] Such newfound support in conservative Republican circles, however, diminished his chances to win the Democratic nomination. Los Angeles, Doherty warned, was a "hotbed of New Dealism," and too prominent an endorsement by California's Old Guard and the state's business community could easily backfire. Johnson's outspoken opposition to the president's leadership in foreign affairs posed yet another complication, especially in the spring of 1940 with the coming of the blitzkrieg and the fall of France; some of his friends began to worry that his candidacy might be swept aside as popular sentiment mounted in support of the White House.[104]

But the most tangible bar to his reelection hopes was Roosevelt himself and the fact that 1940 was a presidential election year. Johnson felt sure that the president would reach out for a third term. Thus in effect Johnson would be asking those Democrats who planned to vote for Roosevelt in November to support his own candidacy in the August primaries. Since he was determined to oppose Roosevelt's third-term bid, he found himself in an awkward position. Strategy dictated a low profile and the postponement of any attack on the White House until his own nomination in the Democratic primary had been decided. But it was a strategy that went against his grain. At first he hesitated to embrace it, for he was unsure whether the Democratic primary could be won and unwilling, as he admitted, to "ride two horses going in opposite directions." Ultimately, however, he acquiesced, ignoring Roosevelt and focusing his energies on organizational efforts rather than on an active personal campaign.[105]

In fact, Johnson had little choice. He could not have physically withstood an extended campaign. He was almost 74 years old, had lost confidence in his speaking abilities, walked uneasily, and tired rapidly after any exertion.[106] In the past, he recalled, his approach had been to "pick up an axe and hew my way through," but that was no longer a viable option. Occasionally he spoke of returning to California, but international events gave him both reason and opportunity to remain "on duty" in Washington, where he prepared two recorded radio addresses, each fifteen minutes in length, which were broadcast in the state on the eve of the primary elections.[107]

Despite his fears, Johnson's reelection was never in serious doubt. Upon the formation of his campaign committees in late May, the strength of his candidacy became obvious. Carefully crafted, nonpartisan in designation, testimonial in character, the committees included representatives of labor, business, agriculture, women, and professional groups, and thus drew support from almost every major segment of the state. It was not always possible to achieve an even balance between Republicans and Democrats, Robert Girvin, his northern California manager explained, in that some prominent Democrats who privately supported his reelection refused to endorse him publicly.[108] But neither of Johnson's two opponents, Los Angeles County Supervisor John Anson Ford, running on Roosevelt's coattails, or Lieutenant Governor Ellis Patterson, running well to the left of Roosevelt on domestic issues and as critical as Johnson of the president's foreign policies, was able to secure anything comparable to the senator's support. Indeed, the California Democratic party, increasingly fractured by personal ambitions and ideological feuds, seemed far less the juggernaut it had been in 1938.[109]

Among Johnson's supporters, some were doubtless drawn to his candidacy in the belief that he could not be dislodged after 24 years of incumbency, others on the basis of past favors. Some stressed his record; others, such as the *San Francisco Chronicle*, ignored it, emphasizing instead his character, his independence, and his reputation for integrity. He secured the endorsement of conservative Democrats such as state senator Peter Myhand of Merced—Johnson, Myhand noted, "will not jump on the bandwagon of every fancy passing political promoter"—but he had the support of liberal Democrats as well. Among them was Manchester Boddy, publisher of the *Los Angeles Daily News*, who disregarded Johnson's more recent defection from the White House to emphasize his past progressive record, his support for the major outlines of the New Deal, and his commitment to national defense.[110] Organized labor, the key element in winning the Democratic nomination, played its part, thanks to the efforts of Johnson's lieutenants to obtain endorsements and to give prominence to labor representatives in the statewide organization. William Green, head of the American Federation of Labor, extended support, as did Dan Tobin, of the Teamsters Union, and C. J. Haggerty, president of the California State Federation of Labor.[111] At Johnson's request, Paul Scharrenberg, the CSFL's legislative liaison, was released from other duties to make the rounds among the undecided. In addition, the Railroad Brotherhoods promoted his reelection. Only the CIO, which was tied to the Patterson candidacy, remained outside the fold.

At first Roosevelt did nothing to impede Johnson's strategy. But in early August, in a prearranged statement at his weekly news briefing, he volunteered that while his affection for the California senator remained strong, Johnson was no longer a liberal.[112] Despite the urgings of almost all his advisers to overlook the president's comment, Johnson characteristically struck back: "Had I followed him in his attempted packing of the Supreme Court and his veiled and un-American deeds leading us down the road to war and dictatorship, I would have been a perfect liberal and progressive, and what glory would be mine. . . . This is just the same old purge; the same old sham expressions of regards and affections, the same old stiletto."[113] During the remaining three weeks of the primary campaign Johnson feared a renewal of the attack, but it never came, and in his prerecorded radio addresses in the week prior to the primary election, he made no mention of the incident save to emphasize that he would be the rubber stamp of no man. Once again, he sought to sidestep the president rather than confront him. To that end he continued to stress his opposition to Roosevelt's policies that risked American civilization in "Europe's mad adventures," but ignored any mention of the third term and stressed too his sympathy toward Britain and his commitment to the president's call for a strong national defense. The United States, he asserted, will never adopt a policy of appeasement and must repair its woefully inadequate forces in order to become so strong that "no roving despot, no totalitarian government will dare attack us."[114]

As predicted, Johnson won the Republican primary with ease, sweeping to victory with a margin of 6 to 1 over the combined total of his Democratic opponents who had cross-filed in the race. The Democratic contest was closer, but there too the strategy of the Johnson organization paid dividends: he made a clean sweep in every county of the state, generating tremendous majorities in the San Joaquin and Sacramento valleys and in San Francisco. Only in Southern California did his tallies fall behind the state average, but never significantly. In the general election he faced the nominal threat of the Communist and Prohibitionist candidates.[115]

With his own reelection assured, Johnson was free to become more outspoken in the presidential campaign, but the Republican presidential choice of Wendell Willkie all but eliminated the possibility that he would play a major role. Willkie, the choice of Republican internationalists, by endorsing both conscription and the recently announced transfer of American destroyers to Britain, made himself only marginally less obnoxious to Johnson than was Roosevelt.[116] When Willkie supporters asked Johnson to accompany the Republican candidate on his California tour, Johnson refused, holding back from any endorsement. Perhaps, he mused, an "innocuous greeting" might be composed, but even that he decided against, and he discouraged the suggestion that Willkie contact him by telephone. He aspired, he noted, to keep his support for the Republican candidate "as mysterious as possible" until the proper time, and vowed that he would assume no responsibility for the campaign in California.[117]

Johnson's reluctance to participate in the national campaign, owing to his dissatisfaction with Willkie, stemmed too from the nonpartisan tactics he had employed during the primary. No one, he privately protested, could have believed that he would support Roosevelt, especially after the president's attack in August. Yet, having kept his silence during the primary, he worried that some of his Democratic sponsors would imply bad faith if he now involved himself in the presidential contest. In the flood of letters he received following his nomination, most encouraged him to speak out for Willkie. A few dissented. "They are trying to make it appear that the vote which you received . . . was a rebuff to the President," one correspondent complained, "but your magnificent vote was due to the fact that the people of California love, honor and respect *you*."[118]

In the end, however, Johnson gave way to Republican solicitations. He agreed to speak from Washington for 30 minutes on a CBS nationwide broadcast in support of Willkie.[119] In his address Johnson acknowledged his disappointment with Willkie's internationalist stand. Unable to forge the election into a national referendum on foreign policy, he used the occasion to condemn Roosevelt's violation of the tradition of forgoing a third term. Abandon that tradition, he argued, and you eliminate an essential safeguard of democracy. In view of the enormous delegations of power to the executive, the "billions of dollars he could disburse at will," the "innumerable boards and commissions" that enforce his will, and the ability to manipulate international events and generate national hysteria at home, no president, especially Roosevelt with his record of attempted court-packing and purges, should be afforded the opportunity to exceed the traditional two-term limitation.[120]

Many who listened to Johnson's address of October 18 believed it one of the best of his career. It had more emotion and feeling, Doherty judged, than any he had ever made.[121] Johnson had been disappointed by his earlier radio speeches during the primary campaign—they sounded "like the yappings of some sanctimonious old dead man," he had commented—but he was pleased by the response to his latest broadcast. Nonetheless he declined to undertake another. A second speech, he reasoned, would be anticlimactic, and in any event Willkie had so circumscribed the campaign by his endorsement of Roosevelt's foreign policies that no other issues remained. Only on the eve of the election did Johnson relent and agree to participate in a radio event staged by the Republican National Committee. He spoke for one minute. Ironically, while waiting to go on the air, he found himself sitting next to CIO president John L. Lewis, whose sit-down strike movement Johnson had excoriated three years before.[122]

Johnson harbored no illusions that Willkie had a chance to win in November—a "gone gosling," he had concluded—and was not surprised by the election results. His own totals, somewhat reduced by the disaffection he had known he would incur because of his endorsement of Willkie, were nevertheless impressive: he swept to victory with over 82 percent of the vote cast in the race.[123]

*　　*　　*

With his new election mandate, Roosevelt pushed hard for American aid to Great Britain, calling for "Lend-Lease" so that the United

States might become the "arsenal of democracy." "We're in the war," Johnson lamented, and only Hitler's restraint prevented actual hostilities.[124] The president's announcement of the "Four Freedoms," the transfer of American destroyers to Britain, and Congress' repeal of the arms embargo were more than ample provocation for Germany to declare war. And with war would come the assault on civil liberties, for the administration would unquestionably move to silence dissenters. "If we can escape the concentration camps we'll be fairly lucky," Johnson remarked.*

Upon returning to Washington after a brief trip to California to visit his ailing grandson, Johnson was again solicited by the Senate's isolationists to organize and manage the campaign against the lend-lease proposal. For once he refused. He would sound his objections but not coordinate the battle. He lacked the energy, and, as he noted, there were just too many "prima-donnas." Watching events unfold, he felt certain he could have done a better job than had his colleagues in cross-examining Hull, Morgenthau, and Knox before the Senate Foreign Relations Committee, but recognized as well that the administration's bill could not be stopped.[125] It had the almost unanimous backing of congressional Democrats and mixed support within Republican circles, including the endorsement of Wendell Willkie. In addition, Roosevelt, in order to build as broad a base of support as possible, showed himself prepared to accept limiting amendments as long as they did not interfere with the bill's central purpose.[126] In early February 1941, by a vote of ten to five, the committee moved to end the hearings on the 11th. It was just as well, Johnson commented; "cranks and crackpots" were waiting in the wings to testify, but in fact the opposition had exhausted its reservoir of respectability. Many once-outspoken isolationists, he complained, had been intimidated by the White House; Edwin Borchard had refused to testify, as had Robert Hutchins, of the University of Chicago, and Henry N. MacCracken, of Vassar.[127]

*HWJ to Hiram Johnson, Jr., Nov. 9, 17, 1940; HWJ to William Phillips Simms, Nov. 24, 1940. Johnson returned to the theme of concentration camps the following year in defending Burton Wheeler against the administration's attacks. "If we must go to a concentration camp, I will go with you, and there will be two of us at least." *Cong. Record,* 77th Cong., 1st sess. (July 28, 1941), p. 6336; HWJ to Hiram Johnson, Jr., July 27, 1941. On the eve of Roosevelt's third inauguration he wrote, "This may be the last ceremony of the inaugiration [*sic*] of a President that we'll ever have." HWJ to Hiram Johnson, Jr., Jan. 19, 1941.

On the floor Johnson unsuccessfully pushed for an amendment to prohibit the dispatching of American troops outside the Western Hemisphere and endorsed any and all amendments that restricted the provisions of the act.[128] Spent by his efforts, he remained virtually silent in floor debate and instead took his protest to the American people via radio. There, he hammered away at the enormous delegation of power, "dictatorial" in scope, that would be extended to the president by the act, and emphasized what the White House and the bill's supporters continued to deny—that the pending Lend-Lease Act was not a substitute for the nation's military presence abroad but a major step toward armed participation. "They purr peace," he charged, but "have a passion for swords and stilettos." Acknowledging his sympathy for Great Britain, he somewhat disingenuously agreed that Britain deserved American aid if such aid did not weaken America's capacity to ensure its own defense. But at the same time, he insisted, the war abroad was not our war, and, whatever the outcome, the United States was not threatened. After the broadcast, thousands of letters poured into his office, twenty to one endorsing his stand; still, he had no illusions. "Our backs are against the wall," he had confessed even as he appealed for popular support. And so they were. In March, by a two to one majority, the Senate passed the Lend-Lease Act. "Last night we did the dirty deed," Johnson lamented. "We assassinated liberty under the pretext of aiding a belligerent in the war."[129]

Certain that a formal declaration of war was only a matter of time, Johnson found himself frustrated by "The Great Dictator," the "pettifogger" in the White House, by the rising tide of popular opinion in support of the president, and by his own infirmities, which made any sustained exertion increasingly wearing.[130] In April, in a futile attempt to regain strength, he and his wife left for a short holiday in Miami. In May, following the president's declaration of an "unlimited national emergency," Johnson turned once again to the radio, this time under the sponsorship of the America First Committee, to repeat his denunciations of the nation's foreign policy. More acrimoniously than in the past, he lashed out at "the little puppets of J. P. Morgan and Co." and at Roosevelt, who "speaks with the confidence of a Hitler or a Mussolini"; stressed the inadequacy of America's defenses; and warned again that the nation would lose its democracy once the United States entered the war.[131] Expressions of support poured in, including encomiums from Herbert Hoover, but nothing changed. "We've already an incipient dictatorship here that is going to ripen, I think, into one that will make Hitler and Mussolini blush," he wrote to a sympathetic Hoover.[132]

In June the war in Europe broadened with Hitler's attack on Russia. Johnson hoped that the two tyrannies would destroy each other, and bemoaned the alacrity with which the administration converted Stalin, "the bloodiest tyrant that ever lived," into a democratic ally.[133] Winston Churchill, he privately complained, was directing American foreign policy, an opinion that was not altered when in August 1941 Roosevelt and Churchill met at sea off the coast of Newfoundland to proclaim the Atlantic Charter.* At almost the same time the administration proposed a one-year extension of service of those inducted under the Selective Service Act. As vigorously as he could, Johnson opposed the extension—a "damned outrage," he wrote, that violated the nation's contract with its draftees—but to no avail. He raged against his own limited power to respond. The Senate gave him its attention, he acknowledged, but he was unequal to the task, his days of fluency and fervor past. Recognizing his inability to alter the course of events, he left the oppressive summer heat of Washington for California in late August. He returned a month later, no more fit than before.[134]

In October 1941 came Roosevelt's call for the repeal of the Neutrality Act to allow American transport of lend-lease materials to belligerent ports, and Johnson wearily attended the closed sessions of the Senate Foreign Relations Committee to oppose the change. The narrowness of the committee vote in support of the administration's proposal afforded him hope that the bill could at least be delayed on the Senate floor. He remained largely on the sidelines, however. Minnie, fearful of the toll on his health, had cautioned him against additional strain, and the fact that he now opposed a return to the traditional concept of neutral rights he had once championed made him reluctant to enter actively into the debate.[135] Even so, he could not help but participate to the extent of voicing his objections

*HWJ to Hiram Johnson, Jr., June 24, Aug. 10, Aug. 17, 1941. The charter, Johnson publicly observed, constituted an "offensive and defensive alliance" between the United States and Great Britain. Out of the war would come "a new order based on righteousness and justice and decency and good government, headed—they do not say so, but I assume—by Mr. Stalin." *Cong. Record*, 77th Cong., 1st sess. (Aug. 19, 1941), pp. 7206–8.

in an NBC radio address and in a brief, emotional appeal to the Senate. On the floor his rancor seemed spent as he urged his colleagues not to plunge the nation into war.[136] Resignedly he watched as the Senate voted 51 to 37 to repeal the Neutrality Act. Perhaps, he privately commented, the war would not be particularly long or fierce, for Hitler's reverses in Russia seemed to spell an end to his dreams of empire. Needing to rest, he and his wife made plans to leave Washington for another holiday in Miami. In the midst of that planning the Japanese struck Pearl Harbor.[137]

★   ★   ★

Johnson joined in the unanimous Senate support for the war declaration against Japan. He was surprised when Germany and Italy responded with their own declarations of war but saw no option save to reply in kind. With our country at war we want to see it win, he affirmed.[138] Cautioning the Senate not to give in to hysteria, he emphasized the need to protect the Bill of Rights and to forsake none of the nation's precious liberties. But for Johnson those liberties clearly did not encompass Pacific Coast residents of Japanese descent, whether aliens or citizens, and he endorsed restrictions that in time led to their removal into relocation centers.[139] Throughout 1942 he worried that Japan would strike a blow on the mainland, his earlier certainty of the nation's invulnerability to attack having deserted him. He hoped that the war would be short, by no means the five to ten years some predicted, but continued to fear its consequences. With the coming of victory, he remarked, the nation might very well find its economy bankrupt and its democratic forms crippled. Congress itself, he noted at one point, might be abolished.[140]

Yet Johnson's deteriorating health made it clear that he would do little more than watch the passing scene. Attendance at morning committee hearings and the regular afternoon Senate sessions became more and more difficult, sustained activity impossible. Minnie, herself increasingly crippled by arthritis, watchfully accompanied him on his rounds, and both sought out diversions from the maelstrom of Washington at war by attending night baseball games. Only rarely was Johnson's voice heard in the Senate. In October 1942, he responded with anger to the administration's proposal to widen the draft to include those between 18 and 20. It was wrong, he argued, to snatch "from the cradle boys who have yet to live their lives." They should be drawn upon only as a last resort. After attending the draft debates well into the evening, he found himself "beastly tired." He had, he lamented to his son, run downhill rather badly.[141]

In December 1942 both Johnson and his wife left for an extended holiday in Miami; they returned in February 1943. The rest did little for his health, and his body continued to betray him. It was impossible, he wrote, to walk more than 50 or 100 yards; his legs just would not work.[142] In early April he began a battery of medical tests at the naval hospital at Bethesda, reporting there each day. He hoped for some improvement but was doubtful of success. At the end of the month his health gave way. Gravely ill, he lapsed into a coma and spent more than two weeks under an oxygen tent in the naval hospital, his prognosis poor. "No one expected me to survive," he remarked; but he gradually improved, and was released from Bethesda in September.[143]

During his hospitalization, Republican leaders, meeting at Mackinac Island, agreed to modify the traditional tenets of American isolationism by endorsing a policy of postwar international cooperation that would have as its goal a "permanent peace with organized justice." Johnson could only observe and recall earlier, more vibrant years when he, Borah, and Reed had fought the good fight. It was sad, he reflected, that he was the only one left.[144] In October 1943, following Johnson's return to Capitol Hill from Bethesda, the Connally resolution pledging American membership in an international "league of free and sovereign nations" came before the Senate. Johnson, complaining that he had neither a voice nor a brain that any longer functioned, vowed to do his best to turn back the "starry-eyed" reformers. His physicians interceded, however, warning him against taking any part in the debate, and Minnie forbade him to participate. Sadly he apologized to the Senate and to the nation for his silence. On November 5, by a vote of 85 to 5, the Senate endorsed the Connally resolution. It was hard, Johnson privately lamented, to see all that he had fought for repudiated, and he could not help but feel that if he had had his health the results would have been different.[145] But his health showed no improvement, and he confessed that he could no longer perform his senatorial duties. He was, he noted, awaiting the day of recovery but doubted its coming.[146]

Johnson and his wife spent the winter and spring of 1944 in Mi-

ami. On their return to Washington in early June, they were met at
the depot with wheelchairs. They secluded themselves at home.[147]
He longed to involve himself in the coming presidential election, he
wrote, but lacked both the voice and the strength. In August Johnson began to attend Senate sessions, but only rarely participated.
Occasionally, the spark of an earlier day returned, as when he voted
against the confirmation of Joseph Grew as under secretary of state.
Grew, he explained to the Senate, was a capable man, but to vote for
him would be to vote for turning over the State Department to the
House of Morgan. He was vocal as well in denouncing British atrocities in Greece and Russian moves in Poland, exhorting Congress to
condemn the actions of its allies and express its sympathy for subject peoples. In the spring of 1945, with memories of earlier battles
still fresh in his mind, he presented the minority report in opposition to the pending treaty with Mexico over water rights and im-
plored his colleagues to look to the nation's interests.[148]

Hearings began on the charter of the United Nations in the summer of 1945. In the Senate Foreign Relations Committee, Johnson
cast the sole vote against ratification, still intent, as he told John
Neylan, on fighting the old fight.[149] But he had no fight left. On July
27, as the Senate debate on the U.N. charter neared its end, he was
readmitted to Bethesda; a few days later he announced his final vote
against the charter from his hospital bed. He died of a stroke in the
early morning of August 6, 1945. In the press, his passing was overshadowed by the bombing of Hiroshima. A new era dawned, spelling
an irrevocable end to America's isolation.[150] Only much later did the
nation begin to assess the impact of that change on the values Johnson had so often stressed.

Accompanied by his wife and his son "Jack," who had been en
route to Washington at the time of his death; by Mary Connor, his
office secretary since 1917; and by the traditional honor guard of
congressmen appointed for the occasion, Johnson's body was returned to San Francisco, where it lay in state in the rotunda of the
City Hall. Three thousand attended the service, to hear Sheridan
Downey deliver the eulogy and Governor Earl Warren and Mayor
Roger Lapham present remarks. Further thousands filed by the cas-
ket to pay their last respects. In the press, the obituary notices and
editorial farewells echoed familiar themes. Most lauded his achievements as governor. Some recalled the incident in 1916 when Charles

Evans Hughes snubbed Johnson at the Virginia Hotel and then lost the presidency, and the episode in 1920 when Johnson turned down his only real chance to become president by refusing to join either Harding or Knox on the national Republican ticket. Almost all emphasized his character, his candor, his integrity, his tenacity of purpose. Always a man of principle, he had fought for his convictions even when it meant standing alone. He had been too much the fighter, some added, but as the *Sacramento Bee* observed, if in his long political life he did sometimes err, his errors were never those of the heart.[151]

Johnson was buried just outside San Francisco, next to his son Archibald, at Cypress Lawn cemetery in Colma. Minnie continued to reside in San Francisco until her own death, in 1955. Hiram Johnson, Jr., died in 1958. All four are interred at Cypress Lawn in a somewhat elaborate marble monument that Minnie helped design.[152]

Reference
Matter

Notes

All letters cited without source identifications are from the Hiram W. Johnson Papers (cited as HWJ Papers), located in the Bancroft Library at the University of California, Berkeley. Johnson's letters to his two sons are also available in Robert E. Burke, ed., *The Diary Letters of Hiram Johnson, 1917–1945,* 7 vols. (New York, 1983). Other manuscript collections consulted include the following:

Arlett, Arthur. Papers. Bancroft Library, University of California, Berkeley.

Arnold, Ralph. Papers. Huntington Library, San Marino, California.

Bancroft, Philip. Papers, Bancroft Library, University of California, Berkeley.

Bard, Thomas Robert. Papers. Huntington Library, San Marino, California.

Dickson, Edward A. Papers. Special Collections Library, University of California, Los Angeles.

Edson, Katherine Philips. Papers. Government and Public Affairs Reading Room, University of California, Los Angeles.

Haynes, John Randolph. Papers. Government and Public Affairs Reading Room, University of California, Los Angeles.

Heney, Francis J. Papers. Bancroft Library, University of California, Berkeley.

Hichborn, Franklin K. "California Politics, 1891–1939." Unpublished manuscript, copies in University of California School of Law, Boalt Hall, Berkeley, and in John R. and Dorah Haynes Foundation Library, Los Angeles.

———. Papers. Government and Public Affairs Reading Room, University of California, Los Angeles.

Huntington, Collis P. Papers. Microfilm edition from the George Arents Research Library, Syracuse University. Microfilming Corporation of America, 1979.

Ickes, Harold L. Papers. Library of Congress.

Jones, Herbert C. Papers. Borel Collection, Stanford University.

Keesling, Francis V. Papers. Borel Collection, Stanford University.

Kent, William. Papers. Yale University Library.

Lissner, Meyer. Papers. Borel Collection, Stanford University.

Lubin, Simon. Papers. Bancroft Library, University of California, Berkeley.

Neylan, John Francis. Papers. Bancroft Library, University of California, Berkeley.

Older, Fremont. Papers. Bancroft Library, University of California, Berkeley.
Pardee, George C. Papers. Bancroft Library, University of California, Berkeley.
Phelan, James D. Papers. Bancroft Library, University of California, Berkeley.
Rowell, Chester. Papers. Bancroft Library, University of California, Berkeley.
Stimson, Marshall. Papers. Huntington Library, San Marino, California.
Works, John D. Papers. Bancroft Library, University of California, Berkeley,
and Borel Collection, Stanford University.

Preface

1. *San Francisco Call*, Nov. 3, 1907.
2. Part III, Carton 8, HWJ Papers.
3. Raymond Moley, *27 Masters of Politics* (New York, 1949), p. 88; HWJ to C. K. McClatchy, Dec. 28, 1930, Mar. 5, Dec. 1, 1931; HWJ to Hiram Johnson, Jr., Dec. 6, 1931; HWJ to Ickes, Mar. 8, 1931; *Cong. Record*, 71st Cong., 1st sess. (Nov. 21, 1929), p. 7871.

Chapter I: The California Years

1. *Sacramento Record-Union*, Oct. 3, 1882. Two-fifths of the assessed land in the city, it was claimed, was owned by railroad employees.
2. Material on Grove Johnson can be found in Irving McKee, "The Background and Early Career of Hiram Warren Johnson, 1866–1910," *Pacific Historical Review* 19:1 (Feb. 1950), pp. 17–30; John James Fitzpatrick III, "Senator Hiram W. Johnson: A Life History, 1866–1945" (Ph.D. diss., University of California, Berkeley, 1975); William L. Willis, *History of Sacramento County California* (Los Angeles, 1913); Winfield J. Davis, *An Illustrated History of Sacramento County, California* (Chicago, 1890); Edward Smith, *A History of Schools of the Syracuse: From Its Early Settlement to January 1, 1893* (Syracuse, 1893). Quincy Adams Johnson was born Jan. 8, 1812, at Lake George, New York, the son of Jonah Johnson, of Massachusetts (b. 1780). He died in Syracuse, Dec. 4, 1856. Grove himself, the second of two sons, was born on March 27, 1841. Grove's mother, Juliette Josephine Redington, the daughter of Jacob Redington, of Connecticut (b. 1759), was born in 1818 and died in 1854. Anne Williamson de-Montfredy was born May 25, 1842, in Onondaga, New York, and died in Sacramento, California, in December 1903. She was one of four children born to Louis deMontfredy, who had immigrated from France in 1824. Her mother was Mary H. Van Courtland, of New York. Her maternal grandfather, Hugh Williamson, of North Carolina, was a member of the Continental Congress, a delegate to the Constitutional Convention, and a member of the House of Representatives in the 1st and 2nd Congresses. Grove Johnson to HWJ, Jan. 12, 17, 1917; Hiram Johnson to Hiram Johnson, Jr., July 2, 1921; *Sacramento Union*, Dec. 9, 1903. Hiram Johnson described his grandfather as a "strange and half demented abolitionist." HWJ to Hiram Johnson, Jr., Feb. 26, 1928. At the time of Quincy's death, the *Syracuse Daily Standard* made no mention either of his partisan involvement or of his abolitionist views, noting only that "his temperament was pecu-

liar, and his indomitable will, strong passions, and taste for debate, often led him into discussions in which considerable acrimony was displayed." *Syracuse Daily Standard*, Dec. 5, 1856.

3. Hiram Johnson was named for one of Grove's uncles. The elder Hiram, who, Johnson recalled, spent much of his life as a seaman on the Great Lakes, retired to a ranch on the outskirts of Sacramento in the late 1870s. Grove Johnson to HWJ, Jan. 12, 29, 1917; Hiram Johnson, Jr., to June K. Hoals, Jan. 24, 1952. Grove Johnson dated his settlement in Sacramento as September 19, 1865. *Sacramento Record-Union*, Nov. 5, 1894. His explanation of the Syracuse imbroglio can be found in *Cong. Record*, 54th Cong., 2nd sess. (Jan. 12, 1897), p. 730. For a contemporary account, see *Syracuse Journal*, Sept. 14, 17, 19, 1863. A listing of the family by age and place of birth can be found in the 1880 U.S. Census, Sacramento County, California, City of Sacramento, 3rd Ward, no. 94.

4. W. Davis, *Sacramento County*, p. 613.

5. *Sacramento Record-Union*, July 20, 22, 26, 27, 29, 31, Aug. 3, 5, 19, 1867, Sept. 1, 1873.

6. *Sacramento Record-Union*, Sept. 7, 9, 1871. Johnson's motives for leaving the Republican party are unclear. Perhaps he was influenced by what seemed to be greater opportunities for advancement within the Democratic party. Perhaps too the decision was linked to the 1867 scandal and what Johnson in all probability took to be the failure of Republican party regulars to come to his defense adequately. Once reestablished in the Republican party, he became a doctrinaire partisan and would never refer to his earlier apostasy.

7. *Sacramento Record-Union*, Aug. 17, 1872, Aug. 6, 7, 28, Sept. 2, 3, 1873, Aug. 20, 25, 28, 31, Sept. 2, 1875; Winfield J. Davis, *History of Political Conventions in California, 1849–1892* (Sacramento, 1893), p. 328.

8. *Sacramento Record-Union*, July 27, Aug. 6, 20, 29, Sept. 12, 1877, Sept. 6, 8, 1879.

9. *Sacramento Record-Union*, Aug. 30, 1879; *Sacramento Bee*, Feb. 21, 1926.

10. *Sacramento Record-Union*, Aug. 6, 1877. See also *Sacramento Record-Union*, Aug. 25, 31, Sept. 2, 3, 1875.

11. *Sacramento Record-Union*, Aug. 4, 5, 7, 10, Oct. 3, 18, 30, Nov. 4, 9, 1882.

12. Willis, *Sacramento County*, p. 501.

13. Grove, one observer wrote, was "suspicious, jealous and small minded. . . . No amount of service rendered him would ever allay a suspicion in his mind that one was his enemy if at the end of a thousand services they should hesitate in the slightest degree at the performance of one." William Mills to Collis P. Huntington, Oct. 23, 1897, Huntington Papers.

14. Draft of article by Hiram Johnson, Jr., Part V, Carton 6, HWJ Papers.

15. HWJ to boys, July 2, 1921; HWJ to Hiram Johnson, Jr., Feb. 5, 1926.

16. E. French Strother, "Hiram W. Johnson, the Man," *California Weekly*, Feb. 25, 1910, pp. 219–22; HWJ to Hiram Johnson, Jr., Mar. 11, 1927; Fitzpatrick, "Senator Hiram W. Johnson," pp. 15–16; draft article by Hiram Johnson, Jr., Part V, Carton 6, HWJ Papers.

17. *Sacramento Bee*, May 25, 1891.

18. *Sacramento Union*, Mar. 29, 1895, Aug. 8, 1902.

19. W. Davis, *Political Conventions in California*, p. 592. Grove Johnson had hoped that the Southern Pacific Railroad would use its power to help him obtain the nomination. Angered by their refusal to provide support, he reiterated his loyalty to the company while expressing his resentment: "I hope and trust that they have received sufficient promise from Mr. Davis, as will justify them in preferring him to me." Grove Johnson to William Mills, July 28, 1892. See also William Mills to Collis P. Huntington, July 29, 1892, both in Huntington Papers. On Anthony Caminetti, see Joseph P. Giovinco, "The California Career of Anthony Caminetti, Italian-American Politician" (Ph.D. diss., University of California, Berkeley, 1973).

20. *Sacramento Record-Union*, Sept. 20, Oct. 3, 15, 16, 18, 20, 24, 27, 29, 31, Nov. 3, 1894.

21. *Sacramento Record-Union*, Nov. 3, 1894. In part, perhaps, Hiram's accusation stemmed from the refusal of the railroad to oppose Caminetti in the 1892 race. "Let Mr. Caminetti alone," Huntington had announced. See A. J. Johnston et al. to Collis P. Huntington, Oct. 28, 1892; Joseph Steffens, J. W. Wilson, and J. D. Coleman to Collis P. Huntington, Oct. 21, 1892, both in Huntington Papers. On Hiram Johnson's involvement in Republican party politics see *Sacramento Record-Union*, Aug. 31, Sept. 5, 1892; Grove Johnson to William Mills, July 28, 1892, Huntington Papers. Lincoln Steffens, who grew up in Sacramento during this time, recalled the Sacramento municipal elections of 1888, when Grove, together with his two sons, with guns drawn, confronted Frank Rhodes, a Republican district boss, in a closed meeting of his henchmen. Although the rivalry between Grove and Rhodes was real, the incident is probably apocryphal. As Steffens notes, there were no outside observers and there is no mention of the event either in the press or in the Johnson papers. Lincoln Steffens, *Autobiography* (New York, 1931), p. 49. See also *Sacramento Record-Union*, Mar. 15, 1888.

22. William H. Mills to Collis P. Huntington, Sept. 22, 1894, Huntington Papers. "If the railroad company stands in the way of doing my duty to the people and to the taxpayers, so much the worse for the railroad company," Johnson had added. *Sacramento Record-Union*, Sept. 20, 1894.

23. *Sacramento Record-Union*, Sept. 20, 1894.

24. William H. Mills to Collis P. Huntington, Oct. 2, 1894, Huntington Papers.

25. R. Hal Williams, *The Democratic Party and California Politics, 1880–1896* (Stanford, Calif., 1973), pp. 216–23.

26. *San Francisco Examiner*, Feb. 1, 11, 15, 16, 21, 1896.

27. *San Francisco Examiner*, Oct. 1, 4, 12, 14, 20, 26, Nov. 1, 1896.

28. *Sacramento Record-Union*, Aug. 13, 16, 1896; *Sacramento Bee*, Aug. 13, Oct. 14, 1896.

29. William Mills to Collis Huntington, Apr. 24, 1896. See also William Mills to Collis Huntington, June 8, 1896, both in Huntington Papers.

30. William Mills to Collis Huntington, Aug. 31, 1896. See also E. B. Willis to William Mills, Oct. 22, 1896, both in Huntington Papers.

31. *Sacramento Record-Union*, Sept. 25, 29, Oct. 23, 24, 26, 28, 30, 31, Nov. 1, 3, 1896; *Sacramento Bee*, Oct. 30, 1896.

32. William Mills to Collis P. Huntington, Oct. 13, 23, Nov. 4, 5, 1896, Huntington Papers. Mills perhaps exaggerated Johnson's personal failings. In the twelve presidential contests between 1864 and 1908, Sacramento County voted Republican in all but one, usually by large majorities. The one exception was the 1896 race, in which Bryan won 50.4 percent of the vote. Running ahead of his party's national ticket in Sacramento, Johnson received 55.4 percent of the vote. Overall, in the fifteen counties composing the Second District, Johnson won 42.3 percent of the vote, only slightly less than the 43 percent he had won in 1894. But then the opposition had been split, with both a Democratic and Populist candidate in the field. With the opposition united, it seems doubtful that Johnson could have won even if he had moderated his railroad stance.

33. *Cong. Record*, 54th Cong., 2nd sess. (Jan. 8, 9, 12, 1897), pp. 590–94, 689, 729–33. The vote was 103 to 168. Supporters of government operation of the railroad included Governor Budd, a majority of the California State Legislature, the San Francisco Chamber of Commerce, the *San Francisco Examiner*, the *Sacramento Bee*, and the *Los Angeles Times*. R. Williams, *Democratic Party and California Politics*, pp. 218–19.

34. *Sacramento Record-Union*, Sept. 23, 1896. Hiram, the *Sacramento Bee* noted, had worked unceasingly in Grove's interests. *Sacramento Bee*, Nov. 3, 1896.

35. *Sacramento Record-Union*, May 31, 1893. When Johnson turned to another threat to the social order—the new immigration from abroad—he sounded more like his father. The nation, he noted, should continue to welcome the immigrant "be he from any part of the world" but should not become "a dumping ground for the scum of the earth." In 1896 Grove had sponsored an amendment to curtail all immigration, *Cong. Record*, 54th Cong., 1st sess. (May 19, 1896), pp. 5420–21.

36. Willis, *Sacramento County*, p. 836.

37. *Sacramento Record-Union*, Nov. 4, 6, 8, 1899, Jan. 8–18, 23, 29, 30, 1900, Feb. 9, 1947. Earlier Johnson had held the same position under the administration of Mayor Hubbard. See *Sacramento Record-Union*, Jan. 7, 21, 1896.

38. *Sacramento Record-Union*, Oct. 26, 1901.

39. *Sacramento Record-Union*, Oct. 17, 1901. See also *Sacramento Record-Union*, Oct. 24, 25, Nov. 2, 1901.

40. *Sacramento Record-Union*, Oct. 23, Nov. 6, 1901.

41. *Sacramento Record-Union*, Aug. 10, 1902.

42. *Sacramento Record-Union*, Aug. 2–5, 11, 1902. No copies of the Clark campaign newsletters remain. It was during this campaign that Grove allegedly referred to his "two chief enemies . . . one, Hiram, full of egotism, and the other Albert, full of booze." Ida Tarbell, notes on interview with Chester Rowell, Apr. 28, 1911, Rowell Papers.

43. *Sacramento Record-Union*, Aug. 1, 1902; *San Francisco Call*, Aug. 1, 1902.

44. *Sacramento Record-Union*, Aug. 6, 7, 9, 13, 1902; *San Francisco Call*, Aug. 2–4, 6, 8–13, 1902.

45. *Sacramento Record-Union*, Aug. 5, 1902. "It took a lot of persuasion upon the part of my father to induce you to take the risk of opening up in San Fran-

cisco," Albert Johnson, Hiram's nephew, long afterwards observed. Albert L. Johnson to HWJ, Jan. 30, 1930.

46. Edgar Williams, "The Man Who Swept California: A Personal Sketch of Hiram W. Johnson," *Outlook*, 114 (Nov. 22, 1916), p. 639. Descriptions of Johnson's courtroom manner can be found in *San Francisco Call*, Jan. 4, 1903, and *San Francisco Chronicle*, Aug. 23, 1904. Classes from Hastings College of Law were often sent into the courtroom to observe Johnson's cross-examination techniques, his son recalled. Draft article by Hiram Johnson, Jr., Part V, Carton 6, HWJ Papers.

47. *San Francisco Chronicle*, Dec. 20, 1905. See also *San Francisco Chronicle*, Sept. 15, 18, 1904. The trial ended with the jury split nine to three for conviction. Collins was ultimately convicted and sentenced to fourteen years at San Quentin. See Hiram Johnson, Jr., to John Dickson, Oct. 21, 1947, for an examination of the particulars of the case.

48. Fremont Older, *My Own Story* (New York, 1926), p. 84. See also John Messing, "Public Lands, Politics, and Progressives: The Oregon Land Fraud Trials, 1903–1910," *Pacific Historical Review* 35:1 (Feb. 1966), pp. 35–66.

49. Walton Bean, *Boss Ruef's San Francisco; The Story of the Union Labor Party, Big Business, and the Graft Prosecution* (Berkeley, 1952).

50. *San Francisco Call*, Aug. 7, 1907.

51. *San Francisco Call*, Oct. 29, 31, Nov. 1, 2, 3, 5, 1907; Strother, "Hiram Johnson, the Man," p. 219; Hiram Johnson, Jr., draft article, Part V, Carton 6, HWJ Papers. Johnson resigned from the prosecution Oct. 28, 1907. *California Weekly*, Nov. 4, 1910, p. 793. Heney, also heavily involved in Langdon's reelection campaign, felt no urge to resign.

52. *San Francisco Call*, Nov. 14, 15, 18, 1908.

53. Ruef was sentenced to 15 years and sent to San Quentin, where he became a model prisoner (#24911) and a spokesman for penal reform. Later, Fremont Older would have second thoughts on the case, describing Ruef as a victim of society rather than its enemy. His efforts to secure Ruef's early release failed when Johnson, now governor, issued a long public statement critical of the move. Ruef was paroled in 1915, after four and one-half years, and was ultimately pardoned by Governor William Stephens, Johnson's successor.

54. George Mowry, *The California Progressives* (Berkeley, 1951), pp. 23–56; Albert Clodius, "The Quest for Good Government in Los Angeles, 1890–1910" (Ph.D. diss., Claremont Graduate School, 1953); Grace L. Miller, "The Origins of the San Diego Lincoln-Roosevelt League, 1905–1909," *Southern California Quarterly* 60:4 (Winter 1978), pp. 421–43.

55. Edward Dickson to Lissner, Feb. 10, 1907, Lissner Papers.

56. Joseph Gregg Layne, "The Lincoln-Roosevelt League: Its Origins and Accomplishments," *Historical Society of Southern California Quarterly* 25 (Sept. 1943), pp. 79–101; Alice Rose, "The Rise of California Insurgency: Origins of the League of Lincoln-Roosevelt Republican Clubs, 1900–1907" (Ph.D. diss., Stanford University, 1942).

57. *Sacramento Union*, Jan. 27, 1909; Franklin Hichborn, *Story of the Session of the California Legislature of 1909* (San Francisco, 1909), p. 206. In 1907 the

San Francisco Bulletin characterized the legislative session of that year as a creature of Grove Johnson and the Southern Pacific. *San Francisco Bulletin*, Jan. 18,
1907. For an examination of the reform career of John R. Haynes, see Tom Sitton,
"California's Practical Idealist: John Randolph Haynes," *California History* 67:1
(Mar. 1988), pp. 2–17.

58. Lissner to Robert La Follette, Dec. 15, 1909, Lissner Papers.

59. *Pacific Outlook*, Jan. 22, 1910, pp. 1–2. See also Spencer C. Olin, Jr.,
"Hiram Johnson, the Lincoln-Roosevelt League, and the Election of 1910," *California Historical Society Quarterly* 45 (Sept. 1966), pp. 225–40.

60. Rowell to HWJ, Jan. 26, 1910, Rowell Papers.

61. Bard Papers, Borel Collection, Stanford University. Johnson received sixteen votes; Charles Belshaw, a legislator from Antioch, secured four. Heney and
Frank Mott, the mayor of Oakland, each received a single vote. See also *California Weekly*, Feb. 11, 1910, p. 185.

62. *San Francisco Call*, Sept. 30, Oct. 8, 23, 26, 27, 30, 31, Nov. 2, 1909.

63. Rowell to Lissner, Jan. 31, 1910, Rowell Papers.

64. Mowry, *California Progressives*, p. 109. Most observers assume that Minnie was won over by the argument that the governorship was the necessary step-
ping stone to Hiram's subsequent election to the U.S. Senate. Yet it seems plain
that she did not relish a political career of any sort for her husband. Although he
actively solicited neither nomination, Hiram himself would almost certainly
have preferred to enter the race for the U.S. Senate. See Hichborn to HWJ, July 14,
1919; HWJ to Hichborn, July 31, 1919, Hichborn Papers.

65. HWJ to Hiram Johnson, Jr., Mar. 10, 1935.

66. HWJ to Allen, Feb. 28, 1910. The executive committee of the Lincoln-
Roosevelt League, by a vote of 21 to 6, made the selection official. See Mowry,
California Progressives, p. 110.

67. HWJ to C. K. McClatchy, Feb. 26, 1910. See also *California Weekly*, Apr.
15, 1910, p. 265; Lissner to HWJ, May 13, 1919, Rowell Papers.

68. Johnson described the event as spontaneous. Versions of the incident differ
in detail. The version quoted here is found in HWJ to H. D. W. English, Dec. 8,
1916. See also *San Francisco Bulletin*, Aug. 6, 1910; Mowry, *California Progressives*, pp. 125–26. The *Los Angeles Times* characterized the outburst as a
"frenzy of vituperation, unspeakably abusive." *Los Angeles Times*, Aug. 6, 1910.

69. HWJ to Lissner, Oct. 28, 1915.

70. HWJ to Rowell, Apr. 19, 1910. It became the practice for Johnson to speak
first when accompanied by Wallace or John Works, the league candidate for the
U.S. Senate. In the aftermath of the primary, Wallace complained that Johnson
had conducted a "selfish" campaign. Unusually contrite, Johnson agreed. HWJ
to Lissner, Aug. 20, 1910.

71. HWJ to C. K. McClatchy, Apr. 19, 1910.

72. McCabe, a stenographer and court reporter, joined the San Francisco District Attorney's Office in 1901 and participated in the graft trials. He was also
involved in the politics of the city, and in 1904 he held the post of secretary of
the California Democratic delegation. He served as Johnson's private secretary
throughout the latter's governorship. See *San Francisco Call*, June 5, 1904; *San*

Francisco Chronicle, Apr. 17, 1950; Marshall Stimson to Rowell, Sept. 7, 1922, Rowell Papers.

73. The itinerary of Johnson's campaign can be followed in the *San Francisco Bulletin*.

74. *Fresno Republican*, Apr. 12, 1910; *San Francisco Bulletin*, Apr. 29, Aug. 12, 1910.

75. Efforts were made to secure Roosevelt's endorsement of the ticket, but although Roosevelt privately sympathized with the movement, he publicly professed his neutrality. See Mowry, *California Progressives*, pp. 122–23; Theodore Roosevelt to Theodore Roosevelt, Jr., Aug. 10, 1910, in Elting Morison, ed., *Letters of Theodore Roosevelt* (Cambridge, Mass., 1954).

76. Johnson was defeated in only 5 of California's 58 counties, and with the exception of San Francisco, where he lost to Curry by more than 3,000 votes, the margins of his defeat rarely exceeded 50 votes. Thus Curry carried Sacramento County by only 42 votes. California Secretary of State, *Statement of Direct Primary Election Vote of California, Aug. 16, 1910*. The one state office the league failed to carry was that of secretary of state, where Florence O'Brien lost to Frank Jordan. Almost from the beginning of Johnson's governorship, he and Jordan would find themselves at loggerheads.

77. *San Francisco Chronicle*, Oct. 26, 1910.

78. *San Francisco Bulletin*, Oct. 14, 1910. See also *California Weekly*, Oct. 14, 1910, p. 744, Oct. 28, 1910, pp. 770, 776.

79. James Phelan to Henry Morgenthau, Aug. 29, 1910, Phelan Papers.

80. George Wallace Milias, "Hiram Johnson's Campaign for the Governorship of California in 1910" (M.A. thesis, Stanford University, 1949).

81. *San Francisco Call*, Sept. 19, 1910; *San Francisco Bulletin*, Oct. 14, 1910.

82. Johnson's endorsement of the Osawatomie address can be found in *San Francisco Bulletin*, Sept. 7, 1910; *San Francisco Call*, Sept. 22, Oct. 12, 23, 1910.

83. *Los Angeles Times*, Nov. 8, 1910. In Los Angeles county, the drop-off was 8,000 votes. Overall, Johnson secured 45.94 percent of the total votes cast in the general election and Bell 40.14 percent. J. Stitt Wilson, the Socialist candidate, received 12.4 percent, while 1.51 percent went to the Prohibitionist candidate. In 1902 Pardee had secured 48.06 percent, and in 1906 Gillett had won with 40.34 percent.

84. A list of the committees and their membership can be found in *California Weekly*, Nov. 18, 1910, pp. 824–25.

85. HWJ to Lissner, Jan. 14, 1911, Lissner Papers; Mowry, *California Progressives*, p. 136; *California Weekly*, Dec. 2, 1910, p. 8.

86. Franklin Hichborn, *Story of the Session of the California Legislature of 1911* (San Francisco, 1911), pp. 18–23. Both George Mowry and Spencer Olin stress the positive contributions made by the conference. Without it, Olin notes, the record of the 1911 legislature "would undoubtedly have been much less impressive." Spencer C. Olin, Jr., *California's Prodigal Sons: Hiram Johnson and the Progressives* (Berkeley, Calif., 1968), p. 33; Mowry, *California Progressives*, p. 136. Given that much of the agenda for 1911 had been defined in the 1909 session, and given Hichborn's comments, it is possible I think to question these

conclusions. It should also be noted that Mowry relies in part on the memory of Edward Dickson, who, in later years, had reason to dislike and belittle Johnson. Dickson's allegation that Johnson was ignorant of the substance of reform legislation proposed during the 1910 campaign is difficult to accept. His allegation that Johnson needed to have the mechanics of the initiative, referendum, and recall explained to him beggars belief. See Mowry, *California Progressives*, p. 135; Edgar A. Luce to George Mowry, Feb. 7, 1953, Neylan Papers.

87. Johnson's inaugural address can be found in Hichborn, *1911*, pp. i–xvi.

88. Hichborn, *1911*, p. 48; William E. Smythe, "Johnson: A Governor Who Has Made Good," *Hampton's Magazine*, July 1911, pp. 91–96.

89. The legislature did, however, balk in implementing Johnson's recommendation to make all state offices appointive save that of the controller, the state's chief fiscal officer; this proposal would have created in effect a cabinet system similar to that at the national level. In all, the legislature passed 956 bills in the 1911 regular session. Of those, Johnson pocketed or vetoed 203 and signed into law the remaining 753. *Sacramento Bee*, May 2, 1911. See also *California Outlook*, May 13, 1911, pp. 6–9.

90. Almost immediately, both the board and Neylan proved their worth by undertaking major audits of the 22 state agencies, exposing graft, and substantially reducing state expenditures.

91. Austin Lewis, "The Day After," *International Socialist Review*, Dec. 1911, p. 358, as quoted in Robert Knight, *Industrial Relations in the San Francisco Bay Area, 1900–1918* (Berkeley, 1960), p. 180.

92. Alexander Saxton, "San Francisco Labor and the Populist and Progressive Insurgencies," *Pacific Historical Review* 34:4 (Nov. 1965), pp. 421–38; Michael Kazin, *Barons of Labor: The San Francisco Building Trades and Union Power in the Progressive Era* (Urbana, Ill., 1987), pp. 177–85. McCarthy had opposed establishing the Union Labor party, but he supported the party after 1905.

93. *San Francisco Call*, Nov. 5, 1907.

94. *Sacramento Bee*, Apr. 18, 1910. In part, Johnson's ebullient praise of labor in Sacramento was intended to offset a publicity handout circulated by the league in which Johnson was incorrectly quoted as having said that the workers in the car shops in Sacramento were all Greeks. It was this incident that gave rise to his remarks about the "Damn Fool" Lincoln-Roosevelt League. HWJ to C. K. McClatchy, Apr. 19, 1910.

95. John L. Shover, "The Progressives and the Working Class Vote in California," *Labor History* 10:4 (Fall 1969), pp. 584–601.

96. Paul Scharrenberg, "Paul Scharrenberg Reminiscences," Transcript of oral history project, Bancroft Library, Berkeley, 1954. Johnson also secured the primary endorsement of Will French, Andrew Furuseth of the Sailors' Union of the Pacific, John Sweeney, past president of the San Francisco Labor Council and Andrew Gallagher of the San Francisco Labor Council. See *California Weekly*, July 22, 1910, p. 553; *San Francisco Examiner*, Aug. 15, 1910.

97. Earl, with Roosevelt's blessing, urged Rowell to telephone Johnson with his objections to the measure, arguing that a bill for a ten-hour day could be secured at the next session. In reply, Johnson confessed that he had already

signed the bill. Only later was it revealed that he had signed the bill during the telephone conversation. *Fresno Republican*, Sept. 27, 1914.

98. *Seamen's Journal*, Apr. 19, 1911. See also California State Federation of Labor, *Proceedings, 1911*, Legislative Report, pp. 80–96.

99. *Labor Clarion*, Apr. 7, 1911, p. 3. That support would be forthcoming in the resolutions passed by the State Federation of Labor meeting at Bakersfield in October 1911. *San Francisco Bulletin*, Oct. 6, 7, 1911.

100. *Labor Clarion*, May 16, 1913, p. 4.

101. Franklin Hichborn, *Story of the Session of the California Legislature of 1913* (San Francisco, 1913); Norris C. Hundley, Jr., "Katherine Philips Edson and the Fight for the California Minimum Wage, 1912–1923," *Pacific Historical Review* 29 (Aug. 1960), pp. 271–85; Samuel E. Wood, "The California State Commission of Immigration and Housing: A Study of Administrative Organization and the Growth of Function" (Ph.D. diss., University of California, Berkeley, 1942); Earl C. Crockett, "The History of California Labor Legislation, 1910–1930" (Ph.D. diss., University of California, Berkeley, 1931).

102. HWJ to Simon Lubin, Aug. 20, 1912, Lubin Papers.

103. "Progressive as our southern city is in most respects, industrially it is archaic," the *California Weekly*, spokesman for Northern California progressives, observed of Los Angeles. *California Weekly*, Dec. 30, 1910; p. 66. See also Rowell to HWJ, Mar. 24, 1917, Rowell Papers.

104. HWJ to Theodore Roosevelt, Aug. 13, 1914.

105. Lissner to HWJ, Mar. 23, 1911.

106. Grace Miller, "The IWW Free Speech Fight: San Diego, 1912," *Southern California Quarterly* 54 : 3 (Fall 1972), pp. 211–38; Ronald Genini, "Industrial Workers of the World and Their Fresno Free Speech Fight, 1910–1911," *California Historical Quarterly* 53 : 2 (Summer 1974), pp. 101–14. For an excellent examination of California agriculture see Cletus E. Daniel, *Bitter Harvest: A History of California Farmworkers, 1870–1941* (Berkeley, 1981).

107. Woodrow C. Whitten, "The Wheatland Episode," *Pacific Historical Review* 17 : 1 (Feb. 1948), pp. 37–42; Cletus E. Daniel, "In Defense of the Wheatland Wobblies: A Critical Analysis of the IWW in California," *Labor History* 19 : 4 (Fall 1978), pp. 485–509; Woodrow C. Whitten, "Criminal Syndicalism and the Law in California: 1919–1927," *Transactions of the American Philosophical Society* 59 : 2 (Mar. 1969), pp. 1–73.

108. HWJ to Charles D. Haywood, Mar. 10, 1914.

109. Conditions in San Diego, Harris Weinstock wrote, reminded him of Czarist Russia. Harris Weinstock, *Report to His Excellency the Governor of California on the Disturbances in the City and County of San Diego in 1912* (Sacramento, 1912), pp. 16–17; Carleton Parker, *A Report to His Excellency Hiram W. Johnson*, reprinted in Carleton Parker, *The Casual Laborer and Other Essays* (New York, 1920), pp. 171–99. Yuba County authorities convicted Richard "Blackie" Ford and Herman Suhr, both associated with the IWW, of conspiracy to commit murder in the Wheatland riot. Each was given a life sentence. Both radicals and moderates within the labor movement rallied to their defense, protesting the unfairness of the trial and conviction. On March 5, 1915, at a pardon

hearing, Johnson promised to review the case, but in the end he refused to intervene, accepting their guilt and explaining that in the face of continued threats, intimidation, and violence on the part of the IWW in support of Ford and Suhr, he would not consider any reduction of sentence. Disappointed, Paul Scharrenberg and the state chapter of the American Federation of Labor, which had led the fight for a rehearing, acquiesced. Refusing to intervene, Scharrenberg wrote, was the only "manly" thing for Johnson to do. See Daniel, "In Defense of Wheatland Wobblies," pp. 499–504.

110. Carey McWilliams, *Factories in the Field: The Story of Migratory Farm Labor in California* (Boston, 1939); Vernon M. Cadys, "California's Plan for Land Settlement," *American Review of Reviews* 58 (Aug. 1918), pp. 182–84. At the same time it should be emphasized that agricultural labor was exempted from the wages and hours legislation afforded their industrial counterparts and that Johnson, while sympathetic to the vision of Mead and Weinstock, made clear that he wanted no plan that would involve major state expenditures. HWJ to Rowell, D. P. Barrows, Harris Weinstock, Feb. 15, 1915; HWJ to Rowell, Mar. 11, 1915, both in Rowell Papers.

111. Rowell to HWJ, Dec. 27, 1916, Rowell Papers.

112. Roger Daniels, *The Politics of Prejudice: The Anti-Japanese Movement in California and the Struggle for Japanese Exclusion* (Berkeley, 1962); Spencer C. Olin, Jr., "European Immigrant and Oriental Alien: Acceptance and Rejection by the California Legislature of 1913," *Pacific Historical Review* 35:3 (Aug. 1966), pp. 303–15.

113. Hichborn, *1911*, pp. 342–44. He was, he assured the Taft administration, willing to veto the legislation if necessary. HWJ to Huntington Wilson, Mar. 24, 1911.

114. HWJ to Theodore Roosevelt, June 21, 1913.

115. Memorandum, "Sacramento Legislative Trip, Jan. 6–7, 1913," Panama Pacific International Exhibition MSS, as quoted in Daniels, *Politics of Prejudice*, pp. 57–58.

116. HWJ to Rowell, Mar. 13, 1913; *Fresno Republican*, Apr. 16, 1913; Hichborn, *1913*, pp. 236–47. Johnson had considered a similar fallback position in 1911.

117. *New York Times*, Apr. 19, 1913. See also Arthur S. Link, *Wilson: The New Freedom* (Princeton, 1956), pp. 289–96.

118. Bryan, Johnson wrote, "presented absolutely nothing that could not have been transmitted within the limits of a night letter, without using all of the allotted words." HWJ to Theodore Roosevelt, June 21, 1913. See also Paolo E. Coletta, "'The Most Thankless Task': Bryan and the California Alien Land Legislation," *Pacific Historical Review* 36:2 (May 1967), pp. 163–87. Bryan "came, talked and—fizzled," the *San Francisco Examiner* reported. *San Francisco Examiner*, Apr. 29, 1913.

119. Hichborn, *1913*, pp. 257–58.

120. HWJ to Theodore Roosevelt, June 21, 1913. The complete text of this letter can be found in Daniels, *Politics of Prejudice*, pp. 112–17.

121. Hichborn, *1913*, pp. 260–74.

122. HWJ to Lissner, June 9, 1913.

123. HWJ to Theodore Roosevelt, June 21, 1913. The embarrassment to California's Democrats, Johnson observed, would prevent any further use of the issue in a partisan way "except as we shall want it to be." In 1915 Johnson worked to ensure that a proposal to prohibit the leasing of agricultural land by alien Japanese would remain bottled in committee. HWJ to Lissner, Jan. 23, 1915; Hichborn, *Story of the Session of the California Legislature of 1915* (San Francisco, 1916), pp. 229–32.

124. Thus in writing to Hichborn, a vocal advocate of moral reform, he referred to *your* red-light bill. HWJ to Hichborn, July 28, 1914, Hichborn Papers. Emphasis mine.

125. HWJ to Lissner, June 9, 1913. See also Gilbert Ostrander, *The Prohibition Movement in California, 1848–1933* (Berkeley, 1957); HWJ to Lissner, Marshall Stimson, Edward Dickson, Sept. 3, 1916.

126. HWJ to Archibald Johnson, Aug. 2, 1917; HWJ to Arthur Arlett, July 7, 1917; *Cong. Record*, 65th Cong., 1st sess. (July 6, 1917), pp. 4756–57; Andrew Sinclair, *Era of Excess: A Social History of the Prohibition Movement* (New York, 1962), p. 157.

127. HWJ to C. K. McClatchy, Aug. 2, 1917. Prohibition, he later wrote, "means prohibition for the poor, while the rich may do as they please." HWJ to boys, Oct. 10, 1921.

128. HWJ to Archibald Johnson, Aug. 2, 1917.

129. *Cong. Record*, 65th Cong., 1st sess. (Aug. 1, 1917), pp. 5651–52.

130. HWJ to W. A. Beasly, Oct. 3, 1932.

131. HWJ to Hiram Johnson, Jr., Sept. 15, 1917; HWJ to Amy Johnson, Feb. 23, 1918. See also Hiram Johnson, Jr., "Notes for Article on Republican National Convention, 1920," Part VI, Carton 6, HWJ Papers.

132. *California Outlook*, Oct. 3, 1914, p. 2. See also Chester Rowell, "More About Hiram Johnson," *Everybody's Magazine*, Nov. 1914, p. 638.

133. Eustace Cullinan, "The Case for Hiram Johnson," *Outlook* 136 (Mar. 19, 1924), p. 481.

134. Rowell to E. A. Forbes, Nov. 28, 1919; Rowell to David Starr Jordan, Oct. 22, 1919; Rowell to Dwight Marvin, July 2, 1919; Rowell to HWJ, Dec. 27, 1916, all in Rowell Papers. On Rowell, see Miles C. Everett, "Chester Harvey Rowell, Pragmatic Humanist and California Progressive" (Ph.D. diss., University of California, Berkeley, 1965).

135. HWJ to George C. Roeding, May 8, 1916; HWJ to Thos. V. Cator, Feb. 15, 1916; HWJ to C. K. McClatchy, Feb. 23, 1925. See also HWJ to Hichborn, July 31, 1919, Hichborn Papers.

136. Rowell to HWJ, Apr. 18, 1916, Rowell Papers. Of his opponents Johnson once remarked: "They wish me not only political annihilation but personal hurt and injury and disaster and ruin. They would like to see me break a leg, or crack my skull, or lose my boy, or in any fashion suffer anguish and sorrow." HWJ to Stanley Washburn, Feb. 11, 1916. Writing in 1922, he noted: "I really believe they would resort to assassination if they dared." HWJ to boys, June 1, 1922.

137. Eshleman to HWJ, Dec. 18, 1913.

138. Rowell to HWJ, July 12, 1916, Rowell Papers.

139. HWJ to T. S. Montgomery, Mar. 9, 1916.

140. Hiram Johnson, Jr., to Norman Hapgood, Apr. 19, 1910; E. Williams, "The Man Who Swept California," p. 640; Elbert F. Baldwin, "Hiram Johnson: His Assets and Liabilities," *Outlook* 124 (Apr. 21, 1920), p. 696. See also Hiram Johnson, Jr., to E. R. Nichols, Nov. 1, 1949.

141. *Nation*, June 5, 1920, p. 748.

142. Rowell to Edson, Oct. 10, 1919, Edson Papers. See also Rowell to E. A. Forbes, Nov. 28, 1919: "It makes Johnson a tremendous crusader to the audience of the moment," Rowell lamented, "but it also makes his speeches almost unquotable to the more critical and infinitely larger audience of print."

143. *California Outlook*, Jan. 20, 1912, p. 8; "Hiram Johnson, Political Revivalist," *American Review of Reviews* 46 (Sept. 1912), pp. 306–9.

144. *California Outlook*, Oct. 3, 1914, pp. 2–3; Baldwin, "Hiram Johnson," pp. 696–98. "A sort of altruism has been introduced that has changed entirely the current of men's thoughts toward government," Johnson wrote in 1914 to explain the progressive currents sweeping the land. And to C. K. McClatchy, he later confessed: "Emotions make us love our fellow beings and fight for them . . . unite men in indissoluble bonds of friendship." HWJ to W. S. Goodrich, Mar. 12, 1914; HWJ to C. K. McClatchy, Oct. 14, 1926.

Chapter II: Armageddon and Back

1. *Sacramento Bee*, Oct. 13, 14, 16, 1911; *Los Angeles Times*, Oct. 14, 16, 17, 1911. Johnson's introduction of Taft at Sacramento lasted little more than a minute. He did not speak at the banquet for Taft in Los Angeles. On Roosevelt's earlier visit see *California Outlook*, Mar. 18, 1911, pp. 3, 8, Mar. 25, 1911, pp. 5, 6, 18, 19; *Los Angeles Express*, Mar. 21, 1911; *Los Angeles Examiner*, Mar. 23, 1911; *San Francisco Examiner*, Mar. 29, 1911.

2. HWJ to Theodore Roosevelt, Oct. 20, 1911, Roosevelt Papers, as quoted in A. Lincoln, "My Dear Governor: Letters Exchanged by Theodore Roosevelt and Hiram Johnson," *California Historical Society Quarterly* 38:3 (Sept. 1959), pp. 233–34.

3. Theodore Roosevelt to HWJ, Oct. 27, 1911; Theodore Roosevelt to Marshall Stimson, Oct. 27, 1910, in Elting Morison, ed., *Letters of Theodore Roosevelt* (Cambridge, Mass., 1954).

4. *San Francisco Bulletin*, Nov. 27, 1911. See also George Mowry, *The California Progressives* (Berkeley, Calif., 1951), pp. 161–64.

5. Theodore Roosevelt to HWJ, Jan. 14, 1912, Roosevelt Papers, in Mowry, *California Progressives*, p. 166; Theodore Roosevelt to HWJ, Jan. 20, 1912, in Morison, *Letters of Theodore Roosevelt*. Publicly, the trip was characterized as a private journey in which Johnson and his wife would visit with their younger son, Archibald, then a law student at Columbia University. See *California Outlook*, Jan. 27, 1912, p. 10.

6. HWJ to Lissner, Feb. 3, 1912, Lissner Papers.

7. *New York Times*, Feb. 4, 5, 6, 1912. In his autobiography, La Follette dis-

missed the episode as minor. "I was not at my best and did not at once get hold of my audience," he explained. *La Follette's Autobiography: A Personal Narrative of Political Experiences* (Madison, Wisc., 1963), p. 259.

8. Mowry, *California Progressives*, pp. 168–73.

9. Johnson's public statement detailing these events can be found in the *San Francisco Bulletin*, Apr. 5, 1912.

10. *California Outlook*, Feb. 12, 1912, p. 10, Mar. 2, 1912, p. 5, Mar. 23, 1912, p. 9.

11. *San Francisco Bulletin*, Mar. 11, 1912; *California Outlook*, Mar. 16, 1912, p. 11.

12. *San Francisco Bulletin*, Mar. 18, 27, Apr. 8, 1912; *California Outlook*, Apr. 13, 1912, pp. 6, 19, May 4, 1912, pp. 6–9, 18.

13. HWJ to Lissner, Apr. 1, 17, 1912; HWJ to Hichborn, Apr. 4, 1912.

14. *San Francisco Bulletin*, Apr. 30, May 1, 13, 1912; *Fresno Republican*, May 7, 1912.

15. Taft won in Calaveras and Inyo counties. La Follette took San Joaquin County, where he had the enthusiastic backing of Irving Martin, publisher of the *Stockton Record*.

16. "The President Aggressive," *Outlook* 100 (Feb. 24, 1912), pp. 376–77; "Mr. Taft's Boston Speech," *Outlook* 100 (Mar. 30, 1912), pp. 706–7; "Taft Fires on His Opponents," *American Review of Reviews* 45 (Mar. 1912), p. 271; "The Republican Feud," *Literary Digest*, Feb. 24, 1912, pp. 357–58; "President Taft's Denunciation of Mr. Roosevelt," *Literary Digest*, May 4, 1912, pp. 922–23.

17. La Follette won in Wisconsin, where the primary was uncontested, and in North Dakota. Taft narrowly squeaked to victory in Massachusetts. Roosevelt won in California, Illinois, Maryland, Nebraska, Oregon, South Dakota, Ohio, Pennsylvania, and New Jersey. All of Roosevelt's victories were landslides except for that in Maryland. Allen Gable, *The Bull Moose Years: Theodore Roosevelt and the Progressive Party* (New York, 1978), p. 14.

18. *Sacramento Bee*, June 10, 12, 1912.

19. Gable, *Bull Moose Years*, p. 17.

20. None today would argue that the Republican party establishment was impartial in its determination of contested delegates. Just as Roosevelt and his predecessors had manipulated the party machinery to their own advantage, so too did Taft. The question is whether an "impartial" settlement of the contending claims would have turned the trick, either in ensuring Roosevelt's nomination or in denying Taft's renomination. There, disagreement continues.

21. *Los Angeles Tribune*, June 12, 1912. See also Edwin Earl to Edward Dickson, June 10, 19, 1912, Dickson Papers.

22. *Sacramento Bee*, June 12, 15, 1912; *California Outlook*, June 15, 1912, p. 7.

23. HWJ to Lissner, June 9, 1912, Lissner Papers. See also HWJ to Matt Sullivan, June 8, 1912; HWJ to Medill McCormick, June 3, 1912; *San Francisco Examiner*, June 21, 22, 1912; Oscar King Davis, *Released for Publication: Some Inside Political History of Theodore Roosevelt and His Times* (New York, 1925), pp. 295, 299; Gable, *Bull Moose Years*, p. 17.

24. George Mowry, "Election of 1912," in Arthur Schlesinger, Jr., ed., *History of American Presidential Elections, 1789–1968*, vol. 3 (New York, 1971), pp. 2135–66.

25. A. Lincoln, "Theodore Roosevelt, Hiram Johnson, and the Vice-presidential Nomination of 1912," *Pacific Historical Review* 28:3 (Aug. 1959), pp. 267–83.

26. Edwin Earl to Theodore Roosevelt, Feb. 15, 1912; Edwin Earl to Edward Dickson, Feb. 8, 1912; Edwin Earl to Brundige, Lissner, Stimson, Mar. 11, 1912, all in Dickson Papers. See also *California Outlook*, Feb. 24, 1912, p. 15, June 8, 1912, pp. 2–4, 7–9, 20.

27. *New York Times*, Mar. 2, 1912.

28. HWJ to Gifford Pinchot, June 3, 1912.

29. HWJ to George Record, July 8, 1912; HWJ to J. C. O'Laughlin, July 11, 1912; HWJ to Medill McCormick, July 11, 1912.

30. HWJ to Al McCabe, Aug. 5, 6, 1912.

31. *California Outlook*, Aug. 17, 1912, p. 7; Gable, *Bull Moose Years*, pp. 108–9.

32. HWJ to P. E. Bowles, Aug. 21, 1912.

33. HWJ to George Perkins, Oct. 1, 1912; *San Francisco Bulletin*, Sept. 19, 1912. Johnson's itinerary can be traced in the *San Francisco Bulletin*. Johnson's irritation with the arrangements, which were largely put together by O. K. Davis, and Davis's irritation with Johnson, are both evident in O. Davis, *Released for Publication*, pp. 345–404. During much of the time Johnson feared that his long absence from California might prompt his enemies to take legal action to call into question his title to the governorship.

34. HWJ to Lissner, Oct. 13, 1912, Lissner Papers; *San Francisco Bulletin*, Oct. 7, 1912.

35. *San Francisco Bulletin*, Nov. 4, 1912.

36. *San Francisco Bulletin*, Sept. 3, 5, 6, Nov. 9, 1912.

37. *San Francisco Bulletin*, Sept. 10, 1912. George West, a reporter for the *San Francisco Bulletin* who had accompanied Johnson through part of his California campaign in 1910, was with him throughout the 1912 campaign.

38. O. Davis, *Released for Publication*, pp. 339–40. Medill McCormick to George Perkins, July 14, 1914, copy in HWJ Papers.

39. *Munsey's Magazine*, Feb. 1913, pp. 729–33; Gable, *Bull Moose Years*, p. 159; HWJ to Stanley Washburn, June 18, 1914; HWJ to Matthew Hale, June 27, 1914.

40. *Sacramento Bee*, Oct. 16, 30, 31, Nov. 10, 1913. Nevertheless, Johnson voiced satisfaction with the second-place showing by Progressives in Massachusetts. He dismissed the results in New Jersey, where the Progressive party ran well behind both the victorious Democrats and the Republican party. There, Edward Stokes, the Republican candidate, had professed his own support for Roosevelt, thus blurring the party division. See Gable, *Bull Moose Years*, p. 176.

41. Lissner to Rowell, June 10, 1913; Lissner to HWJ, July 2, 1913; Lissner to Daniel A. Ryan, Nov. 20, 1913, all in Lissner Papers. The California progressives, Eshleman argued, had cut their ties with the Old Guard, and if they retained the Republican party label they could expect support neither from the standpatters

nor from Democrats who might otherwise affiliate. Not to break with the party, he concluded, would be "inconsistent as well as uncomfortable. . . . The more we allow the rumor to spread that we are weakening the weaker we will become." Eshleman to HWJ, Sept. 30, 1913.

42. *Sacramento Bee*, Nov. 14, 1913.

43. Lissner to Albert Beveridge, Dec. 12, 1913, Lissner Papers. To ease the transition, the 1913 legislature enacted a system of cross-filing that enabled a candidate for political office to file for more than one party nomination.

44. HWJ to Stanley Washburn, Mar. 3, 1914.

45. Lissner to Albert Beveridge, Dec. 12, 1913; Lissner to HWJ, Dec. 20, 1913, Lissner Papers; John R. Haynes to HWJ, Jan. 6, 1914.

46. He did not want to run, Johnson later confessed to Stanley Washburn; but, he continued, "I realize that I would have been unhappy the rest of my days if I had not done just what I am doing now." HWJ to Stanley Washburn, June 18, 1914.

47. Edwin Earl to HWJ, Dec. 2, 1913; Eshleman to HWJ, Dec. 18, 1913; Lissner to HWJ, Dec. 20, 1913, Lissner Papers.

48. Rowell to Lissner, Dec. 19, 1913, Rowell Papers; HWJ to Lissner, Jan. 6, 1914, Lissner Papers. Johnson, William Kent had written earlier, is "thoroughly jealous of Heney and intends keeping him down." William Kent to Hichborn, Aug. 3, 1912, Hichborn Papers. Heney himself was convinced that Johnson had delayed his own announcement in order to freeze Heney out of the running. See Francis Heney to William Kent, Dec. 30, 1913, Kent Papers, as quoted in Mowry, *California Progressives*, p. 209.

49. Rowell to Lissner, Jan. 14, 1914, Lissner Papers; George Stone to Rowell, Dec. 20, 1913; Lissner to Rowell, Jan. 15, 1914, both in Rowell Papers.

50. Registration in Los Angeles, he wrote in his discouragement, demonstrated the persistence of traditional party alignments. Roosevelt, he concluded, had won there in 1912 not because he was a progressive but because he ran on the Republican ticket. HWJ to Lissner, Jan. 19, 1914, Lissner Papers. See also HWJ to Rowell, Apr. 6, 1914, Rowell Papers; Rowell to Lissner, Apr. 11, 1914, Lissner Papers.

51. HWJ to Theodore Roosevelt, Aug. 19, 1914.

52. HWJ to Theodore Roosevelt, June 17, 1914; HWJ to Stanley Washburn, June 18, 1914.

53. *Fresno Republican*, Feb. 25, 1914; *San Francisco Bulletin*, Apr. 27, 1914; *San Diego Union*, Feb. 17, 1914.

54. HWJ to Irving Martin, July 22, 1914; HWJ to Lissner, Aug. 17, 1914, Lissner Papers.

55. For coverage of Fredericks's campaign see *San Diego Union*, Sept. 19, 1914; *Oakland Tribune*, Oct. 11, 23, 1914; *Stockton Record*, Oct. 27, 1914.

56. *San Francisco Bulletin*, Sept. 4, 7, Oct. 24, 1914; *Sacramento Bee*, Oct. 17, 1914.

57. HWJ to Rowell, June 29, 1914.

58. HWJ to Francis Heney, Aug. 31, 1914.

59. At the time of the 1914 general election, Republican registration stood at

510,000, Democratic registration at 277,000, and Progressive registration at 217,000.

60. Johnson's 460,000 votes amounted to 49.7 percent of the turnout for the race. Approximately 78,000 votes went to the Socialist and Prohibitionist candidates. Fredericks won in 5 of the state's 58 counties: San Diego, Kings, Lake, Sutter, and Alpine. California Secretary of State, *Statement of Vote at General Election, November 3, 1914* (Sacramento, 1914).

61. Lissner to Matt Sullivan, Nov. 12, 1914, Lissner Papers; Lissner to HWJ, Jan. 20, 1915. Following the election, Heney charged that Johnson had cut a deal with James Phelan for the San Francisco vote; but as George Mowry suggests, Heney's defeat in San Francisco can be explained in less conspiratorial ways, and the almost 60,000 fall-off in vote totals in the senatorial contest would indicate that distrust of Heney was widespread throughout much of the state. Mowry, *California Progressives*, pp. 215–16. See also Robert E. Hennings, *James D. Phelan and the Wilson Progressives in California* (New York, 1985), pp. 85–100. There is no evidence that Johnson took steps to hurt Heney; what is clear is that he took no steps to help him. Clearly, Johnson did not see Heney's defeat as a serious progressive setback.

62. Gable, *Bull Moose Years*, pp. 207–28; Theodore Roosevelt to Charles J. Bonaparte, Nov. 7, 1914, ibid.

63. HWJ to Lissner, Nov. 17, 1914, Lissner Papers; HWJ to Rowell, Nov. 18, 27, 1914; Lissner to Rowell, Nov. 25, 1914, all in Rowell Papers; HWJ to Benjamin Lindsey, Jan. 23, 1915. See also HWJ to George Perkins, Nov. 17, 1914; HWJ to Medill McCormick, Nov. 18, 1914; HWJ to W. A. Taylor, Nov. 18, 1914.

64. HWJ to Theodore Roosevelt, Feb. 1, 1915. In the summer of 1915, with Roosevelt in California to attend the opening of the Panama-Pacific Exposition, Johnson hoped some sort of strategy could be hammered out. But their talks proved inconclusive, and Johnson's pessimism deepened. HWJ to Macfarlane, July 16, 1915; HWJ to Lissner, Aug. 7, 1915, Lissner Papers. See also Gilson Gardner to HWJ, Mar. 30, 1915; HWJ to Gilson Gardner, Apr. 3, 1915; HWJ to George Perkins, Nov. 22, 1915; Lissner to George Stone, Apr. 23, 1915, Lissner Papers.

65. Gilson Gardner to HWJ, Apr. 9, June 21, 1915; HWJ to Gilson Gardner, June 3, 1915; HWJ memorandum of conversation, May 25, 1915. Gardner nevertheless continued to push Johnson's candidacy. Later, Johnson actively interceded to remove his name from the Indiana and Minnesota Progressive ballots. HWJ to E. M. Lee, Dec. 22, 1915; E. P. Clarke to HWJ, Feb. 17, 1916 (copy), Neylan Papers.

66. Lissner to William Allen White, July 29, 1915; Lissner to George Stone, Aug. 3, 1915; Lissner to Dwight Heard, Dec. 27, 1915; Lissner to E. M. Lee, Feb. 10, 1916; Lissner to Medill McCormick, Nov. 5, 1915, all in Lissner Papers; Lissner to William Allen White, Sept. 21, 1915 (copy); Lissner to Rowell, July 29, 1915, in Rowell Papers; Lissner to HWJ, Aug. 2, 16, 1915.

67. Eshleman to HWJ, Nov. 15, 1915.

68. HWJ to Rowell, Feb. 11, 1916; Lissner to Rowell, Dec. 28, 1915, Lissner Papers. See also HWJ to Theodore Roosevelt, Jan. 22, 1916.

69. HWJ to T. S. Montgomery, Mar. 9, 1916; HWJ to Stanley Washburn, Feb. 11, 1916.

70. HWJ to Benjamin Lindsey, Jan. 23, 1915; HWJ to Edward Dickson, Oct. 28, 1915; HWJ to Rowell, Sept. 15, 1915, Rowell Papers.

71. HWJ to Stanley Washburn, Feb. 11, 1916.

72. Lissner to HWJ, Aug. 3, 9, 19, 1915; HWJ to Lissner, Aug. 7, 1915, Lissner Papers; HWJ to Rowell, Jan. 22, 1916.

73. HWJ to Rowell, Jan. 4, 1916. See also Edward A. Dickson to HWJ, Feb. 9, 1916.

74. Lissner to HWJ, Jan. 5, 13, 1916. See also Edward A. Dickson to HWJ, Jan. 14, 1916.

75. HWJ to Lissner, Jan. 17, 1916. Booth, Johnson continued, was a mental crook, a conscienceless liar, and utterly untrustworthy.

76. Lissner to HWJ, Jan. 25, 1916.

77. *Sacramento Union*, Feb. 20, 22, 1916; Lissner to HWJ, Jan. 25, Feb. 21, 1916; Neylan to E. P. Clarke, Feb. 21, 1916, Neylan Papers.

78. Neylan to Herbert Moody, Irving Martin, E. P. Clarke, Ralph Bull, George Moore, Reginald Fernald, Feb. 10, 1916; Neylan to E. P. Clarke, Feb. 21, 1916; Neylan to Reginald Fernald, Feb. 24, 1916; Charles A. Whitmore to Neylan, Feb. 24, 1916, all in Neylan Papers; HWJ to Rowell, Feb. 11, 1916; HWJ to Edward Dickson, Feb. 11, 14, 1916; Edward Dickson to HWJ, Feb. 9, 1916, Lissner to Edward Dickson, Mar. 9, 1916, Lissner Papers.

79. Lissner to Theodore Roosevelt, Apr. 15, 1916, Lissner Papers; *Fresno Republican*, Feb. 27, 1916; *Sacramento Union*, Feb. 23, 26, 27, Mar. 2, 5, 1916.

80. Rowell to Theodore Roosevelt, May 21, 1916, Rowell Papers.

81. HWJ memo read to Guy Earl, Mar. 8, 1916; Lissner to Edward Dickson, Mar. 9, 1916, Lissner Papers; Rowell to Lissner, Mar. 27, 1916, Rowell Papers.

82. *Sacramento Union*, Apr. 15, 1916. Rowell to HWJ, Mar. 30, Apr. 8, 1916; HWJ to Rowell, Apr. 3, 1916, all in Rowell Papers; Edson to HWJ, Apr. 10, 1916, Edson Papers; HWJ to Lissner, Apr. 21, 1916; Edward Dickson to HWJ, Apr. 28, 1916.

83. *San Diego Union*, May 3, 1916; *Oakland Tribune*, May 5, 7, 1916.

84. Earlier, Johnson had joined with Lissner to suggest that the convention be postponed, for he feared that the Republican convention would dwarf its Progressive counterpart in both numbers and enthusiasm. See Lissner to George Perkins, Dec. 28, 1915; Lissner to Rowell, Dec. 28, 1915, both in Lissner Papers; HWJ to Rowell, Jan. 4, 1916.

85. HWJ to Stanley Washburn, May 26, 1916; HWJ to Fremont Older, May 30, 1916.

86. HWJ to H. Gardner, May 15, 1916. See also Rowell to Samuel M. Lindsay, May 22, 1916, Rowell Papers. On William Crocker, who would head the California delegation, Johnson wrote: "If Crocker didn't have millions, he would be a swamper in a beer saloon, or an attendant in an Insane Asylum. He has neither brains nor power of thought." HWJ to George Perkins, May 12, 1916.

87. HWJ to Fremont Older, May 26, 1916; HWJ to Irving Martin, May 11, 1916. "There is something exceedingly ridiculous to me in running around the

state shouting Hughes when he sits like a sphinx in Washington and declines to have anything to do with us," Johnson complained. HWJ to Eshleman, Feb. 8, 1916.

88. HWJ to Motley Flint, Apr. 17, 1916; HWJ to Stanley Washburn, Feb. 11, 1916; HWJ to Rowell, May 8, 1916, Rowell Papers. See also Irving Martin to HWJ, May 10, 1916; Lissner to Dickson, Aug. 11, 1915, Lissner Papers.

89. Perhaps Lissner was the exception. If it came to a choice between Wilson and Elihu Root, he wrote, he would vote for Root. Lissner to Theodore Roosevelt, Apr. 15, 1916, Lissner Papers. On McClatchy, see C. K. McClatchy to HWJ, Apr. 5, 1915, Jan. 26, 1916. See also HWJ to Theodore Roosevelt, Feb. 7, 1916; HWJ to Gilson Gardner, May 4, 1916.

90. Edwin Earl to George Perkins, Apr. 22, 1916 (copy), HWJ Papers. See also Rowell to P. Richert, May 24, 1916, Rowell Papers.

91. HWJ to Charles S. Bird, Jan. 17, 1916; HWJ to Eshleman, Feb. 8, 1916.

92. *Fresno Republican,* May 7, 1916; HWJ to George Perkins, May 12, 1916. See also Rowell to Samuel Lindsey, May 22, 1916, Rowell Papers.

93. HWJ to Fremont Older, May 26, 1916; HWJ to Irving Martin, May 11, 1916.

94. *San Francisco Bulletin,* June 3, 1916; *Fresno Republican,* June 6, 1916.

95. John A. Garraty, *Right Hand Man: The Life of George W. Perkins* (New York, 1957), p. 337.

96. The Republican team was composed of Murray Crane, Nicholas Murray Butler, Reed Smoot, and A. R. Johnson, all Republican standpatters. Included too was William Borah. Johnson, Perkins, Parker, Horace Wilkerson, and Charles Bonaparte spoke for the Progressives.

97. *Sacramento Union,* June 10, 1916. See also Mowry, *California Progressives,* pp. 233–38, and George Mowry, *Theodore Roosevelt and the Progressive Movement* (Madison, Wis., 1946), pp. 347–57.

98. Garraty, *Right Hand Man,* pp. 347–48.

99. Katherine Philips Edson to HWJ, June 28, 1916, Edson Papers.

100. Rowell to Rowell, June 14, 1916, Rowell Papers; Rowell to Lissner, June 18(?), 1916, Lissner Papers; HWJ to Arthur Brisbane, June 25, 1916. See also Theodore Roosevelt to Lissner, Sept. 10, 1916, in Morison, *Letters of Theodore Roosevelt.*

101. Rowell to Lissner, Nov. 18, 1916, Rowell Papers.

102. Lissner to Medill McCormick, Nov. 5, 1915; Rowell to Lissner, June 15, 18(?), 1916, all in Lissner Papers.

103. Lissner to Theodore Roosevelt, Apr. 15, 1916, Lissner Papers; HWJ to Irving Martin, May 11, 1916; HWJ to C. K. McClatchy, May 15, 1916; HWJ to Edward Dickson, May 15, 1916; Irving Martin to HWJ, May 10, 1916; Edward Dickson to HWJ, May 11, 16, 1916; C. K. McClatchy to HWJ, May 22, 1916.

104. Rowell to Lissner, June 21, 1916, Lissner Papers.

105. HWJ to Edson, June 30, 1916, Edson Papers.

106. Irving Martin to HWJ, May 10, 1916.

107. HWJ to Fremont Older, July 3, 1916; Rowell to J. C. Needham, July 6, 1916, Rowell Papers; *Sacramento Union,* July 8, 1916; *Sacramento Bee,* July 8, 10, 1916.

108. Unissued news release, ca. July 1916, Part II, Carton 43, HWJ Papers.

109. *Sacramento Union*, July 9, 1916; *Sacramento Bee*, July 8–10, 1916. Privately, Johnson contrasted his own willingness to run with Roosevelt's abandonment of a political role at Chicago. See HWJ to Raymond Robins, Aug. 15, 1916; HWJ to E. A. Van Valkenburg, Sept. 5, 1916; HWJ to Arthur Brisbane, July 25, 1916.

110. *Sacramento Bee*, July 8–10, 1916.

111. HWJ to J. C. O'Laughlin, July 13, 1916.

112. Edward Dickson to HWJ, May 9, 1916. See also Lissner to George Perkins, Jan. 3, 1916; Lissner to Rowell, Dec. 28, 1915; Rowell to Percy Long, Jan. 3, 1916, all in Lissner Papers; HWJ to Lissner, May 8, 1916; Lissner to HWJ, May 13, 1916; HWJ to Edward Dickson, May 8, 1916; HWJ to Irving Martin, May 11, 1916; HWJ to Rowell, May 8, 1916, Rowell Papers; *California Outlook*, June 1916, pp. 54–55.

113. HWJ to J. C. O'Laughlin, July 13, 1916. See also HWJ to James Garfield, July 5, 1916; Rowell to HWJ, July 12, 1916; Ickes to Rowell, Aug. 17, 1916, both in Rowell Papers.

114. Rowell to George Perkins, July 12, 14, 1916; Rowell to William Willcox, July 29, 1916, all in Rowell Papers. See also Mowry, *California Progressives*, pp. 246–50.

115. Edwin Earl to HWJ, May 25, 1916. In addition, it had been the southern wing of the party that had played a key role in supporting the senatorial ambitions of Francis Heney over Rowell in the 1914 primary contest. Following his defeat in the general election, Heney, who had been identified with San Francisco and Northern California, moved "bag, baggage and law books" to Los Angeles, where, as Lissner had warned, he remained a force to be reckoned with. Lissner to Edson, Feb. 6, 1915, Lissner Papers.

116. Edwin Earl to HWJ, Jan. 29, Feb. 17, 1913. In fact, the bulk of Johnson's appointments ignored Los Angeles and Southern California.

117. Edwin Earl to HWJ, Jan. 14, June 2, Dec. 2, 1913; HWJ to Edwin Earl, Nov. 3, 1915, Mar. 31, July 3, 1916; HWJ to Marshall Stimson, Nov. 4, 1916. Earl, the *San Francisco Bulletin* observed, had long entertained a secret ambition to lead the Bull Moose by the horns. *San Francisco Bulletin*, Dec. 2, 1916. Lissner later detailed his frosty relations with Earl in Lissner to C. K. McClatchy, Jan. 31, 1920.

118. Lissner to HWJ, Apr. 5, 1916, Lissner Papers. John Works agreed. It was, he observed, an "unwritten law" that the south would control one Senate seat. John Works to HWJ, July 10, 1916, Works Papers. See also John Works to Rowell, July 26, 1916, Works Papers.

119. Lissner to Edson, Feb. 6, 1915; Lissner to HWJ, Mar. 27, Apr. 5, 1916, all in Lissner Papers; William Stephens to Edward Dickson, Jan. 24, Mar. 10, 1916, both in Dickson Papers. See also HWJ to Edward Dickson, May 8, 1916.

120. Edwin Earl to HWJ, May 25, 1916; HWJ to Edwin Earl, May 27, 1916. Eshleman, a victim of tuberculosis, died unexpectedly following a sudden lung hemorrhage. He was 39.

121. HWJ to John R. Haynes, Apr. 14, 1916, Haynes Papers. See also HWJ to E. F. Howe, May 12, 1916; HWJ to George C. Roeding, May 8, 1916.

122. Franklin Hichborn, "California Politics, 1891–1939," vol. 3, p. 1517; Part II, Carton 43, HWJ Papers; Rowell to Edson, Mar. 27, 1916, Rowell Papers.

123. HWJ to C. K. McClatchy, July 20, 26, 1916. Edwin Earl to HWJ, May 25, 1916; HWJ to Edwin Earl, May 23, 1916. Johnson's impression, perhaps inaccurate, was that he was being asked not only to appoint Stephens but to resign immediately from the governorship and devote his attention solely to his candidacy. HWJ to Rowell, Mar. 1, 1917, Rowell Papers. But see also *Los Angeles Examiner*, July 17, 1916.

124. On Dickson's role, see William Stephens to Edward Dickson, Mar. 16, 1916; Edward Dickson to W. A. Avery, Apr. 10, 1916, both in Dickson Papers; Edward Dickson to Edson, June 18, 1916, Edson Papers. See also Edward Dickson to HWJ, July 12, 1916; Lissner to HWJ, Aug. 10, 1916.

125. Walter Bordwell, a Los Angeles judge, was pressured to withdraw from the race. *San Francisco Chronicle*, July 28, 29, Aug. 9, 1916; *Sacramento Union*, July 27, 30, 1916. In 1910 Booth had been one of those under consideration by the Lincoln-Roosevelt League as a possible candidate for the U.S. Senate. See *California Weekly*, Mar. 18, 1910, p. 265.

126. *Los Angeles Times*, Aug. 12, 1916; *San Jose Mercury Herald*, Aug. 25, 1916.

127. Lissner to George Perkins, July 27, 1916; Lissner to O. K. Davis, Aug. 8, 1916, both in Lissner Papers; Ickes to Rowell, Aug. 17, 1916, Rowell Papers.

128. Distancing himself from Rowell, Johnson wrote that joint appearances with Hughes were a "matter of indifference." If he had known beforehand of the proposal, he continued, he would not have endorsed it. HWJ to Raymond Robins, Aug. 15, 1916; HWJ to E. A. Van Valkenburg, Sept. 5, 1916.

129. HWJ to Rowell, Aug. 6(?), 1916, Rowell Papers.

130. HWJ to Raymond Robins, Aug. 15, 1916.

131. Merlo J. Pusey, *Charles Evans Hughes* (New York, 1951), vol. 1, p. 346. See also Spencer C. Olin, Jr., "Hiram Johnson, the California Progressives, and the Hughes Campaign of 1916," *Pacific Historical Review* 31:4 (Nov. 1962), pp. 403–12, and the account by Olin in *California's Prodigal Sons: Hiram Johnson and the Progressives, 1911–1917* (Berkeley, Calif., 1968), pp. 136–43. "It was compatible neither with my personal pride, nor official dignity to make my presence known to him and I did not," Johnson explained. HWJ to E. A. Van Valkenburg, Sept. 5, 1916.

132. Lissner to Ickes, Aug. 2, 1916, Lissner Papers.

133. *California Outlook*, Sept. 1916, p. 126; *San Francisco Bulletin*, Aug. 23, 1916; *San Jose Mercury Herald*, Aug. 27, 1916.

134. Lissner to Ickes, Aug. 22, 1916, Lissner Papers; Lissner to Theodore Roosevelt, Sept. 1, 1916 (copy), Rowell Papers.

135. Upon examining the returns in Los Angeles, Lissner found Johnson strongest in labor districts and among the "moderately well-to-do people who live in their own homes." He was weakest, Lissner continued, in the "silk stocking aristocratic residence districts." Lissner to HWJ, Sept. 8, 1916.

136. *Sacramento Union*, Sept. 12, 13, 1916; *San Francisco Bulletin*, Sept. 19, 1916; C. C. Young to Lissner, Aug. 23, Sept. 1, 1916, Lissner Papers. For the first

time, participation in the Republican State Convention was opened to those who were not registered Republicans if, by cross-filing, they had won the party nomination.

137. *Sacramento Union*, Aug. 14, 1916; C. K. McClatchy to HWJ, Sept. 6, 1916; HWJ to Lissner, Sept. 9, 1916. When news was brought to Johnson that Rowell had urged Crocker to join with him in sending a telegram informing Hughes of Johnson's nomination, Johnson replied: "Please, please do nothing in respect to me in connection with Crocker or men of that sort, without first taking the matter up with me. There is something so much bigger to me than political success, that I would not sacrifice for any office, and that is, independence and my self-respect; and under no circumstances, do I wish to get into a position of being under obligations to any political crook or of asking of any skunk like Crocker any favor at all." HWJ to Rowell, Sept. 4, 1916, Rowell Papers.

138. Lissner to Theodore Roosevelt, Sept. 25, 1916, Lissner Papers; C. K. McClatchy to HWJ, Sept. 6, 1916.

139. *Sacramento Union*, Sept. 20, 21, 1916; *Sacramento Bee*, Sept. 19, 20, 1916; *San Diego Union*, Sept. 20, 22, 1916; *San Francisco Bulletin*, Sept. 20, 1916.

140. Lissner to James McKnight, Oct. 2, 1916, Lissner Papers.

141. See, for example, *Humboldt Times*, Sept. 23, 24, 1916; *Marysville Appeal*, Sept. 29, 1916; *Oroville Daily Mercury*, Sept. 28, 1916; *Chico Record*, Sept. 28, 1916; *Sacramento Bee*, Sept. 29, 1916; *Stockton Record*, Oct. 9, 1916; *Visalia Delta*, Oct. 21, 1916; *San Diego Sun*, Oct. 25, 1916; *Riverside Daily Press*, Oct. 26, 1916; *Los Angeles Express*, Oct. 28, 1916; *Oakland Tribune*, Nov. 3, 1916; *San Francisco Bulletin*, Nov. 4, 1916; *San Francisco Chronicle*, Nov. 4, 1916.

142. HWJ to Ickes, Sept. 11, Oct. 7, 1916; HWJ to E. A. Van Valkenburg, Sept. 5, 1916. Both Rowell and Lissner shared Johnson's original gloomy forecasts. Rowell to George Perkins, Sept. 20, 1916; Lissner to James McKnight, Oct. 2, 1916, both in Lissner Papers. See also Martin Madsen to Ickes, Oct. 28, 1916; Philip Bancroft to George Pinchot, Oct. 31, 1916, Bancroft Papers.

143. *Los Angeles Times*, Nov. 10, 1916; *San Diego Union*, Nov. 11, 12, 1916.

144. Alfred Holman, "The Case of Hiram Johnson: Guilty," *North American Review* 205 (Feb. 1917), pp. 186–202. Frederick Davenport's defense of Johnson, "The Case of Hiram Johnson: Not Guilty," *North American Review* 205 (Feb. 1917), pp. 203–20, was dismissed by George Harvey as lacking the force of logic and "convincingness" found in Holman. It should, said Harvey, be relegated to the "entertainment class." George Harvey, *North American Review* 205 (Feb. 1917), p. 184. See also *California Outlook*, Mar. 1917, pp. 267–69.

145. The *San Diego Union* found no fault with Hughes's tour. His visit to California, it concluded, had been "a grand success." *San Diego Union*, Aug. 30, 1916.

146. Rowell to George Perkins, Sept. 27, 1916; Ickes to Rowell, Oct. 3, 1916, both in Rowell Papers.

147. *San Francisco Bulletin*, Nov. 4, 1916. The *Oakland Tribune*, in a rare

mention of Johnson, conceded that he deserved credit for his direct support of the ticket. *Oakland Tribune*, Nov. 5, 1916.

148. Edson to Mrs. Seward A. Simons, Nov. 17, 1916, Edson Papers. The *Los Angeles Times*, refusing to support Johnson, continued to stress the need for southern representation. The *San Diego Union*, without mentioning Johnson by name, in mid-September endorsed the Republican ticket. The *Oakland Tribune* and the *San Francisco Chronicle* followed suit. Both endorsed the Republican ticket without referring to Johnson's candidacy.

149. "To my surprise and grief," Kent noted, "Johnson, in his senatorial fight, strenuously advocated Hughes, thereby cutting down materially a larger Wilson majority." William Kent to William G. McAdoo, Nov. 21, 1916, as quoted in Seward W. Livermore, *Politics Is Adjourned: Woodrow Wilson and the War Congress, 1916–1918* (Middletown, Conn., 1966), pp. 8–9. See also *California Outlook*, Mar. 1917, pp. 267–69.

150. *Oakland Tribune*, Sept. 10, 1916; *San Francisco Bulletin*, Sept. 28, 1916.

151. Edson to Mrs. L. Van Rensslaer, Dec. 2, 1916, Edson Papers; Lissner to Edson, July 13, 1916, Lissner Papers.

152. Men in positions of trust who refuse to support Hughes, Johnson wrote, would be "false to their trust, and should not be placed in any fiduciary capacity." HWJ to A. W. Posey, Sept. 13, 1916.

153. John Works to Curtis, Sept. 22, 1916, Works Papers. Works, anticipating the charges later made by the *Los Angeles Times*, also predicted that Johnson and Wilson would trade votes.

154. Summing up the attitude of many, Edson confessed: "I am not a Republican in spirit but am still a real progressive and have a very faint heart in this campaign." She could not vote for Wilson, she acknowledged, but found little attraction in Hughes. Edson to Harriet Vittum, Sept. 6, 1916, Edson Papers. In his final assessment, Works too would focus not on betrayal but on the alienation of progressives because of the "abuse and misrepresentation of the 'old guard.'" John Works to Charles Evans Hughes, Nov. 13, 1916, Works Papers.

155. Olin, "Hiram Johnson, the California Progressives, and the Hughes Campaign," p. 404. See also *Oakland Tribune*, Oct. 8, 1916.

156. Edson to Mrs. L. Van Rensslaer, Dec. 2, 1916, Edson Papers.

157. Edson to Florence Kelley, Nov. 18, 1916, Edson Papers.

158. HWJ to Rowell, Nov. 25, 1916. To another correspondent he wrote: "I never thought six years could so completely anchor me that it is well-nigh impossible to cut loose." HWJ to George West, Jan. 31, 1916. See also HWJ to T. S. Montgomery, Dec. 19, 1916; Edson to Raymond Robins, Nov. 29, 1916, Edson Papers.

159. Adding to those suspicions was the refusal of Earl to publish Johnson's scathing denunciation of Otis in answer to the charges that Johnson had betrayed Hughes. To do so, Earl argued, would interfere with a libel suit then in progress. Edward Dickson to HWJ, Nov. 13, 1916; Lissner to HWJ, Nov. 15, 16, 1916; HWJ to Lissner, Nov. 25, 1916, Lissner Papers; Edwin Earl to Fremont Older, Dec. 4, 1916, Dickson Papers.

160. Johnson complained that Dickson, who had neither the "decency" nor

the "courtesy" to call on him, circulated in and out of state offices parceling out jobs for the new administration, solidifying Stephens's support for the 1918 gubernatorial contest and the Senate election of 1920. HWJ to Lissner, Feb. 18, 1917, Lissner Papers. See also Lissner to HWJ, Jan. 31, 1917, Lissner Papers; HWJ to Rowell, Mar. 1, 6, July 10, 1917; Rowell to HWJ, Feb. 8, 1916, in Rowell Papers, *Oakland Tribune*, Dec. 10, 31, 1916.

161. HWJ to Rowell, Nov. 25, 1916.

162. HWJ to Lissner, Feb. 3, 1917.

163. HWJ to Lissner, Feb. 25, 1917, emphasis in original. See also HWJ to Rowell, Mar. 1, 6, 1917, Rowell Papers.

164. HWJ to Rowell, Mar. 16, 1917, Rowell Papers. See also *Sacramento Union*, Mar. 16, 1916; *Oakland Tribune*, Mar. 4, 11, 25, 1916.

165. Franklin Hichborn, *Story of the Session of the California Legislature of 1921* (San Francisco, 1922); Jackson Putnam, "The Persistence of Progressivism in the 1920's: The Case of California," *Pacific Historical Review* 35:4 (Nov. 1966), pp. 395–411.

166. Johnson's ongoing conflict with Stephens can be followed in Rowell to Martin Madsen, Apr. 23, 1917; HWJ to Rowell, Dec. 17, 1917, both in Rowell Papers; Rowell to Lissner, Nov. 24, 1917; Lissner to HWJ, May 7, June 2, 30, Aug. 6, 1917; Lissner to Arthur Arlett, Sept. 27, 1917, all in Lissner Papers; Lissner to HWJ, Feb. 14, 1918; Rowell to HWJ, Mar. 27, Apr. 18, June 2, Aug. 8, 1917; Arthur Arlett to HWJ, Apr. 2, 9, 17, June 30, 1917; William Williams to HWJ, June 16, 1917; Neylan to HWJ, Apr. 12, 23, May 14, 26, 1917; Neylan to Paul Herriott, May 19, 1917, in Neylan Papers; Hiram Johnson, Jr., to HWJ, Feb. 13, 1918; HWJ to Hiram Johnson, Jr., Mar. 13, 1918; HWJ to Al McCabe, Mar. 8, 1918.

Chapter III: War, Peace, and Politics

1. Fred Israel, "Bainbridge Colby and the Progressive Party," *New York History* 40 (Jan. 1959); John Allen Gable, *The Bull Moose Years: Theodore Roosevelt and the Progressive Party* (New York, 1978), p. 249. See also James Oliver Robertson, *No Third Choice: Progressives in Republican Politics, 1916–1921* (New York, 1983).

2. Matthew Hale to HWJ, Nov. 20, Dec. 18, 1916. See also J. A. H. Hopkins to HWJ, Aug. 28, 1916, Jan. 20, Mar. 12, 1917.

3. HWJ to Matthew Hale, Nov. 27, 1916, Jan. 29, Mar. 12, 1917; HWJ to John Parker, Jan. 9, 1917. See also HWJ to Rowell, Jan. 26, 1917, Rowell Papers.

4. HWJ to Rowell, Jan. 31, 1917.

5. HWJ to Ickes, Jan. 26, 1917; HWJ to J. A. H. Hopkins, Mar. 20, 1917; HWJ to Rowell, Dec. 2, 1916, Rowell Papers.

6. "I will not play again with G.W.P.," Johnson wrote of Perkins. HWJ to Rowell, Dec. 2, 1916, Rowell Papers. See also Rowell to Lissner, Nov. 18, 1916, Lissner Papers; Ickes to Rowell, Nov. 22, 1916, Rowell Papers.

7. John A. Garraty, *Right Hand Man: The Life of George W. Perkins* (New York, 1957), pp. 357–58; *California Outlook*, Jan. 1917, pp. 222–23. The Pro-

gressive Leagues, Rowell noted, would be similar to the Lincoln-Roosevelt League. Ickes to Rowell, Dec. 29, 1916, Rowell Papers.

8. HWJ to Rowell, Dec. 26, 1916; HWJ to George Record, Nov. 27, 1916. Lissner agreed. "The only possible way of winning back the Progressives to the Republican party will be the acceptance now, and not several years from now, of a progressive platform and progressive leadership." Lissner to HWJ, Jan. 29, 1917, Lissner Papers. See also William Draper Lewis to Rowell, Dec. 14, 1916, Rowell Papers. Somewhat defensively, Rowell argued that Johnson's prescription, while true to form in demanding confrontation, did not in fact reflect Johnson's own style, which depended less on concrete issues than on a personal appeal that transcended those issues. The only problem, Rowell added, was that the proposal put together in Chicago involved "negotiation instead of defiance." Rowell to HWJ, Dec. 27, 1916, Rowell Papers.

9. *New York Times*, Jan. 19, 1917. Perkins clearly exaggerated his support. Rowell's statement condemning the action of the Republican hierarchy had been an extract from his editorial in the *Fresno Republican* but was given out by Perkins and published without reference to its origins. Similarly, Perkins released a telegram from Johnson but failed to make public the first sentence, in which Johnson disclaimed, albeit rather weakly, any judgment on the immediate controversy. See Rowell to Ickes, Jan. 22, 1917, Rowell Papers.

10. HWJ to Rowell, Jan. 19, 1917.

11. HWJ to Rowell, Jan. 23, Feb. 1, 1917; HWJ to Rowell, Jan. 2, 5, 12, 26, Feb. 21, 1917, all in Rowell Papers. See also Ickes to Rowell, Jan. 6, 9, 19, 1917; Rowell to Ickes, Jan. 24, 1917, all in Rowell Papers. Eighty percent of the Progressive leadership supported the conference plan, Johnson wrote, but 80 percent of the Progressive rank and file supported the independent political action endorsed by Hale. HWJ to Lissner, Jan. 31, 1917, Lissner Papers.

12. Ickes to Rowell, Jan. 22, 1917; HWJ to Rowell, Jan. 29, 1917, both in Rowell Papers.

13. Raymond Robins to HWJ, Mar. 14, 1917; Rowell to HWJ, Mar. 17, 1917, Rowell Papers. Johnson wrote about resuming his law practice in HWJ to Rowell, Jan. 5, 1917, Rowell Papers. Knowing of Johnson's financial worries, Harris Weinstock presented him with a departing gift—a check for $5,000. Johnson, although grateful for Weinstock's words of kindness and tangible support, returned the check. HWJ to Harris Weinstock, Mar. 19, 1917.

14. HWJ to Lissner, Feb. 3, 1917; HWJ to Rowell, Nov. 25, 1916. Johnson had, he noted in his letter to Rowell, been "dumbfounded and more than gratified" by the many press references to his presidential chances. Johnson's self-deprecating remarks with regard to 1920 can be found in HWJ to George Record, Nov. 27, 1916; HWJ to Rowell, Dec. 26, 1916; HWJ to C. K. McClatchy, Apr. 11, 1918; HWJ to Al McCabe, Mar. 18, 1918. But, he acknowledged, "I think that any one of us, who could claim not to desire a nomination by a dominant party for President of the United States would be indulging in mere pretense and hypocrisy." HWJ to T. S. Montgomery, Mar. 9, 1916.

15. Lissner to HWJ, Mar. 23, 1917. The other topics were "Our International Relations," "Labor and Capital," "Social Justice," "Preparedness," "The Tariff,"

and "Government and Big Business." See also Rowell to Lissner, Apr. 13, 1917, Lissner Papers; Lissner to Rowell, May 1, 7, 1917, Rowell Papers; Lissner to HWJ, Apr. 17, May 7, 17, 1917.

16. Ickes to Rowell, Mar. 26, 1917, Rowell Papers; Garraty, *Right Hand Man*, p. 362.

17. HWJ to Rowell, Apr. 10, 1917; HWJ to Hiram Johnson, Jr., Apr. 7, 1917. See also Lissner to HWJ, May 7, 1917.

18. C. K. McClatchy to HWJ, Apr. 2, 1915.

19. C. K. McClatchy to HWJ, Apr. 5, 1915.

20. HWJ to Henry Ford, Nov. 29, 1915. See also Thomas G. Paterson, "California Progressives and Foreign Policy," *California Historical Society Quarterly* 47:4 (Dec. 1968), pp. 329–42.

21. HWJ to Fremont Older, Mar. 24, 1915. On Roosevelt's characterization of Wilson, see Theodore Roosevelt to HWJ, Feb. 22, 1915, in Elting Morison, ed., *Letters of Theodore Roosevelt* (Cambridge, Mass., 1954).

22. HWJ to C. K. McClatchy, Apr. 3, 1915.

23. HWJ to C. K. McClatchy, Jan. 25, 1916.

24. Johnson's only direct criticism of the Wilson administration during the primary campaign focused not on Wilson but on the inefficiency of the nation's military establishment, which had failed to outfit the California National Guard with the arms and materials needed to patrol the Mexican border. In addition, he raised doubts as to whether the National Guard was the proper instrument to conduct such efforts. Privately, he was less circumspect: "The spectacle of a government so weak and so timid that its citizen soldiers must be called into activity to defend . . . the frontier is remarkable." HWJ to Lissner, Apr. 23, 1914.

25. *Visalia Morning Delta*, Oct. 21, 1916; *San Diego Sun*, Oct. 25, 1916; *Riverside Daily Press*, Oct. 26, 1916; *San Francisco Chronicle*, Nov. 4, 1916.

26. *Philadelphia Evening Ledger*, Mar. 31, 1917; *New York Times*, Apr. 1, 1917. "We would only when imperatively compelled by the transgression of our rights, by the destruction of our lives, enter into conflict," Johnson announced. Sharing the platform from which he spoke was Boies Penrose, a stalwart of the Republican Old Guard. Paul Herriott to Hiram Johnson, Jr., Apr. 19, 1917.

27. HWJ to Joe Scott, Apr. 9, 1917. When questioned by the *New York Times*, Johnson replied: "The Republic has spoken through the President and I follow the flag." *New York Times*, Apr. 4, 1917. In the Senate, 6 opposed the war resolution; in the House, 50.

28. HWJ to C. K. McClatchy, Apr. 7, 1917; HWJ to boys, Apr. 3, 1917.

29. HWJ to boys, Apr. 6, 1917; HWJ to Lissner, Apr. 5, 9, 1917. "Nine-tenths of the situation here is sham," Johnson wrote, "and nine-tenths of the other tenth front." HWJ to boys, Apr. 3, 1917.

30. HWJ to boys, Apr. 6, 1917; *Cong. Record*, 65th Cong., 1st sess. (Apr. 28, 1917), p. 1481; speech drafts, St. Louis (June 3, 1917), Philadelphia (Aug. 15, 1917), Pittsburgh (Apr. 6, 1918), Part III, Carton 25, HWJ Papers.

31. HWJ to Archibald Johnson, July 19, 1917.

32. HWJ to C. K. McClatchy, Apr. 7, May 1, 1917; HWJ to boys, Apr. 18, 1917; *Cong. Record*, 65th Cong., 1st sess. (Apr. 23, June 28, 1917), pp. 946–47, 4403; HWJ to Archibald Johnson, July 5, 1917.

33. HWJ to Hiram Johnson, Jr., Aug. 2, 1917.

34. Notes for speech, Washington University, St. Louis, June 2, 1917, Part III, Carton 25, HWJ Papers.

35. *Cong. Record*, 65th Cong., 2nd sess. (Feb. 19, 21, Aug. 1, 1918), pp. 2314–16; 2422; 9191–92. See also HWJ to Lissner, Dec. 20, 1917; HWJ to Archibald Johnson, July 12, 1918; HWJ to C. K. McClatchy, Mar. 18, 1918; Lissner to HWJ, Dec. 11, 1917, Jan. 7, 1918. For Dewey's comments on the "social possibilities of war" see John Dewey, "What Are We Fighting For?" *Independent*, June 22, 1918, p. 480.

36. *Cong. Record*, 65th Cong., 1st sess. (Aug. 11, 1917), p. 5960.

37. *Cong. Record*, 65th Cong., 2nd sess. (May 23, 1918), p. 6959. While governor, Johnson had refused to support a proposed state social insurance program because he was concerned over its costs. In 1918, at Rowell's urging, he endorsed a similar measure. See Rowell to HWJ, Aug. 5, 20, Oct. 8, 1918; Rowell to Ernestine Black, Aug. 20, 1918, all in Rowell Papers.

38. *Cong. Record*, 65th Cong. 1st sess. (Aug. 11, 1917), p. 5960.

39. HWJ to boys, May 17, 1917.

40. HWJ to C. K. McClatchy, Apr. 7, 1917; HWJ to boys, Apr. 7, 1917; HWJ to Lissner, May 22, 1917; Paul Herriott to Hiram Johnson, Jr., Apr. 19, 1917.

41. HWJ to C. K. McClatchy, Apr. 21, 1917.

42. *Cong. Record*, 65th Cong., 1st sess. (Apr. 18, 19, May 5, 1917), pp. 780–81, 840–41, 1869–70; HWJ to boys, Apr. 23, 1917.

43. HWJ to boys, May 17, 1917.

44. *New York World*, May 11, 1917; *Cong. Record*, 65th Cong., 1st sess. (May 11, 1917), pp. 2097–2100; Paul Herriott to Neylan, May 11, 1917, Neylan Papers. Showing unusual restraint, Johnson all but ignored George Creel, who had been selected by Wilson to head the Committee on Public Information. During Johnson's 1914 gubernatorial campaign, Creel, a partisan of Francis Heney, had denied Johnson's progressive credentials, referring to him as "a full-paunched lawyer with the fishy eye of calculation." George Creel, "What About Hiram Johnson of California?," *Everybody's Magazine*, Oct. 1914, p. 458. See also HWJ to Peter Clarke Macfarlane, Feb. 1, 1915.

45. HWJ to Lissner, June 6, 1917. See also Seward W. Livermore, *Politics Is Adjourned; Woodrow Wilson and the War Congress, 1916–1918* (Middletown, Conn., 1966), pp. 32–37.

46. HWJ to Frank Snook, June 6, 1917.

47. *Cong. Record*, 65th Cong., 1st sess. (Apr. 28, 1917), p. 1481.

48. HWJ to boys, Apr. 30, 1917.

49. See David M. Kennedy, *Over Here: The First World War and American Society* (New York, 1980), pp. 148–49; HWJ to Hiram Johnson, Jr., Aug. 7, 1917. Johnson's support of Roosevelt can be found in *Cong. Record*, 65th Cong., 1st sess. (Apr. 23, 28, May 11, 1917), pp. 946–47; 1481–82; 2453–54; HWJ to Henry Cabot Lodge, Apr. 23, 1917; Theodore Roosevelt to HWJ, May 3, 10, 20, 1917; HWJ to Theodore Roosevelt, May 7, 17, 1917. In a sharp, spontaneous response to a bitter attack on Roosevelt by William Stone of Missouri, Johnson lavished praise upon the Colonel. Recalling the breach between the two men after the

1916 Progressive convention, Lissner wrote: "Whatever may be down in your heart concerning the old boy, at least so far as the country is concerned it is now all right—and that is the way it should be." Lissner to HWJ, May 28, 1917.

50. Wilson, Johnson wrote, "would prefer any disaster to permitting Roosevelt to serve our country." HWJ to Harris Weinstock, July 26, 1917. See also *Cong. Record*, 65th Cong., 1st sess. (May 17, 1917), p. 1454; HWJ to Hiram Johnson, Jr., Apr. 12, 1917.

51. HWJ to Hiram Johnson, Jr., July 23, 30, Aug. 2, 1917. Johnson was not eager for either of his sons to serve. Perhaps he would have offered different advice if conscription had not been passed, but as matters stood he urged Archibald, his younger son, to await the draft rather than volunteer. Archibald did not heed the advice. HWJ to Archibald Johnson, June 18, 1917.

52. Crowder, Johnson wrote, "has a fiendish and ghoulish glee when he can wrongfully get a man into [military service]." HWJ to Hiram Johnson, Jr., Aug. 25, 1917. See also HWJ to Hiram Johnson, Jr., June 4, 1918; HWJ to Gen. Enoch Crowder, Aug. 10, 18, 22, 1917; Gen. Enoch Crowder to HWJ, Aug. 14, 23, 1917; HWJ to Woodrow Wilson, Aug. 22, 23, 1917; Woodrow Wilson to HWJ, Aug. 23, 1917; HWJ to Archibald Johnson, Aug. 10, 27, 1917.

53. HWJ to Hiram Johnson, Jr., Aug. 28, 1917; HWJ to Archibald Johnson, Aug. 31, 1917. In the summer of 1918, still protesting his antagonism to the draft, Johnson again accepted its military necessity and supported a widening of the call to include men between the ages of 18 and 45. HWJ to Hiram Johnson, Jr., June 26, Aug. 14, 28, 1918; HWJ to Amy Johnson, June 22, Aug. 10, 1918.

54. HWJ to Joseph Scott, June 25, 1917.

55. John R. Haynes to HWJ, June 12, 1917, Haynes Papers. See also Joseph Scott to HWJ, Apr. 13, 1917; HWJ to boys, Apr. 30, 1917.

56. *Cong. Record*, 65th Cong., 1st sess. (Aug. 20, 31, Sept. 1, 3, 4, 5, 1917), pp. 6183–86, 6479, 6487, 6492–97, 6527, 6568, 6601; *New York Times*, Aug. 10–Sept. 11, 1917; HWJ to Hiram Johnson, Jr., Sept. 5, 1917; HWJ to Theodore Roosevelt, Sept. 8, 1917.

57. HWJ to John S. Chambers, Sept. 15, 1917; HWJ press releases, Sept. 4, 11, 1917, Part III, Carton 25, HWJ Papers.

58. HWJ to Arthur Arlett, Sept. 14, 1917; HWJ to Hiram Johnson, Jr., Sept. 15, 1917; HWJ to Joseph Scott, Sept. 17, 1917; HWJ to C. K. McClatchy, Sept. 17, 1917; HWJ to Katherine Philips Edson, Sept. 17, 1917, Edson Papers; HWJ to Rowell, Sept. 17, 1917, Rowell Papers. See also Lissner to Paul Herriott, Sept. 4, 1917, Lissner Papers.

59. *Cong. Record*, 65th Cong., 2nd sess. (Feb. 19, 1918), pp. 2311–17.

60. *Cong. Record*, 65th Cong., 2nd sess. (Feb. 19, 21, 22, March 13, 1918), pp. 2311–17, 2422, 2511, 3442; HWJ to Hiram Johnson, Jr., Feb. 22, 23, 1918; HWJ to Amy Johnson, Feb. 23, 1918. Johnson was one of eight to vote against the final conference report. That number, he wrote, constituted "the irreducible minimum of radicalism" in the Senate. HWJ to Amy Johnson, Mar. 16, 1918.

61. *Cong. Record*, 65th Cong., 2nd sess. (Feb. 19, 1918), p. 2311; HWJ to Amy Johnson, Feb. 2, 9, 16, 1918. See also *Cong. Record*, 65th Cong., 3rd sess. (Dec. 14, 1918), p. 442; HWJ to Hiram Johnson, Jr., Jan. 3, 1918; HWJ to Archi-

bald Johnson, Jan. 5, 1918; John R. Haynes to HWJ, Feb. 19, 1918, Haynes Papers. As a member of the Senate Commerce Committee, Johnson participated in the Hog Island investigation.

62. HWJ to Archibald Johnson, Sept. 7, 1917; HWJ to Hiram Johnson, Jr., Aug. 18, 1918.

63. HWJ to Hiram Johnson, Jr., July 26, 1917; HWJ to Amy Johnson, Apr. 13, July 8, Aug. 10, 1918; HWJ to Archibald Johnson, June 16, 1918.

64. Speech, San Francisco Ad Club, Nov. 8, 1917, Part III, Carton 19, HWJ Papers; *California Outlook*, Dec. 1917, p. 203.

65. HWJ to Amy Johnson, Feb. 9, Mar. 30, July 15, 1918; HWJ to Archibald Johnson, Mar. 12, June 16, 1918; HWJ to Hiram Johnson, Jr., June 17, 30, 1918.

66. HWJ to Amy Johnson, Mar. 16, 1918. See also HWJ to Amy Johnson, Jan. 26, 1918.

67. HWJ to C. K. McClatchy, Apr. 13, 1918; HWJ to Amy Johnson, Apr. 13, 19, 1918; *Cong. Record*, 65th Cong., 2nd sess. (Apr. 4, 1918), p. 4566. "I would rather have no political future than violate my every idea of liberty," Johnson wrote. HWJ to Hiram Johnson, Jr., Apr. 10, 1918. See also HWJ to Amy Johnson, Apr. 13, 1918. Earlier, Johnson had been one of six to vote against the Trading with the Enemy Act, which gave the executive the power to censor both international communications and the American foreign-language press. *Cong. Record*, 65th Cong., 1st sess. (Sept. 24, 1917), p. 7353.

68. *Cong. Record*, 65th Cong., 2nd sess. (Apr. 24, May 4, 1918), pp. 5542, 5544, 6036–37.

69. *Cong. Record*, 65th Cong., 1st sess. (June 28, 1917), p. 4403. See also HWJ to Archibald Johnson, Apr. 10, 1918.

70. HWJ to Archibald Johnson, June 8, July 12, 1918; HWJ to Amy Johnson, Jan. 12, Apr. 13, 1918. Clearly exaggerating Wilson's power to command events, Johnson described him in early April 1917 as the "absolute dictator and czar. . . . Arbitrarily, dictatorially, and arrogantly, he directs the majority and he has not only a marvellous power here but [by] a look or a word he is able to blight any who oppose him. He does this in spite of the fact that practically nobody loves him and practically everybody hates him." HWJ to Lissner, Apr. 9, 1917. See also HWJ to Hiram Johnson, Jr., Apr. 15, 1917; HWJ to Harris Weinstock, Apr. 16, 1917.

71. HWJ to Amy Johnson, Jan. 26, May 11, 1918; HWJ to Hiram Johnson, Jr., July 26, 1917.

72. HWJ to Amy Johnson, Dec. 29, 1917; HWJ to Hiram Johnson, Jr., Jan. 22, 1918; HWJ to Archibald Johnson, Dec. 29, 1917, Feb. 6, 1918; HWJ to Lissner, Jan. 25, 1918; Theodore Roosevelt to HWJ, Mar. 27, 1918; *Cong. Record*, 65th Cong., 2nd sess. (Feb. 19, Mar. 26, 1918), pp. 2311–12, 4065. Although he was critical of the administration, Johnson nevertheless tempered his remarks, for he was unwilling to support the efforts pushed by the Republican Old Guard, prominent business interests, and the military establishment to discredit and displace Secretary of War Newton Baker. Baker, Johnson wrote, was one of the few safeguards protecting American society from an "unfeeling, inhuman, wooden, military yardstick." HWJ to Amy Johnson, May 5, 1918; HWJ to Archi-

bald Johnson, Jan. 26, 1918; HWJ to Hiram Johnson, Jr., Aug. 2, 1917, July 30, 1918. Earlier, in 1917, Johnson had supported passage of the Weeks-Owen rider to the Lever Act to create a joint congressional committee to oversee the conduct of the war. At Wilson's urging, the rider had been eliminated in conference.

73. HWJ to Amy Johnson, Mar. 23, Apr. 13, May 5, 25, 1918; HWJ to C. K. McClatchy, May 21, 1918. Shortly thereafter, Wilson effectively circumvented an inquiry by the Senate Military Affairs Committee into charges of inefficiency, corruption, and mismanagement in the production of military aircraft by recruiting Charles Evans Hughes to head a Justice Department probe of the matter. HWJ to Amy Johnson, May 18, 25, 1918.

74. HWJ to Amy Johnson, June 8, July 8, 1918; HWJ to Hiram Johnson, Jr., June 30, 1918; *Cong. Record*, 65th Cong., 2nd sess. (June 12, 1918), pp. 7669–72. See also *Cong. Record*, 65th Cong., 2nd sess. (July 6, Aug. 30, 1918), pp. 8746, 9682.

75. HWJ to Amy Johnson, Aug. 31, 1918. See also HWJ to Theodore Roosevelt, July 9, 1918; Livermore, *Politics Is Adjourned*, pp. 105–68. Wilson, Johnson predicted, would prolong the war at least until the spring of 1920, when he would then decide, based upon the political advantages, whether peace should be made prior to or after the elections. HWJ to Amy Johnson, Aug. 17, 1918.

76. HWJ to Amy Johnson, July 27, Aug. 17, 1918; HWJ to Hiram Johnson, Jr., Aug. 28, 1918; HWJ to Lissner, Aug. 14, 1918; HWJ to Rowell, Aug. 13, 1918; Rowell to HWJ, Aug. 27, 1918, both in Rowell Papers.

77. *Cong. Record*, 65th Cong., 2nd sess. (Sept. 5, 1918), pp. 9977–79; HWJ to Amy Johnson, Sept. 7, 1918.

78. HWJ to Hiram Johnson, Jr., Sept. 2, 1917.

79. HWJ to Amy Johnson, June 8, 1918.

80. HWJ to Amy Johnson, Aug. 27, 1918. On Archibald, see Archibald Johnson to HWJ, Sept. 28, 1918; HWJ to Hiram Johnson, Jr., Mar. 5, 1922; HWJ to Archibald Johnson, Mar. 6, 1922. Johnson's tribute to Paul Herriott can be found in *Cong. Record*, 65th Cong., 2nd sess. (May 4, 1918), pp. 6036–37.

81. HWJ to Archibald Johnson, Jan. 8, 1918.

82. HWJ to Rowell, June 8, 1917, Rowell Papers; HWJ to C. K. McClatchy, May 23, 1917; HWJ to boys, May 17, 1917.

83. HWJ to Archibald Johnson, Aug. 2, 27, 1917. Though Johnson was rarely away from the Senate in 1917, he did speak at patriotic rallies in St. Louis in June and in Philadelphia in August. "Making the world safe for democracy," he noted in his Philadelphia address, was both appealing and proper, but it was important as well to focus on specifics. "We deal with a nation where all the people are sovereign, and they should ever have repeated to them the causes for which their sons fight and the reasons for which they are to die." Part III, Carton 25, HWJ Papers; *St. Louis Globe Democrat*, June 4, 1917; *Philadelphia Enquirer*, Aug. 16, 1917.

84. HWJ to Archibald Johnson, Jan. 8, 1918; HWJ to Hiram Johnson, Jr., Jan. 8, 1918; HWJ to C. K. McClatchy, Jan. 8, 1918.

85. HWJ to Hiram Johnson, Jr., Jan. 8, 1918. See also HWJ to Amy Johnson, Jan. 12, 19, 1918. Just prior to Wilson's address, Johnson had voiced similar outrage over the territorial settlement outlined by Lloyd George. On the parallels

between Lloyd George's Caxton Hall address and Wilson's Fourteen-Point Declaration see Lawrence W. Martin, *Peace Without Victory: Woodrow Wilson and the British Liberals* (New Haven, Conn., 1958), pp. 156–59.

86. HWJ to Archibald Johnson, July 27, 1917. Johnson's initial prediction of such a "revolution" came just prior to Senate debate on the tax bill of 1917. He made a similar prediction in the winter of 1917 when coal shortages prompted the government to order a one-week shutdown of eastern factories, and in mid-1918 when discussion began once again on tax legislation. HWJ to Amy Johnson, Jan. 19, Feb. 23, May 11, 1918.

87. HWJ to Amy Johnson, Dec. 29, 1917. See also HWJ to Archibald Johnson, Jan. 25, 1918.

88. HWJ to Paul Herriott, Jan. 28, 1918; HWJ to Amy Johnson, Feb. 9, 23, 1918.

89. HWJ to C. K. McClatchy, Feb. 6, 1918; HWJ to Amy Johnson, Jan. 19, 26, 1918; HWJ to Archibald Johnson, Jan. 11, Feb. 1, 1918; HWJ to Hiram Johnson, Jr., Jan. 11, 1918. Both the *Chicago Tribune* and the Hearst press, Johnson wrote, had promised their support. HWJ to Amy Johnson, Feb. 2, 1918. Just as Johnson disagreed with Charles McClatchy over free speech, so too they differed over the war. Prior to American intervention, McClatchy had defined the conflict in terms of competing economic interests. Once the United States became a participant, he became a crusader. "Personally," he wrote, "I don't believe we should submit to peace until after Hohenzollernism has been whipped to a pulp; and I believe such peace terms should be so severe and so drastic that Prussianism will never rise again. For if it does recover itself and burgeon into strength and into vigor, it will be worse of a menace in forty years than it is today." C. K. McClatchy to HWJ, Aug. 8, 1918.

90. HWJ to Amy Johnson, Feb. 9, 16, 23, 1918. House met with Johnson to sound him out as a possible member of the American delegation to the peace conference. Throughout the luncheon, House reported, Johnson was a model of diplomatic cordiality; he seemed eager to please. House came away with a positive impression. Arthur S. Link, ed., *The Papers of Woodrow Wilson*, vol. 46 (Princeton, N.J., 1984), extracts from diary of Colonel House, Jan. 27, Feb. 10, 1918, pp. 116, 316. On the changes in wording of the Fourteen Points from "must" to "should," see Charles Seymour, ed., *The Intimate Papers of Colonel House*, vol. 3 (Boston, 1928), pp. 329–30.

91. HWJ to C. K. McClatchy, Feb. 13, 1918; HWJ to Amy Johnson, Mar. 30, 1918.

92. HWJ to Amy Johnson, Mar. 9, 1918. See also HWJ to Archibald Johnson, Dec. 10, 1917; HWJ to Hiram Johnson, Jr., Mar. 9, 1918; HWJ to C. K. McClatchy, Mar. 18, 1918; *Cong. Record*, 65th Cong., 2nd sess. (Mar. 5, 1918), p. 3030.

93. HWJ to Amy Johnson, Mar. 23, Apr. 13, June 22, 1918. Johnson took pleasure in his appointment in April 1918 to the Senate Military Affairs Committee. He had not raised a finger to seek the position, he noted, but he wanted it very much. HWJ to Amy Johnson, Apr. 13, 19, 1918; HWJ to Archibald Johnson, Apr. 20, 1918.

94. HWJ to Amy Johnson, June 29, July 8, 20, Aug. 10, 17, 1918; HWJ to Hiram

Johnson, Jr., Aug. 18, 1918. The French, Johnson observed, had invested heavily in Russia and sought to ensure against Russia's repudiation of its debts. But perhaps more importantly, he added, the French hoped that Japanese intervention in Siberia would push Russia into the hands of Germany. If Germany secured control of western Russia, Germany would then return Alsace Lorraine to France and agree to transfer its African colonies to Britain. Peace would be restored at Russia's expense. For similar views see Arno J. Mayer, *Political Origins of the New Diplomacy, 1917–1918* (New Haven, Conn., 1959), p. 273.

95. HWJ to Lissner, Nov. 14, 1918; HWJ to Hiram Johnson, Jr., Nov. 23, Dec. 2, 1918, Jan. 18, 1919. See also *Cong. Record*, 65th Cong., 3rd sess. (Dec. 4, 5, 1918), pp. 71, 130. "Democracy is very, very far behind us when the President does not deign to tell this country why he goes to Europe, when he will not define his peace ideas, upon which the entire future of the Republic may hinge." HWJ to Hiram Johnson, Jr., Dec. 7, 1918.

96. HWJ to Lissner, July 1, 1918; HWJ to Amy Johnson, June 22, July 8, 20, 1918. See also *Cong. Record*, 65th Cong., 2nd sess. (July 13, 1918), pp. 9056–57; Richard Coke Lower, "Hiram Johnson: The Making of an Irreconcilable," *Pacific Historical Review* 46:4 (Nov. 1972), pp. 505–26.

97. Raymond Robins to HWJ, Dec. 3, 10, 1918, Jan. 4, 13, Apr. 2, 1919; HWJ to Hiram Johnson, Jr., Jan. 20, 1919; HWJ to Theodore Roosevelt, Dec. 27, 1918; Minnie Johnson to Hiram Johnson, Jr., ca. Jan. 20, 1919.

98. *Cong. Record*, 65th Cong., 3rd sess. (Dec. 12, 1918), pp. 342–47.

99. HWJ to Hiram Johnson, Jr., Dec. 26, 1918, Jan. 1, 11, Feb. 16, 1919; HWJ to Archibald Johnson, Dec. 14, 20, 25, 1918; HWJ to Lissner, Dec. 18, 1918. Copies of the Robins documents can be found in Part III, Carton 12, HWJ Papers.

100. HWJ to Hiram Johnson, Jr., Jan. 1, 1919; HWJ to Archibald Johnson, Jan. 1, 1919; *Cong. Record*, 65th Cong., 3rd sess. (Jan. 9, 13, 1919), pp. 1163–66, 1313.

101. *Cong. Record*, 65th Cong., 3rd sess. (Jan. 29, 1919), pp. 2261–70; HWJ to Hiram Johnson, Jr., Jan. 11, 24, 1919.

102. *Cong. Record*, 65th Cong., 3rd sess. (Feb. 7, 13, 14, 1919), pp. 2878, 3258–64, 3342; HWJ to Hiram Johnson, Jr., Feb. 1, 8, 12, 16, 1919.

103. *Cong. Record*, 65th Cong. 3rd sess. (Dec. 21, 1918), p. 726. See also Arno J. Mayer, *Politics and Diplomacy of Peacemaking: Containment and Counter-revolution at Versailles, 1918–1919* (New York, 1967), pp. 271–72, 331–37, 447–49.

104. HWJ to Hiram Johnson, Jr., Jan. 24, 1919. With the war at an end, Johnson noted, he would no longer accept "the same old push-button methods of legislation, with the same old rubber-stamp approval by Congress." *Cong. Record*, 65th Cong., 3rd sess. (Jan. 21, 1919), pp. 1797–99. Others opposed food relief for quite different reasons: they were convinced that the carrot was no substitute for the stick as a device to eliminate radicalism. Mayer, *Politics and Diplomacy of Peacemaking*, pp. 260–73.

105. Draft of American University address (St. Louis Advertisers Club), June 2, 1917, Part III, Carton 25, HWJ Papers. In 1916 Johnson echoed the Founding

Fathers, calling for "peace and amity with all nations, entangling alliances with none." Notes for Trinity Auditorium address, Los Angeles, Oct. 27, 1916, Part II, Carton 43, HWJ Papers.

106. Britain, Johnson would have added, was an especial danger, not only because of its skill in diplomacy but also because too many Americans were awed by British ways. Describing the impact of Arthur Balfour on Congress, he noted: "The Anglo maniacs here—and they are many—of course have been in the seventh heaven because they might sit at the feet of an English lord and listen to the inspired words that fell from his lips." Needless to say, Johnson had not been impressed. HWJ to boys, May 17, 1917.

107. *Cong. Record*, 65th Cong., 3rd sess. (Dec. 21, 1918), pp. 723–28; *Cong. Record*, 65th Cong., 2nd sess. (Oct. 28, 1918), pp. 11485–488; Ralph Stone, *The Irreconcilables: The Fight Against the League of Nations* (Lexington, Ky., 1970), pp. 46–48; Lloyd E. Ambrosius, "Wilson, the Republicans, and French Security After World War I," *Journal of American History* 59:2 (Sept. 1972), pp. 341–52.

108. HWJ to Theodore Roosevelt, Dec. 27, 1918; HWJ to Hiram Johnson, Jr., Jan. 18, 1919; *Cong. Record*, 65th Cong., 3rd sess. (Jan. 17, 29, 1919), pp. 1585, 2261–63.

Chapter IV: New Directions

1. *Cong. Record*, 65th Cong., 3rd sess. (Jan. 29, 31, 1919), pp. 2261–63, 2421; HWJ to Hiram Johnson, Jr., Nov. 23, Dec. 2, 7, 1918, Jan. 24, Feb. 16, 1919; HWJ to Archibald Johnson, Dec. 25, 1918. Predictably finding reason to criticize Wilson's conduct abroad, Johnson acidly commented on the president's dinner with the king of England upon a service of solid gold and his attendance by "fifty gorgeously arrayed flunkies and officials, with each backward step indulging in genuflections." Even more irritating were the president's references to "*My* people" and "*My* armies." "He really thinks himself God's anointed," Johnson wrote, "and we have all contributed to the result." HWJ to Archibald Johnson, Dec. 29, 1918; HWJ to Edson, Dec. 28, 1918, Edson Papers; HWJ to Hiram Johnson, Jr., Jan. 1, 1919, emphasis in original.

2. HWJ to Hiram Johnson, Jr., Dec. 7, 1918, Feb. 8, 1919; HWJ to Archibald Johnson, Nov. 26, Dec. 20, 25, 1918; HWJ to Theodore Roosevelt, Dec. 27, 1918.

3. "If I had an adequate understanding of the sort of league of nations the President seeks, I'd be very glad to advocate it upon the floor of the Senate, and to take sharp issue with Lodge," Johnson wrote in late December. And to Lissner he later confessed, "I really wanted to be for it." HWJ to Hiram Johnson, Jr., Dec. 26, 1918, Jan. 24, 1919; HWJ to Lissner, Mar. 14, 1919. See also HWJ to Archibald Johnson, Mar. 16, 1919.

4. HWJ to Hiram Johnson, Jr., Feb. 16, 24, 1919; HWJ to Rowell, Feb. 24, 1919.

5. Minnie Johnson to Hiram Johnson, Jr., Feb. 19, 1919; HWJ to C. K. McClatchy, Feb. 24, 1919.

6. As Ralph Stone notes, the declaration, in failing to specify what changes would be required, was worded to attract the widest support possible. Ralph

Stone, *The Irreconcilables: The Fight Against the League of Nations* (Lexington, Ky., 1970), pp. 70–76.

7. HWJ to A. H. Boynton, Charles C. Moore, Milton H. Esberg, Mar. 12, 1919. See also HWJ to Lissner, Mar. 14, 1919; HWJ to Rowell, Mar. 5, 1919, Rowell Papers.

8. Lincoln Colcord to HWJ, Mar. 3, 1919; HWJ to Lissner, Mar. 14, 1919. What was occurring in Russia, he wrote, "was exactly what we'll have in Europe, Asia and Africa with the League of Nations." HWJ to C. K. McClatchy, Apr. 7, 12, 1919. See John M. Thompson, *Russia, Bolshevism, and the Versailles Peace* (Princeton, N.J., 1966), pp. 178–221, for an examination of these various proposals. On Lincoln Colcord, see Christopher Lasch, *The New Radicalism in America, 1889–1963* (New York, 1965), pp. 225–50.

9. HWJ to Rowell, Mar. 11, 1919; HWJ to Lissner, Mar. 14, 1919; HWJ to C. K. McClatchy, Mar. 14, 22, 1919; HWJ to Archibald Johnson, Mar. 16, 1919.

10. HWJ to Rowell, Mar. 27, 1919. See also HWJ to Archibald Johnson, Apr. 1, 4, 1919.

11. Rowell to HWJ, Feb. 23, Mar. 3, Apr. 3, 1919, Rowell Papers. See also Rowell to C. C. Young, Feb. 27, 1919; Lissner to Rowell, Apr. 15, 1919; Lissner to HWJ, Apr. 15, 1919, all in Rowell Papers. Although Rowell conceded that, literally applied, Article X would do precisely what Johnson feared, he insisted that in practice it would be differently read. Rowell to E. D. Adams, Jan. 22, 1920, Rowell Papers.

12. Johnson estimated on the basis of his correspondence that 80 percent of his constituents favored the league. HWJ to Hiram Johnson, Jr., May 31, 1919. The ministers and church people, he wrote, were the most unreasonable and abusive. "They think they are again worshipping Christ after two years of negation." HWJ to Lissner, Mar. 14, 1919. See also HWJ to Hiram Johnson, Jr., Feb. 24, 1919.

13. Lissner to HWJ, Mar. 8, 26, 1919; Rowell to Lissner, Apr. 17, 1919, Lissner Papers.

14. Rowell to HWJ, May 15, 1919; Rowell to Lissner, May 16, 1919, Rowell Papers. See also Lissner to HWJ, May 16, 1919, Rowell Papers.

15. The death of Theodore Roosevelt, in January 1919, focused the attention of many on the politics of 1920. Perhaps Johnson would have entered the presidential race in any event. Roosevelt, he had earlier written, had made his peace with the Old Guard and would never again get by with the common people. HWJ to Amy Johnson, Jan. 26, 1918. Even so, Roosevelt seemed to many to be the most obvious choice to reunite the Republican factions he had done so much to divide, and it was not until after Roosevelt's death that Johnson began to express interest in the race. Solicitations by various progressives piqued his ambitions. His lieutenants in California, Lissner reported, were "chaffing at the bit." If enough interest was expressed, Johnson admitted, he would run even though his chances were minimal. HWJ to Hiram Johnson, Jr., Jan. 11, 1919. See also HWJ to Hiram Johnson, Jr., Feb. 12, 1919; HWJ to Lissner, Feb. 18, 1919; HWJ to Archibald Johnson, Apr. 24, 1919; Lissner to HWJ, May 13, 1919, Rowell Papers; Lissner to Gifford Pinchot, Jan. 14, 1919, Rowell Papers; Neylan to HWJ, Jan. 15,

1919, Neylan Papers; Lissner to HWJ, Feb. 22, Mar. 8, Apr. 15, 1919; C. K. McClatchy to HWJ, Apr. 29, May 1, 1919.

16. HWJ to C. K. McClatchy, Apr. 24, 1919; HWJ to Archibald Johnson, Apr. 29, 1919.

17. HWJ to Lissner, May 22, 1919, Neylan Papers. See also HWJ to Hiram Johnson, Jr., May 22, 1919. Perhaps too his earlier hope, expressed to McClatchy, that he might be persuaded of the league's merits was shaped by these political concerns.

18. Johnson's predictions can be found in HWJ to Archibald Johnson, Apr. 1, 1919; HWJ to C. K. McClatchy, Apr. 24, 1919; HWJ to Rowell, Apr. 9, 1919, Rowell Papers.

19. *Cong. Record*, 66th Cong., 1st sess. (May 20, 23, 1919), pp. 63, 157–60, 681.

20. *Cong. Record*, 66th Cong., 1st sess. (June 2, 1919), pp. 501–9; *New York Tribune*, June 3, 1919.

21. HWJ to Archibald Johnson, June 6, 1919.

22. The amended Knox resolution, favorably reported, was not brought up for a vote. HWJ to boys, June 12, 1919. See also Stone, *Irreconcilables*, pp. 110–13.

23. Johnson's resolution passed without a roll-call vote on June 6 following the revelation by William Borah that copies of the treaty had found their way to Wall Street. At the time that Borah made the charge, Johnson observed, he totally lacked the evidence to sustain it. *Cong. Record*, 66th Cong., 1st sess. (June 5, 9, 1919), pp. 687, 788–89; HWJ to boys, June 12, 1919. In addition, Johnson continued to focus on the nation's presence in Russia, "just a little war and a little murder," as he described it to Rowell. HWJ to Rowell, July 21, 1919, Rowell Papers. On June 27, by voice vote, the Senate passed his resolution calling on the president to inform the Senate of the reasons for America's continued involvement in Siberia. See *Cong. Record*, 66th Cong., 1st sess. (June 27, 1919), p. 1864.

24. *New York Times*, June 29, 1919; HWJ to boys, July 2, 1919.

25. HWJ to boys, July 16, 1919; HWJ to C. K. McClatchy, July 16, 1919; HWJ to Neylan, July 17, 1919, Neylan Papers. See also Part III, Carton 25, HWJ Papers; *Boston Evening Transcript*, July 8, 12, 1919.

26. Minnie Johnson to boys, Aug. 7, 1919, emphasis in original; *New York Tribune*, Aug. 7, 1919. After Lansing's testimony, Johnson wrote, "I walked over to the office saddened and humiliated, because my country was in the hands of such men, and at the mercy of their dullness, stupidity, and worse." HWJ to Hiram Johnson, Jr., Aug. 7, 1919. See also HWJ to C. K. McClatchy, Aug. 7, 1919. Johnson's questioning and Lansing's sorry performance can be found in U.S. Senate Foreign Relations Committee, 66th Cong., 1st sess., Sen. Document 106, *Hearings of the Committee on Foreign Relations on the Treaty of Peace with Germany* (1919). See especially pp. 161–74, 181–97.

27. U.S. Senate, 66th Cong., 1st sess., Sen. Document 106, *Hearings of the Committee on Foreign Relations on the Treaty of Peace with Germany* (1919). See especially pp. 524–30, 549–50; HWJ to boys, Aug. 15, 1919.

28. Stanley Washburn to HWJ, June 29, 1919; HWJ to Stanley Washburn, July

19, 1919; HWJ to Neylan, July 18, 1919; Neylan to HWJ, July 21, 1919; HWJ to boys, Aug. 1, 15, 1919.

29. HWJ to boys, Sept. 8, 1919. See also HWJ to boys, Aug. 31, Sept. 3, 1919.

30. HWJ to C. K. McClatchy, July 16, 1919; HWJ to boys, July 16, 1919; HWJ to Alex McCabe, July 16, 1919; HWJ to Neylan, July 17, 1919, Neylan Papers.

31. HWJ to boys, Aug. 31, Sept. 8, 22, Nov. 18, 1919; HWJ to Raymond Robins, Sept. 9, 1919; Alex McCabe to HWJ, Aug. 29, 1919.

32. HWJ to Minnie Johnson, Sept. 10, 1919. See also HWJ to Ickes, Sept. 3, 1919; *New York Times*, Sept. 11, 1918.

33. HWJ to Minnie Johnson, Sept. 10, 13, 15, 17, 1919; HWJ to boys, Sept. 21, 1919; Franck Havenner to Minnie Johnson, Sept. 16, 1919; *New York Times*, Sept. 13–21, 1919; *San Francisco Examiner*, Sept. 21, 1919; *San Francisco Call*, Sept. 15, 17–20, 1919; *Sacramento Bee*, Sept. 11–22, 1919. See also "Johnson-Wilson Debate," Part III, Carton 4, HWJ Papers.

34. HWJ to boys, Sept. 22, 1919; *New York Times*, Sept. 19, 20, 1919.

35. HWJ to Archibald Johnson, Sept. 23, 25, 1919; *Cong. Record*, 66th Cong., 1st sess. (Sept. 26, 1919), pp. 5970–71, 5976; *New York Times*, Sept. 23, 26–28, 1919. Rumors that Wilson had captured the state with his rhetoric and that Johnson feared to return doubtless enhanced his determination. See Hichborn to HWJ, Oct. 25, 1919, Hichborn Papers.

36. *San Francisco Examiner*, Oct. 1, 2, 1919. San Francisco's treatment of Wilson, Johnson's son wrote, had been somewhat abusive. Hiram Johnson, Jr., to HWJ, Sept. 18, 1919.

37. Marshall Stimson to Rowell, Oct. 11, 1919, Rowell Papers; *New York Times*, Sept. 29, 1919. In an effort to undercut Johnson, Marshall Stimson sought unsuccessfully to persuade Rowell, who had accompanied Wilson on his California tour, to stump the state, trailing Johnson and answering his charges. When Johnson spoke in Los Angeles, a battery of stenographers and typists from the *Los Angeles Times* sent their texts of his address via motorcycle relays to Stimson's office, where he and members of the League to Enforce Peace dissected the arguments. Both text and dissection appeared the following day. See Marshall Stimson, "President Wilson's League of Nations Los Angeles Visit," League of Nations File, 1961 Misc file, Stimson Papers; Marshall Stimson to Rowell, Sept. 28, 1919; Rowell to Marshall Stimson, Sept. 29, 1919, both in Rowell Papers; Neylan to HWJ, Oct. 17, 1919.

38. *San Francisco Examiner*, Oct. 3–12, 1919; *Sacramento Bee*, Oct. 1–12, 1919.

39. HWJ to boys, Oct. 20, Nov. 1, 1919; HWJ to C. K. McClatchy, Oct. 20, 1919; Minnie Johnson to boys, Oct. 22, 1919; HWJ to James Reed, Oct. 17, 1919; *Cong. Record*, 66th Cong., 1st sess. (Oct. 16, 1919), pp. 7002–4.

40. HWJ to boys, Aug. 7, 16, 1919; HWJ to Lissner, July 25, 1919. On Root, see John Chalmers Vinson, *Referendum for Isolation: Defeat of Article Ten of the League of Nations Covenant* (Athens, Ga., 1961), p. 69. Root, Johnson wrote, was torn between his conscience and his commitment to the designs of Wall Street. HWJ to C. K. McClatchy, July 16, 1919. For Lodge's speech, see *Cong. Record*, 66 Cong., 1st sess. (Aug. 12, 1919), pp. 3778–84.

41. HWJ to C. K. McClatchy, July 16, 1919; HWJ to Albert Beveridge, July 21, 1919; HWJ to Grove Johnson, Aug. 7, 1919; HWJ to Lissner, Aug. 15, 1919; HWJ to Hichborn, Aug. 18, 1919, Hichborn Papers; HWJ to Rowell, July 21, 1919, Rowell Papers.

42. HWJ to boys, Aug. 1, 15, 1919.

43. HWJ to Ickes, June 7, 1919.

44. A second amendment, pushed by Johnson after his first defeat, failed more decisively. See *Cong. Record*, 66th Cong., 1st sess. (Oct. 22–24, 29, 1919), pp. 7327, 7355–60, 7438–39, 7683–87.

45. HWJ to boys, July 16, 24, Aug. 1, 1919; HWJ to Lissner, Aug. 15, 1919.

46. HWJ to Neylan, Nov. 3, 1919.

47. HWJ to boys, Nov. 1, 8, 14, 1919; HWJ to Alex Moore, Nov. 3, 1919; HWJ to Albert Beveridge, Nov. 14, 1919; *Cong. Record*, 66th Cong., 1st sess. (Nov. 6, 10, 15, 18, 1919), pp. 8023, 8196, 8549, 8559, 8718–19, 8731–38, 8753–54.

48. HWJ to boys, Nov. 21, 1919; HWJ to Neylan, Nov. 24, 1919; HWJ to Grove Johnson, Nov. 24, 1919.

49. "Of course, in the Senate when the discussion of the League is up you will be heard and you will talk on the subject," Lissner wrote, "but when you go to the people I don't think that need be the predominant theme." Lissner to HWJ, May 16, 1919, Rowell Papers.

50. HWJ to Archibald Johnson, Apr. 1, 1919; HWJ to Hiram Johnson, Jr., May 22, 1919. Ickes, pointing to the obvious popularity of the league, suggested that critics hold their noses and vote to support American membership. Chiding Ickes, Johnson replied, "I'd prefer to get out of public life than to do something I honestly believe would destroy the Republic, because a vast number of people desired it done." Ickes to HWJ, June 4, 10, 1919; HWJ to Ickes, June 7, 1919.

51. HWJ to C. K. McClatchy, July 16, 1919; HWJ to Neylan, Nov. 3, 1919. See also HWJ to Lissner, July 31, 1919; HWJ to Neylan, July 17, 1919, Neylan Papers.

52. HWJ to Lissner, May 22, 1919.

53. Lissner to HWJ, May 16, 1919, Rowell Papers. Edson herself, though at first opposed to Johnson's stand, would become a convert of sorts after reading John Maynard Keynes's *The Economic Consequences of the Peace* and E. J. Dillon's *The Inside Story of the Peace Conference*. Edson to E. Tolhurst, Apr. 17, 1920, Edson Papers.

54. Marshall Stimson to Rowell, May 10, 1919, Rowell Papers. See also HWJ to Lissner, Aug. 2, 1920, Lissner Papers.

55. Lissner to HWJ, Mar. 26, Apr. 17, 1919; Frank Devlin to HWJ, June 16, 1919; Hichborn to HWJ, July 14, Aug. 7, 1919, Hichborn Papers; H. L. Carnahan to HWJ, July 15, 1919.

56. Among other charges, the *Times* resurrected the 1916 allegations revolving around the Hughes campaign. Dickson, Johnson remarked, was "as foxy as a lavatorial rodent." Lissner to Rowell, Jan. 24, 1920, Rowell Papers; Lissner to C. K. McClatchy, Jan. 31, 1920.

57. Hiram Johnson, Jr., to HWJ, May 21, June 13, 1919; *San Francisco Call*, June 6, 1919.

58. C. K. McClatchy to HWJ, May 27, 1919.

59. Lissner to HWJ, Jan. 18, 1919; Lissner to HWJ, May 20, 1919, Rowell Papers. See also Archibald Johnson to HWJ, May 21, 1919; Rowell to HWJ, May 15, 1919; Rowell to Lissner, May 16, 1919, Lissner Papers.

60. HWJ to Neylan, May 29, 1919, Neylan Papers; HWJ to C. K. McClatchy, June 7, 1919; HWJ to Archibald Johnson, June 1, 1919.

61. HWJ to Hiram Johnson, Jr., June 6, 7, 1919, Most active in directing operations were Hiram Johnson, Jr.; Archibald Johnson; Lissner; Al McCabe; Eustace Cullinan; and John Neylan. Rowell, who was recovering from a leg operation, remained very much in the background. For the names of those in the larger inner circle, see Lissner to Rowell, May 20, 1919, Rowell Papers. See also Hiram Johnson, Jr., to HWJ, May 21, 24, June 2, 17, 1919; Neylan to Hiram Johnson, Jr., June 9, 1919, Neylan Papers.

62. *San Francisco Call*, June 6, 14, 1919; *San Francisco Chronicle*, June 12, 15, 1919; Lissner to Rowell, June 12, 1919, Rowell Papers; Rowell to Lissner, June 13, 1919, Lissner Papers.

63. Hiram Johnson, Jr., to HWJ, June 17, 1919; Irving Martin to HWJ, June 16, 1919; Neylan to HWJ, June 18, 1919.

64. HWJ to boys, June 22, 1919. See also HWJ to Hiram Johnson, Jr., June 16, 1919; HWJ to C. K. McClatchy, June 16, 1919; HWJ to Neylan, June 16, 1919.

65. HWJ to Hiram Johnson, Jr., June 23, 1919; HWJ to Philip Bancroft, June 24, 1919.

66. HWJ to Al McCabe, July 18, 1919; HWJ to Neylan, July 2, 1919; HWJ to boys, July 2, Aug. 16, 1919; Minnie Johnson to Hiram Johnson, Jr., Aug. 21, 1919.

67. Al McCabe to HWJ, Aug. 16, 1919. Johnson himself had urged Frank Flint to delay any organization in Southern California because of the intense sentiment for the league in that area. By December, he regretted that decision. HWJ to boys, July 24, 1919; HWJ to Lissner, July 25, Dec. 3, 1919.

68. HWJ to Lissner, May 12, 1919; Lissner to Rowell, Apr. 22, 1919, both in Rowell Papers; Archibald Johnson to HWJ, June 13, 1919; Al McCabe to HWJ, Aug. 16, 1919. See also Hiram Johnson, Jr., to HWJ, May 21, 1919; Lissner to HWJ, May 13, 1919, Rowell Papers. By February, Johnson's finance committee, while hopeful that they could raise $200,000, had established their minimum goal as $100,000. By March, they had collected $70,000. H. L. Carnahan to HWJ, Feb. 4, 1920; Frank R. Devlin to Philip Bancroft, Mar. 12, 1920, Bancroft Papers. See also Al McCabe to HWJ, Nov. 22, 1920.

69. HWJ to Theodore Roche, Nov. 28, 1919; HWJ to Hiram Johnson, Jr., Dec. 1, 1919; HWJ to C. K. McClatchy, Dec. 8, 12, 1919.

70. HWJ to George Norris, Dec. 30, 1919.

71. HWJ to Philip Bowles, Aug. 9, 1919. One of the qualities said to recommend Wood, Johnson noted, was his ability to point a machine gun. HWJ to Rowell, Dec. 26, 1919, Rowell Papers.

72. HWJ to boys, Feb. 22, 1920. See also HWJ to C. K. McClatchy, Feb. 17, 1920.

73. *New York Times*, Jan. 14, 1920; HWJ to boys, Jan. 16, 1920; 1920 campaign materials, Part III, Carton 10, HWJ Papers.

74. HWJ to Lissner, Mar. 20, 1920; Part III, Cartons 10, 25, HWJ Papers; Row-

ell to Lissner, Mar. 31, 1920; Lissner to Rowell, Apr. 3, 1920, both in Rowell Papers. In an attempt to win converts, Angus McSween, Johnson's New York campaign manager, sent Johnson a program outlined by Saul O. Levinson out of which would come the "outlawry of war" movement. If Johnson would endorse it, McSween noted, the program would be known as the "Johnson Peace Plan." Johnson was not impressed. Angus McSween to HWJ, Apr. 17, 1920.

75. Part III, Cartons 10, 25, HWJ Papers. Despite a rhetoric heavily mired in generalizations, Johnson was, wrote Oswald Garrison Villard, of the *Nation*, the only candidate in the field to voice something of a program. The electorate, the *New Republic* added, read a different meaning into his generalities, regarding them as rooted in his achievements as governor and his liberal record in the U.S. Senate. *Nation*, June 5, 1920, pp. 748–49; *New Republic*, May 19, 1920, pp. 367–69.

76. *New York Times*, Jan. 16–22, 1920.

77. HWJ to boys, Jan. 24, 1920. See also HWJ to Pitman B. Potter, July 31, 1929; Stone, *Irreconcilables*, pp. 151–60. Writing in 1924, Johnson perhaps mistakenly recalled that the meeting had taken place in the rooms used by the Senate Committee on Patents. See "Hiram W. Johnson Newsletter," Dec. 13, 1924, Part III, Carton 25, HWJ Papers.

78. HWJ to Al McCabe, Nov. 2, 1919; HWJ to boys, Feb. 4, 5, 12, 1920; Part III, Carton 4, HWJ Papers.

79. Minnie Johnson to boys, Feb. 6, 10, 1920; HWJ to Rowell, Feb. 16, 1920, Rowell Papers.

80. HWJ to boys, Feb. 22, 1920; HWJ to Hiram Johnson, Jr., Mar. 6, 1920; HWJ to Alex McCabe, Nov. 8, 17, 1919; Alex McCabe to HWJ, Nov. 15, 1919; Hiram Johnson, Jr., to HWJ, Nov. 15, 1919; *New York Times*, Feb. 19–25, 1920; Louise Overacker, *The Presidential Primary* (New York, 1926), pp. 67–68.

81. *Minneapolis Journal*, Mar. 25, 1920; *New York Times*, Mar. 24, 25, 1920; *New Republic*, Apr. 7, 1920, pp. 172–73; HWJ to Hiram Johnson, Jr., Mar. 6, 1920; R. Seldon Wilcox to H. L. Carnahan, Mar. 5, 1920. Johnson's South Dakota campaign expenditures amounted to less than $4,000. Wood spent more than $69,000. Overacker, *Presidential Primary*, p. 156.

82. HWJ to boys, Mar. 18, 1920; HWJ to C. K. McClatchy, Mar. 18, 1920; *New York Times*, Mar. 18, 27, 1920; Overacker, *Presidential Primary*, pp. 206–7.

83. Part III, Carton 4, HWJ Papers; HWJ to boys, Mar. 18, 1920; *Detroit News*, Mar. 28, 1920.

84. *Grand Rapids Herald*, as quoted in *Literary Digest*, Apr. 17, 1920, p. 36.

85. HWJ to Hiram Johnson, Jr., Apr. 23, 1920; Part III, Carton 4, HWJ Papers; Claude Bowers, *Beveridge and the Progressive Era* (Boston, 1932), p. 515.

86. Overacker, *Presidential Primary*, pp. 62–63, 71, 238.

87. *New York Times*, May 2, 1920; Raymond Robins to HWJ, Mar. 23, 1920; HWJ to William Kenyon, Mar. 3, 1920; HWJ to C. K. McClatchy, Mar. 18, 1920; HWJ to Hiram Johnson, Jr., Mar. 20, 1920; H. P. Woodworth to HWJ, Apr. 4, 1920. The Hearst press, of course, was one of Johnson's major backers, and both Neylan and Brisbane urged Johnson to meet personally with Hearst. Johnson declined. He welcomed Hearst's support but "would be no man's . . . candidate."

HWJ to boys, Feb. 5, 12, 1920. Charles McClatchy agreed: "I fear Hearst bearing gifts." C. K. McClatchy to HWJ, Feb. 19, 1920.

88. Gary Dean Best, "The Hoover for President Boom," *Mid America* 53:4 (Oct. 1971), pp. 227–44. Johnson's favorable comments are found in *Cong. Record*, 65th Cong., 1st sess. (June 28, Aug. 6, 1917), pp. 4403, 5818. In fact, Johnson lagged behind both his wife, Minnie, and his secretary, Paul Herriott, in voicing suspicions. Writing to John Neylan, Herriott confessed in the summer of 1917: "The one fellow I have a little sneaking fear of, is Hoover." Hoover, Minnie Johnson observed the following year, was "a pretty slippery guy." Indeed, she added, she had always believed that to be the case. Paul Herriott to Neylan, June 22, 1917, Neylan Papers; Minnie Johnson to Hiram Johnson, Jr., July 27, 1918. See also HWJ to Carlos McClatchy, Nov. 9, 1920.

89. HWJ to Lissner, Feb. 12, 1920. See also HWJ to C. K. McClatchy, Jan. 23, Feb. 12, 1920; HWJ to boys, Jan. 24, Feb. 5, 1920; HWJ to Lissner, Jan. 24, 1920.

90. HWJ to Lissner, Feb. 12, 1920; Lissner to C. K. McClatchy, Jan. 31, 1920; Lissner to Rowell, Feb. 14, 1920, Rowell Papers.

91. Rowell to Edson, Jan. 15, 1920; Rowell to Lissner, Jan. 16, Feb. 16, 1920; Rowell to M. B. Harris, Jan. 23, 1920; Rowell to E. D. Adams, Jan. 23, 1920; Rowell to William Allen White, Mar. 19, 1920, all in Rowell Papers; Rowell to Lissner, Feb. 16, Mar. 13, 1920, Lissner Papers.

92. Rowell to Lissner, Feb. 9, 1920; Rowell to William Kent, Mar. 7, 1920, both in Rowell Papers.

93. Among those who moved was Joe Crail, who confessed to Johnson, "If it were a question of personalities instead of principle, you would still be my candidate." Joe Crail to HWJ, Feb. 17, 1920. See also Ed Fletcher to HWJ, Mar. 17, 1920.

94. Franklin Hichborn, "California Politics, 1891–1939," vol. 3, p. 1764.

95. HWJ to Hiram Johnson, Jr., Mar. 6, 1920; HWJ to C. K. McClatchy, Mar. 6, 1920; HWJ to boys, Mar. 18, 1920; Ed Fletcher to HWJ, Mar. 17, 1920. In fact, Johnson had sent mixed signals to his lieutenants and thus had opened the door to the very outcome he would later condemn. "I am perfectly willing for any sort of harmony you people in California decide upon," he stated to Neylan as the California campaign got under way. "Indeed, I don't think that I ought to attempt to command the personnel of the delegation." HWJ to Neylan, Nov. 24, 1919.

96. HWJ to boys, Mar. 18, 1920. See also HWJ to boys, Mar. 15, Apr. 20, 1920. When solicited for suggestions, Rowell had earlier noted that all were excellent men, and that Fleishhacker and Cochran had become "genuine progressives." Charles McClatchy was more direct. It was far better, he wrote, to have de Young and Crocker on the slate than Rowell. Rowell to H. L. Carnahan, Feb. 27, 1920, Rowell Papers; C. K. McClatchy to HWJ, Mar. 9, 24, 1920.

97. HWJ to C. K. McClatchy, Feb. 12, 1920.

98. HWJ to Archibald Johnson, Feb. 6, 1920; HWJ to C. K. McClatchy, Feb. 17, 1920; HWJ to boys, Apr. 2, 1920. On the possibilities of Hoover's selection by the Democratic party, see the speech by Julius Barnes, one of Hoover's chief advocates, in *New York Times*, Jan. 15, 1920.

99. HWJ to Lissner, Mar. 20, 1920; Rowell to Mark Sullivan, Apr. 29, 1920, Rowell Papers. Much of Rowell's correspondence to Lissner during this period picks at Lissner's subordinate status.

100. On the various predictions, see *New York Times*, May 2, 5, 1920.

101. HWJ to Neylan, May 5, 1920; Lissner to Rowell, May 8, Aug. 7, 1920, Rowell Papers. Johnson lost to Hoover by almost 6,000 votes in Los Angeles's Ninth Congressional District. In addition, Hoover squeaked to narrow victories in Kings and Ventura counties. Divisions within California's Republican camp were not healed following the election. As Ralph Merritt, campaign manager of the Hoover forces, observed in his concession of defeat: "Every vote against him [Johnson] was a vote of protest. The state has not 'made it unanimous.' It has cut his former majority of 300,000 to at least one third. This was done in less than four weeks time by an amateur organization. Like good sportsmen we concede the victory." *Los Angeles Examiner*, May 6, 1920; Part VI, Carton 6, HWJ Papers.

102. *New York Times*, June 3, 1920. See also Part III, Carton 25, HWJ Papers.

103. Walter Lippmann, "Chicago, 1920," *New Republic*, June 23, 1920, pp. 108–10; *New York Times*, June 4, 1920.

104. HWJ to Hiram Johnson, Jr., May 12, 1920; *New York Times*, June 10, 1920.

105. HWJ memo, June 15, 1920, Part III, Carton 4, HWJ Papers; *New York Times*, June 5, 10, 1920.

106. George L. Hart, *Official Report of the Proceedings of the Seventeenth Republican National Convention* (New York, 1920) p. 139; Wesley M. Bagby, *The Road to Normalcy: The Presidential Campaign and Election of 1920* (Baltimore, 1962), p. 32. On Wheeler's selection as speaker see HWJ to Hiram Johnson, Jr., May 8, 1920. Wheeler's speech "succeeded only in driving delegates away from Johnson," wrote Oswald Garrison Villard. The longer he spoke, the worse it got, and by the end Johnson's candidacy had "collapsed in sad fashion." *Nation*, June 19, 1920, p. 820.

107. *New York Times*, June 21, 1920; William Wrigley to HWJ, June 23, 1920; Albert Lasker to HWJ, July 23, Aug. 3, 30, 1920; Warren Harding to HWJ, July 27, Aug. 16, 1920. Harry S. New, head of the Republican party's Speakers Bureau, after examining the requests that flooded into his office, reported that Johnson headed the list of desired speakers. His participation, New concluded, was "indispensable." Harry S. New to Harry M. Daugherty, July 16, 1920, as quoted in Randolph C. Downes, *The Rise of Warren Gamaliel Harding, 1865–1920* (Columbus, 1970), p. 435. See also John Gunther, *Taken at the Flood: The Story of Albert D. Lasker* (New York, 1960). Johnson's comments on the nominating process can be found in *New York Times*, June 24, 1920; Hiram Johnson, "What of the Nation?," *Sunset: The Pacific Monthly*, June, 1920, pp. 21–22, July, 1920, pp. 22–23, Aug. 1920, p. 24, Sept. 1920, p. 23; HWJ to Frederick Landis, Aug. 24, 1920. On the role of Lasker and Wrigley, see HWJ to E. A. Van Valkenburg, Nov. 23, 1923; HWJ to Ralph Strassburger, Nov. 2, 1923.

108. *New York Times*, July 8, 1920; HWJ to Albert Lasker, July 8, 1920.

109. HWJ to C. K. McClatchy, July 17, 1920. After interviewing various per-

sons in San Francisco following Harding's nomination, Lillian Timmonds concluded: "There was an attitude of criticism, even of those most loyal, toward
Senator Johnson should he take the stump in support of the ticket. Indeed, I
should say that those most affectionately attached to him were most insistent
as to this." Lillian Timmonds to Neylan, June 17, 1920, Neylan Papers.

110. *New York Times,* July 20, 1920.

111. HWJ to Albert Beveridge, July 27, 1920; Warren Harding to HWJ, July 27,
1920. See also HWJ to William Borah, July 27, 1920, as quoted in Bagby, *Road to
Normalcy,* p. 137.

112. HWJ to Albert Lasker, Aug. 9, 1920. See also HWJ to Albert Lasker,
Aug. 26, 1920; HWJ to C. K. McClatchy, July 30, 1920; HWJ to Frederick Landis,
Aug. 24, 1920.

113. Albert Lasker to HWJ, Aug. 30, 1920; *New York Times,* Aug. 29, 1920;
Ickes to HWJ, Sept. 3, 1920; Rowell to Herbert Hoover, Aug. 28, 1920, Rowell
Papers.

114. *New York Times,* Sept. 22, 1920; HWJ to Lissner, Sept. 15, 19, 1920,
Lissner Papers; HWJ to Elmer Dover, Sept. 28, 1920; HWJ to Albert Lasker,
Sept. 30, 1920; *San Francisco Examiner,* Sept. 22, 26, 1920.

115. Marshall Stimson to Rowell, Oct. 5, 1920; Rowell to Marshall Stimson,
Oct. 10, 1920, both in Rowell Papers.

116. Bagby, *Road to Normalcy,* pp. 139–41, 158. Johnson's speaking tour included Omaha, Toledo, Cleveland, Milwaukee, Detroit, Baltimore, and Hobo-
ken. See *New York Times,* Oct. 12, 14, 21, 23, 1920.

117. Bagby, *Road to Normalcy,* pp. 159–60; *San Francisco Examiner,* Nov. 4,
1920.

Chapter V: The World at Bay

1. Edson to Mrs. Medill McCormick, Dec. 7, 1920, Edson Papers.

2. HWJ to Lissner, Nov. 27, 1920, Lissner Papers.

3. HWJ to boys, June 25, 1921, Apr. 22, 1922. See also HWJ to Hiram Johnson,
Jr., Mar. 28, 1922; HWJ to Neylan, Mar. 29, 1922; HWJ to Doherty, Mar. 5,
Apr. 4, 1921; Doherty to HWJ, Feb. 17, Mar. 26, 1921. In 1917 Doherty was an
active critic of Johnson. See *Los Angeles Examiner,* Feb. 16, 1917.

4. HWJ to Lissner, Nov. 17, 1920, Lissner Papers.

5. HWJ to Lissner, Nov. 8, 1920. See also HWJ to Albert Lasker, July 8, 1920;
HWJ to C. K. McClatchy, Mar. 9, 1921; HWJ to William Jennings Bryan, Sept. 14,
1920, Bryan Papers.

6. HWJ to William Langer, Sept. 30, 1920.

7. HWJ to Hiram Johnson, Jr., Dec. 24, 1920; HWJ to boys, May 10, 1921. In
1929, on the Senate floor, Johnson remarked: "We are here because we like it,
and because we fight to get here, and because the job is attractive and ministers
to the egotism and the vanity that God put in every one of us. We are here in the
endeavor to do some little service, it is true . . . but we are here, sir, primarily
because we fought with both fists to get here, and every one of us is fighting
with both fists to remain here." *Cong. Record,* 71st Cong., 1st sess. (Nov. 21,
1929), p. 7871.

8. HWJ to Hiram Johnson, Jr., Apr. 7, Sept. 21, 1917; HWJ to Archibald Johnson, Sept. 17, 1917. The hotels included the Willard, Shoreham, Arlington, and Hotel Washington.

9. HWJ to Hiram Johnson, Jr., June 12, 1924. See also HWJ to boys, June 18, 25, July 2, Sept. 10, Nov. 16, 1921, Apr. 17, 1922. For much of this time "Joe" and "Fong," Chinese domestics who had been employed by the Johnsons in California, made up the core staff. On the Johnson home see *New York Times,* Feb. 21, 1926; *Washington Times,* Aug. 21, 25, 1922; Ruth Finney, "Hiram Johnson of California," *American History Illustrated* 1:7 (Nov. 1966), pp. 27–28; HWJ to C. K. McClatchy, Mar. 6, 1926; HWJ to boys, Mar. 6, 1926. The Calvert Mansion is now administered by the Maryland–National Capital Park and Planning Commission.

10. HWJ to Rowell, June 3, 1918, Rowell Papers; HWJ to Hiram Johnson, Jr., Apr. 10, 12, 16, May 5, 1918; HWJ to Archibald Johnson, May 6, 1918. Indeed, there is no record that Johnson ever personally met Hearst. Nevertheless, as Lissner noted, Johnson's defense of Hearst had not made much of a hit in California. Lissner to HWJ, May ?, June 10, 1918. See also Rowell to William Kent, June 12, 1922, Rowell Papers; HWJ to Doherty, July 15, 1922.

11. HWJ to Hiram Johnson, Jr., Feb. 22, Apr. 8, 1922, June 12, 1924, Feb. 6, 1925, Apr. 14, 1926; HWJ to boys, June 18, 23, 1922, Feb. 2, 1927; HWJ to Archibald Johnson, Feb. 13, 1922, Mar. 11, 1927; HWJ to Neylan, Apr. 11, 1921.

12. HWJ to C. K. McClatchy, Mar. 9, 1921; HWJ to Archibald Johnson, Mar. 5, Apr. 4, 1921; HWJ to Fred Bickell, Feb. 13, 1922; HWJ statement, Feb. 25, 1921, Part III, Carton 25, HWJ Papers; *New York Times,* Feb. 23, 1921. Johnson earned $25,000 in the New York traction case. See "1934 Biography," prepared by Hiram Johnson, Jr., in Part III, Carton 24, HWJ Papers. On the New York traction case see *Independent,* Apr. 9, 1921, pp. 376–77.

13. HWJ to boys, June 12, 1921.

14. HWJ to C. K. McClatchy, May 10, 1924. See also HWJ to boys, Dec. 7, 1920; HWJ to Hiram Johnson, Jr., Apr. 8, June 23, 1922, June 12, 1924, Apr. 14, 1926.

15. John W. Owens, "The Tragic Hiram," *American Mercury* 1:1 (Jan. 1924), pp. 57–61. See also Clinton Gilbert, *The Mirrors of Washington* (New York, 1921), pp. 189–91.

16. HWJ to boys, June 1, 1922. See also HWJ to boys, May 24, July 16, 30, Oct. 1, 1921, July 8, 1922; HWJ to Hiram Johnson, Jr., Sept. 22, Oct. 1, Nov. 16, 1921. Johnson dropped from 228 pounds to 189½ by July 1922.

17. For a psychological interpretation of Johnson's behavior see John J. Fitzpatrick, "Senator Hiram W. Johnson: A Life History, 1866–1945" (Ph.D. diss., University of California, Berkeley, 1975), and John J. Fitzpatrick, "Psychoanalytic Considerations on Hiram W. Johnson's Presidential Candidacy in 1920," paper presented to the Western History Association, Oct. 10, 1970.

18. *Riverside Daily Press,* Sept. 27, 1923.

19. See for example, *Sacramento Bee,* Oct. 2, 1919; speech, Excelsior Springs, Missouri, Jan. 27, 1920, Part III, Carton 25, HWJ Papers; *Cong. Record,* 69th Cong., 1st sess. (Jan. 19, 1926), p. 2355.

20. On Wilson, see N. Gordon Levin, *Woodrow Wilson and World Politics: America's Response to War and Revolution* (New York, 1968), and Lloyd E. Ambrosius, *Woodrow Wilson and the American Diplomatic Tradition: The Treaty Fight in Perspective* (New York, 1987). On Hughes, see Betty Glad, *Charles Evans Hughes and the Illusions of Innocence: A Study in American Diplomacy* (Urbana, Ill., 1966). Herbert Hoover's classic endorsement of this theme can be found in Herbert Hoover, *American Individualism* (New York, 1922).

21. *Cong. Record*, 70th Cong., 1st sess. (Jan. 27, 1928), pp. 2126–30; HWJ to Hiram Johnson, Jr., Feb. 20, 1923, Feb. 4, 1933; HWJ to Doherty, Jan. 11, 1923; HWJ to boys, Dec. 18, 1926; HWJ to C. K. McClatchy, May 12, 1928. See also Paul Maxwell Zeis, *American Shipping Policy* (Princeton, N.J., 1938), pp. 115–65; *New York Times*, Feb. 8, 1923.

22. *Cong. Record*, 69th Cong., 2nd sess. (Jan. 3, 1927), pp. 990–97.

23. Johnson elaborated on these points in a series of speeches made in California in the fall of 1923. See *Sacramento Bee*, Sept. 20, 1923; *Fresno Republican*, Oct. 25, 1923; *Stockton Record*, Oct. 28, 1923; *Riverside Daily Press*, Sept. 27, 1923; *Oakland Tribune*, Nov. 1, 1923. See also *New York Tribune*, Jan. 4, 1924.

24. HWJ to Lissner, Nov. 8, 1920.

25. HWJ to Hiram Johnson, Jr., Dec. 24, 1920. See also HWJ to C. K. McClatchy, Jan. 6, 1921.

26. HWJ to boys, Dec. 7, 1920.

27. Neylan to HWJ, Mar. 14, 1921; Doherty to HWJ, Feb. 17, 1921.

28. Johnson continued: "He has no feelings, principle is unknown to him, decency he long since forgot." HWJ to boys, May 29, 1921. See also HWJ to Hiram Johnson, Jr., May 30, 1921; HWJ to Neylan, Aug. 13, 1921; HWJ to Al McCabe, Apr. 16, 1921; Doherty to HWJ, Dec. 6, 1920; HWJ to C. K. McClatchy, Mar. 5, 1923. Writing to Al McCabe, Johnson lamented: "He is for nothing that I am for. . . . He is with me neither on policies, nor legislation, nor on appointments." HWJ to Al McCabe, May 24, 1921. See also HWJ to boys, June 12, 1921; Doherty to HWJ, Dec. 6, 1920; *New York Times*, Sept. 13, 1925. Johnson's letters to Hiram Johnson, Jr.; Doherty; Neylan; and McCabe in this period detail the complexities of the various battles over patronage.

29. Doherty to HWJ, Feb. 17, 1921; Neylan to HWJ, Mar. 14, 1921; Lissner to Rowell, Apr. 18, 1921; Rowell to Lissner, Apr. 19, 1921, both in Rowell Papers.

30. HWJ to boys, Nov. 16, 1921.

31. HWJ to Carlos McClatchy, Nov. 9, 1920.

32. *New York Times*, Feb. 21, 27, 1921.

33. HWJ to C. K. McClatchy, Jan. 6, 1921; HWJ to Frank Devlin, Jan. 6, 1921; Warren Harding to HWJ, Feb. 11, 21, 1921; HWJ to Warren Harding, Feb. 15, 1921; HWJ to Al McCabe, Mar. 7, 1921.

34. HWJ to Neylan, Mar. 9, 1921, Neylan Papers. HWJ press statement, Mar. 4, 1921, Part III, Carton 25, HWJ Papers.

35. Neylan to HWJ, Mar. 14, 1921, Neylan Papers.

36. *Cong. Record*, 67th Cong., 1st sess. (Apr. 15, 1921), pp. 305–10. See also HWJ to Ickes, Mar. 12, 1921; HWJ to Archibald Johnson, Mar. 12, 1921.

37. HWJ to C. K. McClatchy, Apr. 16, 1921; *New York Times*, Apr. 21, 1921.

38. HWJ to boys, May 10, 1921; HWJ to Archibald Johnson, Mar. 12, 1921; HWJ to Jake Newell, May 10, 1921.

39. *Cong. Record*, 67th Cong., 1st sess. (Apr. 15, 1921), p. 305.

40. HWJ to boys, May 1, 1921.

41. HWJ to Ickes, Mar. 12, 1921; HWJ to Al McCabe, Apr. 16, 1921.

42. HWJ to boys, June 18, 1921; HWJ to Raymond Robins, June 18, 1921; *New York Times*, Apr. 4–14, 1921.

43. Those concerns included the assurance of German funding for U.S. occupation forces as well as guarantees that U.S. interests in the disposition of German colonies would not be abridged by the nation's wartime associates.

44. HWJ to C. K. McClatchy, June 21, 1921. See also HWJ to boys, May 10, 1921; HWJ to Hiram Johnson, Jr., Jan. 20, 1923; HWJ to Raymond Robins, June 18, 1921; Ickes to HWJ, May 12, 1921.

45. HWJ to boys, May 10, June 12, 18, 25, 1921.

46. Kurt Wimer and Sarah Wimer, "The Harding Administration, the League of Nations, and the Separate Peace Treaty," *Review of Politics* 29 (1967), pp. 14–15.

47. U.S. Dept. of State, *Papers Relating to the Foreign Relations of the United States, 1921* (Washington, 1936), vol. 2, pp. 29–33.

48. HWJ to boys, Sept. 23, 1921; HWJ to C. K. McClatchy, Oct. 5, 29, 1921.

49. HWJ to boys, Sept. 23, 1921. See also HWJ to Hiram Johnson, Jr., Sept. 22, 1921.

50. *Cong. Record*, 67th Cong., 1st sess. (Oct. 18, 1921), p. 6408; *New York Times*, Oct. 19, 1921; HWJ to boys, Oct. 21, 1921. In addition, Johnson supported amendments proposed by Reed to exempt the United States from obligations arising out of the Versailles treaty and to eliminate any references to that treaty. The amendments were overwhelmingly defeated.

51. HWJ to boys, Oct. 1, 1921. See also HWJ to C. K. McClatchy, Oct. 8, 29, 1921.

52. Wimer and Wimer, "Separate Peace," pp. 23–24.

53. *Cong. Record*, 67th Cong., 1st sess. (Oct. 18, 1921), p. 6409.

54. Harold G. Moulton and Leo Pasvolsky, *World War Debt Settlements* (New York, 1929); Benjamin D. Rhodes, "Reassessing 'Uncle Shylock'; The United States and the French War Debt, 1917–1929," *Journal of American History* 55:4 (Mar. 1969), pp. 787–803.

55. Melvyn Leffler, "The Origins of the Republican War Debt Policy, 1921–1923: A Case Study in the Applicability of the Open Door Interpretation," *Journal of American History* 59:3 (Dec. 1972), pp. 585–601; Joan Hoff Wilson, *American Business and Foreign Policy, 1920–1933* (Lexington, Ky., 1971), pp. 123–56.

56. Ironically, Hoover expressed concerns similar to Johnson's. In the 1920s Hoover criticized "Americans who loved Europe more and America less . . . [and like] our international bankers agitated for cancellation night and day." Quoted in Joan Hoff Wilson, *Herbert Hoover: Forgotten Progressive* (New York, 1975), p. 184.

57. Lawrence W. Levine, *Defender of the Faith: William Jennings Bryan: The Last Decade, 1915–1925* (New York, 1965), pp. 201–2. Harold Ickes was also attracted by the idea. Ickes to HWJ, June 30, 1921.

58. HWJ to boys, Nov. 16, 1921. Johnson had stressed this theme during his 1919 crusade against league membership and would return to it often in the decade of the 1920s. See, for example, *Sacramento Bee*, Sept. 13, 22, 1919; *Fresno Bee*, Nov. 11, 1927; *Cong. Record*, 70th Cong., 2nd sess. (Jan. 31, 1929), p. 2528.

59. HWJ to C. K. McClatchy, June 21, 25, July 23, 1921; HWJ to boys, June 25, July 2, Sept. 10, 1921; HWJ to Raymond Robins, July 21, 1921; HWJ to Fremont Older, June 28, 1921.

60. *Cong. Record*, 67th Cong., 2nd sess. (Jan. 26, 1922), pp. 1753–56. See also *Cong. Record*, 67th Cong., 4th sess. (Jan. 4, Feb. 16, 1923), pp. 1223–24, 3784.

61. *Cong. Record*, 67th Cong., 2nd sess. (Jan. 26, 1922), pp. 1896–97. The guidelines required that interest rates be set at a minimum of 4.25 percent and that the principle be paid in 25 years.

62. *Cong. Record*, 67th Cong., 2nd sess. (Jan. 26, 1922), p. 1753; *Cong. Record*, 69th Cong., 1st sess. (Mar. 30, 1926), p. 6568.

63. "Hiram W. Johnson Newsletter," Feb. 17, 1923, Part III, Carton 25, HWJ Papers; *Cong. Record*, 67th Cong., 4th sess. (Feb. 16, 1923), p. 3786. Payments were to continue over a period of 62 years, with interest at 3.3 percent.

64. *Cong. Record*, 69th Cong., 1st sess. (Mar. 30, Apr. 21, 1926), pp. 6568, 7891–94. Johnson's votes on debt settlement can be found in *Cong. Record*, 69th Cong., 1st sess. (Belgium), p. 8208; (Czechoslovakia), p. 8347; (Italy), p. 7902; (Latvia), p. 8274; (Rumania), p. 8282. See also HWJ to Irving Martin, Dec. 28, 1925; HWJ to Albert Lasker, Feb. 10, 1925; HWJ to Hiram Johnson, Jr., Jan. 20, 1923; *New York Times*, Mar. 26, July 21, 1926. Johnson was especially angered by the ability of the House of Morgan to float a 7 percent loan to Italy after the United States agreed to an interest settlement of 0.4 percent. See *Cong. Record*, 69th Cong., 1st sess. (Dec. 16, 1925, Jan. 6, 1926), pp. 913, 1562. Overall, the 2.1 percent average interest rate on the agreements negotiated reduced the outstanding indebtedness of America's associates by 43 percent. J. Wilson, *American Business and Foreign Policy*, p. 126.

65. Glad, *Charles Evans Hughes*, pp. 220–30. "We have had a hotel full of experts in Paris, who described as 'observers' have really been part of the reparations muddle," Johnson charged in 1923. *New York Times*, Nov. 2, 1923. The administration, he privately wrote, "is owned by the international bankers, and has not the guts to do what they ask." HWJ to boys, Dec. 30, 1922. See also *Cong. Record*, 67th Cong., 4th sess. (Jan. 4, 1923), pp. 1223–24.

66. *Cong. Record*, 68th Cong., 2nd sess. (Feb. 4, 1925), pp. 2984–93; HWJ to Hiram Johnson, Jr., Jan. 29, Feb. 6, 1925; HWJ to boys, Jan. 21, 1925; HWJ to C. K. McClatchy, Jan. 21, 29, Feb. 10, 1925; HWJ to Albert Lasker, Feb. 10, 1925.

67. Harold and Margaret Sprout, *Toward a New Order of Sea Power: American Naval Policy and the World Scene, 1918–1922* (Princeton, N.J., 1946), pp. 74–76.

68. Robert James Maddox, *William E. Borah and American Foreign Policy* (Baton Rouge, 1969), pp. 85–92. Johnson, unlike Borah, supported a broader con-

ference: "If the five great nations of the earth, who constituted the five allied and associated powers in the World War, should meet together and decide upon reduction of armaments, we would have taken the one great step that could be taken toward the promotion of peace and the prevention of all future wars." *Cong. Record*, 66th Cong., 3rd sess. (Dec. 27, 1920), p. 741. But see also *New York Times*, July 12, 1921.

69. J. Chalmers Vinson, *The Parchment Peace: The United States Senate and the Washington Conference, 1921–1922* (Athens, Ga., 1955).

70. The goal of those nations attending the conference, Johnson feared, was to create "something in the nature of an alliance with [the U.S.], or . . . an association not unlike the League of Nations." And it was doubtful, he continued, given the composition of the Senate, that they could be thwarted. HWJ to boys, Oct. 29, 1921. See also HWJ to boys, Aug. 13, 1921; HWJ to C. K. McClatchy, Oct. 5, 1921.

71. HWJ to boys, Nov. 16, 1921; *Cong. Record*, 67th Cong., 1st sess. (Aug. 10, Nov. 8, 1921), pp. 4814, 7536–38.

72. HWJ to boys, Nov. 16, 1921.

73. *New York Times*, Nov. 13, 1921; HWJ to boys, Nov. 16, 19, Dec. 2, 1921.

74. HWJ to C. K. McClatchy, Jan. 15, 1922.

75. HWJ to Hiram Johnson, Jr., Mar. 5, 1922.

76. *Cong. Record*, 67th Cong., 2nd sess. (Feb. 27, 1922), pp. 3093–98.

77. Ibid., p. 3097.

78. *Washington Post*, Dec. 11, 1921.

79. *New York Times*, Jan. 5, 1922; HWJ press statement, Jan. 5, 9, 1922, Part III, Carton 25, HWJ Papers; HWJ to John P. O'Brien, Dec. 29, 1921; HWJ to Neylan, Jan. 4, 1922; HWJ to C. K. McClatchy, Jan. 15, 1922; HWJ to Hichborn, Jan. 17, 1922.

80. HWJ to John P. O'Brien, Mar. 15, 1922.

81. HWJ to C. K. McClatchy, Jan. 15, 1922. The man on the street, Johnson publicly complained, was beginning to wonder whether the election of 1920 had been in vain. *New York Times*, Jan. 14, 1922.

82. HWJ press releases, Jan. 5, 9, 1922, Part III, Carton 25, HWJ Papers; *Cong. Record*, 67th Cong., 2nd sess. (Mar. 13, 1922), p. 3778.

83. *Cong. Record*, 67th Cong., 2nd sess. (Feb. 16, 1922), p. 2638.

84. HWJ to Hiram Johnson, Jr., Feb. 22, 1922; *New York Times*, Feb. 23, 26, 1922. The revised Brandegee reservation denied that the Four-Power pact was an alliance and stipulated that the United States stood under no obligation to help defend Pacific possessions either militarily or by other means.

85. In fact Johnson would describe the agreement between Germany and Russia at Rapallo in April 1922 as the beginning of such an alliance. HWJ to boys, Apr. 22, 1922; HWJ to Hichborn, May 6, 1922.

86. *Cong. Record*, 67th Cong., 2nd sess. (Mar. 13, 17, 27, 1922), pp. 3775–84, 4011–14, 4610–14; HWJ press releases, Jan. 5, 9, 1922, Part III, Carton 25, HWJ Papers.

87. *Cong. Record*, 67th Cong., 2nd sess. (Mar. 13, 1922), p. 3779.

88. HWJ to Archibald Johnson, Feb. 18, 1922; HWJ to Doherty, Mar. 28, 1922.

See also C. Leonard Hoag, *Preface to Preparedness: The Washington Disarmament Conference and Public Opinion* (Washington, D.C., 1941), pp. 142–62.

89. *New York Times*, Mar. 25, 1922. Needing a two-thirds majority, the treaty passed by a 4-vote margin, 67 to 27. Lodge was more than willing to sharpen the perception of a Republican party victory and thus was indifferent to Democratic party opposition as long as it did not threaten ratification. Privately, Lodge reported, he held the pledges of an additional thirteen Democrats to vote his way if necessary. See Vinson, *Parchment Peace*, pp. 192–93.

90. HWJ to boys, Mar. 26, 1922. See also HWJ to W. W. Morrow, Mar. 23, 1922; HWJ to Hichborn, Mar. 27, 1922.

91. HWJ to Doherty, Mar. 16, 1922.

92. *Cong. Record*, 67th Cong., 2nd sess. (Mar. 27, 1922), p. 4620.

93. *Cong. Record*, 67th Cong., 2nd sess. (Mar. 29, 1922), p. 4706.

94. HWJ to boys, Nov. 16, 19, 1921; Theodore Roosevelt, Jr., to HWJ, Jan. 4, 1923.

95. *Cong. Record*, 69th Cong., 1st sess. (Jan. 19, 1926), p. 2350; HWJ to Hiram Johnson, Jr., Feb. 11, 1927.

96. HWJ to C. K. McClatchy, Mar. 19, 1927; C. K. McClatchy to HWJ, Apr. 1, 1927; HWJ to boys, Jan. 8, 1927; HWJ to J. W. Jamieson, Jan. 11, 1927; William Howard Gardiner to HWJ, Jan. 8, 1927.

97. HWJ to boys, Mar. 26, 1922; HWJ to Hichborn et al., Mar. 15, 1922; HWJ to Hiram Johnson, Jr., Mar. 21, 1922; Doherty to HWJ, Mar. 20, 1922.

98. Doherty to HWJ, Mar. 8, 1922.

99. HWJ to Ickes, Nov. 7, 1924. To Charles McClatchy, Johnson observed: Borah is "one of the most cunning men in political life today as well as one of the ablest." HWJ to C. K. McClatchy, Oct. 31, 1924. See also HWJ to C. K. McClatchy, June 4, 1926.

100. HWJ to Doherty, Jan. 2, 1923. "I feel exactly as if I had gone into battle with a man and he had suddenly turned and shot at me," Johnson wrote. HWJ to Richard Tobin, Jan. 9, 1923. See also HWJ to Hiram Johnson, Jr., Dec. 22, 30, 1922; HWJ to C. K. McClatchy, June 4, 22, 1926.

101. *Cong. Record*, 67th Cong., 4th sess. (Dec. 29, 1922), pp. 1046–49. See also HWJ to C. K. McClatchy, Feb. 2, 1923.

102. HWJ to C. K. McClatchy, Dec. 30, 1922. See also Maddox, *Borah and American Foreign Policy*, pp. 131–35.

103. HWJ to Hiram Johnson, Jr., Jan. 13, 1923.

104. *Cong. Record*, 67th Cong., 4th sess. (Jan. 16, 1923), p. 1793; "Why 'Irreconcilables' Keep out of Europe," *New York Times*, Jan. 14, 1923; HWJ to C. K. McClatchy, Feb. 1, 1923.

105. *New York Times*, Feb. 27, 1923; *Cong. Record*, 67th Cong., 4th sess. (Feb. 24, 1923), pp. 4499–4500. See also Robert Accinelli, "Peace Through Law: The United States and the World Court, 1923–1935," *Historical Papers 1972* (Canadian Historical Association, 1974), pp. 247–61; Denna Frank Fleming, *The United States and the World Court, 1920–1966* (New York, 1968), p. 40; Thomas N. Guinsburg, *The Pursuit of Isolationism in the United States Senate: From Versailles to Pearl Harbor* (New York, 1982), pp. 83–109.

106. HWJ speech to the Bronx Board of Trade, Mar. 8, 1923, Part III, Carton 25, HWJ Papers. "The whole scheme," Rowell wrote, "is illogical, impractical, insincere and cowardly. *And I am for it!*" Rowell to HWJ, Feb. 27, 1923, emphasis in original. See also Rowell to HWJ, May 30, 1924.

107. *Cong. Record*, 68th Cong., 2nd sess. (Mar. 3, 1925), p. 5413. The vote was 303 to 28. See also HWJ to boys, Mar. 4, 1925.

108. HWJ to C. K. McClatchy, Dec. 14, 1925, Jan. 7, 1926; HWJ to Hiram Johnson, Jr., Jan. 7, 1926.

109. HWJ to boys, Jan. 16, 23, 1926; HWJ to Albert Lasker, Dec. 19, 1925; HWJ to C. K. McClatchy, Dec. 28, 1925, Jan. 7, 20, 1926. See also HWJ to C. K. McClatchy, Mar. 5, 1923; Ickes to HWJ, Jan. 29, 1926.

110. *Cong. Record*, 69th Cong., 1st sess. (Jan. 19, 1926), pp. 2349–55.

111. *Cong. Record*, 69th Cong., 1st sess. (Jan. 27, 1926), p. 2824. See also HWJ to boys, Jan. 30, 1926; William Hard to HWJ, Jan. 28, 31, 1926; Ickes to HWJ, Jan. 29, 1926.

112. *Cong. Record*, 69th Cong., 1st sess. (Jan. 27, 1926), p. 2825. Shortly thereafter Borah and Reed pledged to campaign in the forthcoming primaries in support of anti-court candidates. Johnson would have no part of a scheme that seemed merely another attempt to bolster Borah's political prospects and that put at risk progressives, such as Norbeck and Norris, who had supported American membership in the court. See *New York Times*, Feb. 10, 1926; HWJ to Ickes, Feb. 1, Mar. 4, 1926.

113. "There is nothing to negotiate about . . . because the President cannot change the Senate reservations and the Senate will not," Johnson observed. HWJ to C. K. McClatchy, Apr. 13, 1928.

114. *Cong. Record*, 67th Cong., 2nd sess. (June 19, 1922), p. 8974. The vote was 9 to 43. See also *New York Times*, Feb. 3, 1921.

115. HWJ speech, Cleveland, Jan. 3, 1924, Part III, Carton 25, HWJ Papers; HWJ to boys, Jan. 8, 1927; HWJ to C. K. McClatchy, Aug. 16, 1924.

116. *Cong. Record*, 76th Cong., 1st sess. (July 24, 25, 1939), pp. 9838–40, 9904–5; *Cong. Record*, 77th Cong., 2nd sess. (Dec. 4, 1942), pp. 9320–22; *New York Times*, Apr. 11, 1936, Mar. 24, July 25, 26, 1939.

117. *Cong. Record*, 75th Cong., 1st sess. (Aug. 9, 1937), p. 8538; *Cong. Record*, 79th Cong., 1st sess. (Mar. 13, 16, 1945), pp. 1945, 2333; *New York Times*, Apr. 12, 1945.

118. HWJ to C. K. McClatchy, Jan. 14, 1927.

119. *Cong. Record*, 70th Cong., 1st sess. (Apr. 25, 1928), p. 7192; *Cong. Record*, 70th Cong., 2nd sess. (Feb. 22, 1929), p. 4047; *New York Times*, Mar. 10, 1927; HWJ to William Hard, Jan. 14, 1927.

120. HWJ to Hiram Johnson, Jr., Jan. 7, 1928; HWJ to Hichborn, Feb. 8, 9, 1927; HWJ to boys, Jan. 17, 1927; HWJ to C. K. McClatchy, Jan. 14, 1927. For Johnson, Coolidge's selection of Dwight Morrow, of the House of Morgan, to negotiate claims with Mexico seemed more than appropriate. It was far better, he cynically noted, to draw upon the talent of Morgan's top man than to rely on his lackeys in the State Department. HWJ to C. K. McClatchy, Sept. 23, 1927.

121. HWJ to Emily E. Dobbin, Apr. 23, 1931; HWJ to Ickes, Apr. 21, May 2, 1931.

122. Robert H. Ferrell, *Peace in Their Time: The Origins of the Kellogg-Briand Pact* (New Haven, Conn., 1952); John Chalmers Vinson, *William E. Borah and the Outlawry of War* (Athens, Ga., 1957). For some, the pact has been seen as evidence of America's unique naïveté in the decade of the 1920s. Yet the fact that both Kellogg and Briand won the Nobel peace prize suggests that the United States had no special claim to that trait.

123. HWJ to Archibald Johnson, Jan. 2, 1928.

124. *Cong. Record*, 70th Cong., 2nd sess. (Jan. 15, 1929), p. 1728; HWJ to Archibald Johnson, Jan. 19, 1923; HWJ to Rowell, Dec. 20, 1928, Jan. 9, 10, 1929; Rowell to HWJ, Dec. 26, 1928, Jan. 9, 1929. The *New York Times* misrepresented Johnson as a champion of the reservation. *New York Times*, Dec. 16, 1928.

125. *Cong. Record*, 70th Cong., 2nd sess. (Jan. 4, 1929), p. 1136. The one dissenter was Senator John Blaine, of Wisconsin.

126. *Cong. Record*, 70th Cong., 2nd sess. (Jan. 31, 1929), pp. 2526–35; HWJ to Hiram Johnson, Jr., Jan. 26, 1929; HWJ to boys, Feb. 2, 1929.

127. *New York Times*, Nov. 2, 16, 1923; *Cong. Record*, 67th Cong., 2nd sess. (Mar. 13, 1922), pp. 3775–76.

128. *New York Times*, Dec. 1, 1923.

129. *Cong. Record*, 67th Cong., 2nd sess. (Mar. 18, 1922), p. 3781.

Chapter VI: At Home

1. HWJ to boys, June 12, Nov. 19, 1921; HWJ to Neylan, May 19, 1921, Neylan Papers; HWJ to Ickes, May 14, 31, July 13, 1921; HWJ to Fremont Older, June 15, 1921; HWJ to Lissner, Sept. 17, 1920, Lissner Papers.

2. *New York Times*, Jan. 10, 1921; HWJ to Fremont Older, Jan. 17, 1921.

3. Edson to Mrs. Medill McCormick, Dec. 7, 1920, Edson Papers; Edwin Layton, "The Better America Federation: A Case Study of Superpatriotism," *Pacific Historical Review* 30 (May 1961), pp. 137–47. See also Lissner to Rowell, June 20, 1917, Rowell Papers; HWJ to Lissner, June 26, 1917.

4. HWJ to Hiram Johnson, Jr., Apr. 10, 1921. See also HWJ to H. H. Timken, June 19, 1922; Hichborn to HWJ, Feb. 11, 1922, Hichborn Papers; Irving Bernstein, *The Lean Years: A History of the American Worker, 1920–1933* (Boston, 1966).

5. HWJ to Al McCabe, Jan. 8, 1921; HWJ to Fremont Older, Jan. 17, 1921; HWJ to Ickes, May 10, 1921. On the erosion of support for the direct primary see Ralph S. Boots, "The Trend of the Direct Primary," *American Political Science Review* 16:3 (Aug. 1922), pp. 412–31; Charles Kettleborough, "Direct Primaries," *Annals of the American Academy of Social Science* 106 (Mar. 1923), p. 11; *Literary Digest*, June 17, 1922, p. 10, July 10, 1926, pp. 10–11; *Outlook*, Sept. 1, 1926, p. 8.

6. HWJ to Hiram Johnson, Jr., Jan. 1, 1919. See also HWJ to Ickes, May 10, 1921; Hichborn to HWJ, June 17, 1926, Hichborn Papers; HWJ to B. S. Rodey, Mar. 30, 1918. Johnson's defense of the direct primary can be found in *Cong. Record*, 69th Cong., 1st sess. (June 15, 1926), p. 11265; *Cong. Record*, 69th Cong., 2nd sess. (Dec. 20, 1926), pp. 759–61; *New York Times*, Oct. 14, Dec. 21, 1926.

7. HWJ to Doherty, July 2, 1922; Michael P. Rogin and John L. Shover, *Political Change in California: Critical Elections and Social Movements, 1890–1966* (Westport, Conn., 1969), pp. 35–89; John L. Shover, "The Progressives and the Working Class Vote in California," *Labor History* 10:4 (Fall 1969), pp. 584–601. See also HWJ to boys, Apr. 22, 1922.

8. HWJ to boys, Sept. 10, 1921; HWJ to Hiram Johnson, Jr., Dec. 16, 1922.

9. HWJ to boys, July 15, 1922.

10. Minnie Johnson to Archibald and Martha Johnson, Mar. 8, 1923; HWJ to boys, May 1, June 12, 1921. See also HWJ to boys, June 25, Aug. 13, Sept. 10, 17, 23, Oct. 21, 1921, June 17, 1922.

11. HWJ to boys, June 12, Oct. 1, Nov. 16, 1921; HWJ to Hiram Johnson, Jr., Sept. 22, 1921.

12. HWJ to boys, May 10, 1921. The Harding presidency began on a note of economic recession, which plagued much of the nation in 1921–22, but the building boom in Los Angeles, high prices for California's specialized agricultural products, and the oil strikes at Signal Hill and Santa Fe Springs muted much of its impact on California. There was, as Frank Doherty observed, little insurgency in the state. Doherty to HWJ, June 19, 1922.

13. *Cong. Record*, 67th Cong., 1st sess. (May 9, 1921), p. 1165; *New York Times*, Feb. 12, 1923. Truman Newberry was accused of excessive campaign expenditures in his 1918 Michigan Senate victory over Henry Ford. After much litigation, Senate progressives moved to deny him his seat. The move failed. A winter storm had delayed Johnson's train en route to Washington from California, causing him, much to his regret, to miss the vote. His critics would later charge that he had purposely ducked the issue because Newberry had stood with him in 1920. See HWJ to C. K. McClatchy, Jan. 15, 1922; HWJ to Doherty, Jan. 19, May 17, 1922; HWJ to Archibald Johnson, Jan. 15, 1922; Al McCabe to HWJ, Jan. 13, 1922; Edgar Luce to HWJ, Feb. 7, 1922.

14. *New York Times*, May 20, 1922; HWJ press statements, May 19, 20, 1922, Part III, Carton 25, HWJ Papers; HWJ to boys, June 25, 1921; HWJ to Ickes, Jan. 22, 1923; *New York Times*, May 20, 1922; *Cong. Record*, 67th Cong., 1st sess. (June 13, 21, 1921), pp. 2479, 2481, 2797. Johnson was instrumental in establishing a second inquiry into conditions in the coalfields in 1928. See *Cong. Record*, 70th Cong., 1st sess. (Feb. 1, 16, 1928), pp. 2306–7, 3086–92; HWJ to Archibald Johnson, Feb. 11, 21, 1928; HWJ to Hiram Johnson, Jr., Feb. 22, 1928, Apr. 20, 1940; John L. Lewis to HWJ, May 17, 1928.

15. HWJ statement, Feb. 3, 1923, Part III, Carton 25, HWJ Papers; *New York Times*, Nov. 3, 1920; *Cong. Record*, 66th Cong., 3rd sess. (Jan. 19, 1921), p. 5726. Johnson continued to oppose similar cuts in the wage standards of government workers during the Coolidge administration. See *Cong. Record*, 68th Cong., 2nd sess. (Jan. 5, 1925), p. 1225; HWJ to boys, Jan. 13, 1925; HWJ to C. K. McClatchy, Feb. 10, 1925.

16. HWJ press statements, May 3, 1921, June 30, 1922, Part III, Carton 25, HWJ Papers; Walter White to HWJ, July 31, 1922; *Cong. Record*, 67th Cong., 1st sess. (May 2, 3, 1921), pp. 928–29, 965. See also *Cong. Record*, 75th Cong., 3rd sess. (Feb. 21, 1938), pp. 2204–5.

17. Rowell to William Kent, July 12, 1922, Rowell Papers. See also Rowell to Martin Madsen, June 18, 1926, Rowell Papers; Chester Rowell, "Why I Shall Vote for Coolidge," *New Republic,* Oct. 29, 1924, pp. 219–21.

18. William Hard, "What Is Progressivism?," *Nation,* Jan. 9, 1924, pp. 27–28; William Hard, "How Many Hirams?," *Nation,* Dec. 12, 1923, pp. 685–86.

19. HWJ to boys, Oct. 1, 29, 1921; HWJ to Ickes, Aug. 13, Sept. 26, 1921.

20. HWJ to boys, Nov. 5, 1921; *Cong. Record,* 67th Cong., 1st sess. (Nov. 7, 1921), p. 7524.

21. HWJ to boys, June 18, July 9, 30, 1921; HWJ to Raymond Robins, June 18, 1921.

22. HWJ to Hiram Johnson, Jr., Jan. 20, 1923.

23. Doherty to HWJ, July 27, Aug. 16, 1921.

24. Rowell to William Kent, June 24, July 12, 1922, Rowell Papers. See also HWJ to Alex Moore, May 2, 1922. California's progressives had always endorsed the principle of protection, even when, as in the 1909 battle over the Payne-Aldrich act, they denounced the excessive rates secured by others. Their core complaint had been that high tariffs enabled big business to monopolize the marketplace. In the 1920s Borah, La Follette, and Norris echoed that complaint and opposed the Fordney-McCumber bill, but they were the only ones on the Republican side to do so. Democratic presidential candidate Winfield Hancock had been correct back in 1880, Johnson later wrote; the tariff was not a matter of principle but was in fact a local issue in which selfishness necessarily prevailed. HWJ to Hiram Johnson, Jr., Mar. 1, 1930.

25. HWJ to Neylan, Aug. 12, 1921, May 20, 1922; HWJ to boys, Aug. 6, 1921; HWJ to Alex Moore, May 2, 1922; HWJ to Doherty, Aug. 6, 1921, Mar. 2, 27, July 6, 1922; HWJ to Al McCabe, May 18, 1922; *Cong. Record,* 67th Cong., 2nd sess. (May 15, 23, July 3, 10, 1922), pp. 6933–38, 6951–61, 7441–43, 9909–12, 9927–30, 10102–4.

26. HWJ to boys, May 11, 19, July 8, 1922; Doherty to HWJ, May 22, 1922; HWJ to Al McCabe, Apr. 16, 1921. The *New York Times* later remarked, "Having befriended 117 crops, Johnson is fortified in all parts of the state." Johnson, the *Times* concluded, was the "business agent of California products." *New York Times,* Aug. 20, 1922, Nov. 17, 1923.

27. Hichborn to HWJ, Jan. 25, Apr. 16, 1922; A. P. Moore to HWJ, Apr. 26, 1922; Doherty to HWJ, June 2, 1922; C. K. McClatchy to HWJ, May 29, 1922; Al McCabe to HWJ, June 10, 1922; Neylan to HWJ, May 1, 25, 1922; Charles A. Whitmore to HWJ, Apr. 13, 1922; Irving Martin to HWJ, May 17, 1922.

28. Rowell to Al McCabe, May 12, 1921, Rowell Papers. See also Rowell to Edson, Dec. 12, 1921, Rowell Papers.

29. HWJ to boys, June 9, 1921; HWJ to Hiram Johnson, Jr., Mar. 21, 1922; HWJ to Raymond Robins, Apr. 7, 1922. See also *Sacramento Bee,* June 4, 1921.

30. Rowell to Lissner, Jan. 11, 1922, Rowell Papers. See also Rowell to Edson, Dec. 12, 1921; Rowell to Hichborn, Jan. 30, 1922, both in Rowell Papers. Johnson well understood the political risks involved in his opposition to the Four-Power pact. "Every rat has come out of his hole, and many who did not dare in the days of my political prosperity . . . are now in full cry," he wrote to Raymond Robins.

HWJ to Raymond Robins, Apr. 7, 1922. See also HWJ to Al McCabe, Jan. 24, Feb. 28, 1922; HWJ to Doherty, Mar. 2, 1922; HWJ to Neylan, Mar. 9, 22, 1922; HWJ to C. K. McClatchy, Jan. 15, Mar. 14, 1922; HWJ to boys, Mar. 26, Apr. 3, 1922; HWJ to Hiram Johnson, Jr., Feb. 28, Mar. 5, 1922.

31. HWJ to Al McCabe, Jan. 24, Feb. 2, May 6, 1922; HWJ to Doherty, Sept. 7, 1921, May 6, June 10, 1922; HWJ to Neylan, Mar. 9, May 8, 11, 1922; HWJ to C. K. McClatchy, Jan. 15, 1922; HWJ to Hiram Johnson, Jr., Apr. 20, 1922; HWJ to boys, Apr. 22, 28, 1922.

32. HWJ to Neylan, May 18, 20, 1922; HWJ to Doherty, May 13, June 22, 1922; HWJ to Hiram Johnson, Jr., June 16, 1922.

33. *Sacramento Bee*, Aug. 8, 10, 19, 22, 25, 26, 29, 1922; *San Francisco Chronicle*, July 29, 31, Aug. 1, 2, 4, 9, 17, 18, 1922; *San Francisco Examiner*, July 31, Aug. 1, 5, 8, 12, 1922; *San Francisco Call*, Aug. 1, 11, 1922; *San Diego Sun*, July 28, 1922; *Bakersfield Echo*, July 30, 1922. See also Part III, Carton 10, HWJ Papers.

34. HWJ speech, Los Angeles, July 28, 1922, Part III, Carton 10, HWJ Papers. See also *Sacramento Bee*, July 29, Aug. 10, 1922; HWJ to Doherty, June 22, 1922.

35. To the regret of Franklin Hichborn, Johnson ignored a proposal then pending before the electorate, Proposition 19, the Water and Power Initiative, which endorsed public ownership of water sources and hydroelectric power. Although it was a "progressive" measure, it was also a divisive one in both the Moore and Johnson camps. Perhaps contributing to Johnson's silence was the observation voiced by both Neylan and Doherty that the state's private utility interests would remain on the sidelines in the senatorial contest if he did not link his candidacy to the measure. Doherty to HWJ, June 2, 1922; Neylan to HWJ, Apr. 17, June 5, 1922. See also HWJ to Al McCabe, July 7, 1922; Hichborn to HWJ, Dec. 22, 1921, Jan. 27, Feb. 11, June 25, 29, 1922, Aug. 11, 1925; HWJ to C. K. McClatchy, Aug. 11, 1924; C. K. McClatchy to HWJ, Aug. 18, 1924; HWJ to Neylan, June 12, 1922; William Kent to Rowell, June 26, 1922, Rowell Papers. In 1924, Johnson again stood aloof. HWJ to C. K. McClatchy, Aug. 11, 1924; C. K. McClatchy to HWJ, Aug. 18, 1924.

36. Lissner to Rowell, Aug. 4, Sept. 6, 1922, Rowell Papers.

37. John Neylan observed, "They have no issue, just a grouch." William Kent, actively pushing the Water and Power Initiative, reluctantly agreed. "I am opposed to Johnson because he is the meanest man I know, and the worst fraud, but as for the issues of the campaign, there really are none for me." Neylan to HWJ, July 13, 1922, Neylan Papers; William Kent to Crosby, July 28, 1922 (copy), Rowell Papers.

38. *New York Times*, June 24, 1922; Marshall Stimson, "Republicans Should Smash Hearst-Johnson Alliance," *Los Angeles Express*, Aug. 28, 1922. See also Part III, Carton 10, HWJ Papers. In addition, Stimson and others exploited Johnson's absence from the Senate when the seating of Truman Newberry was decided. Doherty to HWJ, July 16, 1922.

39. HWJ to Doherty, May 13, 1922. See also HWJ to boys, July 15, 1922; HWJ to Doherty, May 26, 1922. In mid-May, Elmer Dover, acting as Harding's agent, toured California to sound out support for Johnson. Apparently his reports were

favorable. See HWJ to Neylan, May 18, 1922; Neylan to HWJ, May 19, June 30, 1922.

40. Albert Lasker to Lissner, Aug. 1, 1922, Lissner Papers; Albert Lasker to C. C. Teague, Herbert Fleishhacker, Wylie M. Giffen, July 18, 1922. See also Lissner to Rowell, Aug. 4, 1922, Jan. 31, 1923, Rowell Papers; *San Francisco Examiner*, Aug. 8, 1922.

41. *San Francisco Examiner*, Aug. 12, 1922; *Sacramento Bee*, Aug. 12, 1922.

42. *San Francisco Call*, Aug. 4, 1922; *San Francisco Chronicle*, Aug. 29, 30, 1922; *San Francisco Examiner*, July 31, 1922; *Bakersfield Echo*, July 19, 1922. See also Marshall Stimson to Rowell, Sept. 7, 1922, Rowell Papers; Ralph Arnold to Herbert Hoover, Aug. 4, 1922, Arnold Papers.

43. Just prior to the election, the *New York Times*, allowing hope to undermine objectivity, reported: "The defeat of Senator Hiram Johnson looms as a probability in the Republican primary of tomorrow. The sentiment for Charles C. Moore for Senator . . . seems to be sweeping the state." *New York Times*, Aug. 29, 1922. Johnson lost in Kings, Los Angeles, San Diego, and Santa Clara counties. California Secretary of State, *Statement of Vote, Aug. 29, 1922*. From the outset, he had expected to lose Los Angeles, where, as Neylan observed, "every Iowan who step[ped] off the train" was being registered. Neylan to HWJ, May 1, 1922, Neylan Papers. Johnson agreed. As he later noted, elected representatives from Los Angeles were "more imbued with the Iowa spirit than the Californian." HWJ to Ickes, May 18, 1929. Moreover, "Los Angeles hates you for a favor done, and there is nothing so indicative of individual or community character than this singular trait." The city, he observed, was an "over-satisfied, overgrown village." HWJ to boys, May 30, 1929; HWJ to Hiram Johnson, Jr., Dec. 1, 1926. See also HWJ to Al McCabe, Jan. 24, 1922; HWJ to Neylan, Mar. 9, 1922; Hichborn to HWJ, June 3, 1922.

44. *Sacramento Bee*, Sept. 22, 25, 30, 1922. Hichborn to HWJ, Sept. 28, 1922; Albert Boynton to Harry Lutgens, Oct. 23, 1922; Albert Boynton to HWJ, Oct. 24, 1922. But this victory over Richardson was incomplete in that, much to Johnson's despair, Ralph Arnold was elected chairman of the Los Angeles County Republican Central Committee.

45. Herbert Hoover to Warren Harding, Oct. 31, 1922.

46. HWJ to Warren Harding, Nov. 7, 1922. See also *Sacramento Bee*, Oct. 5, Nov. 7, 1922. By way of urging Republican unity, the *Los Angeles Times* sample ballot ignored Johnson's candidacy.

47. *Sacramento Bee*, Oct. 10, 19, 20, 1922. In a four-way senatorial race that included Upton Sinclair on the Socialist ticket and H. Clay Needham as a Prohibitionist, Johnson swept all 58 California counties, winning more than 62 percent of the vote. On his return to the state in 1923, Johnson became more forthright in his assault on Richardson. See Lissner to HWJ, Mar. 2, 1923; *Sacramento Bee*, Nov. 2, 1923.

48. Mary Connor? to Al McCabe, May 15, 1923; HWJ to Hiram Johnson, Jr., Jan. 31, 1923.

49. *New York Times*, Feb. 8, Mar. 19, 1923; HWJ to Hiram Johnson, Jr., Feb. 20, 1923; HWJ to Archibald Johnson, May 15, 1923; Hiram Johnson, Jr., to John Lear, Jan. 25, 1950.

50. *New York Times*, Mar. 16, 26, Apr. 7, June 27, 29, July 3, 6, 1923. Johnson wrote of Mussolini: "I confess an utter lack of sympathy with his destruction of individual liberty and his contempt of the freedom enjoyed by people such as ours." HWJ to C. K. McClatchy, Nov. 17, 1926. See also "Hiram W. Johnson Newsletter," Jan. 13, 1923, Part III, Carton 25, HWJ Papers.

51. *New York Times*, Apr. 2, Apr. 30, 1923.

52. HWJ to Neylan, Feb. 9, 1923, Neylan Papers; HWJ to Doherty, Jan. 11, 1923; HWJ to C. K. McClatchy, Jan. 11, July 30, 1923; HWJ to Raymond Robins, Dec. 13, 1922; HWJ to boys, June 23, 1922.

53. Bert Meek to C. K. McClatchy, July 18, 1923. See also Martin Madsen to C. K. McClatchy, July 20, 1923 (copy), HWJ Papers. Even before the 1922 elections, Charles Michelson, writing in the *New York World*, was to note: "Taken by and large, if the Harding supporters have to take a Progressive it will be Hiram. With the consciousness of the deserving on his face, looking neither to port nor starboard, his stern right arm reaching toward the Progressives and his gentle left arm, with just the suggestion of an embrace, extending toward his friend Harding, a living statue of the graces of compromise. Come to think of it, that is just the attitude of a performer balancing on a slack wire." *New York World*, Sept. 18, 1922.

54. Polis [George Moses], "The Presidency in 1924?" *Forum*, 69 (Mar. 1923), pp. 1308–13.

55. Repeating his refrain of 1920, Charles McClatchy again emphasized Johnson's support among conservatives: "Representatives of great business interests who heretofore have mentioned your name only when accompanied by an oath, are now turning to you as they would turn to a savior . . . the country's only hope of salvation from the more intensely radical Magnus Johnsons [Senator from Minnesota] and La Follettes." C. K. McClatchy to HWJ, July 23, 1923.

56. *Washington Post*, July 24, 1923; *New York Times*, July 22, 24, 1923. See also Mary Connor to Doherty, July 11, 1923; HWJ to boys, Aug. 1, 1923. The *New York Times* estimated that 2,000 were on hand to greet Johnson; the New York police estimated 5,000.

57. HWJ to C. K. McClatchy, July 30, 1923; *New York Times*, July 26, 1923; *Washington Post*, July 26, 1923; "Hiram Johnson's Opening Gun," *Literary Digest*, Aug. 4, 1923, p. 16.

58. HWJ to boys, Aug. 1, 1923; HWJ speech, Waldorf Astoria, July 25, 1923, Part III, Carton 25, HWJ Papers. Johnson began his campaign against American entrance into the World Court in mid-March, prior to his trip abroad. See HWJ speech to the Bronx Board of Trade, Mar. 8, 1923, Part III, Carton 25, HWJ Papers; *New York Times*, Mar. 11, 1923.

59. HWJ to Hiram Johnson, Jr., Aug. 10, 1923.

60. HWJ to boys, Aug. 28, 1923. See also HWJ to Hiram Johnson, Jr., Aug. 10, 1923; Neylan to HWJ, Aug. 7, 1923, Neylan Papers; C. K. McClatchy to HWJ, Aug. 15, 1923; HWJ to C. K. McClatchy, Aug. 9, 10, 1923; HWJ to Alex Moore, Aug. 21, 1923; HWJ to Albert Lasker, Aug. 23, 1923. Johnson had arranged the meeting in HWJ to Albert Lasker, Aug. 21, 1923. On the meeting, see Harold Ickes, *Autobiography of a Curmudgeon* (New York, 1943), pp. 247–51. Lasker

and Wrigley pledged a limit of $25,000 apiece. Thus the *New York Times* was misinformed when it spoke of "huge resources" available to the Johnson campaign. *New York Times*, Nov. 18, 23, 1923.

61. *New York Times*, Nov. 4, 1923. See also *Sacramento Bee*, Sept. 4, 20, Oct. 27, 1923; *Riverside Daily Press*, Sept. 27, 1923; *Fresno Republican*, Oct. 25, 1923; *Stockton Record*, Oct. 26, 1923; *Oakland Tribune*, Nov. 1, 1923.

62. Ickes to HWJ, Oct. 24, 25, 1923, Ickes Papers; *New York Times*, Nov. 16, 1923. See also Albert Lasker to HWJ, Nov. 2, 1923. Two excellent accounts examining Ickes's role in the campaign are Linda J. Lear, *Harold L. Ickes: The Aggressive Progressive, 1874–1933* (New York, 1981), pp. 250–99, and Robert E. Hennings, "Harold Ickes and Hiram Johnson in the Presidential Primary of 1924," in Donald F. Tingley, ed., *Essays in Illinois History in Honor of Glenn Huron Seymour* (Carbondale, 1968), pp. 101–55. See also T. H. Watkins, *Righteous Pilgrim: The Life and Times of Harold Ickes, 1874–1952* (New York, 1990), pp. 205–11.

63. Nevertheless, further embarrassments befell Johnson when one of his private letters was stolen and made public. In it, repeating a familiar refrain, Johnson had rued the dearth of progressivism and the political compromise he had made in 1920: "My weakness today is that I have yielded and given power, position and political strength to the very men I so often formerly denounced." "A Letter from Johnson," *Literary Digest*, Sept. 8, 1923, p. 11; *New York Times*, Aug. 18, Sept. 22, Nov. 23, 1923. See also Walter Jones to HWJ, Aug. 5, 1923; HWJ to C. K. McClatchy, Aug. 23, 1923; Neylan to HWJ, Aug. 16, 1923, Neylan Papers. It had been assumed that if Johnson did run, Moses would direct his campaign. *New York Times*, Sept. 16, 1923. Johnson later characterized Moses as "able, cynical, disreputable, indecent, callous . . . with the gall of a burglar." HWJ to boys, June 9, 1924. See also HWJ to C. K. McClatchy, July 29, 1924. On Moses, see *New York Times*, Nov. 23, 1923; HWJ to Hiram Johnson, Jr., Aug. 10, 1923; HWJ to Albert Lasker, Nov. 3, 1923; *New York Times*, Sept. 2, Nov. 26, 1923.

64. *Current Opinion*, Feb. 1924, pp. 154–55; HWJ to boys, Dec. 10, 1923; *New York Times*, Nov. 27, 1923. Johnson had hoped to obtain Hitchcock as his manager in 1920. Minnie Johnson to boys, ca. Aug. 7, 1919.

65. HWJ to C. K. McClatchy, Nov. 20, 1923; Robert Maddox, *William E. Borah and American Foreign Policy* (Baton Rouge, 1969), p. 153. On Pinchot, see *New York Times*, Jan. 7, 11, 24, 1924. On Borah, see HWJ to Ickes, Oct. 8, 20, 1924.

66. HWJ to Raymond Robins, Oct. 5, 1923. See also HWJ to C. K. McClatchy, Aug. 15, 1924; HWJ to Ickes, Sept. 13, 1924; HWJ to Ickes, June 22, Aug. 6, Oct. 2, 1923, Ickes Papers; HWJ to S. O. Levinson, May 11, 1926; Sister Ann Vincent Meiburger, *The Efforts of Raymond Robins Toward the Recognition of Soviet Russia and the Outlawry of War, 1917–1933* (Washington, D.C., 1958), pp. 115–17; Robert James Maddox, "Keeping Cool with Coolidge," *Journal of American History* 53:4 (Mar. 1967), pp. 772–80.

67. Johnson was especially hurt by Robins's lack of support. Robins, he charged, was "cajoled and seduced by trips [with Coolidge] upon the Mayflower

and promises of future preferment, and never once came near me." His actions represented a betrayal of their long-standing friendship, something Johnson vowed never to forget. HWJ to boys, May 10, 1924. See also HWJ to Ickes, Sept. 13, Oct. 8, 25, 1924; HWJ to Doherty, Oct. 15, 1924; Ickes to HWJ, Nov. 1, 1924.

68. Lissner to Rowell, Jan. 12, 1924, Rowell Papers; HWJ to Albert Lasker, Dec. 18, 1923, Jan. 24, Feb. 9, 1924. See also HWJ to boys, Jan. 6, 1924.

69. *Chicago Tribune*, Feb. 2, 4, 7, 1924; *New York Times*, Feb. 7, 1924.

70. *New York Times*, Nov. 16, 17, 19, 20, 1923; HWJ press release, Nov. 16, 1923; HWJ speech, Chicago, Nov. 27, 1923, both in Part III, Carton 25, HWJ Papers; "Hiram Johnson's Chances," *Literary Digest*, Dec. 1, 1923, p. 18.

71. *New York Times*, Nov. 28, 1923.

72. *New Republic*, Nov. 28, 1923, pp. 4–6. See also *New York Times*, Nov. 17, 1923; *Outlook*, Jan. 16, 1924, pp. 85–86; "Hiram Johnson's Chances," *Literary Digest*, Dec. 1, 1923, pp. 18–19.

73. *Nation*, Nov. 28, 1923, p. 3047, Apr. 23, 1924, p. 465, May 21, 1924, p. 571; *Literary Digest*, Aug. 4, 1923, pp. 8–9; *Current Opinion*, Feb. 1924, p. 137. In the aftermath of the 1924 election, Doherty observed that Johnson could not undercut Coolidge's conservative appeal but was insufficiently radical to appeal to those on the left. Doherty to Franck Havenner, Apr. 9, 1924. "You will agree with me that you have been forced not to say some things which you wanted to say," McClatchy sympathized. C. K. McClatchy to HWJ, Aug. 31, 1924. On the 1922 conference, called by La Follette, Johnson commented: "It is needless to say to you that I would not enter into a La Follette organization, however much I might believe in some of the things he would suggest or do. Indeed, I would not become a member of any organization here which might, in any degree, control my freedom of action in the future." It was a position Johnson maintained throughout his career. HWJ to C. K. McClatchy, Dec. 8, 1922, Dec. 28, 1930, March 5, 1931. See also HWJ to Hiram Johnson, Jr., Dec. 9, 1922, Dec. 6, 1931; HWJ to Doherty, Dec. 9, 1922; Doherty to HWJ, Dec. 14, 1922; HWJ to Ickes, March 8, 1931.

74. *New York Times*, Dec. 10, 13, 1923; *Literary Digest*, Jan. 5, 1924, pp. 14–15; HWJ press statement, Dec. 13, 1923, Part III, Carton 25, HWJ Papers; HWJ to C. K. McClatchy, Dec. 12, 1923, Aug. 17, 1924; HWJ to William Wrigley, Dec. 13, 1923.

75. *New York Times*, Dec. 2, 20, 1923; HWJ to Albert Lasker, Nov. 17, 19, 1923.

76. "The Coolidge Chances for the Nomination," *Literary Digest*, Dec. 22, 1924, pp. 3–6. Upon polling 200 of California's newspapers, the *Digest* reported 60 in favor of Johnson and 127 in favor of Coolidge. *Literary Digest*, Jan. 26, 1924, pp. 5–7. See also the list prepared by Franck Havenner, Feb. 2, 1924, in Part III, Carton 10, HWJ Papers.

77. *New York Times*, Dec. 22, 23, 1923.

78. William Wrigley to HWJ, Dec. 17, 1923. A poll taken by the *Literary Digest* would seem to confirm Wrigley's assessment. *Literary Digest*, Apr. 12, 1924, pp. 10–11. See also HWJ to C. K. McClatchy, Jan. 8, 1926.

79. *New York Tribune*, Jan. 4, 1924. A representative sample of Johnson's initial public statements and addresses is reprinted in *Cong. Record*, 68th Cong., 1st sess., pp. 3142–50. See also Part III, Carton 20, HWJ Papers; "What Johnson Would Do as President," *Literary Digest*, Dec. 22, 1923, p. 8; William Hard, "Johnson Chases Coolidge," *Nation*, Jan. 16, 1924, p. 59; HWJ to William Wrigley, Jan. 11, 1924; HWJ to boys, Jan. 6, 1924.

80. *Cong. Record*, 68th Cong., 1st sess., pp. 3142–50. See also *New York Times*, Jan. 1, 1924; HWJ to C. K. McClatchy, Aug. 16, 1924; HWJ speeches, Cleveland, Jan. 3, 1924, Chicago Broadway Armory, Jan. 18, 1924, in Part III, Carton 25, HWJ Papers.

81. William Wrigley to HWJ, Dec. 17, 1923. Wrigley in fact endorsed the administration's Mexican policy. William Wrigley to HWJ, Jan. 22, 1924. Doherty also advised Johnson to concentrate on domestic issues. Doherty to HWJ, Jan. 30, 1924.

82. *Chicago Tribune*, Mar. 21, 1924.

83. HWJ speech, Chicago, Nov. 27, 1923, Part III, Carton 25, HWJ Papers.

84. *Chicago Tribune*, Feb. 16, 1924; *New York Times*, Feb. 16, 1924; Doherty to HWJ, Jan. 30, 1924. Under the McNary-Haugen plan the domestic prices of specific farm commodities would be artificially set by federal authority and protected against foreign imports by tariffs. The surplus that was not absorbed by the domestic market would be sold abroad at a loss, the costs covered by an "equalization fee" imposed on the producers. Formally introduced in Congress only in January 1924, the plan had widespread backing in much of the nation's wheat belt but had secured only limited endorsement from major farm organizations at the time Johnson gave his backing. See Gilbert C. Fite, *George N. Peek and the Fight for Farm Parity* (Norman, Okla., 1954).

85. Franck Havenner to HWJ, Feb. 6, 1924; HWJ to Franck Havenner, Feb. 25, 1924; E. Forrest Mitchell to Al McCabe, Jan. 18, 1924.

86. *Chicago Tribune*, Feb. 12, 1924; *New York Times*, Feb. 15, 1924; *Cong. Record*, 68th Cong., 1st sess. (Feb. 11, 1924), p. 2243; HWJ press statement, Mar. 30, 1924, Part III, Carton 25, HWJ Papers. See also HWJ to boys, Jan. 21, 1925.

87. Doherty to HWJ, Jan. 30, 1924; Franck Havenner to HWJ, Feb. 6, 1924; *New York Times*, Apr. 3, 1924. See also Bert Noggle, *Teapot Dome: Oil and Politics in the 1920s* (Baton Rouge, 1962). In an unsuccessful effort to silence Johnson, his enemies circulated rumors that one of his two sons might be linked in some way to Edward Doheny, one of the principal conspirators. HWJ to Hiram Johnson, Jr., Feb. 15, 26, 1924; HWJ to Archibald Johnson, Feb. 16, 1924; HWJ to Neylan, Feb. 24, 1924.

88. Ralph Sollitt to HWJ, Mar. 5, 1924; HWJ to Albert Lasker, Feb. 7, Apr. 29, 1924; Oliver H. P. Shelley to Albert Lasker, Feb. 26, 1924; E. Forrest Mitchell to Franck Havenner, Mar. 7, 1924; E. Forrest Mitchell to W. Russell Cole, Feb. 25, 1924; Ickes to Franck Havenner, Mar. 8, 1924; Ickes to Archibald Johnson, Mar. 10, 1924; Oliver H. P. Shelley to Albert Lasker, Feb. 26, 1924; HWJ to boys, Mar. 17, Apr. 7, 1924; HWJ to Albert Lasker, Apr. 11, 1924; HWJ to Frank Hitchcock, Apr. 8, 11, 19, 1924; Frank Hitchcock to HWJ, Apr. 22, 1924.

89. In the aftermath of the contest Frank Hitchcock provided the following breakdown on the use of funds: Indiana, $15,000; Oregon, $10,000; North Dakota, $5,000; South Dakota, $5,000; Ohio, $2,500; Michigan, $2,500; Chicago, $5,000; New York City, $25,000. See HWJ to Albert Lasker, Dec. 29, 1923, Feb. 7, Apr. 29, 1924. See also HWJ to Albert Lasker, Feb. 7, 1924; Ickes to Franck Havenner, Mar. 18, 1924; Ickes to Archibald Johnson, Mar. 10, 1924; HWJ to Franck Havenner, Feb. 25, Mar. 1, 1924.

90. HWJ to Franck Havenner, Feb. 25, Mar. 1, 15, 1924; HWJ to boys, Feb. 28, 1924; HWJ to Neylan, Feb. 24, 1924.

91. R. S. Wilcox to Franck Havenner, Mar. 19, 1924; HWJ to Franck Havenner, Mar. 15, 1924; *New York Times*, Mar. 22, 1924; *Chicago Tribune*, Mar. 17, 1924. Peter Norbeck estimated that the Coolidge forces, in blanketing the state with money, spent $3.00 per vote. See Norbeck statement, Part III, Carton 10, HWJ Papers.

92. *New York Times*, Dec. 5, 1923, Mar. 24, 27, 1924. The itinerary of Johnson's South Dakota campaign can be found in E. Forrest Mitchell to Franck Havenner, Mar. 11, 1924. See also HWJ to boys, Mar. 23, 1924; HWJ to Franck Havenner, Mar. 28, 1924; HWJ to Ickes, May 5, 1924; HWJ to James MacLafferty, Jan. 5, 1925.

93. Doherty to HWJ, Jan. 16, 1924; *New York Times*, Mar. 28, 1924. From the outset, Wrigley's support rested on personal friendship rather than shared convictions, and rumors of his probable defection had long circulated. *New York Times*, Jan. 3, 1924; *Chicago Tribune*, Feb. 2, 4, 1924. Johnson refused to discuss Wrigley's defection. See William Zimmerman to HWJ, Aug. 2, 1932; HWJ to William Zimmerman, Aug. 6, 1932. See also Neylan to HWJ, Dec. 15, 20, 1923; HWJ to Archibald Johnson, Mar. 13, 1931.

94. *Chicago Tribune*, Apr. 10, 1924; *New York Times*, Apr. 8, 9, 14, 1924.

95. HWJ to Doherty, Apr. 11, 1924; HWJ to Franck Havenner, Apr. 10, 1924; Albert Lasker to HWJ, Apr. 24, 1924; HWJ to C. K. McClatchy, Apr. 6, 1924; HWJ to boys, Apr. 7, 1924; Doherty to HWJ, Apr. 12, 1924; *New York Times*, Apr. 11, 17, 18, 24, 26, 1924.

96. *New York Times*, Apr. 26, 1924.

97. On the California campaign, see Frank Snook to HWJ, Dec. 18, 1923; Al McCabe to HWJ, Dec. 16, 1923; Charles A. Whitmore to Franck Havenner, Dec. 12, 1923; E. A. Luce to HWJ, Dec. 25, 1923; Dell Schweitzer to HWJ, Jan. 18, 29, 1924; Theodore Roche to W. T. Ellis, Jan. 29, 1924; Theodore Roche to Alfred Ehrman, Apr. 17, 1924; Archibald Johnson to HWJ, Jan. 8, Feb. 26, Apr. 9, 1924; Frank Devlin et al. to HWJ, Apr. 12, 1924; Franck Havenner to Ickes, Mar. 20, 1924; HWJ to Franck Havenner, Apr. 10, 1924; HWJ to Hiram Johnson, Jr., Apr. 12, 1924; HWJ to Dell Schweitzer, Feb. 1, Mar. 3, 1924; HWJ to boys, Apr. 15, May 1, 1924; HWJ to C. K. McClatchy, Apr. 20, 29, 1924; HWJ to William Hard, May 8, 1924; Hichborn to HWJ, May 29, 1924, Hichborn Papers; Neylan to HWJ, May 29, 1924, Neylan Papers.

98. HWJ to boys, Apr. 15, May 1, 10, 17, 1924; HWJ to Hiram Johnson, Jr., Apr. 28, 1924; HWJ to Doherty, May 9, 1924; HWJ to Ickes, May 1, 1924. In the aftermath of the Nebraska defeat, Johnson lost New Jersey (April 22), Ohio (April 29), California (May 5), Indiana (May 6), and Oregon (May 16).

99. Minnie Johnson to Hiram Johnson, Jr., May ?, 1924. See also HWJ to C. K. McClatchy, May 10, 1924.

100. Roger Daniels, *The Politics of Prejudice: The Anti-Japanese Movement in California and the Struggle for Japanese Exclusion* (Berkeley, 1962), pp. 98–105; *New York Times*, Apr. 10, May 1, 5, 9, 1924; HWJ statements, Apr. 30, May 2, 5, 8, 1924, Part III, Carton 25, HWJ Papers; HWJ to Hiram Johnson, Jr., Apr. 14, 15, 1924. Johnson obviously hoped to breathe at least a bit of life into his faltering California campaign with these efforts. See HWJ to C. K. McClatchy, Neylan, Franck Havenner, May 1, 1924.

101. *Cong. Record*, 68th Cong., 1st sess. (May 24, 1924), pp. 9417–18; HWJ to boys, May 27, 1924; HWJ to Arthur Brisbane, May 27, 1924. See also HWJ to C. K. McClatchy, Aug. 16, 1924.

102. HWJ to Doherty, June 16, 1924. See also *New York Times*, May 23, June 7, 1924. Hoover, Johnson wrote, had "whined, and begged, cried and crawled" for the nomination. HWJ to Doherty, June 16, 1924. To his son he wrote: "This sneak Hoover has been trying to crawl into power in any fashion he could, first with Wilson, then with the Democratic Party, then with the Republican Party, then with Harding, then with Coolidge, and as all of us have known in the last few days, [has been] mad to be vice-president." HWJ to Hiram Johnson, Jr., June 13, 1924. See also HWJ to Archibald Johnson, June 13, 1924.

103. HWJ to boys, July 3, 10, 1924. See also HWJ to Albert Lasker, July 17, 1924.

104. HWJ to C. K. McClatchy, Aug. 28, 1924; HWJ to boys, June 9, July 3, 1924; HWJ to Doherty, Oct. 9, 1924; Doherty to HWJ, Aug. 21, 1924; C. K. McClatchy to HWJ, Aug. 27, Sept. 29, Oct. 12, 1924; HWJ to H. H. Timkin, June 5, 1924.

105. HWJ to C. K. McClatchy, Aug. 16, 1924; HWJ to Doherty, Oct. 9, 1924. In fact, Johnson voiced doubts both about La Follette's physical health and about his mental stability. He would not be surprised, he noted, to see a recurrence of the unpleasantness of 1912. HWJ to boys, June 9, July 3, 1924.

106. Doherty to HWJ, Oct. 13, 1924. See also *New York Times*, June 7, July 19, 1924.

107. Ickes to HWJ, Sept. 9, Oct. 3, 1924; C. K. McClatchy to HWJ, Aug. 14, 1924. McClatchy complained that his endorsement of John W. Davis was precluded by Davis's support of American membership in the League of Nations. La Follette thus became "the choice of three evils."

108. On the various solicitations and Johnson's response, see C. K. McClatchy to HWJ, Aug. 31, Oct. 12, 1924; HWJ to C. K. McClatchy, Sept. 4, 29, 1924; HWJ to Doherty, Oct. 15, 1924; R. G. Fernald to HWJ, Oct. 22, 1924.

109. *New York Times*, Sept. 26, Oct. 1, 1924; HWJ statement, Sept. 25, 1924, Part III, Carton 25, HWJ Papers. See also HWJ to C. K. McClatchy, Aug. 28, Oct. 24, 1924. Johnson would forgo the opportunity to represent the La Follette camp legally in filing for a rehearing. HWJ to C. K. McClatchy, Sept. 29, 1924.

110. Ickes to HWJ, Sept. 9, 1924; HWJ to Ickes, Sept. 13, Oct. 18, 20, 1924; HWJ to C. K. McClatchy, Aug. 16, 17, Sept. 18, 22, Oct. 4, 24, 1924.

111. HWJ to Doherty, Oct. 15, 1924; HWJ to C. K. McClatchy, Sept. 17, 1924.

See also Rowell, "Why I Shall Vote for Coolidge," pp. 219–21; Alan R. Havig, "A Disputed Legacy: Roosevelt Progressives and the La Follette Campaign of 1924," *Mid-America* 53:1 (Jan. 1971), pp. 44–64.

112. HWJ to Ickes, Nov. 10, 1924; HWJ to C. K. McClatchy, Mar. 18, 1925; HWJ to Hiram Johnson, Jr., Dec. 28, 1924.

113. *Cong. Record*, 68th Cong., 2nd sess. (Feb. 23, 1925), p. 4416; *Cong. Record*, 69th Cong., 1st sess. (Mar. 9, 1926), p. 5307.

114. Donald R. McCoy, *Calvin Coolidge: The Quiet President* (New York, 1967), p. 278; Felix A. Nigro, "The Warren Case," *Western Political Quarterly* 11:4 (Dec. 1958), pp. 835–56.

115. HWJ to Archibald Johnson, Mar. 18, 1925; HWJ to C. K. McClatchy, Mar. 17, 1925. See also HWJ to C. K. McClatchy, Jan. 14, 1925.

116. Minnie Johnson to Hiram Johnson, Jr., Feb. 26, 1926; HWJ to Hiram Johnson, Jr., Mar. 1, 1926; HWJ to C. K. McClatchy, Mar. 1, 1926; *Cong. Record*, 69th Cong., 1st sess. (Feb. 10, 1926), p. 3692. For an examination of Senate insurgents in the 1920s, see Erik Olssen, "The Progressive Group in Congress, 1922–1929," *Historian* 42:2 (Feb. 1980), pp. 244–63. Throughout this period, as Olssen notes, Johnson ranked high in progressive circles. Johnson would have agreed. Looking back on his record, he wrote: "Generally speaking, I am with the Progressives. Indeed, if the votes were tallied up, save upon *certain*, and only certain specific items in the Tariff Bill, I think my average would be higher practically than that of any other man in the Senate." HWJ to Ickes, Mar. 8, 1931, emphasis in original.

117. HWJ to C. K. McClatchy, June 22, July 20, 1926. See also *Cong. Record*, 69th Cong., 1st sess. (June 17, 29, 1926), pp. 11427–32, 12195–96, 12202–5; *Cong. Record*, 70th Cong., 1st sess. (Jan. 13, 1928), pp. 1438–39. Although Johnson had moved beyond the progressivism of the prewar years, still it is not clear if he had made his peace with the new liberalism of the 1920s, and he continued to describe the farm proposal as "bizarre." See HWJ to Hiram Johnson, Jr., June 19, 1926.

118. *Cong. Record*, 69th Cong., 1st sess. (June 17, 1926), p. 11427; HWJ to Irving Martin, June 24, 1926; HWJ to Hiram Johnson, Jr., June 26, 1926; HWJ to Archibald Johnson, June 26, 1926.

119. HWJ to C. K. McClatchy, June 22, July 2, 1926; HWJ to boys, July 2, 1926.

120. HWJ to Fremont Older, Mar. 29, 1926.

121. HWJ to Alex McCabe, May 24, 1926. See also HWJ to Hiram Johnson, Jr., Oct. 30, 1926; HWJ to Archibald Johnson, Oct. 30, 1926; HWJ to boys, July 2, 1926; HWJ to C. K. McClatchy, May 22, July 2, 20, 1926; HWJ to Ickes, May 22, 1926.

122. HWJ to Doherty, Nov. 15, 1926. See also HWJ to C. K. McClatchy, Nov. 4, 1926; HWJ to boys, Nov. 6, 13, 20, 1926.

123. Preston J. Hubbard, *Origins of the TVA: The Muscle Shoals Controversy, 1920–1932* (Nashville, 1961).

124. HWJ to Ickes, Mar. 7, 1925.

125. *Cong. Record*, 71st Cong., 3rd sess. (Feb. 20, 1931), pp. 5570–71.

126. HWJ to boys, Jan. 13, 1925.

127. *Cong. Record*, 68th Cong., 2nd sess. (Dec. 19, 1924, Jan. 14, 1925), pp. 817–18, 1797–98. See also HWJ to Hiram Johnson, Jr., Dec. 28, 1924, Jan. 3, 6, 1925; HWJ to Archibald Johnson, Jan. 13, 1925; HWJ to C. K. McClatchy, Jan. 14, 1925.

128. Norris Hundley, Jr., "The Politics of Reclamation: California, the Federal Government, and the Origins of the Boulder Canyon Act—A Second Look," *California Historical Quarterly* 52:4 (Winter 1973), pp. 292–325; Beverley Bowen Moeller, *Phil Swing and Boulder Dam* (Berkeley, 1971). See also HWJ to Doherty, June 5, 1922.

129. Norris Hundley, Jr., *Water and the West: The Colorado River Compact and the Politics of Water in the American West* (Berkeley, 1975); Norris Hundley, Jr., *Dividing the Waters: A Century of Controversy Between the United States and Mexico* (Berkeley, 1966).

130. HWJ to George Young, Dec. 4, 14, 1925; HWJ to Hiram Johnson, Jr., Dec. 4, 12, 1925; HWJ to C. K. McClatchy, Dec. 9, 1925; HWJ to Albert Brisbane, Jan. 2, 1926.

131. Moeller, *Phil Swing and Boulder Dam*, pp. 30, 32, 50, 71–74; "Hiram W. Johnson Newsletter," Dec. 20, 1924, Part III, Carton 25, HWJ Papers.

132. Moeller, *Phil Swing and Boulder Dam*, p. 103. Hoover continued to blame Johnson for California's attachment of the condition—the so-called Finney resolution—but in fact Johnson had played no role, having been at the time uncertain of its merits. HWJ to George Young, Dec. 21, 23, 1925. See also HWJ to Neylan, Feb. 9, 1923; HWJ to Hichborn, June 1, 1926; HWJ to C. K. McClatchy, Oct. 20, 1927; HWJ to George Young, May 22, 1926; Herbert Hoover to Rowell, Apr. 21, Dec. 13, 1926, Rowell Papers; George Young to HWJ, Dec. 22, 1925; HWJ to Neylan, Dec. 10, 1927, Neylan Papers.

133. Herbert Hoover to Rowell, Apr. 11, 1925, Rowell Papers. See also Herbert Hoover to Rowell, Feb. 25, Apr. 21, Dec. 13, 1926, all in Rowell Papers.

134. HWJ to C. K. McClatchy, May 12, 1928. See also HWJ to W. A. Johnstone, May 21, 1926; HWJ to boys, May 8, 1928; HWJ to C. K. McClatchy, Oct. 20, 1927.

135. George Norris to Frank Harrison, May 10, 1926 (copy), HWJ Papers. See also HWJ to C. K. McClatchy, Dec. 28, 1925.

136. HWJ to C. K. McClatchy, Dec. 9, 1925; HWJ to W. A. Johnstone, May 21, 1926; HWJ to Doherty, Oct. 1, 1926. In fact Johnson participated in committee hearings even before his appointment to the committee. See Senate Committee on Irrigation and Reclamation, *Hearings on S. 727, Colorado River Basin*, 68th Cong., 2nd sess. (1925). In October and November 1925, hearings were held in Los Angeles, San Diego, Yuma, Phoenix, and Las Vegas. Senate Committee on Irrigation and Reclamation, *Hearings on Sen. Res. 320, Colorado River Basin*, 69th Cong., 1st sess. (1925). Throughout the hearings, Johnson ably moved to discredit the opposition. See pp. 199–204, 237–39, 251–55, 402–3, 440, 520–21, 538–40, 586–91, 595–97, 608–9, 740–42, 785–94.

137. HWJ to George Young, Jan. 4, 21, Apr. 26, 1926.

138. Moeller, *Phil Swing and Boulder Dam*, pp. 86–90; HWJ to Frank Flint, Feb. 3, 1927 (copy), Neylan Papers; Rowell to Herbert Hoover, Feb. 18, Apr. 9,

1926, Rowell Papers; HWJ to boys, Jan. 16, 1926; HWJ to Hiram Johnson, Jr., Mar. 14, 20, 1926; HWJ to C. K. McClatchy, Mar. 13, 1926; HWJ to Archibald Johnson, Mar. 20, 1926.

139. *New York Times*, Feb. 3, 1927; HWJ to George Young, Apr. 26, May 22, 1926; HWJ to Hiram Johnson, Jr., Apr. 26, 1926; HWJ to George Norris, May 11, 1926; HWJ to Hichborn, May 21, 1926.

140. HWJ to C. K. McClatchy, Jan. 14, 1927. See also HWJ to C. K. McClatchy, Jan. 29, 1927; HWJ to Frank Flint, Feb. 3, 1927; HWJ to boys, Feb. 2, 1927; HWJ to Neylan, Jan. 10, 1927, Neylan Papers.

141. HWJ to C. K. McClatchy, Mar. 5, 1927. See also HWJ to boys, Dec. 3, 1926, Mar. 5, 1927; HWJ to C. K. McClatchy, Oct. 20, 1927; HWJ to Hiram Johnson, Jr., Feb. 11, Mar. 11, 1927; HWJ to George Young, Dec. 14, 1925; HWJ to Neylan, Feb. 16, 1928, HWJ to Frank Flint, Feb. 3, 1927, both in Neylan Papers; Doherty to HWJ, Feb. 8, 1927; Phil Swing to HWJ, Nov. 12, 1927.

142. *New York Times*, Feb. 27, 1927; HWJ to Hiram Johnson, Jr., Mar. 11, 1927; HWJ to Frank Flint, Mar. 7, 1927, copy in Neylan Papers.

143. *New York Times*, Feb. 20, 22–27, 1927; HWJ to C. K. McClatchy, Mar. 5, 1927; HWJ to Hiram Johnson, Jr., Mar. 11, 1927; HWJ to boys, Mar. 5, 1927; HWJ to Frank Flint, Mar. 7, 1927, copy in Neylan Papers.

144. HWJ to C. K. McClatchy, Dec. 31, 1927, Feb. 3, Mar. 2, 17, 1928; HWJ to boys, Jan. 23, Feb. 3, Mar. 2, 1928; Minnie Johnson to Hiram Johnson, Jr., Jan. 28, 1928; HWJ to Archibald Johnson, Jan. 7, 1928.

145. HWJ to Neylan, Feb. 8, 16, 1928, Neylan Papers; HWJ to Dion Holm, Feb. 17, 1928; HWJ to H. R. McLaughlin, Mar. 2, 1928; HWJ to boys, Feb. 25, 1928; *New York Times*, Mar. 22, 1928.

146. *Cong. Record*, 70th Cong., 1st sess. (Apr. 26, May 12, 1928), pp. 7245, 8522–24; HWJ to boys, Apr. 30, May 12, 1928; HWJ to Ickes, June 1, 1928; HWJ to C. K. McClatchy, May 12, June 1, 1928.

147. *New York Times*, Apr. 29, 1928; HWJ to boys, May 31, 1928. In 1927 Dawes was helpful in enabling Johnson to move his project to the Senate floor. See HWJ to Hiram Johnson, Jr., Mar. 11, 1927. Johnson's initial impression of Dawes altered considerably as the vice president showed his independence from Coolidge in this and other battles. Writing in 1925 of Dawes's inauguration address, Johnson described him as "loutish and clownish" in his "unworthy and disgusting exhibition." HWJ to Doherty, Mar. 3, 1925. To Charles McClatchy Johnson remarked: "I really think this man [Dawes] is insane. I never before heard him but the tone of his voice, the occasional shrieks, now and then the hysterical method of expression, his ludicrous gestures were indicative of the hopeless paretic." HWJ to C. K. McClatchy, Mar. 3, 1925. See also HWJ to Ickes, Mar. 7, 1925; HWJ to boys, Mar. 4, 1925, Jan. 30, 1926. At the end of the term, Johnson made an unusual request: he asked Dawes for an autographed photograph. HWJ to Charles Dawes, Feb. 23, 1929.

148. *New York Times*, May 28, 30, 1928.

149. HWJ to C. K. McClatchy, June 1, 1928; HWJ to Ickes, June 1, 1928; HWJ to Ralph Criswell, Aug. 15, 1928.

150. *New York Times*, Dec. 14, 1928; HWJ to boys, Dec. 18, 1928; HWJ to

Doherty, Dec. 27, 1928; HWJ to Ickes, Dec. 27, 1928. On the meaning of the 4.4 million acre-feet limitation see Norris Hundley, Jr., "Clio Nods: Arizona v. California and the Boulder Canyon Act—A Reassessment," *Western Historical Quarterly* 3 : 1 (1972), pp. 17–51.

151. HWJ to C. K. McClatchy, Dec. 18, 1928.

152. HWJ to C. K. McClatchy, Mar. 26, 1930; HWJ to Doherty, Feb. 28, 1930; HWJ to John R. Haynes, Mar. 20, 1930; John R. Haynes to HWJ, Mar. 17, 1930; Phil Swing to Ray Lyman Wilbur, Jan. 25, 1930.

153. Moeller, *Phil Swing and Boulder Dam*, pp. 129–32; HWJ to Doherty, Feb. 28, 1930; John R. Haynes to HWJ, Mar. 17, 1930; HWJ to John R. Haynes, Mar. 23, 1930. If he had had his way, Johnson wrote, he would not have allowed Southern California Edison a single kilowatt. HWJ to C. K. McClatchy, Mar. 26, 1930. Fraser Edwards, of the United News Service, asked Johnson to comment on Wilbur's naming of the dam, but Johnson diplomatically declined. HWJ to Fraser Edwards, Sept. 18, 1930. Johnson pointed to Elwood Mead as the most deserving of tribute. See HWJ to W. B. Mathews, Sept. 19, 1930. On the continuing controversy over the dam's name, see HWJ to William Gibbs McAdoo, Feb. 29, 1936; HWJ to Wesley Barr, Oct. 6, 1936; *Cong. Record*, 71st Cong., 2nd sess. (Jan. 9, 1930), p. 1310.

154. See Hichborn to HWJ, Mar. 1, 1923; Lissner to Rowell, Jan. 12, 1924, Rowell Papers.

155. Russell M. Posner, "The Progressive Voters League, 1923–1926," *California Historical Society Quarterly* 36 : 3 (Sept. 1957), pp. 251–60; Hichborn to Rowell, May 26, 1924, Hichborn Papers.

156. Hichborn to William Kent, Oct. 26, 1923, Hichborn Papers. At approximately the same time the league was formed, many of the same founders created the Roosevelt Club, an organization tied more directly to national politics and to Johnson's cause. It was never much more than a letterhead operation, and its impact was negligible. See Doherty to HWJ, May 22, 1922; HWJ to Doherty, June 16, 1924; Franck Havenner to George Howe, Dec. 7, 1922; Franck Havenner to Herbert C. Jones, Jan. 4, 1923 (copies), HWJ Papers; *Sacramento Bee*, Oct. 28, 1922.

157. *San Francisco Examiner*, July 23, Aug. 23, 1924; *San Francisco Chronicle*, Aug. 15, 1924; HWJ to C. K. McClatchy, May 26, Aug. 11, 19, 1924; C. K. McClatchy to HWJ, May 26, Aug. 19, 31, 1924; HWJ to Hiram Johnson, Jr., Apr. 28, 1924; HWJ to Ickes, Aug. 19, 1924; HWJ to Doherty, May 9, 1924.

158. HWJ press statements, Aug. 13, 23, Sept. 22, 1924, Part III, Carton 25, HWJ Papers; HWJ to C. K. McClatchy, Aug. 20, 1924; Hichborn to HWJ, Aug. 11, 1925; C. K. McClatchy to HWJ, Aug. 19, 31, 1924.

159. C. K. McClatchy to HWJ, Nov. 23, 1925, Jan. 11, 1926; Irving Martin to HWJ, Jan. 16, 1926; Hichborn to HWJ, Jan. 13, 1926, Hichborn Papers; Neylan to HWJ, Apr. 2, 1926, Neylan Papers.

160. HWJ to W. B. Mathews, July 24, 1926; HWJ to Neylan, Oct. 22, 1925; Hichborn to HWJ, Dec. 7, 1925; *New York Times*, Sept. 13, 23, 1925.

161. Hichborn to HWJ, Oct. 23, 1925, June 22, 1926, Hichborn Papers; HWJ to C. K. McClatchy, Feb. 1, 1926; C. K. McClatchy to HWJ, Mar. 3, 1926; Rowell

to Elbert Dille, Jan. 28, 1926, Rowell Papers; Irving Martin to HWJ, Mar. 12, 1926; Hichborn to John R. Haynes, Feb. 17, 1926 (copy), HWJ Papers; Hichborn, "California Politics," vol. 4, p. 2302.

162. HWJ to C. K. McClatchy, Mar. 13, Apr. 9, 1926; HWJ to Neylan, Mar. 29, 1926, Neylan Papers; HWJ to Hiram Johnson, Jr., May 5, 1926; HWJ to boys, July 19, 1926; HWJ to Al McCabe, June 24, 1926; Al McCabe to HWJ, June 1, 1926.

163. *Oakland Post Enquirer*, Aug. 3, 1926; *San Francisco Chronicle*, July 2, 1926. Clarke's position was somewhat undermined when evidence surfaced that he had supported the United States's entrance into the World Court prior to his announcement of candidacy. See *Palo Alto Times*, Mar. 11, 1926; Walter Lineberger to HWJ, Apr. 26, 1926. Johnson's advice to emphasize domestic policies can be found in HWJ to C. K. McClatchy, Oct. 14, 1926; HWJ to W. B. Mathews, July 20, 1926; HWJ to Irving Martin, June 3, 1926; HWJ to George Young, May 13, 1926.

164. Rowell to Martin Madsen, June 18, 1926, Rowell Papers; Doherty to HWJ, July 24, 1926; C. K. McClatchy to HWJ, Sept. 15, 1926; HWJ to C. K. McClatchy, Oct. 14, 26, Dec. 24, 1926; HWJ to Archibald Johnson, Dec. 13, 1926; Hichborn to C. K. McClatchy, Oct. 30, 1926, Hichborn Papers; Hichborn, "California Politics," vol. 4, pp. 2312–15. See also HWJ to Hiram Johnson, Jr., Feb. 4, 1934.

165. HWJ to C. K. McClatchy, Sept. 4, Oct. 1, 14, 26, 1926; *Los Angeles Evening Herald*, Aug. 7, 14, 19, 20, 1926; *San Diego Sun*, Aug. 21, 1926; *Oakland Post-Enquirer*, Aug. 3, 6, 7, 1926; *Sacramento Bee*, Aug. 17, 1926; *San Francisco Examiner*, Aug. 17, 27, 1926; *San Francisco Chronicle*, July 31, Aug. 3, 7, 27, 29, 30, 1926; *New York Times*, Aug. 22, 1926.

166. Martin Madsen to C. K. McClatchy, Feb. 20, 1928; Hichborn to HWJ, Sept. 2, 1926, Hichborn Papers.

167. *San Francisco Chronicle*, Aug. 3, 1926; HWJ to Neylan, July 19, 1926, Neylan Papers; HWJ to C. K. McClatchy, Nov. 17, Dec. 29, 1930.

168. *New York Times*, Sept. 19, Oct. 3, 1926, Mar. 6, 1927; C. K. McClatchy to HWJ, Nov. 3, 1926; HWJ to boys, Dec. 3, 1926; HWJ to Doherty, Feb. 2, Mar. 9, 1929; HWJ to C. K. McClatchy, Sept. 21, Oct. 14, Nov. 17, 24, Dec. 9, 1926, Jan. 29, 1927, Jan. 16, 1929; C. K. McClatchy to Bert Meek, Jan. 5, 1927; Carlos McClatchy to HWJ, Jan. 26, 1929. Johnson judged Young's governorship favorably and expressed willingness to campaign for his reelection in 1930. But the same dynamics were at work, and Johnson was not invited to participate. Young lost the primary to James Rolph, Jr., whom Johnson described as a "sort of tinsel copy" of Jimmy Walker. HWJ to Doherty, Nov. 23, 1929; HWJ to C. K. McClatchy, Jan. 16, 1929, Jan. 22, June 29, July 21, Aug. 7, 11, 1930, Feb. 21, Sept. 23, 1931; HWJ to H. L. Carnahan, Sept. 4, 1930; HWJ to Fraser Edwards, Sept. 8, Oct. 30, 1930; Harriet French to HWJ, Nov. 12, 1932; Doherty to Bert Meek, Nov. 19, 1929.

169. HWJ to Doherty, Nov. 15, 1926; HWJ to C. K. McClatchy, Nov. 17, Dec. 24, 1926.

170. HWJ to Hiram Johnson, Jr., Mar. 11, 1927; *New York Times*, May 27, 1928.

171. *New York Times*, Aug. 3, 1927; HWJ to C. K. McClatchy, June 22, Dec. 7, 1926; HWJ to boys, Nov. 20, 1926.

172. HWJ to C. K. McClatchy, Aug. 11, 19, Oct. 12, Dec. 18, 1927, Feb. 8, 1928; C. K. McClatchy to HWJ, Aug. 16, 1927; Hichborn to C. K. McClatchy, Jan. 6, 1928, Hichborn Papers; Paul Scharrenberg to HWJ, Feb. 7, 1928; Martin Madsen to C. K. McClatchy, Feb. 20, 1928; *New York Times*, Sept. 17, Oct. 4, 1927.

173. Rowell to Herbert Hoover, Aug. 30, 1927, Rowell Papers. See also Rowell to Reginald G. Fernald, Sept. 26, 1927; Rowell to Ernest Harvier, Mar. 9, 1928, all in Rowell Papers.

174. HWJ to C. K. McClatchy, Feb. 3, 8, 18, Mar. 6, 1928; HWJ to Bert Meek, Jan. 16, 1928; HWJ to boys, Jan. 23, 1928; HWJ to Hichborn, Feb. 24, 1930, Hichborn Papers.

175. The five were Charles Curry, Harry Engelbright, Richard Welch, Philip Swing, and Henry Barbour. HWJ to boys, Feb. 3, 25, Mar. 6, 1928; HWJ to C. K. McClatchy, Feb. 3, 1928.

176. HWJ to boys, May 31, June 5, 1928; HWJ to C. K. McClatchy, Mar. 3, 6, Apr. 16, June 1, 1928; C. K. McClatchy to HWJ, Feb. 20, Mar. 20, 1928; Rowell to HWJ, Apr. 20, 1928. See also Archibald Johnson to HWJ, May 14, 1928.

177. HWJ to boys, May 31, 1928. See also HWJ to Hiram Johnson, Jr., Apr. 14, 1926; HWJ to boys, May 12, June 12, 1928; HWJ to C. K. McClatchy, Mar. 17, 1928. Aware of Johnson's hesitancy, George Norris urged Johnson to run and promised his active support in the campaign. Richard Lowitt, *George Norris: The Persistence of a Progressive, 1913–1933* (Urbana, Ill., 1971), p. 408.

178. HWJ to boys, May 31, 1928.

179. Edward Dickson to Joe S. Crail, Feb. 4, 1928, Dickson Papers. Johnson, Dickson wrote, "was one of the outstanding intellects of the Senate," and a forceful representative of California interests. Moreover, Dickson added, less than truthfully, the only thing that had divided Johnson from his past supporters had been his personality and the issue of the League of Nations. On Johnson's concerns about Fitts, see HWJ to C. K. McClatchy, Aug. 29, 1927, Mar. 6, 1928; HWJ to Neylan, Oct. 29, 1927, Neylan Papers. On the need for the Hoover forces to hold Fitts in reserve, see Rowell to Herbert Hoover, Aug. 30, 1927, Rowell Papers.

180. *New York Times*, May 27, June 10, July 8, 1928; HWJ to C. K. McClatchy, June 1, 1928.

181. *New York Times*, July 24, Aug. 2, 1928; *San Francisco Chronicle*, July 24, 1928.

182. *New York Times*, Aug. 4, 1928.

183. C. K. McClatchy to HWJ, May 17, 1928; HWJ to C. K. McClatchy, May 18, 1928; *Los Angeles Evening Herald*, Aug. 1, 2, 1928; *San Francisco Chronicle*, July 30, 1928; *San Diego Union*, Aug. 3, 1928; *Riverside Daily Press*, Aug. 4, 1928. See also Hichborn to C. K. McClatchy, July 2, 1928, Hichborn Papers.

184. California Secretary of State, *Statement of Vote in 1928 Primary Election*. Randall had supported Johnson's 1924 presidential bid. Charles Randall to HWJ, May 5, 1924.

185. Rowell to HWJ, ca. Oct. ?, 1928; Mark Requa to Rowell, Oct. 8, 1928, both in Rowell Papers.

186. HWJ to Doherty, Mar. 9, 1929. Johnson's Democratic opponent was Minor Moore. Overall, Johnson secured more than 74 percent of the vote cast in the senatorial race. His campaign can be traced in the *San Francisco Chronicle,* Sept. 3, Oct. 3–6, 26, 1928; *Sacramento Bee,* Oct. 4, 6, 1928; *Modesto News Herald,* Oct. 23, 1928; *Fresno Bee,* Oct. 24, 26, 27, Nov. 3, 1928; *Bakersfield Californian,* Oct. 26, 1928; *Stockton Record,* Oct. 30, 31, Nov. 2, 1928; *Courier Free Press* (Redding), Sept. 28, Oct. 3, 4, 1928; *Los Angeles Examiner,* Aug. 1, 4, 1928. See also George P. West, "California Is for Hoover," *Nation,* Oct. 10, 1928, pp. 339–40.

Chapter VII: Hoover, Roosevelt, and the New Deal

1. HWJ to boys, Feb. 23, 1929. See also HWJ to boys, Mar. 5, 1929; HWJ to Doherty, Jan. 23, 1929; HWJ to Hiram Johnson, Jr., Feb. 9, 1929; HWJ to Ickes, May 18, 1929.

2. *New York Times,* Nov. 22, 1929. The party breakdown in the new Senate would be 56 Republicans, 39 Democrats, and 1 Farmer-Laborite.

3. HWJ to C. K. McClatchy, Jan. 23, 1929; HWJ to Hiram Johnson, Jr., Apr. 26, 1929; *Cong. Record,* 71st Cong., 1st sess. (May 8, 1929), p. 990. See also HWJ to Carlos McClatchy, June 21, 1929; HWJ to boys, Mar. 5, 1929; HWJ to Edgar Luce, Sept. 5, 1930.

4. *New York Times,* Apr. 7, 1929.

5. HWJ to boys, Mar. 23, May 4, 1929; HWJ to Doherty, Mar. 28, 1929; HWJ to Carlos McClatchy, Mar. 19, 1929; HWJ to C. K. McClatchy, Apr. 4, May 14, 1929.

6. *Cong. Record,* 71st Cong., 1st sess. (May 8, 1929), pp. 989–92. See also HWJ to Carlos McClatchy, June 17, 1929; HWJ to C. K. McClatchy, June 21, 1929; HWJ to Burton A. Towne, June 19, 1929; HWJ to boys, June 7, 1929; HWJ to Doherty, June 17, 1929; HWJ to Ickes, June 3, 1929; HWJ to Hichborn, June 19, 1929, Hichborn Papers; Carlos McClatchy to HWJ, June 20, 1929.

7. HWJ to Hiram Johnson, Jr., June 13, 1929. See also HWJ to boys, May 10, June 7, 1929; HWJ to C. K. McClatchy, May 14, 1929; *New York Times,* May 9, June 7, 12, 1929.

8. HWJ to Carlos McClatchy, June 26, 1929; HWJ to Neylan, Feb. 16, 1929, Neylan Papers; *Cong. Record,* 71st Cong., 1st sess. (June 17, 1929), p. 2975.

9. HWJ to boys, Oct. 18, 1929; *Cong. Record,* 71st Cong., 1st sess. (Nov. 14, 15, 1929), pp. 5581–86, 5593–5600, 5615.

10. "A strict silence is maintained by the individual who should speak most frankly, but all of the little brothers of the press, who constitute the Knights of the Napkin, are told what to do, and they will send out the most poisonous stuff against any man who shows the slightest tendency to rebellion." HWJ to C. K. McClatchy, June 21, 1929.

11. HWJ to boys, Feb. 22, 1930. "The great Mogul in the White House wobbles first on one side, and then the other, and nobody knows, not even himself, what

his opinions are, or what he wishes to do. It is the universally accepted opinion here that there never has been a President so utterly lacking in leadership or decision." HWJ to Hiram Johnson, Jr., Mar. 1, 1930. See also HWJ to Archibald Johnson, Mar. 15, 1930; *Cong. Record,* 71st Cong., 1st sess. (Oct. 28, 1929), p. 4962; *New York Times,* Oct. 29, 1929.

12. *Cong. Record,* 71st Cong., 1st sess. (Oct. 2, 1929), pp. 4118–23; HWJ to C. K. McClatchy, Oct. 10, 1929. Campaigning in California in 1922 at the time the provision for flexibility was adopted, Johnson had voiced his objections but had not emphasized them. See HWJ to C. K. McClatchy, Oct. 10, 1929.

13. *Cong. Record,* 71st Cong., 2nd sess. (Feb. 20, 1930), pp. 3994–95; HWJ statement, Mar. 24, 1930, Part III, Carton 25, HWJ Papers.

14. HWJ to Hiram Johnson, Jr., Feb. 14, 15, 1930. There are, Johnson sarcastically wrote, "three sacrosanct elements in our national and international life now, the Hughes family, the Root office and the House of Morgan. What this nation will do when all the men of these three elements have been depleted in the matter of appointments to the public office and diplomatic posts, God only knows." HWJ to C. K. McClatchy, Feb. 15, 1930.

15. Richard L. Watson, Jr., "The Defeat of Judge Parker: A Study in Pressure Groups and Politics," *Mississippi Valley Historical Review* 50:2 (Sept. 1963), pp. 213–34.

16. HWJ statement, Dec. 10, 1930; HWJ statement (Movietone News) Dec. 13, 1930, HWJ radio address, CBS, Dec. 20, 1930, all in Part III, Carton 25, HWJ Papers; *Cong. Record,* 71st Cong., 3rd sess. (Jan. 5, 1931), pp. 1370–71; HWJ to Hiram Johnson, Jr., Apr. 1, 1929, Jan. 17, Dec. 12, 1930; HWJ to C. K. McClatchy, Apr. 4, 1929, Dec. 22, 1930; HWJ to Ickes, Apr. 11, 1929, Jan. 17, 1930; HWJ to J. T. Adams, Jan. 17, 1930; HWJ to Albert Lasker, Jan. 17, Feb. 24, 1930; HWJ to George Wharton Pepper, Jan. 17, Dec. 13, 31, 1930; HWJ to Fraser Edwards, June 19, 1931; Albert Lasker to HWJ, Jan. 26, Mar. 1, 1930; *New York Times,* Apr. 1, 8, 1929, July 6, Dec. 3, 1930, Nov. 21, 1931.

17. *New York Times,* Mar. 10, 30, 1930; HWJ to Neylan, May 3, 1932.

18. Raymond G. O'Connor, *Perilous Equilibrium: The United States and the London Naval Conference of 1930* (Lawrence, Kans., 1962).

19. HWJ to C. K. McClatchy, May 3, 30, 1930; *New York Times,* Apr. 25, 1930. See also HWJ to Hiram Johnson, Jr., Apr. 19, 1930; Capt. Dudley Knox to HWJ, May 30, June 12, 22, 1930; HWJ to boys, May 3, 17, 24, 1930.

20. Senate Committee on Foreign Relations, *Hearings on Treaty on the Limitation on Naval Armaments,* 71st Cong., 2nd sess. (1930), pp. 35–62, 79–88, 94–95, 115, 134–50, 155–58, 167–68, 176–79, 194–99, 212–13, 219, 235–38, 244, 247–48, 257–61, 267, 273–339; HWJ to Hiram Johnson, Jr., May 30, 1930; HWJ to boys, June 11, 14, 27, 1930; HWJ to C. K. McClatchy, May 30, June 9, 24, 1930. See also *New York Times,* May 15, 16, 23, 27, 30, June 9, 10, 1930.

21. The Senate did agree to call for documents, but also, over Johnson's objections, agreed to limit their request to materials that "were not incompatible with the public interest." Hoover, while willing to allow limited private examination of the documents, refused to make them public. For Johnson's comments, see *Cong. Record,* 71st Cong., Special Session (July 7–10, 1930), pp. 25–32;

49–50, 53, 61–62, 82–85, 90. See also *New York Times*, June 3, 5, 6, 8, 12, 18, July 8–12, 1930.

22. HWJ to Hiram Johnson, Jr., July 4, 1930; HWJ to C. K. McClatchy, June 29, July 4, 12, 21, 1930; *Cong. Record*, 71st Cong., Special Session (July 11, 17, 18, 19, 21, 1930), pp. 110–15, 222–30, 248–59, 295–306, 324–26; *New York Times*, July 6, 12, 15, 1930.

23. *Cong. Record*, 71st Cong., Special Session (July 18, 1930), p. 252.

24. *New York Times*, July 19–22, 1930; HWJ to boys, July 21, 1930; HWJ to C. K. McClatchy, July 21, 1930.

25. Ickes to HWJ, Mar. 9, 1929.

26. HWJ to boys, Oct. 26, 1929. See also HWJ to boys, Nov. 2, 1929; HWJ to Archibald Johnson, Nov. 1, 23, 1929; HWJ to Hiram Johnson, Jr., Nov. 2, 16, 1929.

27. HWJ to Archibald Johnson, Nov. 16, 23, 1929; HWJ to Hiram Johnson, Jr., Nov. 23, 1930; HWJ to James Nourse, Nov. 23, 1929.

28. HWJ to Doherty, Nov. 23, 1929; HWJ to boys, Jan. 15, 1930.

29. HWJ to George Moses, Aug. 14, 1930; HWJ to Edgar Luce, Sept. 5, 1930; HWJ to Hichborn, Oct. 13, 1930, Hichborn Papers.

30. Jordan A. Schwarz, *The Interregnum of Despair; Hoover, Congress, and the Depression* (Urbana, Ill., 1970).

31. HWJ to Hiram Johnson, Jr., Dec. 12, 1930; HWJ to Archibald Johnson, Jan. 2, 7, 1931; HWJ to C. K. McClatchy, Dec. 7, 13, 28, 1930, Jan. 25, 1931.

32. HWJ to Hiram Johnson III, Dec. 30, 1930. See also HWJ to Archibald Johnson, Dec. 6, 1931; HWJ to Hiram Johnson, Jr., Dec. 6, 1931.

33. HWJ to Fraser Edwards, Oct. 3, 1930. To the Senate Johnson stated: "I have read, and read with the utmost interest, aye, with enthusiasm which I could not adequately describe, the statements of gentlemen who came here from various parts of the United States—multi-millionaires—who told us that there was nothing but prosperity in the country, that everything was all right; and the men who had lost their all in the stock market walked the streets afterward with their heads high, perfectly confident in the assurances that they were given in Washington that they were all right, that they were entirely mistaken when they had thought they had lost their fortunes." *Cong. Record*, 71st Cong., 2nd sess. (Mar. 3, 1930), p. 4611.

34. HWJ to C. K. McClatchy, Feb. 21, 1931. See also HWJ American Legion Convention Address, Long Beach, Aug. 31, 1931, Part III, Carton 25, HWJ Papers: "To equivocate about conditions, to pretend prosperity is just around the corner while supinely we watch increased suffering, is not only cruel but cowardly."

35. HWJ to C. K. McClatchy, Mar. 5, 1931.

36. David E. Hamilton, "Herbert Hoover and the Great Drought of 1930," *Journal of American History* 68:4 (Mar. 1982), pp. 850–75.

37. HWJ to Hiram Johnson, Jr., Feb. 8, 15, 1931; HWJ to Archibald Johnson, Feb. 8, 1931; HWJ to C. K. McClatchy, Feb. 8, 15, 1931; HWJ to W. B. Mathews, Feb. 8, 1931. See also *Cong. Record*, 71st Cong., 3rd sess. (Feb. 14, 1931), p. 4899.

38. HWJ to Hiram Johnson, Jr., Jan. 25, 1931; HWJ to C. K. McClatchy, Mar. 5, 1931; HWJ to Archibald Johnson, Jan. 31, 1931.

39. HWJ to Doherty, June 27, Nov. 21, 1931; *San Francisco Examiner*, June 25, 1931; *New York Times*, June 26, Aug. 23, Oct. 16, 1931; HWJ to Mary Connor, Oct. 16, 1931; HWJ statement, Aug. 23, 1931, Part III, Carton 25, HWJ Papers: "Cancellation has been decreed by our international bankers just as they decreed the moratorium. They are the dominant factor, not only in American financial life today, but in American political life. Their ownership extends to the leadership of both political parties. . . . Their political puppets poll-parrot their Pecksniffian phrases of saving Germany and helping America. They do neither. They protect only their own speculations and profits." See also HWJ statement, Oct. 15, 1931, Part III, Carton 25, HWJ Papers; HWJ to George O. MacGregor, July 1, 1931; HWJ to Fraser Edwards, June 27, 1931; HWJ to C. K. McClatchy, Oct. 9, 1931; HWJ to Hichborn, June 26, 1931; HWJ to Ickes, Oct. 29, 1931.

40. *Cong. Record*, 72nd Cong., 1st sess. (Dec. 21, 1931), pp. 1009–13. See also Harry E. Williams to HWJ, Aug. 27, 1931; HWJ to S. D. Meysenburg, Oct. 28, 1931; Prof. William W. Cumberland to HWJ, Nov. 27, 1931.

41. *Cong. Record*, 72nd Cong., 1st sess. (Dec. 21, 22, 1931), pp. 1009–13, 1077–86; HWJ to boys, Dec. 27, 1931, Apr. 17, 1932.

42. HWJ to C. K. McClatchy, Dec. 1, 1931; HWJ to boys, Dec. 12, 19, 1931.

43. HWJ to boys, Dec. 12, 27, 1931; HWJ to Hichborn, Dec. 27, 1931; HWJ statement, ca. Dec. 26, 1931, Part III, Carton 25, HWJ Papers; *New York Times*, Dec. 20, 24, 1931.

44. Senate Committee on Finance, 72nd Cong., 1st sess. (1932), Hearings, *Sale of Foreign Bonds or Securities in the United States*. The hearings lasted from December 1931 into February 1932; Johnson was the dominant figure throughout. See especially his examination of Otto Kahn (pp. 343–400), Clarence Dillon (pp. 458–501), James Speyer (pp. 605–43), Frederick Strauss and Henry Breck (pp. 1268–1326), and Victor Schoepperle (pp. 1623–1681), as well as his examination of H. Freeman Matthews (pp. 1787–1840) and Francis White (pp. 1862–1928), the last two representing the State Department. See also HWJ to boys, Dec. 12, 19, 1931, Jan. 9, 18, 1932; HWJ to Hiram Johnson, Jr., Mar. 21, 1932; HWJ to Archibald Johnson, Mar. 21, 1932; HWJ to Frank Devlin, Mar. 23, 1932; HWJ to C. K. McClatchy, Feb. 2, Mar. 19, 1932; *Cong. Record*, 72nd Cong., 1st sess. (Mar. 15, 1932), pp. 6052–62; *New York Times*, Dec. 10, 1931, Jan. 2, 7–9, 13, 15–17, 20, 21, 28, 29, 1932.

45. HWJ to Irving Martin, Feb. 15, 1932; Michael E. Parrish, *Securities Regulation and the New Deal* (New Haven, Conn., 1970), p. 83. See also HWJ to boys, Dec. 12, 19, 1931; HWJ to Hiram Johnson III, Mar. 27, 1932.

46. HWJ to boys, Jan. 23, 1932. The "damn laws are all made solely for the banks and the Wall Street people," Johnson complained. HWJ to Hiram Johnson, Jr., Feb. 29, 1932. "I cannot find that any of the so-called experts expect permanent results from the Reconstruction Corporation, or the new Federal Reserve Law about to be passed. Some, indeed, fear possible national bankruptcy from them." Hoover's goal, Johnson continued, was to postpone the crisis at least until after the November elections. HWJ to C. K. McClatchy, Feb. 14, 1932. See also HWJ to boys, Feb. 21, 1932.

47. *Cong. Record*, 72nd Cong., 1st sess. (Apr. 14, June 27, 1932), pp. 8205–7,

14016. "The foxy boys of the Republican Party," Johnson wrote, "and the cunning little 'me too's' of the Democratic Party are for the moment playing the Alphonse and Gaston act on governmental economy, from which each side hopes to emerge with some petty political advantage." HWJ to boys, Apr. 10, 24, 1932. See also HWJ to C. K. McClatchy, Apr. 24, 1932; HWJ to Irving Martin, Apr. 26, 1932.

48. *Cong. Record*, 72nd Cong., 1st sess. (June 1, 3, 27, 1932), pp. 11738, 11874–75, 11890–92, 14016; HWJ to boys, June 5, 1932; HWJ to Irving Martin, Apr. 26, 1932. See also *Cong. Record*, 72nd Cong., 2nd sess. (Feb. 6, 1933), pp. 3468–69.

49. HWJ to Hiram Johnson, Jr., Mar. 21, 1932; HWJ to C. K. McClatchy, Feb. 29, Mar. 6, 1932. See also *New York Times*, Aug. 23, 1931. "If ever it could be demonstrated that a party was not fit to govern and it was only fit to follow, that party is the present Democratic party," Johnson grumbled. HWJ to C. K. McClatchy, Feb. 29, 1932.

50. HWJ to C. K. McClatchy, Mar. 25, Apr. 3, 1932; HWJ to boys, Mar. 26, 1932.

51. Johnson observed of Long: "He is the apotheosis of vanity and egotism. He is totally irresponsible and a wholly bloviating blatherskite. He has, however, some shrewdness and some ability, and he has, apparently, one admirable trait, guts." In 1935 Johnson wrote: "He is a dirty fighter, unkempt and uncouth, uncultured and untutored, but as cunning as [a rodent] . . . with the glibness of the battered soap-box spieler." HWJ to C. K. McClatchy, Apr. 30, 1932; HWJ to Hiram Johnson, Jr., Mar. 17, 1935. See also HWJ to C. K. McClatchy, Jan. 16, 1933.

52. HWJ to Hiram Johnson, Jr., May 22, 1932; HWJ to C. K. McClatchy, May 28, 1932; *Cong. Record*, 72nd Cong., 1st sess. (May 26, 1932), pp. 11293, 11296; *New York Times*, May 17, 1932.

53. HWJ to C. K. McClatchy, Feb. 14, 1932; Schwarz, *Interregnum of Despair*, pp. 142–78.

54. *Cong. Record*, 72nd Cong., 1st sess. (Feb. 12, 1932), pp. 3810–12; *New York Times*, Feb. 13, 1932.

55. HWJ to boys, May 14, 1932, HWJ to C. K. McClatchy, May 14, 1932. See also David Burner, *Herbert Hoover: A Public Life* (New York, 1978), pp. 273–83.

56. HWJ to C. K. McClatchy, May 28, June 5, 1932; HWJ to boys, June 5, 12, 1932.

57. HWJ to C. K. McClatchy, June 19, 1932; HWJ to Hiram Johnson, Jr., June 18, 1932, May 13, 1935; HWJ to Archibald Johnson, June 19, 1932.

58. HWJ to C. K. McClatchy, June 19, 1932; HWJ to Archibald Johnson, June 19, 1932; HWJ to Hiram Johnson, Jr., June 18, 1932.

59. Burner, *Hoover*, pp. 273–76.

60. HWJ to C. K. McClatchy, July 17, 1932.

61. HWJ to C. K. McClatchy, May 11, 12, 14, 1932; *Cong. Record*, 72nd Cong., 1st sess. (May 5, 1932), pp. 9644–46.

62. HWJ to C. K. McClatchy, Feb. 2, Apr. 3, 1932; HWJ to Hiram Johnson, Jr., Mar. 21, 1932; HWJ to Frank Devlin, Mar. 23, 1932; HWJ to boys, Apr. 2, 1932.

63. *New York Times*, Nov. 20, 1931; HWJ to Irving Martin, Nov. 30, 1931.

64. HWJ to C. K. McClatchy, Dec. 1, 1931; HWJ to boys, Nov. 22, Dec. 27, 1931; HWJ to Hiram Johnson, Jr., Nov. 29, 1931; HWJ to Archibald Johnson, Nov. 27, 1931.

65. Ickes to HWJ, June 19, Nov. 5, 9, 20, Dec. 7, 11, 1931, Jan. 18, 28, 29, 30, 1932. On Ickes's role, see Linda J. Lear, *Harold L. Ickes: The Aggressive Progressive, 1874–1933* (New York, 1981), pp. 346–49; T. H. Watkins, *Righteous Pilgrim: The Life and Times of Harold L. Ickes, 1874–1952* (New York, 1990), pp. 260–61.

66. Ickes to HWJ, Nov. 9, 20, 28, 1931.

67. Ickes to HWJ, Dec. 14, 1931. See also Ickes to HWJ, Jan. 18, 28, Feb. 3, 6, 8, 9, 16, 1932.

68. Ickes to HWJ, Jan. 29, 1932. Although Ickes was certainly the most forceful advocate of Johnson's candidacy, he was not alone. See also Mary Connor to HWJ, May 13, 1931; Lowell Limpus to HWJ, June 1, 1931; Steve Early to HWJ, May 26, 1931; O. H. P. Shelley to HWJ, June 20, 1931; *New York Times*, Jan. 11, Feb. 2, 1932; *San Francisco Chronicle*, Jan. 12, Nov. 11, 16, 1931.

69. HWJ to boys, Nov. 22, 1931, Jan. 23, 1932.

70. HWJ to Ickes, Nov. 13, 23, Dec. 28, 1931; Ickes to HWJ, Dec. 28, 1931.

71. HWJ to Bert Meek, Doherty, Neylan, Al McCabe, Dec. 26, 1931; HWJ to Hichborn, Dec. 27, 1931.

72. HWJ to Ickes, Dec. 28, 1931; HWJ to boys, Jan. 7, 1932; HWJ to C. K. McClatchy, Feb. 2, 1932; C. K. McClatchy to HWJ, Feb. 8, 1932.

73. HWJ to Doherty, Nov. 5, 1931; Doherty to HWJ, Dec. 28, 1931; HWJ to C. K. McClatchy, Feb. 2, 1932; HWJ to Irving Martin, Nov. 30, 1931, Feb. 15, 1932. If he had the means and the strength, Johnson admitted to McClatchy, he would enter the contest merely for the purpose of putting an end to Hoover's misrule. HWJ to C. K. McClatchy, Aug. 22, 1931.

74. HWJ to boys, Dec. 27, 1931, Jan. 9, Feb. 13, 29, 1932; HWJ to C. K. McClatchy, Feb. 2, 14, Mar. 17, 25, 1932; HWJ to Hiram Johnson, Jr., Feb. 29, 1932; HWJ to Archibald Johnson, Mar. 11, 1932; HWJ to Ickes, Feb. 13, 1932; HWJ to Irving Martin, Feb. 15, 1932.

75. HWJ to Frank Devlin, Mar. 23, 1932; HWJ to Archibald Johnson, Mar. 21, 1932.

76. HWJ to C. K. McClatchy, Feb. 14, Apr. 3, 9, 26, 1932; HWJ to Irving Martin, Apr. 26, 1932.

77. HWJ to C. K. McClatchy, Feb. 14, Apr. 26, June 8, 1932; HWJ to boys, Apr. 15, 17, May 1, 1932; HWJ to Irving Martin, Apr. 26, 1932.

78. As early as 1930 Johnson described Roosevelt as standing apart from the conservative Democratic party leadership. See HWJ to C. K. McClatchy, Dec. 28, 1930; HWJ to Ickes, Oct. 29, 1931. Roosevelt's public disavowal of the league came in February 1932 in a speech before the New York State Grange. Johnson's comments on the primary campaign can be found in HWJ to boys, May 1, 7, 1932; HWJ to C. K. McClatchy, Mar. 17, Apr. 3, 9, 24, 30, May 7, 12, June 5, 26, 1932; HWJ to Frank Devlin, Mar. 23, 1932; HWJ to Archibald Johnson, June 26, 1932.

79. *New York Times*, July 5, 1932; HWJ to C. K. McClatchy, July 8, 1932; HWJ to boys, July 9, 1932.

80. HWJ to C. K. McClatchy, July 3, 1932; HWJ to Hiram Johnson, Jr., July 3, 1932; HWJ to Archibald Johnson, July 3, 1932. See also Marty Hamilton, "Bull Moose Plays an Encore: Hiram Johnson and the Presidential Campaign of 1932," *California Historical Society Quarterly* 41 : 3 (Sept. 1962), pp. 211–21.

81. HWJ to Hiram Johnson, Jr., July 9, 1932; HWJ to C. K. McClatchy, July 8, 1932; HWJ to Ickes, July 9, 1932; *New York Times*, July 8, 1932.

82. *San Francisco Examiner*, Sept. 22, 1932; *San Francisco Chronicle*, July 26, Sept. 23, 1932; HWJ to E. M. Norton, Sept. 26, 1932.

83. *New York Times*, Sept. 23, 24, 1932.

84. HWJ to E. P. Clarke, Oct. 14, 1932; *New York Times*, Oct. 13, 15, 17, 1932.

85. HWJ to George Rockwell Brown, Oct. 21, 1932.

86. Rowell to Philip Bancroft, Oct. 25, 1932, Bancroft Papers. See also Irving Martin to Philip Bancroft, Oct. 25, 1932; Philip Bancroft to M. B. Harris, Oct. 28, 1932, both in Bancroft Papers.

87. *New York Times*, Oct. 29, Nov. 3, 5, 1932; *San Francisco Examiner*, Oct. 29, Nov. 2, 1932; *Sacramento Bee*, Oct. 28, 29, 1932.

88. HWJ to Franklin Roosevelt, Nov. 9, 1932; HWJ to James Farley, Nov. 9, 1932. See also *New York Times*, Nov. 10, 1932.

89. HWJ to William G. McAdoo, Nov. 19, 1932. Johnson had been silent in the senatorial contest, though he confessed privately that he favored the election of Tallant Tubbs, the liberal state senator from San Francisco who had edged out Shortridge in the Republican primary. HWJ to Archibald Johnson, Nov. 3, 5, 1932.

90. HWJ to James Farley, Nov. 14, 1932.

91. *Cong. Record*, 72nd Cong., 2nd sess. (Jan. 4, 9, 1933), pp. 1268–79, 1424–25; *New York Times*, Nov. 30, 1932, Jan. 5, 10, 26, 1933; HWJ to Hiram Johnson, Jr., Jan. 7, 1933; HWJ to C. K. McClatchy, Jan. 9, 15, 1933.

92. "I am extremely anxious to see this administration a success, and short of sacrificing my most cherished principles, I will do anything within my power to aid it," Johnson affirmed. At the same time, he noted, "the Lord, I fear, made me a natural rebel, or as I would prefer to phrase it, with a passionate independence." HWJ to C. K. McClatchy, Dec. 11, 1932. McClatchy agreed: "You have to be a free lance, Hiram, in order to be happy." C. K. McClatchy to HWJ, Dec. 14, 1932. See also HWJ to C. K. McClatchy, Dec. 18, 1932, Feb. 12, 1933; HWJ to boys, Dec. 18, 1932, Jan. 29, 1933.

93. HWJ to Hiram Johnson, Jr., Jan. 22, 1933; HWJ to C. K. McClatchy, Jan. 29, 1933; HWJ to Archibald Johnson, Jan. 21, 1933.

94. HWJ to Ickes, Feb. 1, 1933. See also HWJ to boys, Jan. 29, Feb. 12, 1933; HWJ to Hiram Johnson, Jr., Feb. 4, 1933; HWJ to C. K. McClatchy, Feb. 4, 12, 1933; HWJ to Neylan, Feb. 24, 1933, Neylan Papers.

95. HWJ to boys, Dec. 11, 1932; HWJ to C. K. McClatchy, Dec. 11, 1932, Jan. 29, 1933; HWJ to Hiram Johnson, Jr., Dec. 28, 1932; HWJ to Frank Snook, Jan. 28, 1933.

96. HWJ to boys, Oct. 10, 1921; HWJ to Neylan, Oct. 26, 1921; HWJ to Hichborn, Dec. 1, 1921, Oct. 25, 1926; HWJ to C. K. McClatchy, June 19, 1921, Apr. 14, 1930; HWJ to Ickes, Mar. 8, 1931; Hichborn to HWJ, Nov. 23, 1921; HWJ to Hiram Johnson, Jr., Jan. 18, 1930.

97. Gilman M. Ostrander, *The Prohibition Movement in California, 1848–1933* (Berkeley, 1957). See especially HWJ to Arthur Briggs, Jan. 7, 1930. "I detest the anti-saloon league," Johnson wrote. "I think its leaders, and I differentiate between them and its followers, are not only narrow, bigoted, and intolerant, but utterly corrupt." HWJ to boys, Nov. 13, 1926.

98. HWJ to Archibald Johnson, Apr. 1, 1929, Jan. 18, 1930; HWJ to Hiram Johnson, Jr., Jan. 18, 1930.

99. HWJ to boys, Feb. 19, 1933; HWJ to Hiram Johnson, Jr., May 21, June 12, 1932; HWJ to C. K. McClatchy, May 12, 21, 28, Dec. 11, 18, 1932, Feb. 19, 1933; William Mikulich to HWJ, May 20, June 16, 1932.

100. HWJ to boys, Mar. 5, 1933.

101. HWJ to boys, Mar. 12, 1933; HWJ to Neylan, Mar. 10, 1933.

102. HWJ to Hiram Johnson, Jr., Mar. 14, 1933; Frank Freidel, *Franklin D. Roosevelt: Launching the New Deal* (Boston, 1973), pp. 232–33; Marquis James and Bessie R. James, *Biography of a Bank: The Story of the Bank of America* (New York, 1954), pp. 362–74. See also Russell M. Posner, "The Bank of Italy and the 1926 Campaign in California," *California Historical Society Quarterly* 37:3, 4 (Sept., Dec., 1958), pp. 267–75, 347–58; Russell M. Posner, "A. P. Giannini and the 1934 Campaign in California," *Historical Society of Southern California Quarterly* 39:2 (June 1957), pp. 190–201; Russell Posner, "State Politics and the Bank of America, 1920–1934," (Ph.D. diss., University of California, Berkeley, 1956).

103. HWJ to Hiram Johnson, Jr., Jan. 22, 1933, emphasis in original.

104. HWJ to Hiram Johnson, Jr., Apr. 1, 1933; HWJ to boys, Mar. 19, 1933; HWJ to C. K. McClatchy, Jan. 29, 1933; HWJ to J. Earl Langdon, Mar. 15, 1933; HWJ to Phil Swing, Apr. 30, 1933; HWJ to Edson, Apr. 20, 1933, Edson Papers. "I do not see how any living soul can last physically going the pace that he is going, and mentally any one of us would be a psycopathic [*sic*] case if we undertook to do what he is doing," Johnson wrote. Nevertheless, he added, Roosevelt demonstrated nothing but the utmost good nature. HWJ to boys, Mar. 12, 1933. See also *Cong. Record*, 73rd Cong., 2nd sess. (Mar. 27, 1934), p. 5506.

105. *Cong. Record*, 73rd Cong., 1st sess. (May 31, June 12, 1933), pp. 4651–55, 5738; HWJ to boys, June 16, 1933; HWJ to Hiram Johnson, Jr., June 18, 1933. Earlier, at the time of the passage of the budget bill, Johnson had unsuccessfully joined in support of amendments to moderate its impact.

106. HWJ to Hiram Johnson, Jr., Mar. 31, 1934; HWJ to Neylan, Mar. 30, 1934. See also Ronald L. Feinman, *Twilight of Progressivism: The Western Republican Senators and the New Deal* (Baltimore, 1981); Ronald A. Mulder, *The Insurgent Progressives in the United States Senate and the New Deal, 1933–1939* (New York, 1979).

107. *Cong. Record*, 73rd Cong., 1st sess. (Apr. 5, 1933), pp. 1292–93.

108. Ellis W. Hawley, *The New Deal and the Problem of Monopoly: A Study in Economic Ambivalence* (Princeton, N.J., 1966). In addition, the conference committee had eliminated an amendment, sponsored by La Follette, that required the public disclosure of income tax returns of businesses under code authority.

109. HWJ to boys, Jan. 29, Apr. 16, 23, 1933.

110. HWJ to Hiram Johnson, Jr., Jan. 28, 1934, Feb. 24, 1935; HWJ to boys, Jan. 29, Apr. 23, June 4, 1933; *Cong. Record*, 73rd Cong., 1st sess. (June 3, 1933), pp. 4921, 4927, 4929.

111. *Cong. Record*, 73rd Cong., 1st sess. (May 11, June 6, 1933), pp. 3242–44, 5086–89; HWJ to C. K. McClatchy, Feb. 9, 1934.

112. *Cong. Record*, 73rd Cong., 2nd sess. (May 14, 1934), pp. 8735–39, 8762; *New York Times*, May 13, 15, 1934; HWJ to Franklin Roosevelt, May 28, 1933.

113. *Cong. Record*, 73rd Cong., 2nd sess. (Feb. 2, 5, 1934), pp. 1828–29, 1915–18; HWJ to C. K. McClatchy, Feb. 23, 1934; HWJ to Hiram Johnson, Jr., Feb. 11, 1934; *New York Times*, Feb. 10, 22, 1934. It is this sort of action, Johnson wrote to McClatchy, that endears Roosevelt to me.

114. HWJ to Hiram Johnson, Jr., Apr. 7, 24, May 16, 19, 1934; HWJ to C. K. McClatchy, May 11, 1934; *New York Times*, May 9, 10, 16, 1934.

115. *New York Times*, Jan. 28, 29, Feb. 10, Mar. 23, 1932.

116. HWJ to boys, Apr. 16, 1933; HWJ to Hiram Johnson, Jr., May 14, Aug. 26, 1933; HWJ to FDR, Aug. 26, 1933; Louis Howe to HWJ, June 27, 1934; Richard Washburn Child to FDR, May 11, 1933; Franklin Roosevelt to HWJ, July 31, 1933, Aug. 26, 1934; HWJ to L. E. Hanchett, July 20, Nov. 8, 1933; Parrish, *Securities Regulation*, pp. 87–107; Freidel, *Launching the New Deal*, pp. 349–50; *New York Times*, Apr. 7, 16, 25, May 9, 1933. In its stead, the Foreign Bondholders Protective Council was formed as a private organization under the direction of J. Reuben Clark. It was, as Michael Parrish concludes, a poor substitute.

117. *Cong. Record*, 72nd Cong., 2nd sess. (Jan. 4, 9, 1933), pp. 1268–79, 1424–25. In July 1932, at the Lausanne conference, the European allies agreed to scale down German reparations to less than 10 percent of the original sum due. In return, they demanded comparable relief from Washington. For Johnson's response to the Lausanne conference, see *Cong. Record*, 72nd Cong., 1st sess. (July 12, 1932), pp. 15082–85.

118. HWJ to boys, Apr. 12, 1933. See also HWJ to Hiram Johnson, Jr., Jan. 7, 1933; HWJ to C. K. McClatchy, Dec. 20, 1932, Jan. 29, Feb. 12, 1933, Mar. 11, 1934.

119. A second major modification specifically allowed agencies of the federal government, such as the Export-Import Bank, to extend loans abroad.

120. FDR to Fred I. Kent, May 22, 1934, in Edgar B. Nixon, ed., *Franklin D. Roosevelt and Foreign Affairs* (Cambridge, Mass., 1969), vol. 2, p. 119.

121. HWJ to FDR, Jan. 29, 1934; HWJ to Hiram Johnson, Jr., Feb. 4, 11, Apr. 7, 1934; John Chalmers Vinson, "War Debts and Peace Legislation: The Johnson Act of 1934," *Mid-America* 50:3 (July 1968), pp. 206–22; *New York Times*, June 15, 1933, Jan. 12–14, 18, 30, Feb. 2, 3, Mar. 15, Apr. 1, 4, 5, 1934.

122. *Cong. Record*, 73rd Cong., 2nd sess. (May 30, June 4, 1934), pp. 9959–64; 10370–71, 10386; HWJ to Neylan, Apr. 3, 7, 1934; HWJ to Hiram Johnson, Jr., Mar. 3, Apr. 15, June 2, 1934; HWJ to C. K. McClatchy, Mar. 11, 25, May 11, 1934; HWJ to Raymond Moley, Feb. 19, 1935; *New York Times*, May 19, 31, 1934. Hull, Johnson noted following his selection as secretary of state, was "a pleasant, kindly disposed individual, utterly colorless, wholly without position

in the [Senate]." Press descriptions of him as "a tower of strength," he continued, had elicited laughter from his colleagues. HWJ to C. K. McClatchy, Feb. 26, 1933.

123. HWJ to C. K. McClatchy, June 26, 1932.

124. HWJ to Ickes, July 26, 1933; HWJ to Hiram Johnson, Jr., May 7, 1934.

125. HWJ to Charles McNary, July 28, 1933. See also HWJ to Phil Swing, July 31, 1934; HWJ to C. K. McClatchy, Dec. 6, 1933; HWJ to Major Edmund Wynne, July 14, 1933.

126. Mark Rose to HWJ, July 29, Sept. 12, 1934; W. A. Johnstone to HWJ, Nov. 17, 1933; HWJ to Hiram Johnson, Jr., May 7, 1934.

127. HWJ to Ickes, Oct. 17, 1933; HWJ to Hiram Johnson, Jr., Jan. 2, 1934.

128. HWJ to Phil Swing, Nov. 7, 1933. See also Phil Swing to HWJ, Aug. 30, Oct. 21, Nov. 6, 1933; HWJ to Ickes, Oct. 21, 1933; Ickes to HWJ, Oct. 23, 1933; H. N. Savage to HWJ, Oct. 25, 1933; *The Secret Diary of Harold L. Ickes* (New York, 1953), entry for Oct. 23, 1933.

129. On the project, see FDR to HWJ, Nov. 4, 1935; HWJ to Hiram Johnson, Jr., June 24, 1935; HWJ to Walter Jones, June 26, 1935; HWJ to Ickes, Feb. 16, 1936; HWJ to Ed Hyatt, Mar. 2, 1936; Sacramento Chamber of Commerce to HWJ, June 26, 1935.

130. HWJ to George Young, Oct. 25, 1933; HWJ to Neylan, Jan. 9, 1934; Ickes to HWJ, Nov. 16, 1933; W. A. Johnstone to HWJ, Nov. 17, 1933; *Sacramento Bee*, Nov. 22, 1933.

131. *New York Times*, Nov. 30, 1932; HWJ to Hiram Johnson, Jr., Dec. 4, 1932; HWJ to Ickes, Dec. 2, 1932.

132. HWJ to boys, Mar. 12, 1933; HWJ to C. K. McClatchy, Feb. 26, 1933.

133. HWJ to C. K. McClatchy, Dec. 4, 1932; HWJ to Ickes, Dec. 7, 1932; HWJ to boys, Dec. 11, 1932.

134. HWJ to Hiram Johnson, Jr., July 13, 1935. See also *Cong. Record*, 73rd Cong., 1st sess. (Apr. 28, 1933), p. 2541.

135. FDR to HWJ, Nov. 5, 1933; HWJ to C. K. McClatchy, Nov. 9, 1933. See also FDR to Minnie Johnson, July 16, 1935.

136. HWJ to boys, Feb. 12, Apr. 12, 1933. See also Freidel, *Launching the New Deal*, pp. 384–85.

137. HWJ to Hiram Johnson, Jr., May 21, 1933; HWJ to boys, May 26, 1933; HWJ to Irving Martin, May 28, 1933; *New York Times*, May 22, 1933.

138. Ickes, *Secret Diary*, entries for May 24, 26, 1933.

139. HWJ to boys, June 4, 1933. See also *New York Times*, May 22, 25, 1933; HWJ to Raymond Moley, Dec. 26, 1933; HWJ to Charles McNary, July 28, 1933.

140. HWJ to W. N. Burkhardt, Dec. 22, 1932; HWJ to William Mikulich, Dec. 26, 1932; HWJ to C. K. McClatchy, Jan. 29, 1933; HWJ to boys, Mar. 19, 1933; HWJ to Hiram Johnson, Jr., May 2, 5, 6, 14, 1933; HWJ to Neylan, Feb. 6, Apr. 28, May 1, 19, Oct. 6, 1933; HWJ to J. Earl Langdon, May 14, 1933; Neylan to HWJ, Feb. 2, May 1, 19, 1933, in Neylan Papers.

141. William Mikulich to HWJ, Apr. 9, 15, May 7, 15, 23, 1933; HWJ to William Mikulich, Apr. 1, 1933; HWJ to Hiram Johnson, Jr., Apr. 1, 1933; John D. Elliott to William Gibbs McAdoo, Apr. 25, 1933; *New York Times*, May 14, 21, 1933.

142. William Mikulich to HWJ, May 23, 1933; HWJ to Hiram Johnson, Jr., Jan. 15, 21, 23, 24, 1934; HWJ to Doherty, Oct. 9, Nov. 8, 29, Dec. 8, 1933; HWJ to C. K. McClatchy, Oct. 10, Nov. 14, 24, 1933; Mar. 2, 1934; HWJ to Neylan, Oct. 6, 1933; HWJ to Bert Meek, Jan. 21, 1934; HWJ to Walter Jones, Mar. 2, 1934; Doherty to HWJ, Nov. 28, Dec. 7, 1933; Neylan to HWJ, Jan. 9, 27, 1934.

143. HWJ to Al McCabe, Jan. 28, Feb. 22, 1934; HWJ to Hiram Johnson, Jr., Jan. 28, 29, Feb. 21, 25, 1934; HWJ to C. K. McClatchy, Feb. 1, 1934; *New York Times*, Jan. 27, 31, 1934. Farley had made a similar comment to Ickes much earlier. Ickes, *Secret Diary*, entry for Apr. 12, 1933. In December 1933 Raymond Moley, speaking before the California Democratic Luncheon Club, gave Johnson similar support. *New York Times*, Dec. 2, 1933.

144. HWJ to Hiram Johnson, Jr., Mar. 3, 1934; HWJ to Walter Jones, Mar. 23, 1934.

145. HWJ to Walter Jones, Mar. 12, 23, 1934; HWJ to C. K. McClatchy, Apr. 13, 1934; HWJ to Franck Havenner, May 27, 1934; HWJ to Hiram Johnson, Jr., May 7, 1934.

146. C. K. McClatchy to HWJ, Feb. 26, 1934. See also C. K. McClatchy to HWJ, Dec. 5, 1933, Feb. 5, 1934; HWJ to Hiram Johnson, Jr., Mar. 25, Apr. 15, 29, 1934; HWJ to C. K. McClatchy, Apr. 13, 29, 1934.

147. HWJ to Hiram Johnson, Jr., May 22, 1934, Feb. 19, 1939; HWJ to Neylan, Apr. 13, 1934; Franck Havenner to HWJ, June 1, 6, 1934.

148. Doherty to HWJ, Nov. 11, 1933, June 14, 1934; Franck Havenner to HWJ, Apr. 7, 11, 1934; HWJ to Neylan, Mar. 11, May 27, June 9, 1934; HWJ to Walter Jones, Mar. 2, 12, 1934; Neylan to HWJ, Feb. 23, 1934.

149. HWJ to Hiram Johnson, Jr., June 15, 1934; HWJ to Franck Havenner, May 27, 1934; HWJ to Doherty, June 10, 1934; HWJ to Neylan, May 27, June 9, 12, 1934; HWJ to C. K. McClatchy, June 3, 1934; Franck Havenner to HWJ, June 1, 6, 1934; Neylan to HWJ, June 1, 11, 1934.

150. *New York Times*, June 24, 1934. See also HWJ to Hiram Johnson, Jr., June 23, 1940.

151. By March many Republican officeholders had already endorsed Johnson. See *Sacramento Bee*, Feb. 12, 16, Mar. 4, 1934; *San Francisco Examiner*, Feb. 23, 1934. Louis Mayer, chairman of the Republican State Central Committee, remained silent, but 35 members of the Executive Committee, meeting at the Palace Hotel in San Francisco, extended their overtures to Johnson. Doubtless their solicitations were also shaped by concern over the gubernatorial race. Bert Meek, following conversations with the conservative wing, understood that they would remain inactive if Johnson stayed out of that contest. See HWJ to Hiram Johnson, Jr., Feb. 4, 1934; HWJ to C. K. McClatchy, Feb. 9, Apr. 7, 1934. Characteristically, Johnson dismissed the assurances voiced by his supporters. HWJ to Hiram Johnson, Jr., Feb. 11, 25, 1934; HWJ to Neylan, Mar. 25, 1934; HWJ to C. K. McClatchy, Apr. 29, 1934; C. K. McClatchy to HWJ, Feb. 13, 1934; Neylan to HWJ, Feb. 12, June 11, 1934; Eustace Cullinan to HWJ, May 4, 1934.

152. Percy G. West to Walter Jones, ca. Mar. 7, 1934; Doherty to HWJ, Nov. 11, 1934; Neylan to HWJ, June 11, 1934; HWJ to Hiram Johnson, Jr., Apr. 15, 1934.

153. HWJ to Edgar Luce, Phil Swing, Irving Martin, Walter Jones, William Jerome, H. R. McLaughlin, July 31, 1934.

154. Edgar Luce to HWJ, Aug. 3, 1934; HWJ to Ralph Swing, Aug. 9, 15, 1934; Ralph Swing to HWJ, Aug. 6, 14, 1934.

155. Johnson's Republican opponent was Richard Rust, a onetime Democrat. Even the *Los Angeles Times* stood aloof, making no recommendations, but it did remind its readers that the "record of the pseudo-Republican incumbent, Hiram W. Johnson, is notorious." *Los Angeles Times*, Aug. 28, 1934.

156. James Farley to HWJ, Sept. 27, 1934; *Sacramento Bee*, Sept. 4, 1934; *New York Times*, Sept. 4, 1934; Paul Leake to HWJ, Sept. 9, 1934.

157. HWJ to Mary Connor, Nov. 8, 1934; HWJ to Hiram Johnson, Jr., Apr. 16, May 13, 1935; Huston Thompson to HWJ, June 6, 1935; *New York Times*, Jan. 1, 1935.

158. HWJ to Hiram Johnson, Jr., Dec. 22, 1934; *New York Times*, May 7, 21, 1935.

159. HWJ to George Wharton Pepper, Mar. 19, 24, 1934; HWJ to James Reed, Mar. 24, Apr. 5, 1934; HWJ to John Bassett Moore, Apr. 9, 1934; HWJ to Edwin Borchard, Apr. 16, 25, May 2, 1934; HWJ to Bainbridge Colby, May 3, 1934; HWJ to Neylan, Mar. 25, 1934; HWJ to C. K. McClatchy, Mar. 25, May 11, 1934; Edwin Borchard to HWJ, Apr. 20, 1934.

160. HWJ to Hiram Johnson, Jr., Dec. 22, 1934, Jan. 6, 31, 1935; HWJ to Edwin Borchard, Jan. 8, 1935; HWJ to William Mikulich, Feb. 2, 1935; HWJ to John Bassett Moore, Jan. 8, 1935; *New York Times*, Jan. 13, 1935.

161. HWJ to Edwin Borchard, Jan. 11, 25, 1935.

162. *Cong. Record*, 74th Cong., 1st sess. (Jan. 16, 25, 28, 29, 1935), pp. 479–90, 976–77, 1039–43, 1125; *New York Times*, Jan. 17, 1935.

163. *New York Times*, Feb. 3, 1935; Wayne C. Cole, *Roosevelt and the Isolationists, 1932–45* (Lincoln, Neb., 1983), p. 121. See also *Literary Digest*, Feb. 2, 1935, p. 11.

164. HWJ to Hiram Johnson, Jr., Jan. 6, 25, 26, 1935; HWJ to Edwin Borchard, Jan. 25, 1935.

165. Johnson later claimed that Minnie's complaints to syndicated columnist James Williams helped prompt the Hearst press to play a more forceful role. HWJ to Hiram Johnson, Jr., Jan. 31, 1935.

166. HWJ to Hiram Johnson, Jr., Jan. 31, Feb. 10, 1935; HWJ to William Mikulich, Feb. 2, 1935. Johnson was further displeased by the active role of Eleanor Roosevelt. See HWJ to Hiram Johnson, Jr., Jan. 26, 1935.

167. HWJ to Hiram Johnson, Jr., Jan. 31, 1935; HWJ to J. Reuben Clark, Feb. 3, 1935.

168. Ickes, *Secret Diary*, entry for Jan. 30, 1935.

169. HWJ to Hiram Johnson, Jr., Feb. 10, 24, 1935; HWJ to J. Reuben Clark, Feb. 3, 1935.

170. HWJ to Hiram Johnson, Jr., Dec. 22, 1934, Jan. 6, 26, Feb. 10, Mar. 3, 1935.

171. HWJ to Hiram Johnson, Jr., Apr. 7, 1935. See also *Cong. Record*, 74th Cong., 1st sess. (Feb. 14, 1935), p. 1920.

172. HWJ to Hiram Johnson, Jr., Feb. 24, Mar. 17, 1935.

173. HWJ to Hiram Johnson, Jr., Apr. 7, 1935. See also HWJ to Hiram Johnson, Jr., Apr. 28, May 5, 13, 1935.

174. HWJ to Hiram Johnson, Jr., July 21, 1935. See also HWJ to Hiram Johnson, Jr., May 5, June 14, 1935; *Cong. Record,* 74th Cong., 1st sess. (July 11, 17, 1935), pp. 11028–29, 11281–82.

175. HWJ to Hiram Johnson, Jr., Mar. 3, 10, Apr. 9, June 2, 16, 29, 1935.

176. HWJ to Hiram Johnson, Jr., Aug. 18, 1935.

177. HWJ to Hiram Johnson, Jr., Dec. 27, 1935.

178. HWJ to Hiram Johnson, Jr., Jan. 5, Feb. 2, Mar. 1, 29, Apr. 19, 1936.

179. HWJ to Hiram Johnson, Jr., Feb. 16, Mar. 22, 26, May 9, 1936. Al Smith, Johnson wrote, with his stream of assaults on Roosevelt, had become a "contemptible" figure. HWJ to Hiram Johnson, Jr., Feb. 2, 1936. See also C. K. McClatchy to HWJ, Feb. 22, 1936.

180. HWJ to Hiram Johnson, Jr., Jan. 18, 1936.

181. Minnie Johnson to Hiram Johnson, Jr., Aug. 21, 1936, emphasis in original. See also Minnie Johnson to Hiram Johnson, Jr., Aug. 11, Sept. 8, 1936; Minnie Johnson to Ed Lowry, Sept. 15, 1936; Mary Connor to Grove Fink, July 9, 18, 1936; Mary Connor to George McClellan, Oct. 2, 1936; HWJ to Neylan, July 4, 1936; HWJ to James Reed, Oct. 29, 1936; HWJ to Hiram Johnson, Jr., Aug. 2, Oct. 24, 31, 1936; Mary Connor to Hiram Johnson, Jr., July 7, 27, Aug. 3, 10, 1936.

182. Ickes, *Secret Diary,* entry for May 12, 1937; Minnie Johnson to Hiram Johnson, Jr., Oct. 22, 1936.

183. HWJ to Edward Lowry, Sept. 8, 1936.

184. HWJ to James Farley, Aug. 31, 1936; HWJ to Hiram Johnson, Jr., July 27, Aug. 24, 26, Sept. 6, 28, 1936. See also James Farley to Francis Heney, Sept. 26, 1936, Heney Papers.

185. Minnie Johnson to Hiram Johnson, Jr., Mar. 16, Aug. 26, Sept. 19, Oct. 5, 30, Nov. 9, 1936; Minnie Johnson to Anne Hard, Feb. 18, 1937; Minnie Johnson to Cora Older, May 11, 1937. But even Minnie could have second thoughts: unless Landon perks up, she wrote, she would vote "for the nigger," by whom she meant Roosevelt. Minnie Johnson to Ed Lowry, Aug. 13, 1936.

186. HWJ to Hiram Johnson, Jr., Mar. 15, Oct. 17, 1936. Charles McClatchy, who died before the election, had expressed similar ambivalence. He was for Roosevelt, he acknowledged, but hoped that after the election Roosevelt would "get ride of the Parlor Bolshevists surrounding him and also of the British-Americans in and out of his cabinet." C. K. McClatchy to HWJ, Jan. 7, Feb. 22, 1936.

187. HWJ to Hiram Johnson, Jr., Nov. 2, 1936.

188. HWJ to Hiram Johnson, Jr., Sept. 22, 1936.

189. HWJ to Hiram Johnson, Jr., Oct. 5, 1936.

190. HWJ to Hiram Johnson, Jr., Dec. 22, 1934. To Charles McClatchy, he wrote of the addiction of power: "There is something about power, when once a human being acquires it, that induces the irresistible impulse to acquire more. . . . I am fearful that this may be the effect on our President." HWJ to C. K. McClatchy, Mar. 11, 1934.

191. HWJ to Hiram Johnson, Jr., Nov. 10, 15, 1936.

192. Mary Connor to Hiram Johnson, Jr., Dec. 3, 20, 1936; HWJ to Hiram Johnson, Jr., Nov. 30, 1936, Feb. 6, 1937.

Chapter VIII: In Opposition

1. HWJ to Hiram Johnson, Jr., June 2, 1935, Jan. 11, 1936. In January 1936 Charles K. McClatchy began a campaign in the *Sacramento Bee* for a constitutional amendment to allow the recall of Supreme Court decisions. C. K. Mc-Clatchy to HWJ, Jan. 20, 1936.

2. HWJ to Doherty, Feb. 7, 1937; HWJ to H. L. Baggerly, Sept. 24, 1937; HWJ to Hiram Johnson, Jr., Feb. 14, May 7, 1937; HWJ to Raymond Moley, Mar. 13, 1937.

3. HWJ to Hiram Johnson, Jr., June 5, 23, 1937.

4. HWJ to Neylan, Mar. 26, 1937; HWJ to Hiram Johnson, Jr., June 5, 1937.

5. HWJ to Hiram Johnson, Jr., Feb. 6, Mar. 20, Apr. 9, June 12, 1937, May 28, 1938; HWJ to Neylan, Mar. 26, 1937.

6. *Cong. Record*, 75th Cong., 1st sess. (Mar. 17, 1937), p. 1644; *New York Times*, Mar. 18, 1937; Doherty to HWJ, Feb. 17, 1937; HWJ to Doherty, Feb. 7, 11, 1937.

7. HWJ to Hiram Johnson, Jr., Apr. 16, 1937.

8. *Cong. Record*, 75th Cong., 1st sess. (Mar. 17, Apr. 2, 1937), pp. 2337, 3087; HWJ to Albert Lasker, June 26, 1937; HWJ to Garret McEnerney, Apr. 21, 1937; HWJ to Hiram Johnson, Jr., Apr. 23, 1937; Minnie Johnson to Hiram Johnson, Jr., Mar. 17, 1937.

9. *Cong. Record*, 75th Cong., 1st sess. (Apr. 1, 2, 1937), pp. 3021, 3070.

10. HWJ to Albert Lasker, June 26, 1937; HWJ to Hiram Johnson, Jr., Apr. 9, 1937; *New York Times*, Apr. 2, 1937. The vote was 36 to 48.

11. HWJ to Hiram Johnson, Jr., Feb. 14, 20, 22, Mar. 7, 9, 15, 26, Apr. 9, 23, 1937; HWJ to Neylan, Mar. 26, Apr. 10, 1937. Johnson estimated that by mid-March he had received 20,000 letters, running 7 to 1 against the administration. HWJ to Doherty, Mar. 13, 1937.

12. *Cong. Record*, 75th Cong., 1st sess. (Feb. 26, 1937), p. 1644; HWJ to Neylan, Feb. 26, 1937; HWJ to Hiram Johnson, Jr., Feb. 27, 1937. Johnson was somewhat sympathetic to an amendment proposed by Wheeler that would have allowed Congress, after an intervening election, to override Supreme Court decisions, but, he noted, it was inappropriate to push for the measure during the court-reorganization fight. HWJ to Hiram Johnson, Jr., Feb. 22, 1937.

13. HWJ to Garret McEnerney, May 19, 1937; HWJ to Neylan, Apr. 13, 1937; HWJ to Hiram Johnson, Jr., Apr. 16, 1937.

14. *New York Times*, May 23, 1937; HWJ to Garret McEnerney, May 3, 7, 19, 23, June 26, July 7, 1937; HWJ to Raymond Moley, May 24, 1937; HWJ to Frank Snook, June 7, 1937; HWJ to Hiram Johnson, Jr., May 2, 1937; HWJ to Neylan, May 4, 1937, Neylan Papers.

15. HWJ to Hiram Johnson, Jr., May 21, June 12, 23, July 10, 1937; HWJ to Garret McEnerney, June 26, July 7, 1937.

16. *Cong. Record*, 75th Cong., 1st sess. (July 22, 1937), pp. 7375–82; HWJ to

Hiram Johnson, Jr., July 24, Aug. 1, 1937; *New York Times*, July 23, 1937. See also *New York Times*, Aug. 26, 1937.

17. *Cong. Record*, 75th Cong., 1st sess. (Aug. 12, 1937), p. 8732; HWJ to Hiram Johnson, Jr., Aug. 14, 1937; HWJ to Doherty, Aug. 23, 1937.

18. *Cong. Record*, 75th Cong., 1st sess. (Aug. 17, 1937), pp. 9101–2; HWJ to Garret McEnerney, May 20, 23, 1937; Garret McEnerney to HWJ, May 23, 1937; HWJ to H. C. Kaylor, Oct. 6, 1937; HWJ to Lulu Leppo, Oct. 8, 1937.

19. James T. Patterson, *Congressional Conservatism and the New Deal: The Growth of the Conservative Coalition in Congress, 1933–1939* (Lexington, Ky., 1967); HWJ to Raymond Moley, Mar. 13, 1937.

20. Ickes to Raymond Robins, Sept. 18, 1939, Robins Papers, as quoted in Ronald A. Mulder, *The Insurgent Progressives in the United States Senate and the New Deal, 1933–1939* (New York, 1979), p. 305. See also *The Secret Diary of Harold L. Ickes: The Inside Struggle* (New York, 1954), entry for Feb. 14, 1937.

21. HWJ to Hiram Johnson, Jr., Mar. 5, May 28, 1938.

22. HWJ to Hiram Johnson, Jr., Aug. 1, 1937. See also HWJ to Hiram Johnson, Jr., May 29, 1937.

23. HWJ to Hiram Johnson, Jr., Feb. 26, Mar. 19, 26, Apr. 2, 1938. Even as an enthusiastic "New Dealer," Johnson had been unwilling to allow the president free rein in the reorganization of executive departments. See *Cong. Record*, 73rd Cong., 1st sess. (June 10, 1933), pp. 5600–5602, 5618.

24. HWJ to Doherty, Mar. 22, 24, 1938. The vote was 49 to 42.

25. *Cong. Record*, 75th Cong., 3rd sess. (Mar. 30, 1938), p. 4363.

26. HWJ to Hiram Johnson, Jr., Apr. 2, 1938.

27. HWJ to Doherty, Apr. 11, 1938; HWJ to Hiram Johnson, Jr., Apr. 10, 1938.

28. *Cong. Record*, 75th Cong., 3rd sess. (June 1, 1938), p. 7815. See also *Cong. Record*, 75th Cong., 1st sess. (Aug. 16, 1937), pp. 8950–51; HWJ to Hichborn, July 6, 1938.

29. HWJ to Hiram Johnson, Jr., Apr. 16, June 4, 1938; *Cong. Record*, 75th Cong., 3rd sess. (June 1, 1938), pp. 7826–27.

30. HWJ to Hiram Johnson, Jr., Jan. 28, 1939; HWJ to Doherty, Jan. 30, 1939. See also David L. Porter, *Congress and the Waning of the New Deal* (New York, 1980), pp. 61–88.

31. HWJ to Howard C. Rowley, Aug. 1, 1938; HWJ to Hiram Johnson, Jr., Apr. 16, June 4, 1938.

32. *Cong. Record*, 75th Cong., 2nd sess. (Dec. 7, 10, 17, 1937), pp. 986–87, 1243–45, 1768; 75th Cong., 3rd sess. (Feb. 10, 11, 1938), pp. 1764–65, 1871–73; HWJ to Hiram Johnson, Jr., Dec. 3, 18, 1937; HWJ to Doherty, Dec. 13, 1937; *New York Times*, Dec. 8, 1937.

33. HWJ to Hiram Johnson, Jr., Feb. 12, 1938. In fact Johnson's arguments were similar to those he had expressed during the debate over conscription in 1917. Then too, the issue had been regimentation both of the individual and of society. The McNary amendment failed by a vote of 51 to 25. Among those who stood with Johnson in opposition to the final bill were La Follette, Nye, and Shipstead. The vote was 56 to 31.

34. HWJ to Harry Byrd, Aug. 13, 1938.

35. HWJ to Harry Byrd, Aug. 18, Sept. 2, 14, 1938; HWJ to Charles McNary, Sept. 7, 1938; HWJ to Bennett Champ Clark, Aug. 1, 1938; HWJ to Patrick McCarran, July 18, 1938; HWJ to Frederick Van Nuys, July 15, 1938; HWJ to Gerald Nye, July 12, 1938; HWJ to Hiram Johnson, Jr., June 4, 1938.

36. McAdoo, Johnson wrote, had a "Machiavellian mind." HWJ to Hiram Johnson, Jr., May 13, 1934. See also William Gibbs McAdoo to HWJ, Oct. 11, Nov. 29, 1935; HWJ to Mary Connor, Dec. 14, 1935; HWJ to Doherty, Oct. 23, 1933, Aug. 7, Sept. 11, 1937, June 23, 1938; HWJ to Hiram Johnson, Jr., Jan. 24, May 6, 1938; HWJ to boys, Mar. 19, Apr. 1, 1933; HWJ to Neylan, Mar. 16, 1933; HWJ to William Mikulich, Mar. 18, 24, Apr. 1, 1933; HWJ to C. K. McClatchy, Feb. 1, 1934.

37. Ickes, *Secret Diary*, entry for Mar. 19, 1938; HWJ to William Fitzmaurice, May 14, June 24, 1938. See also HWJ to Hiram Johnson, Jr., May 13, 23, 1938; HWJ to Doherty, Apr. 11, May 13, 1938; HWJ to Neylan, May 13, 1938.

38. HWJ to Walter F. George, July 18, 1938; HWJ to Harry Byrd, Sept. 2, 1938; HWJ to Charles McNary, Sept. 7, 1938. See also Robert E. Burke, *Olson's New Deal for California* (Berkeley, 1953), pp. 21–22; Royce D. Delmatier, "The Rebirth of the Democratic Party in California, 1928–1938" (Ph.D. diss., University of California, Berkeley, 1955), pp. 244–47; and Ronald E. Chinn, "Democratic Party Politics in California, 1920–1956" (Ph.D. diss., University of California, Berkeley, 1958), pp. 115–20.

39. HWJ to Harry Byrd, Aug. 13, Sept. 2, 1938; *New York Times*, Oct. 25, 1938.

40. HWJ to John G. Townsend, Jr., Sept. 20, 1938; HWJ to Philip Bancroft, July 11, 1938; *New York Times*, Dec. 11, 1938. See also HWJ to Hiram Johnson, Jr., May 23, 1938.

41. John G. Townsend, Jr., to HWJ, Sept. 22, Oct. 21, 31, 1938; HWJ to H. L. Carnahan, Oct. 28, 1938; HWJ to Irving Martin, Oct. 3, 1938; HWJ to Walter Jones, Sept. 8, 26, 1938; HWJ to Jesse Steinhart, Oct. 26, 1938; HWJ to John G. Townsend, Jr., Oct. 26, 1938; HWJ to Doherty, Nov. 10, 1938; *San Francisco Chronicle*, Nov. 2, 1938; *New York Times*, Oct. 25, Dec. 11, 1938.

42. *Cong. Record*, 75th Cong., 3rd sess. (May 25, 1938), p. 7461; *Cong. Record*, 76th Cong., 1st sess. (Jan. 23, 1939), pp. 619–21; *New York Times*, Jan. 13, 14, 19, 1938; HWJ to Hiram Johnson, Jr., June 4, 1938, Jan. 14, 21, 28, 1939. Surprisingly, Johnson voted to confirm Frank Murphy as attorney general. Murphy, he noted, was "really not a bad man at all." HWJ to Hiram Johnson, Jr., Jan. 14, 1939.

43. To short-circuit this sort of logic, Edwin Borchard hoped for the repeal of the Kellogg pact. The agreement, he warned, was a "temptation to folly." Edwin Borchard to HWJ, Dec. 28, 1935.

44. HWJ to boys, May 26, 1933; HWJ to C. K. McClatchy, May 19, June 4, 11, 1933; HWJ to John Bassett Moore, May 2, 5, 25, 1933; *New York Times*, May 26, 1933.

45. Davis, Johnson wrote, was "negotiating, manipulating, and controlling our relations with other countries for J. P. Morgan." HWJ to boys, June 4, 1933.

46. Robert A. Divine, *The Illusion of Neutrality* (Chicago, 1962), pp. 81–101.

In international law, contraband goods cannot be supplied to one belligerent except at the risk of seizure by the other.

47. John Bassett Moore to HWJ, Aug. 22, 1935. See also HWJ to J. Reuben Clark, Jr., Feb. 17, 1935; HWJ to John Bassett Moore, Feb. 17, Apr. 14, 15, 1935; HWJ to Edwin Borchard, July 26, 1935.

48. HWJ to Hiram Johnson, Jr., June 10, 1940.

49. HWJ to Edwin Borchard, Dec. 27, 1935.

50. HWJ to John Bassett Moore, Aug. 30, 1935; HWJ to Edwin Borchard, Sept. 24, Oct. 1, 5, 1935.

51. The vote in the Senate was 79 to 2.

52. *Cong. Record*, 74th Cong., 1st sess. (Aug. 24, 1935), pp. 14430–32.

53. Senate Committee on Foreign Relations, *Neutrality: Hearings on S. 3474*, 74th Cong., 2nd sess. (1936), p. 100.

54. John Bassett Moore to HWJ, Jan. 2, 6, 1936. "Dictatorships are all the rage, and we must be in fashion," Moore added. John Bassett Moore to HWJ, Dec. 30, 1935. See also HWJ to John Bassett Moore, Dec. 26, 1935.

55. HWJ to John Bassett Moore, Jan. 8, 10, 14, 16, 31, Feb. 5, 6, 1936; HWJ to Edwin Borchard, Jan. 10, 18, 1936; Edwin Borchard to HWJ, Jan. 20, 24, 1936; Senate Committee on Foreign Relations, *Neutrality: Hearings on S. 3474*, 74th Cong., 2nd sess. (1936), pp. 7–8.

56. HWJ to Hiram Johnson, Jr., Jan. 26, 1936. See also *Cong. Record*, 74th Cong., 2nd sess. (Jan. 16, 1936), p. 507; Senate Committee on Foreign Relations, *Neutrality: Hearings on S. 3474*, 74th Cong., 2nd sess. (1936), pp. 55–56, 64–68, 122–23, 128, 131, 142–43.

57. HWJ to Edwin Borchard, Dec. 27, 29, 1935; HWJ to John Bassett Moore, Jan. 2, 1936; *New York Times*, Jan. 14, 26, 1936. Nye's testimony in support of his measure can be found in Senate Committee on Foreign Relations, *Neutrality: Hearings on S. 3474*, 74th Cong., 2nd sess. (1936), pp. 149–69.

58. HWJ to John Bassett Moore, Jan. 12, 1936; HWJ to Edwin Borchard, Feb. 8, 1936; HWJ to Hiram Johnson, Jr., Jan. 18, 26, Feb. 2, 1936.

59. HWJ to Hiram Johnson, Jr., Feb. 16, 1936; HWJ to John Bassett Moore, Feb. 5, 1936; HWJ to Edwin Borchard, Feb. 11, 1936.

60. HWJ to Hiram Johnson, Jr., Feb. 25, 1936; HWJ to Edwin Borchard, Feb. 21, 1936; HWJ to John Bassett Moore, Feb. 17, 1936.

61. HWJ to Hiram Johnson, Jr., Mar. 1, 1936; Edwin Borchard to HWJ, Feb. 26, 1936; Edwin Borchard to Cyril Wymore, Mar. 30, 1936; Divine, *Illusion of Neutrality*, p. 159.

62. HWJ to C. K. McClatchy, June 4, 1933; HWJ to Hiram Johnson, Jr., Apr. 19, 1935; HWJ to Edwin Borchard, Oct. 3, 1935.

63. HWJ to Edwin Borchard, Oct. 1, 3, 1935; HWJ to John Bassett Moore, Jan. 2, 1936; HWJ to Hiram Johnson, Jr., Feb. 25, 1936.

64. *New York Times*, Feb. 21, 1937; HWJ to John Bassett Moore, Feb. 20, 1937. Borah was absent.

65. *Cong. Record*, 75th Cong., 1st sess. (Mar. 3, 1937), pp. 1778–81. In the 1920s, in response to the "pacifists" and those who argued with Borah for the codification of international law, Johnson had scoffed. In his Senate address of March 3, he described international law as a "living, breathing thing."

66. *New York Times*, Mar. 4, 1937; HWJ to Hiram Johnson, Jr., Mar. 7, 1937. Earlier in the debate, Johnson admitted that he was only fit to listen. *Cong. Record*, 75th Cong., 1st sess. (Mar. 1, 1937), p. 1676.

67. HWJ to John Bassett Moore, Mar. 5, 1937; *Cong. Record*, 75th Cong., 1st sess. (Apr. 29, 1937), pp. 3942–43; *New York Times*, Apr. 20, 1937. In his March 3 address Johnson announced that he was for any and all amendments "no matter what they are." Either this or his own confusion might explain his support of an amendment proposed by Borah that in fact would have enhanced presidential discretion.

68. *New York Times*, June 2, 1937.

69. HWJ to Raymond Moley, Oct. 11, 1937; HWJ to Hiram Johnson, Jr., Apr. 16, 1937.

70. HWJ to John Bassett Moore, Oct. 7, 1937; HWJ to Elizabeth J. Moore, Oct. 7, 1937; HWJ to Edward Devlin, Oct. 22, 1937; HWJ to Joseph Timmons, Oct. 22, 1937.

71. HWJ to Hiram Johnson, Jr., Mar. 29, 1936. See also HWJ to Hiram Johnson, Jr., Mar. 15, 1936, Apr. 21, 1939.

72. HWJ to Hiram Johnson, Jr., Mar. 15, 1936, Feb. 26, 1938, Apr. 21, 1939; *Cong. Record*, 75th Cong., 3rd sess. (Mar. 11, 1938), p. 3246. Appeasement reveals "the realistic policy of Great Britain in all its nakedness," Johnson announced. *New York Times*, Mar. 12, 1938. He returned to this theme in a radio address in October 1939. See *Cong. Record*, 76th Cong., 2nd sess., Appendix, p. 562.

73. *Cong. Record*, 75th Cong., 3rd sess. (Feb. 1, 1938), pp. 1326–27; *New York Times*, Feb. 1–3, 1938. See also *Cong. Record*, 75th Cong., 2nd sess. (Jan. 31, 1938), p. 1263: Referring to Norman Davis, who headed the U.S. delegation to the Brussels conference, Johnson noted: "I want no peripatetic ambassador running around Europe saying over there to various chancelleries whatever may be in his head. At this time, when all the peoples of the world are on edge and jittery, I want no one man to have the right in secrecy to deal with the destiny of my country." See also HWJ to Hiram Johnson, Jr., Feb. 5, 1938.

74. *Cong. Record*, 75th Cong., 3rd sess. (Feb. 7, 1938), p. 1532.

75. *Cong. Record*, 75th Cong., 3rd sess. (Feb. 8, 1938), p. 1622; *New York Times*, Feb. 8, 9, 1938; HWJ to Hiram Johnson, Jr., Feb. 12, 24, 1938, Mar. 5, 1939.

76. *Cong. Record*, 75th Cong., 3rd sess. (Feb. 10, 1938), pp. 1764–65. Johnson repeated his call for the administration to define its foreign policy. See *Cong. Record*, 75th Cong., 3rd sess. (Mar. 11, 1938), p. 3246.

77. HWJ to Edwin Borchard, Apr. 22, June 20, 1938. Being ill at home, Johnson missed the vote and paired in support of naval preparedness. HWJ to Hiram Johnson, Jr., Apr. 29, 1938.

78. HWJ to Edwin Borchard, Feb. 18, June 20, 1938, Jan. 26, 1939; HWJ to Raymond Leslie Buell, July 30, 1938; HWJ to Raymond Moley, Feb. 19, 1938; HWJ to W. F. Prisk, Aug. 3, 1938; HWJ to Hiram Johnson, Jr., Feb. 19, 1938.

79. *New York Times*, Feb. 1, 2, 1939.

80. *Cong. Record*, 76th Cong., 1st sess. (Feb. 1, 1939), pp. 1015–16; HWJ to

Doherty, Feb. 11, 1939; HWJ to Hiram Johnson, Jr., Feb. 4, 11, 19, Apr. 2, 1939; HWJ to Philip Johnson, Apr. 9, 1939.

81. *Cong. Record*, 76th Cong., 1st sess. (May 2, 1939), pp. 4999–5000; HWJ to John Bassett Moore, May 12, 1939. See also HWJ to Philip Bancroft, May 7, 1939; HWJ to Hiram Johnson, Jr., May 6, 27, 1939.

82. HWJ to Hiram Johnson, Jr., Apr. 8, 21, 22, 25, May 13, 1939; HWJ to John Bassett Moore, Feb. 25, Mar. 4, 9, Apr. 5, 6, 9, May 12, 1939; John Bassett Moore to HWJ, Mar. 2, 1939; Senate Committee on Foreign Relations, Hearings, *Neutrality, Peace Legislation, and Our Foreign Policy*, 76th Cong., 1st sess. (Apr.–May 1939), pp. 67–68, 288–89.

83. Divine, *Illusion of Neutrality*, p. 258. By 1939 Johnson once again seemed master of those skills. See for example his exchanges with Henry L. Stimson. Senate Committee on Foreign Relations, Hearings, *Neutrality, Peace Legislation, and Our Foreign Policy*, 76th Cong., 1st sess. (Apr.–May 1939), pp. 17–23.

84. HWJ to Hiram Johnson, Jr., June 17, 1939.

85. *New York Times*, July 8, 9, 1939; HWJ to Hiram Johnson, Jr., July 8, 1939; HWJ to Boake Carter, July 1, 1939.

86. HWJ to Hiram Johnson, Jr., June 3, 17, July 16, 22, 1939. Earlier, Borah had expressed his desire to defeat the bill on the floor rather than bottle it in committee.

87. *Cong. Record*, 74th Cong., 1st sess. (Aug. 24, 1935), p. 14431.

88. HWJ to Hiram Johnson, Jr., Feb. 13, 1932, Apr. 2, 1939; HWJ to Raymond Moley, Oct. 11, 1937; *Cong. Record*, 75th Cong., 3rd sess. (June 16, 1938), p. 9524.

89. HWJ to Hiram Johnson, Jr., Feb. 11, 1938, Feb. 19, Mar. 19, 1939, Jan. 26, 1941. "My sympathies, of course, are wholly with Britain and France, and I pray for their success," Johnson wrote as the Germans launched their spring assault. HWJ to Hiram Johnson, Jr., May 25, 1940. See also HWJ to Sam Rodall, Sept. 7, 1933; HWJ to Hiram Johnson, Jr., June 2, 10, 1940, Mar. 16, June 29, 1941; HWJ to Hichborn, Nov. 16, 1940; HWJ to Doherty, Apr. 15, 1941. To the delight of Johnson's opponents, he and other isolationists were often branded as pro-Nazi. Thus, as the *New York Times* reported on Feb. 21, 1939, Johnson's name was cheered, along with those of Borah, Nye, and Hoover, at a Nazi rally at Madison Square Garden. In time, Johnson would complain of the tendency of the administration to divide people between "patriots" and "sympathizers of Hitler." See HWJ to Hiram Johnson, Jr., Apr. 29, 1939, May 25, 1940.

90. *Cong. Record*, 76th Cong., 1st sess. (Mar. 2, 1939), p. 2137. See also *Cong. Record*, 76th Cong., 2nd sess. (Oct. 20, 1939), p. 631; HWJ to Hiram Johnson, Jr., June 9, 1940.

91. HWJ to Hiram Johnson, Jr., Feb. 11, Mar. 26, May 13, June 10, Nov. 5, 1939, July 6, Sept. 27, 1941.

92. HWJ to Neylan, June 11, 1939; HWJ to Hiram Johnson, Jr., July 30, 1939; *Cong. Record*, 75th Cong., 3rd sess. (June 16, 1938), p. 9524.

93. HWJ to John Bassett Moore, Sept. 24, 1939; HWJ to Hiram Johnson, Jr., Sept. 24, 1939; *New York Times*, Sept. 18, 21, 1939.

94. *New York Times*, Sept. 29, 1939; HWJ to William Borah et al., Oct. 5,

1939; HWJ to Bennett Clark and Robert La Follette, Jr., Oct. 14, 1939; HWJ to Hiram Johnson, Jr., Sept. 30, 1939; *Cong. Record*, 76th Cong., 2nd sess. (Oct. 9, 23, 1939), pp. 203, 745. See also David L. Porter, *The Seventy-sixth Congress and World War II, 1939–1940* (Columbia, Mo., 1979), pp. 55–90.

95. HWJ to Doherty, Oct. 15, 1939; HWJ to Hiram Johnson, Jr., Oct. 15, 21, 28, 1939.

96. *New York Times*, Oct. 21, 1939.

97. *Cong. Record*, 76th Cong., 2nd sess. (Oct. 20, 1939), pp. 628–32. On October 24 Johnson repeated much of his address over NBC radio. See *Cong. Record*, 76th Cong., 2nd sess., Appendix, pp. 561–63. In arguing against the passage of neutrality legislation in 1935 and 1937, Johnson had stressed the need for flexibility, insisting that Congress ought not to anticipate events but rather respond to them. In 1939 he reversed his position, arguing that in responding to the outbreak of war by the repeal of the arms embargo Congress was undertaking an "unneutral" act.

98. *Time*, Oct. 2, 1939, p. 16; *Cong. Record*, 76th Cong., 2nd sess. (Oct. 27, Nov. 3, 1939), pp. 1014–15, 1024, 1356–57.

99. Doherty to HWJ, Nov. 11, 1939.

100. HWJ to Hiram Johnson, Jr., June 23, 1940; HWJ to Manchester Boddy, May 18, June 9, 1939; HWJ to Hiram Johnson, Jr., May 25, June 9, July 15, 1939; HWJ to W. F. Prisk, Aug. 2, 1940; HWJ to Hichborn, Nov. 16, 1940.

101. HWJ to Hiram Johnson, Jr., Sept. 1, 8, 1940; HWJ to Neylan, Sept. 14, 1940; *Cong. Record*, 76th Cong., 3rd sess. (Aug. 9, 26, Sept. 9, 1940), pp. 10090–92, 10898, 11777. In his radio address of October 24, 1939, Johnson had remarked, "A draft law is already prepared, and unquestionably the blanks for the casualty lists are ready." See *Cong. Record*, 76th Cong., 2nd sess., Appendix, p. 561. His comments on Stimson and Knox can be found in HWJ to Hiram Johnson, Jr., June 23, July 4, 1940. See also *New York Times*, June 24, Aug. 4, 1940.

102. Doherty to HWJ, Apr. 14, Nov. 11, 1939, Mar. 11, 1940. See also Robert Girvin to HWJ, May 7, 1940; HWJ to Al McCabe, Feb. 21, 1940. Some Republican endorsements of Johnson prior to the formal opening of his campaign can be found in the *San Francisco Chronicle*, Feb. 12, Mar. 16, Apr. 28, 1940.

103. *Los Angeles Times*, Aug. 26, 1940; Doherty to HWJ, Aug. 19, 1940; H. L. Carnahan to HWJ, Aug. 3, 23, 1940; Al McCabe to HWJ, Sept. 2, 1940. In addition, Johnson had the endorsements of governors Stephens and Young. See *San Francisco Chronicle*, Aug. 16, 1940.

104. Doherty to HWJ, Jan. 9, June 25, 1940.

105. HWJ to Doherty, Mar. 23, July 25, 1940; HWJ to Hiram Johnson, Jr., Mar. 31, Apr. 6, 7, July 19, 1940. Johnson had first announced his opposition to a third term for Roosevelt in 1938. See *New York Times*, Dec. 23, 1938.

106. HWJ to Hiram Johnson, Jr., May 25, July 21, Aug. 11, 1940; Mary Connor? to Doherty, Oct. 26, 1939, June 3, 1940; HWJ to Doherty, Nov. 1, 3, 1939; HWJ to Al McCabe, May 4, 1940.

107. HWJ to Philip Bancroft, June 25, 1939, Bancroft Papers; HWJ to Hiram Johnson, Jr., Aug. 17, 25, 1940.

108. Robert Girvin to HWJ, May 2, 7, 1940; HWJ to Al McCabe, Jan. 11, 1940; HWJ to Hiram Johnson, Jr., Jan. 19, Apr. 7, 1940. See also *San Francisco Chronicle*, May 28, 1940. A Democratic poll announced just prior to the opening of Johnson's campaign showed Johnson in the lead by a substantial majority. *San Francisco Chronicle*, May 27, 1940. An earlier poll by Doherty had also indicated that Johnson had the support of a majority of California's Democrats. Doherty to HWJ, Nov. 1, 1939; HWJ to Doherty, Nov. 3, 1939.

109. See Burke, *Olson's New Deal*, and Chinn, "Democratic Party Politics," pp. 122–28. See also Earl Warren to HWJ, Oct. 23, 1939, Mar. 27, 1940; Doherty to HWJ, June 25, 1940. Patterson, who had begun his campaign in 1939, was the "current darling of Los Angeles radicals," one observer noted. As quoted in *Fortune*, Mar. 1940, p. 140.

110. *San Francisco Chronicle*, Mar. 17, May 2, Aug. 5, 1940. After the election, the *Chronicle* announced that Johnson's victory was an endorsement of the man and not his politics. *San Francisco Chronicle*, Aug. 29, 1940. HWJ to Manchester Boddy, May 18, July 28, 1940. Democratic assemblyman Hugh Burns of Fresno was reported as "100%" for Johnson. In addition, the Solano County Democratic Central Committee gave him their unanimous support. *San Francisco Chronicle*, June 4, 1940; Robert Girvin to HWJ, July 31, 1940.

111. *San Francisco Chronicle*, Apr. 4, Aug. 4, 1940; Doherty to HWJ, Nov. 17, 1939, July 22, 1940; HWJ to Hiram Johnson, Jr., Feb. 24, Apr. 20, July 28, 1940; William Green to Claude McGovern and Alexander Watchman, July 23, 1940 (copy), HWJ Papers. See also *Los Angeles Examiner*, Dec. 6, 1939.

112. *San Francisco Chronicle*, Aug. 3, 1940.

113. *New York Times*, Aug. 4, 1940; *San Francisco Chronicle*, Aug. 4, 1940. David Lawrence, columnist for the *Evening Star* (Washington, D.C.), would author a public rebuke to Roosevelt. Johnson, he wrote, was "the greatest liberal in American public life today." His column can be found in *Cong. Record*, 76th Cong., 3rd sess., Appendix, p. 10069. See also Robert Girvin to HWJ, Aug. 2, 1940; Al McCabe to HWJ, Aug. 2, 1940; HWJ to Hiram Johnson, Jr., Aug. 4, 1940; HWJ to Robert Girvin, Aug. 4, 1940.

114. *San Francisco Chronicle*, Aug. 21, 24, 1940; *Los Angeles Times*, Aug. 26, 1940. Johnson made much the same appeal in a public telegram to Irving Cobb. See *San Francisco Chronicle*, June 15, 1940. Supporting Johnson in radio appeals were Theodore Roche, John Neylan, and Manchester Boddy. *San Francisco Chronicle*, July 29, Aug. 5, 19, 1940; H. L. Carnahan to HWJ, July 29, 1940; Robert Girvin to HWJ, July 31, 1940; HWJ to W. F. Prisk, Aug. 2, 1940.

115. Johnson won 50.3 percent of the Democratic primary vote. Patterson was second with 20.5 percent. Ford received 17.4 percent. Also on the ballot were Samuel Yorty, Richard Otto, and James Meredith.

116. HWJ to Hiram Johnson, Jr., Aug. 30, Sept. 1, 1940; HWJ to Doherty, Aug. 15, Sept. 1, 2, 1940. Johnson's preferred candidate for the Republican nomination had been Thomas Dewey. See HWJ to Hiram Johnson, Jr., July 4, 1940; HWJ to Thomas Dewey, Nov. 14, 1940.

117. HWJ to Hiram Johnson, Jr., Sept. 8, 16, 1940; HWJ to Doherty, Sept. 10, 26, 1940; Al McCabe to HWJ, Sept. 23, 1940; Neylan memo of phone conversation with HWJ, Sept. 17, 1940, Neylan Papers.

118. HWJ to Doherty, Sept. 1, Oct. 4, 10, 1940; Doherty to HWJ, Sept. 3, Oct. 14, 1940; Arthur Kennedy to HWJ, Aug. 29, 1940, emphasis in original.

119. HWJ to Hiram Johnson, Jr., Sept. 29, Oct. 5, 12, 1940; HWJ to Doherty, Oct. 4, 10, 1940; *New York Times*, Oct. 19, 1940.

120. *Cong. Record*, 76th Cong., 3rd sess., Appendix, pp. 6472–74. The address can also be found in *Vital Speeches of the Day* 7:2 (Nov. 1, 1940), pp. 52–55.

121. Doherty to HWJ, Oct. 19, 1940; Philip Bancroft to HWJ, Oct. 19, 1940, Bancroft Papers; Al McCabe to HWJ, Oct. 21, 1940.

122. HWJ to Doherty, Oct. 22, 28, Nov. 4, 7, 1940; HWJ to Hiram Johnson, Jr., Oct. 24, 27, 30, Sept. 1, Nov. 2, 1940; HWJ to Hichborn, Nov. 16, 1940; HWJ to Al McCabe, Nov. 3, 7, 1940.

123. HWJ to Hiram Johnson, Jr., Oct. 5, 30, Nov. 9, 17, 1940. Johnson estimated that his totals were reduced by 100,000 to 200,000 because of his endorsement of Willkie. See HWJ to Doherty, Nov. 7, 1940.

124. HWJ to Hiram Johnson, Jr., Jan. 5, 11, 1941; *New York Times*, Dec. 5, 1940. See also HWJ to Hiram Johnson, Jr., May 5, 1941; HWJ to Hiram Johnson III, July 19, 1941.

125. HWJ to Hiram Johnson, Jr., Jan. 11, Feb. 2, 9, Mar. 16, 1941; HWJ to Doherty, Mar. 2, 1941; HWJ to Philip Bancroft, Mar. 7, 1941, Bancroft Papers. In fact, except for an occasional clash with his committee colleague Tom Connally, Johnson was relatively silent throughout the hearings. See Senate Foreign Relations Committee, *To Promote the Defense of the United States*, Hearings, 77th Cong., 1st sess. (1941).

126. Warren F. Kimball, *The Most Unsordid Act: Lend-Lease, 1939–1941* (Baltimore, 1969). Amendments stipulated that convoys were not authorized, placed a time limit of two years on the duration of the act, and required frequent White House reports to Congress on the administration of the act. In addition, Roosevelt reluctantly accepted an amendment that gave to Congress power to void the Lend-Lease Act by joint resolution. Writing of Willkie, Johnson noted that if it had not been for the issue of the third term he would have gone before the electorate in "sack-cloth and ashes" and apologized for his 1940 endorsement of the Republican candidate. HWJ to Neylan, Jan. 18, 1941; HWJ to Hiram Johnson, Jr., Jan. 19, 26, 1941.

127. HWJ to Hiram Johnson, Jr., Feb. 2, 9, 1941. Borchard, he wrote, had been "frightened out of his skin."

128. *Cong. Record*, 77th Cong., 1st sess. (Mar. 5, 7, 1941), pp. 1813, 1959–62, 1970.

129. *Cong. Record*, 77th Cong., 1st sess., Appendix, pp. A826–A828; HWJ to Hiram Johnson, Jr., Mar. 2, 9, 1941. The vote was 60 to 31.

130. HWJ to Hiram Johnson, Jr., Apr. 17, 25, 1941. Philip Bancroft estimated that Roosevelt had the backing of 75 percent of Californians. Philip Bancroft to HWJ, July 5, 1941, Bancroft Papers.

131. *Cong. Record*, 77th Cong., 1st sess., Appendix, p. A2594. Johnson's address can also be found in *Vital Speeches of the Day* 7:17 (June 15, 1941), pp. 514–17. See also HWJ to Hiram Johnson, Jr., May 11, 24, June 4, 8, 1941.

132. Herbert Hoover to HWJ, June 1, 1941; HWJ to Herbert Hoover, June 4,

1941. See also *Cong. Record,* 77th Cong., 1st sess. (June 5, 1941), p. 4749: "There are secret police forces in many departments of the Government. . . . We learn of them only when somebody steps on our toes."

133. *Cong. Record,* 77th Cong., 1st sess. (July 22, 1941), pp. 6243–44.

134. HWJ to Hiram Johnson, Jr., July 6, 13, Aug. 8, 17, 20, Sept. 27, 1941; *Cong. Record,* 77th Cong., 1st sess. (Aug. 7, 1941), pp. 6847–50; *New York Times,* June 6, July 4, 8, 1941.

135. HWJ to Hiram Johnson, Jr., Oct. 26, Nov. 2, 8, 1941. Senator Joshua Lee, Democrat of Oklahoma, referred to Johnson's reversal in the course of the debate. See *Cong. Record,* 77th Cong., 1st sess. (Nov. 4, 1941), p. 8484. While calling the nation's attention to the inconsistency of an administration that had once sponsored neutrality legislation and now sought its repeal, Johnson refused to admit his own inconsistency publicly.

136. *Cong. Record,* 77th Cong., 1st sess. (Nov. 7, 1941), pp. 8670–71; Appendix, pp. A5040–A5042; *Vital Speeches of the Day* 8:4 (Dec. 1, 1941), pp. 120–24. See also *Cong. Record,* 77th Cong., 1st sess. (Nov. 10, 1941), p. 8695.

137. HWJ to Hiram Johnson, Jr., Nov. 16, Dec. 3, 1941.

138. HWJ to Hiram Johnson, Jr., Dec. 13, 1941. Johnson ascribed the debacle of Pearl Harbor to Japanese malevolence, not to Roosevelt's manipulations. Roosevelt and the State Department, he wrote, were taken for "suckers."

139. *Cong. Record,* 77th Cong., 1st sess. (Dec. 15, 1941), p. 9765; HWJ to Doherty, Feb. 16, 1942.

140. HWJ to Hiram Johnson, Jr., Feb. 19, May 17, June 16, 21, July 10, Aug. 5, Oct. 11, Nov. 5, 1942; HWJ to Hon. Rufus Holman, Feb. 3, 1942; HWJ to Mary Pickford, July 26, 1942; HWJ to Hichborn, July 28, 1942; HWJ to Philip Johnson, Mar. 22, 1942; HWJ to Theodore Roche, June 9, 1942; *Cong. Record,* 77th Cong., 2nd sess. (Feb. 17, 1942), pp. 1332–33.

141. *Cong. Record,* 77th Cong., 2nd sess. (Oct. 23, 24, Nov. 12, 1942), pp. 8566–70, 8651–52, 8794–96; HWJ to Hiram Johnson, Jr., Sept. 5, 1942.

142. HWJ to Hiram Johnson, Jr., Nov. 5, 1942, Mar. 27, 1943.

143. HWJ to Hiram Johnson, Jr., Apr. 15, 27, Mar. 27, July 11, 26, Sept. 20, 1943; HWJ to James E. McCormack, Dec. 15, 1943; *New York Times,* Apr. 30, May 2, 3, 6, 1943. During Johnson's hospital stay, his remaining teeth were pulled to arrest a spreading infection.

144. HWJ to Hiram Johnson, Jr., Sept. 5, 1943. See also Robert A. Divine, *Second Chance: The Triumph of Internationalism in America During World War II* (New York, 1967).

145. HWJ to Hiram Johnson, Jr., Sept. 20, Oct. 14, 1943; *Cong. Record,* 78th Cong., 1st sess. (Nov. 5, 1943), pp. 9210–11. Joining Johnson in opposing the Connally resolution were William Langer of North Dakota; Henrik Shipstead of Minnesota; Burton Wheeler of Montana; and Robert Reynolds of North Carolina.

146. HWJ to Hiram Johnson, Jr., Nov. 21, Dec. 5, 1943. See also Philip Bancroft to HWJ, Nov. 9, 1943, Bancroft Papers; Mary Connor? to Theodore Roche, Nov. 17, 1943.

147. HWJ to Hiram Johnson, Jr., Feb. 15, May 22, June 3, 9, 1944.

148. *Cong. Record*, 78th Cong., 2nd sess. (Dec. 18, 19, 1944), pp. 9648, 9716; *Cong. Record*, 79th Cong., 1st sess. (Mar. 13, 16, 17, 23, Apr. 17, 1945), pp. 1945, 2076, 2333, 2655, 3418–19; *New York Times*, Apr. 12, 1945.

149. *New York Times*, July 15, 1945; HWJ to Neylan, May 1, 1945, Neylan Papers.

150. *New York Times*, Aug. 6, 8, 14, 1945. On the Senate floor, only William Langer of North Dakota and Henrik Shipstead of Minnesota voted no.

151. *San Francisco Chronicle*, Aug. 7, 1945; *Los Angeles Times*, Aug. 7, 1945; *San Diego Union*, Aug. 7, 1945; *Oakland Tribune*, Aug. 6, 1945; *San Francisco Call Bulletin*, Aug. 6, 1945; *Stockton Record*, Aug. 6, 1945; *San Francisco Examiner*, Aug. 7, 1945; *Sacramento Bee*, Aug. 7, 1945.

152. *Sacramento Bee*, Aug. 14, 1945; *San Francisco Chronicle*, Aug. 7, 9, 12, 14, 1945; Hiram Johnson, Jr., to Howard Seidell, Aug. 25, Nov. 17, Dec. 28, 1948, Jan. 7, 17, Apr. 5, 12, 1949; Hiram Johnson, Jr., to R. L. Miller, Jan. 14, 1949; Hiram Johnson, Jr., to E. R. Nichols, Sept. 23, 1949.

Index

In this index an "f" after a number indicates a separate reference on the next page, and an "ff" indicates separate references on the next two pages. A continuous discussion over two or more pages is indicated by a span of page numbers, e.g., "pp. 57–58." *Passim* is used for a cluster of references in close but not consecutive sequence.

A
Bloc
of
One

Library of Congress Cataloging-in-Publication Data

Lower, Richard Coke.
    A bloc of one : the political career of Hiram W.
Johnson / Richard Coke Lower.
        p.   cm.
    Includes bibliographical references and index.
    ISBN 0-8047-2081-9 (cloth : acid-free paper) :
    1. Johnson, Hiram, 1866–1945. 2. United States—
Politics and government—1901–1953. 3. California—
Politics and government—1850–1950. I. Title.
E748.J73L68 1993
973.91′092—dc20
                                    93–6975
                                      CIP